Sunday by Sunday: Music for the Second Service Lectionary, Years A, B & C

Sunday by Sunday

Music for the Second Service Lectionary,
Years A, B & C

RS✦M

CANTERBURY
PRESS
Norwich

The contributors are grateful to Tim Ruffer, Head of Publications at the Royal School of Church Music, for his assistance and support in the preparation of this book.

First published in 2008 by the Canterbury Press Norwich
(a publishing imprint of Hymns Ancient & Modern Limited,
a registered charity)
13–17 Long Lane, London EC1A 9PN

www.scm-canterburypress.co.uk

British Library Cataloguing in Publication data

A catalogue record for this book is available
from the British Library

ISBN 978-1-85311-840-1

Printed and bound by
Biddles Ltd, Kings Lynn, Norfolk

CONTENTS

ABBREVIATIONS

Coding for hymns and songs

Some of the choices relate directly to Scripture readings. This is indicated in the reading column of the grid ('rdg') with the following codes:

ap	Reading from the Apocrypha
g	Gospel reading where provided to be read if the Second Service is a Eucharist
n	New Testament reading
o	Old Testament reading ('1o' and '2o' are occasionally used where there are alternative readings)
ps	Psalm ('1ps' and 2ps' are occasionally used where there is more than one psalm set)
s	Seasonal

When the code is followed by a number, this refers to a verse from the reading.

Some hymns are particularly suitable at certain times of day or certain places in the liturgy. This is indicated in the position column of the grid ('pos') with the following codes:

cm	Particularly suitable for singing during Communion
ga	Gathering hymn
hc	Suitable at some point in a service of Holy Communion
pc	Post-Communion hymn
se	Particularly suitable as worshippers are sent out
mo	Morning
ev	Evening

Coding for psalms, anthems and organ music

*	Indicates optional alternatives for longer psalms (see the *Common Worship* lectionary for details)
*	Indicates organ music for manuals only
(*)	Indicates organ music which may be played with or without pedals
#	Indicates a setting suitable for music groups
(g)	Indicates an anthem related to the Gospel provided for a Eucharist
E/M/D	Indicates the level of difficulty for an average choir or organist (Easy/Medium/Difficult)

For Books and Collections, see pages 372–374.

INTRODUCTION

In 1997 the Royal School of Church Music began to publish a quarterly planner to help those choosing music for services, both within the Church of England and more widely. *Sunday by Sunday*, available only to affiliates and individual members of the RSCM, has since become one of the most widely valued aspects of the organisation's work. It is based on the three-year cycle of readings provided by the *Common Worship* Principal Service Lectionary, which has much in common with the Roman Lectionary and the Revised Common Lectionary.

This new book, covering Sundays and major Festivals throughout Years A, B and C, provides suggestions of music appropriate to the Second Service Lectionary, as used by the Church of England and (with slight variations) by the Methodist Church, the Church of Ireland and others. The music has been chosen by members of the team responsible for the quarterly *Sunday by Sunday* publication and aims for a degree of ecumenical breadth. Some of the designations given to Sundays (for example, immediately before Advent) differ from church to church, while the few differences in readings for the Church of Ireland occur on the Sundays in Ordinary Time before Lent.

Using this book

In many places the Second Service Lectionary will be used at Evensong. In others, the relevant service will be Matins or some other Service of the Word, while there are also churches which use it at a eucharistic service. The lectionary provides a Gospel reading to be used at Holy Communion where the New Testament reading is not from one of the four Gospels; this option is indicated in the readings listed in these pages by italic text. As with any service, those choosing music need to consider not only what relates to the readings but also what is appropriate *liturgically* at any given point and what is appropriate *musically* in the light of local resources.

Where musical suggestions are provided for days on which the Second Service Lectionary allocates only one set of readings to be used in all three years (Christmas Day, Epiphany, the Presentation of Christ in the Temple, Ash Wednesday, Good Friday, Ascension Day, Dedication Festival and All Saints' Day), the lists can be found in the first part of the book, dedicated to Year A. A reference to the relevant pages is provided in the sections covering Years B and C, while extra organ music is listed on pages 364–371. The Dedication Festival (the anniversary of the date of a church's dedication or consecration) may be celebrated on the first Sunday in October or the last Sunday after Trinity where the date of dedication is unknown, or on a suitable date chosen locally. Musical suggestions can be found at the end of the Sundays after Trinity in Year A (pages 120–121).

The editors of this book are well aware that the musical choices are highly selective, particularly at certain seasons, but have tried to provide suggestions in a variety of styles and to meet the needs of different kinds of worshipping communities. We anticipate that the titles listed on any page may alert musicians to other appropriate material which is not mentioned – it would be impossible to provide comprehensive lists, given the constraints of space and the huge range of musical resources currently available. Those who use the book are encouraged to use our lists as a starting point rather than a strait-jacket. Although the situation can alter quite quickly and unpredictably, we have tried on the whole to suggest music from publications which are still in print and which can be ordered from the RSCM's mail order service: RSCM Music Direct, St Mary's Works, St Mary's Plain, Norwich, NR3 3BH (Tel: 0845 021 7726; Fax: 0845 021 8826; Email: musicdirect@rscm.com).

Singing the Psalm

We hope that many congregations and choirs will explore ways of singing the psalms; we have listed settings from a number of psalm-based collections and from hymn and song books, along with items published singly (in which case the publisher, such as OCP, GIA or White Light Publishing, is indicated in brackets). In some cases the music suggested is not a complete setting of the verses allocated by the lectionary; in a few instances a song including only one psalm verse is listed – this might be sung before and after the reading of the psalm in question. An asterisk has been used where the lectionary provides for a shorter portion to be sung; details for Church of England services can be found in *The Christian Year: Calendar, Lectionary and Collects* (Church House Publishing, 1997) on page 96.

Hymns and songs

The list of abbreviations on page vi explains some of the coding used in the hymn tables. Only a few suggestions have been made regarding the 'position' of a hymn or song – since the Second Service Lectionary is used in a wide variety of liturgical contexts it would be unwise to be too prescriptive about where in a service a particular item might best be used. However, some items are especially appropriate at the start or the close of an act of worship, some words are specifically linked with morning or evening gatherings, and some items have a eucharistic focus. We have tried to indicate all such hymns and songs, as well as those which relate principally to the Gospel reading only used at services of Holy Communion; some of the anthems are also marked appropriately.

It has not been considered necessary to list all the variants in the opening lines of hymns. However, where confusion might arise alternatives *have* been given, including some cases where the updating of archaic language affects those looking up a particular hymn in an alphabetical index. Authors are normally given only where two or more writers have used the same opening line. The choice of hymnbooks attempts to represent the breadth of resources used by Anglicans, Methodists and others from various parts of the British Isles. We are aware that some leaders of worship will be disappointed that their own regular hymnbook is not included, but we hope that our suggestions will still be of use, since many hymns are common to most major publications and some congregations will be singing words printed on service sheets or projected on to a screen.

Music from the Taizé Community has been identified in the hymn/song lists. This is partly to alert those who have a mixed vocal and instrumental ensemble at their disposal, since a number of publications offer cantor and instrumental parts for this repertoire. The nature of Taizé chants also means that particular thought needs to be given to how they are used within a broad liturgical context: they may not best serve the worshipping community, for example, by being used as a substitute for a hymn. Some may wish to use them as gathering chants, for a period of reflection after a sermon, as part of the intercessions, or during Holy Communion.

Anthems and vocal music

The lists of anthems and vocal music have been compiled with a variety of contexts in mind, from large choirs with organ accompaniment to small vocal and instrumental ensembles. Many choirs will have access to anthologies and settings not included in our lists, and we hope that the titles mentioned will spark off other ideas as music directors look for repertoire particularly suited to their own context. It may be that groups currently using a relatively narrow repertoire will be encouraged by seeing the pieces listed here to broaden their horizons and explore new material.

Organ music

The suggestions offered for each Sunday or Festival are divided into *Preludes* and *Postludes*. In general the preludes are quieter pieces and the postludes are louder, but there will be occasions when it is desirable to play quieter pieces after the service or to offer a loud processional introit. The selections are mostly written for a 2–manual instrument with pedals. A choice of music without pedals, indicated in the lists by an asterisk *, is given for most Sundays. Where music may be played with the optional use of pedals, or where both 2-stave and 3-stave editions are available, the asterisk is in brackets (*).Whilst much of the organ music suggested is currently available for purchase from music shops, some use has been made of music published by Novello, Paxton, Peters Edition and Oxford University Press in popular anthologies from the past few decades which may no longer be 'in print' but which many parish organists will have in their own library or will find in public libraries. Though the majority of choices are aimed at the average Parish organist, some more difficult music has been included. Marked **D**, this is for players of Grade 8 or diploma standard.

Songs for young people

The section headed 'Songs for Children' gives a very small selection of music which may be suitable at an act of worship when the congregation includes a good number of children and young people, or for a group of children meeting separately. Quite often a hymn or song from the main list is also included in this section, partly to provide additional sources in which it may be found. Other suitable ideas may occasionally emerge from the lists of vocal music.

We hope that this book, used thoughtfully, will prove helpful to all who choose music for their churches and will enrich the worshipping lives of musicians and congregations in many places.

ANNE HARRISON
JOHN HENDERSON
PETER MOGER
DAVID OGDEN

YEAR A

THE FIRST SUNDAY OF ADVENT YEAR A

HYMNS AND SONGS

	pos	rdg	AMNS	CAON	CFE	CH4	CH5	CP	H&P	HTC	LAU	MP	NEH	SG	SOF	TS
Awake, awake: fling off the night!	ga	s	342	57	64			334			851					
Christ is coming! Let creation		s				475										
City of God, Jerusalem		o								187						
Come, thou long-expected Jesus		s	31	128	133	472	119	24	81	52	100	102	3	335		
Creator of the stars of night/ starry height		s	23	135	138	288	121	25			87		1			
Earth was waiting, spent and restless		s								54						
Great is the darkness		s									835			264	742	136
Hark, a herald/thrilling voice is calling/trumpet call is sounding	o,s	s	24	263	243		126	26		192	92		5	436		
Hark the glad sound! The Saviour comes		s	30	265		277	124	27	82	193		210	6	435	154	
Hark what a sound, and too divine		s					127	28	236				600			
Here from all nations		n				466	462			571				455		
Hills of the North, rejoice		s	470	282	255		128	29	237		983		7			
How beauteous/gracious are their feet		o	301					220	449							
How lovely on the mountains (Our God reigns)		o		295	268		129				768	249			192	189
I cannot tell why he, whom angels worship		s		303				54	238	194		266		437	205	199
In a world where people walk in darkness		s					476									
In Christ alone my hope is found		s									1072				1346	1311
In the Lord I'll be ever thankful (Taizé)				929	308	772					944	865		656	817	
Joy to the world!		o		370	335	320	166	57	77	197	156	393		340	314	305
Lo, he comes/Jesus comes with clouds descending	se	s	28	405	373	477	132	31	241	196	109	424	9	438	347	324
Make way, make way, for Christ the king		s		438	479	279	134				819	457			384	349
Revive thy work/your church, O Lord!		o					308		780	515		578				
Sing to God new songs of worship		o		603		173	710			352		600		95	1002	
Take my life, and let it be		o	249	625	677	502	597	581	705	554	874	624		678	519	468
The advent of our God/King	gr	s	25	633				36					14			
The Lord will come and not be slow		s	29	655			140	37	245				15			
Wake, O wake/Wake, awake/ Sleepers, wake	o,s	s	32	703	763	278	142	39	249	199	91		16			
Waken, O sleeper, wake and rise		s		702			143									
When came in flesh the incarnate Word		n											17			
Ye/You servants of the Lord		s	150	757			145	40	248	598			18			
You, living Christ, our eyes behold	of	o	533					333					487			

SONGS FOR CHILDREN

Christmas is coming CH4 282, LAU 93

Make way, make way CAON 438, CFE 479, CH4 279, CH5 134, JP 427, KS 249, LAU 819, MP 457, SOF 384, TS 349

BIBLE READINGS

Psalm 9*
Isaiah 52.1–12
Matthew 24.15–28

SINGING THE PSALM

Psalm 9* CH4, CWP, NPCW

ANTHEMS AND VOCAL MUSIC

Title	Composer	Voices	E/M/D	Book source	Single sheet publisher
UNISON/TWO PART/HIGH VOICES					
Advent Message	How	2/3 part	E	NOEAB	
All the ends of the earth	Haugen, Haas	U#	E	CFE, LAU, VE	GIA
How beautiful are the feet (Messiah)	Handel	S	M		Novello
Litany of the Word	Farrell	U#	E	A, CBL	OCP
Now is the time	Hayward	U	E	TCB	
Rain down justice	Ogden	U/SATB	E	SBS1	RSCM
A Song of Peace	Stanford	U	M		RSCM
A Song of Reflection	Mawby	2 part (SB)	E/M	SBS2	
THREE/FOUR PARTS					
Adventante Deo	Leighton	SATB	D	NNAB	
And the glory of the Lord (Messiah)	Handel	SATB	M	AOAN1 (SAB)	Novello
Creator of the stars of night	Archer	SATB	M	AFC	
E'en so, Lord Jesus, quickly come	Manz	SATB unacc	M	AFC	Morning Star
God hath spoken	Gibbs	SATB	M		RSCM
Holy is the true light	Harris	SATB unacc	E	NCAB, FSB7	Novello
How beautiful upon the mountains	Stainer	SATB	M	AOAN1 (SAMen), BC	RSCM
How lovely are the messengers	Mendelssohn	SATB	M	AFC	Novello
I look from afar	Piccolo	SATB	M/D		RSCM
O pray for the peace of Jerusalem	Howells	SATB	M		OUP
Sleepers, wake	Mendelssohn	SATB	E	AC1	
The bells of waiting Advent ring	Trad arr Iliff	SATB/U	E	TCB	
Wachet auf	Nicolai arr J.S. Bach	SATB	M	AFC, TCB	
Zion, at thy shining gates	Trad arr Guest	SATB	E	AFC	
FIVE OR MORE PARTS					
Matin Responsory	Jackson	SSATB	D	AFC	
Vigilate	Byrd	SATBB unacc	D		Chester

ORGAN MUSIC

PRELUDES

Anon. **Nun komm, der Heiden Heiland** in *120 Chorale Preludes of the 17C & 18C* (Peters) E/M*

Bach J.S. **Nun komm, der Heiden Heiland** BWV 659 of *Eighteen Chorale Preludes* in Novello Vol.17, Bärenreiter Vol.2, Peters Vol.7 M

Bach W.F. **Nun komm, der Heiden Heiland** in *W.F.Bach Organ Works* Bk.2 (Peters) E/M

Bonighton R. **Wachet auf** in *64 Hymn Preludes* and in *Hymn Preludes for the Church Year* Bk.1 (both Mayhew) E

Peeters F. **Creator alme siderum** No.1 of *Thirty Chorale Preludes on Gregorian Themes* Op.75 (Peters) M

POSTLUDES

Chauvet A. **Offertoire for 1st Sunday in Advent** in *Organ Noëls for the Time of Christmas* (Concordia) E/M(*)

Karg-Elert S **Wachet auf** No.33 from *Choral-Improvisationen* Op.65 Vol.3 (Breitkopf) M/D

Merkel G. **Wachet auf** Op.100/4 in *Dresdner Orgelmusik 19 C* (Breitkopf) E/M

Pachelbel J. **Nun komm, der Heiden Heiland** No.1 in *Selected Organ Works* Vol.2 (Kalmus) E/M

HYMNS AND SONGS

	pos rdg	AMNS	CAON	CFE	CH4	CH5	CP	H&P	HTC	LAU	MP	NEH	SG	SOF	TS
Be thou my vision/Lord, be my vision	e	343	70	74/75	465	643	386	378	545	970	51	339	669	42	50
Christ is the world's true light	n	346	100		456	501	396	456	323			494	432		
Hail to the Lord's anointed	n	142	259	241	474	125	87	125	190	102	204	55		150	709
Hark, a herald/thrilling voice is calling/trumpet call is sounding	o,s	24	263	243		126	26		192	92		5	436		
Hark the glad sound! The Saviour comes	s	30	265		277	124	27	82	193		210	6	435	154	
Hark what a sound, and too divine	s					127	28	236				600			
Heaven shall not wait	s		272		362										151
Jesus shall reign where'er the sun	s	143	359		470	97	490	239	516	322	379	388	45	301	1376
Judge eternal, throned in splendour	s		372		264	535	356	409	329		395	490	600		
Lo, God is here!	o							531				209			
Lo, in the wilderness a voice	n	384										170			
Lord of the Church, we pray for our renewing	s					303			499		442		577	1433	
Lord, the light of your love is shining	n		419	388	448	195	513			770	445		614	362	335
O bless the God of Israel	n					706			599						
O Lord, hear my prayer (Taizé)			938	542		620				929	908		246	423	394
On Jordan's bank, the Baptist's cry	n	27	527	575	334	136	34	84	601	94	538	12	339		
Prepare ye the way	n			612											
Restore, O Lord	s		582		469						579		274	483	439
River, wash over me	n										581			487	441
Sing we the praises of the great forerunner	n	315					234								
The kingdom of God is justice and joy	s		646	701			591	139	333	821	651		184		
The race that long in darkness/The people who in darkness		52	656	711	290	199	38	89	71	168		57			
Thou whose almighty word	s	180	684	738	112	324	267	29	506	887	699	466	597	557	
Thy/Your kingdom come, O God	s	177	691			509	607	783	334		949	499	269		
Wait for the Lord (Taizé)	s		949	762	276					88				1575	
Who is on the Lord's side?	o							722			769			607	1066
With my whole heart														611	582
Your love looks after me	o													1145	

SONGS FOR CHILDREN

Lord, the light of your love is shining CAON 419, CFE 388, CG 110, CH 148, CH4 448, CH5 195, CP 513, KS 237, LAU 770, MP 445, SG 614, SOF 362, TS 335
When the time is right CAON 913, KS 379

BIBLE READINGS

Psalms 11 [and 28]
1 Kings 18.17–39
John 1.19–28

SINGING THE PSALM

Psalm 11 CWP, NPCW
Psalm 28 CWP, NPCW

ANTHEMS AND VOCAL MUSIC

Title	Composer	Voices	E/M/D	Book source	Single sheet publisher
UNISON/TWO PART/HIGH VOICES					
Settings of the Benedictus (The Song of Zechariah)	Various	U	E	MCW1, NEP	
Hark! a messenger is calling	Kelly	3 part	E/M	CFL	
How beautiful are the feet (Messiah)	Handel	S	M		Novello
Lord God of Abraham (Elijah)	Mendelssohn	U Men	M		Novello
Prepare ye the way of the Lord	Schwartz arr Ogden	2 part	E	SFL1	
THREE/FOUR PARTS					
Benedictus	Stanford	SATB	M	AFC	
Canite tuba	Guerrero	SATB unacc	M	AFC	
Fuit homo missus a Deo	Palestrina	SATB unacc	M	AFC	
God hath spoken	Gibbs	SATB	M		RSCM
Hark, the glad sound	Walford Davies	SATB	E		RSCM
How beauteous are their feet	Stanford	SATB	M	AOAN1 (SAMen), ASA, NNAB, SC	RSCM
How beautiful upon the mountains	Stainer	SATB	M	AOAN1 (SAMen), BC	RSCM
How lovely are the messengers	Mendelssohn	SATB	M	AFC	Novello
Kindle a light to lighten the darkness	Lloyd	SATB	M		Encore
On Jordan's bank	Trad arr Archer	SATB	E	AFC	
Prepare ye the way of the Lord (Godspell)	Schwartz	SATB	M		Faber
The Spirit of the Lord	Elgar	SATB	M/D	SAEE	RSCM
This is the record of John	Gibbons	SATB + solo A	M/D	OBTA	OUP
This is the record of John	Ives	SATB	M/D	AFC	
Vox clamantis	Esquivel	SATB unacc	M/D		Mapa Mundi
FIVE OR MORE PARTS					
Canite tuba	Palestrina	SSATB unacc	M	CM12	
Vox dicentis, clama	Naylor	SATB + SATB unacc	D		Curwen

ORGAN MUSIC

PRELUDES

Bach J.S.   **Nun freut euch** BWV 734 in Novello Vol.18, Bärenreiter Vol.3, Peters Vol.7 M
Gray A.   **Intermezzo in F** in *An Organ Miscellany* (Mayhew) E
Groves R.   **Dundee** in *Six Scottish Hymn-Tune Preludes* (Novello) E(*)
Hand C.   **Dundee** in *Fifty Hymn Preludes* (Mayhew) E
Peeters F.   **Comfort, comfort ye, my people** in *Hymn Preludes for the Liturgical Year* Op.100 Bk.1 (Peters) E

POSTLUDES

Archer M.   **Merton** in *25 Hymn Preludes: A Year of Praise* and in *40 Christmas Preludes* (Mayhew) M
Chauvet A.   **Offertoire for 2nd Sunday in Advent** in *Organ Noëls for the Time of Christmas* (Concordia) E/M
Parry C.H.H.   **Chorale Prelude 'Dundee'** in *Seven Chorale Preludes* Set 1 (Novello) or in *Preludes and Postludes* (Mayhew) M/D
West J.E.   **Chorale Prelude on 'Winchester New'** (Novello) and in *Romantic Organ Music for Christmas and Advent* (Animus) E/M

THE THIRD SUNDAY OF ADVENT YEAR A

HYMNS AND SONGS

	pos	rdg	AMNS	CAON	CFE	CH4	CH5	CP	H&P	HTC	LAU	MP	NEH	SG	SOF	TS
Break thou the bread of life	cm	g					379	286	467			64			50	
Christ is the King! O friends rejoice		s	345				86	165		492			345	31		
Come, my Way, my Truth, my Life	cm	g		123		579	610	405	254		911		633			
Come, thou long-expected Jesus		s	31	128	133	472	119	24	81	52	100	102	3	335		
Father of mercies, in thy word		g	167							247				224		
God has spoken – by his prophets		g					381		64	248	742	831		225		
God is working his purpose out		s		221	217	235	481	444	769	191	86	189	495	451	135	128
God of love, you freely give us		g		226												
God, we praise you! God, we bless you!		s				120	696	450		341				38		
Hark, a herald/thrilling voice is calling/trumpet call is sounding		s	24	263	243		126	26		192	92		5	436		
Hark, my soul, it is/Christian, do you hear the Lord		g	244	264			569	457	521	472		209	637			
Have faith in God, my heart		n	372	268			458	675	431							
Hills of the North, rejoice		s	470	282	255		128	29	237		983		7			
How beauteous/gracious are their feet		s	301					220	449							
Lord, save thy world; in bitter need		n	397						425							
Make way, make way, for Christ the King		n		438	479	279	134				819	457			384	349
Miserere nobis/Holy Lord, have mercy (Taizé)		s									597			159		
Not far beyond the sea, nor high		g	401					528	477							
Now watch for God's coming		s			514						101					
O bless the God of Israel		n					706			599						
O Christ, the great foundation		n								502	829					
O come, O come, Emmanuel		s	26	480	522	273	135	32	85	66	112	493	11	338	410	
O Day of God, draw nigh		s	405					33								
O for a thousand tongues to sing		s	125	485		352	104	534	744	219		496	415	55	412	383/1452
On Jordan's bank, the Baptist's cry		s	27	527	575	334	136	34	84	601	94	538	12	339		
Prepare the way for the Lord		s												342		
Rejoice! The Lord is king		s	139	580	619	449	281	563	243	180	326	575	443	440	482	948
Rise and hear! The Lord is speaking		g	509				385	321								
Sing we the praises of the great forerunner		s	315					234								
Thanks/Praise to God whose word was spoken		g	423			605	387	584	483	255			438	229		
There's a light upon the mountains		s						246			679					
Wait for the Lord (Taizé)		s		949	762	276					88			1575		
When the King shall come again		s			806					200	90					

SONGS FOR CHILDREN

Lord, you've promised through your Son CAON 864, CH 150, KS 244

Make way, make way CAON 438, CFE 479, CH4 279, CH5 134, JP 427, KS 249, LAU 819, MP 457, SOF 384, TS 349

BIBLE READINGS

Psalms 12 [and 14]
Isaiah 5.8–30
Acts 13.13–41
John 5.31–40

SINGING THE PSALM

Psalm 12 CWP, NPCW
Psalm 14 CWP, NPCW

ANTHEMS AND VOCAL MUSIC

Title	Composer	Voices	E/M/D	Book source	Single sheet publisher
UNISON/TWO PART/HIGH VOICES					
A Song of Peace and Joy	Mawby	U + descant + instr	E	VFLS	
God beyond all names	Farrell	U/SATB#	E	CFE, GBAN, LAU	OCP
Make me a light	Wilby	2 part	E	HP, EAC2	Chester
Praise to you, O Christ our Saviour	Farrell	U#	E	CFE, LAU, RITH, WYP	OCP
Song of Consolation	Jones	U#	E	VE	
THREE/FOUR PARTS					
Call to remembrance	Farrant	SATB unacc	E	NCAB, OBTA	OUP
Canite tuba	Guerrero	SATB unacc	M	AFC	
Fuit homo missus a Deo	Palestrina	SATB unacc	M	AFC	
God has spoken	Trad arr Llewellyn	SATB	E	SWAMS	
In a world where people walk in darkness	Trad arr Harper	SATB	E	LOL	
Jesus, you are the way	Rizza	SATB + solo S#	E	FOL	Mayhew
Matin Responsory	Palestrina	SATB unacc	E/M	CC2, AFC	
The light of the world	Carter	SATB	M	ACA	OUP
The Lord is my light and my salvation	Noon	SATB	M	SBS1	RSCM
The Lord is my light and my salvation	Rutter	SATB + clarinet	M		OUP
The promise which was made	Bairstow	SATB	M		Novello
Thy word is a lantern	Purcell	SATB	M	APA	Novello
FIVE OR MORE PARTS					
Gaudete omnes	Praetorius	SATTB unacc	D		Chester
Matin Responsory	Jackson	SSATB	D	AFC	

ORGAN MUSIC

PRELUDES

Bach J.S.	**Von Gott will ich nicht lassen** BWV 658 in Novello Vol.17, Bärenreiter Vol.2, Peters Vol.7 M
Daniels B.	**Prooemium** ('Veni Emmanuel') in *Lux Mundi: Suite* (Animus) E/M
Forchhammer T.	**Ach Lieber Herre Jesu Christ** ('Breslau') in *Hier Preisen auf der Erd* Vol.1 (Breitkopf) E/M
Moore P.	**Veni Emmanuel** in *Hymn Preludes for the Church Year* Bk.1 (Mayhew) E
Rawsthorne N.	**Veni Emmanuel** in *The Holly and the Ivy* (Mayhew, 2 and 3-stave versions) E/M(*)

POSTLUDES

Andriessen H.	**Veni, veni Emmanuel** in *Advent to Whitsuntide* (Hinrichsen reprint) M
Archer M.	**Winchester New** in *25 Hymn Preludes: A Year of Praise* (Mayhew) E/M
Chauvet A.	**Offertoire for 3rd Sunday in Advent** in *Organ Noëls for the Time of Christmas* (Concordia) E/M(*)
Bairstow E.	**Veni, veni Emmanuel** No.3 from *Three Short Preludes* (Banks) M

HYMNS AND SONGS

	pos	rdg	AMNS	CAON	CFE	CH4	CH5	CP	H&P	HTC	LAU	MP	NEH	SG	SOF	TS
Behold the servant of the Lord		g							788						668	
Bless the Lord, my soul (Taizé)				923	81		1				813			105	676	56
Christ be the Lord of all our days		n								256			*630*			
Christ is the world's true light		n	346	100		456	501	396	456	323			494	432		
Come, let us join our cheerful songs	ga	n	144	120			332	401	810	206		93	349	33	70	
Come, thou long-expected Jesus		s	31	128	133	472	119	24	81	52	100	102	3	335		
Emmanuel, Emmanuel		s										121			83	675
For Mary, mother of our/the Lord		n	360	182			462	238			331		161			
Glorious things of thee are spoken		n	172	205	195	738	646	435	817	494	827	173	362	35	127	691
Great is the darkness		n,s										835		264	742	136
Immanuel, O Immanuel		s										326			233	219
King of glory, King of peace		o	194	375	343		358	494	499	603	715	397	391	178		
Lift up your heads, eternal gates		s				289										
Lift up your heads, O ye gates (Stoodley)		s					337									
Lift up your heads to the coming King		s										418			336	
Lift up your heads, ye mighty gates		s	483		364		131	30	240		105		8			
Long ago, prophets knew	of	s	484	406	375		133	58	83		116		10			867
Magnificat (Rizza)		s		935												
Magnificat (Taizé)		s									335				1445	
Mary, blessed teenage mother		g		442												
Master, speak! Thy servant heareth		o							535			459			386	
No wind at the window		g				287										
O come, O come, Emmanuel	ga/se	g	26	480	522	273	135	32	85	66	112	493	11	338	410	
O holy Mary		g			533											
People look east, the time is near		s		557		281	35									
Soon and very soon		n				749	138					605			1007	460
Tell out, my soul	g,s		422	631	684	286	712	362	86	42	880	631	186	62	520	471
The Lord will come, and not be slow		s	29	655			140	37	245				15			
This child secretly comes in the night		g										690		371	1559	511
We rest on thee/trust in you		n								446		735		510	587	1043
When came in flesh the incarnate Word		g,s											17			
With Mary let my soul rejoice (MCW1)		g														

SONGS FOR CHILDREN

Soon and very soon CH4 749, CH5 138, JP 221, MP 605, SOF 1007, TCB 20, TS 460
When the time is right CAON 913, KS 379

BIBLE READINGS

Psalms 113 [and 126]
1 Samuel 1.1–20
Revelation 22.6–21
Luke 1.39–45

SINGING THE PSALM

Psalm 113 CH4, CRP, CWP, NPCW
    Deiss *Give praise to the Lord* CFE
Psalm 126 CH4, CRP, CWP, H&P, LAU, MCW1, NEP, NPCW
    Farrell *Those who sow in tears* (OCP)#
    Farrell *What marvels the Lord has worked for us* VE#
    Smith *The Lord has done great things for us* (WLP)#
    Ward *What marvels the Lord worked for us* VE#

ANTHEMS AND VOCAL MUSIC

Title	Composer	Voices	E/M/D	Book source	Single sheet publisher
UNISON/TWO PART/HIGH VOICES					
As the deer longs	Hurd	U/SATB#	E	CFE, CG, CH4, LAU	OCP
Come to the well	Farrell	U#	E	GBU	
Jesus Christ, yesterday, today and forever	Toolan	U/SATB	E	LAU	
Maranatha, alleluia!	Ogden	U + descant	E	ACB, CFL, SFL2 (SAMen)	RSCM
The Song of the Tree of Life	Vaughan Williams	U	E	AC2	OUP
THREE/FOUR PARTS					
A tender shoot	Goldschmidt	SATB	M	AFC, TCB	RSCM
Angelus ad virginem	Trad arr Willcocks	SATB	M	CC3	
As the apple tree	Walker	SATB	M		RSCM
As water to the thirsty	Coleman arr Barnard	SATB	E	SC, WIS	
Christ the beginning	P.Moore	SATB	M		Encore
E'en so, Lord Jesus, quickly come	Manz	SATB unacc	M	AFC	Morning Star
Grow in grace	Archer	SATB	E/M	SBS1	RSCM
I am the day	Dove	SATB unacc	M/D		Peters
I heard the voice of Jesus say	Shephard	SATB	M		RSCM
Like as the hart	Croft	SAB	E	CHM	
Like as the hart	Howells	SATB	M	AC4	OUP
Like as the hart	Rawsthorne	SATB	E/M	AWTE	
Sicut cervus	Palestrina	SATB unacc	M	ESM, SL (ATTB)	Chester
Song of Mary	Shephard	SATB	E/M	NOEAB	OUP
Virgin-born, we bow before thee	Waters	SATB	E	NOEAB	
FIVE OR MORE PARTS					
Annunciation	Tavener	SATB + SSAATTBB unacc	M		Chester
Hymn to the Mother of God	Tavener	SSAATTBB unacc	M/D	EAC1	Chester
Hymn to the Virgin	Britten	SSAATTBB unacc	M		B&H

ORGAN MUSIC

PRELUDES

Buxtehude D.   **Four Magnificat Movements** BuxWV 204/205 in *Complete Works* Vol.4 (Bärenreiter) E-M
Caurroy E. du   **Une vierge pucelle** in *The Progressive Organist* Bk.7 (Novello) E/M
Liszt F.   **Ave Maria von Arcadelt** (many editions) E/M
Rawsthorne N.   **The Angel Gabriel** in *The Holly and the Ivy* (Mayhew; 2 and 3-stave versions) E/M(*)
De Grigny N.   **Fugue a 4** (on 'Ave maris stella') p.81 in *Livre d'Orgue* (Kalmus, Schott)

POSTLUDES

Nivers G-G.   **Hymn 'Ave maris stella'** in *Faber Early Organ Series* Vol.8 (Faber) E/M(*)
Chauvet A.   **Offertoire for 4th Sunday in Advent** in *Organ Noëls for the Time of Christmas* (Concordia) E/M(*)
Dupré M.   **For behold, all generations shall call me blessed** No.11 in *Vêpres de Commun de la Sainte Vierge* Op.18 (Gray) M
Ridout A.   **Sortie** ('Salve Regina') from *Messe d'Orgue* (Encore) M

CHRISTMAS DAY YEARS A, B, C

HYMNS AND SONGS

	pos	rdg	AMNS	CAON	CFE	CH4	CH5	CP	H&P	HTC	LAU	MP	NEH	SG	SOF	TS
A great and mighty wonder			43	4			146	41	90	49			21			
Angels from the realms of glory			39	36		324	147	44	92	77	131	35		344	23	631
Away in a manger				776	66	312	149	45	94	72	137	47	22	345	36	36
Behold, the great Creator makes			44	62		308		46		50			23			
Born in the night, Mary's child				80			150		95			62	*602*		1194	
Child in the manger				93	105	314	151			51	141	71				
Child of the stable's secret birth								47	124	53				43		
Christians, awake! Salute the happy morn	mo		36	94				48	96	78		80	24	347	59	653
Cloth for the cradle				107												
Gloria/Glory to God (Taizé)				960		760								110		119
God rest you merry, gentlemen				229	223		158		103	84	129		25	350		
Good Christians all, rejoice with heart				240	229	322	159		104	85	154	196		349	140	
Hark! The herald angels sing			35	266	244	301	160	53	106	59	155	211	26	352	155	144
Holy child, how still you lie										60		236			769	
In the bleak midwinter			42	326	305	305	162	55	107	600	144	337	28	353	243	789
It came upon the midnight clear		n	41	330	314	303	164	56	108	87	135	345	29	354	251	798
Joy to the world!				370	335	320	166	57	77	197	156	393		340	314	305
Let earth and heaven combine									109							1394
Like a candle flame				399								420		370	891	322
Love came down at Christmas				427	397	316	170	59	105	62		451			376	
O come, all ye faithful			34/326	479	520	306	172	61/62	110	597	159	491	30	357	408	380
O little town of Bethlehem			40	508	540	304	174	63	113	88	127	503	32	358	420	393
Of the Father's heart/love/God of God			33/325	486	562	319	175	64/65	79	56	160		33	337		
On Christmas night all Christians sing		n		523	574	294	176		115		134	537				
Once in royal David's city			46	521	577	315	177	66	114	67	128	539	34	359	438	404
See amid the winter's snow/in yonder manger				588	630	313	179	67	117	90	151	588	*604*	360	489	956
See him lying on a bed of straw				589		310		68	118	91		589		361	491	
Silent night/Still the night		n		597	643	309	182	69	112	95	136	597	35	362	498	455
Thou didst leave thy throne			250	683			114	601	154			697	465		555	1015
Thou who wast rich/Lord, you were rich						318	168	72		63		700		356		1018
Unto us a boy is born/is born a son/Jesus Christ the Lord is born				700	755	331	184	73	127	83	152	714	39	355	1574	
What child is this				729	794		202	74			145	749	40		1595	
While shepherds watched			37	745	810	296	188	76	120	94	133	764	42	367	602	1059
Who would think that what was needed				750		295		78								

SONGS FOR CHILDREN

Come and join the celebration CH 247, CH4 321, CH5 152, H&P 97, JP 323, MP 83, SOF 688
Rise up shepherd (There's a star in the east) CAP 116, CH 267

BIBLE READINGS

Morning Psalms 110 and 117
Evening Psalm 8
Isaiah 65.17–25
Philippians 2.5–11 *or* Luke 2.1–20
*(if it has not been used at the
principal service of the day)*

SINGING THE PSALM

Psalm 110 CRP, CWP, NPCW
Psalm 117 CRP, CWP, FGP, NPCW
    Bell *Praise your Maker* PPP
    Berthier *Laudate Dominum* CAON, CFE, CH4, CH5, LAU, TSFP#
    Inwood *Holy is God* HIG, LAU#
    Jakob *Go out to the whole world* C
Psalm 8 CH4, CRP, CWP, FGP, H&P, LAU, NEP, NPCW, PAME
    Bell *O Lord, our Lord, throughout the earth* CH4, PPP
    Walker *I will bless your name* ATNJ# (alternative verses)

ANTHEMS AND VOCAL MUSIC

Title	Composer	Voices	E/M/D	Book source	Single sheet publisher
UNISON/TWO PART/HIGH VOICES					
Christmas Alleluia	Dean	3 part round#	E		OCP
Christmas Gloria	Ledger	U/SATB	E	SBS1	RSCM
Gathering Mass Gloria	Inwood	U#	E	LAU	OCP
Gloria	Salazar	U/SATB#	E		OCP
Glorias 3, 6, 7	Various	U	E	MCW1	
Gloria Carol	Turner	SSA	E	CFL	
Gloria for Christmastide	Proulx	SB#	E		GIA
Gloria of the Bells	Peloquin	U	E		GIA
Gloria round	Brown	U/canon#	E	CFL	
Glory to God/While shepherds watched	Haugen	U/SATB#	E	VE	
THREE/FOUR PARTS					
Fanfare	Shaw	SATB	E		Curwen
Fanfare: Gloria in excelsis Deo	Hubbard	SATB	E		Banks
He came down/Gloria	Trad arr Haugen	SATB/U	E	VE	
Hodie Christus natus est	Poulenc	SATB unacc	D		Salabert
O magnum mysterium	Archer	SATB unacc	M	SC	
On this day earth shall ring	Stewart	SATB	M	AC4	
So long ago one Christmas morn	Scott	SATB unacc	M	SBS1	OUP
The Motcombe Angel's Carol	Ferguson	SATB unacc	M	SBS1	
FIVE OR MORE PARTS					
God is with us	Tavener	SSAATTBBB	M	N	Chester
Hodie	Sweelinck	SSATB unacc	M/D		Novello
Hodie	Whitbourn	SSAATTBB	M		Encore
Hodie Christus natus est	Palestrina	SSAB + ATTB unacc	M/D	CHMO	
On Christmas Day	Rodney Bennett	SAATB unacc	M/D	N	
This day Christ was born	Byrd	SSAATB unacc	M	N	S&B

ORGAN MUSIC

The list of organ music is on page 364.

HYMNS AND SONGS

	pos	rdg	AMNS	CAON	CFE	CH4	CH5	CP	H&P	HTC	LAU	MP	NEH	SG	SOF	TS
A great and mighty wonder		s	43	4			146	41	90	49			21			
A noble flower of Juda		s			5						126					
Above all powers		n										1022			1151	611
All my heart this night rejoices		o						43	91	76						
All praise to thee, for thou, O King divine		n	337	22			684	372	253	204			335			
At/In the name of Jesus		n	148	54	59	458	94	380	74	172	762	41	338	317	32	33
Behold the amazing gift of love		s				478		389	666							
Behold, the great Creator makes		s	44	62		308		46		50			23			
Child in the manger		n,s		93	105	314	151			51	141	71				
Child of the stable's secret birth		s						47	124	53			43			
Cloth for the cradle		s		107												
From east to west, from shore to shore		s		193						99			20			
He came down that we may have love		s				359								116		
In the bleak midwinter		s	42	326	305	305	162	55	107	600	144	337	28	353	243	789
Jesus is the name we honour		n				481						870		122	870	285
Jesus shall take the highest honour		n		360								378		123	302	296
Joy to the world!		s		370	335	320	166	57	77	197	156	393		340	314	305
Laudate omnes gentes/Sing praises, all you peoples (Taizé)											478				1515	
Let earth and heaven combine		s							109							1394
Let us sing to the Lord (Taizé)											689					
Lord, who left the highest heaven		s								97						
Love came down at Christmas		s		427	397	316	170	59	105	62		451			376	
Meekness and majesty		n		448	487	356	228				751	465		395	390	353
Name of all majesty		n		465			102	525		218		481		324	939	
O Christ the same, through all our story's pages		NY		477			103			263			258			
Of the Father's heart/love/God of God		s	33/325	486	562	319	175	64/65	79	56	160		33	337		
The growing limbs of God the Son		g											45			
Thou didst leave thy throne		s	250	683			114	601	154			697	465		555	1015
Thou who wast rich/Lord, you were rich		n,s				318	168	72		63		700		356		1018
Who would think that what was needed		s		750		295		78								

Hymns and songs particularly appropriate for the New Year are marked NY.

SONGS FOR CHILDREN

He came down that we may have love CH4 359, SG 116, VE
O come and join the dance CAON 869, KS2 666, MP 489, TS 381

BIBLE READINGS

Psalm 132
Isaiah 49.7–13
Philippians 2.1–11
Luke 2.41–52

SINGING THE PSALM

Psalm 132 CWP, NPCW

ANTHEMS AND VOCAL MUSIC

Title	Composer	Voices	E/M/D	Book source	Single sheet publisher
UNISON/TWO PART/HIGH VOICES					
At the name of Jesus	Walker	U/SATB#	E	ATNJ	OCP
Bread of life (Christmas verses)	Farrell	U#	E	LAU	OCP
Christ is the world's true light	Stanton	2 part	E	OEAB, OBFA	Banks
Lift on high	Ogden	U/SATB	E		WLP
Love came down at Christmas	Lole	2 part	M		Encore
Love came down at Christmas	Trad arr Grindle	SSSAA unacc	M		Encore
THREE/FOUR PARTS					
Christus factus est	Anerio	SATB unacc	M	ESM, CM1, AWTE	
Grow in grace	Archer	SATB	E/M	SBS1	RSCM
I love the name of Jesus	Thomerson arr Wilson	SATB	E	AWS	
Jesu dulcis memoria	Pott	SATB + solo S unacc	M/D	CN	
Jesu dulcis memoria	Shephard	SATB	E/M		RSCM
Jesu dulcis memoria	Victoria	SATB unacc	M	ESM, NSAC1, NCAB	CMS
Jesu, joy of man's desiring	J.S. Bach	SATB	E	FAB1, NCAB, NOEAB, NSAC1, WFC	RSCM
Jesu, Lamb of God, redeemer	Elgar	SATB	E	OBFA	
Jesu, the very thought of thee	Bairstow	SATB unacc	E/M	FSB7	OUP
Jesu, the very thought of thee	K.Beaumont	SATB unacc	E/M		Encore
Lord, thou hast been our refuge	Bairstow	SATB	D	MTP	
Love came down at Christmas	P.Moore	SATB	E		Encore
The Lamb	Tavener	SATB unacc	M/D	N	Chester
Virgin-born, we bow before thee	Waters	SATB	E	NOEAB	
FIVE OR MORE PARTS					
All hail the power of Jesu's name	Greenhill	SATBB	E/M	SEA2	
Christe adoramus te	Monteverdi	SSATB unacc	M	ESM	
Jesu dulcis memoria	Villette	SSAATTBB unacc	M/D		UMP
O nomen Jesu	Philips	SSATB unacc	M		Mapa Mundi
The Song of Christ's Glory	Ives	SSAATTBB unacc	M/D	WOTC	

ORGAN MUSIC

PRELUDES

Archer J.S.	**Prelude on 'Adeste fideles'** in *Variations on Well-known Hymn Tunes* (Novello) E/M*
Clucas H.	**In dulci jubilo** in *A Coldridge Organ Book* (Animus) E*
Grieg E.	**At the Cradle** Op.68/5 (Peters) E/M
Thiman E.	**Meditation on a theme by Tchaikovsky** in *Four Miniatures* (Schirmer)
Wills A.	**Behold, a virgin shall conceive** No.1 from *Christmas Meditations* (Novello) E/M

POSTLUDES

Chauvet A.	**The Nativity of Our Lord** in *Organ Noëls for the Time of Christmas* (Concordia) E/M*
Fox V.	**Good King Wenceslas** in *At the Organ with Virgil Fox* (Gray) E/M
Moore P.	**Corde natus** in *Christmas Glory* and *Hymn Preludes for the Church Year* Bk.1 (both Mayhew) E/M
West J. E.	**Fantasy on Two Christmas Carols** (Novello) M

HYMNS AND SONGS

	pos	rdg	AMNS	CAON	CFE	CH4	CH5	CP	H&P	HTC	LAU	MP	NEH	SG	SOF	TS
A great and mighty wonder			43	4			146	41	90	49			21			
All my hope on God is founded		NY	336	19	21	192	10	368	63	451	959	16	333	525		620
Angels from the realms of glory	of		39	36		324	147	44	92	77	131	35		344	23	631
Child of the stable's secret birth		s						47	124	53			43			
Christ be the Lord of all our days		NY								256			*630*			
Glorious things of thee are spoken		NY	172	205	195	738	646	435	817	494	827	173	362	35	127	691
God is working his purpose out		NY		221	217	235	481	444	769	191	86	189	495	451	135	128
Great is thy faithfulness		NY		249		153	80	453	66	260		200	*636*	39	147	138
In the bleak midwinter	cm	s	42	326	305	305	162	55	107	600	144	337	28	353	243	789
Laudate Dominum/Sing, praise and bless the Lord (Taizé)				933	346	77	359				698				1514	458
Let earth and heaven combine		s						109								1394
Lord, for the years		NY		409		159	81	81		328	942	428	*619*	602	892	327
Lord, I come to you (Power of your love)		NY										880		689	895	329
Lord, who left the highest heaven										97						
Love came down at Christmas				427	397	316	170	59	105	62		451		376		
O Christ the same, through all our story's pages		NY		477			103			263			258			
O/Our God, our help in ages past		NY	99	494	528	161	537	537	358	37	955	498	417	542	415	905
O Lord of heaven and earth and sea		n	287				363	540	337	287			422	306		
Of the Father's love/heart/God of God		s	33/325	486	562	319	175	64/65	79	56	160		33	337		
Once in royal David's city	ga		46	521	577	315	177	66	114	67	128	539	34	359	438	404
Speak, Lord, in the stillness		n					624			253		608				
Take my life and let it be		NY	249	625	677	502	597	581	705	554	874	624		678	519	468
The first Nowell	of	s		641	692	323	198		119	93	150	644	36		529	974
The love of God comes close		n										940		186		1533
The Son of God his glory hides		n					595									
Thou didst leave thy throne	of		250	683			114	601	154			697		465	555	1015
Thou who wast rich/Lord, you were rich						318	168	72		63		700		356		1018
Through all the changing scenes of life		NY	209	686	740		372	604	73	46		702	467	654	1566	1561
Where is this stupendous stranger?				527				75					41			
Within our darkest night (Taizé)		g		950												

Hymns and songs particularly appropriate for the New Year are marked NY.

SONGS FOR CHILDREN

He came down that we may have love CH4 359, SG 116, VE
See him lying on a bed of straw CAON 589, CH 261, CH4 310, CP 68, H&P 118, HTC 91, JP 214, KS 291, SG 361, SOF 491

BIBLE READINGS

Psalm 135*
Isaiah 41.21 - 42.4
Colossians 1.1–14
Matthew 2.13–23

SINGING THE PSALM

Psalm 135* CWP, NPCW

ANTHEMS AND VOCAL MUSIC

Title	Composer	Voices	E/M/D	Book source	Single sheet publisher
UNISON/TWO PART/HIGH VOICES					
God has chosen me	Farrell arr Weaver	SSA	M	SFL1	
Lully, lullay (g)	Haydn	U/canon	E	CFL	
Out of darkness	Walker	U/SATB#	E	CFE, LAU, OOD	OCP
Peace between nations	Wiggins	2 part	E	OBFA	
Send down the fire of your justice	Haugen	U/SATB#	E	C, TS	GIA
There is a longing in our hearts	Quigley	U/SATB#	E	CH4, LAU, SG	OCP
We rejoice to be God's chosen	Bell	2 part	E	VFLS	
THREE/FOUR PARTS					
Child in the manger	Sanger	SATB (unacc)	E/M	BC, TCB (U + descant)	
Coventry Carol (g)	Trad	SAB unacc	E	CC1	
Lead, kindly light	Harris	SATB	E		OUP
Lully, lulla thou little tiny child (g)	Chilcott	SATB	E/M	BCC	
Lully, lulla, thou little tiny child (g)	Leighton	SATB + solo S unacc	M	N	Novello
O come, ye servants of the Lord	Tye	SATB unacc	E	FAB1	RSCM
O sing unto the Lord	Hinde	SATB + solo SS	M/D	MTP	
Personent hodie (g)	Trad arr Holst	SATB	E	CC2	
Rain down justice (refrain only)	Ogden	SATB	E	SBS1	RSCM
Unto us is born a son (g)	Trad	SATB	E	CC1	
FIVE OR MORE PARTS					
Coventry Carol (g)	Trad arr Allain	SSAATTBB unacc	D	CV	Novello
God has chosen me	Farrell	SSATB unacc	E	GBAN	OCP
Illuminare Jerusalem	Weir	SSAATTBB	D	N	Novello
Nation shall speak peace unto nation	Barry Rose	SSATBB unacc	M	NSAC2	
Vox in Rama (g)	Dering	SATTB	M		CMS/OUP
Vox in Rama (g)	de Wert	SAATB unacc	D		Mapa Mundi

ORGAN MUSIC

PRELUDES

Beechey G.	**Away in a manger** or **Divinum mysterium** in *Six More Easy Carol Preludes* (Fagus) E	
Franck C.	**Offertoire pour la Messe de Minuit** in *Offertoires* (Éditions Marais) E/M	
Luard Selby B.	**A Christmas Pastoral** in *Romantic Organ Music for Christmas and Advent* (Animus) and *Organist's Christmas Album* (Cramer) M	
Marpurg F.	**Trio on 'Ermuntre dich'** in *The Progressive Organist* Bk.6 (Novello) E/M	
Thiman E.	**Christmas Pastorale** ('Quem pastores') in *Times and Seasons* Bk.2 (Novello) E/M	

POSTLUDES

Buttstedt J.H.	**Vom Himmel hoch** in *German Organ and Keyboard Music of the 17th C First Editions* Vol.2 (Bärenreiter) M*	
Buxtehude D.	**Fantasia: Gelobet seist du, Jesu Christ** BuXWV 188 in *Complete Works* Vol.4 (Bärenreiter) M/D	
Kauffmann G.	**Chorale Prelude 'Wir Christenleut'** in *A Graded Anthology for Organ* Bk.4 (Cramer) E*	
Lasky D.	**Trumpet Tune on 'Adeste fideles'** in *An Album of Trumpet Tunes* (Warner) E/M	

HYMNS AND SONGS

	pos	rdg	AMNS	CAON	CFE	CH4	CH5	CP	H&P	HTC	LAU	MP	NEH	SG	SOF	TS
Angels from the realms of glory		s	39	36		324	147	44	92	77	131	35		344	23	631
As with gladness men of old	ga	s	51	49	55	326	189	83	121	99	166	39	47	343	31	639
Behold, the darkness (Arise, shine)		o										36			38	
Bethlehem, of noblest cities/ Earth has many a noble city		s	48	152	79	325	194	85	122		167		48			
Brightest and best of the sons of the morning	se	s	47	85	99	327	190	84	123	338		65	49	346		
Christ is our light!		n				336										
Darkness like a shroud (Arise, shine)		o									110				78	
Eat this bread, drink this cup (Taizé)	cm	n		926	151	661					633				1221	
Hail to the Lord's anointed		s	142	259	241	474	125	87	125	190	102	204	55		150	709
How brightly shines the morning star		s		291	266		192	88					27			
In the bleak midwinter		s	42	326	305	305	162	55	107	600	144	337	28	353	243	789
Jesus come! for we invite you	ga	n								109						
Jubilate Deo, omnis terra (Taizé)		s			336						691					
Laudate omnes gentes/Sing praises, all you peoples (Taizé)		s									478				1515	
Lord, the light of your love is shining		s		419	388	448	195	513			770	445		614	362	335
(O) worship the Lord in the beauty of holiness		o	49	552	560	201	196	89	505	344	169	529	52	204	457	426
One shall tell another (Wine of the kingdom)		n		526	580						541				439	406
Sing of the Lord's goodness		n			654	157	368				713			61		
Songs of thankfulness and praise	ga	n	53	609	661		197	90		98	172		56	376		
The first Nowell		s		641	692	323	198		119	93	150	644	36		529	974
The Lord is my light (Taizé)		s			944											
The race that long in darkness/ The people who in darkness		s	52	656	711	290	199	38	89	71	168		57			
To him we come	of	o								518		709		679	1569	
We come as guests invited	of	n					451			602	630	723				
We three kings of Orient are		s		724	788		201	91			170	740				
We who live by sound and symbol (LFB 108, CG 124)		n														
Why, impious Herod		s											46			
Wise men, they came to look for wisdom		s				328				100				369		

SONGS FOR CHILDREN

He came down that we may have love CH4 359, SG 116, VE
Life for the poor was hard CAON 858, CH 140
Lord, the light of your love is shining CAON 419, CFE 388, CG 110, CH 148, CH4 448, CH5 195, CP 513, KS 237, LAU 770, MP 445, SG 614, SOF 362, TS 335

BIBLE READINGS

Morning Psalms 113 and 132
Evening Psalms 98 and 100
Baruch 4.36 - 5.9 *or* Isaiah 60.1–9
John 2.1–11

SINGING THE PSALM

Psalm 113 CH4, CRP, CWP, NPCW
  Deiss *Give praise to the Lord* CFE
Psalm 132 CWP, NPCW
Psalm 98 BC, CH4, CRP, CWP, FGP, H&P, MCW1, NEH, NPCW, PAME, PFS
  Bell *Sing a new song to the Lord* (GIA)
  Berthier *Psallite Deo* TSFP#
  Berthier *Sing to God* TSFP#
  Foster *All the ends of the earth* VE
  Haas, Haugen *All the ends of the earth* CFE, LAU, VE (GIA)#
  Moore *All the ends of the earth* PCMG
  Wright *All the ends of the earth* VE
Psalm 100 CH4, CRP, CWP, FGP, H&P, LAU, MCW1, NEP, NPCW, PAME
  Berthier *Laudate Dominum* TSFP#
  Deiss *All the earth* C, CFE, LAU #
  Wardle *Enter his gates with thanksgiving* PIW

ANTHEMS AND VOCAL MUSIC

Title	Composer	Voices	E/M/D	Book source	Single sheet publisher
UNISON/TWO PART/HIGH VOICES					
Arise, shine for thy light is come	How	2 part + cong	E/M		Ionian
Brightest and best	Archer	SSA, U	E	ETAS, OBFA	Mayhew
Gather us in (Here in this place)	Haugen	U#	E	CFE, CG, CH4, LAU, SG	GIA
O God, whose loving hand	Self	SB	E		RSCM
The Gentiles shall come	Greene	U	M		RSCM
THREE/FOUR PARTS					
Arise, shine	Shephard	SATB	E/M	SBS1	RSCM
Arise, shine	Stanford	SATB	M	ASA	
Arise, shine, O Jerusalem	Palestrina arr Jackson, Moore	SATB	E	ETAS	
Brightest and best	Thiman	SATB	E	MTH1	Novello
Epiphany Responsory	Lloyd	SATB unacc	E		Encore
From the rising of the sun	Ouseley	SATB	E/M	NCAB, BC	RSCM
Here is the little door	Howells	SATB unacc	M		S&B
Jesus, fount of consolation	Freylinghausen	SATB	E	MTH1	
Look up, sweet babe	Berkeley	SATB + solo S	D		Chester
Magi veniunt ab oriente	Clemens non papa	SATB unacc	M	CM6, ETAS	
O God, who by the leading of a star	Attwood	SATB	M	AC1	
One star	Archer	SATB	E/M	TCB	RSCM
There shall a star from Jacob come	Mendelssohn	SATB	M	NCAB	RSCM
Tribus miraculis	Marenzio	SATB unacc	M	CM1, ETAS	
Tribus miraculis	Palestrina	SATB unacc	M		OUP
FIVE OR MORE PARTS					
Come to the wedding	Whitbourn	SSATB + solo T unacc	E		Encore
Omnes de Saba venient	Handl	SATTB unacc	M	CHMO	RSCM
Surge illuminare	Palestrina	SATB + SATB unacc	M		Joed
Surge illuminare	Simpson	SSAATTBB unacc	M/D	CN	
Videntes stellam	Poulenc	SSAATTBB unacc	D		Salabert
Vinum bonum	Lassus	SSAATTBB unacc	D		Joed

The list of organ music is on page 365.

THE BAPTISM OF CHRIST (THE FIRST SUNDAY OF EPIPHANY) YEAR A

HYMNS AND SONGS

	pos	rdg	AMNS	CAON	CFE	CH4	CH5	CP	H&P	HTC	LAU	MP	NEH	SG	SOF	TS
Awake, awake: fling off the night!		s	342	57	64			334			851					
Baptized in water	gr	g			67	636				381	407			492		
Be thou my vision/Lord, be my vision		s	343	70	74/75	465	643	386	378	545	970	51	339	669	42	50
Breathe on me, breath of God		g	157	84	98	596	293	174	280	226	302	67	342	554	51	57
Christ triumphant, ever-reigning		n		104	113	436	259	398		173	763	77	*613*	319	62	655
Christ, when for us you were baptized		g	442				92	129								
Come down, O love divine	ga	g	156	114	125	489	294	175	281	231	303	89	137	663	1202	71
Crown him with many crowns		g	147	137	139	459	263	166	255	174	321	109	352	321	77	77
Do not be afraid, for I have redeemed you		s		150	147	191					972	115			1213	1183
Fear not, for I am with you		s												105		
God has spoken – by his prophets		n					381		64	248	742	831		225		
God has spoken to his people/Open your ears		s					380			S 13	472	182			131	
Hail to the Lord's anointed		n	142	259	241	474	125	87	125	190	102	204	55		150	709
How firm a foundation		s		292						430		243				186
Laudate Dominum/Sing, praise and bless the Lord (Taizé)				933	346	77	359				698				1514	
Lord of the Church, we pray		s					303			499		442		577	1433	
Name of all majesty		s		465			102	525		218		481		324	939	
No other prophet ever spoke		n												325		901
Now is eternal life		s	402	470			392	152	203				114			
O breath of life, come sweeping through us		g		476		595	305		777	237		488			407	379
O let the Son of God enfold you		g		506								502			419	392
O love, how deep, how broad, how high	of	g	119	516		354	214	118	229				425			
O thou who camest from above		s	233	541	557	625	639	191	745	596		525	431	560	451	416
On Jordan's bank the Baptist's cry	ga/gr	g	27	527	575	334	136	34	84	601	94	538	12	339		
Out of the flowing river		g				335										
River, wash over me		g										581			487	441
Songs of thankfulness and praise				53	609	661	197	90		98	172		56	376		
Spirit divine, attend our prayers		g				583	341	195	327	240		614				
Spirit of the living God (Iverson)	gr	g		615	666	619	310		295	S 23	306	613			510	462
The sinless one to Jordan came		s					200						58			
There is a river		s			722											
To the name of our/that brings salvation		g	121	698	749	471	117	610	80	222			470	72		
When Jesus came to Jordan		g	526				204	93	132							
When John baptized by Jordan's river		g			804						173					

SONGS FOR CHILDREN

Jesus, you're the king KS 222

My God is so big/Our God is so great CAON 547/865/872, CH 169, JP 169, KS 255, SOF 1455, TS 420

BIBLE READINGS

Psalms 46 and 47
Joshua 3.1–8,14–17
Hebrews 1.1–12
Luke 3.15–22

SINGING THE PSALM

Psalm 46 CH4, CWP, H&P, NPCW, PAME
Psalm 47 CH4, CRP, CWP, FGP, H&P, NEH, NPCW, PAME, PFS
Bell *Clap your hands all you nations* CG, MCW1, PPP, SG

ANTHEMS AND VOCAL MUSIC

Title	Composer	Voices	E/M/D	Book source	Single sheet publisher
UNISON/TWO PART/HIGH VOICES					
I'm gonna sing	Trad arr Jones	U/3 part	E	VFLS	
Let the bright seraphim	Handel	S	D		Novello
O for a closer walk with God	Caesar	SSA	M/D	EAC2	
O healing river	Joncas	U/SATB#	E	A, CFE	GIA
The Spirit of the Lord is upon me	Corp	2 part	E	VFLS	
THREE/FOUR PARTS					
Angel voices	Shephard	SATB	M	SC	RSCM
Angels	Lole	SATB	M		Encore
Bless the Lord, all his angels	Frith	SATB	M	FSB7	
Come down, O love divine	Harris	SATB	E/M	FSB9, NCAB, MTH2	Novello
Come down, O love divine	Tadman-Robins	SAMen	E	OBFA	
Deep river	Trad arr Hart	SATB	M	SFC	
Grow in grace	Archer	SATB	E/M	SBS1	RSCM
Holy Spirit, ever dwelling	Howells	SATB	E/M	ETAS	
I heard the voice of Jesus say	Shephard	SATB	M		RSCM
Listen sweet dove	Ives	SATB	M	EAC1, SC	RSCM
O for a closer walk with God	Ives	SATB	M		RSCM
O for a closer walk with God	Stanford	SATB	M	AC1, ASA, BC, OBFA, AOAN1 (SAMen)	RSCM
Spirit of the Lord, come down	Harper	SA(T)B	E	SOTL, SBS1	RSCM
The Baptism of Christ	March	SATB	E	SBS2	
The Spirit of the Lord	Elgar	SATB	M/D	SAEE	RSCM
Tribus miraculis	Marenzio	SATB unacc	M	CM1, ETAS	
FIVE OR MORE PARTS					
Angels	Harvey	SATB + SATB unacc	D		Faber
Deep river (5 Spirituals from 'A Child of our Time')	Tippett	SATB + solo SATB unacc	M/D		Schott
Down to the river to pray	Trad arr Lawson	SATTBB unacc	E/M		Hal Leonard
In splendente nube	Philips	SSATB unacc	M/D		Mapa Mundi

See also the anthems listed for Years B and C (pages 147 and 263).

ORGAN MUSIC

PRELUDES

Bach J.S.	**O Lamm Gottes unschuldig** BWV 618 from the *Orgelbüchlein* (many editions) E
Bach J.S.	**O Lamm Gottes unschuldig** (without BWV) in Bärenreiter Vol.3, Breitkopf Vol.5, Mayhew Vol.2 E/M*
Ley H.G.	**Cradle Song** in *The Oxford Book of Christmas Music* (OUP) E/M
Lloyd Webber W.S.	**Choral 'Jesu dulcis memoria'** in *Four Quiet Interludes* (Bosworth) E/M
Walford Davies H.	**Jesu dulcis memoria** in *A Little Organ Book for Hubert Parry* (Banks) M

POSTLUDES

Bach J.S.	**Christ unser Herr zum Jordan kam** BWV 684 in Novello Vol.16, Bärenreiter Vol.4, Peters Vol.6 M/D
Buxtehude D.	**Christ unser Herr zum Jordan kam** BuxWV 180 in *Complete Works Vol.4* (Bärenreiter) E/M
Pachelbel J.	**O Lamm Gottes unschuldig** in *80 Chorale Preludes* (Peters) E(*)
Peeters F.	**Partita 'Jesu dulcis memoria'** No.5 of *Ten Chorale Preludes on Gregorian Hymns* Op.77 (Peters) M

THE SECOND SUNDAY OF EPIPHANY YEAR A

HYMNS AND SONGS

	pos	rdg	AMNS	CAON	CFE	CH4	CH5	CP	H&P	HTC	LAU	MP	NEH	SG	SOF	TS
A heavenly splendour from on high		n											154			
Behold the Lamb of God (Bell)		g			78						598			190		1145
Captains of the saintly band		n	299	91				212					215			
Come to set us free	gr	n			135						81					
Disposer supreme and judge of the earth		n	298	149				214					216			
Forth in the peace of Christ we go	se		458	187	183	646	454	429		542	853		361	594		
God has spoken – by his prophets		o					381		64	248	742	831		225		
Hail, thou source of every blessing		s											51			
Hail to the Lord's anointed		s	142	259	241	474	125	87	125	190	102	204	55		150	709
How beauteous/gracious are their feet		n	301					220	449							
I cannot tell why he whom angels worship		g		303				54	238	194		266		437	205	199
I come with joy	of	g	473	304		656	421	305	610	408	649		623	469		
I, the Lord of sea and sky (Here I am, Lord)	se	g		332	285	251	581	470			865	857		633	830	246
I will offer up my life		g				503						990		565	851	265
I'll follow my Lord		g											688			
Immortal, invisible, God only wise	ga		199	314	301	132	6	474	9	21	725	327	377	44	234	220
In Christ alone my hope is found		g									1072				1346	1311
Jesus calls us: o'er the tumult		g	312	347		509	584	233	141	104		359	200	668		
Jesus, the name high over all		n		364			99		264	213		385		323	307	298
Just as I am, without one plea	of/cm	g	246	374	339	553	587	308	697	440		396	294	507	316	306
Let earth and heaven combine		s							109							1394
Let us sing to the Lord (Taizé)											689					
Sing of the Lord's goodness					654	157	368				713			61		
Songs of thankfulness and praise		s	53	609	661		197	90		98	172		56	376		
Thanks/Praise to God whose word was spoken		o	423			605	387	584	483	255			438	229		
The eternal gifts of Christ the King		n	297	639							374		213			
Why, impious Herod		s											46			
Will you come and follow me	se	n,g		752	812	533	605	622			877		647	634	1120	
You are the King of glory		g		762	822							790			627	

SONGS FOR CHILDREN

Far and near, hear the call KS 49, MP 982, SG 610, SOF 709, TS 90
Give me joy in my heart/Give me oil in my lamp AMNS 459, CAON 201, CAP 43, CFE 190, CH 55, CH5 570, CP 433, H&P 492, HTC S11, JP 50, KS 66, LAU 722, MP 167, SOF 728

BIBLE READINGS

Psalm 96
Ezekiel 2.1 - 3.4
Galatians 1.11–24
John 1.43–51

SINGING THE PSALM

Psalm 96 CRP, CWP, FGP, H&P, MCW1, NPCW, PAME, PIW
Dean *Proclaim the wonders of the Lord* HG#
Walker *Save us, Lord our God* ATNJ (OCP)

ANTHEMS AND VOCAL MUSIC

Title	Composer	Voices	E/M/D	Book source	Single sheet publisher
UNISON/TWO PART/HIGH VOICES					
A Prayer of St Richard of Chichester	White	2 part	E	BC, OEAB, OBFA	OUP
All that is hidden	Farrell	U/SATB#	E	CFE, LAU, RITH, SFTL	OCP
Centre of my life	Inwood	U/SATB#	E	CFE, CSF, LAU, SG	OCP
Day by day	How	U + 2 part	E	BC, NOEAB (SATB)	RSCM
God has chosen me	Farrell arr Weaver	2 part	E	SFL1	
Make me a light	Wilby	SS	E	EAC2, HP	Chester
Send down the fire of your justice	Haugen	U/SATB#	E	C, TS	GIA
Sent by the Lord am I	Trad arr Weaver	2 part	E	BC	
The Call (Come, my Way)	Vaughan Williams	U	E	NEP	S&B
THREE/FOUR PARTS					
A Prayer of St Richard of Chichester	Archer	SATB	E		RSCM
Come, my Way, my Truth, my Life	Archer	SAB	E/M	AOAN1	Mayhew
Day by day	Godfrey	SATB	E		Encore
Expectans expectavi	Wood	SATB	M		Novello
Go forth and tell!	Ogden	SATB	E/M	SBS2	RSCM
Go forth into the world in peace	Rutter	SATB	E/M	JRA	OUP
Here I am, Lord	Schutte arr Archer	SATB	E	MTH1	
I give you my hands, Lord	Tambling	SAMen unacc	M	AOAN1	
Immortal, invisible	Mold	SATB	E		Encore
Just as I am	Chilcott	SATB	M	BCA	OUP
Light of the world	Elgar	SATB	M/D	AWTE, SAEE	Novello
Now let us from this table rise	Henderson	SATB	E	SBS1	RSCM
Take up your cross	Corp	SATB	E	SBS1, WOTC	RSCM
The Call	Lloyd	SATB unacc	M		RSCM
FIVE OR MORE PARTS					
Beati quorum via	Stanford	SSATBB unacc	M	ASA, WFC	RSCM
The Twelve	Walton	SSAATTBB	D		OUP

ORGAN MUSIC

PRELUDES

Groves R.   **St Denio** in *12 Hymn-Tune Preludes* Set 2 (Novello) E(*)
Hurford P.   **On a Rouen Church Melody** in *Five Chorale Preludes* (OUP) E/M
Praetorius M.   **Christum wir sollen loben schon** in *Complete Works* (Breitkopf) E/M
Walther J.G.   **Christum wir sollen loben schon: Partitas a or b**, No.5 in *Orgelchoräle* (Bärenreiter) E/M*

POSTLUDES

Dyson G.   **Postlude** from *Prelude and Postlude* (Novello) M
Fink C.   **First movement 'Jesu, meine Freude'** from **Sonata No.3** Op.19 in *The Mendelssohn School* (McAfee) M
Groves R.   **Martyrs** in *Six Scottish Hymn-Tune Preludes* (Novello) E(*)
Near G.   **Salzburg** in *Choraleworks* Set 1 (Aureole) E/M
Willan H.   **Prelude on 'Old 104th'** in *Ten Hymn Preludes* Set 2 (Peters) M

HYMNS AND SONGS

	pos	rdg	AMNS	CAON	CFE	CH4	CH5	CP	H&P	HTC	LAU	MP	NEH	SG	SOF	TS
Christ, from whom all blessings flow		u							764	491						
Confitemini Domino (Taizé)				925	137						701					
Give thanks with a grateful heart		g		202	189	180	352					170		108	124	118
God is love, and where true love is		u	465		214		520	441	757		242		513			
God of glory, we exalt your name		g										191			137	130
God of grace and God of glory		g	367	225			533	448	712	324		192		574	139	
Hark, my soul! It is the Lord/Christian, do you hear		g	244	264			569	457	521	472		209	637			
I believe in Jesus (Nelson)		n		301								264		333	203	195
I cannot tell why he, whom angels worship		g		303				54	238	194		266		437	205	199
I come with joy	of	u	473	304		656	421	305	610	408	649		623	469		
Jesus, Lord, we look to thee	gr	u	380				489		759				481			
Jesus shall reign where'er the sun		g	143	359		470	97	490	239	516	322	379	388	45	301	1376
Jesus, the name high over all	ga	g		364			99		264	213		385		323	307	298
Jesus, united by thy grace		u							773							
Laudate Dominum/Sing, praise and bless the Lord (Taizé)				933	346	77	359				698				1514	
Lord of the Church, we pray	of	u					303			499		442		577	1433	
Lord, you are more precious than silver		n										447			368	339
O for a thousand tongues to sing		g	125	485			352	104	534	744	219	496	415	55	412	383/1452
O thou, who at thy Eucharist didst pray/O Christ	of	u	265	540	556	669	438	318	779	420	833		302	476		
One is the body	gr	u				679								280		
Seek ye first the kingdom of God	gr	g		590	633	641	596		138		820	590			493	447
Send me, Lord (Thuma mina)	se	g			636	800							694			
Send me out from here	se	g										594			996	
The Church's one foundation	of	u	170	636	688	739	528	585	515	501	830	640	484	581	525	477
The kingdom of God is justice and joy		g		646	701			591	139	333	821	651		184		
We have a gospel to proclaim	se	s	431	716	778	363	491	612	465	519	852	728	486	331	1583	
We walk by faith		n			789						284					
Why, impious Herod		s											46			
Will you come and follow me	se	g		752	812	533	605	622			877		647	634		1120

Hymns and songs especially suitable for celebrations of the Week of Prayer for Christian Unity are marked 'u'.

SONGS FOR CHILDREN
Come and praise the Lord our king CAP 21, CFE 121, HTC S8, JP 34
The joy of the Lord is my strength JP 240

BIBLE READINGS

Psalm 33*

Ecclesiastes 3.1–11

1 Peter 1.3–12

Luke 4.14–21

SINGING THE PSALM

Psalm 33* CRP, CWP, FGP, H&P, LAU, NEH, NPCW, PAME, PFS

Walker *Lord, be with us* OOD#

ANTHEMS AND VOCAL MUSIC

Title	Composer	Voices	E/M/D	Book source	Single sheet publisher
UNISON/TWO PART/HIGH VOICES					
And I pray thee	Hubbard	SSA	M	SFJ	Banks
My lips shall speak of thy praise	Greene	SS	M		Banks
Praise to you, O Christ our Saviour	Farrell	U#	E	CFE, LAU, RITH, WYP	OCP
Take the word of God with you	Walker	U/SAB#	E	CFE, CIH, LAU	OCP
The Spirit of the Lord is upon me (g)	Corp	2 part	E	VFLS	
THREE/FOUR PARTS					
Blessed be the God and Father	S.S.Wesley	SATB	M	FAB1, NCAB, SC	RSCM
Christ was the Word	Maxim	SATB unacc	E	SBS2	
Go forth and tell!	Ogden	SATB	E	SBS2	
In God's word will I rejoice	Purcell	SAB	M	TPS, SFL2	
O for a thousand tongues	Shephard	SATB	M/D		RSCM
O sing joyfully	Batten	SATB unacc	E	SCAB, WFC	RSCM
Teach me, O God	Camidge	SAB	E	CHM	
Teach me, O Lord	Attwood	SATB	E	NOEAB	RSCM
The heavens declare	Radcliffe	SATB unacc	M		Encore
The Spirit of the Lord (g)	Elgar	SATB	M	SAEE	RSCM
Thy word is a lantern	Purcell	SATB	M	APA	Novello
To everything there is a season	Weaver	SATB + flute	M/D		WLP
Waiting for the word	Skellern	SATB	E/M		RSCM
FIVE OR MORE PARTS					
Open thou mine eyes	Rutter	SSATB unacc	M		OUP
See, see the word is incarnate	Gibbons	SAATB	M		S&B
Sing joyfully	Byrd	SAATB unacc	M/D	OBTA	
Teach me, O Lord	Byrd	SAATB	M	OBTA	OUP

ORGAN MUSIC

Bach/Stockmeier **Jesu, meine Freude** BWV 753 in *The Organ Funeral Album* (Bärenreiter) E*

Bach J.S. **Jesu, meine Freude** BWV 713 in Novello Vol.18, Bärenreiter Vol.3, Peters Vol.6 M/D*

Clérambault L-N. **Duo** *and/or* **Trio** from *Livre d'Orgue: Suite du Deuxième Ton* (Schola Cantorum, Kalmus) E/M*

Langlais J. **Allegretto** No.2 of *Contrastes* (Combre)

Willan H. **Gardiner** (aka 'Fulda') in *36 Short Preludes and Postludes* Set 2 (Peters) E

POSTLUDES

Bach J.S. **Christum wir sollen loben schon** BWV 696 in Novello Vol.18, Bärenreiter Vol.3, Peters Vol.5 E/M

Cavazzoni G. **In Epiphania: Crudelis Herodes** in *Second Organ Book* (Schott, Kalmus) E*

Clérambault L-N. **Caprice sur les grand jeux** from *Livre d'Orgue: Suite du Deuxième Ton* (Schola Cantorum, Kalmus) E/M(*)

Sumsion H. **Procession** in *Gloucester Organ Album* (Novello) M

THE FOURTH SUNDAY OF EPIPHANY YEAR A

HYMNS AND SONGS

	pos	rdg	AMNS	CAON	CFE	CH4	CH5	CP	H&P	HTC	LAU	MP	NEH	SG	SOF	TS
Adoramus te, Domine (Taizé)				921	11		345				667			208		
As Jacob with travel was weary one day		o	435	775				378	444							
At/In the name of Jesus	of	g	148	54	59	458	94	380	74	172	762	41	338	317	32	33
Be still, for the presence of the Lord		g		67	72	189	325	383			720	50	629	7	40	47
Bless the Lord, my soul (Taizé)				923	81		1				813			105	676	56
Brother, sister, let me serve you/ Will you let me be your servant		n		88	813	694	517	393			924			619	54	
Christ is our cornerstone		o,g	161	98			327	395		564			206	14		
Christ is the world's true light			346	100		456	501	396	456	323			494	432		
Come, let us join our cheerful songs	ga		144	120			332	401	810	206		93	349	33	70	
Firmly I believe and truly	of	g	118	174	173		320	426		429	962		360	287		
God is here! As we his people		o	464				330	301	653	560	470					
Hail to the Lord's anointed		s	142	259	241	474	125	87	125	190	102	204	55		150	709
Here in this place (Gather us in)	ga	o			253	623					475			4		
How sweet the name of Jesus sounds	gr	o	122	297		461	92	467	257	211		251	374	42	194/ 782	190/ 1273
I give you all the honour		g		308			574					271			210	203
Jesus Christ is waiting		g		349	323	360					889			624	1381	1360
Jesus, the name high over all		g		364			99		264	264		385		323	307	298
Jesus, we celebrate your victory		n										387			309	299
Join all the glorious names						460		493	78	214		392	639	46	313	848
King of glory, King of peace	gr	g	194	375	343		358	494	499	603	715	397	391	178		
O for a thousand tongues to sing		g	125	485		352	104	534	744	219		496	415	55	412	383/ 1452
O thou who camest from above		n	233	541	557	625	639	191	745	596		525	431	560	451	416
Son of God, eternal Saviour			132				527	573		102			498			
The race that long in darkness/ The people who in darkness		s	52	656	711	290	199	38	89	71	168		57			
There is a Redeemer		g		658		559	112					673		396	544	492
Thine arm, O Lord, in days of old/Your hands		g	285	671				347	397		431		324			
This day the first of days was made													53			
Through all the changing scenes of life		ps	209	686	740		372	604	73	46		702	467	654	1566	1561
Thy/Your hand, O God, has guided		o	171	689	741	511	529	606	784	536	876	705	485	649	1065	
To be in your presence		o		694								951		523	1067	524
We bow down and confess		o										1123		219	1084	1028
We love the place, O God		o	160	718			343	211		558		731	471			
When Christ was lifted from the earth/Dear Christ, uplifted		n	525	142						335				453		

SONGS FOR CHILDREN

As Jacob with travel was weary AMNS 435, CAON 775, CP 378, H&P 444
God is good CAON 214, CH4 178, JP 55, KS 74, MP 185, SOF 132, TS 124

BIBLE READINGS

Psalm 34*
Genesis 28.10–22
Philemon 1–16
Mark 1.21–28

SINGING THE PSALM

Psalm 34* C, CRP, CWP, FGP, H&P, LAU, MCW1, NPCW, PAME
　Bell *I will always bless the Lord* C, CH4, IAMB, OITB
　Dean *Taste and see* CFE, WYP#
　Ogden *Taste and see* (WLP)
　Rizza *I will bless the Lord* LIOD#
　Schutte *Ever on my lips* C (OCP)#
　Walker *Taste and see* CSF (OCP)#

ANTHEMS AND VOCAL MUSIC

Title	Composer	Voices	E/M/D	Book source	Single sheet publisher
UNISON/TWO PART/HIGH VOICES					
Christ is the world's true light	Stanton	2 part	E	OEAB, OBFA	
Eins bitte ich vom Herren	Schütz	2 part	M	AC2	
I was glad	Hubbard	SA	M	SFJ	Banks
The Servant Song	Gillard arr Ogden	U + descant	E	SFL1	
We love the place, O God	Brahms	SS	M		Novello
THREE/FOUR PARTS					
Behold, the tabernacle of God	Harris	SATB	E/M		RSCM
Christ the Word	Vann	SATB	M	STS	
How lovely are thy dwellings	Brahms	SATB	M/D		RSCM
How lovely are thy dwellings	Self	SAB	E		RSCM
I will praise God because of his word	Purcell	SATB	E/M	TPS	
In God's word will I rejoice	Purcell	SAB	M	TPS, SFL2	
Locus iste	Bruckner	SATB unacc	E/M	NCAB	RSCM
O how amiable	Vaughan Williams	SATB	E/M	NCAB, AC4, OEAB	OUP
Teach me, O God	Moger	SAB	E		RSCM
Teach me thy way, O Lord	Purcell	SATB	M	TPS	
Terribilis est locus iste	G. Malcolm	SATB	M		Mayhew
The Doctrine of Wisdom	Mathias	SATB	M		OUP
This is truly the house of God	Rubbra	SATB	M		Lengnick
Thy word is a lantern	Purcell	SATB	M	APA	Novello
Waiting for the word	Skellern	SATB	E		RSCM
We love the place, O God	Sumsion	SATB	M/D		RSCM
Where shall wisdom be found?	Carter	SATB	M/D		OUP
FIVE OR MORE PARTS					
I was glad	Parry	SATB + SATB	M/D		RSCM
I was glad	Purcell	SSATB	M/D	APA	Faber, CMS
In medio Ecclesiae	Joubert	SSAATBB unacc	D	CN	OUP
Lo! God is here!	P.Moore	SSAATTBB	M/D		Faber

See also the anthems listed for the Third Sunday of Epiphany.

ORGAN MUSIC

PRELUDES

Bach J.S.　**Sanctify us by thy goodness** (Cantata 22) in *The Oxford Book of Wedding Music* E/M
Coleman H.　**Quam dilecta** (mistitled 'St Flavian') No.1 of *Two Interludes* (Novello) E/M
Couperin F.　**Dialogue sur le voix humaine** No.XII from *Messe pour les Paroisses* (Kalmus) E/M*
Howells H.　**Psalm-Prelude** Set 1 No.1 (Novello) M
Wesley S.　**Allegretto in D** No.24 in *Organ Works* Vol.10 (Fagus) E*

POSTLUDES

Archer J.S.　**Improvisation on 'Blaenwern'** (Novello) M/D
Buxtehude D.　**Praeludium in C** BuxWV 137 in *Complete Works* Vol.1 (Bärenreiter) M
De Grigny N.　**Dialogue** p.46 in *Livre d'Orgue* (Kalmus, Schott) E/M(*)
Johnson D.　**Trumpet Tune in E flat** in *An Album of Postludes* (OUP) E/M

THE PRESENTATION OF CHRIST IN THE TEMPLE (CANDLEMAS, 2 FEBRUARY) YEARS A, B, C

HYMNS AND SONGS

	pos	rdg	AMNS	CAON	CFE	CH4	CH5	CP	H&P	HTC	LAU	MP	NEH	SG	SOF	TS
Angel voices, ever singing		o,n	163	37	45	498	346	377	484	307	724	34	336	27	24	
Angels from the realms of glory	ga	s	39	36		324	147	44	92	77	131	35		344	23	631
Christ is made the sure foundation/Blessèd city		n	332ii	97	109	200	326	207/208	485	559	456	73	205	572	1199	654
Christ is our cornerstone		n	161	98			327	395		564			206	14		
Christ whose glory fills the skies	mo	s	4	105		578	52	2	457	266	670	79	234	170	1200	
Come and be light for our eyes		s			120											
Come to us, creative Spirit		n				612	453		377	308				621		
Fairest Lord Jesus		s				463	88			209		823	634	199		680
Faithful vigil ended		s	453	157			691	360		55		125	44			
For I'm building a people of power		o		181	174							151			111	109
Glorious things of thee are spoken		n	172	205	195	738	646	435	817	494	827	173	362	35	127	691
Great is the darkness		s									835		264		742	136
Hail, gladdening light	ev	s	8	253		219	699	16	644	275						
Hail to the Lord who comes	of	s	314				191	94	126				157			
Jesus, hope of every nation		s								58				336		
Join all the glorious names		e				460		493	78	214		392	639	46	313	848
Longing for light (Christ, be our light)		s				543					883					1409
Lord, now let your servant		s								611						
Lord, the light of your love is shining		s		419	388	448	195	513			770	445		614	362	335
Lord, who left the highest heaven		s								97						
Misericordias Domini/From age to age (Taizé)					489											
Now, Lord! According to thy word		s				333										
O gladsome light, O grace	ev	s					707	17			677		247			
Of the Father's heart/love/God of God	ga	s	33/325	486	562	319	175	64/65	79	56	160		33	337		
Sing how the age-long promise		s											156			
The/All earth was dark (Lights to the world)		s										8/643				
The light of Christ		s			703						747	652			1026	
The Lord is my light (Taizé)				944												
Virgin-born, we bow before thee		s	311	701			185	244					187			
We bow down and confess	cm	s										1123		219	1084	1028
When candles are lighted		s					203	80								
When Mary brought her treasure		s				332										
Where high the heavenly temple stands		o	130			451	291			184						

SONGS FOR CHILDREN

Born in the night, Mary's child CAON 80, CH 246, CH5 150, H&P 95, JP 313, MP 62, SOF 1194
Lord, the light of your love is shining CAON 419, CFE 388, CG 110, CH 148, CH4 448, CH5 195, CP 513, KS 237, LAU 770, MP 445, SG 614, SOF 362, TS 335

BIBLE READINGS

Morning Psalms 48 and 146
Evening Psalms 122 and 132
Haggai 2.1–9
John 2.18–22

SINGING THE PSALM

Psalm 48 CWP, NPCW
Psalm 146 CRP, CWP, H&P, MCW1, NPCW, PAME
    Dean *Come, Lord, and save us* VE#
    Farrell *Common Psalm* CBL#
    Foster *Come, Lord* VE
Psalm 122 CH4, CRP, CWP, FGP, H&P, LAU, MCW1, NPCW, PAME, PFS
    Cortez *I rejoiced* VE#
    Dean *I rejoiced* SFTL, VE (OCP)#
    Farrell *I rejoiced* CBL, CG, CH4, LAU, MCW1#
    Foley *I rejoiced* VE
    Hurd *Let us go rejoicing* C
    Walker *I rejoiced* OOD (OCP)#
Psalm 132 CWP, NPCW

ANTHEMS AND VOCAL MUSIC

Title	Composer	Voices	E/M/D	Book source	Single sheet publisher
UNISON/TWO PART/HIGH VOICES					
Settings of 'Nunc dimittis' for choir and congregation	Various	U/SATB	E	C, CWP, MCW1, LAU, NEP, VE	
Give us light	Vas	2 part	E	VFLS	
Light of the world	Dankworth	U	E/M	HP	
Make me a light	Wilby	SS	E	EAC2, HP	Chester
O Trinity of blessed light	S. & A.Barrett	U	E	SBS2	RSCM
Prayer for the Blessing of Light	Archer	U	E	ETAS	
This little light of mine	Trad arr Isaacs	2 part	E	VFLS	
THREE/FOUR PARTS					
Behold, the tabernacle of God	Harris	SATB	E/M		RSCM
Ecce beatam lucem	Dove	SATB	M/D		Faber
Hodie beata virgo	Byrd	SATB unacc	M	ETAS	
Lift up your heads	Jackson	SATB	M/D	AC4	
Lift up your heads	Marsh	SAMen	E	NAB2, AOAN1	
Lift up your heads	Mathias	SATB	M/D	AC1	OUP
Light of the world	Elgar	SATB	M/D	AWTE, SAEE	Novello
Lighten our darkness	Stanford	SATB	E/M		RSCM
New light has dawned	Barnard	SATB	E	TCB	
O rex gloriae	Marenzio	SATB unacc	M	CM1	
O thou the central orb	Wood	SATB	M	AC4, AFC, SC	RSCM
Phos hilaron	Flood	SATB	M/D	ETAS	
The Lord of life and glory	Trad arr Barnard	SATB	E	TCB	
The Lord is my light and my salvation	Noon	SATB	M	SBS1	RSCM
FIVE OR MORE PARTS					
Hymn to the Creator of Light	Rutter	SATB + SATB unacc	D		OUP
Lift up your heads, O ye gates	Leighton	SSATB	M/D		Novello
Maria das Jungfräulein/When to the Temple Mary went	Eccard	SSATBB unacc	M	NCAB (English only), ETAS	Novello
Senex puerum portabat	Byrd	SSATB unacc	M	CM2	Chester

The list of organ music is on page 366.

PROPER 1 (SUNDAY BETWEEN 4 AND 10 FEBRUARY INCLUSIVE) YEAR A

(if earlier than the Second Sunday before Lent)

HYMNS AND SONGS

	pos	rdg	AMNS	CAON	CFE	CH4	CH5	CP	H&P	HTC	LAU	MP	NEH	SG	SOF	TS
A stranger once did bless the earth		g	335													
Alleluia! Sing to Jesus	of		262	12	37	445	398	278	592	170	644	207	271	458	153	616
As we are gathered	ga			47		197						38		28		29
At even, ere/when the sun was set		g	9	50			65	12	142	315		43	243	487		
Beauty for brokenness		o		60		259	494					806		263	664	37
Christ for the world we sing!		g	344					394	789							
Christ's is the world in which we move		o		101	115	724					882			252	685	1165
God of freedom, God of justice		o		224		263		447								
Guide me, O thou great Jehovah/Redeemer	se	g	214	252	233	167	647	455	437	528	960	201	368	638	148	708
Heaven shall not wait		o		272		362										151
Help us to help each other/Jesus, united by thy grace	gr	n	374	275			523	461	773	540						
Inspired by love and anger		o		325	311	253										
Jesus, Lord, we look to thee		n	380					489	759				481			
Longing for light (Christ, be our light)		o				543					883					1409
Make me a channel of your peace		n		437	478	528	503	519	776	S 19	898	456		691	381	348
May the mind of Christ my Saviour	gr	n		447		536	636	521	739	550		463		671	1448	887
My Lord, what love is this		n		462	500		230					476		194	398	370
O for a closer walk with God		n	231	483		552	637	532		368		494	414		951	903
O Jesu, King most wonderful		n	120ii				106	539	269	484			386			
O Lord, hear my prayer (Taizé)	ps			938	542		620				929	908		246	423	394
Send down the fire of your justice		o														1495
The kingdom of God is justice and joy		o		646	701			591	139	333	821	651		184		
What does the Lord require?		o	432		796		498		414		893					
When a knight won his spurs		n		731			616								1601	
When I feel the touch of your hand upon my life		g		734								753			594	570
When Jesus walked upon this earth		g								317						
Where love and loving-kindness dwell		n	528				531									
You, living Christ, our eyes behold		g	533					333					487			

SONGS FOR CHILDREN

All of my heart CAON 770, CH 9, KS 6
I am a new creation CAON 298, CFE 270, KS 115, MP 254, SOF 197, TS 191
When a knight won his spurs CAON 731, CAP 50, CP 616, KS 371, SOF 1601

BIBLE READINGS

Psalms [1, 3 and] 4
Amos 2.4–16
Ephesians 4.17–32
Mark 1.29–39

SINGING THE PSALM

Psalm 1 CH4, CRP, CWP, FGP, H&P, MCW1, NPCW, PAME, PIW
  Bell *Happy is the one* PPP
Psalm 3 CWP, NPCW
Psalm 4 CFE, CH4, CRP, CWP, FGP, H&P, LAU, MCW1, NPCW
  Gelineau *A desire fills our being* TSFP#
  Ogden *Lift up the light of your face* (WLP)

ANTHEMS AND VOCAL MUSIC

Title	Composer	Voices	E/M/D	Book source	Single sheet publisher
UNISON/TWO PART/HIGH VOICES					
Create in me a new heart	Ogden	U	E		WLP
Faith, hope and love	Ogden	2 part	E	SBS1	RSCM
Give us a new heart, O God	Walker	U#	E	OOD	OCP
Give us, Lord, a new heart	Farrell	U/SATB#	E/M	LAU, RITH, SLG	OCP
I give you a new commandment	Aston	2 part	E	BC, NOEAB	RSCM
Jesu, Jesu, fill us with your love	Trad arr Weaver	2 part	E	SFL1	
Love one another	S.S.Wesley	S	E	BC	RSCM
Ubi caritas	Lole	SS	E		Encore
THREE/FOUR PARTS					
A new commandment	Anon arr Leddington Wright	SATB	E	SWAMS	
A new commandment	Parshall	SATB unacc	E	WFC	
A new commandment	Shephard	SATB	E	AWTE	RSCM
Give thanks to God	Trad Botswanan arr Bullard	SATB	E	OBFA	
Greater love	Ireland	SATB	M	AC4	S&B
I give to you a new commandment	Nardone	SATB	E/M	SBS1	RSCM
In the heart where love is abiding	Barnard	SATB	E	AWTE, BC	RSCM
O for a thousand tongues (g)	Shephard	SATB	M/D		RSCM
Praise the Lord, my soul	S.S.Wesley	SATB + solo S	M/D	MTP	
Though I speak with the tongues of men	Bairstow	SATB	M	WFC	OUP
Ubi caritas	Ives	SATB unacc	M	SC	
Ubi caritas	Lauridsen	SATB unacc	M		Faber
Ubi caritas	Mawby	SATB	E		Mayhew
We cannot measure how you heal (g)	Bell arr Archer	SATB	E	BC	RSCM
FIVE OR MORE PARTS					
Love one another	Carter	SSAATTBB	M/D		OUP
Ubi caritas	Berkeley	SSATB unacc	D		Chester
Ubi caritas	Duruflé	SAATTBB unacc	M		Durand
When I needed a neighbour	Carter arr Rose	SATB + SATB	E/M	MTH1	

ORGAN MUSIC

PRELUDES

Bédard D. **Andante** No.2 of *Trois Voluntaries* (Cheldar) E/M
Groves R. **Caithness** in *Six Scottish Hymn-Tune Preludes* (Novello) E(*)
Tambling C. **Folk Tune** ('Dream Angus') in *An Organ Miscellany* (Mayhew) E
Wills A. **Elegy** (Fagus) M
Wood C. **Andante** from *A Little Organ Book for Hubert Parry* (Banks) E/M

POSTLUDES

Bédard D. **Allegro** No.3 of *Trois Voluntaries* (Cheldar) E/M
Nixon J. **Hyfrydol** in *Hymn Tune Preludes* (Fagus) E/M
Telemann G.P. **Allein Gott in der Höh' sei Ehr'** in *12 Easy Chorale Preludes* (Kalmus, Peters) E*
Thiman E. **Finale in D minor** in *An Easy Album* (OUP) E/M

PROPER 2 (SUNDAY BETWEEN 11 AND 17 FEBRUARY INCLUSIVE) YEAR A
(if earlier than the Second Sunday before Lent)

HYMNS AND SONGS

	pos	rdg	AMNS	CAON	CFE	CH4	CH5	CP	H&P	HTC	LAU	MP	NEH	SG	SOF	TS
A man there lived in Galilee		g	334	28												
Amazing grace – how sweet the sound				29	40	555	642	375	215	28	846	31	626	26	19	18
As sons of the day and daughters of light		n								490				570		
Awake, awake: fling off the night!	gr	n	342	57	64			334			851					
Awake, my soul, and with the sun	mo	n	1	58		210	51	1	632	264		804	232	618		
Beauty for brokenness		o		60		259	494					806		263	664	37
Christ is the world's true light		n	346	100		456	501	396	456	323			494	432		
Christ whose glory fills the skies	mo	n	4	105		578	52	2	457	266	670	79	234	170	1200	
Christ's is the world in which we move		o		101	115	724					882			252	685	1165
For the healing of the nations		o	361	186	179	706	496	427	402		886			261	1235	
From thee/you all skill and science flow		g	286				512	345	389	310						
God of freedom, God of justice		o		224		263		447								
Great is the darkness		n										835		264	742	136
In God alone my soul (Taizé)															813	
Let us sing to the Lord (Taizé)		n									689					
Light of the world, shine your light		n													342	
Longing for light (Christ, be our light)		o				543					883					1409
O Lord, the clouds are gathering		o				708	538					509		255	429	399
Restore, O Lord, the honour of your name		o		582		469						579		274	483	439
Send down the fire of your justice		o														1495
The/All earth was dark (Lights to the world)		n										8/643				
The kingdom of God is justice and joy		o		646	701			591	139	333	821	651		184		
Thou/God, whose almighty word		n	180	684	738	112	324	267	29	506	887	699	466	597	557	
To God be the glory!				695	745	512	373	609	463	584	719	708		71	559	526
When Jesus walked upon this earth		g								317						
Who can sound the depths of sorrow		o		747								766		257	604	579
Within our darkest night (Taizé)				950												
Ye that know the Lord is gracious		n	175			642	493	628					477			

SONGS FOR CHILDREN

Do what you know is right CAON 791, CH 38, KS2 448
Praise and thanksgiving let everyone bring CAON 878, CH 174, CH4 170, JP 447

BIBLE READINGS

Psalms [7 and] 13
Amos 3.1–8
Ephesians 5.1–17
Mark 1.40–45

SINGING THE PSALM

Psalm 7 CWP, NPCW
Psalm 13 CH4, CWP, NPCW, PAME
Haugen *How long, O God* (GIA)#

ANTHEMS AND VOCAL MUSIC

Title	Composer	Voices	E/M/D	Book source	Single sheet publisher
UNISON/TWO PART/HIGH VOICES					
Christ, be our light	Farrell	U#	E	CBL, CG, CH4, LAU, TS	OCP
Come and be light for our eyes	Haas	U/SAMen	E	CFE	
I'm gonna sing	Trad arr Jones	3 part + descant	E	VFLS	
Let all creation sing	Ogden	U + descant	E/M	SFL2	WLP
Make me a light	Wilby	SS	E	EAC2, HP	Chester
The Spirit of the Lord is upon me	Corp	2 part	E	VFLS	
THREE/FOUR PARTS					
Ad te levavi oculos meos	Palestrina	SATB unacc	M		Joed
As truly as God is our Father	Mathias	SATB	M/D	ETAS	OUP
Be thou my vision	Chilcott	SATB	M	NOEAB, BCA	OUP
Be thou my vision	Rutter	SATB	M		OUP
Exsultate justi	Viadana	SATB	E/M	ESM, SL (ATTB)	
Give thanks to God	Trad Botswanan arr Bullard	SATB	E	OBFA	
In a world where people walk in darkness	Trad arr Harper	SATB unacc	E	LOL	
Let their celestial concerts all unite	Handel	SATB	M		Novello
O Jesus Christ, mein Lebens Licht	J.S. Bach	SATB	M	ESM	
O Master, let me walk with thee	Ledger	SATB	E		Encore
O thou the central orb	Gibbons	SATB	M		S&B
O thou the central orb	Wood	SATB	M	AC4, AFC, SC	RSCM
Out of darkness	Walker	U/SATB#	E	CFE, LAU, OOD	OCP
The Lord is my light and my salvation	Noon	SATB	M	SBS1	RSCM
The secret of Christ	Shephard	SATB	M	NCAB	RSCM
We cannot measure how you heal (g)	Bell arr Archer	SATB	E	BC	RSCM
Wings of the morning	Rutter	SATB	M		OUP
With loving hands (g)	Tredinnick	SATB	E	WIS	
FIVE OR MORE PARTS					
Open thou mine eyes	Rutter	SSATB unacc	M		OUP
Vox Dei	Wilby	SATB + SATB unacc	M/D	EAC1	

ORGAN MUSIC

PRELUDES

Alain J.	**Ballade en mode Phrygien** in *Complete Works* Bk.3 (Leduc) E/M
Gibbons O.	**A Voluntary of Four Parts** in *Organ Music for Manuals* Bk.6 (OUP) M*
Hesford B.	**Amazing grace** (Fentone) E
Schneider J.G.	**Elevation** in *Dresdner Orgelmusik 19 C* (Breitkopf) E/M
Thiman E.	**In-Voluntary for Sunday Morning** ('Morning Hymn') in *Times and Seasons* Bk.2 (Novello) E/M

POSTLUDES

Floyd A.E.   **Sketch in F** in *Musical Miniatures* (Mayhew) E/M
Kellner J.C.   **Präludium in C** in *Orgelmusik um J.S.Bach* (Breitkopf) E/M
Lebègue N.   **Offertoire in B flat** p.26 in *Offertoires from Troisième Livre d'Orgue* (Hawthorns) or p.190 in *Complete Works* Vol.3 (Kalmus) E/M(*)
Peeters F.   **Deus tuorum militum** in *30 Chorale Preludes on Gregorian Hymns* Bk.2 (Peters) M/D

PROPER 3 (SUNDAY BETWEEN 18 AND 24 FEBRUARY INCLUSIVE) YEAR A

(if earlier than the Second Sunday before Lent)

HYMNS AND SONGS

	pos	rdg	AMNS	CAON	CFE	CH4	CH5	CP	H&P	HTC	LAU	MP	NEH	SG	SOF	TS
A mighty fortress/A safe stronghold/God is our fortress		n	114		3	454	668	366	661	523	958	2		637		
And didst thou travel light, dear Lord		g	339					103					*628*			
As we are gathered	ga			47		197						38			28	29
At even, ere/when the sun was set		g	9	50			65	12	142	315		43	243	487		
Be still and know I (John Bell)		g												18	672	
Be still and know II (John Bell)		g			70	754								242		
Be still and know that I am God		g			66	71	755	608			909	48			41	48
Crown him with many crowns		g	147	137	139	459	263	166	255	174	321	109	352	321	77	77
God forgave my sin in Jesus' name		g		212	209		480			S 12	849	181			129	123
God of grace and God of glory		n	367	225			533	448	712	324		192		574	139	
How sweet the name of Jesus sounds		g	122	297		461	92	467	257	211		251	374	42	194/782	190/1273
Immortal love, for ever full		g	133	315			211	475	392	105		328	378	176		
In Christ alone my hope is found		n										1072			1346	1311
In heavenly armour we'll enter the land		n										639			237	228
Jesus Christ is waiting		g		349	323	360					889			624		1360
O changeless Christ, for ever new		g			518					108	745			374		
Oft in danger/Christian soldiers		n	210	487			547	715	524			533	434			
Onward, Christian soldiers		n	333		581	514	659	549	718	532		543	435		442	
Soldiers of Christ, arise	ga	n	219	606		515	487	571	719	533		604	449	643	506	
Soldiers who are Christ's below		n	302	607				228					450			
Spirit of the living God (Iverson)		n		615	666	619	310		295	S 23	306	613			510	462
Stand up, stand up for Jesus		n	221	617			488	578	721	535		617	453	644	513	1517
The Lord is my song (Taizé)				651							929					
The love of God comes close		g										940		186		1533
Thine arm/Your hands, O Lord, in days of old		g	285	671			347	397			431		324			
Thou/God, whose almighty word		g	180	684	738	112	324	267	29	506	887	699	466	597	557	
We cannot measure how you heal		g		712	772	718	514	348			433		490			
We rest on thee/We trust in you		n								446		735		510	587	1043
What a friend we have in Jesus		n		727		547	627		559	373		746		646	593	566
When a knight won his spurs		n		731			616								1601	
Who is on the Lord's side?		n							722			769			607	1066

SONGS FOR CHILDREN

Blessed be the name of the Lord MP 809, SOF 673
When a knight won his spurs CAON 731, CAP 50, CP 616, KS 371, SOF 1601

BIBLE READINGS

Psalm 18.1–20 *or* 18.21–30
Amos 9.5–15
Ephesians 6.1–20
Mark 2.1–12

SINGING THE PSALM

Psalm 18 CRP, CWP, H&P, NPCW
Berthier *In the Lord I'll be ever thankful* TSFP#

ANTHEMS AND VOCAL MUSIC

Title	Composer	Voices	E/M/D	Book source	Single sheet publisher
UNISON/TWO PART/HIGH VOICES					
Be strong in the Lord	Nicholson	SS	E		Curwen
For the beauty of the earth	Rutter	SS	M		OUP
Give us the wings of faith	Archer	2 part	M		Mayhew
Give us the wings of faith	Blatchly	SS	M	HP	
Like a child rests in its mother's arms	Walker	U#	E	LAU, OOD	OCP
Send us as your blessing, Lord	Walker	U/SSATB#	E/M	CFE, HIG	OCP
Teach us, good Lord, to serve thee	Nicholson	U	E		RSCM
THREE/FOUR PARTS					
And didst thou travel light?	Shephard	SATB	M	BC	RSCM
Every time I feel the Spirit	Trad arr Chilcott	SATB	M	SFC	
Fight the good fight	Gardner	SATB	M	MTH1	OUP
Give me the wings of faith	Leighton	SATB	D		Novello
Give us the wings of faith	Bullock	SATB	M	AC4, FSB10	OUP
Go forth and tell!	Ogden	SATB	E	SBS2	RSCM
God the Holy Trinity	Halls	SATB	E	SBS1	RSCM
Holy Spirit, truth divine	Carter	SATB	E/M	ETAS, NOEAB	OUP
If God is building when we build	Trad arr Barnard	SATB	E	SBS2	
In olden time and distant land (g)	Trad arr Mold	SATB	E		Encore
O Lord, give thy Holy Spirit	Harper	SATB	E	SBS2, SOTL	
Praise the Lord, O my soul	Rutter	SATB	M		OUP
We cannot measure how you heal (g)	Bell arr Archer	SATB	E	BC	RSCM
FIVE OR MORE PARTS					
Os justi (g)	Bruckner	SSATTB unacc	M/D	ESM	Peters

ORGAN MUSIC

PRELUDES

Armstrong Gibbs C. **Elegy** No.2 of *Six Sketches* Bk.1 (OUP) E/M
Bédard D. **Consolation** No.4 of *Cinq Pièces Funèbres* (Cheldar) E/M
Puxol L. **Obra de 6º tom** in *Silva Ibérica* Vol.1 (Schott) E*
Rembt J.E. **Trio in B flat** No.1 of *Six Trios* (Schott) M
Vierne L. **Canzona** No.12 of *24 Pièces en Style Libre* Bk.1 Op.31 (Durand) E/M(*)

POSTLUDES

Buxtehude D. **Ein feste Burg ist unser Gott** BuxWV 184 in Peters Vol.2 and Bärenreiter Vol.4 E/M
Thiman E. **Postlude on 'Regent Square'** in *Five Hymn Tune Variants* (Curwen) E/M
Young G. **Fanfare on 'St Gertrude'** in *Eight Organ Voluntaries* (Presser) E/M
Zwart J. First section of **Fantasie 'Een Vaste Burg'** in *Niederländisch-belgische Orgelromantik* (Breitkopf) E/M

THE SECOND SUNDAY BEFORE LENT YEAR A

HYMNS AND SONGS

	pos	rdg	AMNS	CAON	CFE	CH4	CH5	CP	H&P	HTC	LAU	MP	NEH	SG	SOF	TS
All creatures of our God and King	ga	o	105	6	15	147	24	250	329	13	694	7	263	23	645	614
All things bright and beautiful			116	25	27	137	25	251	330	283	685	23	264	294	14	14
All you works of God						151										
Angel voices, ever singing		n	163	37	45	498	346	377	484	307	724	34	336	27	24	
Bless the Lord, creation sings		o								604						
Come, let us join our cheerful songs	ga		144	120			332	401	810	206		93	349	33	70	
Come, ye faithful/Alleluia, raise the anthem	ga	o	145	131			84	409	813	205		103	351	25		
For the fruits of his/all creation			457	185	178	231	39	254	342	286	731	153	*621*	299	1234	685
God, we praise you! God, we bless you!		n				120	696	450		341			38			
God who spoke in the beginning		o	468													
God, whose farm is all creation				370	236	226	41	271	344	282	733			302		
I will worship with all of my heart		n									991			213	859	270
Immortal, invisible, God only wise	ga	o	199	314	301	132	6	474	9	21	725	327	377	44	234	220
Jesus is Lord! Creation's voice				352	326		96	170	260	S 17	324	367			290	284
'Jesus is Lord' – the cry that echoes		o									1078				1387	1367
Let everything that has breath (Redman)											1001			124	880	854
Let us sing to the Lord (Taizé)		ps									689					
Let us with a gladsome mind/Let us gladly			204	392	362	93	30	498	27	23	707	415	397	312	333	
Lord of beauty, thine the splendour			106	415			29	258					265			
Lord of the boundless curves of space			493				31	210	335			405				
Morning has broken	mo	o		450	490	212	58	260	635	265	671	467	237		393	
Nada te turbe/Nothing can trouble (Taizé)		g		937							947			659		
O Lord, my God (How great thou art)				511	568	154	32	262			721	506		56	425	396
O Lord of heaven and earth and sea				287				540	337	287			422	306		
Praise the Lord of heaven				568					507							
The earth is the Lord's (Kendrick)												642			528	
The spacious firmament on high		o	103	665		148	35	265	339				267			
Think of a world without any flowers				900		155	50		572							
Thou/God, whose almighty word		o	180	684	738	112	324	267	29	506	887	699	466	597	557	
Touch the earth lightly						243										
Who can measure heaven and earth?		o								27						
With wonder, Lord, we see your works		o	531					269	353					316		
Worthy, O worthy are you, Lord		n										782			617	585

SONGS FOR CHILDREN

Great is he MP 1048, SOF 1254, TS 705
Seek ye first CAON 590, CFE 633, CH 184, CH4 641, CH5 596, H&P 138, JP 215, LAU 820, MP 590, SOF 493, TS 447
When God made the garden of creation CAON 910, CAP 16, CH 228
When your Father made the world CAON 914, CAP 73, CH 232, CH4 239

BIBLE READINGS

Psalm 148
Proverbs 8.1,22–31
Revelation 4
Luke 12.16–31

SINGING THE PSALM

Psalm 148 CH4, CWP, H&P, NEP, NPCW, PAME, PIW
  Bell *Glory to God above!* CG, CH4, PPP
  Mayhew *All the nations of the earth* PCMG
  Ogden *Let all creation sing* SFL2 (WLP)#

ANTHEMS AND VOCAL MUSIC

Title	Composer	Voices	E/M/D	Book source	Single sheet publisher
UNISON/TWO PART/HIGH VOICES					
Calm me, Lord (g)	Rizza	U/SATB#	E	CAON, CAS, FOLO	
Let nothing trouble you (g)	Farrell	U#	E	CBL	
Let the bright seraphim	Handel	S	D		Novello
O rest in the Lord (Elijah) (g)	Mendelssohn	U	M		RSCM
THREE/FOUR PARTS					
Angel voices	Shephard	SATB	M	SC	RSCM
Angels	Lole	SATB	M		Encore
Come, let us join our cheerful songs	Bullard	SAB	M		RSCM
God omnipotent reigneth	Wood	SATB	E	SBS1	RSCM
Holy, holy, holy	Schubert	SATB unacc	E	NOEAB, OBFA	
Immortal, invisible	Mold	SATB	M		Banks
In the city of the Lord	Harper	SATB	M	LOL	RSCM
Lo, round the throne a glorious band	Ley	SATB	E	NCAB	Novello
Love divine	Lloyd	SAMen	E	AOAN1	
Most glorious Lord of life	Harris	SATB	E/M	AWTE	OUP
Praise to the Lord, the almighty	Stanford	SATB	M	ASA	
Sanctus	Alcock	SATB + solo S	M	NSAC1	
Seek ye the Lord (g)	Varley Roberts	SATB + solo T	M	FAB1	Novello
Worthy is the Lamb (Messiah)	Handel	SATB	M		Novello
FIVE OR MORE PARTS					
Heilig	Mendelssohn	SATB + SATB unacc	M		Collegium
Hymn of the Cherubim	Rachmaninov	SSAATTBB unacc	D	ETAS, RCM	Bailey & Ferguson
O sing unto the Lord	Hinde	SSATB	M	MTP	
The Cherubic Hymn	Glinka	SATTBB unacc	M/D	ESM	
Walk softly (g)	Chilcott	SAATBB	M	BCA	OUP

ORGAN MUSIC

PRELUDES

Bach J.S.   **Vor deinen Thron** BWV 668 in Novello Vol.17, Bärenreiter Vol.2, Peters Vol.7 E/M
Mawby C.   **Montes et omnes colles** in *Gregorian Calendar* (Mayhew) E/M
Gaze N.   **Promenade on 'Bunessan'** in *Matinales* (Fagus) E/M
Groves R.   **Lasst uns erfreuen** in *12 Hymn-Tune Preludes* Set 2 (Novello) E/M(⋆)
Jackson F.   **Prelude on 'East Acklam'** in *Five Preludes on English Hymn Tunes* (Banks) M

POSTLUDES

Bach C.P.E.   **Fugue in D minor** in *Complete Works* Vol.2 (Peters) E/M
Bunk G.   **Tut mir auf die schöne Pforte** ('Unser Herrscher') in *Choralimprovisationen* (Butz) M
Guilain J-A.   **Grand Jeu** from *Suite du Troisième Ton* (Kalmus) E/M(⋆)
Piutti C.   **Gott des Himmels und der Erden** *or* **Die Himmel rühmen des Ewigen Ehre** in *Choralvorspiele* Op.34 Vol.1 (Bärenreiter) E/M and E

HYMNS AND SONGS

	pos	rdg	AMNS	CAON	CFE	CH4	CH5	CP	H&P	HTC	LAU	MP	NEH	SG	SOF	TS
Be still, for the presence of the Lord	gr	n		67	72	189	325	383			720	50	629	7	40	47
Be thou my vision/Lord, be my vision		n	343	70	74/75	465	643	386	378	545	970	51	339	669	42	50
Bright the cloud and bright the glory		n				353										
Children of the heavenly King		o	213							566			344			
Christ upon/Jesus, on the mountain peak	gr	n	441	357			205		155	115			177	322		
Christ whose glory fills the skies	mo	n	4	105		578	52	2	457	266	670	79	234	170	1200	
Come, living God, when least expected		n				609		403								
Come, praise the name of Jesus		n								538						
Confitemini Domino (Taizé)		ps		925	137						701					
From glory to glory advancing	se	n	276	194				299					286			
Here in this place (Gather us in)	ga	n			253	623					475			4		
Immortal, invisible, God only wise	ga		199	314	301	132	6	474	9	21	725	327	377	44	234	220
Jesus, these eyes have never seen	cm	n	245	365				491					389			
Jesus, you are changing me												389			311	
Lord, the light of your love is shining				419	388	448	195	513			770	445		614	362	335
Meekness and majesty		n		448	487	356	228				751	465		395	390	353
My God, how wonderful thou art				102	457	497	7	523	51	369	727	468	410	202	395	896
Name of all majesty		n		465			102	525		218		481		324	939	
O happy band of pilgrims		o	208	497						530			418			
O Lord of hosts, all heaven possessing		n											423			
O raise your eyes on high and see		n	502		551			544			208					
O splendour of God's glory bright		n						7	461							
O vision blest of heavenly light		n											176			
Stay, Master, stay upon this heavenly hill		n						158								
The brightness of God's glory		n							221							
Thee we adore, O hidden Saviour	of/cm		254	640			449	329					308			
'Tis/It's/How good, Lord, to be here	gr	n	318				248	156		209		178				
We declare your majesty		n										726			577	544
When Jesus led his chosen three		n							117							
With glorious clouds encompassed round		n						623	184							
Ye/You holy angels bright	ga	o	198	755		179	376	626	20	353		783	475	76	619	
You, living Christ, our eyes behold			533					333					487			

SONGS FOR CHILDREN

Lord, the light of your love is shining CAON 419, CFE 388, CG 110, CH 148, CH4 448, CH5 195, CP 513, KS 237, LAU 770, MP 445, SG 614, SOF 362, TS 335
When I'm feeling down and sad CH4 568

BIBLE READINGS

Psalm 84
Ecclesiasticus 48.1–10 *or* 2 Kings 2.1–12
Matthew 17.9–23 (*or* 1–23)

SINGING THE PSALM

Psalm 84 CH4, CRP, CWP, H&P, NEH, NPCW, PFS
Dean *They are happy who dwell* LAU
DeBruyn *O how lovely is your dwelling place* CFE, LAU
Haugen *How lovely is your dwelling place* (GIA)#
Walker *How lovely is your dwelling place* CIH# (OCP)

ANTHEMS AND VOCAL MUSIC

Title	Composer	Voices	E/M/D	Book source	Single sheet publisher
UNISON/TWO PART/HIGH VOICES					
Give us the wings of faith	Archer	2 part	M		Mayhew
Give us the wings of faith	Blatchly	SS	M	HP	
We walk by faith	Haugen	U#	E	CFE, LAU	GIA
While faith is with me	Hubbard	U	E	SFJ	Banks
THREE/FOUR PARTS					
Be thou my vision	Chilcott	SATB	E/M	BCA, NOEAB	OUP
Blessings on you from the Lord	Whitbourn	SATB	M		Encore
Christ whose glory fills the skies	Darke	SATB	M	SBS1	RSCM
Father, your steadfast purpose	Tambling	SAB	E	AOAN1	
Firmly I believe and truly	Shephard	SAMen	E	SFL2	
For lo, I raise up	Stanford	SATB	M/D		Cathedral, S&B
Give me the wings of faith	Leighton	SATB	D		Novello
Give us the wings of faith	Bullock	SATB	M	AC4, FSB10	OUP
Grow in grace	Archer	SATB	E/M	SBS1	RSCM
If you believe and I believe	Trad Zimbabwean	SATB unacc	E	C, CG, CH4, RTF, SBTL	
Lord, give me faith	Robson	SATB	E		RSCM
O Lord, increase our faith	Loosemore	SATB unacc	E	SBS1, NCAB	RSCM
O Master, let me walk with thee	Ledger	SATB	M		Encore
Summa	Pärt	SATB unacc	M		Universal
Though you do not now see Christ	Ferguson	SATB unacc	M		Encore
Walking by faith	Marsh	SAB	E	AOAN1	
FIVE OR MORE PARTS					
O nata lux	Tallis	SATTB unacc	M	NSAC2, OBTA, TA	OUP

Some of the anthems suggested for Year B (page 163) are also suitable.

ORGAN MUSIC

PRELUDES

Kiefer H.-M. **Die ganze Welt hast du uns überlassen** (Blues) in *Jazz Inspirations* (Bärenreiter) M
Langlais J. **Glas** No.1 of *Contrastes* (Combre) E/M
Oldroyd G. **My soul hath a desire** No.1 of *Three Liturgical Improvisations* (OUP) E/M
Paolucci G. **Toccata per l'Elevazione** in *Classical Organ Music* Vol.2 (OUP) E/M(*)
Rawsthorne N. **Prelude on 'Be thou my vision'** in *Hymn Preludes for the Church Year* Bk.2 and *Music for Solemn Moments* (both Mayhew) E/M

POSTLUDES

Farrar E. **Chorale Prelude on 'Lord, Thee I'll praise'** Op.7/3 (Animus) E/M
How M. **Maestoso** in *Contrasts* (RSCM) E/M(*)
Peeters F. **O nata lux de lumine** No.10 of *Ten Chorale Preludes on Gregorian Themes* Op.76 (Peters) M/D
Vierne R. **Entrée** from *Messe Basse* Op.8; also on 3 staves in *A Graded Anthology for Organ* Bk.5 (Cramer) M*

HYMNS AND SONGS

	pos	rdg	AMNS	CAON	CFE	CH4	CH5	CP	H&P	HTC	LAU	MP	NEH	SG	SOF	TS
As the deer pants for the water		s		45	54	550	606				965	37			27	27
Be thou my guardian/O Lord, our guardian/Lord, be my guardian		s	217	69			635	385		374			64	512		
Be thou my vision/Lord, be my vision		s	343	70	74/75	465	643	386	378	545	970	51	339	669	42	50
Come, let us to the Lord our God		s				482	206	402	33							
Enter our hearts, O holy Lord		s											606			
Father, hear our prayer		s												157		93
Father of heaven, whose love profound	ga	s	97	165	163	483	319	421	519	359		827	358	144		1201
God forgave my sin in Jesus' name		n		212	209		480			S 12	849	181			129	123
I'll praise my Maker while I've breath		o					357	473	439	20		320		84		
Jesu, lover of my soul	ga/of	o,s	123	343	319	490	553	96	528	438	797	372	383	201	297	838
Just as I am, without one plea		o	246	374	339	553	587	308	697	440		396	294	507	316	306
Lord, as I wake I turn to you	mo	s	485				56		634	267	672		236	561		
Lord God, you love us (Taizé)		n									782					
Lord Jesus, think on me		s	129	412	384	491/2	554	97	533	316	204		70			
Lord of our life and God of our salvation		s		417						529		441	404			
Miserere nobis/Holy Lord, have mercy (Taizé)		s									597			159		
My Jesus, my Saviour		o,s		461		531						1003		129	935	367
My Lord, what love is this		o		462	500		230					476		194	398	370
Not for our sins alone		s	229													
Now is the healing time decreed		s											59			
O for a heart to praise my God		s	230	484			638	533	536	483		495	74	149	411	904
O God of Bethel/Jacob		s	216	491		268	657	536	442	35		907	416	241		
O Lord, hear my prayer (Taizé)		s		938	542		620				929	908		246	423	394
O love, how deep, how broad, how high	of	s	119	516		354	214	118	229			425				
Restore, O Lord, the honour		s		582		469						579		274	483	439
Rock of ages, cleft for me	gr	s	135	584	624	554	557	565	273	593		582	445	150	488	950
Rock of ages (Kendrick)		s													1507	951
Send down the fire of your justice		o														1495
Through the night of doubt and sorrow	pc	s	211	687			661	605	441	466		948	468	544		
To Mercy, Pity, Peace and Love		s											469			
You are merciful to me		s										1018		166	1124	593

SONGS FOR CHILDREN

Father God, I wonder CAON 159, CH4 186, JP 337, KS 52, MP 128, SG 107, SOF 92, TS 91
It's me, it's me, O Lord CAON 838, CFE 316, CH 119, CH4 493, JP 119

BIBLE READINGS

Morning Psalm 38
Evening Psalm 102*
Isaiah 1.10–18
Luke 15.11–32

SINGING THE PSALM

Psalm 38 CWP, NPCW
Psalm 102* CH4, CWP, NPCW
Rizza O Lord, listen to my prayer LIOD#

ANTHEMS AND VOCAL MUSIC

Title	Composer	Voices	E/M/D	Book source	Single sheet publisher
UNISON/TWO PART/HIGH VOICES					
A Song of Hope	Stanford	U	M		RSCM
Amazing grace	Trad arr Jones	U + descant	E	RTF	
Come back to God	Foster	2 part#	E	C	
Create in me	Ogden	U	E		WLP
Lift thine eyes (Elijah)	Mendelssohn	SSA	M		Novello
The Father's Love	Lole	SS	E	EAC2	RSCM
The Prodigal Son	Rusbridge	U	E		WLP
Wash me throughly	Handel	SS	M	AC2	
THREE/FOUR PARTS					
Almighty and everlasting God	Gibbons	SATB (unacc)	E	FAB1, NCAB, OBTA	OUP
Dear Lord and Father of mankind	Carter	SATB	M	ACA	
Give us, Lord, a new heart	Farrell	U/SATB#	E/M	LAU, RITH, SLG	OCP
Hear, O heavens	Pelham Humfrey	SATB	M		Banks
Merciful Lord	March	SATB unacc	M	SBS2	
O for a closer walk with God	Stanford	SATB	M	AC1, ASA, BC, OBFA, AOAN1 (SAMen)	RSCM
Out of the deep	Purcell	SAB	M/D	TPS	
Thou art God	Bourne	SATB	M	NOEAB	OUP
View me, Lord	Lloyd	SATB unacc	E	NNAB, SEA2	Novello
Wash me throughly	Halls	SATB	E	NOEAB	
Wash me throughly	S.S.Wesley	SATB + solo S	M	AWTE, NCAB, SC	Novello
FIVE OR MORE PARTS					
Derelinquit impius	Tallis	SATTB unacc	M	TA	
In ieiunio et fletu	Tallis	SAATB unacc	M	TA	OUP
Miserere	Allegri	SSATB & SSAB unacc	M/D	ESM	Chester (Latin), Novello (English)
Miserere mei	Byrd	SATBB unacc	M/D	OBTA	OUP
Remember, remember not, Lord	Purcell	SSATB unacc	M	APA	Faber

ORGAN MUSIC

PRELUDES

Archer M. **Aus der Tiefe** in *25 Hymn Preludes: A Year of Praise* (Mayhew) E

Bach J.S. **Erbarm' dich** BWV 721 in Novello Vol.18 and Bärenreiter Vol.3 E

Bach J.S. **Ich ruf' zu dir** BWV 639 from the *Orgelbüchlein* (many editions) E/M

Byrd W. **Miserere** 2 settings in *Tallis to Wesley* Bk.8 (Hinrichsen) E/M

Clucas H. **Aus der Tiefe** in *A Coldridge Organ Book* (Animus) E*

Darke H. **Chorale Prelude on 'Heinlein'** from *Chorale Prelude and Fugue on 'Heinlein'* (Anglo-American) E/M

Groves R. **Martyrdom** in *12 Hymn-Tune Preludes* Set 2 (Novello) E*

Hylton Stewart C. **Aberystwyth** from *Five Short and Easy Pieces on Hymn Tunes* (Novello) E

Krebs J.L. **Ach Gott! erhör mein Seufzen** in *Choralvorspiele alter Meister* (Peters) and *C.H.Trevor Organ Book* No.5 (OUP) E/M

The list of organ music is continued on page 367.

THE FIRST SUNDAY OF LENT YEAR A

HYMNS AND SONGS

	pos	rdg	AMNS	CAON	CFE	CH4	CH5	CP	H&P	HTC	LAU	MP	NEH	SG	SOF	TS
All people that on earth do dwell	ga	o	100	21	22	63	683	369	1	14	466	20	334	77	13	13
Amazing grace – how sweet the sound		n		29	40	555	642	375	215	28	846	31	*626*	26	19	18
Be thou my guardian/O Lord, our guardian/Lord, be my guardian			217	69			635	385		374			64	512		
Be thou my vision/Lord, be my vision			343	70	74/75	465	643	386	378	545	970	51	339	669	42	50
Before Jehovah's aweful/awesome throne/Sing to the Lord with joyful voice	ga	o	197					387	61	15						
Faithful Shepherd, feed me	cm	n		156			644			29			282	498		
Father of all, whose laws have stood		o								539				664		
Father of heaven, whose love profound	ga		97	165	163	483	319	421	519	359		827	358	144		1201
Forty days and forty nights			56	190	185	337	207	95	130	103	206	160	67	381		
God forgave my sin in Jesus' name		n,s		212	209		480			S 12	849	181			129	123
I bind unto myself today				302	274	639	322	203	695	5	312		159			757
I will sing the wondrous story		n		337					223	212		315		43	278	821
In heavenly love abiding		n		323		551		478	678	458		331	*638*		238	782
Jesu, lover of my soul			123	343	319	490	553	96	528	438	797	372	383	201	297	838
Lead us, heavenly Father, lead us		s	224	329	351		652	496	68	595	315	400	393	640	321	311
Lord, as I wake I turn to you	mo	s	485				56			634	267	672		236	561	
Lord God, you love us (Taizé)		n											782			
Lord Jesus, think on me		s	129	412	384	491/2	554	97	533	316	204		70			
Loving Shepherd of thy sheep		n	134	434	475		655	517		305	802	888				
Miserere nobis/Holy Lord, have mercy (Taizé)		s									597			159		
My God, how wonderful thou art		o	102	457	497		7	523	51	369	727	468	410	202	395	896
Now is the healing time decreed													59			
O happy band of pilgrims		n	208	497						530			418			
O Jesus, I have promised		o	235	503	536	644	593	538	704	531	875	501	420	676	418	391
Safe in the shadow of the Lord					626	55	595				445	953	583		516	991
Shine thou upon us, Lord		o							560							
The God of love my Shepherd is		n	110	643				587	43				77			
The King of love my Shepherd is		n	126	649	699	462	20	589	69	44	804	649	457	205	533	984
The Lord my pasture shall prepare		n	111	653				593					458			
The Lord's my Shepherd		n	426	654	706	14–16	21	594	70	591	806	660	459	207	537	486
There is a Redeemer		n		658		559	112				673			396	544	492
Thine/Yours for ever, God of love		n	234	673			660	599		556		972	463			
Through the night of doubt and sorrow	se	s	211	687			661	605	441	466		948	468	544		

SONGS FOR CHILDREN

Grace is when God gives us CH4 163, JP 355, KS 92
Oh, once there was a father KS 267
The Good Shepherd SSJ
The Lord is my shepherd JP 244

BIBLE READINGS

Psalm 50.1–15
Deuteronomy 6.4–9,16–25
Luke 15.1–10

SINGING THE PSALM

Psalm 50.1–15 CH4, CRP, CWP, NPCW, PAME
Bell *Let the giving of thanks* PPP
Dean *I will show God's salvation* CRP

ANTHEMS AND VOCAL MUSIC

Title	Composer	Voices	E/M/D	Book source	Single sheet publisher
UNISON/TWO PART/HIGH VOICES					
A Song of Trust	Stanford	U	M		RSCM
God of mercy	Farrell	U + descant	E	C	
The Father's Love	Lole	SS	E/M	EAC2	RSCM
THREE/FOUR PARTS					
Ah, mine heart	G.Jackson	SATB unacc	E/M		OUP
Almighty and everlasting God	Gibbons	SATB (unacc)	E	FAB1, NCAB, OBTA	OUP
Call to remembrance	Farrant	SATB unacc	E/M	NCAB, OBTA	
Give us, Lord, a new heart	Farrell	U/SATB#	E/M	LAU, RITH, SLG	OCP
Help us, O Lord	Copland	SATB	M		B&H
Hide not thou thy face	Farrant	SATB	E	BC, FAB1, NCAB, OBFA (SAMen), OBTA	RSCM
If ye love me	Tallis	SATB unacc	E	NCAB, NOEAB, NSAC1, OBTA, SL (AATB)	OUP
King of glory, King of peace	J.S.Bach arr Harris	SATB	E	NCAB	OUP
King of glory, King of peace	Ives	SATB	M	SBS1	RSCM
King of glory, King of peace	Walford Davies	SATB	M	MTH2, SC	RSCM
Lord, for thy tender mercy's sake	Hilton/Farrant	SATB unacc	E	AWTE, FAB1, NCAB, NOEAB, OBTA	OUP
Lord, who hast formed me	Godfrey	SATB	E	SBS2	
Thee will I love	Howells	SATB	D		Novello
Turn thee again	Attwood	SATB	M		Banks
Turn thy face from my sins	Attwood	SATB	E/M	BC, NCAB, FAB1, TEA	RSCM
View me, Lord	Lloyd	SATB unacc	E	NNAB, SEA2	Novello
FIVE OR MORE PARTS					
I am thine, O save me	S.S.Wesley	SATTB	E/M	MTP	
I love the Lord	Harvey	SATB + solo SSATB, unacc	D	EAC1, MTP	Novello
If ye love me	Chilcott	SSATBB unacc	M	BCA, WFC	OUP
Let my complaint	Greene	SSATB	M		CMS/OUP
O Lord God of hosts	Purcell	SSAATTBB + solo SSATB	M		Novello
Turn thee unto me, O Lord	Boyce	SSATB	E/M		CMS/OUP

Some of the music listed for Ash Wednesday is also suitable.

ORGAN MUSIC

PRELUDES

Best W.T.   **Prelude on 'Halifax'** in *50 Victorian Pieces* (Mayhew) and *English Romantic Classics* (Belwin) E
Bonighton R.   **Southwell** (Damon) in *Preludes on Favourite Hymns* (Mayhew; 2-stave and 3-stave editions available) E
Hesford B.   **Amazing Grace** (Fentone) E
Krebs J.L.   **Herr Gott, dich loben alle wir** ('Old 100th') No. 5 in *Complete Works* Vol.3 (Breitkopf) M
Nixon J.   **Mannheim** in *Meditation* (Mayhew) E/M

POSTLUDES

Bédard D.   **Variations on 'Nous chanterons'** (Old 100th) (Cheldar) M
Joubert J.   **Southwell** in *Six Short Preludes on English Hymn Tunes* Op.125 (Novello) M*
Walther J.G.   **Ach, was soll ich Sünder machen** (Partitas a and/or d) No. 3 in *Orgelchoräle* (Bärenreiter) E/M

Suitable before or after: Movements from Callahan C. **Partita on 'New Britain'** (**Amazing Grace**) (Concordia) E/M-M

Music listed for Ash Wednesday is also suitable.

THE SECOND SUNDAY OF LENT YEAR A

HYMNS AND SONGS

	pos	rdg	AMNS	CAON	CFE	CH4	CH5	CP	H&P	HTC	LAU	MP	NEH	SG	SOF	TS
All that I am, all that I do		n		23	23	505					600					
Bless the Lord, my soul (Taizé)		o		923	81		1				813			105	676	56
Bread of heaven, on thee we feed	cm	o	271	82				284		398			276	464		
Father, hear the prayer we offer		s	113	161	158	255	645	416	436	360	933	132	357	237	1229	
Forgive our sins as we forgive		s	362	180	182	486	550	428	134	111	845		66	145		
God be in my head	cm	n	236	211	205	538	631	439	694	543	914		328	666		
I bind unto myself today/Christ be with me		n		302	274	639	322	203	695	5	312		159/278			757
I heard the voice of Jesus say		s	247	310		540	576	469	136		795	275	376		215	206
I will offer up my life		n				503					990			565	851	265
In the cross of Christ I glory				327		397	225	480	167			338	379			
Light of the minds that know him	se	n		397			588	501		477			400	626		
Lord Jesus, think on me		s	129	412	384	491/2	554	97	533	316	204		70			
Lord of our life and God of our salvation		s		417						529		441	404			
My faith looks up to thee		o		453			590	522	683			469	72			1437
My Jesus, my Saviour		s		461		531						1003		129	935	367
O God of Bethel/Jacob		s	216	491		268	657	536	442	35		907	416	241		
O Jesus, I have promised		n	235	503	536	644	593	538	704	531	875	501	420	676	418	391
O Lord, hear my prayer (Taizé)		s		938	542		620				929	908		246	423	394
O Lord, your tenderness	cm	n		515								511		569	433	402
O my Saviour, lifted		o	248	519			237					516			437	
O worship the King, all glorious above	ga	s	101	551	559	127	34	546	28	24	683	528	433	90	456	425
Praise to the holiest in the height		n	117	572	606	378	108	557	231	140	788	563	439	58	469	
Take up thy cross, the Saviour said		n	237	626		402	599	582		114		935	76	645		
There's a wideness in God's mercy/Souls of men/Restless souls		s	251	662		187	9	598	230	443	810	607/683	461/700	188		
We cannot measure how you heal		o		712	772	718	514	348			433		490			
Who would true valour see/He who would valiant be		s	212	281	248	535	662	621	688	590	862	224	372	639	174	
Will you come and follow me		n		752	812	533	605	622			877		647	634	1120	

SONGS FOR CHILDREN

Do what you know is right CAON 791, CH 38, KS2 448

When I'm feeling down and sad CH4 568

BIBLE READINGS

Psalm 135*
Numbers 21.4–9
Luke 14.27–33

SINGING THE PSALM

Psalm 135* CWP, NPCW

ANTHEMS AND VOCAL MUSIC

Title	Composer	Voices	E/M/D	Book source	Single sheet publisher
UNISON/TWO PART/HIGH VOICES					
A Prayer of St Richard of Chichester	Allain	2 part	E	VFLS	
A Prayer of St Richard of Chichester	White	2 part	E	BC, OBFA, OEAB	OUP
Christ be with me	Rawsthorne	U	E	SBS2	
Christ has no body now but yours	Ogden	2 part	E	LOL, CFAP	RSCM
Day by day	How	U + 2 part	E	BC, NOEAB (SATB)	RSCM
He came singing love	Gibson	2 part	E	VFLS	
Jesu, by thy wounded feet	Ferguson	S	E		Encore
Teach us, good Lord, to serve thee	Nicholson	2 part	E		RSCM
THREE/FOUR PARTS					
A Prayer of St Richard of Chichester	Archer	SATB	E		RSCM
And didst thou travel light	Shephard	SATB	E	BC	RSCM
Be thou my vision	Chilcott	SATB	M	NOEAB, BCA	OUP
Fight the good fight	Gardner	SATB	E	MTH1	OUP
Go forth and tell!	Ogden	SATB	E	SBS2	RSCM
I give you my hands, Lord	Tambling	SAMen unacc	M	AOAN1	
Light of the lonely pilgrim's heart	Nardone	SATB	E		B&H
O for a closer walk with God	Ives	SATB	M		RSCM
O for a closer walk with God	Stanford	SATB	M	BC, AC1, ASA, AOAN1, OBFA (SAMen)	RSCM
O Master, let me walk with thee	Ledger	SATB	M/D		Encore
Take up your cross	Corp	SATB	E	SBS1, WOTC	RSCM
The Grail Prayer	Rizza	SATB + solo S	E	FOLO, LUE	Mayhew
To be a pilgrim	Burt	SAMen	E/M	OBFA	
Wondrous cross	Wilby	SATB	E	OBFA, WOTC	

ORGAN MUSIC

PRELUDES

Elmore R.	**Chorale Prelude 'My faith looks up to thee'** in *Contemporary Chorale Preludes* (Boosey) M
Nixon J.	**St Bernard** in *Hymn Tune Preludes* (Fagus) E/M
Proulx R.	**St Patrick's Breastplate** in *64 Hymn Preludes* and *Hymn Preludes for the Church Year* Bk.2 (both Mayhew) E
Richter E.F.	**Straf mich nicht in deinem Zorn** Op.29/1 in *Organ Music of the Classical & Early Romantic Periods* Vol.6 (Bärenreiter) E/M
Willan H.	**Prelude on 'Martyrdom'** in *Ten Hymn Preludes* Set 2 (Peters) E/M

POSTLUDES

Fedak A.	**The Kingsfold Trumpet** in *An Album of Trumpet Tunes* (Warner) E/M
Krebs J.L.	**Herr, ich habe mißgehandelt** in *Complete Works* Vol.3 (Breitkopf) E/M
Lloyd Webber W.S.	**Prelude on 'Gerontius'** in *Aria* (Mayhew) M/D
Peeters F.	**Jesus, I will ponder now** in *Hymn Preludes for the Liturgical Year* Op.100 Bk.2 (Peters) E

THE THIRD SUNDAY OF LENT YEAR A

HYMNS AND SONGS

	pos	rdg	AMNS	CAON	CFE	CH4	CH5	CP	H&P	HTC	LAU	MP	NEH	SG	SOF	TS
A mighty fortress/A safe stronghold/God is our fortress		o,n	114		3	454	668	366	661	523	958	2		637		
All my hope on God is founded		o	336	19	21	192	10	368	63	451	959	16	333	525		620
Be bold, be strong		o										49			37	38
Be thou my guardian/O Lord, our guardian/Lord, be my guardian			217	69			635	385		374			64	512		
Christ is our cornerstone		g	161	98			327	395		564			206	14		
Come to us, creative Spirit		g				612	453		377	308				621		
Father, hear the prayer we offer			113	161	158	255	645	416	436	360	933	132	357	237	1229	
God forgave my sin in Jesus' name		s		212	209		480			S 12	849	181			129	123
God moves in a mysterious way		o	112	222		158	13	445	65			193	365			700
God of grace and God of glory		n	367	225			533	448	712	324		192		574	139	
God our Father and creator		g								562						
Here is love, vast as the ocean		g					222					987		174	168	164
How sweet the name of Jesus sounds			122	297		461	92	467	257	211		251	374	42	194/782	190/1273
I danced in the morning (Lord of the dance)		g	375	305	275	404	93	468			765		375			
Immortal love, for ever full			133	315			211	475	392	105		328	378	176		
In Christ alone my hope is found		n										1072			1346	1311
In heavenly armour we'll enter the land		n										639			237	228
Lift up your heads, ye gates of brass		o							227	509						
Lord, I have made thy word my choice		o	490					504	475							
Oft in danger/Christian soldiers		n	210	487				547	715	524		533	434			
Onward, Christian soldiers		o,n	333		581	514	659	549	718	532		543	435		442	
Restore, O Lord, the honour		s		582		469				579				274	483	439
Soldiers of Christ, arise	ga	n	219	606		515	487	571	719	533		604	449	643	506	
Soldiers who are Christ's below		n	302	607				228					450			
Spirit of the living God (Iverson)		n		615	666	619	310		295	S 23	306	613			510	462
Stand up, stand up for Jesus		n	221	617			488	578	721	535		617	453	644	513	1517
Wait for the Lord (Taizé)		ps		949	762	276					88				1575	
We love the place, O God		g	160	718			343	211		558		731	471			
We rest on thee/We trust in you		n								446		735		510	587	1043
What a friend we have in Jesus		n		727		547	627		559	373		746		646	593	566
When a knight won his spurs		n		731				616							1601	
Who is on the Lord's side?		n							722			769			607	1066

SONGS FOR CHILDREN

Be bold, be strong JP 14, KS 17, MP 49, SOF 37, TS 38
When a knight won his spurs CAON 731, CAP 50, CP 616, KS 371, SOF 1601
When I'm feeling sad CH4 569

BIBLE READINGS

Psalm 40
Joshua 1.1–9
Ephesians 6.10–20
John 2.13–22

SINGING THE PSALM

Psalm 40 C, CH4, CRP, CWP, FGP, H&P, NPCW, PAME

Bell *I waited, I waited on the Lord* HSNW, SG
Bell *I waited patiently for God* CG, CH4, PPP

ANTHEMS AND VOCAL MUSIC

Title	Composer	Voices	E/M/D	Book source	Single sheet publisher
UNISON/TWO PART/HIGH VOICES					
Bambelela (You must never give up)	Trad South African	U/SATB	E	C	
Give me strength	Chilcott	2 part	E	VFLS	
Lord, be gracious	Hubbard	U	E	SFJ	Banks
O God of mercy	Lole	2 part	E	OBFA	
THREE/FOUR PARTS					
A Clare Benediction	Rutter	SATB (unacc)	E	JRA, OBFA (SAMen)	OUP
Be strong and of good courage	Campbell	SATB	M	FSB7	Novello
Behold, the tabernacle of God (g)	Harris	SATB	E		RSCM
Call to remembrance	Farrant	SATB unacc	E/M	NCAB, OBTA	OUP
Christ is our cornerstone	Ogden	SATB	E	SBS2	
Christ is our cornerstone	Thorne	SATB	E/M	NOEAB	
God is our hope and strength	J.S. Bach	SATB	E	AC1	
God is our hope and strength	Stanford	SATB	M		Novello
Jesus and the traders (g)	Kodaly	SATB unacc	D		Universal Edition
Lord, in thy mercy	Mendelssohn	SAMen	E	OBFA	
Strengthen ye the weak hands	Harris	SATB	M		Novello
Timor et tremor	Poulenc	SATB unacc	M/D		Salabert
Tristis est anima mea	Poulenc	SATB unacc	D		Salabert
Verily, verily I say unto you (g)	Tallis	SATB unacc	E	AC1, TA, SBS2	OUP
FIVE OR MORE PARTS					
Deus noster refugium	Hassler	SAATTB unacc	M/D		CMS/OUP
God is our hope and strength	Blow	SSAATTBB	M		Banks

ORGAN MUSIC

PRELUDES

Kauffmann G. **Kommt her zu mir** in *120 Chorale Preludes of the 17C & 18C* (Peters) E*
Darke H. **Chorale Prelude on 'St Peter'** No.1 of *Three Chorale Preludes* Op.20 (Novello) E/M
Flor C. **Ein feste Burg** in *80 Chorale Preludes* (Peters) E*
Flugel G. **Jesu, meines Lebens Leben** in *Hier Preisen auf der Erd* Vol.1 (Breitkopf) E
Rheinberger J. **Meditation (Canzonetta)** Op.167 No.3 in *A Graded Anthology for Organ* Bk.5 (Cramer, Carus) M

POSTLUDES

Dyson G. **God moves in a mysterious way** in *Variations on Old Psalm Tunes* Bk.1 (Novello) M
Guilain J-A. **Dialogue** from *Suite du Deuxième Ton* (Kalmus) E/M(*)
Hanff J.N. **Ein feste Burg** in *Choralvorspiele alter Meister* (Peters) E/M
Young G. **Fanfare on 'St Gertrude'** in *Eight Organ Voluntaries* (Presser) E/M

THE FOURTH SUNDAY OF LENT YEAR A

HYMNS AND SONGS

	pos	rdg	AMNS	CAON	CFE	CH4	CH5	CP	H&P	HTC	LAU	MP	NEH	SG	SOF	TS
Amazing grace – how sweet the sound		s		29	40	555	642	375	215	28	846	31	626	26	19	18
And can it be that I should gain		g		32	43	396	218	376	216	588	790	33	627	168	21	21
Brother, sister, let me serve you/Will you let me be your servant		n		88	813	694	517	393			924			619	54	
Come, O thou Traveller unknown		n	243					407	434				350			
Drop, drop, slow tears		o		151			548	106					82			
Father, hear the prayer we offer		n	113	161	158	255	645	416	436	360	933	132	357	237		
For God so loved the world		g										149				
Forgive our sins as we forgive		o	362	180	182	486	550	428	134	111	845		66	145		
From heaven you came, helpless babe		g		195	187	374	219	432			749	162		632	120	114
Great God, what do I see and hear		n								189						
Great is thy faithfulness		o		249		153	80	453	66	260		200	636	39	147	138
How deep the Father's love		g				549	224					988		193	780	185
In heavenly love abiding		g		323		551		478	678	458		331	638		238	782
It is a thing most wonderful		g	70	333			226	109	224	131		346	84	557	252	801
Judge eternal, throned in splendour		n		372		264	535	356	409	329		395	490	600		
Lead, kindly light		o	219	378	348		653	495	67		961	399	392			
Lord Jesus, think on me		o	129	412	384	491/2	554	97	533	316	204		70			
Man of sorrows! What a name		g		439			227		228	130		458		383	385	350
My faith looks up to thee		g		453		590	522	683				469	72			1437
Name of all majesty		g		465			102	525		218		481		324	939	
O Lord, your tenderness		n		515								511		569	433	402
O my Saviour, lifted		g	248	519			237					516			437	
O my soul, arise and bless your maker		g										1095			1481	1460
Oh, the mercy of God		g										1099		195	958	914
Praise to the holiest in the height		g	117	572	606	378	108	557	231	140	788	563	439	58	469	
Rejoice! The Lord is king		n	139	580	619	449	281	563	243	180	326	575	443	440	482	948
Rock of ages (Kendrick)		s													1507	951
Rock of ages, cleft for me		s	135	584	624	554	557	565	273	593		582	445	150	488	950
Sing, my tongue		g	59	602	650	398	241	121	177	142	250		78	387		
Sun of my soul	ev	n	11	621			72	21	646				618	251		
Thine arm/Your hands, O Lord, in days of old		n	285	671				347	397		431		324			
Wait for the Lord (Taizé)		n		949	762	276					88				1575	
Within our darkest night (Taizé)				950												
With loving hands at work		g								106			187			

SONGS FOR CHILDREN

Do what you know is right CAON 791, CH 38, KS2 448
Pray at all times KS 285

46

BIBLE READINGS

Psalm 31.1–16 *or* 31.1–8
Micah 7 *or* Prayer of Manasseh
James 5
John 3.14–21
[Principal Service readings may be used if
Mothering Sunday provisions displace them
at the Principal Service itself.]

SINGING THE PSALM

Psalm 31 CRP, CWP, FGP, NEP, NPCW, PAME
  Bell *In you, O Lord, I found refuge* PPP
  Dean *Father, into your hands* RE#
  Foster *Father, into your hands* RE

ANTHEMS AND VOCAL MUSIC

Title	Composer	Voices	E/M/D	Book source	Single sheet publisher
UNISON/TWO PART/HIGH VOICES					
A Song of Hope	Stanford	U	M		RSCM
Community of Christ	Farrell	U + descant#	E	GBU	
Litany to the Holy Spirit (In the hour of my distress)	Hurford	U/SATB	E	AC2, NEP(U), NSAC1, NOEAB (SATB)	OUP
The Song of the Tree of Life	Vaughan Williams	2 part	E	AC2	OUP
THREE/FOUR PARTS					
As Moses lifted up the serpent (g)	Bairstow	SATB	M		Banks
Be thou my vision	Chilcott	SATB + solo S	M	BCA, NOEAB	OUP
Christ is the world's true light	Stanton	SATB	E	OBFA	Banks
Denn alles fleisch (Requiem)	Brahms	SATB	M		Peters
God so loved the world (g)	Bullard	SAMen	E	OBFA	
God so loved the world (g)	Chilcott	SATB + solo S unacc	M	AWTE, BCA	OUP
God so loved the world (g)	Goss	SATB unacc	E	NCAB	
God so loved the world (g)	Ley	ATTB	M	SL	S&B
God so loved the world (g)	Stainer	SAB unacc	E/M	AOAN1	
God so loved the world (g)	Stainer	SATB unacc	E/M	AWTE, FAB1, MHWE, NOEAB, NSAC1	RSCM
I will sing of the Lord's great love	McKinley	SATB	M	SC	
Just as I am	Chilcott	SATB	E	BCA	OUP
O Lord, heal us	Walker	SATB + descant	E	ATNJ	
The Song of Christ's Glory (g)	P.Moore	SATB	E/M		RSCM
Thou God of truth and love	Archer	SATB	M		Mayhew
Verily, verily I say unto you (g)	Tallis	SATB unacc	E	AC1, SBS2, TA	OUP
FIVE OR MORE PARTS					
Ich bin der Auferstehung und das Leben (g)	Schütz	SATB + SATB	M		Peters
In nomine Jesu (g)	Handl	SAATB unacc	M		RSCM
So God loved the world (g)	Gibbons	SAATB	M		Novello
The Song of Christ's Glory (g)	Ives	SSAATTBB unacc	M	WOTC	

Some of the anthems listed for Year B (page 171) are also suitable.

ORGAN MUSIC

PRELUDES

Bryan P.	**St Bernard** in *Hymn Preludes for Lent, Holy Week and Easter* (Mayhew) E/M	
Farrar E.	**Chorale Prelude on 'St Bride'** Op.7/1 (Animus) E	
Lloyd R.	**Lux benigna** in *64 Hymn Preludes* and *Hymn Preludes for the Church Year* Bk.2 (both Mayhew) E/M	
Widor C-M.	**Praeludium** from *Suite Latine* Op.86 (Durand) M	
Wills A.	**Valediction: Drop, drop slow tears** in *Kenneth Leighton Memorial Album* (Banks) E/M	

POSTLUDES

Bach J.S.	**Christ, der du bist der helle Tag** BWV 1120 in *Neumeister Chorale Preludes* (Bärenreiter) E	
Fletcher A.	**St Bernard** in *Hymn Preludes for the Church Year* Bk.1 and *100 Hymn Preludes* (both Mayhew) E/M	
Labor J.	**1st movement** from *Sonata in B minor* Op.15 (Universal) M	
Sechter S.	**Hier legt mein Geist** No.17 of *18 Choralvorspiele* Op. 90 (Doblinger) E/M(*)	

THE FIFTH SUNDAY OF LENT YEAR A
(Passiontide begins)

HYMNS AND SONGS

	pos	rdg	AMNS	CAON	CFE	CH4	CH5	CP	H&P	HTC	LAU	MP	NEH	SG	SOF	TS
Ah, holy Jesu, how hast thou offended		s		5	13	381	215	100	164	123	232		62	378		
All ye who seek for sure relief/a comfort sure		n	64	26	31			101			212		63			
As the deer pants for the water		o		45	54	550	606				965	37			27	27
Bless the Lord, my soul (Taizé)		o		923	81		1				813		105		676	56
Bread of life, hope of the world	cm	n			95	663					78		484			
Brother, sister, let me serve you/ Will you let me be your servant		n		88	813	694	517	393			924			619	54	
Glory be to Jesus		s	66	206	197		220	108		126	750		83	146		
Great is thy faithfulness		o		249		153	80	453	66	260		200	636	39	147	138
Here is love, vast as the ocean		s					222					987		174	168	164
How deep the Father's love		s				549	224					988		193	780	185
I know a place (At the cross)		s										851			802	209
In the cross of Christ I glory		s		327		397	372	480	167			338	379			
It is a thing most wonderful		s	70	333			226	109	224	131		346	84	557	252	801
Jesus Christ (Once again)		s										995	394	865	274	
Lead, kindly light		o	215	378	348		653	495	67		961	399	392			
Lift high the cross, the love of Christ proclaim		s	72	394	363		484	499	170	508	389	417	*641*	601	1418	
Misericordias Domini/From age to age (Taizé)		ps			489											
Morning glory, starlit sky/Open are the gifts		s	496			390		259					*608*			
My Lord, you wore no royal crown		n								118				628		
My song is love unknown		s	63	463	503	399	231	112	173	136	752	478	86	384	400	897
New every morning is the love	mo	o	2	467		214	59	6	636	270		480	238			
O/Our God, our help in ages past		o	99	494	528	161	537	537	358	37	955	498	417	542	415	905
Praise to the holiest in the height		s	117	572	606	378	108	557	231	140	788	563	439	58	469	
The royal banners forward go		s	58	663	712		243	122	179		252		79			
The steadfast love of the Lord never ceases		o										666			549	505
Through all the changing scenes of life		o	209	686	740		372	604	73	46		702	467	654	1566	1561
Victim divine, thy grace we claim	cm	n							629				309			
We sing the praise of him who died		s	138	723		405	248	125	182	146		738	94	390		
When all thy mercies, O my God		o	109	732			374	617	573	39		751	472	73		
When I survey the wondrous cross		s	67	738	801	392	247	127	180	147	756	755/ 1126	95	680	596	572

SONGS FOR CHILDREN
I'm special JP 106, KS 162, MP 325, SOF 236, TS 222
Jesu, Jesu, fill us with your love CFE 318, CH5 495, IECS, H&P 145, LAU 241, SFL1 18

BIBLE READINGS

Psalm 30
Lamentations 3.19–33
Matthew 20.17–34

SINGING THE PSALM

Psalm 30 CH4, CRP, CWP, NEP, NPCW

Inwood *I will praise you, Lord* CSF (OCP)#
O'Carroll *I will praise you, Lord* RE
Ogden *Keep me by your side, Lord* (WLP)#
Ridge *I will praise you, Lord* RE#

ANTHEMS AND VOCAL MUSIC

Title	Composer	Voices	E/M/D	Book source	Single sheet publisher
UNISON/TWO PART/HIGH VOICES					
Amazing grace	Trad arr How	U/SSA	E	SOS	
Amazing grace	Trad arr Jones	U + descant	E	RTF	
Be light for our eyes	Haas	U/SAB#	E	CFE	GIA
Bread of life (Lent verses)	Farrell	U	E	HIG, RITH	OCP
Christ, be our light	Farrell	U#	E	CBL, CG, CH4, LAU, TS	OCP
Lift on high	Ogden	U/SATB#	E		WLP
Make me a light	Wilby	SS	E	EAC2, HP	Chester
The Servant Song	Gillard arr Ogden	2 part	E	SFL1	
The Spirit of the Lord is upon me	Corp	2 part	E	VFLS	
Word of God, burn within us	Hurd	U#	E	C	
THREE/FOUR PARTS					
Ad te levavi oculos meos	Palestrina	SATB unacc	M		Joed
Be thou my vision	Chilcott	SATB	E/M	BCA, NOEAB	OUP
Be thou my vision	Rutter	SATB	M		OUP
I heard the voice of Jesus say	Shephard	SATB	M		RSCM
In a world where people walk in darkness	Trad arr Harper	SATB	E	LOL	
O thou the central orb	Wood	SATB	M	AC4, AFC, SC	RSCM
Oculi omnium	Wood	SATB unacc	E	NSAC1	RSCM
Open our eyes	Reith	SATB (unacc)	E	C	
Out of darkness	Walker	U/SATB#	E	CFE, LAU, OOD	OCP
The Lord is my light and my salvation	Noon	SATB	M	SBS1	RSCM
The Lord is my light and my salvation	Rutter	SATB + clarinet	M		OUP
The Servant King	Kendrick	SATB	E	SWAMS	
The Spirit of the Lord	Elgar	SATB	M	SAEE	RSCM
Wings of the morning	Rutter	SATB	M		OUP
FIVE OR MORE PARTS					
Oculi omnium	Cleobury	SSAATTBB unacc	M		Encore
Open thou mine eyes	Rutter	SSATB unacc	M		OUP

ORGAN MUSIC

PRELUDES

Archer M.   **Caswall** in *25 Hymn Preludes: A Year of Praise* (Mayhew) E
Bovet G.   **O Lamm Gottes unschuldig** in *Nouveau Cahier de Pièces* (Cantate Domino) E/M
Brahms J.   **O Welt, ich muß dich lassen** No.11 of *Eleven Chorale Preludes* Op.122 E/M
Karg-Elert S.   **O Welt, ich muß dich lassen** No.21 from *Choral-Improvisationen* Op.65 (Breitkopf) and in *14 Choral-Improvisationen* E/M
Telemann G.P.   **O Lamm Gottes unschuldig** in *Organ Music for Manuals* Bk.3 (OUP); another in *Seasonal Chorale Preludes for Manuals* Bk.1 (OUP) E*

POSTLUDES

Bach J.S.   **Ach Herr, mich armen Sünder** BWV 742 in *Neumeister Choral Preludes* (Bärenreiter) E/M*
Carter A.   **St Wilfrid's Suite: Procession on 'Crucifer'** in *Carter Organ Album* (OUP) M
Reger M.   **O Haupt voll Blut und Wunden** WoO p.157 in *Complete Organ Works* Vol.7 (Breitkopf) E/M

Suitable before or after: Movements from Bach J.S. **Partita 'Sei gegrüsset'** BWV 768 in Novello Vol.19, Bärenreiter Vol.1, Peters Vol.5 E-D

PALM SUNDAY YEAR A

(Readings for the Liturgy of Palms are found only in the Principal Service Lectionary.)

HYMNS AND SONGS

	pos	rdg	AMNS	CAON	CFE	CH4	CH5	CP	H&P	HTC	LAU	MP	NEH	SG	SOF	TS
Ah, holy Jesu, how hast thou offended		n		5	13	381	215	100	164	123			62	378		
All praise to thee, for thou, O King divine		n	337	22			684	372	253	204			335			
And now, O Father, mindful of the love	of/cm	n	260	34			400	279	593	392			273	459		
Broken for me, broken for you	cm	n		87			404	287		S 6		66		485	53	58
From heaven you came, helpless babe		n		195	187	374	219	432			749	162		632	120	114
Hail, thou once despisèd Jesus		n		258			268	168	222	175		203		149		
He gave his life in selfless love		n					417			405		214	467			
Here is love, vast as the ocean		n					222					987		174	168	164
How deep the Father's love		n				549	224					988		193	780	185
I am the vine and you the branches (LFB p.52)		o														
I cannot tell why he, whom angels worship		s		303				54	238	194		266		437	205	199
I know a place (At the cross)		n										851			802	209
I will sing the wondrous story		s		337					223	212		315		43	278	821
In the cross of Christ I glory		n		327		397	225	480	167			338	379			
It is a thing most wonderful		n	70	333			226	109	224	131		346	84	557	252	801
Jesus Christ (Once again)		n										995		394	865	274
Jesus, remember me (Taizé)		s		931		775	617				253			875		294
Meekness and majesty		n		448	487	356	228				751	465		395	390	353
Morning glory, starlit sky/Open are the gifts			496			390		259					608			
My Lord, what love is this		n		462	500		230					476		194	398	370
My Lord, you wore no royal crown		s								118				628		
My song is love unknown		n	63	463	503	399	231	112	173	136	752	478	86	384	400	897
No scenes of stately majesty		n												427	1463	375
O Lord, hear my prayer (Taizé)		s		938	542		620				929	908		246	423	394
O love divine, how sweet thou art			124				621	541					424			
O love, how deep, how broad, how high		s	119	516		354	214	118	229			425				
O sacred head		n	68	535	552	382	235	119/120	176	139	237	520	90	385	446	928
Praise to the holiest in the height		n	117	572	606	378	108	557	231	140	788	563	439	58	469	
Thou didst leave thy throne		s	250	683			114	601	154			697	465		555	1015
We sing the praise of him who died		n	138	723		405	248	125	182	146		738	94	390		
When I survey the wondrous cross		n	67	738	801	392	247	127	180	147	756	755/1126	95	680	596	572
Who is this, so weak and helpless		n		748									474			
You are the vine (Daniels)		o										792			629	
You are the vine (O'Hara)		o			824											

SONGS FOR CHILDREN

Each of us is a living stone CAON 793, CH 41

BIBLE READINGS

Psalm 80

Isaiah 5.1–7

Matthew 21.33–46

SINGING THE PSALM

Psalm 80 CH4, CWP, H&P, MCW1, NEP, NPCW, PAME

Haugen *Lord, make us turn to you (Let us see your face)* VE (GIA)#

Sharpe *Let your face shine on us* CRP

ANTHEMS AND VOCAL MUSIC

Title	Composer	Voices	E/M/D	Book source	Single sheet publisher
UNISON/TWO PART/HIGH VOICES					
Christ has no body now but yours	Ogden	U + descant	E	CFAP, LOL	RSCM
Ex ore innocentium	Ireland	SS	M/D	NSAC2	B&H
I see his blood upon the rose	Ogden	U	M	SFL2	
My song is love unknown	Archer	SS	M	EAC2	RSCM
When I survey the wondrous cross	R.Jones	2 part#	E	MHWE	
THREE/FOUR PARTS					
Christus factus est	Anerio	SATB unacc	M	ESM, CM1, AWTE	
Christus factus est	Bruckner	SATB unacc	M/D	ESM	RSCM
Christus factus est	Ridout	SATB unacc	E		Encore
God so loved the world	Bullard	SAMen	E	OBFA	
It is a thing most wonderful	P.Moore	SATB	M	SC, WOTC	RSCM
Jesu, grant me this I pray	Gibbons	SATB	E/M	AWTE	
O Saviour of the world	Goss	SATB	M	FAB1, NCAB, NOEAB	
O Saviour of the world	Somervell	SATB	E	NCAB	
Solus ad victimam	Leighton	SATB	M	AC1, NCAB, SC	Banks
Surely thou hast tasted that the Lord is good	Bernard Rose	SATB unacc	M/D	EAC1	
The Lamentation	Bairstow	SATB	M	AWTE	OUP
The Song of Christ's Glory	P.Moore	SATB	E		RSCM
What wondrous love is this?	Trad arr Weaver	SAB	E	LOL, SBS1, SFL2	
Wondrous cross	Wilby	SATB	E	OBFA, WOTC	
FIVE OR MORE PARTS					
Crucifixus a 6	Lotti	SSAATB unacc	M	WOTC	
Crucifixus pro nobis	Leighton	SATB div	D		Novello
Salvator mundi	Blow	SSATB	D		CMS/OUP
Salvator mundi	Tallis	SAATB unacc	M/D	OBTA, SC, TA	RSCM
Vinea mea electa	Gesualdo	SSATTB unacc	M/D		Carus
Vinea mea electa	Poulenc	SATBB unacc	D		Salabert

Settings of 'God so loved the world' listed for the Fourth Sunday of Lent (page 47) are also suitable.

ORGAN MUSIC

PRELUDES

Bach J.S.   **An Wasserflüssen Babylon** BWV 653 in Novello Vol.17, Bärenreiter Vol.2, Peters Vol.6 M

Near G.   **O Welt, ich muß dich lassen** in *Choraleworks* Set 1 (Aureole) E

Nixon J.   **Caswall** in *Hymn Tune Preludes* (Fagus) E/M

Reger M.   **Passion** Op.145 No.4 (Breitkopf) M

Telemann G.P   **Christus, der uns selig macht** in *12 Easy Chorale Preludes* (Kalmus, Peters) E/M*

POSTLUDES

Bach J.S.   **Wo soll ich fliehen** BWV 646 in Novello Vol.16, Bärenreiter Vol.1, Peters Vol.7 M

Rowley A.   **Triumph Song: Alleluia** (Novello) E/M

van Eyken J.   **First movement of Sonata 1** ('O sacred head') in *The Mendelssohn School* (McAfee) M/D

Suitable before or after: Movements from Pachelbel J. **Partita 'Herzlich thut mich verlangen'** in *Selected Works* Vol.4 (Kalmus) E-E/M*

GOOD FRIDAY YEARS A, B, C

HYMNS AND SONGS

	pos	rdg	AMNS	CAON	CFE	CH4	CH5	CP	H&P	HTC	LAU	MP	NEH	SG	SOF	TS
A purple robe				39						122				379		1120
Alone thou goest forth, O Lord								102								
At the cross her station keeping			69	51	57	387		104			223		97			
At the foot of the cross – I can hardly												805			662	32
Beneath the cross of Jesus				65			561	105	165			55			39	45
Come and see, come and see				109								85		393	67	70
Come, wounded Healer				130											1210	1176
Crucem tuam adoramus (Taizé)											222					
Drop, drop, slow tears				151			548	106					82			
Glory be to Jesus			66	206	197		220	108		126	750		83	146		
He was pierced for our transgressions												222			173	169
Here hangs a man discarded						385										
How deep the Father's love						549	224					988		193	780	185
Lord Christ, we praise your sacrifice			487						532	132				627		
Mary, blessed grieving mother				441												
Morning glory, starlit sky/Open are the gifts			496			390		259					608			
My Lord, what love is this				462	500		230					476		194	398	370
My song is love unknown			63	463	503	399	231	112	173	136	752	478	86	384	400	897
Nature with open volume stands			497				232	113	174				87			
No weight of gold or silver										138				181		
O come and mourn with me awhile					521			114			226					
O come and stand beneath the cross													98			
O sacred head			68	535	552	382	235	119/120	176	139	237	520	90	385	446	928
On the blood-stained ground																922
Rock of ages, cleft for me			135	584	624	554	557	565	273	593		582	445	150	488	950
Sing, my tongue			59	602	650	398	241	121	177	142	250		78	387		
The head that once was crowned with thorns			141	644	696	438	285	172	209	182	290	647	134	442	531	979
The Love that clothes itself in light						384										
There is a green hill far away			137	657	721	380	244	123	178	148	809	674	92	388	542	990
There is a Redeemer				658		559	112					673		396	544	492
This is your coronation						391										
Were you there?			523	721	791	403	246	126	181		225	745	93		1589	1592
When I survey the wondrous cross			67	738	801	392	247	127	180	147	756	755/1126	95	680	596	572
Where high the heavenly temple stands			130			451	291				184					
While Mary was watching						383										

SONGS FOR CHILDREN

I danced in the morning AMNS 375, CAON 305, CAP 22, CFE 275, CH 96, CH4 404, CH5 93, CP 468, JP 91, LAU 765, NEH 375, SOF 1310
Jesus, thank you for the cross KS 214

BIBLE READINGS (Morning)

Psalm 69

Genesis 22.1–18

A part of John 18 –19 (if not used at the Principal Service) *or* Hebrews 10.1–10

BIBLE READINGS (Evening)

Psalms 130 and 143

Lamentations 5.15–22

John 19.38–42 *or* Colossians 1.18–23

SINGING THE PSALM

Psalm 69 CRP, CWP, H&P, NPCW, PAME, WOTC

Psalm 130 C, CH4, CRP, CWP, FGP, H&P, LAU, MCW1, NPCW, PIW, PAME

Bell *In deep distress my soul declares* (GIA)

Bell *Out of the direst depths* LAU, PPP

Smith *From the depths I call to you* (WLP)

Psalm 143 CH4, CWP, FGP, NPCW, PAME

ANTHEMS AND VOCAL MUSIC

Title	Composer	Voices	E/M/D	Book source	Single sheet publisher
UNISON/TWO PART/HIGH VOICES					
Answer me (The Reproaches)	Quigley	U#	E	RE	
O my people (The Reproaches)	Jones	U#	E	EM, MHWE	OCP
Stabat mater	Pergolesi	SS	M	SFL2, AC2	
St John Passion	Plainchant	2 part	E		Music Makers
The Reproaches	Bramma	U + speaker	E	PSRB	
THREE/FOUR PARTS					
Crux fidelis	John IV of Portugal	SATB unacc	E	AWTE, ESM, NCAB	OUP
O my people (The Reproaches)	Lundy arr Walker	U/SATB	E/M	RE	OCP
O vos omnes	Correa	SATB unacc	E	NOEAB	
O vos omnes	Croce	SATB unacc	E	AWTE, MHWE	
O vos omnes	Daley	SATB unacc	M	SC	
O vos omnes	Victoria	SATB unacc	M	ESM, AC3	
Popule meus	Victoria	SATB unacc	E	AWTE	OUP
The Reproaches	Llewellyn, Rose	SATB, cong	E	PSRB	
Vexilla regis	Bruckner	SATB unacc	M		Peters
Were you there?	Trad arr Chilcott	SATB	M	AWTE	
Were you there?	Trad arr Hart	SATB	M/D	SFC	
Were you there?	Trad arr Ogden	SATB + soli unacc	E	SBS1, WOTC	
Were you there?	Trad arr Shephard	SATB	M		RSCM
FIVE OR MORE PARTS					
Christe adoramus te	Monteverdi	SSATB unacc	M	ESM	
Crucifixus	Caldara	SSSSAAAATTTTBBBB	M		OUP
Crucifixus	Lotti	SSAATTBB unacc	M/D	ESM, NSAC1	RSCM
In manus tuas	Creese	SSAATBB unacc	D		Encore
In manus tuas	Tallis	SATTB unacc	M	TA	OUP
Stabat mater	Palestrina	SATB + SATB unacc	D		Chester
Surely he died on Calvary	Trad arr Jennings	SSAATTBB unacc	D	SFC	

The Passiontide music listed for Palm Sunday is also appropriate.

The list of organ music is on page 368.

EASTER DAY YEAR A

HYMNS AND SONGS

	pos	rdg	AMNS	CAON	CFE	CH4	CH5	CP	H&P	HTC	LAU	MP	NEH	SG	SOF	TS
At your feet we fall		n										45			34	35
Christ has risen while earth slumbers		s				430										
Christ is alive, with joy we sing		s			107						270					
Christ the Lord is risen again		s	79	103			258	141	192	153			105	400		1166
Christus resurrexit (Taizé)		s									265					
Come, ye faithful/Alleluia, raise the anthem	ga	s	145	131			84	409	813	205		103	351	25		
Come, ye faithful, raise the strain/Spring has come	ga	s	76	132		414	262	143	194	160			106			
Comes Mary to the grave		g				407				152				401		
From the very depths of darkness		g		198												
God, we praise you! God, we bless you!		s				120	696	450		341				38		
Good Christians all, rejoice and sing		s	85	241	230			145	191	154			107	404		
Good Joseph had a garden		g					265	146	195							
Hail thee, festival day (Easter)	ga	s		257							255		109			
Hallelujah, my Father	cm	s		261			216					206			152	143
Jesus Christ is risen: the feast		g											111			
Jesus Christ is risen today/Christ the Lord	ga	s	77	348	322	410	271	147	193	155	267	357	110	408	285	276
Jesus, Jesus, holy and anointed one		s										872		215	293	286
Jesus lives! Thy terrors now		s	82	354			272	148	198	156		373	112	409	296	
Led like a lamb to the slaughter		g		380			273					402		424	322	312
Light's glittering morn bedecks the sky	ga	g	329				274	149		157						
Love's redeeming work is done/Christ the Lord is risen/All creation		s	83	433		411	277	150	193	150		76	113	412		
Now is Christ risen from the dead		s										901				
Now is eternal life	se		402	470			392	152	203				114			
Now the green blade riseth		g	501	475	513	417	278	153	204				115	414		
O sons and daughters, let us sing/Alleluia!		g	74			431	279	154	205		280		125			
See, what a morning!		g										1105				1494
The day of resurrection		s	75	637	690	413	283	157	208	161	283		117	415		
The Lord is risen indeed!		s	84	652				158					118			
The strife is o'er/past		s	78	667		412	286	159	214	163	275	670	119	416		
Thine/Yours be the glory	se	s	428	672	728	419	288	160	212	167	287	689	120	417	551	510
This joyful Eastertide		s		680	735	415	289	161	213	165	286		121			
Walking in a garden		g	518	705			290						123			
When Easter to the dark world came		g							200							
Ye/You choirs of new Jerusalem		s	73	754	818		292	162	823	168	279		124	419		

Seasonal hymns and songs listed for Years B and C (pages 176 and 292) are also appropriate.

SONGS FOR CHILDREN

No more weeping SG 426
Risen! Risen! KS 289
They crucified my Saviour CH4 406

BIBLE READINGS

Morning Psalms 114 and 117
Evening Psalms 105 *or* 66.1–11
Song of Solomon 3.2–5; 8.6,7
John 20.11–18 (*if not used at the*
Principal Service) *or* Revelation 1.12–18

SINGING THE PSALM

Psalm 114 CFE, CWP, NPCW, PAME
Psalm 117 CRP, CWP, FGP, NPCW
    Bell *Praise your Maker* PPP
    Berthier *Laudate Dominum* CAON, CFE, CH4, CH5, LAU, TSFP#
    Inwood *Holy is God* HIG, LAU#
    Jakob *Go out to the whole world* C
Psalm 105 CRP, CWP, NPCW, PAME
    Dean *He, the Lord, is our God* VE
Psalm 66.1–11 CRP, CWP, NPCW
    Deiss *All you nations* CFE

ANTHEMS AND VOCAL MUSIC

Title	Composer	Voices	E/M/D	Book source	Single sheet publisher
UNISON/TWO PART/HIGH VOICES					
Bright morning	Dean	U#	E	RE	
I have seen the Lord	Hurd	U#	E		OCP
I know that my Redeemer lives	Ogden	U#	E		WLP
Lift your hearts this Easter morning	Walsh	U	E	RE	
Surgens Jesus	Monteverdi	SAA unacc	M	AC3	
The angel rolled the stone away	Trad arr Weaver	2 part	E	SFL1	
Victimae Paschali laudes	Plainsong	U	E	RE	
We walk by faith	Haugen	U#	E	CFE, LAU	GIA
THREE/FOUR PARTS					
Arise, my love	Martinson	SATB unacc	M/D	WFC	
Comes Mary to the grave	N.Warren	SATB	E	WIS	
Greater love	Ireland	SATB	M	AC4	S&B
Here, O my Lord, I see thee	Whitlock	SATB	E/M	NSAC2	OUP
I know that my Redeemer liveth	Morley	SATB	M		Fagus
Lord, give me faith	Robson	SATB	E		RSCM
O filii et filiae	Trad arr Sanger	SATB	M/D		Banks
O sons and daughters, let us sing	Trad arr Walford Davies	SATB	E	MTH2	RSCM
O voice of the beloved	Ives	SATB	M	SBS2	RSCM
Out of the stillness	Shephard	SATB	M	SBS2	RSCM
Set me as a seal	Carpenter	SATB + solo S	M		WLP
Set me as a seal	Walton	SATB	M/D	AC4, WFC	OUP
When Mary through the garden went	Stanford	SATB unacc	E	ASA	S&B
Woman, why weepest thou?	Schütz	SATB	M		Concordia
FIVE OR MORE PARTS					
Surrexit Christus hodie	Scheidt	SATB + SATB (unacc)	M/D	AWTE	OUP
Surgens Jesus	Lassus	SSATB unacc	M/D		Mapa Mundi
Surgens Jesus	Philips	SSATB unacc	M/D	NCAB	
Victimae Paschali	Byrd	SSATB unacc	M/D		Joed
Victimae Paschali	Victoria	SATB + SATB unacc	M/D		Joed

ORGAN MUSIC

PRELUDES

Albrechtsberger, J. G.   **Fuge in D minor** ('Christus ist erstanden') in *Albrechtsberger Vier Fugen* (Doblinger) E/M(*)
Beechey G.   **Variations on an old French carol** (Noël nouvelet) (Fagus) E/M
Dupré M.   **At the Lamb's royal feast** No.7 from *Le Tombeau de Titelouze* Op.38 (Gray) M
Händel G. F.   **I know that my redeemer liveth** (many arrangements) E/M
Lemmens J-N.   **Second movement** ('O filii') from *2nd Sonata* (Forberg, or Novello reprint) E/M

POSTLUDES

Archer M.   **St Albinus** in *25 Hymn Preludes: A Year of Praise* and *Preludes on the Great Hymns of Lent, Holy Week and Easter* (Mayhew) E/M
Bach J.S.   **Christ ist erstanden** BWV 627 from the *Orgelbüchlein* (many editions) M/D
Guilmant A.   **Paraphrase on 'Judas Maccabeus'** Op.90/16 from *18 Nouvelles Pièces* Op.90 (Vol.4 of the *Complete Works*; Belwin-Mills) E/M
Faulkes W.   **Alleluya: Festal Postlude on the Easter Hymn** (Novello) M

THE SECOND SUNDAY OF EASTER YEAR A

HYMNS AND SONGS

	pos	rdg	AMNS	CAON	CFE	CH4	CH5	CP	H&P	HTC	LAU	MP	NEH	SG	SOF	TS
Be bold, be strong		o										49			37	38
Bless the Lord, my soul (Taizé)				923	81		1				813			105	676	56
Christ is risen as he said		n					256									
Christ is risen! Raise your voices		n											399			
Christ the Lord is risen again		n	79	103			258	141	192	153			105	400		1166
Christus resurrexit (Taizé)		s									265					
Come, ye faithful/Alleluia, raise the anthem	ga	s	145	131			84	409	813	205		103	351	25		
Come, ye faithful, raise the strain/Spring has come	ga	s	76	132		414	262	143	194	160			106			
Do not be afraid, for I have redeemed you		o		150	147	191					972	115			1213	1183
God, we praise you! God, we bless you!		s				120	696	450		341				38		
Good Christians all, rejoice and sing		n	85	241	230			145	191	154			107	404		
He has risen		n										839			753	155
Here in this place (Gather us in)		o			253	623					475			4		
In heavenly armour we'll enter the land		o										639			237	228
Jesus lives! Thy terrors now		n	82	354			272	148	198	156		373	112	409	296	
Love's redeeming work is done/ Christ the Lord is risen/All creation		n	83	433		411	277	150	193	150		76	113	412		
Most glorious Lord of life		n		452		215		151					255			
Now is eternal life	se	s	402	470			392	152	203				114			
Sing of the Lord's goodness		o			654	157	368				713			61		
Stand up, stand up for Jesus		o	221	617			488	578	721	535		617	453	644	513	1517
The day of resurrection		n	75	637	690	413	283	157	208	161	283		117	415		
The Lamb's high banquet we await		s											101			
The Lord is risen indeed!		n	84	652				158					118			
The strife is o'er/past		n	78	667		412	286	159	214	163	275	670	119	416		
Thine/Yours be the glory	se	n	428	672	728	419	288	160	212	167	287	689	120	417	551	510
Through all the changing scenes of life		o	209	686	740		372	604	73	46		702	467	654	1566	1561
Walk with me, O my Lord		o			765						966					
Who would true valour see/He who would valiant be		o	212	281	248	535	662	621	688	590	862	224	372	639	174	
Ye/You choirs of new Jerusalem		n	73	754	818		292	162	823	168	279		124	419		

SONGS FOR CHILDREN

Christ is risen as he said CH5 256
No more weeping SG 426
They crucified my Saviour CH4 406

BIBLE READINGS

Psalm 30.1–5
Daniel 6.1–23 *or* 6.6–23
Mark 15.46 - 16.8

SINGING THE PSALM

Psalm 30.1–5 CH4, CRP, CWP, NEP, NPCW
Inwood *I will praise you, Lord* CSF (OCP)#
O'Carroll *I will praise you, Lord* RE
Ogden *Keep me by your side, Lord* (WLP)#
Ridge *I will praise you, Lord* RE#

ANTHEMS AND VOCAL MUSIC

Title	Composer	Voices	E/M/D	Book source	Single sheet publisher
UNISON/TWO PART/HIGH VOICES					
Daniel Jazz	Chappell	U	E		Novello
Didn't my Lord deliver Daniel?	Trad arr Weaver	2 part	E	CFAP	
I know that my Redeemer lives	Dean	U	E		Decani
Let all creation sing (Easter verses)	Ogden	U + descant	E	SFL2	WLP
Out of darkness	Walker	U/SATB#	E	CFE, LAU, OOD	OCP
Song of the Risen One	Haas	U/SATB#	E/M		GIA
THREE/FOUR PARTS					
Christ the Lord is risen again	Rutter	SATB	M	AC1, AWTE	OUP
Comes Mary to the grave	N.Warren	SATB	E	WIS	
Here, O my Lord, I see thee	Barry Rose	SATB	E/M	MTH2	
Here, O my Lord, I see thee	Whitlock	SATB	E/M	NSAC2	OUP
Love's redeeming work is done	Ogden	SATB/U	E	SBS1	RSCM
O filii et filiae	Trad arr Sanger	SATB	M/D		Banks
O sons and daughters, let us sing	Trad arr Walford Davies	SATB	E	MTH2	RSCM
O voice of the beloved	Ives	SATB	M	SBS2	RSCM
Out of the stillness	Shephard	SATB	M	SBS2	RSCM
Sing choirs of heaven!	Shephard	SATB	E	AWTE, BC, NEP	RSCM
Sing ye to the Lord	Bairstow	SATB	M/D	NNAB	Novello
The strife is o'er	Armstrong Gibbs	SATB	M	OEAB	Banks
The strife is o'er	Ley	SATB	E	NCAB	OUP
The strife is o'er	Shephard	SATB	M		OUP
When Mary through the garden went	Stanford	SATB unacc	E	ASA	S&B
Ye choirs of new Jerusalem	Shephard	SATB	D	EAC1	OUP
Ye choirs of new Jerusalem	Stanford	SATB	M	AC1, AWTE, FAB1	RSCM
FIVE OR MORE PARTS					
Didn't my Lord deliver Daniel?	Trad arr Hart	SSAATTBB (unacc)	M/D	SFC	
Easter Propers	Byrd	SSATB unacc	M/D		Chester
Surrexit Christus hodie	Scheidt	SATB + SATB (unacc)	M/D	AWTE	Collegium

ORGAN MUSIC

PRELUDES

Bédard D. **Méditation sur 'O filii et filiae'** (Cheldar) E/M
Böhm G. **Christ lag in Todesbanden** No.9 in *Complete Works* (Breitkopf) E/M
Fischer J.K. **Chorale Prelude 'Christ ist erstanden'** in *80 Chorale Preludes* (Peters) and *The Organ Funeral Album* (Bärenreiter) E(*)
Peeters F. Movements from **King Jesus hath a Garden** No.10 of *Ten Organ Chorales* Op.39 (Schott) M-D
Reger M. **Christ ist erstanden** Op.79b No.8 in *Complete Organ Works* Vol.7 (Breitkopf) E/M

POSTLUDES

Archer J.S. **Postlude on 'Easter Hymn'** in *Variations on Well-known Hymn Tunes* (Novello) E/M*
Bédard D. **Choral sur 'O filii et filiae'** No.5 of *Six Paraphrases Grégoriennes* (Cheldar) E/M
Tambling C. **Maccabeus** in *Preludes on Favourite Hymns* (Mayhew; 2-stave and 3-stave editions available) M(*)
Thiman E. **Toccatina for Easter Day** ('Easter Hymn') in *Times and Seasons* Bk.2 (Novello) M

THE THIRD SUNDAY OF EASTER YEAR A

HYMNS AND SONGS

	pos	rdg	AMNS	CAON	CFE	CH4	CH5	CP	H&P	HTC	LAU	MP	NEH	SG	SOF	TS
All people that on earth do dwell	ga	o	100	21	22	63	683	369	1	14	466	20	334	77	13	13
Before Jehovah's aweful/awesome throne/Sing to the Lord with joyful voice	ga	o	197					387	61	15						
Christ is made the sure foundation/Blessèd city		n	332ii	97	109	200	326	207/208	485	559	456	73	205	572	1199	654
Christ is our cornerstone		g	161	98			327	395		564			206	14		
Come down, O love divine		n	156	114	125	489	294	175	281	231	303	89	137	663	1202	71
Come to us, creative Spirit		g				612	453		377	308			621			
Come, ye faithful/Alleluia, raise the anthem	ga	s	145	131			84	409	813	205		103	351	25		
God, who hast caused to be written		o	467						472							
Great is the Lord and most worthy		ps		248			354					199		113	145	137
He is Lord, he is Lord		s		274	246	443	91		256	S 7	761	220			165	158
Here is love, vast as the ocean		g					222					987		174	168	164
Jesus lives! Thy terrors now		s	82	354			272	148	198	156		373	112	409	296	
Laudate Dominum/Sing, praise and bless the Lord (Taizé)				933	346	77	359				698				1514	458
Let us build a house (All are welcome)		n				198					458					
Light's glittering morn bedecks the sky	ga	g	329				274	149		157						
My hope is built on nothing less		n								462		473		537		365
O sons and daughters, let us sing/Alleluia!		g	74			431	279	154	205		280		125			
Restore, O Lord, the honour		o		582		469						579		274	483	439
Son of God, eternal Saviour		o	132			468	527	573		102			498			
Take my life and let it be		o	249	625	677	502	597	581	705	554	874	624		678	519	468
The Church of God a kingdom is		n	169	635				325					483			
The Church's one foundation		n	170	636	688	739	528	585	515	501	830	640	484	581	525	477
The Lamb's high banquet we await		s											101			
We rest on thee/We trust in you		n								446		735		510	587	1043
Ye/You choirs of new Jerusalem		s	73	754	818		292	162	823	168	279		124	419		

SONGS FOR CHILDREN

Allundé, allundé CFAP, IECS
Each of us is a living stone CAON 793, CG 41
I want to serve the purpose of God MP 859, SOF 260, TS 256

BIBLE READINGS

Psalm 48

Haggai 1.13 - 2.9

1 Corinthians 3.10–17

John 2.13–22

SINGING THE PSALM

Psalm 48 CWP, NPCW

ANTHEMS AND VOCAL MUSIC

Title	Composer	Voices	E/M/D	Book source	Single sheet publisher
UNISON/TWO PART/HIGH VOICES					
Alleluia, Jesus, risen Lord of life	Farrell	U#	E	CH4, LAU, MHWE, SG, TS	
Gather us in (Here in this place)	Haugen	U#	E	CFE, CG, CH4, LAU, SG	GIA
THREE/FOUR PARTS					
And I saw a new heaven	Archer	SATB	E	NOEAB	
And I saw a new heaven	Bainton	SATB	M/D	FSB4	Novello
Angel voices	Shephard	SATB	E/M	SC	RSCM
Behold, the tabernacle of God	Harris	SATB	E		RSCM
Behold, the tabernacle of God	Rutter	SATB	M/D		OUP
Blessed city, heavenly Salem	Bairstow	SATB	D		Banks
Christ is our cornerstone	Ogden	SATB	E/M	SBS2	RSCM
Christ is our cornerstone	Rawsthorne	SATB	M		Mayhew
Christ is our cornerstone	Thorne	SATB	E/M	NOEAB	
How lovely are thy dwellings	Brahms	SATB	M/D		RSCM
How lovely are thy dwellings	Self	SAB	E		RSCM
Jesus and the traders (g)	Kodaly	SATB	D		Universal Edition
Surely thou hast tasted that the Lord is good (g)	Bernard Rose	SATB unacc	D	EAC1	Cathedral
We wait for thy loving kindness	McKie	SATB	E	AC4, NSAC2	OUP
Verily, verily I say unto you (g)	Tallis	SATB unacc	E	AC1, SBS2, TA	OUP
FIVE OR MORE PARTS					
Christ is the morning star	Carter	SSAATTBB	D		OUP

ORGAN MUSIC

PRELUDES

Beechey G. **Würtemburg** in *Easter Preludes* (Fagus) E

Magnus E. **Auf, auf mein Herz** in *Hier Preisen auf der Erd* Vol.1 (Breitkopf) M

Nagel M. **For You** ('Christ ist erstanden') in *The Organ Funeral Album* (Bärenreiter) E/M*

Near G. **Ad coenam agni providi** or **Aurora lucis rutilat** in *Chantworks* Set 2 (Aureole) E/M

POSTLUDES

Herzog J.G. **Maestoso from Easter Sonata** in *Passiontide and Easter* (Bärenreiter) E/M

Pachelbel J. **Herr Gott, dich loben alle wir** ('Old 100th') in *80 Chorale Preludes* (Peters) and No.11 in *Orgelwerke* Vol.2 (Peters) E/M

Smith A. **Trumpet Tune on 'Westminster Abbey'** in *Ten Hymn-Tune Preludes* (Animus) E/M

Willan H. **Prelude on 'O fillii et filiae'** in *Ten Hymn Preludes* Set 1 (Peters) M

Suitable before or after: Movements from Pachelbel J. **Partita 'Alle Menschen müssen sterben'** in *Selected Works* Vol.4 (Kalmus) E/M-M*

THE FOURTH SUNDAY OF EASTER YEAR A

HYMNS AND SONGS

	pos	rdg	AMNS	CAON	CFE	CH4	CH5	CP	H&P	HTC	LAU	MP	NEH	SG	SOF	TS
All over the world the Spirit is moving		n		20							984	18			12	12
All people that on earth do dwell	ga	o	100	21	22	63	683	369	1	14	466	20	334	77	13	13
Christ is made the sure foundation/Blessèd city		n	332ii	97	109	200	326	207/208	485	559	456	73	205	572	1199	654
Christ is our cornerstone		n	161	98			327	395		564			206	14		
Christ is the King! O friends rejoice		s	345				86	165		492			345	31		
Earth was waiting, spent and restless		g								54						
For I'm building a people of power		n		181	174							151			111	109
From all that dwell/From all who live		o	98	192		146	351	431	489	580				82	119	
Gloria/Glory to God (Taizé)		ps		960		760								110		119
Glory in the highest to the God of heaven		g					693	300		582			363	37		
God of freedom, God of justice		g		224		263		447								
God, we praise you! God, we bless you!		s				120	696	450		341				38		
He wants not friends that hath thy love		n	183					459	495				371			
I will enter his gates with thanksgiving	ga	g		336			334					307			268	262
In Christ there is no east or west		n	376	319	303	624	522	477	758	322	831	329	480	575		
Jesus put this song into our hearts		n		851		692						376			299	292
Laudate Dominum/Sing, praise and bless the Lord (Taizé)		o		933	346	77	359				698				1514	458
New songs of celebration render		g	498	468	509		705	527	491	343				87		
O heaven is in my heart		n		499											416	388
Peace, perfect peace, in this dark world		n		554	598		675	553		467		555			977	
Praise him on the trumpet		o		561	600		364					558			464	
Pray that Jerusalem may have		g				82	506	560	510				441			
Sing of the Lord's goodness		o			654	157	368				713			61		
The Church's one foundation		n	170	636	688	739	528	585	515	501	830	640	484	581	525	477
The Lamb's high banquet we await		s											101			
The Spirit came as promised		n					313			244				450		
To God be the glory!		n		695	745	512	373	609	463	584	719	708		71	559	526
Turn our hearts to one another		n											589			531
When I needed a neighbour		n	433	736	800	544	499				888				1604	

SONGS FOR CHILDREN

Each of us is a living stone CAON 793, CG 41
Give thanks to the Lord, our God and King MP 1046, SOF 1241, TS 688
Praise him on the trumpet CAON 561, CFE 600, CH5 364, JP 200, KS 284, MP 558, SOF 464

BIBLE READINGS

Psalm 29.1–10
Ezra 3.1–13
Ephesians 2.11–22
Luke 19.37–48

SINGING THE PSALM

Psalm 29.1–10 CRP, CWP, NEP, NPCW, PAME

Feeley *The Lord will bless his people with peace* VE

Gregory Murray, Gelineau *The Lord will bless his people with peace* VE

Rees *The Lord will bless his people with peace* PCMG

ANTHEMS AND VOCAL MUSIC

Title	Composer	Voices	E/M/D	Book source	Single sheet publisher
UNISON/TWO PART/HIGH VOICES					
All glory, all honour (g)	Toolan	U#	E	RE	
Let all the world	Lang	2 part	M		OUP
The Lord bless you and keep you	Rutter	2 part	E	EAC2	OUP
When in our music God is glorified	Haugen	U#	E		GIA
THREE/FOUR PARTS					
A Gaelic Blessing	Rutter	SATB	E	NCAB	RSCM
And when the builders	Shephard	SATB	M/D		Banks
Behold, the tabernacle of God	Harris	SATB	E		RSCM
Behold, the tabernacle of God	Rutter	SATB	M/D		OUP
Christians, shout for joy and gladness	Trad German	SAB	E	OBFA	
Hosanna to the Son of David (g)	Hutchings	SATB unacc	E/M	AWTE	Novello
I will sing of the Lord's great love	McKinley	SATB	M	SC	
In the heart where love is abiding	Barnard	SATB	E	AWTE, BC	RSCM
Lift up your heads(g)	Mathias	SATB	M/D	AC1	OUP
Lift up your heads (g)	Marsh	SAMen	E	AOAN1	
Lift up your heads (g)	Jackson	SATB	M/D	AC4	
One in body, heart and mind	Walker	SATB/U#	E	ATNJ, SFL2 (SAB)	OCP
Peace be to this congregation	Cadden arr Grindle	SATB	E/M		Encore
Surely thou hast tasted that the Lord is good	Bernard Rose	SATB unacc	D	EAC1	Cathedral
There's a wideness in God's mercy	Bevan	SATB	E/M	LD, MTH1, NEP, NOEAB	
Ubi caritas	Hurd	SATB#	E	MUC	OCP
FIVE OR MORE PARTS					
Hosanna to the Son of David (g)	Gibbons	SSAATTBB unacc	M/D	OBTA	OUP
Hosanna to the Son of David (g)	Weelkes	SSATBB unacc	M	OBTA	OUP
Lift up your heads, O ye gates (g)	Leighton	SSATB	M/D		Novello
Ubi caritas	Berkeley	SSATB unacc	D		Chester
Ubi caritas	Duruflé	SAATTBB unacc	M		Durand

ORGAN MUSIC

PRELUDES

Bach J.B.   **Du Friedefürst, Herr Jesu Christ** in *Choralvorspiele alter Meister* (Peters) M*
Karg-Elert S.   **Ich will dich lieben** No.18 from *Chorale-Improvisations* Op.65 Bk.2 (Breitkopf) E/M
Kellner J.P.   **Chorale Prelude 'Wer nur den lieben Gott'** in *Orgelmusik um J.S.Bach* (Breitkopf) M
Tambling C.   **Chorale on 'York'** in *An Organ Miscellany* (Mayhew) E/M
Wolfrum P.   **Ich will dich lieben** in *Hier Preisen auf der Erd* Vol.1 (Breitkopf) E/M

POSTLUDES

Bach J.S.   **Ich hab' mein Sach Gott heimgestellt** BWV 1113 in *Neumeister Chorale Preludes* (Bärenreiter) E*
Hollins A.   **Trumpet Minuet** (Novello); also in *A Victorian Organ Album* (OUP) M/D
Homilius G.A.   **Chorale Prelude 'Erschienen ist der herrlich Tag'** in *Complete Chorale Preludes* (Breitkopf) M
Morhardt P.   **Du Friedefürst, Herr Jesu Christ** in *120 Chorale Preludes of the 17C & 18C* (Peters) E/M

THE FIFTH SUNDAY OF EASTER YEAR A

HYMNS AND SONGS

	pos	rdg	AMNS	CAON	CFE	CH4	CH5	CP	H&P	HTC	LAU	MP	NEH	SG	SOF	TS
All shall be well!		s								149				397		1110
Christ is made the sure foundation/Blessèd city		n	332ii	97	109	200	326	207/208	485	559	456	73	205	572	1199	654
Christ on whom the Spirit rested		n								228						
Christ whose glory fills the skies	mo	g	4	105		578	52	2	457	266	670	79	234	170	1200	
City of God, Jerusalem		n								187						
Fairest Lord Jesus		g				463	88			209		823	634	199		680
Glorious things of thee are spoken		n	172	205	195	738	646	435	817	494	827	173	362	35	127	691
God is our strength and refuge		n		219			12	443		527		188		650		699
Hail thee, festival day (Easter)	ga	s		257							255		109			
Hail, gladdening light	ev	g	8	253		219	699	16	644	275						
Holy Spirit, truth divine		o		289		626	300	184	289	235						
How bright those glorious spirits shine		n	306			745	467	221		572			227			
Jerusalem the golden		n	184	340	317	747	670	482		573	991		381			
Jesus, Jesus, holy and anointed one		n										872		215	293	286
Laudate omnes gentes/Sing praises, all you peoples (Taizé)		ps									478				1515	
Light's glittering morn bedecks the sky	ga	s	329				274	149		157						
Longing for light (Christ be our light)		g				543					883					1409
Lord, the light of your love is shining		g		419	388	448	195	513			770	445		614	362	335
Now the green blade riseth		s	501	475	513	417	278	153	204				115	414		
O holy City, seen of John		n	409													
O love that wilt not let me go		n		517		557	592	542	685	486		515			434	917
Soon and very soon		n				749	138					605			1007	460
Surrexit Dominus vere (Taizé)		s				794										
The Lamb's high banquet we await		s											101			
The Lord is my light (Taizé)		n		944												
Then I saw a new heaven and earth		n										669		456		
There is a land of pure delight		n	190				681	597	822	575			460			
There's a place (Because of you)		n										1011		457	1041	498
We know that Christ is raised		n				635				389						

SONGS FOR CHILDREN

Have you heard the raindrops CAON 817, CH 78, CAP 2, CH4 525, JP 71, KS 99
I danced in the morning AMNS 375, CAON 305, CAP 22, CFE 275, CH 96, CH4 404, CH5 93, CP 468, JP 91, LAU 765, NEH 375, SOF 1310
No, not by might TS 376

BIBLE READINGS

Psalm 147.1–12
Zechariah 4.1–10
Revelation 21.1–14
Luke 2.25–32[33–38]

SINGING THE PSALM

Psalm 147.1–12 CH4, CRP, CWP, H&P, NPCW

Bell *Sing to God with joy* MCW1, PPP

ANTHEMS AND VOCAL MUSIC

Title	Composer	Voices	E/M/D	Book source	Single sheet publisher
UNISON/TWO PART/HIGH VOICES					
Settings of 'Nunc dimittis' for choir and congregation (g)	Various	U/SATB	E	C, CWP, LAU, MCW1, NEP, VE	
As the deer longs	Hurd	U/SATB#	E	CFE, CG, CH4, LAU	OCP
Just like the deer	Ogden	U#	E/M		WLP
O Trinity of blessed light (g)	S. &A.Barrett	U	E	SBS2	RSCM
The Song of the Tree of Life	Vaughan Williams	2 part	E	AC2	OUP
Water of life	Dean	U#	E	CFE, CSF, LAU, NEP	OCP
THREE/FOUR PARTS					
And I saw a new heaven	Archer	SATB	E	NOEAB	
And I saw a new heaven	Bainton	SATB	M/D	FSB4	Novello
As water to the thirsty	Coleman arr Barnard	SATB	E	SC, WIS	
Christ the beginning	P.Moore	SATB	M		Encore
Ecce beatam lucem (g)	Dove	SATB	M/D		Faber
Hallelujah (Messiah)	Handel	SATB	M	WFC	Novello
Hodie beata virgo (g)	Byrd	SATB unacc	M	ETAS	
I am the day	Dove	SATB	M/D		Peters
Like as the hart	Howells	SATB	M	AC4	OUP
Like as the hart	Rawsthorne	SATB	E/M	AWTE	RSCM
Lighten our darkness (g)	Stanford	SATB	E/M		RSCM
O pray for the peace of Jerusalem	Howells	SATB	M		OUP
O rex gloriae (g)	Marenzio	SATB unacc	M	CM1	
Pray that Jerusalem	Stanford	SATB	E	ASA	RSCM
Worthy is the Lamb (Messiah)	Handel	SATB	M		Novello
FIVE OR MORE PARTS					
Living in a holy city	Trad arr Hatfield	SSATB unacc	M		B&H
Maria das Jungfräulein/When to the Temple Mary went	Eccard	SSATBB unacc	M	NCAB (English only), ETAS	Novello
Senex puerum portabat (g)	Byrd	SSATB unacc	M	CM2	Chester

ORGAN MUSIC

PRELUDES

Buxtehude D.	**Danket dem Herren** BuxWV 181 in *Complete Works* Vol.4 (Bärenreiter) M	
Fink C.	**Jesus, meine Zuversicht** Op.2/1 in *The Mendelssohn School* (McAfee)	
Hancock G.	**Paraphrase on 'St Elizabeth'** (OUP) M	
Harker C.	**Prelude on 'Westminster Abbey'** (Bosworth) E/M	
Young G.	**Benedictus on 'Sicilian Mariners'** in *Eight Organ Voluntaries* (Presser) E/M	

POSTLUDES

Bach J.S.	**Christ lag in Todesbanden** BWV 718 in Novello Vol.18, Bärenreiter Vol.3, Peters Vol.6 M	
Callahan C.	**Fanfare on 'Abbot's Leigh'** in *Two English Voluntaries* (Concordia) E/M	
Marchand L.	**Basse de trompette** p.245 in *Organ Compositions* (Kalmus K4148) E*	
Near G.	**Westminster Abbey** in *Choraleworks* Set 1 (Aureole) E/M	

THE SIXTH SUNDAY OF EASTER YEAR A

HYMNS AND SONGS

	pos	rdg	AMNS	CAON	CFE	CH4	CH5	CP	H&P	HTC	LAU	MP	NEH	SG	SOF	TS
Christ is made the sure foundation/Blessèd city		n	332ii	97	109	200	326	207/208	485	559	456	73	205	572	1199	654
Christ is surely coming		o										75				
Christ on whom the Spirit rested		n								228						
City of God, Jerusalem		n								187						
Glorious things of thee are spoken		n	172	205	195	738	646	435	817	494	827	173	362	35	127	691
God has spoken to his people/Open your ears		o			582		380			S 13	472	182			131	
God is our strength and refuge		n		219			12	443		527		188		650		699
God is working his purpose out		o		221	217	235	481	444	769	191	86	189	495	451	135	128
How bright those glorious spirits shine		n	306			745	467	221		572			227			
Jerusalem the golden		n	184	340	317	747	670	482		573	991		381			
Jesus, Jesus, holy and anointed one		n										872		215	293	286
Lead us, heavenly Father, lead us		g	224	379	351		652	496	68	595	315	400	393	640	321	311
Lord God, you love us (Taizé)											782					
Lord, you have come to the lakeside/seashore		g			395	532					871					
My God, I love thee; not because		g	65	458	498		229	524	171	479			73			
O Day of God, draw nigh		o	405				33									
O holy City, seen of John		n	409													
O love that wilt not let me go		n		517		557	592	542	685	486		515			434	917
Open our eyes, Lord		g		532								545			443	1468
Soon and very soon		n				749	138					605			1007	460
The Lamb's high banquet we await		s											101			
The Lord is my light (Taizé)		n		944												
Then I saw a new heaven and earth		n										669		456		
There is a land of pure delight		n	190				681	597	822	575			460			
There's a place (Because of you)		n										1011		457	1041	498
Will you come and follow me		g		752	812	533	605	622			877		647	634	1120	
You are the King of glory		o		762	822							790			627	

SONGS FOR CHILDREN

All heaven declares CAON 17, CFE 20, CH4 426, KS 4, LAU 760, MP 14, SG 420, SOF 10, TS 8
Have you heard the raindrops CAON 817, CH 78, CAP 2, CH4 525, JP 71, KS 99
Haven't you heard that Jesus is risen? CG 46, CH4 433

BIBLE READINGS

Psalms 87 and 36.5–10
Zechariah 8.1–13
Revelation 21.22 - 22.5
John 21.1–14

SINGING THE PSALM

Psalm 87 CWP, NPCW
Psalm 36.5–10 CH4, CWP, NPCW, PAME
  Taizé *With you, O Lord* TSFP#
  Wardle *Your love, O Lord, reaches to the heavens* PIW

ANTHEMS AND VOCAL MUSIC

Title	Composer	Voices	E/M/D	Book source	Single sheet publisher
UNISON/TWO PART/HIGH VOICES					
A Song of Peace	Stanford	U	M		RSCM
How beautiful are the feet (Messiah)	Handel	U	E/M		Novello
If there is to be peace	Shephard	2 part	E	VFLS	
Peace between nations	Wiggins	2 part	E	OBFA	
Prayer for Peace	Rizza	U/SATB#	E	ROP	
THREE/FOUR PARTS					
As truly as God is our Father	Mathias	SATB	M/D	ETAS	
Be strong and of good courage	Campbell	SATB	M	FSB7	Novello
God is our hope and strength	J.S.Bach	SATB	E	AC1	
God is our hope and strength	Stanford	SATB	M		Novello
Lord, make me an instrument of your peace	Aston	SATB	E/M		RSCM
Lord, make me an instrument of your peace	Rutter	SATB	M/D		RSCM
Make me a channel of your peace	Temple arr Wilson	SATB	E	AWS	
O pray for the peace of Jerusalem	Blow	SATB	M	FSB2	Novello
O pray for the peace of Jerusalem	Goss	SATB	E	AC1	
O pray for the peace of Jerusalem	Howells	SATB	M		OUP
O pray for the peace of Jerusalem	Tomkins	SATB	M	SCAB	
On this mountain	Ridout	SAMen	E	AOAN1	
Prayer of St Francis	Kelly	SATB	M/D		Encore
Pray that Jerusalem	Stanford	SATB	E	ASA	RSCM
The peace of God	Rutter	SATB	E	JRA, NOEAB	OUP
The Prayer of Peace	Carter	SATB	M	EAC1	OUP
FIVE OR MORE PARTS					
Deus noster refugium	Hassler	SAATTB unacc	M/D		CMS/OUP
God is our hope and strength	Blow	SSAATTBB	M		Banks
Nation shall speak peace unto nation	Barry Rose	SSATBB unacc	M	NSAC2	

ORGAN MUSIC

PRELUDES

Moore P.	**St Francis Xavier** in *50 Hymn Preludes* (Mayhew) E	
Near G.	**Liebster Jesu** in *Choraleworks* Set 2 (Aureole) E/M	
Redford J.	**Aurora lucis with a meane** in *The Mulliner Book* (Stainer) E*	
Rembt J.E.	**Trio in F** No.3 of *Six Trios* (Schott) M	
Von Paradis M.	**Sicilienne** in *Ceremonial Music* (OUP) E/M	

POSTLUDES

Bédard D.   **Ouverture** from *Triptyque* (Cheldar) E/M
Boëllmann L.   **Sortie I** from *Heures Mystiques* Op.30 (Kalmus, Enoch, Bärenreiter), 3-stave version in *Tryptique* (Fentone) E/M*
Dubois T.   **Entrée du cortège** from *Messe de Mariage* (Kalmus) M
Nagel M.   **Give us peace (Jazz Variations)** in *Jazz Inspirations* (Bärenreiter) E/M

ASCENSION DAY YEARS A, B, C

HYMNS AND SONGS

	pos	rdg	AMNS	CAON	CFE	CH4	CH5	CP	H&P	HTC	LAU	MP	NEH	SG	SOF	TS
Adoramus te, Domine (Taizé)				921	11		345				667			208		
All hail the power of Jesus' name		s	140	16	19	457	250	163	252	587	323	13	332	24	9	7
All heaven declares	gr			17	20	426					760	14		420	10	8
Alleluia! Sing to Jesus	of	s	262	12	37	445	398	278	592	170	644	207	271	458	153	616
At/In the name of Jesus		s	148	54	59	458	94	380	74	172	762	41	338	317	32	33
Blessing and honour (Ancient of days)		o				442						976		106	675	54
Christ is the King! O friends rejoice	se		345				86	165		492			345	31		
Christ triumphant, ever reigning	ga/se	s		104	113	436	259	398		173	763	77	*613*	319	62	655
Clap your hands, all you nations													79			
Come, let us join our cheerful songs	ga		144	120			332	401	810	206		93	349	33	70	
Crown him with many crowns		s	147	137	139	459	263	166	255	174	321	109	352	321	77	77
Hail the day that sees him rise	ga	s	87	255	240		266	167	197	176	291	202	130	434		
Hail thee, festival day (Ascension)		s		256									109			
Hark how the adoring hosts above		o				744										
He is exalted		s		273		437						217		117	164	156
Jesus is King, and I will extol him		s										366			289	283
'Jesus is Lord' – the cry that echoes		s										1078			1387	1367
Jesus shall reign where'er the sun	se		143	359		470	97	490	239	516	322	379	388	45	301	1376
Jesus, we enthrone you		s										388			310	300
King of kings, majesty		s										1000			1404	309
Laudate Dominum/Sing, praise and bless the Lord (Taizé)				933	346	77	359				698				1514	458
Look, ye saints, the sight is glorious		s				439	275	171	201	179		426			349	869
Lord, enthroned in heavenly splendour	of		263	408	379		431	311	616	416	769	431	296	52	352	870
Majesty, worship his majesty		s		436	477		276				767	454			379	346
Make way, make way for Christ the King	ga			438	479	279	134				819	457			384	349
Meekness and majesty		s		448	487	356	228				751	465		395	390	353
Name of all majesty		s		465			102	525		218		481		324	939	
Out of sight, the Lord has gone		a				444										869
Rejoice! The Lord is king	se	s	139	580	619	449	281	563	243	180	326	575	443	440	482	948
See the conqueror mounts in triumph			88	591						181			132			
Sing alleluia forth ye saints on high		s					568						446			
The head that once was crowned with thorns	se	s	141	644	696	438	285	172	209	182	290	647	134	442	531	979/1528
The Lord ascendeth up on high		s				440		173	210			135				

SONGS FOR CHILDREN

All heaven declares CAON 17, CFE 20, CH4 426, KS 4, LAU 760, MP 14, SG 420, SOF 10, TS 8
He is the King of kings CAON 818, CH 80, TS 1244

BIBLE READINGS

Morning Psalm 110
Evening Psalm 8
Song of the Three 29–37 *or* 2 Kings 2.1–15
Revelation 5
Year A: Mark 16.14–20
Years B and C: Matthew 28.16–20

SINGING THE PSALM

Psalm 110 CRP, CWP, NPCW
Psalm 8 CH4, CRP, CWP, FGP, H&P, LAU, NEP, NPCW, PAME
  Bell *O Lord, our Lord, throughout the earth* CH4, PPP
  Walker *I will bless your name* ATNJ# (alternative verses)

ANTHEMS AND VOCAL MUSIC

Title	Composer	Voices	E/M/D	Book source	Single sheet publisher
UNISON/TWO PART/HIGH VOICES					
God is ascended (from 'An Easter Sequence')	Leighton	U	D		Banks
King of glory, King of peace	Sanders	SSAA	M/D		Encore
The heavenly aeroplane	Rutter	2 part	M		OUP
The Lord ascendeth	Praetorius	2 part/SATB	E	OBFA	
THREE/FOUR PARTS					
Ascendens Christus	Handl	SATB unacc	M	ETAS	
Ascension	Moore	SATB	M		Ramsey
Forsaking chariots of fire	Ives	SATB	M	LOL	
Glorious and powerful God	Wood	SATB	E/M	SC	Cathedral
God is gone up	Finzi	SATB	D		B&H
God is gone up	Hutchings	SATB unacc	M	MTP	Novello
God omnipotent reigneth	Wood	SATB	E	SBS1	RSCM
I will not leave you comfortless	Joule	SATB	M/D		RSCM
In the city of the Lord	Harper	SATB	M	LOL	
Jesus shall take the highest honour	Bowater	SATB	E/M	WIS	
Lo, round the throne a glorious band	Ley	SATB	E	NCAB	Banks
Most glorious Lord of life	Harris	SAMen	E/M	AWTE	OUP
O clap your hands	Rutter	SATB	M/D	AC4	OUP
O clap your hands	Vaughan Williams	SATB	M/D	AC4	S&B
The Lord goes up	Archer	SATB	M	NOEAB	
Worthy is the Lamb (Messiah)	Handel	SATB	M		Novello
FIVE OR MORE PARTS					
Ascendit Deus	Philips	SAATTB unacc	M/D	OBTA	OUP
Coelos ascendit hodie	Stanford	SATB + SATB unacc	M/D	ASA	B&H
Ecce vicit Leo	Philips	SATB + SATB unacc	D		Joed
God is gone up	Croft	SSAATB	E/M		Novello
O clap your hands	Gibbons	SSAATTBB unacc	D	OBTA	OUP

The list of organ music is on page 369.

THE SEVENTH SUNDAY OF EASTER (THE SUNDAY AFTER ASCENSION DAY) YEAR A

HYMNS AND SONGS

	pos	rdg	AMNS	CAON	CFE	CH4	CH5	CP	H&P	HTC	LAU	MP	NEH	SG	SOF	TS
All hail the power of Jesus' name		s	140	16	19	457	250	163	252	587	323	13	332	24	9	7
All heaven declares	gr			17	20	426					760	14		420	10	8
Alleluia! Sing to Jesus	of	s	262	12	37	445	398	278	592	170	644	207	271	458	153	616
As the bridegroom to his chosen		o	340						30							
At/In the name of Jesus		n	148	54	59	458	94	380	74	172	762	41	338	317	32	33
Blessing and honour (Ancient of days)						442						976		106	675	54
Christ is the King! O friends rejoice				345			86	165		492			345	31		
Christ triumphant, ever reigning		n		104	113	436	259	398		173	763	77	*613*	319	62	655
Christ whose glory fills the skies	mo	o	4	105		578	52	2	457	266	670	79	234	170	1200	
Come, let us join our cheerful songs	ga		144	120			332	401	810	206		93	349	33	70	
Crown him with many crowns		n	147	137	139	459	263	166	255	174	321	109	352	321	77	77
Hail the day that sees him rise		n	87	255	240		266	167	197	176	291	202	130	434		
I see the Lord (Falson)		n													824	238
Jesus shall reign where'er the sun	se		143	359		470	97	490	239	516	322	379	388	45	301	1376
Jesus shall take the highest honour				360								378		123	302	296
Jesus, we enthrone you		s										388			310	300
King of kings, majesty		s										1000			1404	309
Laudate Dominum/Sing, praise and bless the Lord (Taizé)				933	346	77	359				698				1514	458
Lord, enthroned in heavenly splendour		n	263	408	379		431	311	616	416	769	431	296	52	352	870
Majesty, worship his majesty		s		436	477		276				767	454			379	346
Make way, make way for Christ the King	ga			438	479	279	134				819	457			384	349
Mine eyes have seen the glory		o		449	488	476			242		987					
Now let us learn of Christ		n								503						
O Christe Domine Jesu (Taizé)					519						757					
Oh, the mercy of God		n										1099		195	958	914
Rejoice! The Lord is king		n	139	580	619	449	281	563	243	180	326	575	443	440	482	948
The head that once was crowned with thorns		n	141	644	696	438	285	172	209	182	290	647	134	442	531	979/1529
The Lord ascendeth up on high		s				440		173	210				135			
Thy/Your kingdom come, O God		o	177	691			509	607	783	334		949	499	269		
We declare your majesty		n										726			577	544
You are mighty		n												428	1125	594

SONGS FOR CHILDREN

Jesus Christ is alive today JP 129, MP 358
Make way, make way CAON 438, CFE 479, CH4 279, CH5 134, JP 427, KS 249, LAU 819, MP 457, SOF 384, TS 349
Out of sight, the Lord has gone CH4 444

BIBLE READINGS

Psalm 47
2 Samuel 23.1–5
Ephesians 1.15–23
Mark 16.14–20

SINGING THE PSALM

Psalm 47 CH4, CRP, CWP, FGP, H&P, NEH, NPCW, PAME, PFS
Bell *Clap your hands all you nations* CG, MCW1, PPP, SG

ANTHEMS AND VOCAL MUSIC

Title	Composer	Voices	E/M/D	Book source	Single sheet publisher
UNISON/TWO PART/HIGH VOICES					
At the name of Jesus	Walker	U/SATB#	E	ATNJ	OCP
Christ whose glory fills the skies	Shephard	S	M	HP	
God is ascended (from 'An Easter Sequence') (g)	Leighton	U	D		OUP
Rejoice, the Lord is king	Weaver	2 part	E/M	CFAP	
THREE/FOUR PARTS					
Christ our God descends from heaven	Bullard	SAMen	E	SBS2	
Christ whose glory fills the skies	Darke	SATB	M	SBS1	RSCM
King of glory, King of peace	Ives	SATB	M	SBS1	RSCM
Let all mortal flesh keep silence	Trad arr Covey-Crump	SATB unacc	M	MTH1	
Let all the world	Dyson	SATB	E	MTH1	Novello
Let all the world	Halsey	SATB	E	BC	RSCM
Let all the world	Leighton	SATB	D	EAC1	Novello
Let all the world	Vaughan Williams	SATB	M/D		S&B
Lo, round the throne a glorious band	Ley	SATB	E	NCAB	Banks
O Christ, who art the light and day	Whyte	SATB unacc	E	AC1	
O God, the King of glory	Purcell	SATB	E/M	ETAS, APA	OUP
O thou that art the light	G.Jackson	SATB unacc	E/M		OUP
Rejoice, the Lord is king	Archer	SATB	M		Mayhew
Rejoice, the Lord is king	Kelly	SATB	M/D	NNAB, MTH1	
Rejoice, the Lord is king	Weaver	SATB	M	SC	
The Spirit of the Lord	Elgar	SATB	M	SAEE	RSCM
FIVE OR MORE PARTS					
Christ is the morning star	Carter	SSAATTBB	D		OUP
Let all mortal flesh keep silence	Bairstow	SSAATTBB unacc	D	AC4	S&B

See also the anthems listed for Ascension Day.

ORGAN MUSIC

PRELUDES

Karg-Elert S. **Pastorale (My inmost heart now raises)** No.2 from *Choral-Improvisationen* Op.65 (Breitkopf) E/M

Pachelbel J. **Was Gott tut, das ist wohlgetan** in *The Organ Funeral Album* (Bärenreiter) E*

Redford J. **Glorificamus** in *The Mulliner Book* (Stainer) E*

Sechter S. **Mir nach, spricht Christus** in *18 Choralvorspiele* Op. 90 (Doblinger) E*

POSTLUDES

Bédard D. **Dialogue sur 'Te Deum'** No.1 of *Six Paraphrases Grégoriennes* (Cheldar) E/M

Couperin F. **Offertoire sur les grands jeux** No.XV from *Messe pour les Couvents* (Kalmus) M

Kunkel L. **Aus meines Herzens Grunde** in *Jazz Inspirations* (Bärenreiter) E(*)

Nixon J. **St Helen** or **Hyfrydol** in *Hymn Tune Preludes* (Fagus) E/M

Suitable before or after: Movements from Callahan C. **Partita on 'Hyfrydol'** (Concordia) E-M

DAY OF PENTECOST (WHIT SUNDAY) YEAR A

HYMNS AND SONGS

	pos	rdg	AMNS	CAON	CFE	CH4	CH5	CP	H&P	HTC	LAU	MP	NEH	SG	SOF	TS
All over the world the Spirit is moving		o		20							984	18			12	12
Be still, for the presence of the Lord	gr			67	72	189	325	383			720	50	629	7	40	47
Born by the Holy Spirit's breath		s							279	225		61		446		
Breathe on me, breath of God		o	157	84	98	596	293	174	280	226	302	67	342	554	51	57
Christ on whom the Spirit rested		s								228						
Christians, lift up your hearts (Praise for the Spirit)		s	444	95			399			229						
Come down, O love divine	ga	s	156	114	125	489	294	175	281	231	303	89	137	663	1202	71
Come, gracious Spirit, heavenly dove		s	153	116		587	295	176					347			
Come, Holy Ghost, our souls inspire	ga	s	93	118		586	296	178	283	589		90	138	555		
Come, Holy Spirit, come! Inflame		s		119		594		179								
Come, Holy Spirit, descend on us		s				589					304	818		19		1168
Come, thou/most/O Holy Spirit, come		s	92	127			297	180	284	227			139	20		
Creator Spirit, by whose aid		s							285							
Filled with the Spirit's power		s	359	170			298	425	314	233				593		
Hail thee, festival day! (Pentecost)		s				581			302		255					
Holy Spirit, come, confirm us	se	s	471	288		640	299	183	288		311		140			
Laudate Dominum/Sing, praise and bless the Lord (Taizé)				933	346	77	359				698				1514	458
Let every Christian pray		s	478				301		305	230			640	576		
Like the murmur of the dove's song		s				592		185						17		
Lord of the Church, we pray		s					303			499		442		577	1433	
Lord, the light of your love is shining		s		419	388	448	195	513			770	445		614	362	335
O breath of life, come sweeping through us	gr			476		595	305		777	237		488		407	379	
O holy dove of God descending		s				591										
O King enthroned on high		s	158	504				189	311				421			
O thou who camest from above		s	233	541	557	625	639	191	745	596		525	431	560	451	416
On the day of Pentecost		s		504				192								
Our Lord, his Passion ended		s	91					194	323				611			
Sing to him in whom creation		s							324				142			
Spirit of God, unseen as the wind		s				600	386						612	233		
Spirit of God within me		s		612	665			196	294	243	310			677		
Spirit of mercy, truth and love		o	89	613				197					143			
Spirit of the living God (Iverson)	gr	s		615	666	619	310		295	S 23	306	613			510	462
There's a spirit in the air		s	515	661		616	314	198	326	245				69		
Wind of God, dynamic Spirit		s												681		

Seasonal hymns and songs listed for Years B and C (pages 190 and 306) are also appropriate.

SONGS FOR CHILDREN

Holy Spirit, fill our hearts CH4 611
Holy Spirit (pour your power) KS 515
Jesus is Lord, alleluia! LAU 294
Wa wa wa emimimo A 103, IECS, SFL1 13, MAG

BIBLE READINGS

Morning Psalm 87
Evening Psalms 67 and 133
Joel 2.21–32
Acts 2.14–21[22–38]
Luke 24.44–53

SINGING THE PSALM

Psalm 87 CWP, NPCW
Psalm 67 CH4, CRP, CWP, FGP, H&P, MCW1, NPCW, PAME
    Dean *O God, be gracious* VE#
    Rizza *O God, be gracious* AIL
Psalm 133 CWP, NPCW, PAME

ANTHEMS AND VOCAL MUSIC

Title	Composer	Voices	E/M/D	Book source	Single sheet publisher
UNISON/TWO PART/HIGH VOICES					
Give us, Lord, a new heart	Farrell	U/SATB#	E/M	LAU, RITH, SLG	OCP
Veni Creator	Berlioz	SSA + solo SSA unacc	M/D	AC3	
Veni lumen cordium	Rizza	U/SATB#	E	CAON, CAS, FOL	
Veni Sancte Spiritus	Walker	U + cantor#	E	WYP	OCP
THREE/FOUR PARTS					
Be still, for the presence of the Lord	Evans arr Shephard	SAMen	E	OBFA	
Behold how good and joyful	Clarke-Whitfield	SATB	E	AC1	
Come down, O love divine	Tadman-Robins	SAMen	E	OBFA	
Come down, O love divine	Harris	SATB	E/M	FSB9, NCAB, MTH2	Novello
Come, Holy Ghost	Attwood	SATB	E	FAB1, NCAB, NNAB, NSAC2, AOAN1 (SAB)	Novello
Come, Holy Ghost	Heron	SAB or SATB	E		RSCM
Come, Holy Ghost, our souls inspire	Carter	SATB	D		OUP
Fear not, O Lord	Elgar	SATB	M		Novello
Listen sweet dove	Ives	SATB	M	EAC1, SC	RSCM
Song 34: To the Holy Spirit	Gibbons	SATB	E	AC1, MEA (SAB)	
Spirit of the Lord, come down	Harper	SA(T)B	E	SBS1, SOTL	RSCM
FIVE OR MORE PARTS					
Come down, O love divine	Rutter	SATB + SATB unacc	M/D		OUP
Come, Holy Ghost	Harvey	SSAATTBB unacc	D		Faber
Dum complerentur dies pentecostes	Palestrina	SAATTB unacc	M		Joed

ORGAN MUSIC

PRELUDES

Alberti J.   **Der du bist drei in Einigkeit** (verse 1 and/or verse 3) in *Choralvorspiele alter Meister* (Peters) E/M
Archer J.S.   **Meditation on 'Veni creator'** in *Variations on Well-known Hymn Tunes* (Novello) E/M*
Byrd W.   **Veni Creator Spiritus** 2 settings in *Tallis to Wesley* Bk.8 (Hinrichsen) E/M*
Pachelbel J.   **Komm, Gott Schöpfer, Heiliger Geist** in *120 Chorale Preludes of the 17C & 18C* (Peters) E*
Sumsion H.   **Chorale Prelude on 'Down Ampney'** (Paraclete) E/M

POSTLUDES

Bach J.S.   **Komm, Heiliger Geist, Herre Gott** BWV 651 in *Eighteen Chorale Preludes*, Novello Vol.17, Bärenreiter Vol.2, Peters Vol.7 M
Bédard D.   **Toccata et Grand Choeur sur 'Veni Creator'** No.6 of *Six Paraphrases Grégoriennes* (Cheldar) E/M
Piutti C.   **Komm, Gott Schöpfer, Heiliger Geist** in *Choralvorspiele* Op.34 Vol.2 (Bärenreiter) E
Telemann G.P.   **Komm, Heiliger Geist, Herre Gott** in *12 Easy Chorale Preludes* (Kalmus, Peters) E/M*

HYMNS AND SONGS

	pos	rdg	AMNS	CAON	CFE	CH4	CH5	CP	H&P	HTC	LAU	MP	NEH	SG	SOF	TS
Adoramus te, Domine (Taizé)				921	11		345					667		208		
Angel voices, ever singing		o	163	37	45	498	346	377	484	307	724	34	336	27	24	
Born by the Holy Spirit's breath		n							279	225		61		446		
Bright the vision that delighted		o	96	86			316	392	445	578			343	29		
Father eternal, Lord of the ages		s								1			356			
Father most holy, merciful and tender/loving		s	94	164	162			419	5	3			144			
Father of heaven, whose love profound			97	165	163	483	319	421	519	359		827	358	144		1201
Father, we adore you, lay our lives	cm	s		166	164		568	297		S 5	718	139			99	
Father, we love you, we worship		s		167	167		348					142			102	103
Forth in the peace of Christ we go	se	o	458	187	183	646	454	429		542	853		361	594		
Give to our God immortal praise		s	460	203			353	434	22	31		171		83		
God, we praise you! God, we bless you!		o				120	696	450		341			38			
Holy, holy, holy is the Lord		o		285			355				714	239		182		
Holy, holy, holy, Lord God almighty	mo	s	95	286	259	111	331	202	7	594	468	237	146	290	183	177
Holy Spirit, truth divine		n		289		626	300	184	289	235						
How shall I sing that majesty		s	472	296		128	468	466	8				373/ 699			
I bind unto myself today/Christ be with me		s		302	274	639	322	203	695	5	312		159 / 278			757
I see the Lord (Falson)		o												824	238	
I, the Lord of sea and sky (Here I am, Lord)	se	o		332	285	251	581	470			865	857		633	830	246
Immortal, invisible, God only wise		o	199	314	301	132	6	474	9	21	725	327	377	44	234	220
Lead us, heavenly Father, lead us		s	224	379	351		652	496	68	595	315	400	393	640	321	311
May the grace of Christ our Saviour	gr	s	181	446			524	520	762	370			298	579		
My God, how wonderful thou art		o	102	457	497		7	523	51	369	727	468	410	202	395	896
Sent by the Lord am I	se	o			638	250					855		616			
Spirit of God within me		n		612	665			196	294	243	310		677			
Strengthen for service, Lord/ Make strong	pc	o	421	619			446	323	626	423			306	473		
The God of Abraham praise		o	331	642		162	323	586	452	9	712	645	148	66	530	975
Thou/God, whose almighty word		s	180	684	738	112	324	267	29	506	887	699	466	597	557	
We give immortal praise		s	520	713				206	18	11						
Ye/You holy angels bright		o	198	755		179	376	626	20	353		783	475	76	619	

SONGS FOR CHILDREN

Because of who he is KS 18, TS 642
Father in heaven/Loving Creator CH4 116, H&P 3, HTC 2, LAU 313, SBTL, SG 200
Here I am, Lord KS 104

BIBLE READINGS

Morning Psalm 86.8–13
Evening Psalms 93 and 150
Isaiah 6.1–8
John 16.5–15

SINGING THE PSALM

Psalm 86.8–13 CRP, CWP, FGP, H&P, NPCW
Psalm 93 CH4, CRP, CWP, H&P, MCW1, NEP, NPCW, PAME
Psalm 150 CH4, CWP, H&P, LAU, MCW1, NEP, NPCW, PIW
Berthier *Let us sing to the Lord* TSFP#

ANTHEMS AND VOCAL MUSIC

Title	Composer	Voices	E/M/D	Book source	Single sheet publisher
UNISON/TWO PART/HIGH VOICES					
Duo seraphim	Dering	SS	M/D	AC2	CMS
Duo seraphim	Victoria	SSAA unacc	M		Joed
O Trinity of blessed light	S. & A.Barrett	U	E	SBS2	RSCM
Praise to the Trinity/Laus Trinitati	Hildegard of Bingen	U unacc	E	ETAS (Latin), OBFA	
THREE/FOUR PARTS					
As truly as God is our Father	Mathias	SATB	M/D	ETAS	OUP
Firmly I believe and truly	Shephard	SAMen	E	SFL2	
God the Holy Trinity	Halls	SATB	E	SBS1	RSCM
Holy, holy, holy, Lord God almighty	A.Smith	SAMen	M	OBFA	
Holy God, faithful and unchanging	Marks	SAMen	E	SBS2	
Holy, holy, holy	Schubert	SATB unacc	E	NOEAB, OBFA	
Holy Spirit, truth divine	Carter	SATB	E	ETAS, NOEAB	OUP
Hymn to the Trinity	Harper	SATB	E	SOTL	
Hymn to the Trinity	Leighton	SATB unacc	D	AC4	
If ye love me	Ledger	SATB	E	ETAS	
If ye love me	Tallis	SATB unacc	E	FAB1, NCAB, NOEAB, NSAC1, OBTA, SL (AATB), TA	OUP
O Trinity, most blessed light	Archer	SATB	E	ETAS	
Sanctus	Alcock	SATB + solo S	M	NSAC1	
FIVE OR MORE PARTS					
Benedicta sit sancta Trinitas	Philips	SSAATTBB unacc	M/D		Cathedral
Duo seraphim	Guerrero	SATB + SATB + SATB unacc	M		Joed
Heilig	Mendelssohn	SATB + SATB unacc	M		Collegium
Hymn of the Cherubim	Rachmaninov	SSAATTBB unacc	D	ETAS, RCM	Bailey & Ferguson (English)
I saw the Lord	Stainer	SATB + SATB	M		RSCM
If ye love me	Chilcott	SSATBB unacc	M	BCA, WFC	
The Cherubic Hymn	Glinka	SATTBB unacc	M/D	ESM	
Vox Dei	Wilby	SSAATTBB unacc	D	EAC1	Chester

Anthems suggested for Years B and C (pages 193 and 309) are also suitable.

ORGAN MUSIC

PRELUDES

Bach J.S.   **Kyrie, Gott Vater in Ewigkeit** BWV 672 in Novello Vol.16, Bärenreiter Vol.4, Peters Vol.7 E*
Cameron J.G.   **Capetown** in *Six Preludes on Hymn Tunes* (Novello) E/M
Praetorius M.   **O Lux beata Trinitas** in *Complete Works* (Breitkopf) E/M
Simonds B.   **Prelude on 'Iam sol recedit igneus'** (OUP) M/D

POSTLUDES

Blitheman J.   **Gloria tibi Trinitas** in *The Mulliner Book* (Stainer, 6 settings) and in *Early Organ Music* Vol.1 (Faber, 1 setting) E/M*-D*
Hurford P.   **Processional** (Ps.93) from *Suite: Laudate Dominum* (OUP) E/M
Langlais J.   **Le Père** No.1 of *Trois Méditations sur la Sainte Trinité* (Combre) E/M
Peeters F.   **Holy God, we praise thy name** ('Hursley') Op. 70/10 in *30 Chorale Preludes* Vol.3 (Peters) E/M
Thiman E.   **Postlude on 'Redhead 46'** No.3 of *Six Pieces* Set 1 (Curwen) E/M

PROPER 4 (SUNDAY BETWEEN 29 MAY AND 4 JUNE INCLUSIVE) YEAR A
(if after Trinity Sunday)

HYMNS AND SONGS

	pos	rdg	AMNS	CAON	CFE	CH4	CH5	CP	H&P	HTC	LAU	MP	NEH	SG	SOF	TS
As the bridegroom to his chosen		n	340						30							
Beyond all mortal praise		o		71									340			
Father of mercies, in thy word		n	167							247				224		
For the fruits of all/his creation		n	457	185	178	231	39	254	342	286	731	153	*621*	299	1234	685
From all that dwell/From all who live		n	98	192		146	351	431	489	580				82	119	
From the sun's rising		n		197								164			122	116
Happy are they, they that love God		n	176	262			649	456	711	473			369			
Jesus shall reign where'er the sun		n	143	359		470	97	490	239	516	322	379	388	45	301	1376
Lord, as I wake I turn to you	mo	n	485				56		634	267	672		236	561		
Lord, thy word abideth/your word shall guide us		n	166	420	390		384	515	476	251	977/8	446	407			
May the mind of Christ my Saviour		n		447		536	636	521	739	550		463		671	1448	887
My God, and/now is thy table spread/My God, your table		n	259	456	496		433	313		418	651		474			
O God of Bethel/Jacob		o	216	491		268	657	536	442	35		907	416	241		
Now let us from this table rise	pc		403	472		675	436	315	619	419	647		475			
Now thank we all our God		o	205	474	512	182	361	530	566	33	945	486	413	54	405	
Praise, my soul, the King of heaven	ga	o	192	565	602	160	366	555	13	38	807	560	436	93	466	433
Psallite Domino (Taizé)					614											
Rejoice! The Lord is king		n	139	580	619	449	281	563	243	180	326	575	443	440	482	948
Safe in the shadow of the Lord		o			626	55	595			445	953	583		516	991	
Thanks/Praise to God whose word was spoken		n	423			605	387	584	483	255			438	229		
The day thou gavest, Lord, is ended	ev	n	16	638	691	220	73	22	648	280	679	641	252	65	527	
Unless a (single) grain of wheat shall fall		n			754	347					748					
Wait for the Lord (Taizé)				949	762	276						88			1575	
Ye/You servants of the Lord		n	150	757			145	40	248	598			18			
Your word is a lamp unto my feet		n												234		

SONGS FOR CHILDREN
Colours of day CAP 55, CFE 118, CH 33, JP 28, KS2 433, LAU 764, MP 1039, SOF 64, TS 69
In our lives plant seeds of hope CH4 349

BIBLE READINGS

Psalm 33*
Ruth 2.1–20a
Luke 8.4–15

SINGING THE PSALM

Psalm 33* CRP, CWP, FGP, H&P, LAU, NEH, NPCW, PAME, PFS
Walker *Lord, be with us* OOD#

ANTHEMS AND VOCAL MUSIC

Title	Composer	Voices	E/M/D	Book source	Single sheet publisher
UNISON/TWO PART/HIGH VOICES					
Listen to the Spirit	Dean	U#	E	C	
Listen	Nazareth arr Archer	2 part	E	BC	
Praise to you, O Christ our Saviour	Farrell	U#	E	CFE, LAU, RITH, WYP	OCP
Take the word of God with you	Walker	U/SAB#	E	CFE, CIH, LAU	OCP
THREE/FOUR PARTS					
Christ was the Word	Maxim	SATB unacc	E	SBS2	
I will praise God because of his word	Purcell	SATB	E/M	TPS	
In God's Word	Purcell	SAB	M	TPS, SFL2	
Lord, be thy word my rule	Wood	2 part	E	SEA2	
O Word of God	Manalo	SATB#	E	C	
Teach me, O God	Camidge	SAB	E	CHM	
Teach me, O Lord	Attwood	SATB	E	NOEAB	RSCM
The Lord bless you and keep you	Rutter	2 part	E	EAC2	OUP
Thy word is a lantern	Purcell	SATB	M	APA	Novello
Word of God	Farrell	SATB unacc	E	GBU	
You visit the land and water it	Corp	SAMen	E/M	SFL2	
FIVE OR MORE PARTS					
Hymn to the Word of God	Maxwell Davies	SATTBB + solo T	D		Chester
Teach me, O Lord	Byrd	SAATB	M	OBTA	OUP

ORGAN MUSIC

PRELUDES

Adams T.   **Adagio** from **Voluntary No.4** in *Organ Works Vol.5: Six Organ Voluntaries* (Fagus) E/M*
De Grigny N.   **Quoniam tu solus** p.30 in *Livre d'Orgue* (Kalmus, Schott) M
Groves R.   **Praise my soul** in *12 Hymn-Tune Preludes* Set 1 (Novello) E(*)
Piutti C.   **Gottes Sohn ist kommen** ('Ravenshaw') in *Choralvorspiele* Op.34 Vol.1 (Bärenreiter) E
Thalben-Ball G. **Illsley** No.41 of *113 Variations on Hymn Tunes* (Novello) E

POSTLUDES

Couperin G.F.   **Rondo** in *Couperin: Pièces pour Orgue* (Chanvrelin) E/M*
Dubois T.   **Entrée en forme de carillon** from *Ten Pieces* (Schirmer); also in *Complete Works* Vol.1 (Bärenreiter) M
Howells H.   **Psalm-Prelude** Set 2 No.3 (Novello) D
Vann S.   **Prelude on 'Solothurn'** in *Six Preludes* (Mayhew) E/M

PROPER 5 (SUNDAY BETWEEN 5 AND 11 JUNE INCLUSIVE) YEAR A

(if after Trinity Sunday)

HYMNS AND SONGS

	pos	rdg	AMNS	CAON	CFE	CH4	CH5	CP	H&P	HTC	LAU	MP	NEH	SG	SOF	TS
Be bold, be strong		o										49			37	38
Be still and know I (John Bell)		n												18	672	
Be still and know II (John Bell)		n			70	754								242		
Be still and know that I am God		n		66		71	755	608			909	48			41	48
Be still, for the presence of the Lord		n		67	72	189	325	383			720	50	*629*	7	40	47
Bless the Lord, my soul (Taizé)				923	81		1				813			105	676	56
Broken for me, broken for you	cm	n		87			404	287		S 6		66		485	53	58
Come, wounded healer		n		130											1210	1176
Dear Lord and Father of mankind			115	144	143	485	549	411	673	356	934	111	353	497	79	79
Father, hear the prayer we offer		o	113	161	158	255	645	416	436	360	933	132	357	237	1229	
Father, we praise thee now the night is over	mo				168	209	53	3	633				149			
From thee/you all skill and science flow		n	286				512	345	389	310						
Have faith in God, my heart		n	372	268				458	675	431						
Immortal love, for ever full		n	133	315			211	475	392	105		328	378	176		
Jesu, thou joy of loving hearts			255	369		662	425	486	258	413		383	292	471		839
Lord, come and heal your church													427		351	
Lord Jesus Christ, lover of all		n									437					
Lord of all, to whom alone		n	492					509								
Misericordias Domini/From age to age (Taizé)					489											
O Christ the healer, we have come		n				717	513	346			430			489		
O let the Son of God enfold you		n		506									502		419	392
Saviour, again to thy dear name we raise	ev	n	15	587		221	71	20	643	281		584	250			
Sing of the Lord's goodness		o			654	157	368				713			61		
Soldiers of Christ, arise	o,n		219	606		515	487	571	719	533		604	449	643	506	
Stand up, stand up for Jesus	o		221	617			488	578	721	535		617	453	644	513	1517
The kingdom is upon you!		n	512					590					*650*			
There is no other friend															1037	
Thine arm/Your hands, O Lord, in days of old		n	285	671				347	397		431		324			
We cannot measure how you heal		n		712	772	718	514	348			433			490		
We give God thanks for those who knew		n			777					318	434					
Who would true valour see/He who would valiant be	o		212	281	248	535	662	621	688	590	862	224	372	639	174	
Your will for us and others, Lord		n						398								

SONGS FOR CHILDREN

Be bold, be strong JP 14, KS 17, MP 49, SOF 37, TS 38

Jesus' hands were kind hands CH4 351, CH5 213, H&P 393, JP 134, KS 194

BIBLE READINGS

Psalms [39 and] 41
1 Samuel 18.1–16
Luke 8.41–56

SINGING THE PSALM

Psalm 39 CWP, NPCW
Psalm 41 CRP, CWP, NPCW

ANTHEMS AND VOCAL MUSIC

Title	Composer	Voices	E/M/D	Book source	Single sheet publisher
UNISON/TWO PART/HIGH VOICES					
Amazing grace	Trad arr Jones	U + descant	E	RTF, VFLS	
Listen to the Spirit	Dean	U#	E	C	
Litany to the Holy Spirit (In the hour of my distress)	Hurford	U	E	AC2, NEP	OUP
On eagle's wings	Joncas	U#	E	CFE, LAU	OCP
There is a longing in our hearts	Quigley	SATB/U#	E	CH4, LAU, SG	OCP
THREE/FOUR PARTS					
A touching place (Christ's is the world)	Bell	SATB	E	CG, IAMB, LFB, WGIR, WIS	GIA
As water to the thirsty	Coleman arr Barnard	SATB	E	SC, WIS	
Evening prayers (Three Prayers of Dietrich Bonhoeffer)	P.Moore	SATB unacc	D		B&H
Hear my prayer	Batten	SATB + solo B	E		OUP
Hear my prayer	Mendelssohn	SATB	M		RSCM
I heard the voice of Jesus say	Shephard	SATB	M		RSCM
In a world where people walk in darkness	Trad arr Harper	SATB unacc	E	LOL	
In olden time and distant land	Mold	SATB	E		Encore
Just as I am	Chilcott	SATB	M	BCA	OUP
Litany to the Holy Spirit	Hurford	SATB	E	NOEAB, NSAC1	OUP
Now go in peace	Trad arr Jeffcoat	SATB	E	PSA, SC	
O Lord, heal us	Walker	SATB + descant	E	ATNJ	
O most merciful	Wood	SATB	E		RSCM
Strengthen ye the weak hands	Harris	SATB	M		Novello
There's a wideness in God's mercy	Bevan	SATB	E	LD, MTH1, NEP, NOEAB	
Thou God of truth and love	Archer	SATB	M		Mayhew
We cannot measure how you heal	Bell arr Archer	SATB	E	BC	RSCM
With loving hands	Tredinnick	SATB	E	WIS	
FIVE OR MORE PARTS					
Blessing	Allwood	SATBB unacc	E	NSAC2	

ORGAN MUSIC

PRELUDES

Bédard D.   **Entrée** from *Suite Liturgique* (Cheldar) E/M
Bridge F.   **Allegro ben moderato** No.6 of *Six Organ Pieces* (Boosey) M
Couperin G.F.   **Elévation in B flat minor** in *Couperin: Pièces pour Orgue* (Chanvrelin) E/M*
Vann S.   **Prelude on 'Song 1'** in *Six Preludes* (Mayhew) E/M
Vierne L.   **Arabesque** from *24 Pièces en Style Libre* Bk.2 (Masters, Durand) E(*)

POSTLUDES

Bédard D.   **Postlude** from *Quatre Pièces en Forme de Messe* (Cheldar) M
Dupré M.   **Lauda Sion** No.6 of *Eight Short Preludes on Gregorian Themes* (Summy-Birchard) E/M*
Gaze N.   **Toccata on 'Christe Sanctorum'** in *Matinales* (Fagus) M/D
Thalben-Ball G.   **Wolvercote** *or* **Monk's Gate** in *113 Variations on Hymn Tunes* (Novello) E/M

PROPER 6 (SUNDAY BETWEEN 12 AND 18 JUNE INCLUSIVE) YEAR A

(if after Trinity Sunday)

HYMNS AND SONGS

	pos	rdg	AMNS	CAON	CFE	CH4	CH5	CP	H&P	HTC	LAU	MP	NEH	SG	SOF	TS
A mighty fortress/A safe stronghold/God is our fortress		o,n	114		3	454	668	366	661	523	958	2			637	25
Be bold, be strong		o,n										49			37	38
Be thou my vision/Lord, be my vision		o	343	70	74/75	465	643	386	378	545	970	51	339	669	42	50
Behold the servant of the Lord		n							788						668	
Christ on whom the Spirit rested		o								228						
Christ triumphant, ever reigning		n		104	113	436	259	398		173	763	77	*613*	319	62	655
Crown him with many crowns		n	147	137	139	459	263	166	255	174	321	109	352	321	77	77
Do not be afraid, for I have redeemed you		o		150	147	191					972	115			1213	1183
Father, hear the prayer we offer		o	113	161	158	255	645	416	436	360	933	132	357	237	1229	
God is our strength from days of old		o,n		220												
God moves in a mysterious way		o	112	222		158	13	445	65			193	365			700
God of grace and God of glory		o	367	225			533	448	712	324		192		574	139	
Happy are they, they that love God		n	176	262			649	456	711	473			369			
Here in this place (Gather us in)	hc	o			253	623					475			4		
Jesus shall take the highest honour		n		360								378		123	302	296
King of kings, majesty		n										1000			1404	309
O taste and see that the Lord is good (Rogers)		o													447	
Sing of the Lord's goodness		o			654	157	368				713			61		
Soldiers of Christ, arise		n	219	606		515	487	571	719	533		604	449	643	506	
Soldiers who are Christ's below		n	302	607				228					450			
Spread, O spread, thou mighty word		o											482			
Stand up, stand up for Jesus		n	221	617			488	578	721	535		617	453	644	513	1517
The kingdom is upon you!		n	512					590					*650*			
The kingdom of God is justice and joy		n		646	701			591	139	333	821	651		184		
The Lord is my light (Taizé)				944												
Through all the changing scenes of life		o	209	686	740		372	604	73	46		702	467	654	1566	1561
Thy/Your kingdom come, O God		n	177	691			509	607	783	334		949	499	269		
Thy/Your kingdom come! On bended knee		n	178	690		473		608					500			
Who would true valour see/He who would valiant be		o	212	281	248	535	662	621	688	590	862	224	372	639	174	
Within our darkest night (Taizé)				950												

SONGS FOR CHILDREN

Be bold, be strong JP 14, KS 17, MP 49, SOF 37, TS 38
Be the centre of my life CAON 778, CH 21, KS 20

BIBLE READINGS

Psalms [42 and] 43
1 Samuel 21.1–15
Luke 11.14–28

SINGING THE PSALM

Psalms 42 and/or 43 CRP, CWP, H&P, LAU, NEH, NPCW, PAME, PFS
Bell *Just as a lost and thirsty deer* LFB, PPP
Berthier *De noche iremos (By night we hasten)* TSFP#
Hurd *As the deer longs* CFE, CG, CH4, LAU#
Farrell *O God, for you I long* C, GBAN#
Miffleton *As the deer* C#
Rizza *Oculi mei* AIL#
Walker *We love this place, O God* ATNJ
Walsh *Why so sad, O my soul?* C

ANTHEMS AND VOCAL MUSIC

Title	Composer	Voices	E/M/D	Book source	Single sheet publisher
UNISON/TWO PART/HIGH VOICES					
Community of Christ	Farrell	U#	E	GBU	OCP
Give ear unto me	Marcello	SS	E/M	AC2	
In the land	Farrell	U#	E	GBAN	
There is a longing	Quigley	U/SATB#	E	CH4, LAU, SG	OCP
THREE/FOUR PARTS					
Be thou my vision	Chilcott	SATB	M	NOEAB, BCA	OUP
Be thou my vision	Rutter	SATB	M		OUP
Christ the Word	Vann	SATB	M	STS	
Christ was the Word	Maxim	SATB unacc	E	SBS2	
Fight the good fight	Gardner	SATB	M	MTH1	OUP
God has spoken	Trad arr Llewellyn	SATB	E	SWAMS	
Gustate et videte	Isaac	SATB unacc	E	CM5	
How lovely are the messengers	Mendelssohn	SATB	M	AFC	Novello
I will praise God because of his word	Purcell	SATB	E/M	TPS	
In God's Word	Purcell	SAB	M	TPS, SFL2	
Lord of our Fathers	Mawby	SAMen	E	AOAN1	
O sing joyfully	Batten	SATB unacc	E	SCAB, WFC	RSCM
O taste and see	Vaughan Williams	SATB unacc	E	AC4, NOEAB, NSAC1	OUP
Taste and see	Walker	U/SATB#	E	CSF	
Teach me, O God	Camidge	SAB	E	CHM	
Teach me, O Lord	Attwood	SATB	E	NOEAB	RSCM
To be a pilgrim	Burt	SAMen	E/M	OBFA	
Waiting for the word	Skellern	SATB	E/M		RSCM
The will of God	Warren	SAMen	E	NAB2, AOAN1	
FIVE OR MORE PARTS					
Teach me, O Lord	Byrd	SAATB	M	OBTA	OUP

ORGAN MUSIC

PRELUDES

Buxtehude D.   **Ein feste Burg ist unser Gott** BuxWV 184 in Peters Vol.2 and Bärenreiter Vol.4 E/M
Couperin G.F.   **Récit de hautbois** (either or both settings) in *Couperin: Pièces pour Orgue* (Chanvrelin) E/M
Harwood B.   **Eventide** No.2 of *8 Short Pieces* Op.58 in *Complete Works* Vol.2 (Stainer) E/M
Tambling C.   **Slane** in *100 Hymn Preludes* (Mayhew) E
Willan H.   **Prelude on 'Irish'** in *36 Short Preludes and Postludes* Set 2 (Peters) E

POSTLUDES

Bennett J.   **Voluntary No.5 in A** in *Ten Voluntaries* Bk.1 (Fagus) M*
Kittel J.C.   **Präludium in C** in *The Progressive Organist* Bk.5 (Novello) E/M
Thalben-Ball G.   **Wiltshire** No.110 of *113 Variations on Hymn Tunes* (Novello) E
Zwart J.   First section of **Fantasie 'Een Vaste Burg'** in *Niederländisch-belgische Orgelromantik* (Breitkopf) E/M

PROPER 7 (SUNDAY BETWEEN 19 AND 25 JUNE INCLUSIVE) YEAR A

(if after Trinity Sunday)

HYMNS AND SONGS

	pos	rdg	AMNS	CAON	CFE	CH4	CH5	CP	H&P	HTC	LAU	MP	NEH	SG	SOF	TS
Bread of the world in mercy broken	cm	n	270	83	97		403	285	599	396			277	465		
Bring to the Lord a glad new song		n				106				336	705			78		
Christian, seek not yet repose		o								355						
Come, let us join our cheerful songs	ga		144	120			332	401	810	206		93	349	33	70	
Come, my Way, my Truth, my Life	cm	n		123		579	610	405	254		911		*633*			
Come, sinners, to the gospel feast		n							460							
Confitemini Domino (Taizé)				925	137						701					
For everyone born, a place at the table		n				685										
Glory, love, and praise, and honour	pc	n	461	207				436	35				287			
Great is the Lord and most worthy of praise		o		248			354					199		113	145	137
Here in this place (Gather us in)	ga	n			253	623					475			4		
Here, O my Lord, I see thee face to face	cm	n	274	279		664	418	304	608	406		230		468		
How long, O Lord, will you forget		o				7					848		651			
I, the Lord of sea and sky (Here I am, Lord)		n		332	285	251	581	470			865	857		633	830	246
In God alone my soul (Taizé)															813	
Jesus, humble was your birth		n	379					488								
Let God arise		o										405			323	
Let us build a house (All are welcome)		n				198					458					
Lord of our life and God of our salvation		o		417						529		441	404			
My God, and/now is thy table spread/My God, your table		n	259	456	496		433	313		418	651		474			
Rock of ages (Kendrick)		o												1507	951	
Rock of ages, cleft for me		o	135	584	624	554	557	565	273	593		582	445	150	488	950
Safe in the shadow of the Lord		o			626	55	595			445	953	583		516	991	
Tell out, my soul		n	422	631	684	286	712	362	86	42	880	631	186	62	520	471
The King of love my Shepherd is	o,n	126	649	699	462	20	589	69	44	804	649	457	205	533	984
The trumpets sound, the angels sing		n					448					667			550	506
Thy/Your hand, O God, has guided		n	171	689	741	511	529	606	784	536	876	705	485	649	1065	
We come as guests invited		n					451			602	630	723				
We rest on thee/We trust in you		o								446		735		510	587	1043

SONGS FOR CHILDREN

God is so good JP 53, KS 78, SOF 732, TS 1223
Know that God is good (Mungu ni mwema) CH4 788, OITB

BIBLE READINGS

Psalms 46 [and 48]

1 Samuel 24.1–17

Luke 14.12–24

SINGING THE PSALM

Psalm 46 CH4, CWP, H&P, NPCW, PAME

Psalm 48 CWP, NPCW

ANTHEMS AND VOCAL MUSIC

Title	Composer	Voices	E/M/D	Book source	Single sheet publisher
UNISON/TWO PART/HIGH VOICES					
Bread for the world	Farrell	U#	E	GBAN	
Bread for the world broken	Walker	U/SAB#	E	CFE, WYP	
Community of Christ	Farrell	U + descant	E	GBU	
Gather us in (Here in this place)	Haugen	U#	E	CFE, CH4, LAU	GIA
Now in this banquet	Haugen	U	E	CFE, LAU	GIA
O sacrum convivium	Leighton	SSA	M/D	EAC2	Banks
Send down the fire of your justice	Haugen	U/SATB#	E	C, TS	GIA
Table of plenty (Come to the feast)	Schutte	U#	E	LAU	OCP
Take my gifts	Farrell	U	E	GBU	
The bread which you do not use	Moore	2 part	E	BFH	
The Call (Come, my Way)	Vaughan Williams	U	E	NEP	S&B
THREE/FOUR PARTS					
Blessed is he that considereth the poor and needy	Wise	SATB	M	NCAB	
Bread of the world in mercy broken	Aston	SATB	E/M	SBS2	
Bread of the world in mercy broken	Baldwin	SAMen	E	SBS2	
Broken for me	Lunt	SATB	E	SWAMS	
Come among us, Lord	Sheldon	SATB	E	WIS	
Come, my Way, my Truth, my Life	Archer	SAB	E/M	AOAN1	Mayhew
Come my Way, my Truth my Life	Harris	SATB	M	NNAB	
Give almes of thy goods	Tye	SATB unacc	E	AC1, OBTA	OUP
I heard the voice of Jesus say	Shephard	SATB	M		RSCM
Now let us from this table rise	Henderson	SATB	E	SBS1	RSCM
O sacrum convivium	Messiaen	SATB unacc	D		UMP
Strengthen ye the weak hands	Harris	SATB	M		Novello
The Call	Lloyd	SATB unacc	M		RSCM
FIVE OR MORE PARTS					
O sacrum convivium	Tallis	SAATB unacc	M/D	TA	OUP

ORGAN MUSIC

PRELUDES

Bingham S.   **Chorale Prelude 'Ajalon'** (Rock of Ages) No.1 of *12 Hymn Preludes* Op.38 Set 1 (Gray) E

Bull J.   **Voluntary** in *A Graded Anthology for Organ* Bk.5 (Cramer) E*

Dubois T.   **Marcietta** from **Seven Pieces** (Butz, Kalmus); also in *Complete Works* Vol.1 (Bärenreiter) E/M

Dupré M.   **No.1** of *Trois Élévations* (Combre) E

Noble T.T.   **Chorale Prelude on 'Rockingham'** (OUP reprint) E/M

POSTLUDES

Archer M.   **A Thornbury Fanfare** in *New Music for Organ* Bk.2 and *The Organ Music of Malcolm Archer* (both Mayhew) M

Bridge F.   **Allegro con spirito in B flat** from *Three Pieces (1905)* (Novello) M

Marsh J.   **Voluntary II** from *Eighteen Voluntaries* Vol.1 (Animus) E*

Thalben-Ball G.   **Woodlands** in *113 Variations on Hymn Tunes* (Novello) E

PROPER 8 (SUNDAY BETWEEN 26 JUNE AND 2 JULY INCLUSIVE) YEAR A

HYMNS AND SONGS

	pos	rdg	AMNS	CAON	CFE	CH4	CH5	CP	H&P	HTC	LAU	MP	NEH	SG	SOF	TS
All my hope on God is founded			336	19	21	192	10	368	63	451	959	16	333	525		620
At/In the name of Jesus		n	148	54	59	458	94	380	74	172	762	41	338	317	32	33
Beyond all mortal praise		o		71									340			
Christ triumphant, ever reigning		n		104	113	436	259	398		173	763	77	*613*	319	62	655
Come and see the shining hope		n		110						188		86		454		
Come, worship God who is worthy of honour		o					690			18						
Delight yourselves in the Lord		o										113				
Great is the darkness		n										835		264	742	136
Hark what a sound, and too divine		n					127	28	236				*600*			
Jesus is the name we honour		n				481						870		122	870	285
Jesus, remember me (Taizé)				931		775	617				253			875	294
Jesus shall take the highest honour		n		360								378		123	302	296
Lord of all power, I give you my will/Lord of creation		n	395			500	594	508	699	547	869	440				
Love divine, all loves excelling		n	131	428	398	519	634	516	267	217	801	449	408	179	377	343
My Jesus, my Saviour		n		461		531						1003		129	935	367
Reign in me		n										570			478	437
Sent by the Lord am I	se	o			638	250					855			616		
Soon and very soon		n				749	138					605			1007	460
The kingdom is upon you!		n	512					590					*650*			
The kingdom of God is justice and joy		n		646	701			591	139	333	821	651		184		
Through the darkness of the ages		n											538			
Thy/Your kingdom come, O God		n	177	691			509	607	783	334		949	499	269		
Thy/Your kingdom come! On bended knee		n	178	690		473		608					500			
When came in flesh the incarnate Word		n											17			
When peace, like a river		n										757				574
When the Lord in glory comes		n								201		758				

SONGS FOR CHILDREN

Soon and very soon CH4 749, CH5 138, JP 221, MP 605, SOF 1007, TCB 20, TS 460
When the time is right CAON 913, KS 379

BIBLE READINGS

Psalm 50*
1 Samuel 28.3–19
Luke 17.20–37

SINGING THE PSALM

Psalm 50* CH4, CRP, CWP, NPCW, PAME
Bell *Let the giving of thanks* PPP

ANTHEMS AND VOCAL MUSIC

Title	Composer	Voices	E/M/D	Book source	Single sheet publisher
UNISON/TWO PART/HIGH VOICES					
Settings of the Lord's Prayer	Various	U/SATB	E	MCW1	
At the name of Jesus	Walker	U/SATB#	E	ATNJ	OCP
King of glory, King of peace	Harris	SSA	M		OUP
King of glory, King of peace	Sanders	SSAA	M/D		Encore
Soon and very soon	Trad arr Iliff	U/SATB	E	TCB	
THREE/FOUR PARTS					
Above all praise	Mendelssohn	SATB	E	NCAB, OEAB	RSCM
Christus factus est	Anerio	SATB unacc	M	AWTE, CM1, ESM	
Christus factus est	Bruckner	SATB unacc	M/D	ESM	RSCM
Glorious and powerful God	Wood	SATB	E/M	SC	Cathedral
In the city of the Lord	Harper	SATB	M	LOL	
Jesus shall take the highest honour	Bowater	SATB	E/M	WIS	
King of glory, King of peace	J.S.Bach arr Harris	SATB	E	NCAB	OUP
King of glory, King of peace	Ives	SATB	M	SBS1	RSCM
Light of the lonely pilgrim's heart	Nardone	SATB	E		B&H
O how glorious	Harwood	SATB	M/D		Banks
O quam gloriosum	Byrd	SATB unacc	M	OBTA	Banks
O quam gloriosum	Vaet	SATB unacc	M	ETAS	
O quam gloriosum	Victoria	SATB unacc	M	ESM, NCAB	Chester
Rejoice, the Lord is king	Archer	SATB	M		Mayhew
Rejoice, the Lord is king	Kelly	SATB	M/D	NNAB, MTH1	
Rejoice, the Lord is king	Weaver	SATB	M	SC	
The Song of Christ's Glory	P.Moore	SATB	E		RSCM
FIVE OR MORE PARTS					
All hail the power of Jesu's name	Greenhill	SATBB	E/M		Novello
Glorious in heaven	Whitlock	SATBB unacc	E/M	ETAS	Banks
God has chosen me	Farrell	SSATB unacc	E	GBAN	OCP
O nomen Jesu	Philips	SSATB unacc	M		Mapa Mundi
The Song of Christ's Glory	Ives	SSAATTBB unacc	M	WOTC	

ORGAN MUSIC

PRELUDES

Alain J.   **Petite pièce** in *Complete Works* Bk.3 (Leduc) E/M*
Callahan C.   **Prelude on 'Michael'** in *Two English Voluntaries* (Concordia) E/M
Dyson G.   **Prelude** from *Prelude and Postlude* (Novello) E/M
Eben P.   **Theme** *and/or* **Vars. 1 & 2** from *Choralpartita 'O Jesu, all mein Leben bist du'* (Universal) E
Tambling C.   **Interlude on 'Irish'** in *An Organ Miscellany* (Mayhew) E

POSTLUDES

Willan H.   **Prelude on 'Slane'** (Peters) E/M
Eben P.   **Final** (Var.5) from *Choralpartita 'O Jesu, all mein Leben bist du'* (Universal) M
Guridi J.   **Himno** No.4 in *Escuela Española de Organo* (UME) E/M
Long S.   **Voluntary in D minor** in *Old English Organ Music for Manuals* Bk.6 (OUP) E*

HYMNS AND SONGS

	pos	rdg	AMNS	CAON	CFE	CH4	CH5	CP	H&P	HTC	LAU	MP	NEH	SG	SOF	TS
All my hope on God is founded	o		336	19	21	192	10	368	63	451	959	16	333	525		620
All ye who seek for sure relief/a comfort sure		n	64	26	31			101			212		63			
Be bold, be strong		o										49			37	38
Christ is the One who calls		n										813				
Come, praise the Lord, he is life		n													1206	1173
Deck thyself, my soul, with gladness/Soul, array thyself		n	257	146			445	295	606	400			280			
God forgave my sin in Jesus' name		n		212	209		480			S 12	849	181			129	123
He gave his life in selfless love		n					417			405		214		467		
Head of thy church triumphant		n							818							
I come with joy		n	473	304		656	421	305	610	408	649		623	469		
I heard the voice of Jesus say		n	247	310		540	576	469	136		795	275	376		215	206
Immortal love, for ever full		n	133	315			211	475	392	105		328	378	176		
Jesus Christ is waiting		n		349	323	360					889			624	1381	1360
Just as I am, without one plea		n	246	374	339	553	587	308	697	440		396	294	507	316	306
My Lord, you wore no royal crown		n								118				628		
Nada te turbe/Nothing can trouble (Taizé)				937							947			659		
O bless the God of Israel		o					706			599						
O Christe Domine Jesu (Taizé)					519						757					
O for a closer walk with God		n	231	483		552	637	532		368		494	414		951	903
O love, how deep, how broad, how high		n	119	516		354	214	118	229				425			
These are the days of Elijah		o					141					1012			1047	503
This is the day the Lord hath/has made		n	22	677				9	577	379			257	70		
When Christ was lifted from the earth/Dear Christ, uplifted		n	525	142						335				453		
When the Spirit of the Lord is within my heart		o		912											598	
Who would true valour see/He who would valiant be		o	212	281	248	535	662	621	688	590	862	224	372	639	174	
Will you come and follow me		n		752	812	533	605	622			877		647	634	1120	
You, living Christ, our eyes behold		n	533				333					487				

SONGS FOR CHILDREN

Zacchaeus SSJ
Zacchaeus was a very little man CAON 919, CH 243, JP 300

BIBLE READINGS

Psalms 56 [and 57]
2 Samuel 2.1–11; 3.1
Luke 18.31 - 19.10

SINGING THE PSALM

Psalm 56 CWP, NPCW
 Bell *In my day of fear* PPP
Psalm 57 CWP, NPCW, PIW

ANTHEMS AND VOCAL MUSIC

Title	Composer	Voices	E/M/D	Book source	Single sheet publisher
UNISON/TWO PART/HIGH VOICES					
Amazing grace	Trad arr Jones	U + descant	E	RTF	
Lift thine eyes	Mendelssohn	SSA	M		Novello
The Spirit of the Lord is upon me	Corp	2 part	E	VFLS	
THREE/FOUR PARTS					
Ad te levavi oculos meos	Palestrina	SATB unacc	M		OUP
Be thou my vision	Chilcott	SATB	E/M	BCA, NOEAB	OUP
Be thou my vision	Rutter	SATB	M		OUP
I heard the voice of Jesus say	Shephard	SATB	M		RSCM
In a world where people walk in darkness	Trad arr Harper	SATB	E	LOL	
Just as I am	Chilcott	SATB	E	BCA	OUP
O thou the central orb	Wood	SATB	M	AC4, SC, AFC	RSCM
Open our eyes	Reith	SATB (unacc)	E	C	
Oculi omnium	Wood	SATB unacc	E	NSAC1	
Out of darkness	Walker	U/SATB#	E	CFE, LAU, OOD	OCP
Save me, O God	Blow	SATB unacc	M		Broude
The Lord is my light and my salvation	Noon	SATB	M	SBS1	RSCM
The Lord is my light and my salvation	Rutter	SATB + clarinet	M		OUP
The Spirit of the Lord	Elgar	SATB	M	SAEE	RSCM
To be a pilgrim	Burt	SAMen	E/M	OBFA	
We cannot measure how you heal (g)	Bell arr Archer	SATB	E	BC	RSCM
Wings of the morning	Rutter	SATB	M		OUP
FIVE OR MORE PARTS					
I am thine, O save me	S.S.Wesley	SATTB	E/M	MTP	
Oculi omnium	Cleobury	SSAATTBB unacc	M		Encore
Open thou mine eyes	Rutter	SSATB unacc	M		OUP
Save me, O God	Byrd	SSAATB unacc	M		Joed

ORGAN MUSIC

PRELUDES

Dubois T. **Offertoire** No.3 of *Ten Pieces* (Schirmer); also in *Complete Works* Vol.1 (Bärenreiter) E/M
Marchand L. **Basse de trompette ou de cromorne** p.82 in *Selected Compositions* Vol.1 (Kalmus) E*
Nixon J. **St Bernard** in *Hymn Tune Preludes* (Fagus) E/M
Sumsion H. **Allegretto** (RSCM) M
Vierne L. **Madrigal** No.9 of *24 Pièces en Style Libre* Bk.1 (Masters, Durand) E/M(*)

POSTLUDES

Corrette G. **Dialogue à deux choeurs** p.22 in *Messe du 8o ton* (Kalmus, Masters, Schola Cantorum) E*
Fedak A. **The Kingsfold Trumpet** in *An Album of Trumpet Tunes* (Warner) E/M
Stanford C.V. **Funeral March from Becket** (Stainer) M
Tambling C. **Fugue and Chorale** in *An Organ Miscellany* (Mayhew) E/M

PROPER 10 (SUNDAY BETWEEN 10 AND 16 JULY INCLUSIVE) YEAR A

HYMNS AND SONGS

	pos	rdg	AMNS	CAON	CFE	CH4	CH5	CP	H&P	HTC	LAU	MP	NEH	SG	SOF	TS
All my hope on God is founded		o	336	19	21	192	10	368	63	451	959	16	333	525		620
All praise to thee, for thou, O King divine		n	337	22			684	372	253	204			335			
Beyond all mortal praise		o		71									340			
Christ is the King! O friends rejoice		n	345				86	165		492			345	31		
Earth was waiting, spent and restless		n								54						
Father, we praise thee now the night is over	mo				168	209	53	3	633				149			
God is my great desire		2ps		218	216						912					
God of freedom, God of justice		n		224		263		447								
Great is the Lord and most worthy of praise		o		248			354					199		113	145	137
Great is thy faithfulness		o		249		153	80	453	66	260		200	636	39	147	138
Holy, holy, holy, Lord God almighty	mo	o	95	286	259	111	321	202	7	594	468	237	146	290	183	177
Jesus Christ is waiting		n		349	323	360				889				624	1381	1360
Judge eternal, throned in splendour		n		372		264	535	356	409	329		395	490	600		
Let us go to the house of the Lord		n												331		
My God, how wonderful thou art		o	102	457	497		7	523	51	369	727	468	410	202	395	896
O God of earth and altar		n		492	527			358	426		935		492			
O Lord, hear my prayer (Taizé)				938	542		620				929	908		246	423	394
Pray that Jerusalem may have		n				82	506	560	510				441			
Saviour, again to thy dear name we raise	ev		15	587		221	71	20	643	281		584	250			
Sing of the Lord's goodness		o			654	157	368				713			61		
Son of God, eternal Saviour		n	132				527	573		102			498			
Thy/Your kingdom come, O God		n	177	691			509	607	783	334		949	499	269		
Who is this so weak and helpless		n		748									474			

SONGS FOR CHILDREN

O Lord, I want to sing your praises MP 904, SOF 961

BIBLE READINGS

Psalm 60 [and 63]
2 Samuel 7.18–29
Luke 19.41 - 20.8

SINGING THE PSALM

Psalm 60 CWP, NPCW
Psalm 63 CRP, CWP, H&P, LAU, NEH, NPCW, PFS
    Bell *O God, you are my God alone* CG, CH4, PPP
    Haugen *Your love is finer than life* CFE, LAU (GIA)#
    Hurd *My heart is searching* C#
    Taizé *Jesus, your Spirit in us* C#
    Walker *O Lord, I will sing* OOD (OCP)#

ANTHEMS AND VOCAL MUSIC

Title	Composer	Voices	E/M/D	Book source	Single sheet publisher
UNISON/TWO PART/HIGH VOICES					
Eins bitte ich vom Herren	Schütz	2 part	M	AC2	
God of the living	Tamblyn	U/SATB#	E	SFTL	
I was glad	Hubbard	SA	M	SFJ	Banks
THREE/FOUR PARTS					
A Gaelic Blessing	Rutter	SATB	E	NCAB	RSCM
And when the builders	Shephard	SATB	M/D		Banks
Behold, the tabernacle of God	Harris	SATB	E		RSCM
Behold, the tabernacle of God	Rutter	SATB	M/D		OUP
Christ is our cornerstone	Ogden	SATB	E	SBS2	
Christ is our cornerstone	Thorne	SATB	E/M	NOEAB	
Christians shout for joy and gladness	Trad German	SAB	E	OBFA	
God is our hope and strength	J.S.Bach	SATB	E	AC1	
Jesus and the traders	Kodaly	SATB unacc	D		Universal Edition
Judge eternal	Archer	SATB	E/M		Mayhew
O pray for the peace of Jerusalem	Blow	SATB	M	FSB2	OUP
O pray for the peace of Jerusalem	Howells	SATB	M		OUP
Peace be to this congregation	Cadden arr Grindle	SATB	E/M		Encore
Pray that Jerusalem	Chilcott	SATB	E/M		OUP
Pray that Jerusalem	Stanford	SATB	E	ASA	RSCM
Surely thou hast tasted that the Lord is good	Bernard Rose	SATB unacc	D	EAC1	Cathedral
There's a wideness in God's mercy	Bevan	SATB	E/M	LD, MTH1, NEP, NOEAB	
FIVE OR MORE PARTS					
Civitas sancti tui	Byrd	SAATBB unacc	M		Chester
God is our hope and strength	Blow	SSAATTBB	M		Banks

ORGAN MUSIC

PRELUDES

Bédard D.	**Dialogue** from *Suite du Premier Ton* (Cheldar) E/M
Berkeley L.	**Andantino** Op.21 No.2 (Cramer) E/M
Lloyd Webber W.S.	**Arietta** in *Eight Varied Pieces* (Bosworth) M
Whitlock P.	**Dolcezza** from *Reflections*, now in *Whitlock: Complete Shorter Works* (OUP) E/M
Willan H.	**Prelude on 'Nicea'** in *36 Short Preludes and Postludes* Set 1 (Peters) E*

POSTLUDES

Archer M.	**Noel nouvelet** in *Fifty Hymn Preludes* (Mayhew) M
Beauvarlet-Charpentier J.J.	**Grand Choeur in G minor** in *Pièces pour Orgue* (Chanvrelin) E/M
Marsh J.	**Voluntary V** from *Eighteen Voluntaries* Vol.1 (Animus) E*
Smith A.	**Toccata-Rondo** (Escorial) E/M

PROPER 11 (SUNDAY BETWEEN 17 AND 23 JULY INCLUSIVE) YEAR A

HYMNS AND SONGS

	pos	rdg	AMNS	CAON	CFE	CH4	CH5	CP	H&P	HTC	LAU	MP	NEH	SG	SOF	TS
At even ere the sun was set		g	9	50			65	12	142	315		43	243	487		
At/In the name of Jesus		n	148	54	59	458	94	380	74	172	762	41	338	317	32	33
Be thou my vision/Lord, be my vision		o	343	70	74/75	465	643	386	378	545	970	51	339	669	42	50
Christ is made the sure foundation/Blessèd city		n	332ii	97	109	200	326	207/208	485	559	456	73	205	572	1199	654
Christ is our cornerstone		n	161	98			327	395		564			206	14		
Christ is the world's light		n	440	99	111		87	213	455	321	744			591		
Dear Lord and Father of mankind		g	115	144	143	485	549	411	673	356	934	111	353	497	79	79
Forth in thy name, O Lord, I go	se	o	239	188	184	529	567	430	381	306	861	159	235	623	1237	
Hail, thou once despised/our once rejected Jesus		n		258			268	168	222	175		203			149	
How sweet the name of Jesus sounds		n	122	297		461	92	467	257	211		251	374	42	194/782	190/1273
Immortal love, for ever full		g	133	315			211	475	392	105		328	378	176		
In Christ alone my hope is found		n									1072				1346	1311
Jesus is the name we honour		n				481					870			122	870	285
Jesus, the name high over all		n		364			99		264	213	385			323	307	298
Jesus, where'er thy people meet/Lord Jesus, when your people	ga	n	162	367			336	492	549	371			390	16		844
Laudate omnes gentes/Sing praises, all you peoples (Taizé)												478		1515		
Let us sing to the Lord (Taizé)												689				
Lord God, you love us (Taizé)												782				
Lord Jesus Christ, lover of all		g										437				
Lord of all power, I give you my will/Lord of creation		o	395			500	594	508	699	547	869	440				
Lord of beauty, thine the splendour		o	106	415			29	258					265			
Lord, we come to ask your healing		g		422												
Quiet my mind, Lord		g													983	
Shout for joy, loud and long		n								348						
The King of love my shepherd is		g	126	649	699	462	20	589	69	44	804	649	457	205	533	984
The Lord's my shepherd		g	426	654	706	14–16	21	594	70	591	806	660	459	207	537	486
The Lord's my shepherd (Townend)		g										1008		206	1030	988
Thine arm/Your hands, O Lord, in days of old		g	285	671			347	397			431		324			
We cannot measure how you heal		g		712	772	718	514	348			433			490		
We have a gospel to proclaim		n	431	716	778	363	491	612	465	519	852	728	486	331	1583	

SONGS FOR CHILDREN

Each of us is a living stone CAON 793, CH 41

BIBLE READINGS

Psalms 67 [and 70]
1 Kings 2.10–12; 3.16–28
Acts 4.1–22
Mark 6.30–34,53–56

SINGING THE PSALM

Psalm 67 CH4, CRP, CWP, FGP, H&P, MCW1, NPCW, PAME
   Dean *O God, be gracious* VE#
   Rizza *O God, be gracious* AIL#
Psalm 70 CWP, NPCW, PAME

ANTHEMS AND VOCAL MUSIC

Title	Composer	Voices	E/M/D	Book source	Single sheet publisher
UNISON/TWO PART/HIGH VOICES					
I know that my Redeemer lives	Dean	U	E		Decani
Psalm 23 (g)	Mawby	U	M		RSCM
The Lord is my shepherd (g)	Greene	SS	M	AC2	
The Lord is my shepherd (g)	Schubert	SSAA	M/D	ESM	
THREE/FOUR PARTS					
Brother James' Air (g)	Bain arr Bullard	SATB	E	NOEAB	
Christ is our cornerstone	Ogden	SATB	E/M	SBS2	RSCM
Christ is our cornerstone	Thorne	SATB	E/M	NOEAB	
Christus factus est	Bruckner	SATB unacc	M/D	ESM	RSCM
God so loved the world	Bullard	SAMen	E	OBFA	
God so loved the world	Stainer	SATB unacc	E/M	AWTE, FAB1, MHWE, NOEAB, NSAC1	RSCM
God so loved the world (g)	Stainer	SAB unacc	E/M	AOAN1	
I know that my Redeemer liveth	Morley	SATB	M		Fagus
The God of Love (g)	Thalben Ball	SATB	E/M		Banks
The Lord is my shepherd (g)	Berkeley	SATB	D	MTP	Chester
The Lord is my shepherd (g)	Carter	SATB	M	ACA	OUP
The Lord is my shepherd (g)	Goodall	SATB	E		Faber
The Lord is my shepherd (g)	Rutter	SATB	M		OUP
The Lord is my shepherd (g)	Stanford	SATB	M/D	ASA	Novello
The Song of Christ's Glory	P.Moore	SATB	E/M		RSCM
We cannot measure how you heal (g)	Bell arr Archer	SATB	E	BC	RSCM
Where shall wisdom be found?	Carter	SATB	M/D		OUP
FIVE OR MORE PARTS					
Ich bin der Auferstehung und das Leben (g)	Schütz	SATB + SATB	M		Peters
The Song of Christ's Glory	Ives	SSAATTBB unacc	M	WOTC	
Where shall wisdom be found?	Boyce	SSATB	M		Novello

ORGAN MUSIC

PRELUDES

Armstrong Gibbs C.	**Folk-Song** No.2 of *Six Sketches* Bk.2 (OUP) E/M	
Bach J.S.	**Adagio** from BWV564 in Novello Vol.9, Bärenreiter Vol.6, Peters Vol.3 E/M	
Callahan C.	**Prelude** or **Chaconne** from *Suite in G* (MorningStar) E	
Gant A.	**Westminster Abbey** in *100 Hymn Preludes* (Mayhew) E	
Vierne L.	**Introit** from *Messe Basse* (Schola Cantorum) E*	

POSTLUDES

Callahan C.   **The Rejoicing** from *Suite in G* (MorningStar) E/M
Elgar E.   **Carillon** Op.75 in *Elgar Organ Album* Bk.1 (Novello) M/D
Phillips G.   **Trumpet Tune** from *Tower Hill Suite* (Animus) E/M
Rawsthorne N.   **Sortie: Forth in thy name** ('Song 34') in *50 Hymn Preludes* and in *Hymn Preludes for the Church Year* Bk.2 (both Mayhew) M

HYMNS AND SONGS

	pos	rdg	AMNS	CAON	CFE	CH4	CH5	CP	H&P	HTC	LAU	MP	NEH	SG	SOF	TS
Adoramus te, Domine (Taizé)				921	11		345				667			208		
All heaven waits with bated breath		n										15			11	9
All is ready for the Feast!		g				373										
All people that on earth do dwell	ga		100	21	22	63	683	369	1	14	466	20	334	77	13	13
And can it be that I should gain		n		32	43	396	218	376	216	588	790	33	*627*	168	21	21
Angel voices, ever singing		o	163	37	45	498	346	377	484	307	724	34	336	27	24	
Be still and know I (John Bell)		g												18	672	
Be still and know II (John Bell)		g			70	754							242			
Bread of heaven, on thee we feed	cm	g	271	82				284		398			276	464		
Christ is made the sure foundation/Blessèd city		n	332ii	97	109	200	326	207/208	485	559	456	73	205	572	1199	654
Christ the prisoner		n											*631*			
Come to us, creative Spirit		o				612	453		377	308				621		
Eternal Father, strong to save		g	292	153	152	260	612	413	379	285	963	122	354	235	1222	
Faithful Shepherd, feed me	cm	g		156			644		29				282	498		
Fierce raged the tempest		n	225							144						
Guide me, O thou great Jehovah/Redeemer	se	g	214	252	233	167	647	455	437	528	960	201	368	638	148	708
Here in this house of the great King		o														726
Here in this place (Gather us in)		o,g			253	623					475			4		
Jesus shall reign where'er the sun		n	143	359		470	97	490	239	516	322	379	388	45	301	1376
Let us break bread together		g	480	387	359		428		615			414			330	
Let us build a house (All are welcome)		n				198					458					
Lift up your heads, ye mighty gates		o	483		364		131	30	240	509	105		8			
Misericordias Domini/From age to age (Taizé)					489											
O for a thousand tongues to sing		n	125	485		352	104	534	744	219		496	415	55	412	383/1452
Prayer is the soul's sincere desire		n				546	625	561	557	372		567	442			
Saints of God! Lo, Jesu's people		n											179			
We love the place, O God		o	160	718			343	211		558		731	471			
When prison walls extend their reach (LUR 155)		n														

SONGS FOR CHILDREN

5000+ hungry folk KS 2, SOF 719, TS 107
If you believe and I believe C 70, CG 62, CH4 771, RTF, SBTL
Two little fishes CH4 504

BIBLE READINGS

Psalms 75 [and 76]
1 Kings 6.11–14,23–38
Acts 12.1–17
John 6.1–21

SINGING THE PSALM

Psalm 75 CWP, NPCW
Psalm 76 CWP, NPCW

ANTHEMS AND VOCAL MUSIC

Title	Composer	Voices	E/M/D	Book source	Single sheet publisher
UNISON/TWO PART/HIGH VOICES					
Bread for the world	Farrell	U#	E	GBAN	OCP
Give us the wings of faith	Blatchly	SS	M	HP	
O sacrum convivium (g)	Leighton	S/SS	M/D	EAC2	
The bread which you do not use (g)	Moore	2 part	E	BFH	
You are Peter	Aston	2 part	E		RSCM
THREE/FOUR PARTS					
Bread of the world in mercy broken	Baldwin	SAMen	E	SBS2	
Christ is our cornerstone	Ogden	SATB	M	SBS2	RSCM
Give me the wings of faith	Leighton	SATB	D		Novello
Give us the wings of faith	Bullock	SATB	M	AC4, FSB10	OUP
Hail, glorious spirits, heirs of light	Tye	SATB unacc	E		RSCM
Holy is the true light	Harris	SATB unacc	E/M	FSB7, SL (ATTB)	Novello
Hymn to St Peter	Britten	SATB	D		B&H
If God is building when we build	Trad arr Barnard	SATB	E	SBS2	
O taste and see	Vaughan Williams	SATB unacc	E	AC4, NOEAB, NSAC1	OUP
O sacrum convivium (g)	Messiaen	SATB unacc	D		UMP
O sacrum convivium (g)	Byrd	SATB unacc	M	SBS2	
Surely thou hast tasted that the Lord is good	Bernard Rose	SATB unacc	M/D	EAC1	
The Church triumphant	Shephard	SATB	E	SBS1	RSCM
To be a pilgrim	Burt	SAMen	E/M	OBFA	
Tu es Petrus	Duruflé	SATB unacc	M		Salabert
Tu es Petrus	Hassler	SATB unacc	M	CM4	
We love the place, O God	Sumsion	SATB	M/D		RSCM
FIVE OR MORE PARTS					
Let all mortal flesh keep silence (g)	Bairstow	SSAATTBB unacc	M/D	AC4	S&B
O sacrum convivium (g)	Tallis	SAATB unacc	M/D	TA	OUP
Tu es Petrus	Palestrina	SSATBB unacc	M	ESM	

ORGAN MUSIC

PRELUDES

Bach A.W.   **Trio in E flat** in *Berliner Orgelmusik des 19 Jahrhunderts* (Breitkopf) M/D
Barr J.   **Prelude on 'Cwm Rhondda'** in *Three Preludes on Hymn Tunes* (Gray) M
Camidge M.   **Gavotte (from a concerto)** in *Old English Organ music for Manuals* Bk.1 (OUP) E*
Coleman H.   **Quam dilecta** (mistitled 'St Flavian') No.1 of *Two Interludes* (Novello) E/M

POSTLUDES

Beranek J.   **Fugue in G minor** in *Easy Organ Pieces from the 19th C* (Bärenreiter) E/M
Clucas H.   **Melita** in *A Coldridge Organ Book* (Animus) E*
Frey R.   **Trumpet Procession** (Hope) E/M
Guilmant A. **Grand Chœur in March Form** Op.52 No.2 in *The Practical Organist: Complete Works* Vol.5 (Belwin) E/M
Terry D.   **Angel Voices** in *Preludes on Favourite Hymns* (Mayhew; both 2-stave and 3-stave editions available) E/M

PROPER 13 (SUNDAY BETWEEN 31 JULY AND 6 AUGUST INCLUSIVE) YEAR A

HYMNS AND SONGS

	pos	rdg	AMNS	CAON	CFE	CH4	CH5	CP	H&P	HTC	LAU	MP	NEH	SG	SOF	TS
Be thou my vision/Lord, be my vision		o	343	70	74/75	465	643	386	378	545	970	51	339	669	42	50
Bread of life, hope of the world	cm	g			95	663					78			484		
Break thou the bread of life	cm	g					379	286	467			64			50	
Christian, dost thou see them		n	55										65			
Come, risen Lord, and deign		g	349	126			408	293	605	399			279			
Create in me a clean heart, O God		o										108			76	
Deck thyself, my soul, with gladness/Soul, array thyself		g	257	146			445	295	606	400			280			
Draw near/nigh and take the body of the Lord	cm	g			150		411	296		401	628		281			
Eat this bread/Jesus Christ, bread of life (Taizé)				926	151	661					633				1221	
Eternal light, shine in my heart		o					613	415		339						
Facing a task unfinished		n										126			88	
For this purpose Christ was revealed		n										155			114	111
Forth in thy name, O Lord, I go	se	o	239	188	184	529	567	430	381	306	861	159	235	623	1237	
From glory to glory advancing	se	g	276	194				299					286			
God of grace and God of glory		o	367	225			533	448	712	324		192		574	139	
I am the bread of life		g		299	271/2		420		611		629	261			200	
Immortal, invisible, God only wise		o	199	314	301	132	6	474	9	21	725	327	377	44	234	220
In her house there is a table (CG 147)		o														
Jesu, thou joy of loving hearts		g	255	369		662	425	486	258	413		383	292	471		839
Jesus, stand among us in thy risen power	ev	n		362			338		530	364		380		304		
Let all mortal flesh keep silence		g	256	381	355	666	427	309	266	61	607		295	472	1413	
Lord, enthroned in heavenly splendour		g	263	408	379		431	311	616	416	769	431	296	52	352	870
May the mind of Christ my Saviour		o		447		536	636	521	739	550		463		671	1448	887
Now is eternal life		g	402	470			392	152	203				114			
O thou, who at thy Eucharist didst pray/O Christ		g	265	540	556	669	438	318	779	420	833		302	476		
Ostende nobis, Domine (Taizé)		ps		583							839					
Sing to him in whom creation		o							324				142			
When morning gilds the skies	mo	n	146	739	805		344	619	276	223		756	473	74	597	1054
Who can measure heaven and earth		o								27						

SONGS FOR CHILDREN

One more step along the world I go CAON 525, CAP 47, CH 166, CH4 530, CH5 658, CP 548, H&P 746, JP 188, KS 273, SOF 1483

Send me, Lord (Thuma mina) CFE 636, CG129, CH4 800, IECS, SG 694

BIBLE READINGS

Psalm 80*
1 Kings 10.1–13
Acts 13.1–13
John 6.24–35

SINGING THE PSALM

Psalm 80* CH4, CRP, CWP, H&P, MCW1, NEP, NPCW, PAME
Haugen *Let us see your face* (GIA)#
Sharpe *Let your face shine on us* CRP#

ANTHEMS AND VOCAL MUSIC

Title	Composer	Voices	E/M/D	Book source	Single sheet publisher
UNISON/TWO PART/HIGH VOICES					
Ave verum	Fauré	SS	M/D	MEA, SFL2	
Bread for the world (g)	Farrell	U#	E	GBAN	
Bread of life from heaven	Argentinian arr Haugen	U#	E	C	GIA
Christ has no body now but yours	Ogden	U + descant	E	CFAP, LOL	RSCM
Give us the wings of faith	Blatchly	SS	M	HP	
Send us as your blessing, Lord	Walker	U/SSATB#	E	CFE, HIG	OCP
Sent by the Lord am I	Trad arr Weaver	2 part	E	BC	
THREE/FOUR PARTS					
Be thou my vision	Chilcott	SATB	E/M	BCA, NOEAB	OUP
Bread of the world (g)	Scottish trad arr Bullard	SAMen	E	OBFA	
Bread of the world in mercy broken (g)	Baldwin	SAMen	E	SBS2	
Christ our God descends from heaven (g)	Bullard	SAB	E/M	SBS2	
Ego sum panis vivus (g)	Palestrina	SATB unacc	M	CM1	Chester
Give me the wings of faith	Leighton	SATB	D		Novello
Give us the wings of faith	Bullock	SATB	M	AC4, FSB10	OUP
Go forth and tell!	Ogden	SATB	E	SBS2	RSCM
Go forth into the world in peace	Rutter	SATB	E	JRA	OUP
Let all mortal flesh keep silence (g)	Trad arr Covey-Crump	SATB unacc	M	MTH1	
Panis angelicus (g)	Franck	SATB	M	ESM	
The Spirit of the Lord	Elgar	SATB	M	SAEE	RSCM
To be a pilgrim	Burt	SAMen	E/M	OBFA	
Verily, verily I say unto you (g)	Tallis	SATB unacc	E	AC1, SBS2, TA	OUP
FIVE OR MORE PARTS					
Ave verum (g)	Mawby	SSAATTBB unacc	M/D		Mayhew
Let all mortal flesh keep silence (g)	Bairstow	SSAATTBB unacc	M/D	AC4	S&B
Panis angelicus (g)	Villette	SSAATTBB unacc	M/D		UMP

ORGAN MUSIC

PRELUDES

Lloyd Webber W.S.   **Introit** in *Eight Varied Pieces* (Bosworth) E/M
Marpurg F.W.   **Chorale Prelude 'Schmücke dich'** in *A Graded Anthology for Organ* Bk.4 (Cramer) E/M
Papperitz R.   **Schmücke dich, O liebe Seele** in *Leipziger Orgelmusik des 19 C* (Breitkopf) M
Rowley A.   **Picardy** in *Hymn Tune Voluntaries* (OUP) E
Vierne L.   **Élégie** from *24 Pièces en Style Libre* Bk.2 (Masters, Durand) E/M(*)

POSTLUDES

Benoist F.   **Offertoire No.6** in *Benoist: Pièces pour Orgue* (Chanvrelin) E/M
Boëllmann L.   **Introduction and Minuet Gothique** from *Suite Gothique* (many editions) M
Gilbert N.   **Epilogue** in *An Album of Praise* (OUP) E/M
Nixon J.   **St Helen** in *Hymn Tune Preludes* (Fagus) E/M

HYMNS AND SONGS

	pos	rdg	AMNS	CAON	CFE	CH4	CH5	CP	H&P	HTC	LAU	MP	NEH	SG	SOF	TS
All creatures of our God and King		n	105	6	15	147	24	250	329	13	694	7	263	23	645	614
All hail the power of Jesus' name		o	140	16	19	457	250	163	252	587	323	13	332	24	9	7
All-creating heavenly giver		n							489				662			
Author of life divine	cm	g	258	56				281	596	395			274			
Clothed with splendour and majesty		n														657
Earth was waiting, spent and restless		o								54						
Eat this bread/Jesus Christ, bread of life (Taizé)		g		926	151	661					633				1221	
Father of mercy, God of consolation		n					511						323			
For the fruits of his/all creation		n	457	185	178	231	39	254	342	286	731	153	*621*	299	1234	685
God is love, let heaven adore him		g	365	217		123	3	442	36		811	187	364			
God, who made the earth		n		235			4									
Great is thy faithfulness		n		249		153	80	453	66	260		200	*636*	39	147	138
Let all mortal flesh keep silence	cm	g	256	381	355	666	427	309	266	61	607		295	472	1413	
Let us with a gladsome mind/Let us gladly		n	204	392	362	93	30	498	27	23	707	415	397	312	333	
Lord of beauty, thine the splendour		n	106	415			29	258					265			
O God of earth and altar		o		492	527			358	426		935		492			
O/Our God our help in ages past		o	99	494	528	161	537	537	358	37	955	498	417	542	415	905
O Lord, hear my prayer (Taizé)		ps		938	542		620				929	908	246	423	394	
Of the glorious body telling		g	252	473	563	667	437	316			246		268			
Praise, O praise our God and King		n	288	566			45	273	359							
Soul of my Saviour		g		612	663		444	322			938		305			
Thee we adore		g	254	640			449	329					308			
Thine arm/Your hands, O Lord, in days of old		n	285	671				347	397		431		324			
Thou/God, whose almighty word		n	180	684	738	112	324	267	29	506	887	699	466	597	557	
Thy/Your hand, O God, has guided		o	171	689	741	511	529	606	784	536	876	705	485	649	1065	
We cannot measure how you heal		n		712	772	718	514	348			433		490			
With wonder, Lord, we see your works		n	531					269	353				316			

SONGS FOR CHILDREN

When the road is rough and steep JP 279, SOF 1612

BIBLE READINGS

Psalm 86
1 Kings 11.41 - 12.20
Acts 14.8–20
John 6.35,41–51

SINGING THE PSALM

Psalm 86 CRP, CWP, FGP, H&P, NPCW, PAME

ANTHEMS AND VOCAL MUSIC

Title	Composer	Voices	E/M/D	Book source	Single sheet publisher
UNISON/TWO PART/HIGH VOICES					
Ave verum (g)	Fauré	SS	M/D	MEA, SFL2	
Bread of life	Farrell	U/SATB#	E	HIG, LAU, RITH	OCP
Bread of life from heaven	Argentinian arr Haugen	U#	E	C	GIA
Song of the Body of Christ (g)	Haas	U#	E	C	GIA
THREE/FOUR PARTS					
Ave verum (g)	Byrd	SATB unacc	M	NCAB, NSAC2, OBTA	OUP
Ave verum (g)	Elgar	SATB	M	BC, NCAB	RSCM
Bow down thine ear, O Lord	Blow	SATB	M		Banks
Ego sum panis vivus (g)	Byrd	SATB unacc	M		Chester
Ego sum panis vivus (g)	Palestrina	SATB unacc	M	CM1	Chester
Fight the good fight	Gardner	SATB	M	MTH1	OUP
Greater love	Ireland	SATB	M/D	AC4	S&B
Holy is the true light	Harris	SATB	E/M	FSB7, SL (ATTB)	Novello
I am the bread of life (g)	Lole	SATB	E	SBS1, WIS, BC (U + descant)	RSCM
I am the bread of life	Rawsthorne	SAMen	E	AOAN1	
I am the bread of life (g)	Toolan arr Wilson	SATB	E	AWS	
Tantum ergo (g)	De Séverac	SATB unacc	M	AWTE	RSCM
Tantum ergo (g)	Duruflé	SATB unacc	M		Durand
Teach me thy way, O Lord	Fox	SATB unacc	E	FSB7, SBS1	Novello
Therefore we before him bending (g)	Pearsall	SATB	E		CMS/OUP
Verily, verily, I say unto you (g)	Tallis	SATB unacc	E	AC1, SBS2, TA	OUP
FIVE OR MORE PARTS					
Ave verum (g)	Lassus	SSATTB unacc	M	ESM	
Ave verum (g)	Mawby	SSAATTBB unacc	M/D		Mayhew
O salutaris hostia (g)	Tallis	SATBB unacc	M	SC, TA	OUP

ORGAN MUSIC

PRELUDES

Archer M.	**Monkland** in *100 Hymn Preludes* (Mayhew) E
Bairstow E.	**Evening Song** (Lengnick) M
Watson R.	**Meditation on 'East Acklam'** (Escorial) M
Wesley S.S.	**Prelude in C minor** in *50 Victorian Pieces* (Mayhew) E*

POSTLUDES

Archer J.S.	**Improvisation on 'St Anne'** in *Variations on Well-known Hymn Tunes* (Novello) E/M*
Bédard D.	**Variations sur 'Lasst uns erfreuen'** (Cheldar) E/M
Guilain J-A.	**Basse de trompette** from *Suite du Deuxième Ton* (Kalmus) E*
Ireland J.	**Alla marcia** in *John Ireland Organ Works* (Novello) E/M
Viner A.	**March for an Occasion** from *100 Processionals and Recessionals* (Mayhew) M

PROPER 15 (SUNDAY BETWEEN 14 AND 20 AUGUST INCLUSIVE) YEAR A

HYMNS AND SONGS

	pos	rdg	AMNS	CAON	CFE	CH4	CH5	CP	H&P	HTC	LAU	MP	NEH	SG	SOF	TS
Affirm anew the threefold name		n						200								
All for Jesus, all for Jesus		n		13	16			277	251	469			272	661		
All praise to our redeeming Lord		o						371	753			19				
Be known to us in breaking bread/O Lord, you gave	cm	g					401	282	597		410				669	
Bless the Lord, my soul (Taizé)				923	81		1				813			105	676	
Christ for the world we sing		n	344					394	789							
Come, ye faithful/Alleluia, raise the anthem		g	145	131			84	409	813	205		103	351	25		
Draw near/nigh and take the body of the Lord	cm	g			150		411	296		401	628		281			
Eat this bread/Jesus Christ, bread of life (Taizé)		g		926	151	661					633				1221	
Faithful Shepherd, feed me	cm	g		156			644		29				282	498		
Glory to God, the source of all our mission		n												595		
Go forth and tell!		n		238			478	437	770	505		178		596	738	
God has spoken – by his prophets		o					381		64	248	742	831		225		
God is working his purpose out		n		221	217	235	481	444	769	191	86	189	495	451	135	128
Great Shepherd of thy people, hear		n	164	250			614	454	490	363			238			
Jesus, we thus obey	hc	n	477				307	614								
Lift up your heads, ye mighty gates		n	483		364		131	30	240	509	105		8			
Lord, enthroned in heavenly splendour	of	g	263	408	379		431	311	616	416	769	431	296	52	352	870
My God, and/now is thy table spread?		g	259	456	496		433	313		418	651		474			
Now is eternal life		o,g	402	470			392	152	203				114			
Now let us from this table rise	pc	g	403	472		675	436	315	619	419	647		475			
One more step along the world I go	se	n		525		530	658	548	746						1483	
Our Lord, his Passion ended		n	91					194	323				611			
The Son of God rides out to war		n								577						
We have a gospel to proclaim		n	431	716	778	363	491	612	465	519	852	728	486	331	1583	
When peace, like a river		o										757				574
Ye servants of God, your master proclaim		n	149	756	819	130	492	627	278	520		784	476	75	620	1074
Ye that know the Lord is gracious		n	175			642	493	628					477			

SONGS FOR CHILDREN

One more step along the world I go CAON 525, CAP 47, CH 166, CH4 530, CH5 658, CP 548, H&P 746, JP 188, KS 273, SOF 1483

The Church is wherever God's people are praising CH4 522

BIBLE READINGS

Psalm 90*
2 Kings 4.1–37
Acts 16.1–15
John 6.51–58

SINGING THE PSALM

Psalm 90* CH4, CRP, CWP, FGP, H&P, NPCW, PAME, PFS
Farrell *Restless is the heart* RITH, SFTL (OCP)#

ANTHEMS AND VOCAL MUSIC

Title	Composer	Voices	E/M/D	Book source	Single sheet publisher
UNISON/TWO PART/HIGH VOICES					
All that is hidden	Farrell	U/SATB#	E	CFE, LAU, RITH, SFTL	OCP
Christ has no body now but yours	Ogden	U + descant	E	CFAP, LOL	RSCM
Day by day	How	U + 2 part	E	BC	RSCM
Give us the wings of faith	Blatchly	SS	M	HP	
Lift on high	Ogden	U/SATB	E		WLP
The Call (Come, my Way)	Vaughan Williams	U	E	NEP	S&B
THREE/FOUR PARTS					
A Prayer of St Richard of Chichester	Archer	SATB	E		RSCM
Be thou my vision	Chilcott	SATB	E/M	BCA, NOEAB	OUP
Day by day	Godfrey	SATB	E		Encore
Give me the wings of faith	Leighton	SATB	D		Novello
Give us the wings of faith	Bullock	SATB	M	AC4, FSB10	OUP
Go forth and tell!	Ogden	SATB	E	SBS2	RSCM
Go forth into the world in peace	Rutter	SATB	E	JRA	OUP
Just as I am	Chilcott	SATB	M	BCA	OUP
Light of the world	Elgar	SATB	M/D	AWTE	Novello
Now let us from this table rise	Henderson	SATB	E	SBS1	RSCM
Out of darkness	Walker	U/SATB#	E	CFE, LAU, OOD	OCP
Take up your cross	Corp	SATB	E	SBS1, WOTC	RSCM
The Call	Lloyd	SATB unacc	M		RSCM
The Spirit of the Lord	Elgar	SATB	M	SAEE	RSCM
To be a pilgrim	Burt	SAMen	E/M	OBFA	
Verily, verily, I say unto you (g)	Tallis	SATB unacc	E	AC1, SBS2, TA	OUP
FIVE OR MORE PARTS					
Beati quorum via	Stanford	SSATBB unacc	M	ASA, WFC	RSCM
The Twelve	Walton	SSAATTBB	D		OUP

Some of the anthems listed for Proper 13 (page 93) are also appropriate.

ORGAN MUSIC

PRELUDES

Ashdown F.   **Pastor pastorum** from *Two Meditations on the 23rd Psalm* E/M
Clucas H.   **All for Jesus** in *A Coldridge Organ Book* (Animus) E*
Dallier H.   **Monstra te esse matrem** No.3 of *Cinq Invocations* (Lemoine) M
Dupré M.   **Antiphon III** or **V** of *Fifteen Pieces on Antiphons* Op.18 (Gray, Masters) M & E/M
Whitlock P.   **Folk-Tune** from *Five Short Pieces*: in *Whitlock: Complete Shorter Works* (OUP) E/M

POSTLUDES

Bunk G.   **Tut mir auf die schöne Pforte** ('Unser Herrscher') in *Choralimprovisationen* (Butz) M
Buxtehude D.   **Partita 'Auf meinen lieben Gott'** BuxWV 179 in *Complete Works* Vol.4 (Bärenreiter) M/D*
Plum J-M.   **Toccatina** in *Niederländisch-belgische Orgelromantik* (Breitkopf) E/M
Vann S.   **Prelude on 'Solothurn'** in *Six Preludes* (Mayhew) E/M

PROPER 16 (SUNDAY BETWEEN 21 AND 27 AUGUST INCLUSIVE) YEAR A

HYMNS AND SONGS

	pos	rdg	AMNS	CAON	CFE	CH4	CH5	CP	H&P	HTC	LAU	MP	NEH	SG	SOF	TS
And did those feet in ancient time		o	294	33	44			353					488			
As we break the bread		g		48						393				460		
Author of life divine	cm	g	258	56				281	596	395			274			
Broken for me, broken for you		g		87			404	287		S 6		66		485	53	58
Come, now is the time to worship	ga	n				196						1040		10	1205	662
Eat this bread/Jesus Christ, bread of life (Taizé)		g		926	151	661					633				1221	
God moves in a mysterious way		o	112	222		158	13	445	65			193	365			700
I am the bread of life		g		299	271/2		420		611		629	261			200	
I come with joy, a child of God		g	473	304		656	421	305	610	408	649		623	469		
In Christ alone my hope is found		g										1072			1346	1311
Jesus is the name we honour		n				481						870		122	870	285
Let us sing to the Lord (Taizé)		ps									689					
Lord Jesus Christ, you have come to us		g	391	411	383		429	505	617	417	772	435	297	670	357	
Lord of the Church, we pray for our renewing		n					303			499		442		577	1433	'
Lord, I lift your name on high		n				558						881		126	897	330
O/Our God our help in ages past		o	99	494	528	161	537	537	358	37	955	498	417	542	415	905
O God, you search me and you know me		n				97					779			514		1454
O thou, who at thy Eucharist didst pray/O Christ		g	265	540	556	669	438	318	779	420	833		302	476		
Surrexit Christus (Taizé)		n		943	672		282/711				266					
The highest and the holiest place		n											165			
There is no moment of my life		n					19		428					185		
This is the body of Christ		g				799										
Through all the changing scenes of life		o	209	686	740		372	604	73	46		702	467	654	1566	1561
Thy/Your hand, O God, has guided		o	171	689	741	511	529	606	784	536	876	705	485	649	1065	
We have a gospel to proclaim		n	431	716	778	363	491	612	465	519	852	728	486	331	1583	
We pray thee, heavenly Father		g	264	720			331						311			
Ye servants of God, your master proclaim		n	149	756	819	130	492	627	278	520		784	476	75	620	1074
Ye watchers and ye holy ones		n	532	758			476	230					478			
You are before me, God/Thou art before me, Lord		n				96			543							
You are the King of glory				762	822							790			627	

SONGS FOR CHILDREN

Come and praise the Lord our king CAP 21, CFE 121, HTC S8, JP 34
Let us sing to the God of salvation SG 86

BIBLE READINGS

Psalm 95
2 Kings 6.8–23
Acts 17.15–34
John 6.56–69

SINGING THE PSALM

Psalm 95 CH4, CRP, CWP, FGP, H&P, LAU, MCW1, NPCW, PAME
Berthier *Let us sing to the Lord* TSFP#
Inwood *Ring out your joy* CSF#
O'Hara *O that today you would listen* CRP#
Trad arr Foster *Come, ring out your joy* C

ANTHEMS AND VOCAL MUSIC

Title	Composer	Voices	E/M/D	Book source	Single sheet publisher
UNISON/TWO PART/HIGH VOICES					
Bread for the world (g)	Farrell	U#	E	GBAN	
Gospel Greeting (g)	Farrell	U/SATB#	E	C, CBL	OCP
My song is in sighing	Dalby	S	M/D	HP	
Table of plenty (Come to the feast) (g)	Schutte	U#	E	LAU	OCP
We walk by faith	Haugen	U#	E	CFE, LAU	GIA
Your words are spirit and life (g)	Farrell	U#	E	CBL, LAU	
THREE/FOUR PARTS					
Author of life divine (g)	Archer	SATB unacc	E		Mayhew
Come , let us rejoice	Amner	SATB unacc	E	FSB7	RSCM
Christ was the Word (g)	Maxim	SATB unacc	E	SBS2	
Ego sum panis vivus (g)	Byrd	SATB unacc	M		Chester
Ego sum panis vivus (g)	Esquivel	SATB unacc	M	CM3	Chester
Ego sum panis vivus (g)	Palestrina	SATB unacc	M	CM1	Chester
Fight the good fight	Gardner	SATB	M	MTH1	OUP
Firmly I believe and truly	Shephard	SAMen	E	SFL2	
I am the bread of life (g)	Lole	SATB	E	SBS1, WIS, BC (U + descant)	RSCM
I am the bread of life (g)	Rawsthorne	SAMen	E	AOAN1	
If ye be risen again with Christ	Gibbons	SATB + solo SSA	M		Novello
O come, let us sing unto the Lord	Piccolo	SATB	M	NCAB	OUP
Tantum ergo (g)	De Séverac	SATB unacc	M	AWTE	RSCM
Tantum ergo (g)	Duruflé	SATB unacc	M		Durand
The Spirit of the Lord	Elgar	SATB	M	SAEE	RSCM
Verily, verily I say unto you (g)	Tallis	SATB unacc	E	AC1, SBS2, TA	OUP
Waiting for the word	Skellern	SATB	E/M		RSCM
FIVE OR MORE PARTS					
Death is swallowed up	Tomkins	SAATB + solo SSAABB	M		Cathedral
Surrexit Christus	O'Regan	SSAATTBB unacc	D	CN	

ORGAN MUSIC

PRELUDES

Best W.T.   **Prelude on 'London New'** in *50 Victorian Pieces* (Mayhew) and in *English Romantic Classics* (Belwin) E
Dubois T.   **Communion funèbre** No.2 in *Complete Works* Vol.1 (Bärenreiter) E*
Rawsthorne N.   **London New** in *50 Hymn Preludes* and in *Hymn Preludes for the Church Year* Bk.2 (both Mayhew) E
Whitlock P.   **Pazienza** from *Reflections*, now in *Whitlock: Complete Shorter Works* (OUP) E/M
Williamson M.   **Communion** or **Gradual** from *Mass of a Medieval Saint* (Marks, Belwin) E/M

POSTLUDES

Lloyd R.   **Church Parade** in *New Music for Organ* Bk.2 (Mayhew) E
Sumsion H.   **Ceremonial March** in *Oxford Book of Ceremonial Music* (OUP) M
Williamson M.   **Sortie** from *Mass of a Medieval Saint* (Marks, Belwin) M
Young G.   **Recessional on 'St Anne'** in *Eight Organ Voluntaries* (Presser) E

PROPER 17 (SUNDAY BETWEEN 28 AUGUST AND 3 SEPTEMBER INCLUSIVE) YEAR A

HYMNS AND SONGS

	pos	rdg	AMNS	CAON	CFE	CH4	CH5	CP	H&P	HTC	LAU	MP	NEH	SG	SOF	TS
Be thou my vision/Lord, be my vision			343	70	74/75	465	643	386	378	545	970	51	339	669	42	50
Blessed Jesus, at your word/Dearest Jesu, we are here		n	269	143	87		410	294								
Blest are the pure in heart		g	238	77	88		630	391	724	110	908		341	372		
Christ on whom the Spirit rested		n								228						
Colours of day dawn into the mind		n		108	118						764	1039			64	69
Create in me a clean heart, O God		g										108			76	
Dear Lord and Father of mankind		g	115	144	143	485	549	411	673	356	934	111	353	497	79	79
Do not be afraid, for I have redeemed you		n		150	147	191					972	115			1213	1183
Fear not, for I am with you		n												105		
Go forth and tell!	se	n		238			478	437	770	505			178		596	738
God is here, as we his people	ga	n	464				330	301	653	560	470					
In Adam we have all been one		g	474						420							
In the Lord I'll be ever thankful (Taizé)		o		929	308	772					944	865		656	817	
Laudate omnes gentes/Sing praises, all you peoples (Taizé)												478			1515	
Lord, thy Church on earth is seeking		n						514	774							
My God, accept my heart this day		g	279	455	495			338	701	551	872		318	559		
New every morning is the love	mo		2	467		214	59	6	636	270		480	238			
O come, thou/Come, O thou all-victorious Lord		g							418	441						
O/Our God, our help in ages past		o	99	494	528	161	537	537	358	37	955	498	417	542	415	905
Purify my heart		g		574			640					921		163	475	436
River, wash over me		g										581			487	441
Send me, Lord (Thuma mina)	se	n,g			636	800							694			
Thanks/Praise to God whose word was spoken		n	423			605	387	584	483	255			438	229		
The day thou gavest, Lord, is ended	ev		16	638	691	220	73	22	648	280	679	641	252	65	527	
Through all the changing scenes of life		o	209	686	740		372	604	73	46		702	467	654	1566	1561
Through the darkness of the ages		o												538		
Thy/Your hand, O God, has guided		o	171	689	741	511	529	606	784	536	876	705	485	649	1065	
To the name of our/that brings salvation		n	121	698	749	471	117	610	80	222			470	72		
When we walk with the Lord		n		741			603		687			760			599	1618
Ye servants of God, your master proclaim		n	149	756	819	130	492	627	278	520		784	476	75	620	1074

SONGS FOR CHILDREN

Our God is an awesome God MP 1005, SOF 453, TS 418

BIBLE READINGS

Psalm 105.1–15
2 Kings 6.24–25; 7.3–20
Acts 18.1–16
Mark 7.1–8,14,15, 21–23

SINGING THE PSALM

Psalm 105.1–15 CRP, CWP, NPCW, PAME
    Dean *He, the Lord, is our God* VE

ANTHEMS AND VOCAL MUSIC

Title	Composer	Voices	E/M/D	Book source	Single sheet publisher
UNISON/TWO PART/HIGH VOICES					
Centre of my life	Inwood	U/SATB#	E	CFE, CSF, LAU, SG	OCP
Give ear unto me (g)	Marcello	SS	M	AC2	
I lift up my eyes	Ogden	U	E		WLP
I will lift up mine eyes	Mawby	S	E		RSCM
Lord, what love have I (g)	Croft	SS	M	AC2	
O God, you search me	Farrell	U/SATB#	E	CBL, CH4, LAU, MCW1, SG, TS	OCP
THREE/FOUR PARTS					
Amen, amen, it shall be so!	Bell	SATB + cantor	E	LAA	
Be thou my vision	Chilcott	SATB	E/M	BCA, NOEAB	OUP
Blessed are they (g)	S.S.Wesley	SAB	M		S&B
Dear Lord and Father of mankind	Carter	SATB	M	ACA	
I lift up my eyes (**Requiem**)	Howells	SATB unacc	M/D		Novello
I will lift up my eyes	Rutter	SATB	M		OUP
If ye love me (g)	Tallis	SATB unacc	E	FAB1, NCAB, NSAC1, OBTA, TA	OUP
O sing joyfully (g)	Batten	SATB unacc	E	SCAB, WFC	RSCM
Teach me, O God	Camidge	SAB	E	CHM	
Teach me thy way, O Lord (g)	Fox	SATB	E	FSB7, SBS1	
The Beatitudes (g)	Chilcott	SATB	M		OUP
The Beatitudes (g)	Pärt	SATB	D		Universal
FIVE OR MORE PARTS					
Beati quorum via	Stanford	SSATBB unacc	M	ASA, WFC	RSCM
I am thine, O save me (g)	S.S.Wesley	SATTB	M	MTP	Novello
If ye love me (g)	Chilcott	SSATB unacc	M	BCA, WFC	
Os justi (g)	Bruckner	SSATTBB unacc	M/D	ESM	Peters
Sing joyfully (g)	Byrd	SAATB unacc	M	OBTA	OUP

ORGAN MUSIC

PRELUDES

Carvalho J.de	**Allegro** in *Silva Ibérica* Vol.1 (Schott) E*
Dubois T.	**Verset de Procession** in *Douze Pièces* (Leduc, Bärenreiter) M
Lefébure-Wély A.	**Andante in F 'The Hymn of Nuns'** No.7 in *Meditaciones Religiosas* (Harmonia) E/M
Rawsthorne N.	**Prelude on 'Be thou my vision'** in *Hymn Preludes for the Church Year* Bk.2 and in *Music for Solemn Moments* (both Mayhew) E/M

POSTLUDES

Boëllmann L.	**Marche religieuse** No.3 of *Douze Pièces* Op.16 (Leduc, Masters); also in *Complete Works* Vol.1 (Bärenreiter) M
Lind R.	**Triumphant March** (Paraclete)
Lefébure-Wély A.	**Offertoire (Grand choeur) in G minor** No.2 in *Meditaciones Religiosas* (Harmonia) M

Suitable before or after: Movements from Callahan C. **Partita on 'Slane'** (Concordia) E-M

PROPER 18 (SUNDAY BETWEEN 4 AND 10 SEPTEMBER INCLUSIVE) YEAR A

HYMNS AND SONGS

	pos	rdg	AMNS	CAON	CFE	CH4	CH5	CP	H&P	HTC	LAU	MP	NEH	SG	SOF	TS
All people that on earth do dwell	ga		100	21	22	63	683	369	1	14	466	20	334	77	13	13
Baptized in water		n			67	636				381	407		492			
Come down, O love divine		n	156	114	125	489	294	175	281	231	303	89	137	663	1202	71
Come, gracious Spirit, heavenly dove		n	153	116		587	295	176					347			
Dear Lord and Father of mankind		g	115	144	143	485	549	411	673	356	934	111	353	497	79	79
Earth was waiting, spent and restless		o								54						
God forgave my sin in Jesus' name		n		212	209		480			S 12	849	181			129	123
God has spoken – by his prophets		o				381		64		248	742	831		225		
How beauteous/gracious are their feet		o	301					220	449							
I believe in Jesus		g		301								264		333	203	195
I heard the voice of Jesus say		g	247	310		540	576	469	136		795	275	376		215	206
I receive your love		g										290			248	236
In the Lord I'll be ever thankful (Taizé)				929	308	772					944	865		656	817	
Inspired by love and anger		o		325	311	253										
Lord of beauty, thine the splendour		o	106	415			29	258					265			
Lord, thy word abideth/your word shall guide us		o	166	420	390		384	515	476	251	977/8	446	407			
Misericordias Domini/From age to age (Taizé)					489											
O breath of life, come sweeping through us		n		476		595	305		777	237		488			407	379
O for a thousand tongues to sing		g	125	485		352	104	534	744	219		496	415	55	412	383/1452
O let the Son of God enfold you		n,g		506								502			419	392
O my Saviour, lifted		g	248	519			237					516			437	
Restore, O Lord, the honour		g		582		469						579		274	483	439
Saviour, again to thy dear name we raise	ev		15	587		221	71	20	643	281		584	250			
Spirit of the living God, fall afresh on me (Iverson)		n		615	666	619	310		295	S 23	306	613			510	462
Thou/God, whose almighty word		g	180	684	738	112	324	267	29	506	887	699	466	597	557	
Thy/Your kingdom come! On bended knee		o	178	690		473		608				500				

SONGS FOR CHILDREN

Send me, Lord (Thuma mina) CFE 636, CG 129, CH4 800, IECS, SG 694
Sent by the Lord am I CFE 638, CG 105, CH4 250, IECS, LAU 855, SBTL, SG 616

BIBLE READINGS
Psalm 108 [and 115]
Ezekiel 12.21 - 13.16
Acts 19.1–20
Mark 7.24–37

SINGING THE PSALM
Psalm 108 CWP, NPCW
Psalm 115 CH4, CWP, NPCW

ANTHEMS AND VOCAL MUSIC

Title	Composer	Voices	E/M/D	Book source	Single sheet publisher
UNISON/TWO PART/HIGH VOICES					
Give us, Lord, a new heart	Farrell	U/SATB#	E/M	LAU, RITH, SLG	OCP
O for a closer walk with God	Caesar	SSA	M/D	EAC2	
The Spirit of the Lord is upon me	Corp	2 part	E	VFLS	
Veni Creator	Berlioz	SSA + solo SSA unacc	M/D	AC3	
Veni lumen cordium	Rizza	U/SATB#	E	CAON, CAS, FOL	
THREE/FOUR PARTS					
A touching place (Christ's is the world) (g)	Bell	SATB	E	CG, IAMB, LFB, WGIR, WIS	GIA
Come down, O love divine	Harris	SATB	E/M	FSB9, NCAB, MTH2	Novello
Come down, O love divine	Tadman-Robins	SAMen	E	OBFA	
Come, Holy Ghost, our souls inspire	Carter	SATB	D		OUP
Grow in grace	Archer	SATB	E/M	SBS1	RSCM
Holy Spirit, ever dwelling	Howells	SATB	E/M	ETAS	
Jesus, fount of consolation (g)	Freylinghausen	SATB	E	MTH1	
Listen sweet dove	Ives	SATB	M	EAC1, SC	RSCM
O for a closer walk with God	Stanford	SATB	M	AC1, ASA, BC, OBFA	RSCM
O for a closer walk with God	Ives	SATB	M		RSCM
O for a thousand tongues (g)	Shephard	SATB	M/D		RSCM
O Holy Spirit, Lord of grace	Tye	SATB unacc	E		RSCM
The Spirit of the Lord	Elgar	SATB	M/D	SAEE	RSCM
Tribus miraculis	Marenzio	SATB unacc	M	CM1, ETAS	
Veni Sancte Spiritus	Harper	SATB (unacc)	E	SOTL	
Veni Sancte Spiritus	Kelly	SATB	D	EAC1	
We cannot measure how you heal (g)	Bell arr Archer	SATB	E	BC	RSCM
FIVE OR MORE PARTS					
Come down, O love divine	Rutter	SSAATTBB unacc	D		OUP
Come, Holy Ghost	Harvey	SSAATTBB unacc	D		Faber
God has chosen me	Farrell	SSATB unacc	E	GBAN	OCP

ORGAN MUSIC

PRELUDES
Betteridge L.   **Gregorian Prelude** (Paraclete) E/M
Dupont G.   **Meditation** in *French Masterworks* (Belwin Mills) M
Pachelbel J.   **Nun lob, mein Seel** in *Orgelwerke* Vol.2 (Peters) or Vol.3 (Kalmus) E/M
Vierne R.   **Entrée** No.1 of *Dix Pièces de Différents Styles* (Kalmus) E/M*
Walmisley T.A.   **Larghetto in F minor** in *An Organ Miscellany* (Mayhew) E/M

POSTLUDES
Battishill J.   **Voluntary in B flat** in *Old English Organ Music for Manuals* Bk.2 (OUP) E*
Beauvarlet-Charpentier J.J.   **Grand Choeur in D minor** in *Pièces pour Orgue* (Chanvrelin) M
Buttstedt J.H.   **Gottes Sohn ist kommen** ('Ravenshaw') in *120 Chorale Preludes of the 17C & 18C* (Peters) E/M
Forchhammer T.   **Postlude on 'Nun lob, mein Seel'** ('Old 100th') in *Praise and Thanks* (Bärenreiter) E/M

PROPER 19 (SUNDAY BETWEEN 11 AND 17 SEPTEMBER INCLUSIVE) YEAR A

HYMNS AND SONGS

	pos	rdg	AMNS	CAON	CFE	CH4	CH5	CP	H&P	HTC	LAU	MP	NEH	SG	SOF	TS
A charge to keep I have		n							785							
At/In the name of Jesus		n	148	54	59	458	94	380	74	172	762	41	338	317	32	33
Forth in thy name, O Lord, I go	se	n	239	188	184	529	567	430	381	306	861	159	235	623	1237	
God be with you till we meet again	se	n			206			440								
Happy are they, they that love God		n	176	262			649	456	711	473			369			
Holy Spirit, come, confirm us		n	471	288		640	299	183	288		311		140			
Holy Spirit, ever dwelling/living		n				615			303				141			
I, the Lord of sea and sky (Here I am, Lord)		g		332	285	251	581	470			865	857		633	830	246
I will follow you to the cross		g												849		
I'm not ashamed to own/name my Lord		g		316		645			677	448		323		532		
Just as I am, without one plea		g	246	374	339	553	587	308	697	440		396	294	507	316	306
Lord, for the years		g		409		159	81	81		328	942	428	*619*	602	892	327
Loving Shepherd of thy sheep		n	134	434	475		655	517		305	802	888				
O God of earth and altar		o		492	527			358	426		935		492			
O God, you search me and you know me		o				97					779			514		1454
O Jesus, I have promised		g	235	503	536	644	593	538	704	531	875	501	420	676	418	391
Rejoice! The Lord is king		o	139	580	619	449	281	563	243	180	326	575	443	440	482	948
Take my life and let it be		g	249	625	677	502	597	581	705	554	874	624		678	519	468
The Church's one foundation		n	170	636	688	739	528	585	515	501	830	640	484	581	525	477
The highest and the holiest place		n											165			
The Lord is my song (Taizé)				651							929					
There is a Redeemer		g		658		559	112					673		396	544	492
There is no moment of my life		o					19		428				185			
This is the day the Lord hath made		n	22	677				9	577	379			257	70		
Thy/Your hand, O God, has guided		n	171	689	741	511	529	606	784	536	876	705	485	649	1065	
Thy/Your kingdom come, O God		n	177	691			509	607	783	334		949	499	269		
To God be the glory!		n		695	745	512	373	609	463	584	719	708		71	559	526
We sing the glorious conquest		n	313					237					155			
Will you come and follow me		g		752	812	533	605	622			877		*647*	634	1120	
Within our darkest night (Taizé)				950												
You are before me, God/Thou art before me, Lord		o				96			543							

SONGS FOR CHILDREN

Be the centre of my life CAON 778, CH 21, KS 20

BIBLE READINGS

Psalm 119.41–48[49–64]
Ezekiel 20.1–8,33–44
Acts 20.17–38
Mark 8.27–38

SINGING THE PSALM

Psalm 119.41–48[49–64] CWP, NPCW

ANTHEMS AND VOCAL MUSIC

Title	Composer	Voices	E/M/D	Book source	Single sheet publisher
UNISON/TWO PART/HIGH VOICES					
Christ has no body now but yours	Ogden	2 part	E	CFAP, LOL	RSCM
Give us, Lord, a new heart	Farrell	U/SATB#	E/M	LAU, RITH, SLG	OCP
Ex ore innocentium (g)	Ireland	SS	M/D	NSAC2	B&H
My song is love unknown (g)	Archer	SS	M	EAC2	RSCM
Take my life, Lord	Rizza	U/SATB#	E	FOLO	Mayhew
THREE/FOUR PARTS					
And didst thou travel light (g)	Shephard	SATB	E/M	BC	RSCM
Christus factus est (g)	Anerio	SATB unacc	M	AWTE, CM1, ESM	
Christus factus est (g)	Bruckner	SATB unacc	M/D	ESM	RSCM
Greater love	Ireland	SATB	M	AC4	S&B
Grow in grace	Archer	SATB	E/M	SBS1	RSCM
Holy Spirit, ever dwelling	Howells	SATB	E	ETAS	
Lead me, Lord	S.S.Wesley	SATB	E	AC1, NCAB, NOEAB, NSAC1	Novello
Lord, for thy tender mercy's sake	Hilton/Farrant	SATB unacc	E	AWTE, FAB1, NOEAB, OBTA, NCAB	OUP
Solus ad victimam (g)	Leighton	SATB	M	AC1, SC	OUP
Take up your cross (g)	Corp	SATB	E	SBS1, WOTC	RSCM
The Song of Christ's Glory (g)	P.Moore	SATB	E		RSCM
Thou art the way (g)	Steel	SATB	M	NNAB, MTH2	
View me, Lord	Lloyd	SATB unacc	E	NNAB	Novello
We rejoice to be God's chosen	Bell	STB + flute	E		GIA
What wondrous love is this? (g)	Trad arr Weaver	SAB	E	LOL, SBS1, SFL2	
Wondrous cross (g)	Wilby	SATB	E	OBFA, WOTC	
FIVE OR MORE PARTS					
O nomen Jesu	Philips	SSATB unacc	M		Mapa Mundi
The Song of Christ's Glory (g)	Ives	SSAATTBB unacc	M	WOTC	

ORGAN MUSIC

PRELUDES

Bédard D.	**Plein jeu** from *Suite du Premier Ton* (Cheldar) E	
Clucas H.	**All for Jesus** in *A Coldridge Organ Book* (Animus) E*	
Du Mage P.	**Récit** from *Première Livre d'Orgue* (Kalmus) E/M*	
Stanford C.V.	**Fantasia on Parry's 'Intercessor'** (Cathedral Music) E/M	
Whitlock P.	**Werde Munter** in *Shorter Organ Works* (OUP) M	

POSTLUDES

Archer M.   **A Thornbury Fanfare** in *New Music for Organ* Bk.2 and in *The Organ Music of Malcolm Archer* (both Mayhew) M

Bach J.S.   **Alle Menschen müssen sterben** BWV 1117 in *Neumeister Chorale Preludes* (Bärenreiter) M*

Du Mage P.   **Plein Jeu** *and/or* **Fugue** from *Première Livre d'Orgue* (Kalmus) E(*)

Telemann G.P.   **Nun danket alle Gott** in *120 Chorale Preludes of the 17C & 18C* (Peters) E/M*

PROPER 20 (SUNDAY BETWEEN 18 AND 24 SEPTEMBER INCLUSIVE) YEAR A

HYMNS AND SONGS

	pos	rdg	AMNS	CAON	CFE	CH4	CH5	CP	H&P	HTC	LAU	MP	NEH	SG	SOF	TS
A man there lived in Galilee		g	334	28												
And now, O Father, mindful of the love	hc	g	260	34			400	279	593	392			273	459		
Be thou my vision/Lord, be my vision		n	343	70	74/75	465	643	386	378	545	970	51	339	669	42	50
Because the Lord is my shepherd		o			77					948				513		
Brother, sister, let me serve you/ Will you let me be your servant		g		88	813	694	517	393			924			619	54	
Colours of day dawn into the mind		n		108	118						764	1039			64	69
Faithful Shepherd, feed me		o		156			644		29				282	498		
From heaven you came, helpless babe		g		195	187	374	219	432			749	162		632	120	114
Great/Lord God, your love has called us here		g	489	246		484	416	133	500	480						
I will sing the wondrous story		o		337					223	212		315		43	278	821
In God alone my soul (Taizé)														813		
Jesus, hope of every nation		n							58					336		
Let the round world with songs rejoice		n											214			
Lord of the Church, we pray for our renewing		n					303			499		442		577	1433	
Lord, thy Church on earth is seeking		n						514	774							
My faith looks up to thee		n		453			590	522	683			469	72			1437
My God, how wonderful thou art		n	102	457	497		7	523	51	369	727	468	410	202	395	896
My song is love unknown		g	63	463	503	399	231	112	173	136	752	478	86	384	400	897
The God of love my shepherd is		o	110	643				587	43				77			
The King of love my shepherd is		o	126	649	699	462	20	589	69	44	804	649	457	205	533	984
The Lord is my light (Taizé)				944												
The Lord my pasture shall prepare		o	111	653				593					458			
The Lord's my shepherd		o	426	654	706	14–16	21	594	70	591	806	660	459	207	537	486
The Lord's my shepherd (Townend)		o										1008		206	1030	988
Thou Shepherd of Israel and mine		o							750							
Through the darkness of the ages		n												538		
We sing the glorious conquest		n	313					237					155			
What a friend we have in Jesus		g		727		547	627		559	373		746		646	593	566
Ye that know the Lord is gracious		n	175			642	493	628				477				
You laid aside your majesty		n										795			633	601

SONGS FOR CHILDREN

Tell me the stories of Jesus CH5 110, H&P 153, JP 228, MP 629, TS 152
You are my hiding place MP 793, SOF 625, TS 1080

BIBLE READINGS

Psalm 119.113–136*
Ezekiel 33.23,30 - 34.10
Acts 26.1,9–25
Mark 9.30–37

SINGING THE PSALM

Psalm 119.113–136* CWP, NPCW

ANTHEMS AND VOCAL MUSIC

Title	Composer	Voices	E/M/D	Book source	Single sheet publisher
UNISON/TWO PART/HIGH VOICES					
Settings of the Jubilate	Various	U/SATB	E	CWP, MCW1	
Brother James' Air	Bain arr Archer	U + descant	E	BC	
Like a child rests in its mother's arms (g)	Walker	U#	E	LAU, OOD	OCP
My song is love unknown (g)	Archer	SS	M	EAC2	RSCM
On another's sorrow (g)	Ferguson	S unacc	M		Encore
Psalm 23	How	U/SSS	M		Weinberger
Psalm 23	Mawby	U	M		RSCM
Shepherd of souls	Barnard	2 part	E	BFH	
The Call (Come, my Way)	Vaughan Williams	U	E	NEP	S&B
The Lord is my shepherd	Kelly	S	M		Encore
The Lord is my shepherd	Schubert	SSAA	M/D	ESM	
THREE/FOUR PARTS					
An Affirmation (g)	Carter	SATB unacc	M	ACA	OUP
Come, my Way, my Truth, my Life	Harris	SATB	M	NNAB	
Holy Spirit, truth divine	Carter	SATB	E/M	ETAS, NOEAB	OUP
Loving Shepherd of thy sheep	Ledger	SATB	E	NOEAB	
Morning glory, starlit sky(g)	Barry Rose	SATB + solo S/T	E/M	MTH2	
The Call	Lloyd	SATB unacc	M		RSCM
The God of love (Elegy)	Thalben- Ball arr Seivewright	SATB	M		Banks
The Lord is my shepherd	Berkeley	SATB	D	MTP	Chester
The Lord is my shepherd	Carter	SATB	M	ACA	OUP
The Lord is my shepherd	Goodall	SATB	E		Faber
The Lord is my shepherd	Rutter	SATB	M		OUP
The Lord is my shepherd	Stanford	SATB	M/D	ASA	Novello
We are his children	Kendrick arr Tambling	SATB	E/M	WSCC1	

ORGAN MUSIC

PRELUDES

Couperin F.   **Tierce en taille** No.XVIII from *Messe pour les Couvents* (Kalmus) E/M

Pachelbel J.   **Der Herr ist mein getreuer Hirt** No.8 in *Selected Works* Vol.3 (Kalmus), No.6 in *Orgelwerke* Vol.2 (Peters), p.84 in *Organ Works* (Dover) E/M(*)

Vierne R.   **Prière** No.3 of *Dix Pièces de Différents Styles* (Kalmus); also in *French Masterworks* (Belwin Mills) E/M*

Vaughan Williams R. **Prelude on 'Rhosymedre'** in *Three Preludes on Welsh Hymn Tunes* (OUP) E/M

Wesley S.S.   **Andante in G (1868)** No.2 in *English Organ Music* Vol.10 (Novello) and in *A Second Set of 3 Pieces* (Animus) M

POSTLUDES

Kirnberger J.P.   **Lobe den Herren** in *120 Chorale Preludes of the 17C & 18C* (Peters) E/M*

Stanford C.V.   **Postlude in D minor** No.6 of *Six Short Preludes and Postludes* (Set 2) Op.105 (Stainer); also in *Preludes and Postludes* (Mayhew) M

Vierne R.   **Postlude in D minor** No.6 of *Dix Pièces de Différents Styles* (Kalmus) M*

Suitable before or after: Movements from Coates R. **Partita on 'Converse'** in *Festmusikk 11* (Cantando) E-M

PROPER 21 (SUNDAY BETWEEN 25 SEPTEMBER AND 1 OCTOBER INCLUSIVE) YEAR A

HYMNS AND SONGS

	pos	rdg	AMNS	CAON	CFE	CH4	CH5	CP	H&P	HTC	LAU	MP	NEH	SG	SOF	TS
Be thou my vision/Lord, be my vision		n	343	70	74/75	465	643	386	378	545	970	51	339	669	42	50
Bless the Lord, my soul (Taizé)				923	81		1				813			105	676	56
Bread of heaven, on thee we feed	cm	n	271	82				284		398			276	464		
Bright the vision that delighted		o	96	86			316	392	445	578			343	29		
Dear Lord and Father of mankind		g	115	144	143	485	549	411	673	356	934	111	353	497	79	79
Father God, I wonder		n		159		186						128		107	92	91
Father of heaven, whose love profound		g	97	165	163	483	319	421	519	359		827	358	144		1201
For the beauty of the earth		g	104	184	177	181	350	253	333	298	726	152	285	298	112	
I am a new creation		n		298	270							254			197	191
I am the vine and you the branches (LFB p.52)		n														
I bind unto myself today/Christ be with me		n		302	274	639	322	203	695	5	312		159/278			757
I heard the voice of Jesus say		g	247	310		540	576	469	136		795	275	376		215	206
In heavenly love abiding		n		323		551	478		678	458		331	638		238	782
Jesu, lover of my soul		n	123	343	319	490	553	96	528	438	797	372	383	201	297	838
Judge eternal, throned in splendour		o		372		264	535	356	409	329		395	490	600		
Let your word run freely		n													889	
Lord, for the years		o		409		159	81	81		328	942	428	619	602	892	327
Loving Shepherd of thy sheep		o	134	434	475		655	517		305	802	888				
O God of earth and altar		o		492	527			358	426		935		492			
O let the Son of God enfold you		g		506								502			419	392
O love divine, how sweet thou art		n	124				621	541					424			
O love that wilt not let me go		n		517		557	592	542	685	486		515			434	917
Praise, my soul, the King of heaven	ga	g	192	565	602	160	366	555	13	38	807	560	436	93	466	433
Purify my heart		g		574			640					921		163	475	436
Son of God, eternal Saviour		g	132			468	527	573		102			498			
Strengthen for service, Lord/Make strong	pc	g	421	619			446	323	626	423			306	473		
These are the days of Elijah		o					141					1012			1047	503
Thou Shepherd of Israel and mine		o								750						
When all thy mercies, O my God		g	109	732			374	617	573	39		751	472	73		

SONGS FOR CHILDREN

Father God, I wonder CAON 159, CH4 186, JP 337, KS 52, MP 128, SG 107, SOF 92, TS 91
God's not dead CAON 810, CH 72, JP 60, KS 85, TS 133

BIBLE READINGS

Psalms [120, 123 and] 124
Ezekiel 37.15–28
1 John 2.22–29
Mark 9.38–50

SINGING THE PSALM

Psalm 120 CWP, NPCW
Psalm 123 CRP, CWP, NPCW
Psalm 124 CH4, CWP, NPCW, PAME

ANTHEMS AND VOCAL MUSIC

Title	Composer	Voices	E/M/D	Book source	Single sheet publisher
UNISON/TWO PART/HIGH VOICES					
Settings of the Creed	Various	U/SATB	E	MCW1	
A Song of Peace and Joy	Mawby	2 part	E	VFLS	
Bring forth the kingdom (g)	Haugen	U	E	CFE, LAU	GIA
I have loved you with an everlasting love	Ogden	U	E		WLP
I know that my redeemer lives	Dean	U	E		Decani
Now go in peace	Trad arr Mair	U	E	VFLS	
We believe	Walker	U/SATB#	E	HIG, LAU	
THREE/FOUR PARTS					
A Gaelic Blessing (g)	Rutter	SATB	E	NCAB	RSCM
Be strong and of good courage	Campbell	SATB	M	FSB7	Novello
Bless, O Lord, us thy servants	Harper	U/SATB	E	PSA	RSCM
Blessed be the God and Father	S.S.Wesley	SATB	M	NCAB, FAB1, SC	RSCM
E'en so, Lord Jesus, quickly come	Manz	SATB unacc	M	AFC	Morning Star
Go forth and tell!	Ogden	SATB	E	SBS2	RSCM
God is our hope and strength	J.S. Bach	SATB	E	AC1, FSB4	
God is our hope and strength	Stanford	SATB	M		Novello
If ye be risen again with Christ	Gibbons	SATB + solo SSA	M		Novello
If ye love me	Tallis	SATB unacc	E	NOEAB, NSAC1, OBTA, TA, SL (AATB)	OUP
Now is eternal life	Lloyd	SAMen	M	AOAN1, NAB2	
Now the God of peace (g)	Knight	SATB	E/M	SBS1	RSCM
O pray for the peace of Jerusalem (g)	Howells	SATB	M		OUP
Prayer of St Francis (g)	Kelly	SATB	M/D		Encore
Walking by faith	Marsh	SAB	E	AOAN1	
FIVE OR MORE PARTS					
Deep peace	Carter	SSATB + solo SA	M	ACA, WFC	OUP
If ye love me	Chilcott	SSATBB unacc	M	BCA, WFC	
Nation shall speak peace unto nation (g)	Barry Rose	SSATBB unacc	M	NSAC2	

ORGAN MUSIC

PRELUDES

Archer M.	**Dix** in *25 Hymn Preludes: A Year of Praise* (Mayhew) E/M
Buxtehude D.	**Wär Gott nicht mit uns diese Zeit** BuxWV 222 in *Complete Works* Bk.5 (Bärenreiter) E/M
Couperin F.	**Tierce en taille** No.XI from *Messe pour les Paroisses* (Kalmus) E/M
Sumsion H.	**Intermezzo** (RSCM) E/M
Zachau F.	**Wo Gott der Herr nicht bei uns hält** in *Organ Music for Manuals* Bk.2 (OUP) E*

POSTLUDES

Bach J.C.	**Wo Gott der Herr nicht bei uns hält** in *120 Chorale Preludes of the 17C & 18C* (Peters) E(*)
Lemmens J-N.	**Marche Pontificale** from *Sonata Pontificale* (Forberg) M/D
Pachelbel J.	**Wo Gott der Herr nicht bei uns hält** in *120 Chorale Preludes of the 17C & 18C* (Peters) E*
Stanford C.V.	**On an old Irish church melody** No.5 of *Six Short Preludes and Postludes* (Set 1) Op.101 (Stainer); also in *Preludes and Postludes* (Mayhew) E/M

PROPER 22 (SUNDAY BETWEEN 2 AND 8 OCTOBER INCLUSIVE) YEAR A

HYMNS AND SONGS

	pos	rdg	AMNS	CAON	CFE	CH4	CH5	CP	H&P	HTC	LAU	MP	NEH	SG	SOF	TS
A man there lived in Galilee		n	334	28												
Abide with me	ev	n	13	2	9	580	62	10	665	425	907	4	331	495	2	2
Be thou my guardian/O Lord, our guardian/Lord, be my guardian		n	217	69			635	385					64			
Be thou my vision/Lord, be my vision		o	343	70	74/75	465	643	386	378	545	970	51	339	669	42	50
Blest are the pure in heart		g	238	77	88		630	391	724	110	908		341	372		
Breathe on me, breath of God		n	157	84	98	596	293	174	280	226	302	67	342	554	51	57
Christ is the world's light		n	440	99	111		87	213	455	321	744			591		
Confitemini Domino (Taizé)		ps		925	137						701					
Eternal light, shine in my heart		o					613	415		339						
Forth in thy name, O Lord, I go	se	o	239	188	184	529	567	430	381	306	861	159	235	623	1237	
Glorious things of thee are spoken		n	172	205	195	738	646	435	817	494	827	173	362	35	127	691
God has spoken to his people		o					380		S 13	472	182				131	
Happy are they, they that love God		g	176	262			649	456	711	473			369			
Happy the home that welcomes you		g							366	300						
I know that my Redeemer lives, what joy		n		311			270		196	169			278		406	
Immortal, invisible, God only wise	ga	o	199	314	301	132	6	474	9	21	725	327	377	44	234	220
Jesu, grant me this, I pray		n	136	342			212	110					382			
Lead us, heavenly Father, lead us		g	224	379	351		652	496	68	595	315	400	393	640	321	311
Lord Jesus Christ, you have come to us		g	391	411	383		429	505	617	417	772	435	297	670	357	
Lord of beauty, thine the splendour		o	106	415			29	258					265			
Love divine, all loves excelling		g	131	428	398	519	634	516	267	217	801	449	408	179	377	343
Now thank we all our God		g	205	474	512	182	361	530	566	33	945	486	413	54	405	
O Jesus, I have promised		n	235	503	536	644	593	538	704	531	875	501	420	676	418	391
Seek ye first the kingdom of God		g		590	633	641	596		138		820	590			493	447
The works of the Lord are created in wisdom		o						266	26							
Ubi caritas/Living charity (Taizé)		n		946		801	530				245				1573	
Who can measure heaven and earth?		o								27						
Will you come and follow me		g		752	812	533	605	622			877		647	634	1120	

SONGS FOR CHILDREN

I am a lighthouse JP 87, KS 114, SOF 196
Jesus' hands were kind hands CH4 351, CH5 213, H&P 393, JP 134, KS 194

BIBLE READINGS

Psalm 136*
Proverbs 2.1–11
1 John 2.1–17
Mark 10.2–16

SINGING THE PSALM

Psalm 136* CH4, CWP, FGP, LAU, NEP, NPCW, PAME, PFS

ANTHEMS AND VOCAL MUSIC

Title	Composer	Voices	E/M/D	Book source	Single sheet publisher
UNISON/TWO PART/HIGH VOICES					
A Song of Wisdom	Stanford	U	M		RSCM
Faith, hope and love	Ogden	2 part	E	SBS1	RSCM
Father God, bless this family	Schiavone	U#	E	LAU	
I give you a new commandment	Aston	2 part	E	BC, EAC2, NOEAB	RSCM
Like a child rests in its mother's arms (g)	Walker	U#	E	LAU, OOD	OCP
Live in the light	Ogden	U	E/M		WLP
Love one another	S.S.Wesley	S	E	BC	RSCM
Love will find out the way (g)	Goodall	2 part	E/M	SFL2	RSCM
Ubi caritas	Lole	SS	M		Encore
THREE/FOUR PARTS					
A new commandment	Parshall	SATB unacc	E	WFC	
I give to you a new commandment	Nardone	SATB	E/M	SBS1	RSCM
Jesu, joy of man's desiring	J.S.Bach	SATB	E	FAB1, NCAB, NOEAB, NSAC1, WFC	RSCM
Love divine	Goodall	SATB	E		Faber
Love divine	Willcocks	SATB	E	NOEAB	
O sapientia	Philips	SATB unacc	M	CM5	
Set me as a seal (g)	Walton	SATB unacc	M/D	AC4, WFC	OUP
The Doctrine of Wisdom	Mathias	SATB	M		OUP
Thy perfect love (g)	Rutter	SATB	E	NOEAB	OUP
Ubi caritas	Ives	SATB unacc	M	SC	
Ubi caritas	Lauridsen	SATB unacc	M		Faber
Ubi caritas	Mawby	SATB	E		Mayhew
Where shall wisdom be found?	Carter	SATB	M/D		OUP
FIVE OR MORE PARTS					
O where shall wisdom be found?	Boyce	SSATB	M		Novello
Ubi caritas	Berkeley	SSATB unacc	D		Chester
Ubi caritas	Duruflé	SAATTBB unacc	M		Durand

ORGAN MUSIC

PRELUDES

Floyd A.E.   **Chorale Prelude on 'Song 13'** in *Musical Miniatures* and in *Hymn Preludes for the Church Year* Bk.2 (both Mayhew) E/M

Lang C.S.   **Chorale Prelude 'Abridge'** No.2 of *Three Chorale Preludes* Op.77 (OUP reprint) M

Lloyd Webber W.S.   **Verset** in *Aria* (Mayhew) E/M

Tambling C.   **A Voluntary for Evensong** ('Eventide') in *Music for Manuals* (Mayhew) E*

Thiman E.   **Prelude on 'Franconia'** in *Five Hymn Tune Variants* (Curwen) E

POSTLUDES

Gulbins M.   **Dankfest II** ('Nun danket') in *Praise and Thanks* (Bärenreiter) E/M

Kellner J.P.   **Nun danket alle Gott** in *120 Chorale Preludes of the 17C & 18C* (Peters) M

Langlais J.   **Pasticcio** No.X from *Organ Book* (Elkan-Vogel) M

Thiman E.   **Postlude on 'Regent Square'** in *Five Hymn Tune Variants* (Curwen) E/M

HYMNS AND SONGS

	pos	rdg	AMNS	CAON	CFE	CH4	CH5	CP	H&P	HTC	LAU	MP	NEH	SG	SOF	TS
All I once held dear		g		18		506						799		562	646	11
Awake, my soul, and with the sun	mo,ga	o	1	58		210	51	1	632	264		804	232	618		
Be still and know I (John Bell)		g												18	672	
Be still and know II (John Bell)		g			70	754								242		
Be still and know that I am God		g		66	71	755	608				909	48			41	48
Be thou my guardian/O Lord, our guardian/Lord, be my guardian		n	217	69			635	385					64			
Behold the amazing gift of love		n				478		389	666							
Christ the Way of life possess me		o						397				78				
Christ, from whom all blessings flow		o							764	491						
Father God, I wonder		n		159		186						128		107	92	91
Father, hear the prayer we offer		n	113	161	158	255	645	416	436	360	933	132	357	237	1229	
Father of heaven, whose love profound		n	97	165	163	483	319	421	519	359		827	358	144		1201
For this purpose Christ was revealed		n										155			114	111
God is our strength and refuge		n		219			12	443		527		188		650		699
Hark, my soul, it is/Christian, do you hear the Lord		o	244	264			569	457	521	472		209	637			
I am trusting thee, Lord Jesus		o		300						433		258			202	
I cannot tell why he, whom angels worship		n		303				54	238	194		266		437	205	199
I vow to thee, my country		o	295		286	704		355					620			
I, the Lord of sea and sky (Here I am, Lord)		g		332	285	251	581	470			865	857		633	830	246
Jesus calls us: o'er the tumult		g	312	347		509	584	233	141	104		359	200	668		
Lord, speak to me that I may speak		n				542	589	512	553	510		444				
My Lord, what love is this		n		462	500		230					476		194	398	370
O God, you search me and you know me		ps				97					779			514		1454
O Jesus, I have promised		g	235	503	536	644	593	538	704	531	875	501	420	676	418	391
Purify my heart		n		574			640					921	163	475	436	
Seek ye first the kingdom of God		o		590	633	641	596		138		820	590			493	447
Take my life and let it be		g	249	625	677	502	597	581	705	554	874	624		678	519	468
The works of the Lord are created in wisdom		o						266	26							
Ubi caritas/Living charity (Taizé)		n		946		801	530				245				1573	
What a friend we have in Jesus		n		727		547	627		559	373		746		646	593	566
Within our darkest night (Taizé)				950												

SONGS FOR CHILDREN

Come on and celebrate CAON 125, CH 35, CH5 328, JP 325, KS 34, MP 99, SOF 73, TS 75
Father God, I wonder CAON 159, CH4 186, JP 337, KS 52, MP 128, SG 107, SOF 92, TS 91
Heaven is singing for joy LAU 690

BIBLE READINGS

Psalm 139.1–18*
Proverbs 3.1–18
1 John 3.1–15
Mark 10.17–31

SINGING THE PSALM

Psalm 139.1–18* CH4, CWP, H&P, NPCW, PAME, PFS
Berthier *Lord Jesus Christ* TSFP#
Farrell *O God, you search me* CBL, CH4, LAU, MCW1, SG, TS (OCP)#
Schutte *Yawheh, I know you are near* LAU, CFE
Walsh *You know me, Lord* LAU, SFTL#

ANTHEMS AND VOCAL MUSIC

Title	Composer	Voices	E/M/D	Book source	Single sheet publisher
UNISON/TWO PART/HIGH VOICES					
A Song of Wisdom	Stanford	U	M		RSCM
Faith, hope and love	Ogden	2 part	E	SBS1	RSCM
In thee, O Lord, I put my trust	Handel	2 part	E		RSCM
Love one another	S.S.Wesley	S	E	BC	RSCM
O rest in the Lord (Elijah)	Mendelssohn	U	E		Novello
THREE/FOUR PARTS					
A new commandment	Parshall	SATB unacc	E	WFC	
Greater love	Ireland	SATB	M	AC4	S&B
I give to you a new commandment	Nardone	SATB	E/M	SBS1	RSCM
I give you a new commandment	Shepherd	TTBB unacc	E		CMS/OUP
Just as I am (g)	Chilcott	SATB	E/M	BCA	OUP
Jesu, joy of man's desiring	J.S. Bach	SATB	E	FAB1, NCAB, NOEAB, NSAC1, WFC	RSCM
O Lord, increase our faith	Loosemore	SATB (unacc)	E	NCAB, SBS1	RSCM
O sapientia	Philips	SATB unacc	M	CM5	
The Doctrine of Wisdom	Mathias	SATB	M		OUP
The Lord bless you and keep you	Rutter	SATB	E	JRA, EAC1, WFC, OBFA (SAMen)	OUP
Trust in the Lord	Moore	SATB	M		Encore
Ubi caritas	Ives	SATB unacc	M	SC	
Where shall wisdom be found?	Carter	SATB	M/D		OUP
FIVE OR MORE PARTS					
Delight thou in the Lord (g)	Thurlow	SSAATTBB	M/D		Encore
Jesu meine Freude (g)	J.S.Bach	SSATB unacc	D		Bärenreiter
Love one another	Carter	SSAATTBB	M/D		OUP
O where shall wisdom be found?	Boyce	SSATB	M		Novello
Ubi caritas	Berkeley	SSATB unacc	D		Chester
Ubi caritas	Duruflé	SAATTBB unacc	M		Durand

ORGAN MUSIC

PRELUDES

Berthier J.   **Imploration I, II or III** from *Ten Liturgical Meditations* (Mayhew) E*
Guilmant A.   **Méditation-Prière** Op.90 No.12 from *18 Nouvelles Pièces* Op.90 (Schott); also in *Complete Works* Vol.4 (Belwin-Mills) E/M
Howells H.   **Psalm-Prelude Set 2 No.2** (Novello) M
Krebs J.L.   **Was Gott tut, das ist wohlgetan** in *The Progressive Organist* Bk.3 (Novello) E*
Stanford C.V.   **Intermezzo on an Irish Air** Op.189/4 (Novello); also in *The Victorian Collection* (McAfee) E/M

POSTLUDES

Archer M.   **Merton** in *25 Hymn Preludes: A Year of Praise* and in *40 Christmas Preludes* (both Mayhew) M
Best W.T.   **Fugue on a Trumpet Fanfare** in *Organ Music for Manuals Only* (Dover) M*
Du Mage P.   **Plein jeu** *and/or* **Fugue** from *Première Livre d'Orgue* (Kalmus) E(*)
Lang C.S.   **Procession** from *Album of Postludes* (OUP) E/M

PROPER 24 (SUNDAY BETWEEN 16 AND 22 OCTOBER INCLUSIVE) YEAR A

HYMNS AND SONGS

	pos	rdg	AMNS	CAON	CFE	CH4	CH5	CP	H&P	HTC	LAU	MP	NEH	SG	SOF	TS
A/The new commandment		n		35	4		515			S 26	920	1			22	23
All praise to thee, for thou, O King divine		g	337	22			684	372	253	204			335			
Almighty Father, who for us thy Son didst give		n	338				374		401							
Among the gods there is none like you		o													653	19
Be thou my vision/Lord, be my vision		o	343	70	74/75	465	643	386	378	545	970	51	339	669	42	50
Brother, sister, let me serve you/Will you let me be your servant		g		88	813	694	517	393			924			619	54	
Christ whose glory fills the skies	mo	o	4	105			578	52	2	457	266	670	79	234	170	1200
Eternal light, shine in my heart		o					613	415		339						
Father of heaven, whose love profound		n,g	97	165	163	483	319	421	519	359		827	358	144		1201
Forth in thy name, O Lord, I go	se	o	239	188	184	529	567	430	381	306	861	159	235	623	1237	
From heaven you came, helpless babe		g		195	187	374	219	432			749	162		632	120	114
God, we praise you! God, we bless you!		g				120	696	450		341			38			
Here is love, vast as the ocean		g					222				987			174	168	164
How deep the Father's love		g				549	224				988			193	780	185
I will sing the wondrous story		n		337					223	212	315			43	278	821
Jesus Christ (Once again)		g									995			394	865	274
Let there be love shared among us		n		386	358		525				411				329	317
Love divine, all loves excelling		n	131	428	398	519	634	516	267	217	801	449	408	179	377	343
My Lord, what love is this		g		462	500		230				476			194	398	370
My Lord, you wore no royal crown		g								118				628		
O Lord, hear my prayer (Taizé)		o		938	542		620				929	908		246	423	394
O love divine, how sweet thou art		n	124				621	541					424			
Praise, my soul, the King of heaven	ga	g	192	565	602	160	366	555	13	38	807	560	436	93	466	433
Remember, remember your mercy, Lord		o			621						843		154			
Spirit of holiness, wisdom and faithfulness		o					576			246		611		449	1010	
Teach me thy way, O Lord		o										626				969
The works of the Lord are created in wisdom		o						266	26							
Thine for ever, God of love		n	234	673			660	599		556		972	463			
Ubi caritas/Living charity (Taizé)		n		946		801	530				245				1573	
Who can measure heaven and earth?		o								27						

SONGS FOR CHILDREN

We will walk with God/We are on the Lord's road (Sizohamba naye) C 198, CH4 803, IECS, OITB, SFL1 21, SG 138, VFLS 40

When I needed a neighbour AMNS 433, CAON 736, CAP 65, CFE 800, CH 229, CH4 544, CH5 499, JP 275, LAU 888, SOF 1604

BIBLE READINGS

Psalms 142 [and 143.1–11]
Proverbs 4.1–18
1 John 3.16 - 4.6
Mark 10.35–45

SINGING THE PSALM

Psalm 142 CWP, NPCW
   Dean *You are my refuge, Lord* C#
   Walker *You are my refuge* C#
Psalm 143.1–11 CH4, CWP, FGP, NPCW, PAME

ANTHEMS AND VOCAL MUSIC

Title	Composer	Voices	E/M/D	Book source	Single sheet publisher
UNISON/TWO PART/HIGH VOICES					
Christ has no body now but yours	Ogden	U + descant	E	LOL, CFAP	RSCM
O for a closer walk with God	Caesar	SSA	M/D	EAC2	
The Servant Song	Gillard arr Ogden	2 part	E	SFL1	
When I needed a neighbour	Carter arr Burt	2 part	M	SFL1	
THREE/FOUR PARTS					
Blessed are those that are undefiled in the way	Greene	SATB + SS	M/D		CMS/OUP
Come down, O love divine	Harris	SATB	E/M	NCAB	Novello
Come down, O love divine	Tadman-Robins	SAMen	E	OBFA	
Greater love (g)	Ireland	SATB	M	AC4	S&B
Grow in grace	Archer	SATB	E/M	SBS1	RSCM
Holy is the true light	Harris	SATB unacc	E	FSB7, NCAB, NSAC2, SL (ATTB)	Novello
If ye love me	Tallis	SATB unacc	E	FAB1, NCAB, NOEAB, NSAC1, OBTA, TA	OUP
Lord, for thy tender mercy's sake	Hilton/Farrant	SATB unacc	E	AWTE, FAB1, NCAB, NOEAB, OBTA	OUP
O for a closer walk with God	Ives	SATB	M		RSCM
O for a closer walk with God	Stanford	SATB	M	AC1, ASA, BC, OBFA, AOAN1 (SAMen)	RSCM
O Master, let me walk with thee	Ledger	SATB	M/D		Encore
So they gave their bodies	Aston	SATB	M	NCAB	RSCM
Teach me, O God	Attwood	SATB	E	NOEAB	RSCM
The Grail Prayer	Rizza	SATB + solo S	E	FOLO	Mayhew
Though I speak with the tongues of men	Bairstow	SATB	M	FSB10, NCAB, WFC	OUP
What wondrous love is this? (g)	Trad arr Weaver	SAB	E	LOL, SBS1, SFL2	
FIVE OR MORE PARTS					
Beati quorum via	Stanford	SSATBB unacc	M	ASA, WFC	RSCM
If ye love me	Chilcott	SSATB unacc	M	BCA, WFC	
Teach me, O Lord	Byrd	SAATB	M	OBTA	OUP
When I needed a neighbour	Carter arr Rose	SATB + SATB	E/M	MTH1	

ORGAN MUSIC

PRELUDES

Bonnet J.	**Romance sans Paroles** Op.7 No.8 (Leduc) E/M	
Cima G.P.	**Ricercar à quattro** No.8 in *Faber Early Organ* Vol.17 E/M*	
Hunt D.	**Love divine** in *100 Hymn Preludes* and in *Hymn Preludes for the Church Year* Bk.2 (both Mayhew) E	
Warren N.	**A new commandment** in *Preludes on Favourite Hymns* and in *Preludes on Favourite Hymns for Manuals* (both Mayhew) E(*)	
Watson R.	**Elegie in memoriam Herbert Howells** (Fagus) M	

POSTLUDES

Archer M.	**Festive Scherzo** from *100 Processionals and Recessionals* (Mayhew) M	
Callahan C.	**Voluntary on 'Engelberg'** (MorningStar) M	
Johnson D.	**Trumpet Tune in D** (Augsburg Fortress) E/M	
Young G.	**Tambourine Toccata** from *Suite Mediévale* (Flammer) E/M	

PROPER 25 (SUNDAY BETWEEN 23 AND 29 OCTOBER INCLUSIVE) YEAR A

HYMNS AND SONGS

	pos	rdg	AMNS	CAON	CFE	CH4	CH5	CP	H&P	HTC	LAU	MP	NEH	SG	SOF	TS
Abide with me	ev	o	13	2	9	580	62	10	665	425	907	4	331	495	2	2
And can it be that I should gain		g		32	43	396	218	376	216	588	790	33	627	168	21	21
Awake, my soul, and with the sun	mo,ga	o	1	58		210	51	1	632	264		804	232	618		
By your side I would stay		g		90								810			55	60
Disposer supreme and judge of the earth		n	298	149				214					216			
Eternal light, shine in my heart		o					613	415		339						
Fight the good fight		n	220	169	171	517	566	423	710	526	860	143	359	635	107	
God forgave my sin in Jesus' name		g		212	209		480			S 12	849	181			129	123
I want to walk with Jesus Christ		g					580			S 16		302			261	
I will offer up my life		g				503						990		565	851	265
Immortal, invisible, God only wise	ga	o	199	314	301	132	6	474	9	21	725	327	377	44	234	220
Jesus calls us: o'er the tumult		g	312	347		509	584	233	141	104		359	200	668		
Just as I am, without one plea		g	246	374	339	553	587	308	697	440		396	294	507	316	306
New every morning is the love	mo	o	2	467		214	59	6	636	270		480	238			
O God beyond all praising		o		489			362			36	728			53	953	
O/Our God, our help in ages past		o	99	494	528	161	537	537	358	37	955	498	417	542	415	905
O thou who camest from above		g	233	541	557	625	639	191	745	596		525	431	560	451	416
Oft in danger/Christian soldiers		n	210	487			547		715	524		533	434			
Onward, Christian soldiers		n	333		581	514	659	549	718	532		543	435		442	
Powerful in making us wise to salvation		o							479	252			228			
Soldiers of Christ, arise		n	219	606		515	487	571	719	533		604	449	643	506	
Soldiers who are Christ's below		n	302	607			228						450			
Stand up, stand up for Jesus		n	221	617			488	578	721	535		617	453	644	513	1517
Teach me, my God and King		o	240	629			601	583	803				456			
The Lord is my song (Taizé)				651							929					
To him we come		n								518		709		679		1569
We rest on thee/trust in you		n								446		735		510	587	1043
Will you come and follow me		g		752	812	533	605	622			877		647	634	1120	
Will your anchor hold in the storms of life?		o		753		737	680		689			770				

SONGS FOR CHILDREN

Be bold, be strong JP 14, KS 17, MP 49, SOF 37, TS 38

BIBLE READINGS

Psalm 119.89–104
Ecclesiastes 11, 12
2 Timothy 2.1–7
Mark 12.28–34

SINGING THE PSALM

Psalm 119.89–104 CWP, NPCW, PFS

ANTHEMS AND VOCAL MUSIC

Title	Composer	Voices	E/M/D	Book source	Single sheet publisher
UNISON/TWO PART/HIGH VOICES					
Bambelela (You must never give up)	Trad South African	U/SATB	E	C	
Be strong in the Lord	Nicholson	SS	E		Curwen
Christ has no body now but yours	Ogden	U + descant#	E	CFAP, LOL	RSCM
Creator God	Rizza	U/SATB + descant#	E	ROP	
Ex ore innocentium	Ireland	S	M/D	NSAC2	B&H
Give me strength	Chilcott	2 part	E	VFLS	
I give you a new commandment	Aston	2 part	E	BC, EAC2, NOEAB	RSCM
No greater love	Joncas	U/SATB	E/M	MHWE	GIA
THREE/FOUR PARTS					
A new commandment (g)	Parshall	SATB unacc	E	WFC	
Be strong and of good courage	Campbell	SATB	M	FSB7	Novello
Fight the good fight	Gardner	SATB	E	MTH1	OUP
God is our hope and strength	Stanford	SATB	M		Novello
Greater love	Ireland	SATB	M	AC4	S&B
I give to you a new commandment (g)	Nardone	SATB	E/M	SBS1	RSCM
Jesu, grant me this I pray	Gibbons	SATB	E/M	AWTE	
Prayer before the Crucifix	P. Moore	SATB	E/M		Banks
Solus ad victimam	Leighton	SATB	M	NCAB, AC1, SC	
There's a wideness in God's mercy	Bevan	SATB	E	LD, MTH1, NEP, NOEAB	
Ubi caritas (g)	Ives	SATB unacc	M	SC	
Ubi caritas (g)	Mawby	SATB	E		Mayhew
Wondrous cross	Wilby	SATB	E	OBFA, WOTC	
FIVE OR MORE PARTS					
Deus noster refugium	Hassler	SAATTB unacc	M/D		CMS/OUP
God is our hope and strength	Blow	SSAATTBB	M		Banks
Ubi caritas (g)	Berkeley	SSATB unacc	D		Chester
Ubi caritas (g)	Duruflé	SAATTBB unacc	M		Durand

ORGAN MUSIC

PRELUDES

Guilmant A.	**Oraison No.3** from *Trois Oraisons* Op.94 in *Selected Works* Vol.3 (Bärenreiter) E
Karg-Elert S.	**Introitus** from *8 Short Pieces for the Organ* Op.154 (Cathedral Music) E/M
Kerll J.K.	**Toccata IV cromatica con durezza, e ligature** No.4 in *Faber Early Organ* Vol.15 (Faber) E/M*
Parry C.H.H.	**Chorale Prelude 'Eventide'** in *Seven Chorale Preludes* Set 1 (Novello); also in *Preludes and Postludes* (Mayhew) E/M
Thiman E.	**In-Voluntary for Sunday Morning** ('Morning Hymn') in *Times and Seasons* Bk.2 (Novello) E/M

POSTLUDES

Lloyd Webber W.S.	**Epilogue** in *Eight Varied Pieces* (Bosworth) M
Pachelbel J.	**Ein feste Burg ist unser Gott** in *80 Chorale Preludes* (Peters) E/M
Watson R.	**Pageant (Ionian)** *or* **March (Aeolian)** from *In the Mode* (Fagus) E/M*
Young G.	**Fanfare on 'St Gertrude'** in *Eight Organ Voluntaries* (Presser) E/M

THE LAST SUNDAY AFTER TRINITY (IF OBSERVED AS BIBLE SUNDAY) YEAR A

HYMNS AND SONGS

	pos	rdg	AMNS	CAON	CFE	CH4	CH5	CP	H&P	HTC	LAU	MP	NEH	SG	SOF	TS
All who are thirsty, come to the Lord		o												546		
Break thou the bread of life		o					379	286	467			64			50	
Christ is our cornerstone		n	161	98			327	395		564			206	14		
Father of mercies, in thy word		o	167							247				224		
God has spoken – by his prophets		s					381		64	248	742	831		225		
God of glory, we exalt your name		n										191			137	130
God of grace and God of glory		n	367	225			533	448	712	324		192		574	139	
God, who has caused to be written		s	467						472							
How sure the Scriptures are!		s								249				227		
In the Lord I'll be ever thankful (Taizé)				929	308	772					944	865		656	817	
Jesus shall reign where'er the sun		n	143	359		470	97	490	239	516	322	379	388	45	301	1376
Lord, be thy word/make your word my rule		o	232				383	209		250						
Lord, I have made thy word my choice		s	490					504	475							
Lord, thy word abideth/your word shall guide us		o	166	420	390		384	515	476	251	977/8	446	407			
May the mind of Christ my Saviour		s		447		536	636	521	739	550		463		671	1448	887
My Lord, you wore no royal crown		n								118				628		
Not far beyond the sea, nor high		s	401					528	477							
O for a thousand tongues to sing		n	125	485		352	104	534	744	219		496	415	55	412	383/1452
Open thou mine eyes		s										546				
Powerful in making us wise to salvation		s							479	252				228		
Rise and hear! The Lord is speaking		o	509				385	321								
Seek ye first the kingdom of God		o		590	633	641	596		138		820	590			493	447
Thanks/Praise to God whose word was spoken		s	423			605	387	584	483	255			438	229		
The kingdom of God is justice and joy		n		646	701			591	139	333	821	651		184		
Thou/God, whose almighty word		s	180	684	738	112	324	267	29	506	887	699	466	597	557	
We have a gospel to proclaim		s	431	716	778	363	491	612	465	519	852	728	486	331	1583	
Will you come and follow me	se	n		752	812	533	605	622			877		647	634	1120	
Your word is a lamp unto my feet		s												234		

SONGS FOR CHILDREN

Have you heard the raindrops CAON 817, CH 78, CAP 2, CH4 525, JP 71, KS 99
The word of the Lord is planted in my heart JP 473, KS 338

118

BIBLE READINGS

Psalm 119.89–104

Isaiah 55.1–11

Luke 4.14–30

SINGING THE PSALM

Psalm 119.89–104 CWP, NPCW, PFS

ANTHEMS AND VOCAL MUSIC

Title	Composer	Voices	E/M/D	Book source	Single sheet publisher
UNISON/TWO PART/HIGH VOICES					
As the deer longs	Hurd	U/SATB#	E	CFE, CG, CH4, LAU	OCP
Ho, everyone who thirsts (Come to the feast)	Haugen	U	E	LAU	GIA
May the Word of God strengthen us	Walker	U/2 part#	E	C	
Praise to you, O Christ our Saviour	Farrell	U#	E	CFE, LAU, RITH, WYP	OCP
Water of life	Dean	U#	E	CFE, CSF, LAU, NEP	OCP
Word of God, burn within us	Hurd	U#	E	C	
THREE/FOUR PARTS					
As water to the thirsty	Coleman arr Barnard	SATB	E	SC	
Blessed be the God and Father	S.S.Wesley	SATB	M	FAB1, NCAB, SC	RSCM
Christ was the Word	Maxim	SATB unacc	E	SBS2	
I heard the voice of Jesus say	Shephard	SATB	M		RSCM
I will praise God because of his word	Purcell	SATB	E/M	TPS	
Like as the hart	Howells	SATB	M	AC4	OUP
O sing joyfully	Batten	SATB unacc	E	SCAB, WFC	RSCM
Sicut cervus	Palestrina	SATB unacc	M	ESM, SL (ATTB)	Chester
Teach me, O God	Camidge	SAB	E	CHM	
Teach me, O Lord	Attwood	SATB	E	NOEAB	RSCM
The Spirit of the Lord	Elgar	SATB	M	SAEE	RSCM
Thy word is a lantern	Purcell	SATB	M	APA	Novello
Waiting for the word	Skellern	SATB	E/M		RSCM
FIVE OR MORE PARTS					
Beati quorum via	Stanford	SSATBB unacc	M	ASA, WFC	RSCM
Deus, Deus meus	R.Panufnik	SSAATTBB + solo S	D		Universal
I am thine, O save me	S.S.Wesley	SATTB	M	MTP	Novello
Os justi	Bruckner	SSATTB unacc	M/D	ESM	Peters
Sing joyfully	Byrd	SAATB unacc	M	OBTA	OUP
Teach me, O Lord	Byrd	SAATB	M	OBTA	OUP

ORGAN MUSIC

PRELUDES

Anon.	**Erhalt uns, Herr, bei deinem Wort** in *120 Chorale Preludes of the 17C & 18C* (Peters) E/M
Bach J.S.	**Herr Jesu Christ, dich zu uns wend** BWV 632 from the *Orgelbüchlein* (many editions) M
Böhm G.	**Erhalt uns, Herr, bei deinem Wort** in *Complete Works* (Breitkopf) E/M
Roe B.	**Eden** in *The Organist's Liturgical Year* (Mayhew) E
Willan H.	**Gardiner** (aka 'Fulda') in *36 Short Preludes and Postludes* Set 2 (Peters) E

POSTLUDES

Bach J.C.	**Erhalt uns, Herr, bei deinem Wort** in *120 Chorale Preludes of the 17C & 18C* (Peters) E(*)
Buxtehude D.	**Es spricht der Unweisen Mund wohl** BuxWV 187 in *Complete Works* Vol.4 (Bärenreiter) M
Karg-Elert S.	**Herr Jesu Christ, dich zu uns wend'** No.9 of *20 Preludes and Postludes* Op.78 (Breitkopf) E/M
Piutti C.	**Liebster Jesu, wir sind hier** in *Choralvorspiele* Op.34 Vol.2 (Bärenreiter) E/M

DEDICATION FESTIVAL YEARS A, B, C
(Observed on the First Sunday in October or the last Sunday after Trinity if the date is not known)

HYMNS AND SONGS

	pos	rdg	AMNS	CAON	CFE	CH4	CH5	CP	H&P	HTC	LAU	MP	NEH	SG	SOF	TS
Adoramus te, Domine (Taizé)				921	11		345				667		208			
Angel voices, ever singing		s	163	37	45	498	346	377	484	307	724	34	336	27	24	
Be still, for the presence of the Lord		s		67	72	189	325	383			720	50	*629*	7	40	47
Blessèd city, heavenly Salem		s	332				326	208	485				204			
Christ is made the sure foundation		s	332ii	97	109	200		207		559	456	73	205	572	1199	654
Christ is our cornerstone		s	161	98			327	395		564			206	14		
Christians, lift up your hearts (This is the house)		s	445													
Forth in the peace of Christ we go	se		458	187	183	646	454	429		542	853		361	594		
Glorious things of thee are spoken		s	172	205	195	738	646	435	817	494	827	173	362	35	127	691
God is here! As we his people		s	464				330	301	653	560	470					
Here in this place (Gather us in)		s			253	623					475			4		
Here to the house of God we come		s				195										
Here within this house of prayer		s								563						
How lovely are thy dwellings fair		s					333									
How lovely is thy dwelling place		s				52						247			191	
How lovely is your dwelling place (Redman)		s													781	188
I rejoiced to hear them say		s												6		
I rejoiced when I heard them say		s				83					992					
In our day of thanksgiving		s	284	324			469	351	660				208			
Let us build a house (All are welcome)		o				198					458					
Longing for light (Christ be our light)		o				543					883					1409
Lord, for the years		s		409		159	81	81		328	942	428	*619*	602	892	327
Rejoice today with one accord		s			620					347			444			
Sing and be glad, for this is God's house!		s					340									
The Church's one foundation		s	170	636	688	739	528	585	515	501	830	640	484	581	525	477
Thy/Your hand, O God, has guided		s	171	689	741	511	529	606	784	536	876	705	485	649	1065	
We have a gospel to proclaim		s	431	716	778	363	491	612	465	519	852	728	486	331	1583	
We love the place, O God		s	160	718			343	211		558		731	471			
Ye that know the Lord is gracious		s	175			642	493	628					477			

SONGS FOR CHILDREN

Each of us is a living stone CAON 793, CH 41
Praise the Lord with the sound of trumpet CH4 169
Zacchaeus SSJ
Zacchaeus was a very little man CAON 919, CH 243, JP 300

BIBLE READINGS Year A

Morning Psalms 48 and 150
Evening Psalm 132
Jeremiah 7.1–11
1 Corinthians 3.9–17
Luke 19.1–10

BIBLE READINGS Years B and C

Morning Psalms 48 and 150
Evening Psalm 132
Jeremiah 7.1–11
Luke 19.1–10

SINGING THE PSALM

Psalm 48 CWP, NPCW
Psalm 150 CH4, CWP, H&P, LAU, MCW1, NEP, NPCW, PIW
   Berthier *Let us sing to the Lord* TSFP#
Psalm 132 CWP, NPCW

ANTHEMS AND VOCAL MUSIC

Title	Composer	Voices	E/M/D	Book source	Single sheet publisher
UNISON/TWO PART/HIGH VOICES					
How lovely is your dwelling place	Walker	U/SATB#	E/M	CIH	
I was glad	Hubbard	SA	M	SFJ	Banks
Im Himmelreich	Reger	SSAA unacc	M	AC3	
We love the place, O God	Brahms	SS	M		Novello
THREE/FOUR PARTS					
Behold, the tabernacle of God (A)	Harris	SATB	E/M		RSCM
Behold, the tabernacle of God (A)	Rutter	SATB	M/D		OUP
Blessed city, heavenly Salem	Bairstow	SATB	D		Banks
Christ is our cornerstone	Thorne	SATB	E/M	NOEAB	
I was glad	Bertalot	SATB	M	NAB3	
If God is building when we build	Trad arr Barnard	SATB	E	SBS2	
Locus iste	Bruckner	SATB unacc	E/M	NCAB, ESM	RSCM
Locus iste	O'Regan	SATB unacc	M		OUP
How lovely are thy dwellings	Brahms	SATB	M/D		RSCM
How lovely are thy dwellings	Self	SAB	E		RSCM
How lovely is your dwelling place	Hubbard	SATB	M	GAW	Banks
O how amiable	Vaughan Williams	SATB	E/M	NCAB, AC4, OEAB	OUP
Pray that Jerusalem	Stanford	SATB	E	ASA	RSCM
Surely thou hast tasted that the Lord is good	Bernard Rose	SATB unacc	M/D	EAC1	
The Church triumphant	Shephard	SATB	E/M	SBS1	RSCM
This is truly the house of God	Rubbra	SATB	M		Lengnick
We love the place, O God	Sumsion	SATB	M/D		RSCM
FIVE OR MORE PARTS					
Christ is the morning star	Carter	SSAATTBB	D		OUP
Lo! God is here!	P.Moore	SSAATTBB	M/D		Faber
I was glad	Parry	SATB + SATB	M/D		RSCM
I was glad	Purcell	SSATB	M/D	APA	Faber, CMS

The list of organ music is on page 370.

HYMNS AND SONGS

	pos	rdg	AMNS	CAON	CFE	CH4	CH5	CP	H&P	HTC	LAU	MP	NEH	SG	SOF	TS
Adoramus te, Domine (Taizé)				921	11		345				667			208		
Author of faith, eternal Word		n						381	662							
Blest are the pure in heart	gr	s	238	77	88		630	391	724	110	908		341	372		
Christ, from whom all blessings flow	gr	n							764	491						
Faithful one, so unchanging		n					2					825		547	89	89
Fight the good fight with all thy might	se	n	220	169	171	517	566	423	710	526	860	143	359	496	107	
For all the saints who from their labours rest	ga	s	305	177	176	740	459	232	814	567	371	148	197	636	109	684
For all the saints who showed your love		s									387					
For all thy saints, O Lord		s	308	179			461	215					224			
From thee/you all skill and science flow		o	286				512	345	389	310						
Give me/us the wings of faith		s	324	204				216	815				225			
Give thanks with a grateful heart		n		202	189	180	352					170		108	124	118
Glory in the highest to the God of heaven		n					693	300		582			363	37		
Glory to you, O God, for all your saints		n				741										
God, we praise you! God, we bless you!		n				120	696	450		341				38		
He gave his life in selfless love		n					417			405		214	467			
How bright these glorious spirits shine!		s	306			745	467	221		572			227			
Join all the glorious names		s				460		493	78	214		392	639	46	313	848
Let saints on earth/Come, let us join our friends		s	182	384				222	812	574		409	396	578		
Light of the minds that know him	se	s		397			588	501		477			400	626		
Lord of the Church, we pray		n					303			499		442		577	1433	
May the mind of Christ my Saviour		n		447		536	636	521	739	550		463		671	1448	887
O what their joy and their glory must be	se	s	186	550				225					432			
Palms of glory, raiment bright		s	307					226					230			
Sing alleluia forth ye saints on high		n					568						446			
Such love, pure as the whitest snow		n		620								619		216	514	465
Thanks be to God for his saints		s												64		
There is a land of pure delight		s	190				681	597	822	575			460			
There's a place (Because of you)		s										1011		457	1041	498
We walk by faith		n			789						284					
Who are these, like stars appearing		s	323	746			475	229					231			
Ye/You holy angels bright	ga	n	198	755		179	376	626	20	353			783	475	76	619
Ye watchers and ye holy ones		s	532	758			476	230					478			

SONGS FOR CHILDREN

Don't be lazy SOF 701
O when the saints CAON 876, CFE 571, CH 163, JP 195, VFLS 20

BIBLE READINGS

Morning Psalms 15, 84 and 149
Evening Psalms 148 and 150
Isaiah 65.17–25
Hebrews 11.32 - 12.2

SINGING THE PSALM

Psalm 15 CRP, CWP, H&P, NEP, NPCW
    Bell *Lord, who may enter your house?* CH4, OITB
Psalm 84 CH4, CRP, CWP, H&P, NEH, NPCW, PFS
    Dean *They are happy who dwell* LAU
    DeBruyn *O how lovely is your dwelling place* CFE, LAU
    Haugen *How lovely is your dwelling place* (GIA)#
    Walker *How lovely is your dwelling place* CIH# (OCP)
Psalm 149 CWP, NPCW, PAME
    Trad *Blest be God* OITB
Psalm 148 CH4, CWP, H&P, NEP, NPCW, PAME, PIW
    Bell *Glory to God above!* CG, CH4, PPP
    Mayhew *All the nations of the earth* PCMG
    Ogden *Let all creation sing* SFL2 (WLP)#
Psalm 150 CH4, CWP, H&P, LAU, MCW1, NEP, NPCW, PIW
    Berthier *Let us sing to the Lord* TSFP#

ANTHEMS AND VOCAL MUSIC

Title	Composer	Voices	E/M/D	Book source	Single sheet publisher
UNISON/TWO PART/HIGH VOICES					
Settings of the Te Deum	Various	U/SATB	E	CWP, MCW1	
Alleluia Beati	Walker	U/2 part#	E	C	
Gaudent in coelis	Dering	2 part	M	AC2, SFL2	Schott
Give us the wings of faith	Blatchly	SS	M	HP	
Happy Land	Chilcott	SS	E		OUP
Let saints on earth	Ridout	U	E	AC2	
Saints of God in glory	Farrell	U	E	GBAN	
The souls of the righteous	Nares	SS	M	AC2	OUP
THREE/FOUR PARTS					
And I saw a new heaven	Archer	SATB	M	NOEAB	
And I saw a new heaven	Bainton	SATB	M/D	FSB4	Novello
Fight the good fight	Gardner	SATB	M	MTH1	OUP
For all thy saints	Bullard	SATB	E/M	NOEAB	
In the city of the Lord	Harper	SATB	M/D	LOL	
Justorum animae	Berkeley	SATB unacc	D		Chester
Justorum animae	Stanford	SATB unacc	M	ASA	S&B
Lo, round the throne	Ley	SATB	E	FSB3, NCAB	OUP
O King all glorious	Willan	SATB unacc	E/M	ETAS	
O quam gloriosum	Byrd	SATB unacc	M	OBTA	Banks
O quam gloriosum	Vaet	SATB unacc	M	ETAS	
O quam gloriosum	Victoria	SATB unacc	M	ESM, NCAB	Chester
Praise his name in the dance	Kelly	SATB	M/D		Encore
When the saints go marching in	Rutter	SATB	M		OUP
FIVE OR MORE PARTS					
Beati mundo corde	Byrd	SSATB unacc	M/D	ETAS	CMS/OUP
Christ is the morning star	Carter	SSAATTBB	D		OUP
Christus est stella	Todd	SSAATTBB unacc	D	CN	
Glorious in heaven	Whitlock	SATBB unacc	E/M	ETAS	
Justorum animae	Byrd	SSATB unacc	M/D	OBTA	OUP

The list of organ music is on page 371.

HYMNS AND SONGS

	pos	rdg	AMNS	CAON	CFE	CH4	CH5	CP	H&P	HTC	LAU	MP	NEH	SG	SOF	TS
Blessing and honour (Ancient of days)		o				442						976		106	675	54
Blest are the pure in heart		n	238	77	88		630	391	724	110	908		341	372		
Come, let us join our cheerful songs	ga	o	144	120			332	401	810	206		93	349	33	70	
For all the saints who from their labours rest		s	305	177	176	740	459	232	814	567	371	148	197	636	109	684
Give me/us the wings of faith		n	324	204			463	216	815				225			
Great God, what do I see and hear		o								189						
Happy are they, they that love God		n	176	262			649	456	711	473			369			
How bright those glorious spirits shine		s	306			745	467	221		572			227			
How shall I sing that majesty		o	472	296		128	468	466	8				373/699			
Immortal, invisible, God only wise		o	199	314	301	132	6	474	9	21	725	327	377	44	234	220
Jesu, the very thought of thee		n	120	368	321	560	101	485	265	478	798	386	385	534	308	
Jesus Christ is waiting		n		349	323	360					889			624		1360
Jesus shall take the highest honour		o		360									378	123	302	296
Laudate Dominum/Sing, praise and bless the Lord (Taizé)		ps		933	346	77	359				698				1514	458
O worship the King, all glorious above	ga	o	101	551	559	127	34	546	28	24	683	528	433	90	456	425
Sun of my soul	ev	n	11	621			72	21	646			618	251			
Take this moment, sign and space		n			680	501	598				850					
The God of Abraham praise		o	331	642		162	323	586	452	9	712	645	148	66	530	975
There is a land of pure delight		s	190				681	597	822	575			460			
There's a place (Because of you)		s										1011		457	1041	498
Who are these, like stars appearing		s	323	746			475	229					231			
Ye/You servants of God, your master proclaim		o	149	756	819	130	492	627	278	520		784	476	75	620	1074
Ye watchers and ye holy ones		s	532	758			476	230					478			

SONGS FOR CHILDREN

Great is he MP 1048, SOF 1254, TS 705

The kingdom of heaven CAON 647, CFE 702, LAU 816

BIBLE READINGS

Psalms 111 and 117
Daniel 7.1–18
Luke 6.17–31

SINGING THE PSALM

Psalm 111 CWP, H&P, NEP, NPCW
Psalm 117 CRP, CWP, FGP, NPCW

Bell *Praise your Maker* PPP
Berthier *Laudate Dominum* CAON, CFE, CH4, CH5, LAU, TSFP#
Inwood *Holy is God* HIG, LAU#
Jakob *Go out to the whole world* C

ANTHEMS AND VOCAL MUSIC

Title	Composer	Voices	E/M/D	Book source	Single sheet publisher
UNISON/TWO PART/HIGH VOICES					
Alleluia! Raise the Gospel	Farrell	U/SATB#	E	C, GBU	OCP
Benedictus/The Beatitudes	Rizza	U/SATB#	E	ROP	
Blest are they	Haas	U#	E	CH4, LAU	GIA
Love one another	S.S.Wesley	S	E	BC	RSCM
THREE/FOUR PARTS					
A touching place (Christ's is the world)	Bell	SATB	E	CG, IAMB, LFB, WGIR, WIS	GIA
Amen, amen, it shall be so!	Bell	SATB + cantor	E	LAA	
Blessed are they	S.S.Wesley	SAB	M		S&B
Blest are the pure in heart	Walford Davies	SATB unacc	E	MTH1, NCAB	RSCM
Judge eternal	Archer	SATB	E/M		Mayhew
O for a thousand tongues	Shephard	SATB	M/D		RSCM
Teach me, O God	Moger	SAB	E		RSCM
Teach me, O Lord	Attwood	SATB	E	NOEAB	RSCM
Teach me thy way, O Lord	Fox	SATB unacc	E	FSB7, SBS1	RSCM
Teach me thy way, O Lord	Purcell	SATB	M	TPS	
The Beatitudes	Chilcott	SATB	M		OUP
The Beatitudes	Pärt	SATB	D		Universal
The Beatitudes	Watson Henderson	SATB	M/D	SC	RSCM
Ubi caritas	Ives	SATB unacc	M	SC	
We cannot measure how you heal	Bell arr Archer	SATB	E	BC	RSCM
FIVE OR MORE PARTS					
Beati mundo corde	Byrd	SSATB unacc	M/D	ETAS	CMS/OUP
Teach me, O Lord	Byrd	SAATB	M	OBTA	OUP
Ubi caritas	Berkeley	SSATB unacc	D		Chester
Ubi caritas	Duruflé	SAATTBB unacc	M		Durand

ORGAN MUSIC

PRELUDES

Fletcher A.   **Franconia** in *Hymn Preludes for the Church Year* Bk.1 (Mayhew) E
Noble T.T.   **Chorale Prelude 'Stracathro'** (OUP reprint) E/M
Saint-Saëns C.   **No.1** of *Sept Improvisations* Op.150 (Durand, Butz) M
Trevor C.H.   **Study on 'Franconia'** in *The Progressive Organist* Bk.5 (Novello) E
Watson R.   **Scherzetto (Dorian)** No.2 from *In the Mode* (Fagus) E/M*

POSTLUDES

Boyce W.   **Voluntary No.1 in D** (many editions) E/M*
Lebègue N.   **Autre Offertoire in C** p.16 in *Offertoires from Troisième Livre d'Orgue* (Hawthorns); also p.181 in *Complete Works* Vol.3 (Kalmus) E/M(*)
Peeters F.   **Chorale Fantasie 'Lasst uns erfreuen'** in *Festal Voluntaries: Easter* (Novello) M
Spedding A.   **Carillon ('Leoni')** in *Recuerdos* (IAO) E/M

THE THIRD SUNDAY BEFORE ADVENT YEAR A

HYMNS AND SONGS

	pos	rdg	AMNS	CAON	CFE	CH4	CH5	CP	H&P	HTC	LAU	MP	NEH	SG	SOF	TS
A/The new commandment		n		35	4		515			S 26	920	1			22	23
Be still and know I (John Bell)		o												18	672	
Be still and know II (John Bell)		o			70	754							242			
Be still and know that I am God		o		66	71	755	608				909	48			41	48
Christian, dost thou see them		o	55										65			
Come down, O love divine		n	156	114	125	489	294	175	281	231	303	89	137	663	1202	71
Deck thyself, my soul, with gladness/Soul, array thyself	cm	n	257	146			445	295	606	400			280			
Disposer supreme and judge of the earth		o	298	149				214					216			
God is love, and where true love is		n	465		214		520	441	757		242		513			
Great/Lord God, your love has called us here		n	489	246		484	416	133	500	480						
Here is love, vast as the ocean		n				222					987			174	168	164
In heavenly armour we'll enter the land		o									639			237	228
In heavenly love abiding		n		323		551		478	678	458		331	638		238	782
Lord, I come to you (Power of your love)		n										880		689	895	329
Love divine, all loves excelling		n	131	428	398	519	634	516	267	217	801	449	408	179	377	343
O Jesus, I have promised		n	235	503	536	644	593	538	704	531	875	501	420	676	418	391
Take my life and let it be		n	249	625	677	502	597	581	705	554	874	624		678	519	468
The race that long in darkness/The people who in darkness		o	52	656	711	290	199	38	89	71	168		57			
The Son of God proclaim		n	427				328	627	415	650			482			
There's a spirit in the air		n	515	661		616	314	198	326	245			69			
Ubi caritas/Living charity (Taizé)		n		946		801	530				245				1573	
What a friend we have in Jesus		n		727		547	627		559	373		746		646	593	566

SONGS FOR CHILDREN

God has chosen me CFE 212, LAU 858, MP 830, SFL1 24, SG 612
God's love is for everybody CH4 765

BIBLE READINGS

Psalms [20 and] 82
Judges 7.2–22
John 15.9–17

SINGING THE PSALM

Psalm 20 CH4, CWP, NPCW
Psalm 82 CWP, NPCW

ANTHEMS AND VOCAL MUSIC

Title	Composer	Voices	E/M/D	Book source	Single sheet publisher
UNISON/TWO PART/HIGH VOICES					
A Song of St Francis	Hurd	SSA	M/D	EAC2	
Faith, hope and love	Ogden	2 part	E	SBS1	RSCM
Jesu, Jesu, fill us with your love	Trad arr Weaver	2 part	E	IECS, SFL1	
Love one another	S.S.Wesley	S	E	BC	RSCM
Prayer of St Benedict	Payne	2 part	E	VFLS	
The Father's love	Lole	SS	E/M	EAC2	RSCM
Ubi caritas	Lole	SS	M		Encore
The Servant Song	Gillard arr Ogden	2 part	E	SFL1	
THREE/FOUR PARTS					
Anima mea	M. de Rivafrecha	SATB unacc	E/M	CM3	Chester
Arise, my love	Martinson	SATB unacc	M/D	WFC	
Beloved, let us love	Aston	SATB unacc	D		RSCM
God is always there	Plainsong arr Bullard		E	OBFA	
Greater love	Ireland	SATB	M	AC4	S&B
In the heart where love is abiding	Barnard	SATB	E	AWTE, BC	RSCM
Lord, make me an instrument	Aston	SATB (unacc)	E/M		RSCM
Love divine	Willcocks	SATB	E	NOEAB	
Love one another	Carter	SATB	D		OUP
My beloved is mine	Lole	SATB unacc	M		Encore
Set me as a seal	Walton	SATB	M/D	AC4, WFC	OUP
Strengthen ye the weak hands	Harris	SATB	M		Novello
Though I speak with the tongues of men	Bairstow	SATB	M	FSB10, NCAB, WFC	OUP
Thy perfect love	Rutter	SATB	E/M	NOEAB	OUP
Ubi caritas	Ives	SATB unacc	M	SC	
FIVE OR MORE PARTS					
Ubi caritas	Berkeley	SSATB unacc	D		Chester
Ubi caritas	Duruflé	SAATTBB unacc	M		Durand

ORGAN MUSIC

PRELUDES

Bach J.S.	**Schmücke dich** BWV 654 in Novello Vol.17, Bärenreiter Vol.2, Peters Vol.7 M
Langlais J.	**Poem of Peace** (Elkan-Vogel) E/M
Thalben-Ball G.	**Elegy in B flat** (Novello) E/M
Warren N.	**A new commandment** in *Preludes on Favourite Hymns* and in *Preludes on Favourite Hymns for Manuals* (both Mayhew) E(*)
Widor C-M.	**Adagio** 5th movement of *4th Symphonie* (Kalmus, Hamelle) M

POSTLUDES

Clérambault L-N.	**Basse de cromorne** from *Livre d'Orgue: Suite du Deuxième Ton* (Schola Cantorum, Kalmus) E*
Hopkins E.J.	**Postlude on 'Love divine'** in *A Canterbury Organ Album* (Novello) M
Lefébure-Wély A.	**Marche funèbre** No.9 in *Meditaciones Religiosas* (Harmonia) E/M
Parry C.H.H.	**Chorale Prelude 'Old 104th'** in *Seven Chorale Preludes* Set 1 (Novello) and in *Preludes and Postludes* (Mayhew) M

THE SECOND SUNDAY BEFORE ADVENT YEAR A

HYMNS AND SONGS

	pos	rdg	AMNS	CAON	CFE	CH4	CH5	CP	H&P	HTC	LAU	MP	NEH	SG	SOF	TS
All hail the power of Jesus' name		s	140	16	19	457	250	163	252	587	323	13	332	24	9	7
At/In the name of Jesus		n	148	54	59	458	94	380	74	172	762	41	338	317	32	33
At your feet we fall		n										45			34	35
Blessing and honour (Ancient of days)		n				442						976		106	675	54
Christ is the King! O friends rejoice		s	345				86	165		492			345	31		
Christ triumphant, ever reigning		s		104	113	436	259	398		173	763	77	613	319	62	655
Crown him with many crowns		s	147	137	139	459	263	166	255	174	321	109	352	321	77	77
Forth in the peace of Christ we go	se	n	458	187	183	646	454	429		542	853		361	594		
Holy, holy, holy, Lord God almighty	mo	n	95	286	259	111	331	202	7	594	468	237	146	290	183	177
I lift my eyes to the quiet hills		g		312			14					281		515	804	
Jesus is the name we honour		n				481						870		122	870	285
Jesus, remember me (Taizé)		n		931		775	617				253			875		294
Jesus shall reign where'er the sun		s	143	359		470	97	490	239	516	322	379	388	45	301	1376
Jesus shall take the highest honour		n		360								378		123	302	296
Judge eternal, throned in splendour		s		372		264	535	356	409	329		395	490	600		
Majesty, worship his majesty		s		436	477		276				767	454			379	346
O worship the King, all glorious above	ga	s	101	551	559	127	34	546	28	24	683	528	433	90	456	425
Rejoice! The Lord is king		s	139	580	619	449	281	563	243	180	326	575	443	440	482	948
Send me, Lord (Thuma mina)		g			636	800							694			
Sent by the Lord am I	se	g			638	250					855		616			
The kingdom of God is justice and joy		s		646	701			591	139	333	821	651		184		
To God be the glory!		n		695	745	512	373	609	463	584	719	708		71	559	526
We have a gospel to proclaim		g	431	716	778	363	491	612	465	519	852	728	486	331	1583	
Ye/You servants of God, your master proclaim		g	149	756	819	130	492	627	278	520		784	476	75	620	1074

SONGS FOR CHILDREN

Sent by the Lord am I CFE 638, CG 105, CH4 250, IECS, LAU 855, SBTL, SG 616
Soon and very soon CH4 749, CH5 138, JP 221, MP 605, SOF 1007, TCB 20, TS 460

BIBLE READINGS

Psalm 89.19–37*
1 Kings 1.15–40 (*or* 1–40)
Revelation 1.4–18
Luke 9.1–6

SINGING THE PSALM

Psalm 89.19–37* CWP, NPCW

ANTHEMS AND VOCAL MUSIC

Title	Composer	Voices	E/M/D	Book source	Single sheet publisher
UNISON/TWO PART/HIGH VOICES					
God of the living	Tamblyn	U/SATB#	E	SFTL	
Jesus Christ, yesterday, today and forever	Toolan	U/SATB	E	LAU	
Maranatha, alleluia!	Ogden	U + descant	E	ACB, CFL, SFL2 (SAMen)	RSCM
Send down the fire of your justice (g)	Haugen	U/SATB#	E	C, TS	GIA
Sent by the Lord am I (g)	Trad arr Weaver	2 part	E	BC, IECS	
The Song of the Tree of Life	Vaughan Williams	2 part	E	AC2	OUP
THREE/FOUR PARTS					
Adventante Deo	Leighton	SATB	D	NNAB	
Be strong and of good courage	Campbell	SATB	M	FSB7	Novello
Christ the beginning	P.Moore	SATB	M		Encore
E'en so, Lord Jesus, quickly come	Manz	SATB unacc	M	AFC	Morning Star
Go forth and tell! (g)	Ogden	SATB	E	SBS2	RSCM
God is our hope and strength	J.S. Bach	SATB	E	AC1	
I am hope	Goodall	SAMen	M	SFL2	RSCM
I am the day	Dove	SATB unacc	M/D		Peters
If we believe that Jesus died	Goss	SATB	E		Novello
Never weather-beaten sail	Shepherd	SATB	M		RSCM
Never weather-beaten sail	Wood	SATB	M	NCAB	Banks
Now go in peace (g)	Trad arr Jeffcoat	SATB	E	PSA, SC	
Out of the stillness	Shephard	SATB	E/M	SBS2	RSCM
The true glory	Aston	SATB	M		RSCM
There is an old belief	Parry	SATB unacc	M/D		Banks
FIVE OR MORE PARTS					
All hail the power of Jesu's name	Greenhill	SATBB	E/M		Novello
The Twelve (g)	Walton	SSAATTBB	D		OUP
Zadok the Priest	Handel	SSAATBB	M/D	NCAB	Novello

ORGAN MUSIC

PRELUDES

Guilmant A.   **Lamento** from *18 Nouvelles Pièces* Op.90 (Schott); also in *Complete Works* Vol.4 (Belwin-Mills)) E
Stainer J.   **Adagio ma non troppo in E flat** No.3 of *Six Pieces for Organ* Set 1 (Butz, Novello) E/M
Thiman E.   **Air and Variation in the Old English style** No.2 of *Six Pieces* Set 1 (Curwen) E/M
Widor C.-M.   **Méditation** from *1st Symphonie* (Hamelle, Kalmus, Dover) E/M
Zipoli D.   **Canzona in F** in *Sonate d'Intavolature* (Süddeutscher Musikverlag) M*

POSTLUDES

Chauvet A.   **Grand Choeur in E flat** No.7 of *20 Morceaux* (Publimuses) M
Frescobaldi G.   **Altro Ricercare** No.32 in *Fiori Musicali* (Bärenreiter, Peters) E/M
Lebègue N.   **Offertoire in G** p.16 in *Offertoires from Troisième Livre d'Orgue* (Hawthorns); also p.181 in *Complete Works* Vol.3 (Kalmus) E/M*
Willan H.   **Postlude in D** in *An Album of Praise* (OUP) E/M

CHRIST THE KING (THE SUNDAY NEXT BEFORE ADVENT) YEAR A

HYMNS AND SONGS

	pos	rdg	AMNS	CAON	CFE	CH4	CH5	CP	H&P	HTC	LAU	MP	NEH	SG	SOF	TS
Adoramus te, Domine (Taizé)				921	11		345				667			208		
All hail the power of Jesus' name		s	140	16	19	457	250	163	252	587	323	13	332	24	9	7
All heaven declares	gr			17	20	426					760	14		420	10	8
Alleluia! Sing to Jesus	of	s	262	12	37	445	398	278	592	170	644	207	271	458	153	616
As the bridegroom to his chosen		o	340					30								
At/In the name of Jesus		s	148	54	59	458	94	380	74	172	762	41	338	317	32	33
Blessing and honour (Ancient of days)		s				442						976		106	675	54
Christ is the King! O friends rejoice		S	345				86	165		492			345	31		
Christ triumphant, ever reigning		s		104	113	436	259	398		173	763	77	*613*	319	62	655
Christ whose glory fills the skies	mo	o	4	105		578	52	2	457	266	670	79	234	170	1200	
Christians, lift up your hearts (Praise for the Spirit)		n	444	95			399			229						
Crown him with many crowns		s	147	137	139	459	263	166	255	174	321	109	352	321	77	77
Jesus shall reign where'er the sun		s	143	359		470	97	490	239	516	322	379	388	45	301	1376
Jesus shall take the highest honour		s		360								378		123	302	296
Jesus, we enthrone you		s										388		310	300	
Judge eternal, throned in splendour		s		372		264	535	356	409	329		395	490	600		
King of kings, majesty		s										1000			1404	309
Majesty, worship his majesty		n,s		436	477		276				767	454			379	346
Make way, make way for Christ the king	ga			438	479	279	134				819	457			384	349
Mine eyes have seen the glory		o		449	488	476			242		987					
O Christe Domine Jesu (Taizé)					519						757					
O Spirit of the living God		n					306	190	322	513				606		
O worship the King, all glorious above	ga	s	101	551	559	127	34	546	28	24	683	528	433	90	456	425
Rejoice! The Lord is king		s	139	580	619	449	281	563	243	180	326	575	443	440	482	948
The kingdom of God is justice and joy		s		646	701		591	139	333		821	651		184		
The Lord ascendeth up on high		s				440		173	210				135			
Thou/God, whose almighty word		n	180	684	738	112	324	267	29	506	887	699	466	597	557	
Thy/Your kingdom come! On bended knee		s	178	690		473		608				500				
Thy/Your kingdom come, O God		s	177	691			509	607	783	334		949	499	269		

SONGS FOR CHILDREN

All heaven declares CAON 17, CFE 20, CH4 426, KS 4, LAU 760, MP 14, SG 420, SOF 10, TS 8

Come, children, join and sing CH4 185

Go out to the whole world CFE 201, LAU 998

Make way, make way CAON 438, CFE 479, CH4 279, CH5 134, JP 427, KS 249, LAU 819, MP 457, SOF 384, TS 349

BIBLE READINGS

Morning Psalms 29 and 110
Evening Psalms 93 [and 97]
2 Samuel 23.1–7
or 1 Maccabees 2.15–29
Matthew 28.16–20

SINGING THE PSALM

Psalm 29 CRP, CWP, NEP, NPCW, PAME
    Feeley *The Lord will bless his people with peace* VE
    Gregory Murray, Gelineau *The Lord will bless his people with peace* VE
    Rees *The Lord will bless his people with peace* PCMG
Psalm 110 CRP, CWP, NPCW
Psalm 93 CH4, CRP, CWP, H&P, MCW1, NEP, NPCW, PAME
Psalm 97 CRP, CWP, FGP, MCW1, NPCW, PAME

ANTHEMS AND VOCAL MUSIC

Title	Composer	Voices	E/M/D	Book source	Single sheet publisher
UNISON/TWO PART/HIGH VOICES					
Alleluia to the end of time	Inwood	U#	E		OCP
God beyond all names	Farrell	U/SATB#	E	CFE, GBAN, LAU	OCP
Christ whose glory fills the skies	Knight	S	M		RSCM
THREE/FOUR PARTS					
Above all praise	Mendelssohn	SATB	E	NCAB, OEAB	RSCM
As the bridegroom to his chosen	Rutter	SATB	E		OUP
Christ whose glory fills the skies	Darke	SATB	M	SBS1	RSCM
Christus vincit	Mawby	SATB	D		Mayhew
Forsaking chariots of fire	Ives	SATB	M	LOL	
Go forth and tell!	Ogden	SATB	E	SBS2	RSCM
Hallelujah (Messiah)	Handel	SATB	M	WFC, AOAN1 (SAMen)	Novello
I will not leave you comfortless	Joule	SATB	M/D		RSCM
Jesus shall take the highest honour	Bowater	SATB	E/M	WIS	
Lo, round the throne a glorious band	Ley	SATB	E	NCAB	Novello
Now go in peace	Trad arr Jeffcoat	SATB	E	PSA, SC	
O clap your hands	Rutter	SATB	M/D	AC4	OUP
O clap your hands	Vaughan Williams	SATB	M/D	AC4	OUP
Rejoice, the Lord is king	Archer	SATB	M		Mayhew
Rejoice, the Lord is king	Kelly	SATB	M/D	NNAB, MTH1	
Rejoice, the Lord is king	Weaver	SATB	M	SC	
Worthy is the Lamb (Messiah)	Handel	SATB	M		Novello
FIVE OR MORE PARTS					
O clap your hands	Gibbons	SSAATTBB unacc	D	OBTA	OUP
Omnes gentes	Gabrieli	SSAT + SATB + ATBB + SATB	D		Peters
The Lord is King	Radcliffe	SATBB	M		Encore

ORGAN MUSIC

PRELUDES

d'Indy V.   **Verset 'Qui sequitur me non ambulat in tenebris'** in *St Cecilia Organ Library* Vol.1 (Cramer) E/M
Fletcher A.   **Prelude: Angels, help us to adore him** in *Inspiration* (Mayhew; manuals-only edition also available) E
Reger M.   **Wunderbarer König** Op.135a/30 in *Complete Works* Vol.7 (Breitkopf) E
Tambling C.   **Chorale on 'O King of might and splendour'** in *Music for Manuals* (Mayhew) E*

POSTLUDES

Chaminade C.   **Offertoire au Christ-Roi** in *La Nef Sacrée* (Enoch) E/M(*)
Gigault N.   **Fugue à 3 Domine Deus** p.17 in *Organ Book* Vol.1 (Kalmus) E*
Krebs J.L.   **O König, dessen Majestät** in *Complete Works* Vol.3 (Breitkopf) M
Stirling E.   **Choral and Fugue 'Es ist gewisslich'** No.4 of *Six Pedal Fugues* (McAfee) M/D
Tambling C.   **Trumpet Voluntary on 'Luckington'** in *Music for Manuals* (Mayhew) E*

YEAR B

THE FIRST SUNDAY OF ADVENT YEAR B

HYMNS AND SONGS

	pos	rdg	AMNS	CAON	CFE	CH4	CH5	CP	H&P	HTC	LAU	MP	NEH	SG	SOF	TS
Awake, awake: fling off the night!	ga	s	342	57	64			334			851					
Bless the Lord, my soul (Taizé)				923	81		1				813			105	676	56
Come, thou long-expected Jesus		s	31	128	133	472	119	24	81	52	100	102	3	335		
Creator of the stars of night/ starry height		s	23	135	138	288	121	25			87		1			
Great is the darkness		s										835		264	742	136
Hills of the North, rejoice		s	470	282	255		128	29	237		983		7			
How lovely on the mountains (Our God reigns)		s		295	268		129				768	249			192	189
I cannot tell why he, whom angels worship		s		303				54	238	194		266		437	205	199
I'll praise my Maker while I've breath		o					357	473	439	20		320		84		
Jesu, lover of my soul		o	123	343	319	490	553	96	528	438	797	372	383	201	297	838
Just as I am, without one plea		o	246	374	339	553	587	308	697	440		396	294	507	316	306
Lift up your heads, eternal gates		s				289										
Lift up your heads, O ye gates (Stoodley)		s					337									
Lift up your heads to the coming King		n										418			336	
Lift up your heads, ye gates of brass		n							227	509						
Lift up your heads, ye mighty gates		n	483		364		131	30	240	509	105		8			
Lo, he comes with clouds descending/Jesus comes		s	28	405	373	477	132	31	241	196	109	424	9	438	347	324
Make way, make way, for Christ the king		n		438	479	279	134				819	457			384	349
My Lord, what love is this		o		462	500		230					476		194	398	370
O Day of God, draw nigh		o	405					33								
Purify my heart		o		574			640					921		163	475	436
Send down the fire of your justice		o														1495
Strengthen for service, Lord/ Make strong	pc	o	421	619			446	323	626	423			306	473		
Swing wide the gates		n										621			517	
The Lord will come and not be slow		s	29	655			140	37	245				15			
Wake, O wake/Wake, awake/ Sleepers, wake!		s	32	703	763	278	142	39	249	199	91		16			
Waken, O sleeper		s		702			143									
You are the King of glory		n		762	822							790			627	

SONGS FOR CHILDREN

Christmas is coming CH4 282, LAU 93
King of kings and Lord of lords CAON 376, CH 132, JP 148, MP 398, TS 307, VFLS 5
Make way, make way CAON 438, CFE 479, CH4 279, CH5 134, JP 427, KS 249, LAU 819, MP 457, SOF 384, TS 349

BIBLE READINGS

Psalm 25*

Isaiah 1.1–20

Matthew 21.1–13

SINGING THE PSALM

Psalm 25* CH4, CRP, CWP, FGP, MCW1, NEH, NPCW, PAME, PFS

Bell *I lift my soul to you, O God* MCW1, PPP

Berthier *In te confido* TSFP#

Dean *To you, O Lord, I lift my soul* VE#

Foster *Jesus, Saviour* C#

Haugen *To you, O God* (GIA)#

Haugen *To you, O Lord, I lift my soul* C, VE#

Inwood *Remember, remember your mercy, Lord* CFE, LAU, SG, SLG (OCP)#

Kendrick *To you, O Lord* SG, SOF, TS

Ogden *Here I am* (WLP)#

O'Hara *In your love remember me* CFE

ANTHEMS AND VOCAL MUSIC

Title	Composer	Voices	E/M/D	Book source	Single sheet publisher
UNISON/TWO PART/HIGH VOICES					
Settings of the Benedictus (Blessed is he who comes)	Various	U	E	MCW1	
Alleluia! Hurry, the Lord is near	Sands arr Inwood, Peacock	U/2 part#	E	TCB	
Benedictus qui venit	Berthier	U/canon#	E	VE	
Come to Jerusalem	Israeli trad	U#	E	RE, LAU, MHWE	
Let all mortal flesh keep silence	Trad arr Cleobury	2 part	E	AFC	
Maranatha, alleluia!	Ogden	U + descant	E	ACB, CFL, SFL2 (SAMen)	RSCM
Remember, remember your mercy, Lord	Inwood	U/SATB#		CFE, LAU, SG, SLG	OCP
THREE/FOUR PARTS					
Come, thou Redeemer of the earth	Trad arr Lumsden	SATB	E		Encore
Ingrediente Domino	Malcolm	SATB unacc	M	NAB3, AWTE	
Hark, the glad sound	Walford Davies	SATB	E		RSCM
Lift up your heads (Messiah)	Handel	SATB	M		Novello
Lift up your heads	Marsh	SAMen	E	AOAN1	
Lift up your heads	Mathias	SATB	M/D	AC1	OUP
Rejoice, the Lord is king	Weaver	SATB	M	SC	
The Lord will come and not be slow	Tye	SATB unacc	E/M		RSCM
Zion, at thy shining gates	Trad arr Guest	SATB	E	AFC	Dean
FIVE OR MORE PARTS					
Civitas sancti tui	Byrd	SAATBB unacc	M		Chester
Let all mortal flesh keep silence	Bairstow	SSAATTBB unacc	M	AC4	S&B
Let all mortal flesh keep silence	Trad arr Jackson	SSSAATTBB	M/D	MTH2	

ORGAN MUSIC

PRELUDES

Demessieux J.   **Rorate Coeli: Choral orné** from *12 Chorale Preludes on Gregorian Chant Themes* (Summy-Birchard) E

Lemmens J-N.   **Creator alme siderum** in *St Cecilia Organ Library* Vol.1 (Cramer) E

Sweelinck J.   **Nun komm, der Heiden Heiland** in *Three Chorale Variations* (Peeters) M/D*

Von Herzogenberg H.   **Nun komm, der Heiden Heiland** in *Seasonal Chorale Preludes with Pedals* Bk.1 (OUP) E/M

Walther J.G.   **Wachet auf** in *Seasonal Chorale Preludes for Manuals* Bk.1 (OUP) and *80 Chorale Preludes* (Peters) E/M

POSTLUDES

Bach J.S.   **Wachet auf** BWV 645 in Novello Vol.16, Bärenreiter Vol.1, Peters Vol.7 E/M

Leighton K.   **Veni Emmanuel** No.5 from *Six Fantasies on Hymn Tunes* Op.72 (Ramsey) M/D

Tambling C.   **Fugue and Chorale on 'Helmsley'** in *Fifty Hymn Preludes* (Mayhew) E/M

Titelouze J.   **3rd Verset on 'Conditor alme siderum'** in *Hymnes de l'Église* (Kalmus, Schott) M

THE SECOND SUNDAY OF ADVENT YEAR B

HYMNS AND SONGS

	pos	rdg	AMNS	CAON	CFE	CH4	CH5	CP	H&P	HTC	LAU	MP	NEH	SG	SOF	TS
Christ is the King! O friends rejoice		n	345				86	165		492			345	31		
Creator of the stars of night/ starry height		s	23	135	138	288	121	25			87		1			
God, we praise you! God, we bless you!		g				120	696	450		341				38		
God, who hast caused to be written		e	467						472							
Great God, what do I see and hear		g								189						
Great is the darkness		s										835		264	742	136
Hark the glad sound! The Saviour comes		s	30	265		277	124	27	82	193		210	6	435	154	
Hark what a sound, and too divine		s					127	28	236				600			
Heaven shall not wait		s		272		362										151
How beauteous/gracious are their feet		n	301					220	449							
In heavenly love abiding		n		323		551		478	678	458		331	638		238	782
Jesus shall reign where'er the sun		s	143	359		470	97	490	239	516	322	379	388	45	301	1376
Jesus, the name high over all		g		364			99		264	213		385		323	307	298
Judge eternal, throned in splendour		s		372		264	535	356	409	329		395	490	600		
Let the desert sing		g								198						
Lord, thy word abideth/your word shall guide us		n	166	420	390		384	515	476	251	977/8	446	407			
May the mind of Christ my Saviour		n		447		536	636	521	739	550		463		671	1448	887
Now in reverence and awe	gr	e										902		232	1468	
O Day of God, draw nigh		s	405					33								
O for a thousand tongues to sing		g	125	485		352	104	534	744	219		496	415	55	412	383/ 1452
Sing we the praises of the great forerunner		g	315					234								
Thanks/Praise to God whose word was spoken		n	423			605	387	584	483	255			438	229		
The kingdom of God is justice and joy		g		646	701			591	139	333	821	651		184		
There's a wideness in God's mercy/Souls of men/ Restless souls		o	251	662		187	9	598	230	443	810	607/ 683	461/ 700	188		
Thou/God, whose almighty word		g	180	684	738	112	324	267	29	506	887	699	466	597	557	
Thy/Your kingdom come, O God		s	177	691			509	607	783	334		949	499	269		
Wait for the Lord (Taizé)		s		949	762	276					88				1575	
When the King shall come again		g			806					200	90					

SONGS FOR CHILDREN

The joy of the Lord is my strength JP 240
When the time is right CAON 913, KS 379

BIBLE READINGS

Psalm 40*
1 Kings 22.1–28
Romans 15.4–13
Matthew 11.2–11

SINGING THE PSALM

Psalm 40* C, CH4, CRP, CWP, FGP, H&P, NPCW, PAME
Bell *I waited, I waited on the Lord* HSNW, SG
Bell *I waited patiently for God* CG, CH4, PPP

ANTHEMS AND VOCAL MUSIC

Title	Composer	Voices	E/M/D	Book source	Single sheet publisher
UNISON/TWO PART/HIGH VOICES					
Settings of the Benedictus (The Song of Zechariah)	Various	U	E	MCW1, NEP	
A Song of Peace	Stanford	U	M		RSCM
A Song of Peace and Joy	Mawby	U + descant + instr	E	VFLS	
A tender shoot	Goode	SSA unacc + cello	D	CFL	
All are welcome (Let us build a house)	Haugen	U#	E	CG, CH4, LAU	GIA
Hark! a messenger is calling	Kelly	3 part	E/M	CFL	
He comes, the Way that all may tread	Llewellyn	3 part	E	CFL	
Send down the fire of your justice	Haugen	U#	E	C, TS	GIA
Song of Consolation	Jones	U	E	VE#	
The Spirit of the Lord is upon me (g)	Corp	2 part	E	VFLS	
THREE/FOUR PARTS					
A tender shoot	Goldschmidt	SATB	M	AFC, TCB	RSCM
And the glory of the Lord (Messiah)	Handel	SATB	M		Novello
Benedictus	Stanford	SATB	M	AFC	
Canite tuba	Guerrero	SATB unacc	M	AFC	
Come, thou Redeemer of the earth	Praetorius arr Lumsden	SATB	E		Encore
Come, thou Redeemer of the earth	Praetorius arr Parnell	ATBB	M	SL	
Hark, the glad sound	Walford Davies	SATB	E		RSCM
How lovely are the messengers	Mendelssohn	SATB	M	AFC	Novello
I am hope	Goodall	SAB	E	SFL2	RSCM
O for a thousand tongues (g)	Shephard	SATB	M		RSCM
On Jordan's bank	Trad arr Archer	SATB	E	AFC	
The Spirit of the Lord (g)	Elgar	SATB	M	SAEE	RSCM
Virga Jesse floruit	Bruckner	SATB unacc	D	AFC, CHMO	Peters
FIVE OR MORE PARTS					
Vox dicentis, clama	Naylor	SATB + SATB unacc	D		Curwen

ORGAN MUSIC

PRELUDES

Bach J.S.   **Gottes Sohn ist kommen** ('Ravenshaw') BWV 724 in Novello Vol.18, Bärenreiter Vol.3, Peters Vol.6 E/M
Brosig M.   **Nun komm der Heiden Heiland** in *Hier Preisen auf der Erd* Vol.2 (Breitkopf) E/M
Groves R.   **Bristol** in *12 Hymn-Tune Preludes* Set 2 (Novello) E*
Karg-Elert S.   **Mit Ernst, O Menschenkinder** No.9 from *Choral-Improvisationen* Op.65 Vol.1 (Breitkopf) M
Rinck J.C.H.   **Gottes Sohn ist kommen** ('Ravenshaw') in *Hier Preisen auf der Erd* Vol.1 (Breitkopf) E

POSTLUDES

Dyson G.   **Hark the glad sound** in *Variations on Old Psalm Tunes* Bk.3 (Novello) E/M
Kauffmann G.   **Chorale Prelude 'Nun freut euch, lieben'** in *A Graded Anthology for Organ* Bk.2 (Cramer) E/M*
Lloyd Webber W.S.   **Winchester New** in *Six Interludes on Passion Hymns* (Novello) and *Aria* (Mayhew) E/M
Willan H.   **Prelude on 'Bristol'** in *Ten Hymn Preludes* Set 2 (Peters) E/M

THE THIRD SUNDAY OF ADVENT YEAR B

HYMNS AND SONGS

	pos	rdg	AMNS	CAON	CFE	CH4	CH5	CP	H&P	HTC	LAU	MP	NEH	SG	SOF	TS
Clear the road (Prepare the way)	o														63	
Come, thou long-expected Jesus	s		31	128	133	472	119	24	81	52	100	102	3	335		
Creator of the stars of night/starry height	s		23	135	138	288	121	25			87		1			
God is in his temple/God reveals his presence	o						331		494			186				
God is working his purpose out	s			221	217	235	481	444	769	191	86	189	495	451	135	128
Hark, a herald/thrilling voice is calling/trumpet call is sounding	s		24	263	243		126	26		192	92		5	436		
Here in this place (Gather us in)	o				253	623					475			4		
How beauteous/gracious are their feet	s		301					220	449							
I will rest in Christ	n													549	854	
In the Lord I'll be ever thankful (Taizé)	n			929	308	772					944	865		656	817	
Like a mighty river flowing	n			400	367		16			32	897	419		51		
Love divine, all loves excelling	o		131	428	398	519	634	516	267	217	801	449	408	179	377	343
Make way, make way, for Christ the king	o			438	479	279	134				819	457			384	349
May the mind of Christ my Saviour	n			447		536	636	521	739	550		463		671	1448	887
O come, O come, Emmanuel	s		26	480	522	273	135	32	85	66	112	493	11	338	410	
O Day of God, draw nigh	s		405					33								
O for a thousand tongues to sing	s		125	485		352	104	534	744	219		496	415	55	412	383/1452
On Jordan's bank, the Baptist's cry	s		27	527	575	334	136	34	84	601	94	538	12	339		
Prepare the way for the Lord	s													342		
Purify my heart	o			574			640					921		163	475	436
Rejoice! the Lord is king	s		139	580	619	449	281	563	243	180	326	575	443	440	482	948
Restore, O Lord, the honour	o			582		469						579		274	483	439
Sing a new song to the Lord	n				645	62			57	349		599				
Sing we the praises of the great forerunner	s		315					234								
To God be the glory	n			695	745	512	373	609	463	584	719	708		71	559	526
Wait for the Lord (Taizé)	n			949	762	276					88				1575	
What a friend we have in Jesus	n			727		547	627		559	373		746		646	593	566
Within our darkest night (Taizé)	g			950												
Within the busy rush of life	n													648		

SONGS FOR CHILDREN

Make way, make way CAON 438, CFE 479, CH4 279, CH5 134, JP 427, KS 249, LAU 819, MP 457, SOF 384, TS 349
Rejoice in the Lord always CAON 578, CAP 95, CH 180, CFE 617, JP 208, MP 577, SOF 1506, VFLS 7

BIBLE READINGS

Psalm 68.1–19*

Malachi 3.1–4; 4

Philippians 4.4–7

Matthew 14.1–12

SINGING THE PSALM

Psalm 68.1–19* CRP, CWP, NPCW, PAME

ANTHEMS AND VOCAL MUSIC

Title	Composer	Voices	E/M/D	Book source	Single sheet publisher
UNISON/TWO PART/HIGH VOICES					
Advent Prose	Trad arr Cleobury	U	E	AFC	
A Song of Peace and Joy	Mawby	U + descant + instr	E	VFLS	
He came singing love	Gibson	2 part	E	VFLS	
He comes, the Way that all may tread	Llewellyn	3 part	E	CFL	
If there is to be peace	Shephard	2 part	E/M	VFLS	
Song of Consolation	Jones	U#	E	VE	
There is a longing	Quigley	U/SATB#	E	CH4, LAU, SG	OCP
THREE/FOUR PARTS					
Canite tuba	Guerrero	SATB unacc	M	AFC	
Come, thou Redeemer of the earth	Trad arr Lumsden	SATB	E		Encore
E'en so, Lord Jesus, quickly come	Manz	SATB unacc	M	AFC	Morning Star
For you shall go out with joy	Grotenhuis	SATB	M		Dean
How lovely are the messengers	Mendelssohn	SATB	M	AFC	Novello
Now the God of peace	Knight	SATB	E	SBS1	RSCM
On Jordan's bank	Trad arr Archer	SATB	E	AFC	
Rejoice in the Lord alway	Anon arr Le Huray	SATB unacc	E	AFC	OUP
Rejoice in the Lord alway	Carter	SATB	M/D	ACA	OUP
Rejoice in the Lord always	Purcell	SATB	E	NCAB, APA	Novello
The Lord will come and not be slow	Tye	SATB unacc	E/M		RSCM
The peace of God	Rutter	SATB	E	JRA, NOEAB	OUP
Tollite hostias	Saint-Saëns	SAB	E	AOAN1	
You shall go out with joy	Geiser Rubin arr Meacock	SATB	E	SWAMS	
FIVE OR MORE PARTS					
Gaudete omnes	Praetorius	SATTB unacc	D		Chester

ORGAN MUSIC

PRELUDES

Gaze N.   **No.1** from *An Advent Triptych on 'Veni Emmanuel'* (Fagus) E/M

Harker C.   **Meditation on 'Veni, veni Emmanuel'** in *Three Pieces based on Plainsong Themes* (Bosworth) M

Lane P.   **Veni Emmanuel** in *Fifty Hymn Preludes* (Mayhew) E/M

Marpurg F.W. **Von Gott will ich nicht lassen** in *The Progressive Organist* Bk.7 (Novello) E/M

Rawsthorne N. **This is the truth sent from above** 2 settings in *The Holly and the Ivy: 48 Carol Improvisations* (Mayhew) E/M

POSTLUDES

Bach J.S.   **Lob sei dem allmächtigen Gott** BWV 602 from the *Orgelbüchlein* (many editions) E/M

Hurford P.   **Exurgat Deus** from *Suite: Laudate Dominum* (OUP) M

Pachelbel J.   **Mag ich Unglück** in *Choralvorspiele alter Meister* (Peters) E/M

Whitlock P.   **Sortie** (Ps. 68) No.7 of *Seven Sketches from the Psalms* (OUP) M/D

THE FOURTH SUNDAY OF ADVENT YEAR B

HYMNS AND SONGS

	pos	rdg	AMNS	CAON	CFE	CH4	CH5	CP	H&P	HTC	LAU	MP	NEH	SG	SOF	TS
Behold the servant of the Lord		n							788						668	
Come, thou long-expected Jesus		s	31	128	133	472	119	24	81	52	100	102	3	335		
Creator of the stars of night/starry height		s	23	135	138	288	121	25			87		1			
Emmanuel, Emmanuel		s										121			83	675
For Mary, mother of our/the Lord		n	360	182			462	238			331		161			
Great is the darkness		s										835		264	742	136
Hark the glad sound! The Saviour comes		s	30	265		277	124	27	82	193		210	6	435	154	
Immanuel, O Immanuel		s										326			233	219
Jesus, the name high over all		s		364			99		264	213		385		323	307	298
Let all mortal flesh keep silence	cm	n	256	381	355	666	427	309	266	61	607		295	472	1413	
Lift up your heads, eternal gates		s				289										
Lift up your heads, O ye gates (Stoodley)		s					337									
Lift up your heads to the coming King		s										418			336	
Lift up your heads, ye mighty gates		s	483		364		131	30	240	509	105		8			
Long ago, prophets knew		s	484	406	375		133	58	83		116		10			867
Magnificat (Rizza)		n		935												
Magnificat (Taizé)		n									335				1445	
Mary, blessed teenage mother		n		442												
Master, speak! Thy servant heareth		n							535			459			386	
Misericordias Domini/From age to age (Taizé)		o			489											
O come, O come, Emmanuel	ga/se	s	26	480	522	273	135	32	85	66	112	493	11	338	410	
O holy Mary		n			533											
People look east, the time is near		s		557		281		35								
Tell out, my soul		n,s	422	631	684	286	712	362	86	42	880	631	186	62	520	471
There's a light upon the mountains		s							246			679				
This child secretly comes in the night		n										690		371	1559	511
To the name of our/that brings salvation		s	121	698	749	471	117	610	80	222			470	72		
When came in flesh the incarnate Word		n,s											17			
With Mary let my soul rejoice (MCW1)		n														
Ye who own the faith of Jesus/All who keep/claim		n		759	29			231			359		188			

SONGS FOR CHILDREN

Alleluia! Hurry, the Lord is near CH4 280, TCB 2
Christmas is coming CH4 282, LAU 93
Rejoice in the Lord always CAON 578, CAP 95, CH 180, CFE 617, JP 208, MP 577, SOF 1506, VFLS 7

BIBLE READINGS

Psalms 113 [and 131]
Zechariah 2.10–13
Luke 1.39–55

SINGING THE PSALM

Psalm 113 CH4, CRP, CWP, NPCW

    Deiss *Give praise to the Lord* CFE

Psalm 131 CRP, CWP, FGP, NPCW

    Bell *For you, the pride from my heart is banished* CH4, PPP

    Deiss *My soul is longing for your peace* CFE, LAU

    Rizza *O Lord, my heart is not proud* CAS, FOL#

    Smith *Guard my soul* (WLP)#

    Walker *Like a child rests* LAU, OOD (OCP)#

ANTHEMS AND VOCAL MUSIC

Title	Composer	Voices	E/M/D	Book source	Single sheet publisher
UNISON/TWO PART/HIGH VOICES					
Settings of the Magnificat	Various	U/SATB	E	C, CWP, MCW1, LAU, NEP	
Ave Maria	Holst	SSSSAAAA unacc	D		Novello
Ave Maria	Lindley	U/2 part	E	EAC2	Ramsey
Hail, holy queen	Le Poidevin	U	E		WLP
Quam pulchra es	Dunstable	SAA unacc	M	AC3	
Tota pulchra es	Duruflé	SSA unacc	M		Salabert
THREE/FOUR PARTS					
Ave Maria	Arcadelt	SATB unacc	E	AOAN1 (SAB), NOEAB, SEA1	Novello
Ave Maria	Archer	SATB	E	AFC	
Ave Maria	Bruckner	SATB unacc	M/D	ESM	Peters
Ave Maria	Elgar	SATB	E/M		RSCM
Ave Maria	Gounod	SAMen	E	AOAN1	
Ave Maria	Josquin	SATB unacc	D	ESM	UMP
Ave Maria	Palestrina	SATB unacc	M		OUP
Ave Maria	Rachmaninov	SATB unacc	D	ESM	RSCM
Ave Maria	Stravinsky	SATB unacc	M	ESM	B&H
Ave Maria	Verdi	SATB unacc	D	ESM	
Ave Maria	Victoria	SATB unacc	M/D	ESM	RSCM
Nova! Nova!	Chilcott	SATB unacc	M/D	AFC	OUP
Salve regina	Poulenc	SATB unacc	M	ESM	
Sancta Maria	Dunstable	ATB unacc	M	SL	
Song of Mary	Shephard	SATB	E/M	NOEAB	OUP
FIVE OR MORE PARTS					
Ave Maria (Angelus Domini)	Biebl	TTB + TTBB unacc	M	SL	
Ave maris stella	Elgar	SSATB	M		RSCM
Ave maris stella	Grieg	SSAATTBB unacc	M	ESM	OUP
Bogoroditsye Dyevo	Pärt	SSAATTBB unacc	M	AFC	Universal

Anthems suggested for Year C (page 257) are also appropriate.

ORGAN MUSIC

PRELUDES

Berlioz H.   **Sérénade agreste à la Madone** from *Three Pieces* in *Organ Music for Manuals Only* (Dover)

Boëllmann L.   **Prière à Notre-Dame** from *Suite Gothique* (many editions), also in *Complete Works* Vol.2 (Bärenreiter) E/M

Hoyer K.   **Es kommt ein Schiff** in *Hier Preisen auf der Erd* Vol.1 (Breitkopf) E/M

Ridout A.   **Procession** from *Messe d'Orgue* (Encore) E/M

Willan H.   **Ave maris stella** from *Five Preludes on Plainchant Melodies* (OUP Archive complete or singly) E/M

POSTLUDES

Anon.   **Gloria de Sancta Maria Vergine** (9 movements) from *The Buxheimer Orgelbuch* Vol. 1 (Hinrichsen) E*-M*

Bach J.S.   **Fugue on the Magnificat** BWV 733 in Novello Vol.18, Bärenreiter Vol.3, Peters Vol.7 M/D

Bonighton R.   **Advent Reflections** ('Personent hodie') in *The Organist's Liturgical Year* (Mayhew) E/M

Hakim N.   **Danse** (on 'Ave maris stella') from *Mariales* (UMP) E/M

THE FIRST SUNDAY OF CHRISTMAS YEAR B

(For Christmas Day, see Year A, page 10.)

HYMNS AND SONGS

	pos	rdg	AMNS	CAON	CFE	CH4	CH5	CP	H&P	HTC	LAU	MP	NEH	SG	SOF	TS
A great and mighty wonder	o,s		43	4			146	41	90	49			21			
A noble flower of Juda	s				5					126						
Adoramus te, Domine (Taizé)				921	11		345				667		208			
All my heart this night rejoices	s							43	91	76						
At/In the name of Jesus	n		148	54	59	458	94	380	74	172	762	41	338	317	32	33
Be bold, be strong	o											49			37	38
Behold the amazing gift of love	s					478		389	666							
Behold, the great Creator makes	s		44	62		308		46		50			23			
Child in the manger	s			93	105	314	151			51	141	71				
Child of the stable's secret birth	s							47	124	53			43			
Cloth for the cradle	s			107												
From east to west, from shore to shore	s			193					99				20			
He came down that we may have love	s					359								116		
I hunger and I thirst	o							306	730	409			470			
In the bleak midwinter	s		42	326	305	305	162	55	107	600	144	337	28	353	243	789
Joy to the world!	o,s			370	335	320	166	57	77	197	156	393		340	314	305
Jubilate Deo, omnis terra (Taizé)	o			336							691					
Let earth and heaven combine	s								109							1394
Let the desert sing	o									198						
Lord, who left the highest heaven	s									97						
Love came down at Christmas	s			427	397	316	170	59	105	62		451			376	
O Christ the same, through all our story's pages	NY			477			103			263			258			
Of the Father's heart/love/God of God	s		33/325	486	562	319	175	64/65	79	56	160		33	337		
The growing limbs of God the Son	g												45			
Thou didst leave thy throne	s		250	683			114	601	154			697	465		555	1015
Thou who wast rich/Lord, you were rich	s					318	168	72		63		700		356		1018
When the King shall come again	o				806					200	90					
Who is this, so weak and helpless	n			748								474				
Who would think that what was needed	s			750		295		78								

Hymns and songs particularly appropriate for the New Year are marked NY.

SONGS FOR CHILDREN

Be bold, be strong JP 14, KS 17, MP 49, SOF 37, TS 38
He came down that we may have love CH4 359, SG 116, VE
It was on a starry night CH4 302, JP 396, KS2 571, SOF 1365

BIBLE READINGS

Psalm 132
Isaiah 35
Colossians 1.9–20 *or* Luke 2.41–52

SINGING THE PSALM

Psalm 132 CWP, NPCW

ANTHEMS AND VOCAL MUSIC

Title	Composer	Voices	E/M/D	Book source	Single sheet publisher
UNISON/TWO PART/HIGH VOICES					
Let all creation sing	Ogden	U/SATB	E	SFL2	WLP
Love came down at Christmas	Lole	2 part	M		Encore
Love came down at Christmas	Trad Irish arr Grindle	SSSAA unacc	M		Encore
Unfinished story	Godfrey	2 part	E	VFLS	
THREE/FOUR PARTS					
And the glory of the Lord (Messiah)	Handel	SATB	M		Novello
Be thou my vision	Chilcott	SATB	E/M	BCA, NOEAB	OUP
Christ the beginning	P.Moore	SATB	M		Encore
Grow in grace	Archer	SATB	E/M	SBS1	RSCM
I am hope	Goodall	SAMen	M	SFL2	
Jesu dulcis memoria	Pott	SATB + solo S unacc	M/D	CN	
Jesu dulcis memoria	Shephard	SATB	E/M		RSCM
Jesu dulcis memoria	Victoria	SATB unacc	M	ESM, NSAC1, NCAB	CMS
Jesu, the very thought of thee	Bairstow	SATB unacc	E/M	FSB7	OUP
Jesu, the very thought of thee	K.Beaumont	SATB unacc	M		Encore
Jesus Christ, yesterday, today and forever	Toolan	SATB	E	LAU	
O for a thousand tongues	Shephard	SATB	M		RSCM
Seek him out	Bryden	SATB + solo S	E/M		Encore
Strengthen ye the weak hands	Harris	SATB	M		Novello
The Wilderness	Goss	SATB	M		Novello
The Wilderness	S.S.Wesley	SATB	M		Novello
Verbum caro factum est	Halsey	SATB	M	SBS2	
FIVE OR MORE PARTS					
Jesu dulcis memoria	Villette	SSAATTBB unacc	M/D		UMP
O nomen Jesu	Philips	SSATB unacc	M		Mapa Mundi
So said the angel	Skellern	SSATB unacc	M/D	N	Novello

ORGAN MUSIC

PRELUDES

Bach J.S.   **Vom Himmel hoch (fughetta)** BWV 701 in Novello Vol.19, Bärenreiter Vol.3, Peters Vol.7 E*
Caurroy E. du   **Une vierge pucelle** in *The Progressive Organist* Bk.7 (Novello) E/M
Mulet H.   **Noël** from *Esquisses Byzantines* (Leduc) E/M
Piutti C.   **Nun singet und seid froh** ('In dulci jubilo') in *Hier Preisen auf der Erd* Vol.2 (Breitkopf) E/M
Wesley S.   **The Old Christmas Carol** ('God rest ye, merry') in *Ten Short Pieces for Organ* (Animus) E*

POSTLUDES

Blair H.   **Fantasy on Old Christmas Carols** in *Romantic Organ Music for Christmas and Advent* (Animus) E/M
Chauvet A.   **Offertoire for the First Sunday after Christmas** in *Organ Noëls for the Time of Christmas* (Concordia) E/M*
Milford R.   **Pastorale Dance on 'On Christmas Night'** No.3 of *Three Christmas Pieces* (Cathedral Music or OUP reprint) M
Wills A.   **And suddenly there was with the angel** No.2 from *Christmas Meditations* (Novello) E/M

THE SECOND SUNDAY OF CHRISTMAS YEAR B

HYMNS AND SONGS

	pos	rdg	AMNS	CAON	CFE	CH4	CH5	CP	H&P	HTC	LAU	MP	NEH	SG	SOF	TS
All my hope on God is founded		NY	336	19	21	192	10	368	63	451	959	16	333	525		620
Angels from the realms of glory	of	s	39	36		324	147	44	92	77	131	35		344	23	631
As we are gathered		n		47		197						38			28	29
Be still and know that I am God		o		66	71		608				909	48			41	48
Child of the stable's secret birth		s					47	124	53				43			
Christ be the Lord of all our days		NY								256			*630*			
From east to west, from shore to shore		s		193					99				20			
Glorious things of thee are spoken		NY	172	205	195	738	646	435	817	494	827	173	362	35	127	691
God is working his purpose out		NY		221	217	235	481	444	769	191	86	189	495	451	135	128
Great is thy faithfulness		NY		249		153	80	453	66	260		200	*696*	39	147	138
Help us to help each other/Jesus, united by thy grace		n	374	275			523	461	773	540						
Holy Spirit, come, confirm us		n	471	288		640	299	183	288		311		140			
I will offer up my life		n				503						990		565	851	265
In the bleak midwinter	cm	s	42	326	305	305	162	55	107	600	144	337	28	353	243	789
Let earth and heaven combine		s							109							1394
Lord, for the years		NY		409		159	81	81		328	942	428	*619*	602	892	327
Lord, I come to you		NY										880		689	895	329
Lord, who left the highest heaven										97						
Love came down at Christmas				427	397	316	170	59	105	62		451			376	
My Jesus, my Saviour		o		461		531						1003		129	935	367
O Christ the same, through all our story's pages		NY		477			103			263			258			
O/Our God, our help in ages past		NY	99	494	528	161	537	537	358	37	955	498	417	542	415	905
Of the Father's love/heart/God of God		s	33/325	486	562	319	175	64/65	79	56	160		33	337		
Once in royal David's city	ga		46	521	577	315	177	66	114	67	128	539	34	359	438	404
Take my life and let it be		NY	249	625	677	502	597	581	705	554	874	624	678	519		468
The first Nowell	of	s		641	692	323	198		119	93	150	644	36		529	974
Thou didst leave thy throne	of		250	683			114	601	154			697	465		555	1015
Thou who wast rich/Lord, you were rich						318	168	72		63		700	356			1018
Through all the changing scenes of life		NY	209	686	740		372	604	73	46		702	467	654	1566	1561
Where is this stupendous stranger?			527					75					41			
Within our darkest night (Taizé)		g		950												

Hymns and songs particularly appropriate for the New Year are marked NY.

SONGS FOR CHILDREN

All of my heart CAON 770, CH 9, KS 6
From the darkness came light CAP 29

BIBLE READINGS

Psalm 135*
Isaiah 46.3–13
Romans 12.1–8
Matthew 2.13–23

SINGING THE PSALM

Psalm 135* CWP, NPCW

ANTHEMS AND VOCAL MUSIC

Title	Composer	Voices	E/M/D	Book source	Single sheet publisher
UNISON/TWO PART/HIGH VOICES					
Lully, lullay (g)	Haydn	U/canon	E	CFL	
Out of darkness	Walker	U/SATB#	E	CFE, LAU, OOD	OCP
Take my gifts	Farrell	U#	E	GBU	
THREE/FOUR PARTS					
Coventry Carol (g)	Trad	SAB	E	CC1	
Greater love	Ireland	SATB	M	AC4	S&B
Lully, lulla thou little tiny child (g)	Chilcott	SATB	E/M	BCC	
Lully, lulla, thou little tiny child (g)	Leighton	SATB + solo S unacc	M	N	Novello
One in body, heart and mind	Walker	SATB/U#	E	SFL2(SAB), ATNJ	OCP
Personent hodie (g)	Trad arr Holst	SATB	E	CC2	
Surely thou hast tasted that the Lord is good	Bernard Rose	SATB unacc	M	EAC1	Cathedral
Take this moment	Bell	SATB	E	CG, IAMB, LFB, OITB, WIS	GIA
Unto us is born a son (g)	Trad	SATB	E	CC1	
FIVE OR MORE PARTS					
Coventry Carol (g)	Trad arr Allain	SSAATTBB unacc	D	CV	Novello
Illuminare Jerusalem	Weir	SSAATTBB	D	N	Novello
Vox in Rama (g)	Dering	SATTB	M		CMS/OUP
Vox in Rama (g)	de Wert	SAATB unacc	D		Mapa Mundi

ORGAN MUSIC

PRELUDES

Best W.T.	**Quem vidistis, pastores?** in *Romantic Organ Music for Christmas and Advent* (Animus) E/M
Chauvet A.	**Offertoire for the Sunday between Circumcision and Epiphany** in *Organ Noëls for the Time of Christmas* (Concordia) E*
Milford R.	**Come, all you worthy gentlemen** in *A Christmas Collection* (Novello) E/M
Schneider F.	**Der Tag, der ist so freudenreich** in *Sechs Pastoralestücke* (Doblinger) M*
Willan H.	**Prelude on 'This endris night'** in *Ten Hymn Preludes* Set 2 (Peters) E/M

POSTLUDES

Bach J.S.	**Vom Himmel hoch** BWV 700 in Novello Vol.19, Bärenreiter Vol.3, Peters Vol.7 E/M
Gilbert N.	**Christmas Fantasia** in *Pieces for Four Seasons* (Novello) M
Joulain J.	**Noël flamand** in *Christmas Music by Various French Composers* (Kalmus) M
Walther J.G.	**Allein Gott in der Höh sei Ehr'** 2 settings in *Orgelchoräle* (Bärenreiter) E/M

THE BAPTISM OF CHRIST (THE FIRST SUNDAY OF EPIPHANY) YEAR B

(For Epiphany, see Year A, page 16.)

HYMNS AND SONGS

	pos	rdg	AMNS	CAON	CFE	CH4	CH5	CP	H&P	HTC	LAU	MP	NEH	SG	SOF	TS
Awake, awake: fling off the night!		s	342	57	64			334			851					
Baptized in water	gr	g			67	636				381	407			492		
Be thou my vision/Lord, be my vision		s	343	70	74/75	465	643	386	378	545	970	51	339	669	42	50
Bless the Lord, my soul (Taizé)		n		923	81		1				813			105	676	56
Breathe on me, breath of God		g	157	84	98	596	293	174	280	226	302	67	342	554	51	57
Christ, when for us you were baptized		g	442					92	129							
Come down, O love divine	ga	g	156	114	125	489	294	175	281	231	303	89	137	663	1202	71
Crown him with many crowns		g	147	137	139	459	263	166	255	174	321	109	352	321	77	77
Do not be afraid, for I have redeemed you		s		150	147	191					972	115			1213	1183
Fear not, for I am with you		s												105		
God has spoken to his people/Open your ears		s				380				S 13	472	182			131	
Hail to the Lord's anointed		g	142	259	241	474	125	87	125	190	102	204	55		150	709
How firm a foundation		s		292						430		243				186
Lord of the Church, we pray		s					303			499		442		577	1433	
Name of all majesty		s		465			102	525		218		481		324	939	
Now is eternal life		n	402	470			392	152	203				114			
O breath of life, come sweeping through us		g		476		595	305		777	237		488			407	379
O let the Son of God enfold you		g		506								502			419	392
O love, how deep, how broad, how high	of	g	119	516		354	214	118	229				425			
O thou who camest from above		s	233	541	557	625	639	191	745	596		525	431	560	451	416
Out of the flowing river		g				335										
River, wash over me		g										581			487	441
Songs of thankfulness and praise		s	53	609	661		197	90		98	172		56	376		
Spirit divine, attend our prayers		g				583	341	195	327	240		614				
Spirit of the living God (Iverson)	gr	g		615	666	619	310		295	S 23	306	613			510	462
The sinless one to Jordan came		s					200						58			
There is a river		s			722											
To the name of our/that brings salvation		g	121	698	749	471	117	610	80	222			470	72		
When Jesus came to Jordan		g	526				204	93	132							
When Jesus comes to be baptized	o,g										171					
When John baptized by Jordan's river		g			804						173					

SONGS FOR CHILDREN

Father welcomes all his children CAON 797, CH 48
Light a flame CH 255, SOF 339

BIBLE READINGS

Psalms 46 [and 47]
Isaiah 42.1–9
Ephesians 2.1–10
Matthew 3.13–17

SINGING THE PSALM

Psalm 46 CH4, CWP, H&P, NPCW, PAME
Psalm 47 CH4, CRP, CWP, FGP, H&P, NEH, NPCW, PAME, PFS
Bell *Clap your hands all you nations* CG, MCW1, PPP, SG

ANTHEMS AND VOCAL MUSIC

Title	Composer	Voices	E/M/D	Book source	Single sheet publisher
UNISON/TWO PART/HIGH VOICES					
Breathe on me	Hubbard	S	E/M	SFJ	Banks
Come down, O love divine	Hand	SSA	M	NAB1	
I'm gonna sing	Trad arr Jones	U/3 part	E	VFLS	
O for a closer walk with God	Caesar	SSA	M/D	EAC2	
The Spirit of the Lord is upon me	Corp	2 part	E	VFLS	
THREE/FOUR PARTS					
Breathe on me, breath of God	Wilby	SATB + solo S	E/M		RSCM
Come down, O love divine	Tadman-Robins	SAMen	E	OBFA	
God so loved the world	Chilcott	SATB + solo S unacc	M	BCA, AWTE	OUP
God so loved the world	Stainer	SAB unacc	E/M	AOAN1	
God so loved the world	Stainer	SATB unacc	E/M	AWTE, FAB1, MHWE, NOEAB, NSAC1	RSCM
Greater love	Ireland	SATB	M	AC4	S&B
Grow in grace	Archer	SATB	E/M	SBS1	RSCM
Holy Spirit, ever dwelling	Howells	SATB	E/M	ETAS	
Listen sweet dove	Ives	SATB	M	EAC1, SC	RSCM
O for a closer walk with God	Stanford	SATB	M	AC1, ASA, BC, OBFA, AOAN1 (SAMen)	RSCM
Since by man came death (Messiah)	Handel	SATB	M		Novello
Spirit of the Lord, come down	Harper	SA(T)B	E	SOTL, SBS1	RSCM
The Baptism of Christ	March	SATB	E	SBS2	
The dove descending breaks the air	Stravinsky	SATB	D		B&H
The Spirit of the Lord	Elgar	SATB	M/D	SAEE	RSCM
Tomorrow shall be my dancing day	Gardner	SATB	M	N	OUP
Tribus miraculis	Marenzio	SATB unacc	M	CM1, ETAS	
FIVE OR MORE PARTS					
Come down, O love divine	Rutter	SSAATTBB unacc	D		OUP
Gracious Spirit	Forbes	SSATB unacc	D	NNAB	
In splendente nube	Philips	SSATB unacc	M/D		Mapa Mundi
The dove descending	Harvey	SATB + SATB	D		Novello

See also the anthems listed for Years A and C (pages 19 and 263).

ORGAN MUSIC

PRELUDES

Bach J.S.	**Christ unser Herr zum Jordan kam** BWV 685 in Novello Vol.16, Bärenreiter Vol.4, Peters Vol.6 E/M
Beechey G.	**Jesu dulcis memoria** in *The Cross of Christ* (Fagus) E/M
Elmore R.	**Chorale Prelude 'Jesus, the very thought'** in *Contemporary Chorale Preludes* (Boosey) E
Reger M.	**O Lamm Gottes unschuldig** Op.67/33 in *Complete Organ Works* Vol.7 (Breitkopf) E
Stanford C.V.	**Jesu dulcis memoria** (Cathedral Music) E/M

POSTLUDES

Bach J.S.	**O Lamm Gottes unschuldig** BWV 1095 in *Neumeister Chorale Preludes* (Bärenreiter) E/M(*)
Dandrieu J-F.	**Quand le Sauveur Jésus Christ** in *Noëls* (Kalmus) M*
Ireland J.	**The Holy Boy** in *The Oxford Book of Christmas Organ Music* (OUP) E/M
Pachelbel J.	**Christ unser Herr zum Jordan kam** No.3 in *Selected Works* Vol.3 (Kalmus), also p.81 in *Organ Works* (Dover) E/M

HYMNS AND SONGS

	pos	rdg	AMNS	CAON	CFE	CH4	CH5	CP	H&P	HTC	LAU	MP	NEH	SG	SOF	TS
Angels from the realms of glory		g	39	36		324	147	44	92	77	131	35		344	23	631
As with gladness men of old		o	51	49	55	326	189	83	121	99	166	39	47	343	31	639
Author of life divine	cm	g	258	56				281	596	395			274			
Brightest and best of the sons of the morning		s	47	85	99	327	190	84	123	338		65	49	346		
Eternal Light, shine in my heart		n					613	415		339						
Faithful one, so unchanging		n					2					825		547	89	89
Forth in the peace of Christ we go	se		458	187	183	646	454	429		542	853		361	594		
Give me/us the wings of faith		n	324	204			463	216	815				225			
Glory, love, and praise, and honour	pc	g	461	207				436	35				287			
God has spoken – by his prophets		n					381		64	248	742	831		225		
Hail, thou source of every blessing		s										51				
Hail to the Lord's anointed		s	142	259	241	474	125	87	125	190	102	204	55		150	709
He's got the whole (wide) world in his hands		o		819	249				25		973	225				
Jerusalem, my happy home/thou city blest		o	187	339			481			569	373		228			
Jerusalem the golden		o	184	340	317	747	670	482		573	991		381			
Jesus, these eyes have never seen		n	245	365			491						389			
Let earth and heaven combine		s						109								1394
Light's abode, celestial Salem		o	185	398			672	502					401			
Lord, enthroned in heavenly splendour		n	263	408	379		431	311	616	416	769	431	296	52	352	870
(O) worship the Lord in the beauty of holiness	ga	s	49	552	560	201	196	89	505	344	169	529	52	204	457	426
Rejoice and be glad! The Redeemer has come		o						207			573					1490
Sing of the Lord's goodness					654	157	368				713			61		
Songs of thankfulness and praise		s	53	609	661		197	90		98	172		56	376		
The Lord is my light (Taizé)		o		944												
The race that long in darkness/The people who in darkness		s	52	656	711	290	199	38	89	71	168		57			
Why, impious Herod		s											46			
Ye that know the Lord is gracious	of	o	175			642	493	628					477			

SONGS FOR CHILDREN

He's got the whole (wide) world in his hands CAON 819, CAP 19, CFE 249, CH 82, H&P 25, JP 78, KS2 508, LAU 973, MP 225

We're a bright light together CAON 906, KS 362, TS 1040

BIBLE READINGS

Psalm 96
Isaiah 60.9–22
Hebrews 6.17 - 7.10
Matthew 8.5–13

SINGING THE PSALM

Psalm 96 CRP, CWP, FGP, H&P, MCW1, NPCW, PAME, PIW
Dean *Proclaim the wonders of the Lord* HG#
Walker *Save us, Lord our God* ATNJ (OCP)

ANTHEMS AND VOCAL MUSIC

Title	Composer	Voices	E/M/D	Book source	Single sheet publisher
UNISON/TWO PART/HIGH VOICES					
Author of life divine	McDowall	2 part	E	OBFA	
Light of the world	Dankworth	U	E/M	HP	
Listen to the Spirit	Dean	U#	E	C	
Litany to the Holy Spirit (In the hour of my distress)	Hurford	U	E	AC2, NEP	OUP
THREE/FOUR PARTS					
A touching place (Christ's is the world) (g)	Bell	SATB	E	CG, IAMB, LFB, WGIR, WIS	GIA
Author of life divine	Archer	SATB unacc	E		Mayhew
Bread of the world	Aston	SATB	E/M	SBS2	
Dixit Dominus	Mozart	SATB	M		Novello
He shall feed his flock (Messiah)	Handel arr Hand	SAMen	M	AOAN1	
I heard the voice of Jesus say	Shephard	SATB	M		RSCM
In the city of the Lord	Harper	SATB	M/D	LOL	RSCM
Just as I am	Chilcott	SATB	E	BCA	OUP
Light of the lonely pilgrim's heart	Nardone	SATB	E		B&H
Lord of all hopefulness	Trad arr Rose	SATB + solo S	E/M	MTH2	
O Lord, increase our faith	Loosemore	SATB (unacc)	E	NCAB, SBS1	RSCM
O thou that art the light	G.Jackson	SATB unacc	E/M		OUP
Take my life, Lord	Rizza	SATB#	E	FOLO	Mayhew
The Lord is my light and my salvation	Noon	SATB	M	SBS1	RSCM
The Lord is my light and my salvation	Rutter	SATB + clarinet	M		OUP
The secret of Christ (g)	Shephard	SATB	M	NCAB	RSCM
There is a longing in our hearts	Quigley	SATB/U#	E	CH4, LAU, SG	OCP
There's a wideness in God's mercy	Bevan	SATB	E	LD, MTH1, NEP, NOEAB	
We cannot measure how you heal (g)	Bell arr Archer	SATB	E	BC	RSCM
FIVE OR MORE PARTS					
Blessing (g)	Allwood	SATBB unacc	E	NSAC2	
Deus noster refugium	Hassler	SAATTB unacc	M/D		CMS/OUP

ORGAN MUSIC

PRELUDES

Karg-Elert S. **O Gott, du frommer Gott** No.50 in Vol.5 of *Choral-Improvisationen* Op.65 and in *14 Choral-Improvisationen* (both Breitkopf) E/M

Kellner J.C. **Jesu meine Freude** in *Orgelmusik um J.S.Bach* (Breitkopf) E/M

Peeters F. **Hostis Herodes Impie** No.5 of *30 Chorale Preludes* Set 3 Op.70 (Peters) E/M

Piutti C. **Christ, der du bist der helle Tag** in *Choralvorspiele* Op.34 Vol.1 (Bärenreiter) E/M

Walther J.G. **Jesu meine Freude** in *80 Chorale Preludes* (Peters) E*

POSTLUDES

Alain J. **2ème Fantaisie** in *Complete Works* Bk.3 (Leduc) M

Dubois T. **Postlude-Cantique** from *Seven Pieces* (Butz/Kalmus); also in *Complete Works* Vol.1 (Bärenreiter) M

Krebs J.L. **Jesu meine Freude** No.3 in *Complete Works Vol.4: Clavierübung* (Breitkopf) E/M*

Suitable before or after: Variations from Bach J.S. **Partita 'Christ, der du bist der helle Tag'** BWV 766 E(*)-D or **Partita 'O Gott, du frommer Gott'** BWV 767 in Novello Vol.19, Bärenreiter Vol.1, Peters Vol.5 E/M*-M*

THE THIRD SUNDAY OF EPIPHANY YEAR B

HYMNS AND SONGS

	pos	rdg	AMNS	CAON	CFE	CH4	CH5	CP	H&P	HTC	LAU	MP	NEH	SG	SOF	TS
Christ, from whom all blessings flow		u							764	491						
Give thanks with a grateful heart		g		202	189	180	352					170		108	124	118
God is love, and where true love is		u	465		214		520	441	757		242		513			
God of glory, we exalt your name		g										191			137	130
God of grace and God of glory		g	367	225			533	448	712	324		192		574	139	
Hark, my soul! It is the Lord/ Christian, do you hear		g	244	264			569	457	521	472		209	637			
I come with joy	of	u	473	304		656	421	305	610	408	649		623	469		
I lift my eyes to the quiet hills		o		312			14					281		515	804	
Jesus, Lord, we look to thee	gr	u	380				489	759				481				
Jesus shall reign where'er the sun		g	143	359		470	97	490	239	516	322	379	388	45	301	1376
Jesus shall take the highest honour		g		360								378		123	302	296
Jesus, united by thy grace		u							773							
Laudate Dominum/Sing, praise and bless the Lord (Taizé)		ps		933	346	77	359				698				1514	
Look, ye saints, the sight is glorious		n				439	275	171	201	179		426			349	
Lord of the Church, we pray	of	u					303			499		442		577	1433	
Nature with open volume stands		n	497				232	113	174				87			
O for a thousand tongues to sing		g	125	485		352	104	534	744	219		496	415	55	412	383/ 1452
O thou, who at thy Eucharist didst pray/O Christ	of	u	265	540	556	669	438	318	779	420	833		302	476		
One is the body	gr	u				679							280			
Rejoice! The Lord is king		n	139	580	619	449	281	563	243	180	326	575	443	440	482	948
Seek ye first the kingdom of God		g		590	633	641	596		138		820	590			493	447
The Church's one foundation		u	170	636	688	739	528	585	515	501	830	640	484	581	525	477
The kingdom of God is justice and joy		g		646	701			591	139	333	821	651		184		
The Spirit lives to set us free		n		666			490				771	664			1555	
Wait for the Lord (Taizé)		n		949	762	276					88				1575	
When peace, like a river		n										757				574
Why, impious Herod		s											46			
Will you come and follow me	se	g		752	812	533	605	622			877		647	634	1120	

Hymns and songs especially suitable for celebrations of the Week of Prayer for Christian Unity are marked 'u'.

SONGS FOR CHILDREN
Come and praise the Lord our king CAP 21, CFE 121, HTC S8, JP 34
Far and near, hear the call KS 49, MP 982, SG 610, SOF 709, TS 90

150

BIBLE READINGS

Psalm 33*

Jeremiah 3.21 - 4.2

Titus 2.1–8,11–14

Matthew 4.12–23

SINGING THE PSALM

Psalm 33* CRP, CWP, FGP, H&P, LAU, NEH, NPCW, PAME, PFS

Walker *Lord, be with us* OOD#

ANTHEMS AND VOCAL MUSIC

Title	Composer	Voices	E/M/D	Book source	Single sheet publisher
UNISON/TWO PART/HIGH VOICES					
A Prayer of St Richard of Chichester	White	2 part	E	OEAB, BC, OBFA	OUP
Christ has no body now but yours	Ogden	2 part	E	CFAP, LOL	RSCM
Christ whose glory fills the skies	Shephard	S	M	HP	
Day by day	How	U + 2 part	E	BC	RSCM
Dear Lord and Father of mankind	Parnell	SS	E/M		Encore
God has chosen me	Farrell arr Weaver	2 part	E	SFL1	
Make me a light	Wilby	SS	E	EAC2, HP	Chester
Prayer of St Benedict	Payne	2 part	E	VFLS	
Sent by the Lord am I	Trad arr Weaver	2 part	E	BC	
THREE/FOUR PARTS					
A Prayer of St Richard of Chichester	Archer	SATB	E		RSCM
Christ whose glory fills the skies	Archer	SATB	M		Mayhew
Christ whose glory fills the skies	Darke	SATB	M	SBS1	RSCM
Day by day	Godfrey	SATB	E		Encore
Day by day	How	SATB	E	NOEAB	
Dear Lord and Father of mankind	Carter	SATB	M	ACA	
Give us the wings of faith	Bullock	SATB	M	AC4	OUP
Go forth and tell!	Ogden	SATB	E/M	SBS2	RSCM
I give you my hands, Lord	Tambling	SAMen	M	AOAN1	
Lead me, Lord	S.S.Wesley	SATB	E	AC1, FAB1, NCAB, NOEAB, NSAC1	Novello
Light of the world	Elgar	SATB	M/D	AWTE, SAEE	Novello
Now let us from this table rise	Henderson	SATB	E	SBS1	RSCM
O Master, let me walk with thee	Ledger	SATB	M		Encore
Take up your cross	Corp	SATB	E	SBS1, WOTC	RSCM
The light of the world	Carter	SATB	M	ACA	OUP
FIVE OR MORE PARTS					
Beati quorum via	Stanford	SSATBB unacc	M	ASA, WFC	RSCM
The Twelve	Walton	SSAATTBB	D		OUP

ORGAN MUSIC

PRELUDES

Bach J.S.   **Liebster Jesu, wir sind hier** BWV 633 or 634 from the *Orgelbüchlein* (many editions) E/M

Dupré M.   **From whence the sun rises** Op.38/3 from *Le Tombeau de Titelouze* Op.38 (Gray) E

Guilmant A.   **Allegro moderato e Pastorale** Op.57 No.1 in *Complete Works* Bk.5 (Belwin); also in *An Organ Miscellany* (Mayhew) E/M

Schneider J.   **Chorale Prelude 'Mein Gott, das Herze bring ich dir'** in *Orgelmusik um J.S.Bach* (Breitkopf) M

Telemann G.P.   **Herr Christ, der einig Gotts Sohn** in *The Progressive Organist* Bk.7 (Novello) E*

POSTLUDES

Buxtehude D.   **Herr Christ, der einig Gotts Sohn** BuxWV 191 in *Complete Works* Vol.4 (Bärenreiter) E/M

Franck C.   **Quasi marcia** Op.22 in *Organ Music for Manuals Only* (Dover) E/M*

Rheinberger J.   **Monologue in F minor** Op.162/10 *Monologues* (Carus) and in *Free Organ Music for the Worship Service* (Carus) M

Titelouze J.   **A solis ortus/Crudelis Herodes** 3 settings in *Hymnes de l'Église* (Kalmus, Schott) E-M

THE FOURTH SUNDAY OF EPIPHANY YEAR B

HYMNS AND SONGS

	pos	rdg	AMNS	CAON	CFE	CH4	CH5	CP	H&P	HTC	LAU	MP	NEH	SG	SOF	TS
Be still and know I (John Bell)		o												18	672	
Be still and know II (John Bell)		o			70	754								242		
Be still and know that I am God		o		66	71	755	608				909	48			41	48
Christ triumphant, ever reigning				104	113	436	259	398		173	763	77	613	319	62	655
Come, let us join our cheerful songs	ga		144	120			332	401	810	206		93	349	33	70	
Crown him with many crowns			147	137	139	459	263	166	255	174	321	109	352	321	77	77
Dear Lord and Father of mankind		o	115	144	143	485	549	411	673	356	934	111	353	497	79	79
Forth in the peace of Christ we go	se		458	187	183	646	454	429		542	853		361	594		
Glory in the highest to the God of heaven							693	300		582			363	37		
God of glory, we exalt your name												191			137	130
Hail to the Lord's anointed		s	142	259	241	474	125	87	125	190	102	204	55		150	709
Hail, thou source of every blessing		s											51			
How beauteous/gracious are their feet		g	301				220	449								
Hushed was the evening hymn		o							523			253				
Immortal, invisible, God only wise	ga		199	314	301	132	6	474	9	21	725	327	377	44	234	220
Lord, speak to me that I may speak		o			542	589	512	553	510		444					
Master, speak! Thy servant heareth		o						535			459			386		
Misericordias Domini/From age to age (Taizé)	ps			489												
One is the body		n				679							280			
Rise and hear! The Lord is speaking		g	509				385	321								
Seek ye first the kingdom of God		g		590	633	641	596		138		820	590			493	447
Songs of thankfulness and praise		s	53	609	661		197	90		98	172		56	376		
The kingdom of God is justice and joy		s		646	701			591	139	333	821	651		184		
The race that long in darkness/The people who in darkness		s	52	656	711	290	199	38	89	71	168		57			
Through all the changing scenes of life	ps		209	686	740		372	604	73	46		702	467	654	1566	1561
Why, impious Herod		s											46			

SONGS FOR CHILDREN

God is good CAON 214, CH4 178, JP 55, KS 74, MP 185, SOF 132, TS 124
I am the church! CH4 204, CH5 521, JP 367

BIBLE READINGS

Psalm 34*
1 Samuel 3.1–20
1 Corinthians 14.12–20
Matthew 13.10–17

SINGING THE PSALM

Psalm 34* C, CRP, CWP, FGP, H&P, LAU, MCW1, NPCW, PAME
  Bell *I will always bless the Lord* C, CH4, IAMB, OITB
  Dean *Taste and see* CFE, WYP#
  Ogden *Taste and see* (WLP)
  Rizza *I will bless the Lord* LIOD#
  Schutte *Ever on my lips* C (OCP)#
  Walker *Taste and see* CSF (OCP)#

ANTHEMS AND VOCAL MUSIC

Title	Composer	Voices	E/M/D	Book source	Single sheet publisher
UNISON/TWO PART/HIGH VOICES					
Give ear unto me	Marcello	SS	M	AC2	
God be in my head	How	U + divisions	E		RSCM
Here I am, Lord	Schutte arr Weaver	SA	E	SFL1	
Listen	Nazareth arr Archer	2 part	E	BC	
The Call (Come, my Way)	Vaughan Williams	U	E	NEP	S&B
THREE/FOUR PARTS					
Ad te levavi oculos meos	Palestrina	SATB unacc	M		OUP
Be still, for the presence of the Lord	Evans arr Tambling	SATB	E	WSCC1	
Christ whose glory fills the skies	Darke	SATB	M	SBS1	RSCM
Come, my Way, my Truth, my Life	Archer	SAB	E/M	AOAN1	Mayhew
Expectans expectavi	Wood	SATB	M		Banks
God be in my head	Carter	SATB	M	ACA	OUP
God be in my head	Lloyd	ATTB unacc	M		Encore
God be in my head	Rutter	SATB unacc	E	JRA, NCAB, WFC	OUP
God be in my head	Walford Davies	SATB unacc	E	NCAB, NOEAB, NSAC2	RSCM
God be in my head	Wilby	SATB	M	NOEAB	
Here I am, Lord	Schutte arr Langford	SATB	E/M	WIS	
I will sing with the spirit	Goodenough	SATB	E	SBS2	
I will sing with the spirit	Rutter	SATB	E/M	JRA	OUP
Lead me, Lord	S.S.Wesley	SATB	E	AC1, FAB1, NCAB, NOEAB, NSAC1	Novello
Oculi omnium	Wood	SATB unacc	E	NSAC1	RSCM
Spiritus intus alit	B.Ferguson	SATB	M	ETAS	
The Call	Lloyd	SATB unacc	M		RSCM
FIVE OR MORE PARTS					
Oculi omnium	Cleobury	SSAATTBB unacc	M		Encore
Open thou mine eyes	Rutter	SSATB unacc	M		OUP

ORGAN MUSIC

PRELUDES

Bach C.P.E.	**Adagio in D minor** in *Complete Works* Vol.2 (Peters) E/M
Hindemith P.	**2nd Sonata: 2nd movement** (Schott) E/M
Howells H.	**Psalm-Prelude** Set 1 No.1 (Novello) M
Rinck J.C.H.	**Adagio in F** in *Easy Organ Pieces from the 19th C* (Bärenreiter) E*
Santo Elias M.de	**Sonata** in *Silva Ibérica* Vol.1 (Schott) E/M*

POSTLUDES

Couperin F.	**Dialogue en trio** No.XIII from *Messe pour les Paroisses* (Kalmus) M
Near G.	**Salzburg** in *Choraleworks* Set I (Aureole) E/M
Russell W.	**Voluntary I: Gracioso and Allegro moderato** in *Twelve Voluntaries* Set 1 (Fagus) E/M*
Whitlock P.	**Hymn Prelude 'St Denio'** in *Whitlock: Complete Shorter Works* (OUP) M/D

PROPER 1 (SUNDAY BETWEEN 4 AND 10 FEBRUARY INCLUSIVE) YEAR B

(if earlier than the Second Sunday before Lent)

(For the Presentation of Christ in the Temple, see Year A, page 26.)

HYMNS AND SONGS

	pos	rdg	AMNS	CAON	CFE	CH4	CH5	CP	H&P	HTC	LAU	MP	NEH	SG	SOF	TS
Almighty Father, who for us thy Son didst give		n	338					374	401							
At/In the name of Jesus		n	148	54	59	458	94	380	74	172	762	41	338	317	32	33
Awake, my soul, and with the sun	mo,ga	n	1	58		210	51	1	632	264		804	232	618		
Blessed Jesu, at your word/Dearest Jesu, we are here		n,g	269	143	87		410	294								
Dear Lord and Father of mankind		g	115	144	143	485	549	411	673	356	934	111	353	497	79	79
Fight the good fight		n	220	169	171	517	566	423	710	526	860	143	359	635	107	
Forth in thy name, O Lord, I go	se	n,g	239	188	184	529	567	430	381	306	861	159	235	623	1237	
Hark, my soul! It is the Lord/Christian, do you hear		g	244	264			569	457	521	472		209	637			
How deep the Father's love		n				549	224					988		193	780	185
How sure the Scriptures are		n								249			227			
I, the Lord of sea and sky (Here I am, Lord)	se	g		332	285	251	581	470			865	857		633	830	246
I want to walk with Jesus Christ		g					580			S 16		302		261		
Inspired by love and anger		g		325	311	253										
Jesus calls us: o'er the tumult		g	312	347		509	584	233	141	104		359	200	668		
Lord, as I wake I turn to you	mo	ps	485				56		634	267	672		236	561		
My Lord, you wore no royal crown		n								118			628			
O Lord, hear my prayer (Taizé)		ps		938	542		620				929	908		246	423	394
O thou who camest from above		n	233	541	557	625	639	191	745	596		525	431	560	451	416
O Word of God/Christ the Word incarnate		n					531	478				527				
Praise to the Lord, the almighty	ga	n	207	573	608	124	365	558	16	40	706	564	440	59	470	945
Saviour, again to thy dear name we raise	ev	g	15	587			71	20	643	281		584	250			
Speak, Lord, in the stillness		n					624			253		608				
Spread, O spread, thou mighty word		n											482			
Thanks/Praise to God whose word was spoken		n,g	423			605	387	584	483	255			438	229		
There is a land of pure delight		o	190				681	597	822	575			460			
We love the place, O God		n	160	718			343	211		558		731	471			
Who would true valour see/He who would valiant be		o	212	281	248	535	662	621	688	590	862	224	372	639	174	
Will you come and follow me	se	g		752	812	533	605	622			877		647	634	1120	

SONGS FOR CHILDREN

Praise and thanksgiving let everyone bring CH4 170

We're a bright light together TS 1040

BIBLE READINGS

Psalm 5
Numbers 13.1–2,27–33
Philippians 2.12–28
Luke 5.1–11

SINGING THE PSALM

Psalm 5 CH4, CWP, NPCW, PFS

ANTHEMS AND VOCAL MUSIC

Title	Composer	Voices	E/M/D	Book source	Single sheet publisher
UNISON/TWO PART/HIGH VOICES					
All that is hidden	Farrell	U/SATB#	E	CFE, LAU, RITH, SFTL	OCP
Centre of my life	Inwood	U/SATB#	E	CFE, CSF, LAU, SG	OCP
Give us light	Vas	2 part	E	VFLS	
Give us the wings of faith	Blatchly	SS	M	HP	
God be in my head	How	U + divisions	E		RSCM
Make me a light	Wilby	SS	E	EAC2, HP	Chester
This little light of mine	Trad arr Isaacs	2 part	E	VFLS	
You are the centre	Rizza	U/SATB#	E	FOL	Mayhew
THREE/FOUR PARTS					
Christ whose glory fills the skies	Darke	SATB	M	SBS1	RSCM
Dear Lord and Father of mankind	Carter	SATB	M	ACA	
Ecce beatam lucem	Dove	SATB	M/D		Faber
Firmly I believe and truly	Shephard	SAMen	E	SFL2	
Give us the wings of faith	Bullock	SATB	M	AC4, FSB10	OUP
God be in my head	Armstrong Gibbs	SAMen	E	OBFA	
God be in my head	Nicholson	SATB	E		RSCM
Light of the world	Elgar	SATB	M/D	AWTE, SAEE	Novello
Lord, give me faith	Robson	SATB	E		RSCM
O hearken thou	Elgar	SATB	M	MTP, SAEE	
O Lord, increase our faith	Loosemore	SATB (unacc)	E	SBS1, NCAB	RSCM
Praise the Lord, my soul	S.S.Wesley	SATB + solo S	M/D	MTP	
Prayer of St Patrick	Rutter	SATB unacc	E/M	JRA	OUP
The Lord is my light and my salvation	Noon	SATB	M	SBS1	RSCM
Wings of the morning	Rutter	SATB	M		OUP
FIVE OR MORE PARTS					
Let there be light	Joubert	SSSAAATTTBBB unacc	D		Novello
The Twelve	Walton	SSAATTBB	D		OUP

ORGAN MUSIC

PRELUDES

Clérambault L.-N.	**Basse et dessus de trompette** from *Livre d'Orgue: Suite du Premier Ton* (Schola Cantorum, Kalmus) E(*)
Langlais J.	**No.2** of *Trois Offertoires* (Combre) M
Michel J.M.	**Lobe den Herren** (melancholy jazz) in *Jazz Inspirations* (Bärenreiter) E/M
Stanford C.V.	**On a theme of Orlando Gibbons** No.1 of *Six Short Preludes and Postludes* (Set 2) Op.105 (Stainer) and in *Preludes and Postludes* (Mayhew) E/M
Thiman E.	**In-Voluntary for Sunday Morning** ('Morning Hymn') in *Times and Seasons* Bk.2 (Novello) E/M

POSTLUDES

Clérambault L.-N.	**Dialogue sur le grands jeux** from *Livre d'Orgue: Suite du Premier Ton* (Schola Cantorum, Kalmus) E(*)
Guilmant A.	**Grand Chœur in March Form** Op.52 No.2 in *The Practical Organist: Complete Works* Vol.5 (Belwin) E/M
Rawsthorne N.	**Sortie: Forth in thy name** ('Song 34') in *50 Hymn Preludes* and *Hymn Preludes for the Church Year* Bk.2 (both Mayhew) M
Sechter S.	**Nun lob, mein Seel, den Herren** in *18 Choralvorspiele* Op. 90 (Doblinger) E/M*

PROPER 2 (SUNDAY BETWEEN 11 AND 17 FEBRUARY INCLUSIVE) YEAR B
(if earlier than the Second Sunday before Lent)

HYMNS AND SONGS

	pos	rdg	AMNS	CAON	CFE	CH4	CH5	CP	H&P	HTC	LAU	MP	NEH	SG	SOF	TS
And can it be that I should gain		n		32	43	396	218	376	216	588	790	33	*627*	168	21	21
Beneath the cross of Jesus		n		65			561	105	165			55			39	45
Come with all joy to sing to God	ga	o								16						
Father, hear the prayer we offer		o	113	161	158	255	645	416	436	360	933	132	357	237	1229	
Fight the good fight		n	220	169	171	517	566	423	710	526	860	143	359	635	107	
From heaven you came, helpless babe		n		195	187	374	219	432			749	162		632	120	114
Happy are they, they that love God		g	176	262			649	456	711	473			369			
Here, O my Lord, I see thee face to face	cm	n	274	279			418	304	608	406		230		468		
In Christ alone my hope is found		n									1072				1346	1311
In the cross of Christ I glory		n		327		397	225	480	167			338	379			
In the Lord I'll be ever thankful (Taizé)		n		929	308	772					944	865		656	817	
Jesu, the very thought of thee		n, g	120	368	321	560	101	485	265	478	798	386	385	534	308	
Jesus Christ is waiting		g		349	323	360					889			624	1381	1360
Light of the minds that know him	se	n		397			588	501		477			400	626		
Lord Jesus, once you spoke to men		g	392							112						
Lord, for the years		n		409		159	81	81		328	942	428	*619*	602	892	327
My hope is built on nothing less		n								462		473		537		365
My Lord, what love is this		n		462	500		230					476		194	398	370
O Lord, hear my prayer (Taizé)	ps			938	542		620				929	908		246	423	394
O Word of God incarnate/O Christ the Word		o						531	478			527				
Remember, remember your mercy, Lord		g			621									154		
Sun of my soul	ev	g	11	621			72	21	646			618	251			
Take our bread, we ask you	cm	g			678						610					
The love of God comes close		g										940		186		1533
There is a Redeemer		n		658		559	112					673		396	544	492
We sing the praise of him who died		n	138	723		405	248	125	182	146		738	94	390		
When I survey the wondrous cross		n	67	738	801	392	247	127	180	147	756	755/1126	95	680	596	572
You shall cross the barren desert		g			830		22				964					

SONGS FOR CHILDREN

Give me joy in my heart/Give me oil in my lamp AMNS 459, CAON 201, CAP 43, CFE 190, CH 55, CH5 570, CP 433, H&P 492, HTC S11, JP 50, KS 66, LAU 722, MP 167, SOF 728
The joy of the Lord is my strength JP 240

BIBLE READINGS

Psalm 6
Numbers 20.2–13
Philippians 3.7–21
Luke 6.17–26

SINGING THE PSALM

Psalm 6 CWP, NPCW

Bell *Hear me, Lord, and draw near* LFB, PPP

ANTHEMS AND VOCAL MUSIC

Title	Composer	Voices	E/M/D	Book source	Single sheet publisher
UNISON/TWO PART/HIGH VOICES					
Come to the well	Farrell	U#	E	GBU	
God of the living	Tamblyn	U/SATB#	E	SFTL	
I know that my Redeemer lives	Ogden	U	E		WLP
I saw water flowing	Davis	U	E	MHWE	
Most glorious Lord of life	Harris	2 part	E/M	OEAB	OUP
Springs of water, bless the Lord	Haugen	2 part + descant#	E	LAU, RE	GIA
The Lord is my light	Bell	U	E	VFLS	
THREE/FOUR PARTS					
Amen, amen, it shall be so! (g)	Bell	SATB + cantor	E	LAA	
As water to the thirsty	Coleman arr Barnard	SATB	E	SC, WIS	
Blessed are they (g)	S.S.Wesley	SAB	M		S&B
Blest are the pure in heart (g)	Gower	SATB	E		Encore
Blest are the pure in heart (g)	Walford Davies	SATB unacc	E	MTH1, NCAB	
God is our hope and strength	J.S. Bach	SATB	E	AC1	
I know that my Redeemer liveth	Morley	SATB	E/M		Fagus
If ye be risen again with Christ	Gibbons	SATB + solo SSA	M		Novello
Jesus is the brightest light	Freylinghausen	SATB unacc	E	MTH1	
Most glorious Lord of life	Harris	SATB	E	AWTE	OUP
Out of the stillness	Shephard	SATB	E/M	SBS2	RSCM
The Beatitudes (g)	Chilcott	SATB	M		OUP
The Beatitudes(g)	Pärt	SATB	D		Universal
The Beatitudes (g)	Watson Henderson	SATB	M	SC	RSCM
FIVE OR MORE PARTS					
Beati mundo corde (g)	Byrd	SSATB unacc	M/D	ETAS	CMS/OUP
Go down, Moses (5 Spirituals from 'A Child of our Time')	Trad arr Tippett	SSAATTBB unacc	M/D		Schott
God is our hope and strength	Blow	SSAATTBB	M		Kings
Libera plebem	Joubert	SAATBB unacc	D		Novello

ORGAN MUSIC

PRELUDES

Adlung J.   **Trio in A minor** in *Orgelmusik um J.S.Bach* (Breitkopf) M
Elgar E.   **No.5** from *Vesper Voluntaries* (Faber) E*
Jackson F.   **Prelude for a Solemn Occasion** in *The Modern Organist* (Banks) E/M
Nixon J.   **Rockingham** in *Hymn Tune Preludes* (Fagus) E/M
Vierne L.   **Légende** from *24 Pièces en Style Libre* Bk.2 (Masters, Durand) M(*)

POSTLUDES

Bédard D.   **Allegro** No.1 of *Trois Voluntaries* (Cheldar) E/M
Guilain J-A.   **Dialogue** from *Suite de Magnificat du Premier Ton* (Kalmus) E/M(*)
Peeters F.   **Holy God, we praise thy name** ('Hursley') Op. 70/10 in *30 Chorale Preludes* Vol.3 (Peters) E/M
Stanford C.V.   **Song 22** No.2 of *Six Short Preludes and Postludes* (Set 2) Op.105 (Stainer); also in *Preludes and Postludes* (Mayhew) E/M

PROPER 3 (SUNDAY BETWEEN 18 AND 24 FEBRUARY INCLUSIVE) YEAR B

(if earlier than the Second Sunday before Lent)

HYMNS AND SONGS

	pos	rdg	AMNS	CAON	CFE	CH4	CH5	CP	H&P	HTC	LAU	MP	NEH	SG	SOF	TS
All creatures of our God and King	ga	n	105	6	15	147	24	250	329	13	694	7	263	23		614
Blest are the pure in heart		g	238	77	88		630	391	724	110	908		341	372		
Father, I place into your hands		n		162	159		565				971	133			97	97
Glory in the highest to the God of heaven		n					693	300		582			363	37		
God be in my head		o	236	211	205	538	631	439	694	543	914		328	666		
God! When human bonds are broken		g		234												
He that is down needs fear no fall		n	218						676							
I am trusting thee, Lord Jesus		n		300						433		258			202	
I know that my Redeemer lives, what joy		n		311			270		196	169		278		406		
In Christ alone my hope is found		n										1072			1346	1311
Jehovah Jireh, my provider		n										354			284	
Lord of all hopefulness		n	394	413	386	166	618	507	552	101	969	882	239	509	902	
Lord, speak to me that I may speak		o					589	512	553	510		444				
Lord, thy word abideth/your word shall guide us		g	166	420	390		384	515	476	251	977/8	446	407			
Nada te turbe/Nothing can trouble (Taizé)		n		937							947			659		
O God in heaven, whose loving plan		n	407					535	369							
Ostende nobis, Domine (Taizé)		ps		583							839					
Praise to the Lord, the almighty	ga	n	207	573	608	124	365	558	16	40	706	564	440	59	470	945
Rejoice! Rejoice! Christ is in you		n			618						818	572			480	438
Send me out from here	se	n										594			996	
Soldiers of Christ, arise		n	219	606		515	487	571	719	533		604	449	643	506	
Take this moment, sign and space		g			680	501	598				850					
Teach me, my God and King		n	240	629			601	583	803			456				
Thine for ever, God of love		n	234	673			660	599		556		972	463			
What a friend we have in Jesus		n		727		547	627		559	373		746		646	593	566
When morning gilds the skies	mo	n	146	739	805		344	619	276	223		756	473	74	597	1054
You are my hiding place		n										793			625	1080

SONGS FOR CHILDREN

Father, I place into your hands CAON 162, CFE 159, CH 44, CH5 565, JP 42, KS2 457, LAU 971, MP 133, SOF 97, TS 97

I can do all things KS 124, SOF 1301

You are my hiding place MP 793, SOF 625, TS 1080

BIBLE READINGS

Psalm 10
Numbers 22.21 - 23.12
Philippians 4.10–20
Luke 6.27–38

SINGING THE PSALM

Psalm 10 CWP, NPCW

ANTHEMS AND VOCAL MUSIC

Title	Composer	Voices	E/M/D	Book source	Single sheet publisher
UNISON/TWO PART/HIGH VOICES					
Bambelela (You must never give up)	Trad South African	U/SATB	E	C	
Gather us in (Here in this place)	Haugen	U#	E	CFE, CG, CH4, LAU, SG	GIA
Give me strength	Chilcott	2 part	E	VFLS	
Love one another (g)	S.S.Wesley	S	E	BC	RSCM
O praise the Lord	Boyce	U	E/M		Curwen
Prayer of St Benedict (g)	Payne	2 part	E	VFLS	
The Father's love (g)	Lole	SS	E/M	EAC2	RSCM
Ubi caritas (g)	Lole	SS	M		Encore
THREE/FOUR PARTS					
Be strong and of good courage	Campbell	SATB	M	FSB7	Novello
Blessed is he that considereth the poor (g)	Wise	SATB	M	NCAB	
Give almes of thy goods (g)	Tye	SATB unacc	E	AC1, OBTA	OUP
God is our hope and strength	Stanford	SATB	M		Novello
Just as I am	Chilcott	SATB	E/M	BCA	OUP
Strengthen ye the weak hands	Harris	SATB	M		Novello
Though I speak with the tongues of men (g)	Bairstow	SATB	M	NCAB	OUP
FIVE OR MORE PARTS					
Deus noster refugium	Hassler	SAATTB unacc	M/D		CMS/OUP
God is our hope and strength	Blow	SSAATTBB	M		Banks
Ubi caritas (g)	Berkeley	SSATB unacc	D		Chester
Ubi caritas (g)	Duruflé	SAATTBB unacc	M		Durand
When I needed a neighbour (g)	Carter arr Rose	SATB + SATB	E/M	MTH1	

ORGAN MUSIC

PRELUDES

Bach J.S.   **Gottes Sohn ist kommen** ('Ravenshaw') BWV 703 in Novello Vol.18, Bärenreiter Vol.3, Peters Vol.5 E*
Couperin F.   **Tierce en taille** No.XVIII from *Messe pour les Couvents* (Kalmus) E/M
Bédard D.   **Lamento** from *Suite* (Cheldar) E/M
Walther J.G.   **Lobe den Herren** in *80 Chorale Preludes* (Peters) E/M
Willan H.   **Prelude on 'Slane'** (Peters) E/M

POSTLUDES

Benoist F.   **Grand Chœur No.1** in *Benoist: Pièces pour Orgue* (Chanvrelin) E/M
Clucas H.   **Melita** in *A Coldridge Organ Book* (Animus) E*
Stainer J.   **Fughetta in C** No.2b of *Six Pieces for Organ* Set 1 (Butz, Novello)
Walther J.G.   **Prelude with Fugue in D minor** in *A Graded Anthology for Organ* Bk.5 (Cramer) M

THE SECOND SUNDAY BEFORE LENT YEAR B

HYMNS AND SONGS

	pos	rdg	AMNS	CAON	CFE	CH4	CH5	CP	H&P	HTC	LAU	MP	NEH	SG	SOF	TS
All creatures of our God and King	ga	o	105	6	15	147	24	250	329	13	694	7	263	23	645	614
All things bright and beautiful			116	25	27	137	25	251	330	283	685	23	264	294	14	14
Bless the Lord, creation sings		o								604						
Come, let us join our cheerful songs	ga		144	120			332	401	810	206		93	349	33	70	
Come, let us with our Lord arise	ga		449				142	575	375				254			
Come, ye faithful/Alleluia, raise the anthem	ga	o	145	131			84	409	813	205		103	351	25		
Fierce raged the tempest o'er the deep		n	225						144				635			
For the fruits of his/all creation			457	185	178	231	39	254	342	286	731	153	621	299	1234	685
Give to our God immortal praise			460	203			353	434	22	31		171		83		
God who spoke in the beginning		o	468													
God, whose farm is all creation			370	236		226	41	271	344	282	733			302		
Great is the darkness		n									835			264	742	136
Immortal, invisible, God only wise	ga	o	199	314	301	132	6	474	9	21	725	327	377	44	234	220
In the Lord I'll be ever thankful (Taizé)				929	308	772					944	865		656	817	
'Jesus is Lord' – the cry that echoes		o									1078				1387	1367
Let everything that has breath (Redman)											1001		124	880	854	
Let us with a gladsome mind/Let us gladly			204	392	362	93	30	498	27	23	707	415	397	312	333	
Light of the minds that know him		n		397			588	501		477			400	626		
Lord of beauty, thine the splendour			106	415			29	258					265			
Lord of the boundless curves of space			493				31	210	335				405			
Morning has broken	mo	o		450	490	212	58	260	635	265	671	467	237		393	
Name of all majesty		o		465			102	525		218		481		324	939	
New every morning is the love			2	467		214	7	6	636	270		480	238			
O Lord, my God (How great thou art)				511	568	154	32	262			721	506		56	425	396
The spacious firmament on high		o	103	665		148	35	265	339				267			
Think of a world without any flowers				900		155	50		572							
This is the day the Lord has made (Milligan)													618			
Thou/God, whose almighty word		o	180	684	738	112	324	267	29	506	887	699	466	597	557	
Touch the earth lightly						243										
With wonder, Lord, we see your works		o	531					269	353					316		
You shall cross the barren desert		n			830		22				964					

Some of the hymns and songs listed for Years A and C (pages 34 and 276) are also appropriate.

SONGS FOR CHILDREN

God, who made the earth CAON 325, CAP 10, CH5 4, JP 63
He made the earth SOF 756
When your Father made the world CAON 914, CAP 73, CH 232, CH4 239
Who put the colours in the rainbow? CAON 915, CAP 12, CH 235, CH4 143, JP 288, KS 386, SOF 1624

BIBLE READINGS

Psalm 65

Genesis 2.4b-25

Luke 8.22–35

SINGING THE PSALM

Psalm 65 CH4, CRP, CWP, H&P, NEP, NPCW, PAME, PFS

Schutte *Glory and praise to our God* CFE (OCP)#

ANTHEMS AND VOCAL MUSIC

Title	Composer	Voices	E/M/D	Book source	Single sheet publisher
UNISON/TWO PART/HIGH VOICES					
A Gaelic Blessing	Rutter	U/SSA	E	BC (U), EAC2 (SSA)	RSCM
All creatures of our God and King	Harris	SATB	M		RSCM
Badgers and hedgehogs	Carter	2 part	E	CFTW	
Calm me, Lord (g)	Rizza	U/SATB#	E	CAON, CAS, FOLO	
Morning has broken	Trad arr Nelson	SSA	E		Banks
Sing of the Lord's goodness	Sands	U + descant#	E	CFE, CG, CH4, CH5, LAU, SFL1, SG, SLG	OCP
THREE/FOUR PARTS					
A Gaelic Blessing	Rutter	SATB	E	NCAB	RSCM
Adam and his helpmate	Trad arr Gower	SATB	E		Encore
Be still, my soul	Sibelius	SATB	E		Breitkopf & Hartel
Be still, my soul	Whitlock	SATB	M		Banks
How can I keep from singing?	Lowry arr Weaver	SAB	E	SFL2	
Immortal, invisible	Mold	SATB	M		Banks
Look at the world	Rutter	SATB	E	JRA	OUP
O Lord of every constellation	Leddington Wright	SATB	E		Hinshaw
O Lord, our Governor	Barry Rose	SATB	M	MTP	
Praise to the Lord, the almighty	Archer	SATB	E/M		Mayhew
Praise to the Lord, the almighty	Stanford	SATB	M	ASA	
The heavens are telling (Creation)	Haydn	SATB	M		Novello
The Lord at first did Adam make	Trad arr Cleobury	SATB unacc	E		OUP
They that go down to the sea in ships	Sumsion	SATB	M		RSCM
FIVE OR MORE PARTS					
Ascendente in naviculum	De Wert	SSATB unacc	D		Mapa Mundi
Deep peace	Carter	SSATB + solo SA	M	ACA, WFC	OUP
O Lord, our Governor	Hawes	SATB + SATB	M		Novello

ORGAN MUSIC

PRELUDES

Archer M.   **Monkland** in *100 Hymn Preludes* (Mayhew) E

Buxtehude D.   **Durch Adams Fall** BuxWV 183 in *Complete Works* Vol.4 (Bärenreiter) E/M

Dubois T.   **Prelude** in *Douze Pièces* (Leduc, Bärenreiter) E/M

Edwards P.   **Siciliana** from *Northampton Miniatures* (Fagus) E*

Willan H.   **Prelude on 'Melcombe'** in *Ten Hymn Preludes* Set 1 (Peters) E

POSTLUDES

Pachelbel J.   **Durch Adams Fall** No.6 in *Selected Works* Vol.3 (Kalmus); also p.89 in *Organ Works* (Dover) M*

Kunkel L.   **Erfreue dich, Himmel** (Blues) in *Jazz Inspirations* (Bärenreiter) E/M

Rawsthorne N. **Alleluias** (Lasst uns erfreuen) in *Twelve Miniatures for Festive Occasions* (Mayhew; manuals-only edition also available) E

Walther J.G.   **Gott des Himmels und der Erden** in *80 Chorale Preludes* (Peters) M

THE SUNDAY NEXT BEFORE LENT YEAR B

HYMNS AND SONGS

	pos	rdg	AMNS	CAON	CFE	CH4	CH5	CP	H&P	HTC	LAU	MP	NEH	SG	SOF	TS
Be still, for the presence of the Lord	gr	n,g		67	72	189	325	383			720	50	*629*	7	40	47
Be thou my vision/Lord, be my vision		n,g	343	70	74/75	465	643	386	378	545	970	51	339	669	42	50
Bright the cloud and bright the glory		n,g				353										
Christ upon/Jesus, on the mountain peak	gr	n,g	441	357			205		155	115			177	322		
Christ whose glory fills the skies	mo	n,g	4	105		578	52	2	457	266	670	79	234	170	1200	
Come, living God, when least expected		n,g				609		403								
Come, praise the name of Jesus		n,g								538						
Dear Lord and Father of mankind		o	115	144	143	485	549	411	673	356	934	111	353	497	79	79
From glory to glory advancing	se	n,g	276	194				299					286			
Give me/us the wings of faith		o	324	204			463	216	815				225			
Here in this place (Gather us in)	ga	n,g			253	623					475			4		
Immortal, invisible, God only wise	ga		199	314	301	132	6	474	9	21	725	327	377	44	234	220
Jesus, these eyes have never seen	cm	n,g	245	365				491					389			
Jesus, you are changing me												389			311	
Lord Jesus, let these eyes of mine		o								549						
Lord, the light of your love is shining				419	388	448	195	513			770	445		614	362	335
Lord, you sometimes speak in wonders		o				606										
Meekness and majesty		n,g		448	487	356	228				751	465		395	390	353
My God, how wonderful thou art			102	457	497		7	523	51	369	727	468	410	202	395	896
Name of all majesty		n,g		465			102	525		218		481		324	939	
O Lord of hosts, all heaven possessing		n,g											423			
O raise your eyes on high and see		n,g	502		551			544				208				
O splendour of God's glory bright		n,g						7	461							
O vision blest of heavenly light		n,g											176			
Speak, Lord, in the stillness		o					624			253		608				
Stay, Master, stay upon this heavenly hill		n,g							158							
The brightness of God's glory		n,g								221						
Thee we adore, O hidden Saviour	of/cm		254	640			449	329					308			
'Tis/It's/How good, Lord, to be here	gr	n,g	318				248	156			209		178			
We declare your majesty		n,g										726			577	544
When Jesus led his chosen three		n,g								117						
With glorious clouds encompassed round		n,g						623	184							
Within our darkest night (Taizé)				950												
You, living Christ, our eyes behold			533					333					487			

SONGS FOR CHILDREN

Lord, the light of your love is shining CAON 419, CFE 388, CG 110, CH 148, CH4 448, CH5 195, CP 513, KS 237, LAU 770, MP 445, SG 614, SOF 362, TS 335
When I'm feeling down and sad CH4 568

BIBLE READINGS

Psalms 2 [and 99]
1 Kings 19.1–16
2 Peter 1.16–21
Mark 9.[2–8]9–13

SINGING THE PSALM

Psalm 2 CWP, NPCW, PAME
Psalm 99 CWP, NEP, NPCW, PAME

ANTHEMS AND VOCAL MUSIC

Title	Composer	Voices	E/M/D	Book source	Single sheet publisher
UNISON/TWO PART/HIGH VOICES					
All that is hidden	Farrell	U/SATB#	E	CFE, LAU, RITH, SFTL	OCP
Christ whose glory fills the skies	Shephard	S	M	HP	
Glory of the God of Israel	Fletcher	2 part	M		Mayhew
God of the living	Tamblyn	U/SATB#	E	SFTL	
I'm goin' up a yonder	Hawkins	2 part	E	RTF	
Like as the hart	Goode	SSS	M		Encore
THREE/FOUR PARTS					
Be thou my vision	Chilcott	SATB	E/M	BCA, NOEAB	OUP
Be thou my vision	Rutter	SATB	M		OUP
Christ whose glory fills the skies	Archer	SATB	M		Mayhew
Christ whose glory fills the skies	Darke	SATB	M	SBS1	RSCM
For lo, I raise up	Stanford	SATB	D		Cathedral
Glorious and powerful God	Stanford	SATB unacc	M	NCAB	S&B
God hath spoken	Gibbs	SATB	M		RSCM
I saw him standing	O'Regan	SATB + solo Bar	M		OUP
Immortal, invisible	Mold	SATB	E/M		Banks
Like as the hart	Howells	SATB	M	AC4	Novello
Lord of all hopefulness	Trad arr Rose	SATB + solo S	E/M	MTH2	
My eyes for beauty pine	Howells	SATB	E	NOEAB	OUP
On this mountain	Ridout	SAMen	M	AOAN1	
FIVE OR MORE PARTS					
Christ is the morning star	Carter	SSAATTBB	D		OUP
In splendente nube	Philips	SSATB unacc	M/D		Mapa Mundi
O nata lux	Tallis	SATTB unacc	M	NSAC2, OBTA, TA	OUP

ORGAN MUSIC

PRELUDES

Bach J.S.	**Aria** from **Pastorale** BWV 590 in Novello Vol.12, Bärenreiter Vol.7, Peters Vol.1 E*
Couperin F.	**Récit de chromhorne** No.3 from *Messe pour les Couvents* (Kalmus) E*
Howells H.	**Siciliano for a High Ceremony** (Novello) M
Willan H.	**Prelude on 'Carlisle'** in *36 Short Preludes and Postludes* Set 2 (Peters) E
Young G.	**Prelude on 'Slane'** in *Eight Organ Voluntaries* (Presser) E/M

POSTLUDES

Couperin F.	**Dialogue** No.5 from *Messe pour les Couvents* (Kalmus) E
Dubois T.	**Laus Deo** from *Messe de Mariage* (Kalmus) M
Vann S.	**Versets on a Choral Melody** in *New Music for Organ* Bk.2 (Mayhew) E/M
Whitlock P.	**Prelude on 'Darwall's 148th'** in *Whitlock: Complete Shorter Works* (OUP) M/D

THE FIRST SUNDAY OF LENT YEAR B

(For Ash Wednesday, see Year A, page 38.)

HYMNS AND SONGS

	pos	rdg	AMNS	CAON	CFE	CH4	CH5	CP	H&P	HTC	LAU	MP	NEH	SG	SOF	TS
A mighty fortress/A safe stronghold/God is our fortress		s	114		3	454	668	366	661	523	958	2		637		
Ah, holy Jesu, how hast thou offended		g		5	13	381	215	100	164	123	232		62	378		
All hail the power of Jesus' name		o,n	140	16	19	457	250	163	252	587	323	13	332	24	9	7
And can it be that I should gain		o,n		32	43	396	218	376	216	588	790	33	*627*	168	21	21
Be thou my guardian/O Lord, our guardian/Lord, be my guardian		s	217	69			635	385		374			64	512		
Be thou my vision/Lord, be my vision			343	70	74/75	465	643	386	378	545	970	51	339	669	42	50
Christian, dost thou see them		s	55										65			
Father, hear the prayer we offer		s	113	161	158	255	645	416	436	360	933	132	357	237	1229	
Father of heaven, whose love profound	ga	s	97	165	163	483	319	421	519	359		827	358	144		1201
Forty days and forty nights		s	56	190	185	337	207	95	130	103	206	160	67	381		
He lives in us, the Christ of God		s								457				173		
I am a new creation		n		298	270							254			197	191
I am trusting thee, Lord Jesus		n		300						433		258			202	
Jesu, grant me this, I pray		s	136	342			212	110				382				
Jesu, lover of my soul		s	123	343	319	490	553	96	528	438	797	372	383	201	297	838
Lead us, heavenly Father, lead us		s	224	379	351		652	496	68	595	315	400	393	640	321	311
Lord, as I wake I turn to you	mo	s	485				56		634	267	672		236	561		
Lord Jesus, think on me		s	129	412	384	491/2	554	97	533	316	204		70			
Miserere nobis/Holy Lord, have mercy (Taizé)		s								597						
Now is the healing time decreed		s											59			
O Jesus, I have promised	se	o	235	503	536	644	593	538	704	531	875	501	420	676	418	391
O lift us up, strong Son of God		o								427						
O love, how deep, how broad, how high		g	119	516		354	214	118	229				425			
Praise to the holiest in the height		o,n	117	572	606	378	108	557	231	140	788	563	439	58	469	
Pray that Jerusalem may have		g				82	506	560	510				441			
Restore, O Lord, the honour		o		582		469							579	274	483	439
Safe in the shadow of the Lord		s			626	55	595			445	953	583		516	991	
Through the night of doubt and sorrow	se	s	211	687			661	605	441	466		948	468	544		
Walking in a garden		o	518	705			290						123			
What a friend we have in Jesus		s		727		547	627		559	373		746		646	593	566
With joy we meditate the grace		s	530					624	235			774				

SONGS FOR CHILDREN

Grace is when God gives us CH4 163, JP 355, KS 92

I am a new creation CAON 298, CFE 270, KS 115, MP 254, SOF 197, TS 191

BIBLE READINGS

Psalm 119.17–32
Genesis 2.15–17; 3.1–7
Romans 5.12–19 *or* Luke 13.31–35

SINGING THE PSALM

Psalm 119.17–32 CWP, NPCW
Dean *You have laid down your precepts* HG#

ANTHEMS AND VOCAL MUSIC

Title	Composer	Voices	E/M/D	Book source	Single sheet publisher
UNISON/TWO PART/HIGH VOICES					
Settings of Kyrie eleison/Lord, have mercy	Various	U/SATB	E	C, MCW1, LAU, RE	
Carol of the Atonement	Trad	U	E	TEA	
Dear Lord and Father of mankind	Parnell	SS	E/M		Encore
Go before us	Farrell	U + descant#	E	GBU	OCP
On eagle's wings	Joncas	U#	E	CFE, LAU	OCP
You are the centre	Rizza	U/SATB#	E	FOL, CAON, CAS	Mayhew
THREE/FOUR PARTS					
Adam and his helpmate	Trad arr Gower	SATB	E		Encore
Bow down thine ear, O Lord	Purcell	SATB	M		OUP
Forty days and forty nights	Oxley	SATB	E/M	MTH2	
Have mercy upon me, O God	Tomkins	SAB	E		Banks
Hear my prayer	Mendelssohn	SATB	M		RSCM
Lord, who hast formed me	Godfrey	SATB	E/M	SBS2	
Morning Prayers (Three Prayers of Dietrich Bonhoeffer)	P.Moore	SATB + solo A unacc	M/D		B&H
O Lord, my God	S.S.Wesley	SATB unacc	E	SBS1	RSCM
Prayers in Time of Distress (Three Prayers of Dietrich Bonhoeffer)	P.Moore	SATB unacc	M/D		B&H
Purge me, O Lord	Tallis	SATB unacc	E/M	SBS1, TA	OUP, RSCM
The Lord at first did Adam make	Trad arr Cleobury	SATB unacc	E		OUP
The will of God	Warren	SAMen	E	AOAN1	
Wings of the morning	Rutter	SATB	M		OUP
FIVE OR MORE PARTS					
Civitas sancti tui (g)	Byrd	SATBB unacc	M		Chester
Let my complaint	Greene	SSATB	M		CMS/OUP
Pray that Jerusalem (g)	Chilcott	SATB unacc	E/M		OUP
Pray that Jerusalem (g)	Stanford	SATB	E	ASA	RSCM
Turn thee unto me, O Lord	Boyce	SSATB	M		CMS/OUP

Some of the music listed for Year A (page 41) and for Ash Wednesday (page 39) is also suitable.

ORGAN MUSIC

PRELUDES

Fletcher A.   **Mannheim** in *100 Hymn Preludes* and in *Hymn Preludes for the Church Year* Bk.2 (both Mayhew) E

Joubert J.   **Abridge** in *Six Short Preludes on English Hymn Tunes* Op.125 (Novello) E/M*

Vaughan Williams R.   **Prelude on Song 13** (OUP) E/M

Willan H.   **Southwell** in *36 Short Preludes and Postludes* Set 3 (Peters) E

Wood C.   **Prelude on 'York Tune'** No.5 of *Sixteen Preludes on Melodies from the English and Scottish Psalters* Vol.1 (FitzSimons) M

POSTLUDES

Bach J.S.   **Machs mit mir, Gott** BWV 957 in *Neumeister Chorale Preludes* (Bärenreiter) E/M*

Nixon J.   **Procession on 'Salzburg'** in *Easter Glory* (Mayhew) M

Cameron J.G.   **Windsor** in *Six Preludes on Hymn Tunes* (Novello) E/M

Suitable before or after: Movements from Coates R. **Partita on 'Converse'** in *Festmusikk 11* (Cantando) E/M

Music listed for Ash Wednesday is also suitable (pages 39 and 367).

HYMNS AND SONGS

	pos	rdg	AMNS	CAON	CFE	CH4	CH5	CP	H&P	HTC	LAU	MP	NEH	SG	SOF	TS
Author of faith, eternal Word		n						381	662							
Blessèd assurance		o		74	84	561	562	390	668			59			44	52
Brother, sister, let me serve you/Will you let me be your servant		n		88	813	694	517	393			924			619	54	
Christ is made the sure foundation/Blessèd city		n	332ii	97	109	200	326	207/208	485	559	456	73	205	572	1199	654
Colours of day dawn into the mind		n		108	118						764	1039			64	69
Father, hear the prayer we offer		s	113	161	158	255	645	416	436	360	933	132	357	237	1229	
Glorious things of thee are spoken		n	172	205	195	738	646	435	817	494	827	173	362	35	127	691
God who spoke in the beginning		o	468													
Guide me, O thou great Jehovah/Redeemer		n	214	252	233	167	647	455	437	528	960	201	368	638	148	708
How beauteous/gracious are their feet		n	301					220	449							
Jerusalem, my happy home/thou city blest		n	187	339				481		569			228			
Jerusalem the golden		n	184	340	317	747	670	482		573	991		381			
Laudate omnes gentes/Sing praises, all you peoples (Taizé)		ps									478				1515	
Lord Jesus, think on me		s	129	412	384	491/2	554	97	533	316	204		70			
My Jesus, my Saviour		n		461		531						1003		129	935	367
My soul, there is a country		n	191	464			261						412			
O God of Bethel/Jacob		n	216	491		268	657	536	442	35		907	416	241		
O/Our God, our help in ages past		n	99	494	528	161	537	537	358	37	955	498	417	542	415	905
O happy band of pilgrims		n	208	497						530			418			
O what their joy		n	186	550			225						432			
One more step along the world I go	se	n		525		530	658	548	746						1483	
Thanks/Praise to God whose word was spoken		n	423			605	387	584	483	255			438	229		
The God of Abraham praise	o,n,g		331	642		162	323	586	452	9	712	645	148	66	530	975
There is a land of pure delight		n	190				681	597	822	575			460			
There's a place (Because of you)		n										1011		457	1041	498
There's a wideness in God's mercy/Souls of men/Restless souls		s	251	662		187	9	598	230	443	810	607/683	461/700	188		
Through all the changing scenes of life			209	686	740		372	604	73	46		702	467	654	1566	1561
Through the night of doubt and sorrow		n	211	687			661	605	441	466		948	468	544		
Walk with me, oh my Lord		o			765						966					
Who would true valour see/He who would valiant be		s	212	281	248	535	662	621	688	590	862	224	372	639	174	

SONGS FOR CHILDREN

Forward in faith CAON 800

One more step along the world I go CAON 525, CAP 47, CH 166, CH4 530, CH5 658, CP 548, H&P 746, JP 188, KS 273, SOF 1483

BIBLE READINGS

Psalm 135*
Genesis 12.1–9
Hebrews 11.1–3,8–16
John 8.51–59

SINGING THE PSALM

Psalm 135* CWP, NPCW

ANTHEMS AND VOCAL MUSIC

Title	Composer	Voices	E/M/D	Book source	Single sheet publisher
UNISON/TWO PART/HIGH VOICES					
Centre of my life	Inwood	U/SATB#	E	CFE, CSF, LAU, SG	OCP
Christ whose glory fills the skies	Knight	S	M		RSCM
Give us the wings of faith	Blatchly	SS	M	HP	
God of Abraham	Farrell	U/SATB + cantor#	E	GBAN	OCP
Loving God	Aston	2 part	E	BC	
O rest in the Lord (Elijah)	Mendelssohn	U	E		Novello
We have hope	Perera	U#	E	VE	
We walk by faith	Haugen	U#	E	CFE, LAU	GIA
While faith is with me	Hubbard	U	E	SFJ	Banks
You are the centre	Rizza	U/SATB#	E	CAS, FOL	Mayhew
THREE/FOUR PARTS					
Christ is our cornerstone	Thorne	SATB	E/M	NOEAB	
Christ is our cornerstone	Ogden	SATB	E	SBS2	
Christ whose glory fills the skies	Darke	SATB	M	SBS1	RSCM
Firmly I believe and truly	Shephard	SAMen	E	SFL2	
Give me the wings of faith	Leighton	SATB	D		Novello
Give us the wings of faith	Bullock	SATB	M	AC4, FSB10	OUP
Grow in grace	Archer	SATB	E/M	SBS1	RSCM
If you believe and I believe	Trad Zimbabwean	SATB unacc	E	C, CG, CH4, IECS, RTF, SBTL	
Lord, give me faith	Robson	SATB	E		RSCM
My soul, there is a country	Parry	SATB unacc	D	SC	RSCM
O Lord, increase our faith	Loosemore	SATB (unacc)	E	NCAB, SBS1	RSCM
Thou, O Jehovah, abideth forever	Copland	SATB unacc	M/D		B&H
Though you do not now see Christ	Ferguson	SATB unacc	M		Encore
Walking by faith	Marsh	SAB	E	AOAN1	

ORGAN MUSIC

PRELUDES

Cameron J.G. **Martyrdom** in *Six Preludes on Hymn Tunes* (Novello) E/M

Homilius G.A. **Straf mich nicht in deinem Zorn** in *Chorale Preludes* (Breitkopf) E/M

Near G. **Jam, Christe, sol justitiae** in *Chantworks* Set 2 (Aureole) E/M

Pachelbel J. **Allein zu dir, Herr Jesu Christ** in *Choralvorspiele alter Meister* (Peters) and *Organ Funeral Album* (Bärenreiter) E/M

Willan H. **Prelude on 'Windsor'** in *Ten Hymn Preludes* Set 3 (Peters) E

POSTLUDES

Bach J.S. **Allein zu dir, Herr Jesu Christ** BWV 1100 in *Neumeister Chorale Preludes* (Bärenreiter) E/M*

Krebs J.L. **Warum betrübst du dich, mein Herz** in *Complete Works* Vol.3 (Breitkopf) E/M

Thalben-Ball G. **Monk's Gate** No. 59 of *113 Variations on Hymn Tunes* (Novello) E

Thomas M. **Ramoth** in *Six Preludes on Welsh Hymn Tunes* (Mansel Thomas Trust) M

THE THIRD SUNDAY OF LENT YEAR B

HYMNS AND SONGS

	pos	rdg	AMNS	CAON	CFE	CH4	CH5	CP	H&P	HTC	LAU	MP	NEH	SG	SOF	TS
And can it be that I should gain		n		32	43	396	218	376	216	588	790	33	*627*	168	21	21
Be thou my guardian/O Lord, our guardian/Lord, be my guardian		s	217	69			635	385		374			64	512		
Beneath the cross of Jesus		n		65			561	105	165			55		39	45	
Can we/man by searching find out God		n	438				11	201	76	426			496			
Fight the good fight		n	220	169	171	517	566	423	710	526	860	143	359	635	107	
From heaven you came, helpless babe		n		195	187	374	219	432			749	162		632	120	114
God forgave my sin in Jesus' name		s		212	209		480			S 12	849	181			129	123
God of freedom, God of justice		o		224		263		447								
Here, O my Lord, I see thee face to face	cm	n	274	279			418	304	608	406		230		468		
How sweet the name of Jesus sounds		s	122	297		461	92	467	257	211		251	374	42	194/782	190/1273
In Christ shall all be made alive		n								459				533		
In heavenly love abiding		s		323		551		478	678	458		331	*638*		238	782
In the cross of Christ I glory		n		327		397	225	480	167			338	379			
Jesu, the very thought of thee/O Jesu, King most wonderful		n	120	368	321	560	101	485	265	478	798	386	385	534	308	
Jesu, thou joy of loving hearts		n	255	369		662	425	486	258	413		383	292	471		839
Jesu, thy/Jesus, your blood and righteousness		n					671	111	225	460				177		841
Light of the minds that know him	se	n		397			588	501		477			400	626		
Lord, for the years	se	n		409		159	81	81		328	942	428	*619*	602	892	327
My hope is built on nothing less		n								462		473		537		365
O happy band of pilgrims		n	208	497						530			418			
The God of Abraham praise		o	331	642		162	323	586	452	9	712	645	148	66	530	975
Thou hidden source of calm repose		n						603	275							
To God be the glory!		n		695	745	512	373	609	463	584	719	708		71	559	526
Wait for the Lord (Taizé)				949	762	276					88				1575	
We rest on thee/We trust in you		s								446		735		510	587	1043
We sing the praise of him who died		n	138	723		405	248	125	182	146		738		94	390	
When I survey the wondrous cross		n	67	738	801	392	247	127	180	147	756	755/1126	95	680	596	572

SONGS FOR CHILDREN

If you believe and I believe C 70, CG 62, CH4 771, IECS, RTF, SBTL
When I'm feeling sad CH4 569
When Israel was in Egypt's land CFE 803, CH5 679, JP 276

BIBLE READINGS

Psalms 11 and 12
Exodus 5.1 - 6.1
Philippians 3.4b–14 *or* Matthew 10.16–22

SINGING THE PSALM

Psalm 11 CWP, NPCW
Psalm 12 CWP, NPCW

ANTHEMS AND VOCAL MUSIC

Title	Composer	Voices	E/M/D	Book source	Single sheet publisher
UNISON/TWO PART/HIGH VOICES					
Christ is the world's true light	Stanton	U + descant	E	OBFA, OEAB	Banks
Freedom is coming	Trad arr Perona-Wright	SSAA unacc	E	RTF	
Give us the wings of faith	Blatchly	SS	M	HP	
God has chosen me (g)	Farrell arr Weaver	2 part	E	SFL1	
Jesu, by thy wounded feet	B.Ferguson	S	E		Encore
Let my people go	Trad arr Weaver	2 part	E	RTF	
Long since in Egypt's plenteous land	Parry	S + solo SS	E	NSAC1	
On another's sorrow	B.Ferguson	S	M		Encore
Send us as your blessing, Lord (g)	Walker	U/SSATB#	E/M	CFE, HIG	OCP
Sent by the Lord am I (g)	Trad arr Weaver	2 part	E	BC	
THREE/FOUR PARTS					
Firmly I believe and truly	Shephard	SAMen	E	SFL2	
Freedom is coming	Trad arr Ogden	SAB	E	SFL2	
Give me the wings of faith	Leighton	SATB	D		Novello
Give us the wings of faith	Bullock	SATB	M	AC4, FSB10	OUP
Go forth into the world in peace (g)	Rutter	SATB	M	JRA	OUP
Hamba nath'inkululi wethu (Go with us, Lord)	Trad arr Weaver	SAB	E	SFL2	
O Lord, increase our faith	Loosemore	SATB (unacc)	E	SBS1, NCAB	RSCM
Prayer before the Crucifix	P.Moore	SATB	E/M		Banks
Solus ad victimam	Leighton	SATB	M	NCAB, AC1, SC	Banks
Take up your cross (g)	Corp	SATB	E	SBS1, WOTC	RSCM
The Summons (g)	Bell arr Whitbourn	SATB	E	AWS	
To be a pilgrim	Burt	SAMen	E/M	OBFA	RSCM
FIVE OR MORE PARTS					
Domine tu jurasti	Byrd	SATBB + B solo unacc	M		Procter
Go down, Moses (5 Spirituals from 'A Child of our Time')	Trad arr Tippett	SSAATTBB unacc	M		Schott

ORGAN MUSIC

PRELUDES

Anon.	**Ach Gott, vom Himmel** in *Choralvorspiele alter Meister* (Peters) E/M
Smart H.	**Andante in F** in *50 Victorian Pieces* (Mayhew) M
Spedding A.	**Elegy** ('St Peter') in *Recuerdos* (IAO) E
Telemann G.P.	**Fugue** No.7 in *The Progressive Organist* Bk.4 (Novello) E/M
Walther J.G.	**Ach Gott, vom Himmel sich darein** in *Orgelchoräle* (Bärenreiter) E*

POSTLUDES

Beauvarlet-Charpentier J.J.	**Grand Choeur in E minor** in *Pièces pour Orgue* (Chanvrelin) E*
Burney C.	**Fugue in F minor** in *Old English Organ Music for Manuals* Bk.1 (OUP) E/M*
Françaix J.	**Entrée** No.1 of *Messe de Mariage* (Schott) E/M
Richter E.F.	**Prelude and Fugue in C minor** Op.21/1 in *Leipziger Orgelmusik des 19 C* (Breitkopf) M

THE FOURTH SUNDAY OF LENT YEAR B

HYMNS AND SONGS

	pos	rdg	AMNS	CAON	CFE	CH4	CH5	CP	H&P	HTC	LAU	MP	NEH	SG	SOF	TS
Amazing grace – how sweet the sound		s		29	40	555	642	375	215	28	846	31	626	26	19	18
Bread of heaven, on thee we feed		n	271	82				284		398			276	464		
Brother, sister, let me serve you/ Will you let me be your servant		g		88	813	694	517	393			924			619	54	
Come down, O love divine		n	156	114	125	489	294	175	281	231	303	89	137	663	1202	71
From heaven you came, helpless babe		g		195	187	374	219	432			749	162		632	120	114
How deep the Father's love		s				549	224					988		193	780	185
How good a thing it is		g							497				585			
I am a new creation		n		298	270							254			197	191
In heavenly love abiding		n		323		551		478	678	458		331	638		238	782
Jesu, lover of my soul		s	123	343	319	490	553	96	528	438	797	372	383	201	297	838
Jesu, my Lord, my God, my all	cm	n			329		583	483		476			384			
Lord God, you love us (Taizé)		n									782					
Lord of the cross of shame		n								548		443		558		
My God, I love thee; not because		n	65	458	498		229	524	171	479			73			
Nada te turbe/Nothing can trouble (Taizé)				937							947			659		
Not what these hands/I bless the Christ of God		n								435		487		175		
Now is the healing time decreed		s											59			
O love divine, how sweet thou art		g	124				621	541					424			
O love, how deep, how broad, how high	of	s	119	516		354	214	118	229				425			
Praise to the holiest in the height		s	117	572	606	378	388	557	231	140	788	563	439	58	469	
Rock of ages (Kendrick)		s													1507	951
Rock of ages, cleft for me		s	135	584	624	554	557	565	273	593		582	445	150	488	950
Soften my heart, Lord		g										606			505	459
There is a line of women (OITB p.60)		g														
Through all the changing scenes of life		n	209	686	740		372	604	73	46		702	467	654	1566	1561
We cannot measure how you heal		n		712	772	718	514	348			433		490			

SONGS FOR CHILDREN

I am a new creation CAON 298, CFE 270, KS 115, MP 254, SOF 197, TS 191
The voice from the bush CAON 896, CH 199
When Israel was in Egypt's land CFE 803, CH5 679, JP 276

BIBLE READINGS

Psalms 13 and 14
Exodus 6.2–13
Romans 5.1–11
John 12.1–8
[Principal Service readings may be used if
Mothering Sunday provisions displace them
at the Principal Service itself.]

SINGING THE PSALM

Psalm 13 CH4, CWP, NPCW, PAME
 Haugen *How long, O God* (GIA)#
Psalm 14 CWP, NPCW

ANTHEMS AND VOCAL MUSIC

Title	Composer	Voices	E/M/D	Book source	Single sheet publisher
UNISON/TWO PART/HIGH VOICES					
Christ is the world's true light	Stanton	U + descant	E	OBFA, OEAB	Banks
Come down, O love divine	Hand	SSA	M	NAB1	
Drop, drop slow tears (g)	Gibbons	SSA	E	AC3	
Freedom is coming	Trad arr Perona-Wright	SSAA unacc	E	RTF	
Let my people go	Trad arr Weaver	2 part	E	RTF	
Long since in Egypt's plenteous land	Parry	S + solo SS	E	NSAC1	
The Freedom Train	Trad	U	E	SFL2	
THREE/FOUR PARTS					
A Litany (Drop, drop slow tears) (g)	Walton	SATB unacc	D	AC4	OUP
Come down, O love divine	Harris	SATB	E/M	FSB9, MTH2, NCAB	Novello
Come down, O love divine	Tadman-Robins	SAMen	E	OBFA	
Drop, drop slow tears (g)	Andrew	SAMen/3part Men	E	OBFA	
Drop, drop slow tears (g)	Gibbons	SATB	E	NOEAB, MEA (SAB)	
Drop, drop slow tears (g)	Leighton	SATB	D		Novello
Freedom is coming	Trad arr Ogden	SAB	E	SFL2	
Hamba nath'inkululi wethu (Go with us, Lord)	Trad arr Weaver	SAB	E	SFL2	
Holy Spirit, truth divine	Carter	SATB	E	ETAS, NOEAB	OUP
The Lord bless you and keep you	Rutter	SATB	E	JRA, EAC1, WFC, OBFA (SAMen)	OUP
FIVE OR MORE PARTS					
Come down, O love divine	Rutter	SSAATTBB unacc	D		OUP
Drop, drop slow tears (g)	Gibbons	SAATB unacc	E	NCAB	
Go down, Moses (5 Spirituals from 'A Child of our Time')	Trad arr Tippett	SSAATTBB unacc	M		Schott
Libera plebem	Joubert	SAATBB unacc	D		Novello

Some of the anthems listed for Year A (page 47) are also suitable.

ORGAN MUSIC

PRELUDES

Bach J.S.	**Ach Gott und Herr** BWV 714 in Novello Vol.18, Bärenreiter Vol.3, Peters Vol.9 E
Buxtehude D.	**Ich ruf zu dir** BuxWV 196 in *Complete Works* Vol.4 (Bärenreiter) M
Ley H.G.	**Prelude on 'Down Ampney'** (OUP) E
Walther J.G.	**Mach's mit mir, Gott** in *A Graded Anthology for Organ* Bk.3 (Cramer) E*
Watson R.	**Jesu, lover of my soul** in *At Your Service* (Fagus) E

POSTLUDES

Bestel E.	**Allein zu dir, Herr Jesu Christ** in *The Progressive Organist* Bk.5 (Novello) E/M*
Callahan C.	**Postlude on Two Spirituals** ('Go down, Moses', 'I want to be ready') from *Suite on Afro-American Hymn Tunes* (Concordia) E/M
Pachelbel J.	**Ich ruf zu dir** No.12 in *Orgelwerke* Vol.2 (Peters) E/M
Piutti C.	**Nicht so traurig, nicht so sehr** in *Choralvorspiele* Op.34 Vol.2 (Bärenreiter) E/M

THE FIFTH SUNDAY OF LENT YEAR B
(Passiontide begins)

HYMNS AND SONGS

	pos	rdg	AMNS	CAON	CFE	CH4	CH5	CP	H&P	HTC	LAU	MP	NEH	SG	SOF	TS
All hail the power of Jesus' name		n	140	16	19	457	250	163	252	587	323	13	332	24	9	7
An upper room did our Lord prepare	ga/of	g	434	38	42		399	130	594		248					
And can it be that I should gain		n		32	43	396	218	376	216	588	790	33	627	168	21	21
And now, O Father, mindful of the love	of/ cm	s	260	34			400	279	593	392			273	459		
As the bridegroom to his chosen		o	340						30							
Bless the Lord, my soul (Taizé)		n		923	81		1				813			105	676	56
Come, wounded healer		s		130											1210	1176
Glorious things of thee are spoken		o	172	205	195	738	646	435	817	494	827	173	362	35	127	691
Glory be to Jesus		n	66	206	197		220	108		126	750		83	146		
Here is love, vast as the ocean		s					222					987		174	168	164
How deep the Father's love		s				549	224					988		193	780	185
How sweet the name of Jesus sounds		o	122	297		461	92	467	257	211		251	374	42	194/ 782	190/ 1273
I heard the voice of Jesus say		o	247	310		540	576	469	136		795	275	376		215	206
I hunger and I thirst		o						306	730	409			470			
I know a place (At the cross)		s										851			802	209
In the cross of Christ I glory		s		327		397	225	480	167			338	379			
It is a thing most wonderful		s	70	333			226	109	224	131		346	84	557	252	801
Jesus Christ (Once again)		s										995		394	865	274
Lift high the cross, the love of Christ proclaim		s	72	394	363		484	499	170	508	389	417	641	601	1418	
Morning glory, starlit sky/Open are the gifts		s	496			390		259					608			
My song is love unknown		s	63	463	503	399	231	112	173	136	752	478	86	384	400	897
Praise to the holiest in the height		s	117	572	606	378	108	557	231	140	788	563	439	58	469	
The royal banners forward go		s	58	663	712		243	122	179		252		79			
We sing the praise of him who died		s	138	723		405	248	125	182	146		738	94	390		
When I survey the wondrous cross		s	67	738	801	392	247	127	180	147	756	755/ 1126	95	680	596	572

SONGS FOR CHILDREN

Grace is when God gives us CH4 163, JP 355, KS 92
I'm special JP 106, KS 162, MP 325, SOF 236, TS 222
When Israel was in Egypt's land CFE 803, CH5 679, JP 276

BIBLE READINGS

Psalm 34*
Exodus 7.8–24
Romans 5.12–21
Luke 22.1–13

SINGING THE PSALM

Psalm 34* C, CRP, CWP, FGP, H&P, LAU, MCW1, NPCW, PAME
   Bell *I will always bless the Lord* C, CH4, IAMB, OITB
   Dean *Taste and see* CFE, WYP#
   Ogden *Taste and see* (WLP)
   Rizza *I will bless the Lord* LIOD#
   Schutte *Ever on my lips* C (OCP)#
   Walker *Taste and see* CSF (OCP)#

ANTHEMS AND VOCAL MUSIC

Title	Composer	Voices	E/M/D	Book source	Single sheet publisher
UNISON/TWO PART/HIGH VOICES					
Dear Lord and Father of mankind	Parnell	SS	E/M		Encore
Let my people go	Trad arr Weaver	2 part	E	RTF	
Long since in Egypt's plenteous land	Parry	S + solo SS	E	NSAC1	
You are the centre	Rizza	U/SATB#	E	FOL, CAON, CAS	Mayhew
THREE/FOUR PARTS					
Almighty and everlasting God	Gibbons	SATB unacc	M	FAB1, NCAB, NSAC1, OBTA	OUP
Asperges me	Victoria	SATB unacc	E/M		Joed
Bread of the world in mercy broken	Baldwin	SAMen	E	SBS2	
Come down, O love divine	Harris	SATB	E/M	FSB9, MTH2, NCAB	Novello
Come down, O love divine	Tadman-Robins	SAMen	E	OBFA	
Hamba nath'inkululi wethu (Go with us, Lord)	Trad arr Weaver	SAB	E	SFL2	
Hide not thou thy face	Hilton/Farrant	SATB unacc	E/M	BC, FAB1, NCAB, NSAC2, OBFA (SAMen), OBTA	RSCM, OUP
How lovely are the messengers	Mendelssohn	SATB	M	AFC	Banks
Inter vestibulum et altare	Morales	SATB unacc	M		Faber
Lord, for thy tender mercy's sake	Hilton	SATB unacc	E	AWTE, FAB1, NCAB, NOEAB, OBTA	OUP
Lord, who hast formed me	Godfrey	SATB	E/M	SBS2	
Our lives are laid open before you	March	SATB unacc	E/M	SBS2	
Purge me, O Lord	Tallis	SATB unacc	E/M	SBS1, TA	RSCM
Turn thy face from my sins	Attwood	SATB	E/M	BC, FAB1, NCAB, TEA	RSCM
View me, Lord	Lloyd	SATB unacc	E	NNAB, NSAC1	Novello
Wash me throughly	S.S.Wesley	SATB + solo S	M	AWTE, NCAB, SC	Novello
FIVE OR MORE PARTS					
Go down, Moses (5 Spirituals from 'A Child of our Time')	Trad arr Tippett	SSAATTBB unacc	M		Schott
Let my complaint	Greene	SSATB	M		CMS/OUP
O Lord God of hosts	Purcell	SSAATTBB + SSATB soli	M		Novello
Remember, remember not, Lord	Purcell	SSATB unacc	M	APA	Faber
Turn thee unto me, O Lord	Boyce	SSATB	M		CMS/OUP

ORGAN MUSIC

PRELUDES

Byrd W.   **Clarifica me, Pater** 3 settings in *Early Organ Music* Vol.1 (Faber) E/M*
Demessieux J. **Berceuse 'Domine Jesu'** from *12 Chorale Preludes on Gregorian Chant Themes* (Summy-Birchard) E
Howells H.   **Psalm-Prelude** Set 1 No.1 (Novello) M
Parry C.H.H.   **Chorale Prelude 'St Mary'** in *Seven Chorale Preludes* Set 2 (Novello); also in *Preludes and Postludes* (Mayhew) E/M
Walther J.G.   **O Welt, ich muß dich lassen** in *80 Chorale Preludes* (Peters) E

POSTLUDES

Bach W.F.   **Wir danken dir, Herr Jesu Christ** in *W.F.Bach Organ Works* Bk.2 (Peters) and *Choralvorspiele alter Meister* (Peters) E/M
Buxtehude D.   **Ach Herr, mich armen Sünder** BuxWV 178 in *Complete Works* Vol.4 (Bärenreiter) E/M
Krebs J.L.   **Ach Herr, mich armen Sünder** in *Complete Works* Vol.3 (Breitkopf) M
Parry C.H.H.   **Chorale Prelude 'Rockingham'** in *Seven Chorale Preludes* Set 1 (Novello); also in *Preludes and Postludes* (Mayhew) M

PALM SUNDAY YEAR B

(Readings for the Liturgy of Palms are found only in the Principal Service Lectionary.)

HYMNS AND SONGS

	pos	rdg	AMNS	CAON	CFE	CH4	CH5	CP	H&P	HTC	LAU	MP	NEH	SG	SOF	TS
Ah, holy Jesu, how hast thou offended		n		5	13	381	215	100	164	123			62	378		
All praise to thee, for thou, O King divine		n	337	22			684	372	253	204			335			
And now, O Father, mindful of the love	of/cm	n	260	34			400	279	593	392			273	459		
Broken for me, broken for you	cm	n		87			404	287		S 6		66		485	53	58
From heaven you came, helpless babe		n		195	187	374	219	432			749	162		632	120	114
Hail, thou once despisèd Jesus		n		258			268	168	222	175		203			149	
He gave his life in selfless love		n					417			405		214	467			
Here is love, vast as the ocean		n					222					987		174	168	164
How deep the Father's love		n				549	224					988		193	780	185
I am the vine and you the branches (LFB p.52)		o														
I cannot tell why he, whom angels worship		s		303				54	238	194		266		437	205	199
I know a place (At the cross)		n										851			802	209
I will sing the wondrous story		s		337					223	212		315		43	278	821
In the cross of Christ I glory		n		327		397	225	480	167			338	379			
It is a thing most wonderful		n	70	333			226	109	224	131		346	84	557	252	801
Jesus Christ (Once again)		n										995		394	865	274
Jesus, remember me (Taizé)		s		931		775	617				253			875		294
Meekness and majesty		n		448	487	356	228				751	465		395	390	353
Morning glory, starlit sky/Open are the gifts			496			390		259					608			
My Lord, what love is this		n		462	500		230					476		194	398	370
My Lord, you wore no royal crown		s								118			628			
My song is love unknown		n	63	463	503	399	231	112	173	136	752	478	86	384	400	897
No scenes of stately majesty		n											427	1463	375
O Lord, hear my prayer (Taizé)		s		938	542		620				929	908		246	423	394
O love divine, how sweet thou art			124				621	541				424				
O love, how deep, how broad, how high		s	119	516		354	214	118	229			425				
O sacred head		n	68	535	552	382	235	119/120	176	139	237	520	90	385	446	928
Praise to the holiest in the height		n	117	572	606	378	108	557	231	140	788	563	439	58	469	
Thou didst leave thy throne		s	250	683			114	601	154			697	465		555	1015
We sing the praise of him who died		n	138	723		405	248	125	182	146		738	94	390		
When I survey the wondrous cross		n	67	738	801	392	247	127	180	147	756	755/1126	95	680	596	572
Who is this, so weak and helpless		n		748									474			
You are the vine (Daniels)		o										792			629	
You are the vine (O'Hara)		o			824											

SONGS FOR CHILDREN

Each of us is a living stone CAON 793, CH 41

BIBLE READINGS

Psalm 69.1–20
Isaiah 5.1–7
Mark 12.1–12

SINGING THE PSALM

Psalm 69.1–20 CRP, CWP, H&P, NPCW, PAME

ANTHEMS AND VOCAL MUSIC

Title	Composer	Voices	E/M/D	Book source	Single sheet publisher
UNISON/TWO PART/HIGH VOICES					
Christ has no body now but yours	Ogden	U + descant	E	CFAP, LOL	RSCM
Ex ore innocentium	Ireland	SS	M/D	NSAC2	B&H
I see his blood upon the rose	Ogden	U	M	SFL2	
My song is love unknown	Archer	SS	M	EAC2	RSCM
When I survey the wondrous cross	R.Jones	2 part#	E	MHWE	
THREE/FOUR PARTS					
Christus factus est	Anerio	SATB unacc	M	ESM, CM1, AWTE	
Christus factus est	Bruckner	SATB unacc	M/D	ESM	RSCM
Christus factus est	Ridout	SATB unacc	E		Encore
God so loved the world	Bullard	SAMen	E	OBFA	
It is a thing most wonderful	P.Moore	SATB	M	SC, WOTC	RSCM
Jesu, grant me this I pray	Gibbons	SATB	E/M	AWTE	
O Saviour of the world	Goss	SATB	M	FAB1, NCAB, NOEAB	
O Saviour of the world	Somervell	SATB	E	NCAB	
Solus ad victimam	Leighton	SATB	M	AC1, NCAB, SC	Banks
Surely thou hast tasted that the Lord is good	Bernard Rose	SATB unacc	M/D	EAC1	
The Lamentation	Bairstow	SATB	M	AWTE	OUP
The Song of Christ's Glory	P.Moore	SATB	E		RSCM
What wondrous love is this?	Trad arr Weaver	SAB	E	SFL2	
Wondrous cross	Wilby	SATB	E	OBFA, WOTC	
FIVE OR MORE PARTS					
Crucifixus a 6	Lotti	SSAATB	M	WOTC	
Crucifixus pro nobis	Leighton	SATB div	D		Novello
Salvator mundi	Blow	SSAATB	D		CMS/OUP
Salvator mundi	Tallis	SAATB unacc	M/D	OBTA, SC, TA	RSCM
Vinea mea electa	Gesualdo	SSATTB unacc	M/D		Carus
Vinea mea electa	Poulenc	SATBB unacc	D		Salabert

Settings of 'God so loved the world' listed for the Baptism of Christ (page 147) are also suitable.

ORGAN MUSIC

PRELUDES

Bach J.S.	**Christe, du Lamm Gottes** BWV 619 from the *Orgelbüchlein* (many editions) E/M
Couperin F.	**Benedictus: Chromhorne sur la taille** No.XVIII from *Messe pour les Paroisses* (Kalmus) E/M
Dupré M.	**Audi, benigne Conditor** No.4 in *Tombeau de Titelouze* Op.38 (Gray) M
Kauffmann G.	**Chorale Prelude 'Ach Herr, mich armen Sünder'** in *A Graded Anthology for Organ* Bk.2 (Cramer) E
Torres E.	**Saeta IV** in *An Organ Album for Manuals Only* Bk.2 (Banks) E/M

POSTLUDES

Couperin F.	**Dialogue sur les grands jeux** No.XIV from *Messe pour les Paroisses* (Kalmus) M*
Kellner J.P.	**Herzlich tut mich verlangen** in *Choralvorspiele alter Meister* (Peters) M
Langlais J.	**Mon âme cherche une fin paisible** No.7 of *Neuf Pièces* (Bornemann, Leduc) E/M
Walther J.G.	**Herzlich thut mich verlangen** in *80 Chorale Preludes* (Peters) and *The Organ Funeral Album* (Bärenreiter) E*

EASTER DAY YEAR B

(For Good Friday, see Year A, page 52.)

HYMNS AND SONGS

	pos	rdg	AMNS	CAON	CFE	CH4	CH5	CP	H&P	HTC	LAU	MP	NEH	SG	SOF	TS
Abide with me	ev	n	13	2	9	580	62	10	665	425	907	4	331	495	2	2
All shall be well!		s								149				397		1110
Alleluia, alleluia, give thanks to the risen Lord	gr	s		8	32		252	136	250	S 3	268	30			6	4
Alleluia, alleluia, Jesus, risen Lord	gr	s				428								421		1102
Alleluia! Jesus is risen		n				429										
As we walked home at close of day		n					253									
At the Lamb's high feast we sing	of	s	81	53	58		254	138			269		104			
Be known to us in breaking bread	cm	n					401	282	597	410				669		
Christ is alive! Let Christians sing		s		96		416	260	140	190		272			32		
Christ is alive, with joy we sing		s			107						270					
Christ the Lord is risen again		s	79	103			258	141	192	153			105	400		1166
Come, risen Lord	of	n	349	126			408	293	605	399			279			
Come, ye faithful/Alleluia, raise the anthem	ga	s	145	131			84	409	813	205		103	351	25		
Come, ye faithful, raise the strain/Spring has come	ga	s	76	132		414	262	143	194	160			106			
Finished the strife of battle now		s	455	173			264	144					*610*			
God, we praise you! God, we bless you!		s				120	696	450		341				38		
Good Christians all, rejoice and sing		s	85	241	230			145	191	154			107	404		
Hail thee, festival day (Easter)	ga	s		257							255		109			
He has risen		s											839	753		155
He is Lord, he is Lord		s			246	443			256	S 7			220		165	158
I am the bread of life	of			299	272		420		611		629	261		200		
I know that my Redeemer lives, what joy		s		311			270		196	169			278	406		
Jesus Christ is risen today	ga	s	77	348	322	410	271	147	193	155	267	357	110	408	285	276
Jesus lives! Thy terrors now	se	s	82	354			272	148	198	156		373	112	409	296	
Light of the minds that know him		n		397			588	501		477			400	626		
Love's redeeming work is done/Christ the Lord is risen/All creation		s	83	433		411	277		193			76	113			
Low in the grave he lay		s		435					202	158		453		411	378	345
Most glorious Lord of life		s		452		215	151					255				
Now is eternal life	se	s	402	470			392	152	203			114				
Now lives the Lamb of God		s					703			159			413			
O thou who this mysterious bread		n							621							
Surrexit Christus (Taizé)		s		943	672		282/711				266					
The Lamb's high banquet we await		s										101				
Ye/You choirs of new Jerusalem		s	73	754	818		292	162	823	168	279		124	419		

Seasonal hymns and songs listed for Years A and C (pages 54 and 292) are also appropriate.

SONGS FOR CHILDREN

Haven't you heard that Jesus is risen? CG 46, CH4 433
No more weeping SG 426
Risen! Risen! KS 289

BIBLE READINGS

Morning Psalms 114 and 117
Evening Psalms 105 *or* 66.1–11
Ezekiel 37.1–14
Luke 24.13–35

SINGING THE PSALM

Psalm 114 CFE, CWP, NPCW, PAME
Psalm 117 CRP, CWP, FGP, NPCW
  Bell *Praise your Maker* PPP
  Berthier *Laudate Dominum* CAON, CFE, CH4, CH5, LAU, TSFP#
  Inwood *Holy is God* HIG, LAU#
  Jakob *Go out to the whole world* C
Psalm 105 CRP, CWP, NPCW, PAME
  Dean *He, the Lord, is our God* VE
Psalm 66.1–11 CRP, CWP, NPCW
  Deiss *All you nations* CFE

ANTHEMS AND VOCAL MUSIC

Title	Composer	Voices	E/M/D	Book source	Single sheet publisher
UNISON/TWO PART/HIGH VOICES					
I am the bread of life	Lole	U + descant	E	BC	RSCM
Jesus, you are the bread	Farrell	U/SATB#	E	C, RITH	
Let all mortal flesh keep silence	Trad arr Greening	2 part	E	TEA	
On the journey to Emmaus	Haugen	U#	E	LAU	GIA
Risen Lord	Barry Rose	2 part	E	HP	
Shepherd of souls	Barnard	2 part	E	BFH	
THREE/FOUR PARTS					
Bread is blessed and broken	Bell	SATB	E	CAON, CG, LFB, WIS	
Bread of the world in mercy broken	Baldwin	SAMen	E	SBS2	
Broken for me	Lunt	SATB	E	SWAMS	
Christ, our God, descends from heaven	Bullard	SAMen	E	SBS2	
Christ was the Word	Maxim	SATB unacc	E	SBS2	
Ego sum panis vivus	Byrd	SATB unacc	M		OUP
Ego sum panis vivus	Palestrina	SATB unacc	M	CM1	
Here, O my Lord, I see thee	Barry Rose	SATB	E/M	MTH2	
Here, O my Lord, I see thee	Whitlock	SATB	E/M	NSAC2	OUP
I am the bread of life	Lole	SATB	E	SBS1, WIS	RSCM
Let all mortal flesh keep silence	Cleobury	SAMen	E	OBFA	
Let all mortal flesh keep silence	Trad arr Covey-Crump	SATB unacc	M	MTH1	
O for a closer walk with God	Ives	SATB	M		RSCM
O for a closer walk with God	Stanford	SATB	M	AC1, ASA, BC, OBFA (SAB)	RSCM
O taste and see	Vaughan Williams	SATB	E	AC4, NOEAB, NSAC1	OUP
The walk to Emmaus	Walford Davies	SATB	M		RSCM
FIVE OR MORE PARTS					
Let all mortal flesh keep silence	Bairstow	SSAATTBB unacc	M/D	AC4	S&B

ORGAN MUSIC

PRELUDES

Beauvarlet-Charpentier J-J.	**'O filii' avec des variations** in *Pièces pour Orgue* (Chanvrelin) E/M*
Cogen P.	**Offrande pour Pâques** (Combre) E/M
Peeters F.	**Alleluia, O sons and daughters** in *Hymn Preludes for the Liturgical Year* Op.100 Bk.2 (Peters) E/M
Rawsthorne N.	**Gelobet sei Gott** in *Easter Glory* (Mayhew) E/M
Stanford C.V.	**At Eastertide** in *Six Occasional Pieces* Bk.1 (Stainer) E/M

POSTLUDES

Archer M.	**Noel nouvelet** in *Fifty Hymn Preludes* and in *Preludes on the Great Hymns of Lent, Holy Week and Easter* (both Mayhew) E/M
Bach J.S.	**Erschienen ist de herrliche Tag** BWV 628 or 629 from the *Orgelbüchlein* (many editions) E/M
Shearing G.	**I know that my redeemer lives** in *Sacred Sounds from George Shearing* (SMP) E/M
Slater G.	**Easter Alleluia** (OUP) D

THE SECOND SUNDAY OF EASTER YEAR B

HYMNS AND SONGS

	pos	rdg	AMNS	CAON	CFE	CH4	CH5	CP	H&P	HTC	LAU	MP	NEH	SG	SOF	TS
At your feet we fall		s										45			34	35
Blessed be the name of the Lord (Prosch, Daniels)		o										808			46	53
Christ is risen! Raise your voices		n											399			
Christ the Lord is risen again		n	79	103			258	141	192	153			105	400		1166
Come, let us with our Lord arise	ga	n	449					142	575	375			254			
Come, ye faithful/Alleluia, raise the anthem	ga	s	145	131			84	409	813	205		103	351	25		
Come, ye faithful, raise the strain/Spring has come	ga	n	76	132		414	262	143	194	160			106			
Glorious things of thee are spoken		o	172	205	195	738	646	435	817	494	827	173	362	35	127	691
God is our strength and refuge		o		219			12	443		527		188		650		699
God, we praise you! God, we bless you!		s				120	696	450		341				38		
Good Christians all, rejoice and sing		n	85	241	230			145	191	154			107	404		
He has risen		n										839			753	155
Jerusalem, my happy home/thou city blest		o	187	339				481		569	373		228			
Jesus lives! Thy terrors now		n	82	354			272	148	198	156		373	112	409	296	
Laudate omnes gentes/Sing praises, all you peoples (Taizé)		o								478					1515	
Like a mighty river flowing		o		400	367		16			32	897	419		51		
Love's redeeming work is done/Christ the Lord is risen/All creation		s	83	433		411	277	150	193	150		76	113	412		
Most glorious Lord of life		n		452		215		151					255			
Now is eternal life	se	s	402	470			392	152	203				114			
O Lord, hear my prayer (Taizé)		ps		938	542		620			929	908			246	423	394
Psallite Domino (Taizé)		o			614											
Rejoice, O land, in God thy might		o	296	579			539	359		331			493			
Rock of ages (Kendrick)		o													1507	951
Rock of ages, cleft for me		o	135	584	624	554	557	565	273	593		582	445	150	488	950
The day of resurrection		n	75	637	690	413	283	157	208	161	283		117	415		
The Lamb's high banquet we await		s											101			
The Lord is risen indeed!		n	84	652				158					118			
The strife is o'er/past		n	78	667		412	286	159	214	163	275	670	119	416		
Thine/Yours be the glory	se	n	428	672	728	419	288	160	212	167	287	689	120	417	551	510
This joyful Eastertide		s		680	735	415	289	161	213	165	286		121			
Ye/You choirs of new Jerusalem		n	73	754	818		292	162	823	168	279		124	419		

SONGS FOR CHILDREN

Christ is risen as he said CH5 256
Jesus is risen from the grave CH4 434
No more weeping SG 426

BIBLE READINGS

Psalm 143.1–11
Isaiah 26.1–9,19
Luke 24.1–12

SINGING THE PSALM

Psalm 143.1–11 CH4, CWP, FGP, NPCW, PAME

ANTHEMS AND VOCAL MUSIC

Title	Composer	Voices	E/M/D	Book source	Single sheet publisher
UNISON/TWO PART/HIGH VOICES					
An Easter Sequence	Leighton	SSAA	D		Banks
Christo resurgenti	Couperin	SS	M	AC2	
Most glorious Lord of life	Harris	2 part	E/M	OEAB	OUP
Risen Lord	Barry Rose	2 part	E	HP	
Song of the Risen One	Haas	U/SATB#	E/M		GIA
THREE/FOUR PARTS					
Away with gloom, away with doubt	Ferguson	SATB unacc	E	BC	RSCM
But thanks (Messiah)	Handel	SATB	M		Novello
Comes Mary to the grave	N.Warren	SATB	E	WIS	
Easter Anthems	Carter	SATB	E	*Palm Sunday to Easter*	RSCM
Easter Anthems	Scott	SATB	M	AWTE	
He is risen	Cope	SATB	E	OBFA, OEAB	Banks
He is risen	Whitlock	SATB	E/M	AWTE	Banks
Most glorious Lord of life	Harris	SATB	E	AWTE	OUP
O filii et filiae	Trad arr Sanger	SATB	M/D		Banks
O God of my righteousness	Greene	SATB + solo ST	M/D		CMS/OUP
O sons and daughters, let us sing	Trad arr Walford Davies	SATB	E	MTH2	RSCM
The strife is o'er	Armstrong Gibbs	SATB	M	OEAB	Banks
The strife is o'er	Ley	SATB	E	NCAB	OUP
Thou wilt keep him in perfect peace	Sumsion	SATB	M		RSCM
When Mary through the garden went	Stanford	SATB unacc	E	ASA	S&B
Ye choirs of new Jerusalem	M.Rose	SATB	M		Banks
Ye choirs of new Jerusalem	Shephard	SATB	D	EAC1	OUP
Ye choirs of new Jerusalem	Stanford	SATB	M	AC1, AWTE, FAB1	RSCM
FIVE OR MORE PARTS					
Haec dies	Byrd	SSATTB unacc	D	OBTA	OUP
Haec dies	Howells	SSATB unacc	D		OUP
Thou wilt keep him in perfect peace	S.S.Wesley	SATBB	M	NCAB	Novello

ORGAN MUSIC

PRELUDES

Beechey G.	**St John Damascene** in *Easter Preludes* (Fagus) E/M	
Dupré M.	**Christ lag in Todesbanden** No.12 of *79 Chorals* Op.28 (Gray) E	
Lindeman L.M.	**Wer nur den lieben Gott** in *The Organ Funeral Album* (Bärenreiter) E/M*	
Reger M.	**Jesus, meine Zuversicht** Op.67/22 or Op. 135a/13, both in *Complete Works* Bk.7 (Breitkopf) E/M	
Vann S.	**Savannah** in *Preludes on the Great Hymns of Lent, Holy Week and Easter* (Mayhew) E	

POSTLUDES

Buxtehude D.	**Erschienen ist der herrliche Tag** BuxWV 224 in *Complete Works* Vol.5 (Bärenreiter) E/M	
Langlais J.	**Fugue on 'O filii'** from *Folkloric Suite* (FitzSimons) M/D	
Lebègue N.	**Offertoire sur le Chant d'O filii et filiæ** in *Complete Works* Vol.3 (Kalmus) and *Offertoires from Troisième Livre d'Orgue* (Hawthorns) M*	
Sechter S.	**Jesus, meine Zuversicht** in *18 Choralvorspiele* Op.90 (Doblinger) E*	

THE THIRD SUNDAY OF EASTER YEAR B

HYMNS AND SONGS

	pos	rdg	AMNS	CAON	CFE	CH4	CH5	CP	H&P	HTC	LAU	MP	NEH	SG	SOF	TS
As water to the thirsty		g						252		470		803		553	659	
At even, ere/when the sun was set		n	9	50			65	12	142	315		43	243	487		
At your feet we fall		n										45			34	35
Bless the Lord, my soul (Taizé)		o		923	81		1				813			105	676	56
Christ, when for us you were baptized		n	442				92		129							
Come, ye faithful/Alleluia, raise the anthem	ga	s	145	131			84	409	813	205		103	351	25		
Faithful Shepherd, feed me	cm	o		156			644			29			282	498		
Father of mercies, in thy word		g	167							247			224			
Fight the good fight		n	220	169	171	517	566	423	710	526	860	143	359	635	107	
For all the saints who from their labours rest		n	305	177	176	740	459	232	814	567	371	148	197	636	109	684
For the healing of the nations		g	361	186	179	706	496	427	402		886			261	1235	
From thee/you all skill and science flow		n	286				512	345	389	310						
God of freedom, God of justice		n		224		263	447									
Jesus lives! Thy terrors now		s	82	354			272	148	198	156			373	112	409	296
Let the poor man say (Let the river flow)		n													1414	859
Lord God, you love us (Taizé)		o									782					
My Lord of light who made the worlds		n								4						
O thou not made with hands		n	174						656				430			
Rejoice! The Lord is king		n	139	580	619	449	281	563	243	180	326	575	443	440	482	948
Tell out, my soul		g	422	631	684	286	712	362	86	42	880	631	186	62	520	471
The Church of God a kingdom is		n	169	635			325						483			
The Lamb's high banquet we await		s											101			
When I needed a neighbour		g	433	736	800	544	499				888				1604	
Who would true valour see/He who would valiant be		n	212	281	248	535	662	621	688	590	862	224	372	639	174	
Worthy, O worthy are you, Lord		o										782			617	585
Ye/You choirs of new Jerusalem		s	73	754	818		292	162	823	168	279		124	419		

SONGS FOR CHILDREN

The Lord is risen from the dead CH4 797

When I needed a neighbour AMNS 433, CAON 736, CAP 65, CFE 800, CH 229, CH4 544, CH5 499, JP 275, LAU 888, SOF 1604

BIBLE READINGS

Psalm 142
Deuteronomy 7.7–13
Revelation 2.1–11
Luke 16.19–31

SINGING THE PSALM

Psalm 142 CWP, NPCW

ANTHEMS AND VOCAL MUSIC

Title	Composer	Voices	E/M/D	Book source	Single sheet publisher
UNISON/TWO PART/HIGH VOICES					
Like the murmur of a dove's song	A.Smith	2 part	E	OBFA	
Listen	Nazareth arr Archer	2 part	E	BC	
Listen to the Spirit	Dean	U#	E	C	
My lips shall speak of thy praise	Greene	SS	M		OUP
The Tree	Harvey	SSSS	D		OUP
THREE/FOUR PARTS					
Blessed are those who are undefiled in the way	Greene	SATB + solo SS	M		RSCM
Christ whose glory fills the skies	Darke	SATB	M	SBS1	RSCM
Dives and Lazarus (g)	Trad arr Carter	SATB	M		OUP
Firmly I believe and truly	Shephard	SAMen	E	SFL2	
Give almes of thy goods (g)	Tye	SATB unacc	E	AC1, OBTA	OUP
I call on the Lord	Ridout	SAMen	E	NAB2	
If ye love me	Tallis	SATB unacc	E	FAB1, NCAB, NOEAB, NSAC1, OBTA, TA, SL (AATB)	OUP
In God's Word	Purcell	SAB	M	TPS, SFL2	
Lord, give me faith	Robson	SATB	E		RSCM
O Lord, increase our faith	Loosemore	SATB (unacc)	E	NCAB, SBS1	RSCM
Teach me, O God	Moger	SAB	E		RSCM
Teach me, O Lord	Attwood	SATB	E	NOEAB	RSCM
Teach me thy way, O Lord	Fox	SATB unacc	E	FSB7, SBS1	RSCM
Verily, verily I say unto you (g)	Tallis	SATB unacc	E	AC1, SBS2, TA	OUP
FIVE OR MORE PARTS					
Beati quorum via	Stanford	SSATBB unacc	M	ASA, WFC	RSCM
If ye love me	Chilcott	SSATBB unacc	M	BCA, WFC	OUP
Open thou mine eyes	Rutter	SSATBB unacc	M		OUP
Teach me, O Lord	Byrd	SAATB	M	OBTA	OUP

ORGAN MUSIC

PRELUDES

Buxtehude D. **Mensch, willt du leben seliglich** BuxWV 206 in *Complete Works* Vol.4 (Bärenreiter) E/M
Homilius G.A. **Christ lag in Todesbanden** in *Eight Chorale Preludes* (Harmonia) E/M
Near G. **Jesus, meine Zuversicht** in *Choraleworks* Set 3 (Aureole) E/M
Pachelbel J. **Alle Menschen müssen sterben** in *Seasonal Chorale Preludes for Manuals* Bk.2 (OUP) E*
Titelouze J. **2ème Verset 'Ad coenam agni'** in *Hymnes de l'Église* (Kalmus, Schott) E/M*

POSTLUDES

Dubois T. **Alleluia** from *Douze Pièces Nouvelles* (Masters, Leduc) M/D
Nixon J. **St Albinus** in *Hymn Tune Preludes* (Fagus) E/M
Titelouze J. **4ème Verset 'Ad coenam agni'** in *Hymnes de l'Église* (Kalmus, Schott) E/M*
Sumsion H. **Toccata on 'University'** (RSCM) M

THE FOURTH SUNDAY OF EASTER YEAR B

HYMNS AND SONGS

	pos	rdg	AMNS	CAON	CFE	CH4	CH5	CP	H&P	HTC	LAU	MP	NEH	SG	SOF	TS
At the Lamb's high feast we sing		s,o	81	53	58		254	138			269		104			
At your feet we fall		n										45			34	35
Bread of heaven, on thee we feed		g	271	82				284		398			276	464		
Bread of life, hope of the world	cm	g			95	663					78			484		
Break thou the bread of life	cm	g					379	286	467			64		50		
Christ triumphant, ever reigning		s		104	113	436	259	398		173	763	77	*613*	319	62	655
Christ whose glory fills the skies	ga	o	4	105		578	52	2	457	266	670	79	234	170	1200	
Come, risen Lord		g	349	126			408	293	605	399			279			
Come, ye faithful/Alleluia, raise the anthem	ga	s	145	131			84	409	813	205		103	351	25		
Dear Lord and Father of mankind		o	115	144	143	485	549	411	673	356	934	111	353	497	79	79
Deck thyself, my soul, with gladness/Soul, array thyself		g	257	146			445	295	606	400			280			
Draw near/nigh and take the body of the Lord	cm	g			150		411	296		401	628		281			
Eat this bread, drink this cup (Taizé)		o,g		926	151	661					633				1221	
From glory to glory advancing	pc	g	276	194				299					286			
Glorious things of thee are spoken		o	172	205	195	738	646	435	817	494	827	173	362	35	127	691
Guide me, O thou great Jehovah/Redeemer	se	o	214	252	233	167	647	455	437	528	960	201	368	638	148	708
I am the bread of life		o,g		299	272		420		611		629	261			200	
I hunger and I thirst		o						306	730	409				470		
Jesu, thou joy of loving hearts		g	255	369		662	425	486	258	413		383	292	471		839
Light of the minds that know him	se	o		397			588	501		477			400	626		
Lord, enthroned in heavenly splendour		s,g	263	408	379		431	311	616	416	769	431	296	52	352	870
Now is eternal life	se	s,g	402	470			392	152	203				114			
Shepherd divine, our wants relieve		n	228					566	558							
The Lamb's high banquet we await		s,o											101			
The strife is o'er/past		s	78	667		412	286	159	214	163	275	670	119	416		
You, living Christ, our eyes behold		n	533					333					487			

SONGS FOR CHILDREN

Allundé, allundé CFAP, IECS
Come on and celebrate CAON 125, CH 35, CH5 328, JP 325, KS 34, MP 99, SOF 73, TS 75
I will sing a song of love VFLS 18

BIBLE READINGS

Psalm 81.8–16
Exodus 16.4–15
Revelation 2.12–17
John 6.30–40

SINGING THE PSALM

Psalm 81.8–16 CRP, CWP, FGP, NPCW

ANTHEMS AND VOCAL MUSIC

Title	Composer	Voices	E/M/D	Book source	Single sheet publisher
UNISON/TWO PART/HIGH VOICES					
Bread for the world	Farrell	U#	E	GBAN	OCP
Bread of life	Farrell	U/SATB#	E	CFE, CH4, HIG, LAU, RITH, SG	OCP
Panis angelicus	Franck	SS	M		Ashdown
Unless a grain of wheat	Farrell	U/SATB#	E	CFE, LAU, RITH, WYP	OCP
THREE/FOUR PARTS					
Bread for the world broken	Walker	U/SAB#	E	CFE, WYP	
Bread of the world	Scottish trad arr Bullard	SAMen	E	OBFA	
Bread of the world in mercy broken	Aston	SATB	M	SBS2	
Bread of the world in mercy broken	Baldwin	SAMen	E	SBS2	
Broken for me	Lunt	SATB	E	SWAMS	
Christ our God descends from heaven	Bullard	SAB	E/M	SBS2	
Ego sum panis vivus	Byrd	SATB unacc	M		OUP
Ego sum panis vivus	Palestrina	SATB unacc	M	CM1	
I am the bread of life	Lole	SATB	E	SBS1, WIS, BC (U + descant)	RSCM
I am the bread of life	Toolan arr Wilson	SATB	E	AWS	
Let all mortal flesh keep silence	Trad arr Covey-Crump	SATB unacc	M	MTH1	
Panis angelicus	Franck	SATB	M	ESM, OBFA, WFC	RSCM
Panis angelicus	Saint-Saëns	SATB	E	NCAB	
Shepherd of souls	Barnard	SATB	E/M	SC	RSCM
Take and eat	Joncas	SATB#	E		GIA
Take and eat	Ogden	SATB unacc	E		WLP
Verily, verily, I say unto you	Tallis	SATB unacc	E	AC1, TA, SBS2	OUP
FIVE OR MORE PARTS					
Let all mortal flesh keep silence	Bairstow	SSAATTBB unacc	M/D	AC4	S&B
Panis angelicus	Villette	SSAATTBB unacc	M/D		UMP

ORGAN MUSIC

PRELUDES

Dyson G.	**O Word Immortal** in *Variations on Old Psalm Tunes* Bk.3 (Novello) E/M
Fraser I.	**Bread of heaven** in *Ten Hymn-Tune Preludes* (Animus) E
Hurford P.	**Schmücke dich** in *Five Chorale Preludes* (OUP) E
Rawsthorne N.	**Prelude on 'Bread of heaven'** in *A Second Organ Miscellany* and *Consecration* (Mayhew) E
Reger M.	**Schmücke dich** Op.67/36 in *Complete Chorale Preludes* (Breitkopf) E/M

POSTLUDES

Bach J.S.	**Schmücke dich** BWV 654 in Novello Vol.17, Bärenreiter Vol.2, Peters Vol.7 M
Nixon J.	**St Helen** in *Hymn Tune Preludes* (Fagus) E/M
Sanders J.	**Toccata** in *Gloucester Organ Album* (Novello) M
Scheidt S.	**Christ lag in Todesbanden** in *Choralvorspiele alter Meister* (Peters) E/M

HYMNS AND SONGS

	pos	rdg	AMNS	CAON	CFE	CH4	CH5	CP	H&P	HTC	LAU	MP	NEH	SG	SOF	TS
Alleluia, alleluia, give thanks		g		8	32		252	136	250	S 3	268	30			6	4
Awake, awake: fling off the night!		o	342	57	64			334			851					
Christ whose glory fills the skies	mo	o	4	105		578	52	2	457	266	670	79	234	170	1200	
City of God, Jerusalem		o								187						
Come, O thou Traveller unknown		n	243					407	434				350			
Darkness like a shroud (Arise, shine)		o									110				78	
Great is the darkness		o									835			264	742	136
Hail thee, festival day (Easter)	ga	s,g		257							255		109			
How bright these glorious spirits shine		n	306			745	467	221		572			227			
I'm not ashamed to own/name my Lord		n		316		645			677	448		323/992		532		
Jerusalem the golden		n	184	340	317	747	670	482		573	991		381			
Jerusalem, my happy home/thou city blest		n	187	339			481			569	373		228			
Jesus shall take the highest honour		g		360								378		123	302	296
Jubilate Deo omnis terra (Taizé)		ps			336						691					
Longing for light (Christ be our light)		o				543					883					1409
Lord, the light of your love is shining		o		419	388	448	195	513			770	445		614	362	335
O for a heart to praise my God		n	230	484			638	533	536	483		495	74	149	411	904
O holy City, seen of John		n	409													
O sons and daughters, let us sing/Alleluia!		g	74			431	279	154	205		280		125			
Out of darkness God has called us		o			591						835					
Psallite Domino (Taizé)					614											
Revive thy work/your church, O Lord!		n					308		780	515		578				
The Lamb's high banquet we await		s											101			
There's a light upon the mountains		o							246			679				
We have a gospel to proclaim		g	431	716	778	363	491	612	465	519	852	728	486	331	1583	
We love the place, O God		n	160	718			343	211		558		731	471			
Where high the heavenly temple stands		n	130			451	291			184						

SONGS FOR CHILDREN

Allundé, allundé CFAP, IECS
I danced in the morning AMNS 375, CAON 305, CAP 22, CFE 275, CH 96, CH4 404, CH5 93, CP 468, JP 91, LAU 765, NEH 375, SOF 1310
I will sing a song of love VFLS 18

BIBLE READINGS

Psalm 96
Isaiah 60.1–14
Revelation 3.1–13
Mark 16.9–16

SINGING THE PSALM

Psalm 96 CRP, CWP, FGP, H&P, MCW1, NPCW, PAME, PIW
  Dean *Proclaim the wonders of the Lord* HG#
  Walker *Save us, Lord our God* ATNJ (OCP)

ANTHEMS AND VOCAL MUSIC

Title	Composer	Voices	E/M/D	Book source	Single sheet publisher
UNISON/TWO PART/HIGH VOICES					
All that is hidden	Farrell	U/SATB#	E	CFE, LAU, RITH, SFTL	OCP
Arise, shine for thy light is come	How	2 part + cong	E/M		Ionian
Christ has no body now but yours	Ogden	U + descant	E	CFAP, LOL	RSCM
Go out to the whole world	Jakob	U	E	C	
Like the murmur of a dove's song	A.Smith	2 part	E	OBFA	
Listen	Nazareth arr Archer	2 part	E	BC	
Send us as your blessing, Lord	Walker	U/SSATB#	E	HIG	OCP
Sent by the Lord am I	Trad arr Weaver	2 part	E	BC	
THREE/FOUR PARTS					
Arise, shine	Shephard	SATB	E/M	SBS1	RSCM
Arise, shine	Stanford	SATB	M	ASA	
Arise, shine O Jerusalem	Palestrina arr Jackson & Moore	SATB	E	ETAS	
Arise, shine for your light has come	Mathias	SATB	M		Banks
Ascribe unto the Lord	S.S.Wesley	SATB	M		Banks, Novello
Ascribe unto the Lord	Travers	SATB + solo TB	M		Novello
Be thou my vision	Chilcott	SATB	E	BCA, NOEAB	OUP
Cantate Domino	Hassler	SATB unacc	M	CM4	Carus
Go forth into the world in peace	Rutter	SATB	E	JRA	OUP
Go forth and tell!	Ogden	SATB	E	SBS2	RSCM
Here I am, Lord	Schutte arr Archer	SATB	E	MTH1	
Jesus, you are the way	Rizza	SATB + solo S#	E	FOL	Mayhew
Light of the lonely pilgrim's heart	Nardone	SATB	E		B&H
Now go in peace	Trad arr Jeffcoat	SATB	E	PSA, SC	
O sing unto the Lord a new song	Purcell	SATB	M		Novello
To be a pilgrim	Burt	SAMen	E/M	OBFA	
FIVE OR MORE PARTS					
Surge illuminare	Palestrina	SATB + SATB unacc	M		Chester
Surge illuminare	Simpson	SSAATTBB unacc	M/D	CN	

ORGAN MUSIC

PRELUDES

Bach J.S. **In dich hab' ich gehoffet, Herr** BWV 712 in Novello Vol.18, Bärenreiter Vol.3, Peters Vol.6 M*
Bédard D. **Offertoire** from *Suite Liturgique* (Cheldar) E
Elmore R. **In vernali tempore** in *Contemporary Chorale Preludes* (Boosey) E/M
Lemmens J.-N. **Second movement** ('O filii') from *2nd Sonata* (Forberg, or Novello reprint) E/M
Lloyd Webber W.S. **Prelude on 'Stracathro'** in *Aria* (Mayhew) E

POSTLUDES

Krebs J.L. **Christ lag in Todesbanden** in *The Progressive Organist* Bk.4 (Novello) E/M
Rawsthorne N. **Jubilate** in *Twelve Miniatures for Festive Occasions* (Mayhew; manuals-only edition also available) E
Sweelinck J. **Toccata** in *Organ Music for Manuals* Bk.1 (OUP) E/M*
Vierne R. **Canzona** No.10 of *Dix Pièces de Différents Styles* (Kalmus) E/M*
West J.E. **Variations on 'O filii'** (Novello) M

THE SIXTH SUNDAY OF EASTER YEAR B

HYMNS AND SONGS

	pos	rdg	AMNS	CAON	CFE	CH4	CH5	CP	H&P	HTC	LAU	MP	NEH	SG	SOF	TS
Adoramus te, Domine (Taizé)				921	11		345				667			208		
At/In the name of Jesus		o	148	54	59	458	94	380	74	172	762	41	338	317	32	33
Be known to us in breaking bread/O Lord, you gave	cm	n					401	282	597	410					669	
Christ triumphant, ever reigning		g		104	113	436	259	398		173	763	77	*613*	319	62	655
From heaven you came, helpless babe		g		195	187	374	219	432			749	162		632	120	114
God of freedom, God of justice		o		224		263	447									
God of grace and God of glory		n	367	225			533	448	712	324		192		574	139	
God, we praise you! God, we bless you!		s				120	696	450		341				38		
Gracious Spirit, Holy Ghost/Holy Spirit, gracious guest		o	154	245		627	312	182	301	474		198	367	556		
Hark, my soul! It is the Lord/Christian, do you hear		o,n	244	264			569	457	521	472		209	*637*			
Jesus is King and I will extol him		g										366			289	283
Jesus, Jesus, holy and anointed one		s										872		215	293	286
Jesus lives! Thy terrors now		n,s	82	354			272	148	198	156		373	112	409	296	
Just as I am, without one plea		n	246	374	339	553	587	308	697	440		396	294	507	316	306
Meekness and majesty		g		448	487	356	228				751	465		395	390	353
Morning glory, starlit sky/Open are the gifts		g	496			390		259					*608*			
My Lord, you wore no royal crown		g								118				628		
Now the green blade riseth		o,s	501	475	513	417	278	153	204				115	414		
O Holy Ghost, thy people bless/O Holy Spirit, come		o	155	500				187		238						
O Jesu, King most wonderful		n	120ii				106	539	269	484			386			
O love divine, how sweet thou art		o	124				621	541					424			
Rock of ages (Kendrick)		n													1507	951
Rock of ages, cleft for me		n	135	584	624	554	557	565	273	593		582	445	150	488	950
Stand up, stand up for Jesus		n	221	617			488	578	721	535		617	453	644	513	1517
The Lamb's high banquet we await		s											101			
Ubi caritas/Living charity (Taizé)		o		946		801	530				245				1573	
Who is on the Lord's side?		n							722			769			607	1066

SONGS FOR CHILDREN

Here I stand CAYP, EOA

Praise him, praise him (God is love) CAON 563, CH5 367, H&P 565, HTC S21, JP 201

BIBLE READINGS

Psalm 45

Song of Solomon 4.16 - 5.2; 8.6,7

Revelation 3.14–22

Luke 22.24–30

SINGING THE PSALM

Psalm 45 CWP, NEP, NPCW, PAME

ANTHEMS AND VOCAL MUSIC

Title	Composer	Voices	E/M/D	Book source	Single sheet publisher
UNISON/TWO PART/HIGH VOICES					
Faith, hope and love	Ogden	2 part	E	SBS1	RSCM
God is always there	Plainsong arr Bullard	2 part	E	OBFA	
Jesu, Jesu, fill us with your love	Trad arr Weaver	2 part	E	IECS, SFL1	
Listen	Nazareth arr Archer	2 part	E	BC	
Listen to the Spirit	Dean	U#	E	C	
Love one another	S.S.Wesley	S	E	BC	RSCM
The Servant Song	Gillard arr Ogden	2 part	E	SFL1	
THREE/FOUR PARTS					
Anima mea	M.de Rivafrecha	SATB unacc	E/M	CM3	Chester
Arise, my love	Martinson	SATB unacc	M/D	WFC	
Beloved, let us love	Aston	SATB unacc	D		RSCM
Greater love	Ireland	SATB	M	AC4	S&B
In the heart where love is abiding	Barnard	SATB	E	AWTE, BC	RSCM
Love divine	Lloyd	SAMen	E	AOAN1	
Love divine	Willcocks	SATB	E	NOEAB	
Love one another	Carter	SATB	D		OUP
Morning glory, starlit sky	Barry Rose	SATB + solo S/T	E/M	MTH2	
My beloved is mine	Lole	SATB unacc	M		Encore
Now let us from this table rise	Henderson	SATB	E	SBS1	RSCM
O voice of the beloved	Ives	SATB	M	SBS2	RSCM
Set me as a seal	Carpenter	SATB + solo S	M		WLP
Set me as a seal	Walton	SATB	M/D	AC4, WFC	OUP
The Light of the World	Carter	SATB	M	ACA	OUP
Though I speak with the tongues of men	Bairstow	SATB	M	FSB10, WFC	OUP
Ubi caritas	Mawby	SATB	E		Mayhew
Ubi caritas	Ives	SATB unacc	M	SC	
FIVE OR MORE PARTS					
Ubi caritas	Duruflé	SAATTBB unacc	M		Durand

ORGAN MUSIC

PRELUDES

Floyd A.E.   **Chorale Prelude on 'Petra'** in *Musical Miniatures* and in *Hymn Preludes for the Church Year* Bk.2
(both Mayhew) E/M

Nixon J.   **Capetown** or **Saffron Walden** in *Hymn Tune Preludes* (Fagus) E/M

Vann S.   **Prelude on 'Song 13'** in *Six Preludes* (Mayhew) E/M

Whitlock P.   **Song 13** in *Whitlock: Complete Shorter Works* (OUP) E/M

Willan H.   **Sicilienne on 'Capetown'** in *Ten Hymn Preludes* Set 1 (Peters) E/M

POSTLUDES

Edwards P.   **Overture** from *Northampton Miniatures* (Fagus) E*

Groves R.   **St Albinus/Passion Chorale** in *12 Hymn-Tune Preludes* Set 1 (Novello) E(*)

Vierne L.   **Cortège** No.3 of *Trois Improvisations* (Durand) M

Willan H.   **Prelude on 'Old 124th'** in *Ten Hymn Preludes* Set 2 (Peters) E/M

THE SEVENTH SUNDAY OF EASTER (THE SUNDAY AFTER ASCENSION DAY) YEAR B

(For Ascension Day, see Year A, page 66.)

HYMNS AND SONGS

	pos	rdg	AMNS	CAON	CFE	CH4	CH5	CP	H&P	HTC	LAU	MP	NEH	SG	SOF	TS
All hail the power of Jesus' name		s	140	16	19	457	250	163	252	587	323	13	332	24	9	7
All heaven declares	gr	s		17	20	426					760	14		420	10	8
Alleluia! Sing to Jesus	of	s	262	12	37	445	398	278	592	170	644	207	271	458	153	616
Blessing and honour (Ancient of days)		s				442						976		106	675	54
Christ is the King! O friends rejoice		s	345				86	165		492			345	31		
Christ triumphant, ever reigning		s		104	113	436	259	398		173	763	77	*613*	319	62	655
Come, let us join our cheerful songs	ga	s	144	120			332	401	810	206		93	349	33	70	
Crown him with many crowns		s	147	137	139	459	263	166	255	174	321	109	352	321	77	77
God is working his purpose out		o		221	217	235	481	444	769	191	86	189	495	451	135	128
God of grace and God of glory		n	367	225			533	448	712	324		192		574	139	
Hail the day that sees him rise		s	87	255	240		266	167	197	176	291	202	130	434		
Hail to the Lord's anointed		o	142	259	241	474	125	87	125	190	102	204	55		150	709
I see the Lord (Falson)		s													824	238
In the Lord I'll be ever thankful (Taizé)		o		929	308	772					944	865		656	817	
Jesus shall reign where'er the sun		o,n	143	359		470	97	490	239	516	322	379	388	45	301	1376
Jesus shall take the highest honour		s		360								378		123	302	296
Jesus, the name high over all		n		364			99		264	213		385		323	307	298
Jesus, we enthrone you		s										388		310	300	
King of kings, majesty		s										1000		1404	309	
Lord, enthroned in heavenly splendour		s	263	408	379		431	311	616	416	769	431	296	52	352	870
Majesty, worship his majesty		s		436	477		276				767	454			379	346
Make way, make way for Christ the King	ga	s		438	479	279	134				819	457			384	349
O Christe Domine Jesu (Taizé)					519						757					
O for a thousand tongues to sing		n	125	485		352	104	534	744	219		496	415	55	412	383/1452
Rejoice! The Lord is king		s	139	580	619	449	281	563	243	180	326	575	443	440	482	948
Thanks/Praise to God whose word was spoken		n	423			605	387	584	483	255			438	229		
The head that once was crowned with thorns		s	141	644	696	438	285	172	209	182	290	647	134	442	531	979/1528
The kingdom of God is justice and joy		n		646	701			591	139	333	821	651		184		
The Lord ascendeth up on high		s				440		173	210			135				
Thou/God, whose almighty word		o	180	684	738	112	324	267	29	506	887	699	466	597	557	
Will you come and follow me	se	n		752	812	533	605	622			877		*647*	634	1120	

SONGS FOR CHILDREN

All heaven declares CAON 17, CFE 20, CH4 426, KS 4, LAU 760, MP 14, SG 420, SOF 10, TS 8
Breathe on me, Spirit of Jesus SOF 677
God has chosen me CFE 212, LAU 858, MP 830, SFL1 24, SG 612

BIBLE READINGS

Psalm 147.1–12

Isaiah 61

Luke 4.14–21

SINGING THE PSALM

Psalm 147.1–12 CH4, CRP, CWP, H&P, NPCW

Bell *Sing to God with joy* MCW1, PPP

ANTHEMS AND VOCAL MUSIC

Title	Composer	Voices	E/M/D	Book source	Single sheet publisher
UNISON/TWO PART/HIGH VOICES					
Breathe on me	Hubbard	S	E	SFJ	Banks
Like the murmur of the dove's song	A.Smith	2 part	E	OBFA	
Listen to the Spirit	Dean	U#	E	C	
O breath of life	Trad arr Bullard	2 part/SB	E	OBFA	
The Spirit of the Lord	Corp	SS	E	VFLS	
When the Spirit of the Lord	Trad arr Jones	2 part	E	VFLS	
THREE/FOUR PARTS					
Breathe on me, breath of God	Wilby	SATB + solo S	E/M		RSCM
Come down, O love divine	Harris	SATB	E/M	FSB9, NCAB, MTH2	Novello
Come down, O love divine	Tadman-Robins	SAMen	E	OBFA	
Come, Holy Ghost	Attwood	SATB	E	FAB1, NCAB, NNAB, NSAC2, AOAN1 (SAB)	Novello
Come, Holy Ghost	Heron	SAB or SATB	E		RSCM
Grow in grace	Archer	SATB	E/M	SBS1	RSCM
Holy Spirit, truth divine	Carter	SATB	E/M	ETAS, NOEAB	OUP
If ye love me	Tallis	SATB unacc	E	FAB1, NCAB, NOEAB, NSAC1, OBTA, TA, SL (AATB)	OUP
O Lord, give thy Holy Spirit	Harper	SATB	E	SBS2, SOTL	
The Spirit of the Lord	Elgar	SATB	M	SAEE	RSCM
FIVE OR MORE PARTS					
If ye love me	Chilcott	SSATB unacc	M	BCA, WFC	
Veni Sancte Spiritus	Rutter	SSAATTBB unacc	M/D	CN	OUP
Veni Sancte Spiritus	Victoria	SATB + SATB unacc	M		Joed

See also the anthems listed for Ascension Day (page 67).

ORGAN MUSIC

PRELUDES

Couperin G.F. **Récit de cromorne ou hautbois** in *Couperin: Pièces pour Orgue* (Chanvrelin) E/M*

Karg-Elert S. **Herzlich lieb hab ich dir'** No.15 from *Choral-Improvisationen* Op.65 Vol.2 (Breitkopf) E/M

Near G. **Freu dich sehr** in *Choraleworks* Set 2 (Aureole) E/M

Pachelbel J. **Nun lob, mein Seel** in *Orgelwerke* Vol.2 (Peters) or Vol.3 (Kalmus) E/M

POSTLUDES

Leighton K. **Toccata on 'Hanover'** No.6 from *Six Fantasies on Hymn Tunes* Op.72 (Ramsey) M/D

Rawsthorne N. **Exultemus** in *Twelve Miniatures for Festive Occasions* (Mayhew; manuals-only edition also available) E

Vann S. **Prelude on 'Hanover'** in *Six Preludes* (Mayhew) E/M

Willan H. **Prelude on 'Hyfrydol'** in *Ten Hymn Preludes* Set 1 (Peters) E/M

Suitable before or after: Movements from Böhm G. **Partita 'Freu dich sehr, O meine Seele'** in *Complete Works* (Breitkopf) E-M(*)

DAY OF PENTECOST (WHIT SUNDAY) YEAR B

HYMNS AND SONGS

	pos	rdg	AMNS	CAON	CFE	CH4	CH5	CP	H&P	HTC	LAU	MP	NEH	SG	SOF	TS
All over the world the Spirit is moving		o		20							984	18			12	12
As pants the hart/As longs the deer		o	226	44		32	607	379	416		450		337			
As the deer pants for the water		o		45	54	550	606				965	37			27	27
Be still and know		g		66	71	755	608				909	48				
Be still and know I (John Bell)		g												18	672	
Be still and know II (John Bell)		g			70	754								242		
Be still, for the presence of the Lord	gr	g		67	72	189	325	383			720	50	629	7	40	47
Bless the Lord, my soul (Taizé)				923	81		1				813			105	676	56
Blessed Thomas, doubt no longer		g											173			
Born by the Holy Spirit's breath		s						279	225			61			446	
Breathe on me, breath of God		g	157	84	98	596	293	174	280	226	302	67	342	554	51	57
Breathe on me, Spirit of Jesus		g													677	
Christ on whom the Spirit rested		s								228						
Come down, O love divine	ga	s	156	114	125	489	294	175	281	231	303	89	137	663	1202	71
Come, Holy Spirit, come! Inflame		s		119		594		179								
Come, Holy Spirit, gracious heavenly dove		s				758										
Filled with the Spirit's power		s	359	170			298	425	314	233				593		
Hail thee, festival day! (Pentecost)		s				581			302		255					
Holy Spirit, come, confirm us	se	s	471	288		640	299	183	288		311		140			
Holy Spirit, ever dwelling/living		s				615			303				141			
Jesus, stand among us at the meeting		g		361			424					381			303	
Jesus, stand among us in thy risen power		g		362			338		530	364		380			304	
Let every Christian pray		s	478				301		305	230			640	576		
Like the murmur of the dove's song		s				592		185						17		
O breath of life, come sweeping through us	gr	s		476		595	305		777	237		488			407	379
O holy dove of God descending		s				591										
O King enthroned on high		s	158	504				189	311				421			
Open our eyes, Lord	gr	g		532								545			443	1468
Our Lord, his Passion ended		s	91					194	323				611			
Spirit of God, unseen as the wind		s				600	386						612	233		
Spirit of God within me		s		612	665			196	294	243	310			677		
Spirit of mercy, truth and love		o	89	613				197					143			
The Spirit lives to set us free		g		666			490				771	664			1555	
There's a spirit in the air		s	515	661		616	314	198	326	245				69		

Seasonal hymns and songs listed for Years A and C (pages 70 and 306) are also appropriate.

SONGS FOR CHILDREN

Breathe on me, Spirit of Jesus SOF 677
Holy Spirit, fill our hearts CH4 611
Holy Spirit (pour your power) KS 515
Wa wa wa emimimo A 103, IECS, MAG, SFL1 13

BIBLE READINGS

Morning Psalm 145
Evening Psalm 139.1–11[13–18,23–24]
Ezekiel 36.22–28
Acts 2.22–38
John 20.19–23

SINGING THE PSALM

Psalm 145 CH4, CRP, CWP, H&P, LAU, NEH, NPCW, PAME, PFS
    Walker *I will bless your name* ATNJ
Psalm 139 CH4, CWP, H&P, NPCW, PAME, PFS
    Berthier *Lord Jesus Christ* TSFP#
    Farrell *O God, you search me* CBL, CH4, LAU, MCW1, SG, TS (OCP)#
    Schutte *Yawheh, I know you are near* CFE
    Walsh *You know me, Lord* SFTL#

ANTHEMS AND VOCAL MUSIC

Title	Composer	Voices	E/M/D	Book source	Single sheet publisher
UNISON/TWO PART/HIGH VOICES					
As the deer longs	Hurd	U/SATB#	E	CFE, CG, CH4, LAU	OCP
Breathe on me	Hubbard	S	E	SFJ	Banks
Create in me	Ogden	U	E		WLP
Give me a new heart, O God	Walker	U#	E	OOD	
Give us, Lord, a new heart	Farrell	U/SATB#	E/M	LAU, RITH, SLG	OCP
Just like the deer	Ogden	U	E/M		WLP
Litany to the Holy Spirit (In the hour of my distress)	Hurford	U	E	AC2, NEP	OUP
THREE/FOUR PARTS					
Breathe on me, breath of God	Wilby	SATB + solo S	E/M		RSCM
Like as the hart	Howells	SATB	M	AC4	OUP
O God, you search me	Farrell	U/SATB#	E	CBL, CH4, LAU, MCW1, SG, TS	OCP
O Holy Spirit, Lord of grace	Tye	SATB unacc	E		RSCM
Sicut cervus	Palestrina	SATB unacc	M	ESM, SL (ATTB)	Chester
The dove descending breaks the air	Stravinsky	SATB	D		B&H
The Spirit's gift	McKinley	SATB	M/D	LOL	
Veni Sancte Spiritus	Fenton	SATB	M		B&H
Veni Sancte Spiritus	Harper	SATB (unacc)	E	SOTL	
Veni Sancte Spiritus	Kelly	SATB	D	EAC1	
FIVE OR MORE PARTS					
Deus, Deus meus	R.Panufnik	SSAATTBB + solo S	D		Universal
Dum complerentur dies pentecostes	Palestrina	SAATTB unacc	M		Novello
Gracious Spirit	Forbes	SSATB unacc	D	NNAB	
Loquebantur variis linguis	Tallis	SAATB unacc	M/D		Cathedral

ORGAN MUSIC

PRELUDES

Armsdorf A.   **Komm, Heiliger Geist, Herre Gott** in *80 Chorale Preludes* (Peters) E*
Buxtehude D.   **Nun bitten wir den Heiligen Geist** BuxWV 208 in *Complete Works* Vol.5 (Bärenreiter) E/M
Ley H.G.   **Prelude on 'Down Ampney'** (OUP) E
Peeters F.   **Komm, Heiliger Geist** in *Hymn Preludes for the Liturgical Year* Op.100 Bk.3 (Peters) E/M
Reger M.   **Pfingsten** Op.145/6 (Breitkopf) M

POSTLUDES

Clucas H.   **Variations on 'Veni creator'** (Fagus) E/M*
Near G.   **Komm, Gott Schöpfer, Heiliger Geist** in *Choraleworks* Set 3 (Aureole) M
Homilius G.A.   **Komm, Heiliger Geist, Herre Gott** in *Chorale Preludes* (Breitkopf) M
Walther J.G.   **Nun bitten wir den Heiligen Geist** in *80 Chorale Preludes* (Peters) E/M

TRINITY SUNDAY YEAR B

HYMNS AND SONGS

	pos	rdg	AMNS	CAON	CFE	CH4	CH5	CP	H&P	HTC	LAU	MP	NEH	SG	SOF	TS
Angel voices, ever singing		n	163	37	45	498	346	377	484	307	724	34	336	27	24	
Come, let us join our cheerful songs	ga			144	120		332	401	810	206		93	349	33	70	
Father eternal, Lord of the ages		s								1			356			
Father most holy, merciful and tender/loving		s	94	164	162			419	5	3			144			
Father of heaven, whose love profound		s	97	165	163	483	319	421	519	359		827	358	144		1201
Father, we adore you, lay our lives	cm	s		166	164		568	297		S 5	718	139			99	
Father, we love you, we worship		s		167	167		348					142		102	103	
Give to our God immortal praise		s	460	203			353	434	22	31		171		83		
God, we praise you! God, we bless you!		n				120	696	450		341			38			
Holy, holy, holy is the Lord		s		285			355				714	239			182	
Holy, holy, holy, Lord God almighty	m	s	95	286	259	111	321	202	7	594	468	237	146	290	183	177
How shall I sing that majesty		s	472	296		128	468	466	8				373/699			
I bind unto myself today/Christ be with me		s		302	274	639	322	203	695	5	312		159/278			757
I, the Lord of sea and sky (Here I am, Lord)	se	s		332	285	251	581	470			865	857		633	830	246
I will worship with all of my heart		n										991		213	859	270
Immortal, invisible, God only wise	ga	n	199	314	301	132	6	474	9	21	725	327	377	44	234	220
Lead us, heavenly Father, lead us		s	224	379	351		652	496	68	595	315	400	393	640	321	311
Let us sing to the Lord (Taizé)											689					
Lord of all being, throned afar		o				125		506	11			439	403			
May the grace of Christ our Saviour	gr	s	181	446			524	520	762	370			298	579		
My God, how wonderful thou art		s	102	457	497		7	523	51	369	727	468	410	202	395	896
The God of Abraham praise		s	331	642		162	323	586	452	9	712	645	148	66	530	975
Thou/God, whose almighty word		s	180	684	738	112	324	267	29	506	887	699	466	597	557	
We give immortal praise		s	520	713				206	18	11						
Worthy, O worthy are you, Lord		n										782			617	585
Ye/You holy angels bright		n	198	755		179	376	626	20	353		783	475	76	619	
You, living Christ, our eyes behold		o	533				333						487			

SONGS FOR CHILDREN

Because of who he is KS 18, TS 642
Father in heaven/Loving Creator CH4 116, H&P 3, HTC 2, LAU 313, SBTL, SG 200
Great is he MP 1048, SOF 1254, TS 705

BIBLE READINGS

Morning Psalm 33.1–12
Evening Psalm 104.1–10
Ezekiel 1.4–10,22–28a
Revelation 4
Mark 1.1–13

SINGING THE PSALM

Psalm 33.1–12 CRP, CWP, FGP, H&P, LAU, NEH, NPCW, PAME, PFS
  Walker *Lord, be with us* OOD#
Psalm 104.1–10 CRP, CWP, H&P, MCW1, NEH, NPCW, PFS
  Dean *Send forth your Spirit, O Lord* RE
  Nazareth *Send forth your Spirit, O Lord* PCMG#
  Rizza *Bless the Lord, my soul* LIOD#
  Rizza *Send forth your Spirit, O Lord* CAS, FOL#

ANTHEMS AND VOCAL MUSIC

Title	Composer	Voices	E/M/D	Book source	Single sheet publisher
UNISON/TWO PART/HIGH VOICES					
Breathe on me	Hubbard	S	E/M	SFJ	Banks
Praise to the Trinity/Laus Trinitati	Hildegard of Bingen	U	E	ETAS (Latin), OBFA	
The Spirit of the Lord is upon me (g)	Corp	2 part	E	VFLS	
THREE/FOUR PARTS					
God the Holy Trinity	Halls	SATB	E	SBS1	RSCM
Holy God, faithful and unchanging	Marks	SAMen	E	SBS2	
Holy, holy, holy	Schubert	SATB unacc	E	NOEAB, OBFA	
Holy, holy, holy, Lord God almighty	A.Smith	SAMen	M	OBFA	
Holy Spirit, ever dwelling (g)	Howells	SATB	E/M	ETAS	
Hymn to the Trinity	Tchaikovsky	SATB	M	NCAB, NNAB	Novello
Listen sweet dove (g)	Ives	SATB	M	EAC1, SC	RSCM
Love divine	Lloyd	SAMen	E	AOAN1	
Love divine	Willcocks	SATB	E	NOEAB	
Sanctus	Alcock	SATB + solo S	M	NSAC1	
The dove descending breaks the air (g)	Stravinsky	SATB	D		B&H
The Spirit of the Lord (g)	Elgar	SATB	M/D	SAEE	RSCM
Where thou reignest	Schubert	SATB	M	NCAB	
Worthy is the Lamb (Messiah)	Handel	SATB	M		Novello
FIVE OR MORE PARTS					
Alleluia, I heard a voice	Weelkes	SATBB unacc	D	OBTA	OUP
A Vision of Aeroplanes	Vaughan Williams	SSAATTBB	D		OUP
Holy, holy, holy	Gowers	SATB + SATB	M/D		RSCM
Libera me	Tavener	SSAATTBB unacc	D		OUP
The Cherubic Hymn	Glinka	SATTBB unacc	M/D	ESM	
The Cherubic Hymn	Grechaninov	SSAATTBB unacc	M	RCM	
The dove descending (g)	Harvey	SATB + SATB	D		Novello
Tibi laus	Philips	SSATB unacc	M/D		Banks

Anthems suggested for Years A and C (pages 73 and 309) are also suitable.

ORGAN MUSIC

PRELUDES

Bach J.S.	**Allein Gott in der Höh' sei Ehr'** BWV 711 and/or BWV 717 in Novello Vol.18, Bärenreiter Vol.3, Peters Vol.6 E/M and M*
Harper J.	**Triptych of the Holy Trinity** in *The IAO Millennium Organ Book* (IAO) E/M
Pachelbel J.	**Gott der Vater wohn uns bei** in *Complete Works* Vol.2 (Barenreiter) E/M*
Peeters F.	**St Patrick's Breastplate** in *Hymn Preludes for the Liturgical Year* Op.100 Bk.3 (Peters) E
Tallis T.	**Gloria tibi Trinitas** in *A Graded Anthology for Organ* Bk.2 (Cramer) and *Complete Works* (Peters) E*

POSTLUDES

Archer M.	**Laus Deo** in *25 Hymn Preludes: A Year of Praise* and in *Hymn Preludes for the Church Year* Bk.2 (both Mayhew) E/M
Bach J.S.	**Wir glauben all' an einen Gott, Schöpfer** BWV 680 in Novello Vols.2 & 16, Bärenreiter Vol.4, Peters Vol.7 E/M
Karg-Elert S.	**Allein Gott in der Höh** No.1 from *20 Preludes and Postludes* Op.78 and in *Hier Preisen auf der Erd* Vol.1 (Breitkopf) M
Piutti C.	**Kyrie, Gott Vater in Ewigkeit** in *Choralvorspiele* Op.34 Vol.2 (Bärenreiter) E

PROPER 4 (SUNDAY BETWEEN 29 MAY AND 4 JUNE INCLUSIVE) YEAR B
(if after Trinity Sunday)

HYMNS AND SONGS

	pos	rdg	AMNS	CAON	CFE	CH4	CH5	CP	H&P	HTC	LAU	MP	NEH	SG	SOF	TS
All I once held dear		g		18		506						799		562	646	11
Amazing grace – how sweet the sound		n		29	40	555	642	375	215	28	846	31	626	26	19	18
Beauty for brokenness		o		60		259	494					806		263	664	37
Forgiveness is your gift		n				361										
Give thanks with a grateful heart		n		202	189	180	352					170		108	124	118
God forgave my sin in Jesus' name		n		212	209		480			S 12	849	181			129	123
Have faith in God, my heart		g	372	268				458	675	431						
I walk by faith (Falson)		g												519	839	253
Jesu, lover of my soul		n	123	343	319	490	553	96	528	438	797	372	383	201	297	838
Lord, in thy name thy servants plead		o											126			
Miserere nobis/Holy Lord, have mercy (Taizé)												597		159		
My faith looks up to thee		g		453			590	522	683			469	72			1437
My spirit longs for thee		g	57					99					299			
Not far beyond the sea, nor high		g	401					528	477							
O God of earth and altar		o		492	527			358	426		935		492			
O lift us up, strong Son of God		n							427							
Ostende nobis, Domine (Taizé)				583							839					
Rejoice! Rejoice! Christ is in you		g			618						818	572			480	438
Sing of the Lord's goodness		n			654	157	368				713			61		
The kingdom is upon you!		g	512					590					650			
The kingdom of God is justice and joy		o		646	701			591	139	333	821	651	184			
The strife is o'er/past		n	78	667		412	286	159	214	163	275	670	119	416		
Thine arm/Your hands, O Lord, in days of old		g	285	671			347		397		431		324			
We cannot measure how you heal		g		712	772	718	514	348			433			490		
We rest on thee/We trust in you		n,g								446		735		510	587	1043
Will you come and follow me		g		752	812	533	605	622			877		647	634	1120	

SONGS FOR CHILDREN
Give me peace, O Lord CFE 191, CAON 802
I'm sorry for the wrong I've done KS 161

BIBLE READINGS

Psalm 35*
Jeremiah 5.1–19
Romans 7.7–25
Luke 7.1–10

SINGING THE PSALM

Psalm 35* CWP, NPCW

ANTHEMS AND VOCAL MUSIC

Title	Composer	Voices	E/M/D	Book source	Single sheet publisher
UNISON/TWO PART/HIGH VOICES					
Give ear unto me	Marcello	SS	E/M	AC2	
My spirit longs for thee	Godfrey	2 part	E	SBS2	
We walk by faith	Haugen	U#	E	CFE, LAU	GIA
THREE/FOUR PARTS					
Almighty and everlasting God	Gibbons	SATB unacc	M	FAB1, NCAB, OBTA	OUP
Come down, O love divine	Harris	SATB	E/M	FSB9, NCAB, MTH2	Novello
Firmly I believe and truly (g)	Shephard	SAMen	E	SFL2	
I heard the voice of Jesus say	Shephard	SATB	M		RSCM
If you believe and I believe (g)	Trad Zimbabwean	SATB unacc	E	C, CG, CH4, RTF, SBTL	
Lord, for thy tender mercy's sake	Hilton/Farrant	SATB unacc	E	AWTE, FAB1, NCAB, NOEAB, OBTA	OUP
Lord, give me faith (g)	Robson	SATB	E		RSCM
My spirit longs for thee	Lole	SATB unacc	E	SBS2	
O Lord, increase our faith (g)	Loosemore	SATB (unacc)	E	NCAB, SBS1	RSCM
O sing joyfully	Batten	SATB unacc	E	SCAB, WFC	RSCM
Teach me, O God	Camidge	SAB	E	CHM	
Teach me, O Lord	Moger	SAB	E		RSCM
Teach me, O Lord	Attwood	SATB	E	NOEAB	RSCM
The Spirit of the Lord	Elgar	SATB	M/D	SAEE	RSCM
The will of God	Warren	SAMen	E	NAB2, AOAN1	
We cannot measure how you heal	Bell arr Archer	SATB	E	BC	RSCM
FIVE OR MORE PARTS					
Beati quorum via	Stanford	SSATBB unacc	M	ASA, WFC	RSCM
Delight thou in the Lord	Thurlow	SSAATTBB + T unacc	M/D		Encore
Deus, Deus meus	R.Panufnik	SSAATTBB + solo S	D		Universal
I am thine, O save me	S.S.Wesley	SATTB	M	MTP	
Os justi	Bruckner	SSATTB unacc	M/D	ESM	Peters
Sing joyfully	Byrd	SAATB unacc	M	OBTA	OUP
Teach me, O Lord	Byrd	SAATB	M	OBTA	OUP

ORGAN MUSIC

PRELUDES

Darke H.   **Retrospection** in *Retrospection* (Novello) M
Elmore R.   **Chorale Prelude 'My faith looks up to thee'** in *Contemporary Chorale Preludes* (Boosey) M
Fletcher A.   **Doncaster** in *Preludes on the Great Hymns of Lent, Holy Week and Easter* (Mayhew) E/M
Hesford B.   **Amazing grace** (Fentone) E

POSTLUDES

Grace H.   **Toccatina on 'Kings Lynn'** in *Ten Compositions* Vol.1 (Schott) M
Rawsthorne N.   **Gelobet sei Gott** in *Easter Glory* (Mayhew) E/M
Taverner J.   **In nomine** in *The Mulliner Book* (Stainer) E/M*
Thiman E.   **Hanover** in *Four Chorale Improvisations* (Novello) M

Suitable before or after: Movements from Callahan C. **Partita on 'New Britain' (Amazing Grace)** (Concordia) E/M-M

PROPER 5 (SUNDAY BETWEEN 5 AND 11 JUNE INCLUSIVE) YEAR B
(if after Trinity Sunday)

HYMNS AND SONGS

	pos	rdg	AMNS	CAON	CFE	CH4	CH5	CP	H&P	HTC	LAU	MP	NEH	SG	SOF	TS
An army of ordinary people		n		31								32			20	20
Awake, my soul, and with the sun	mo,ga	1		58		210	51	1	632	264		804	232	618		
Born of the water		n								382						
Christ triumphant, ever reigning				104	113	436	259	398		173	763	77	*613*	319	62	655
Eternal Light, shine in my heart		g					613	415		339						
Glory to thee my God, this night/All praise	ev		10	208	200	223	63	14	642	274		176	244	502		
I am the bread of life (Konstant)		g			271											
I am the bread of life (Toolan)	of	g		299	272		420		611		629	261			200	
Jesus, the name high over all		g		364			99		264	213		385		323	307	298
Lord, for the years		o		409		159	81	81		328	942	428	*619*	602	892	327
Lord, I was blind, I could not see		g							423	437		433				
Lord of the Church, we pray for our renewing		n					303			499		442		577	1433	
My heart is full of Christ, and longs		n							799							
Now is eternal life		g	402	470			392	152	203				114			
Now the green blade riseth		g	501	475	513	417	278	153	204		278		115	414		
O bless the God of Israel		g					706			599						
O God of earth and altar		o		492	527			358	426		935		492			
O Lord of heaven and earth and sea		n	287				363	540	337	287			422	306		
Rejoice, O land, in God thy might		o	296	579			539	359		331			493			
Restore, O Lord, the honour		n		582		469						579		274	483	439
The God of Abraham praise		n	331	642		162	323	586	452	9	712	645	148	66	530	975
Thine arm/Your hands, O Lord, in days of old		g	285	671			347	397		431		324				
Wait for the Lord (Taizé)		s		949	762	276					88			1575		
We cannot measure how you heal		g		712	772	718	514	348			433		490			
We rest on thee/We trust in you		o								446		735		510	587	1043
Worthy, O worthy are you, Lord		n										782		617	585	
Ye who own the faith of Jesus/All who claim/keep		n		759	29			231			359		188			

SONGS FOR CHILDREN

Give me peace, O Lord CFE 191, CAON 802
We will walk with God/We are on the Lord's road (Sizohamba naye) C 198, CH4 803, IECS, OITB, SFL1 21, SG 138, VFLS 40

BIBLE READINGS

Psalm 37.1–11[12–17]
Jeremiah 6.16–21
Romans 9.1–13
Luke 7.11–17

SINGING THE PSALM

Psalm 37.1–11[12–17] CWP, NPCW

ANTHEMS AND VOCAL MUSIC

Title	Composer	Voices	E/M/D	Book source	Single sheet publisher
UNISON/TWO PART/HIGH VOICES					
Most glorious Lord of life	Harris	2 part	E/M	OEAB	OUP
O for a closer walk with God	Caesar	SSA	M/D	EAC2	
Risen Lord	Barry Rose	2 part	E	HP	
We walk by faith	Haugen	U#	E	CFE, LAU	GIA
THREE/FOUR PARTS					
Blessed are those that are undefiled in the way	Greene	SATB + SS	M/D		CMS/OUP
Go forth and tell!	Ogden	SATB	E	SBS2	RSCM
Holy God	March	SATB unacc	E	SBS2	
If ye be risen again with Christ	Gibbons	SATB + solo SSA	M		Novello
Lead me, Lord	S.S.Wesley	SATB	E	AC1, NCAB, NOEAB, NSAC1	Novello
Lord, for thy tender mercy's sake	Hilton/Farrant	SATB unacc	E	AWTE, FAB1, NCAB, NOEAB, OBTA	OUP
Now the green blade riseth (g)	Trad arr Lindley	SATB	E/M	AWTE	Banks
Now the green blade riseth (g)	Trad arr Lumsden	SATB	M		Encore
O for a closer walk with God	Ives	SATB	M		RSCM
O for a closer walk with God	Stanford	SATB	M	AC1, ASA, BC, OBFA, AOAN1 (SAMen)	RSCM
O Master, let me walk with thee	Ledger	SATB	E		Encore
Purest and highest	Stanford	SATB	E	ASA	RSCM
Since by man came death (Messiah) (g)	Handel	SATB	M		Novello
To be a pilgrim	Burt	SAMen	E/M	OBFA	
Verily, verily I say unto you (g)	Tallis	SATB unacc	E	AC1, TA, SBS2	OUP
Walking by faith	Marsh	SAB	E	AOAN1	
FIVE OR MORE PARTS					
Beati quorum via	Stanford	SSATBB unacc	M	ASA, WFC	RSCM
I want Jesus to walk with me	Trad arr Williams	SSATB	M	SFC	
Now the green blade riseth (g)	Trad arr Moore	SAATBB unacc	M/D		Encore
Open thou mine eyes	Rutter	SSATB unacc			OUP
Walk softly (g)	Chilcott	SAATBB	M	BCA	OUP

ORGAN MUSIC

PRELUDES

Bach J.S.	**Liebster Jesu, wir sind hier** BWV 706 (i), BWV 730 or BWV 731 in Novello Vol.18, Bärenreiter Vol.3, Peters Vol.5 E
Burkhardt M.	**Now the green blade rises** in *5 Easter Season Hymn Improvisations* Set 2 (MorningStar) E/M
Gaze N.	**Terzet on 'Morning Hymn'** in *Matinales* (Fagus) M/D
Howells H.	**Psalm-Prelude** Set 1 No.2 (Novello) M
Willan H.	**Prelude on 'Wareham'** in *Ten Hymn Preludes* Set 2 (Peters) E/M

POSTLUDES

Archer M.	**Noel nouvelet** in *Fifty Hymn Preludes* and in *Preludes on the Great Hymns of Lent, Holy Week and Easter* (both Mayhew) E/M
Lang C.S.	**Chorale Prelude 'Leoni'** No.3 of *Three Chorale Preludes* Op.77 (OUP reprint) M
Lebègue N.	**Offertoire du 3ème ton** p.8 in *Offertoires from Troisième Livre d'Orgue* (Hawthorns) E/M*
Near G.	**Leoni** in *Choraleworks* Set 2 (Aureole) E/M

PROPER 6 (SUNDAY BETWEEN 12 AND 18 JUNE INCLUSIVE) YEAR B

(if after Trinity Sunday)

HYMNS AND SONGS

	pos	rdg	AMNS	CAON	CFE	CH4	CH5	CP	H&P	HTC	LAU	MP	NEH	SG	SOF	TS
All I once held dear		g		18		506						799		562	646	11
All my hope on God is founded		o	336	19	21	192	10	368	63	451	959	16	333	525		620
Forgiveness is your gift		g				361										
God forgave my sin in Jesus' name		g		212	209		480			S 12	849	181			129	123
God is love, let heaven adore him		o	365	217		123	3	442	36		811	187	364			
God of freedom, God of justice		o		224		263		447								
How sweet the name of Jesus sounds		g	122	297		461	92	467	257	211		251	374	42	194/782	190/1273
I bind unto myself today/Christ be with me		g		302	274	639	322	203	695	5	312		159/278			757
In Christ there is no east or west		n	376	319	303	624	522	477	758	322	831	329	480	575		
Jesu, lover of my soul		g	123	343	319	490	553	96	528	438	797	372	383	201	297	838
Jesus Christ is waiting		o		349	323	360					889			624	1381	1360
Jesus, you are changing me		n										389			311	
Join all the glorious names		n				460		493	78	214		392	639	46	313	848
Judge eternal, throned in splendour		o		372		264	535	356	409	329		395	490	600		
Miserere nobis/Holy Lord, have mercy (Taizé)											597		159			
O God of earth and altar		o		492	527			358	426		935		492			
O Lord, hear my prayer (Taizé)		ps		938	542		620				929	908		246	423	394
Oh, the mercy of God		g										1099		195	958	914
Open our eyes, Lord		g		532								545			443	1468
Ostende nobis, Domine (Taizé)				583							839					
Rock of ages (Kendrick)		g													1507	951
Rock of ages, cleft for me		g	135	584	624	554	557	565	273	593		582	445	150	488	950
Saviour, again to thy dear name we raise	ev		15	587		221	71	20	643	281		584	250			
Such love, pure as the whitest snow		g		620								619		216	514	465
The kingdom of God is justice and joy		o		646	701			591	139	333	821	651		184		
The Lord is king! Lift up thy voice		n	107	650		129	8	592	58	183		656		98		
What shall I do my God to love		n							47							
When morning gilds the skies	mo		146	739	805		344	619	276	223		756	473	74	597	1054
Who can sound the depths of sorrow		o		747								766		257	604	579

SONGS FOR CHILDREN

Do what you know is right CAON 791, CH 38, KS2 448

Lord, I pray, if today CH4 541

BIBLE READINGS

Psalm 39
Jeremiah 7.1–16
Romans 9.14–26
Luke 7.36 - 8.3

SINGING THE PSALM

Psalm 39 CWP, NPCW

ANTHEMS AND VOCAL MUSIC

Title	Composer	Voices	E/M/D	Book source	Single sheet publisher
UNISON/TWO PART/HIGH VOICES					
Settings of Kyrie eleison/Lord have mercy	Various	U/SATB	E	C, LAU, MCW1, RE	
Community of Christ	Farrell	U + descant	E	GBU	
Creator God	Rizza	U/SATB + descant#	E	ROP	
Drop, drop slow tears (g)	Gibbons	SSA	E	AC3	
Send down the fire of your justice	Haugen	U/SATB#	E	C, TS	GIA
Sent by the Lord am I	Trad arr Weaver	2 part	E	BC	RSCM
THREE/FOUR PARTS					
A Litany (Drop, drop, slow tears) (g)	Walton	SATB unacc	D	AC4	OUP
Almighty and everlasting God	Gibbons	SATB unacc	M	FAB1, NCAB, OBTA	OUP
Amen, amen, it shall be so!	Bell	SATB + cantor	E	LAA	
Blessed are they	S.S.Wesley	SAB	E		S&B
Blest are the pure in heart	Walford Davies	SATB unacc	E	MTH1, NCAB	
Drop, drop slow tears (g)	Gibbons	SATB	E	NOEAB, MEA (SAB)	
Drop, drop slow tears (g)	Leighton	SATB	D		Novello
Have mercy upon me, O God	Tomkins	SAB	E		Banks
Hide not thou thy face	Farrant	SATB unacc	E/M	NCAB, OBFA, OBTA, BC	
Lord, for thy tender mercy's sake	Hilton/Farrant	SATB unacc	E	AWTE, FAB1, NCAB, NOEAB, OBTA	OUP
The Beatitudes	Chilcott	SATB	M		OUP
The Beatitudes	Pärt	SATB	D		Universal
The Beatitudes	Watson Henderson	SATB	M/D	SC	RSCM
There's a wideness in God's mercy	Bevan	SATB	E	LD, MTH1, NOEAB, NEP	
Turn thy face from my sins	Attwood	SATB	E/M	BC, FAB1, NCAB, TEA	RSCM
FIVE OR MORE PARTS					
Drop, drop slow tears (g)	Gibbons	SAATB unacc	E	NCAB	
Miserere mei	Byrd	SATBB unacc	M/D	OBTA	OUP
Remember, remember not, Lord	Purcell	SSATB unacc	M	APA	Faber

ORGAN MUSIC

PRELUDES

Adams T.   **Andante** from **Voluntary No.6** in *Organ Works Vol.5: Six Organ Voluntaries* (Fagus) M(*)
Archer M.   **St Peter** in *25 Hymn Preludes: A Year of Praise* (Mayhew) E
Boëllmann L. **Andantino** from *Deuxième Suite* (Kalmus, Butz, Durand) and in *Complete Works* Vol.2 (Bärenreiter) E/M
Callahan C.   **Prelude on 'Michael'** in *Two English Voluntaries* (Concordia) E/M
Darke H.   **Elegy** in *A Book of Simple Organ Voluntaries* (OUP Archive) E/M

POSTLUDES

Marchand L.   **Grand jeu** p.226 in *Organ Compositions* (Kalmus K4148) E(*)
Mathias W.   **Chorale** in *Easy Modern Organ Music* Bk.1 (OUP) E/M
Stanford C.V. **Final: St Patrick's Breastplate** *Finale of Sonata Celtica* (No.4) (Cathedral Music) D

Suitable before or after: Movements from Callahan C. **Partita on 'Hyfrydol'** (Concordia) E-M

PROPER 7 (SUNDAY BETWEEN 19 AND 25 JUNE INCLUSIVE) YEAR B

(if after Trinity Sunday)

HYMNS AND SONGS

	pos	rdg	AMNS	CAON	CFE	CH4	CH5	CP	H&P	HTC	LAU	MP	NEH	SG	SOF	TS
All the ends of the earth will remember		o													648	
Bless the Lord, my soul (Taizé)				923	81		1				813			105	676	56
Can we/man by searching find out God		n	438				11	201	76	426				496		
Dear Lord and Father of mankind		g	115	144	143	485	549	411	673	356	934	111	353		497	79
Deck thyself, my soul, with gladness/Soul, array thyself		n	257	146			445	295	606	400			280			
Father, we praise thee now the night is over	mo	o			168	209	53	3	633				149			
Father, whose everlasting love		n						107	520							
God forgave my sin in Jesus' name		g		212	209		480			S 12	849	181			129	
God is a name my soul adores		n						255	24							
God moves in a mysterious way		n	112	222		158	13	445	65			193	365			700
Hail thee, festival day! (Pentecost)		n				581			302		255					
Have faith in God, my heart		n	372	268			458	675	431							
How good/This, this is the God we adore		n		293				464		450		244		41		1270
Let earth and heaven combine		n							109							1394
Lord Jesus, think on me		g	129	412	384	491/2	554	97	533	316	204		70			
Meekness and majesty		n		448	487	356	228				751	465		395	390	353
My God, how wonderful thou art		n	102	457	497		7	523	51	369	727	468	410	202	395	896
Nature with open volume stands		n	497				232	113	174				87			
Praise the One who breaks the darkness		g				348										
Praise to the holiest in the height		n	117	572	606	378	108	557	231	140	788	563	439	58	469	
Praise, my soul, the King of heaven	ga	o	192	565	602	160	366	555	13	38	807	560	436	93	466	433
Rock of ages (Kendrick)		g													1507	951
Rock of ages, cleft for me		g	135	584	624	554	557	565	273	593		582	445	150	488	950
There's a wideness in God's mercy/Souls of men/Restless souls		n	251	662		187	9	598	230	443	810	683	461/700	188		
To God be the glory		g		695	745	512	373	609	463	584	719	708		71	559	526
We cannot measure how you heal		g		712	772	718	514	348			433		490			
We give immortal praise		n	520	713				206	18	11						
Worthy, the Lord is worthy		n													618	
You are beautiful beyond description		n		760								788			621	589

SONGS FOR CHILDREN

Fishes of the ocean CAON 799, CH 49

My God is so big/Our God is so great CAON 547/865/872, CH 169, JP 169, KS 255, SOF 1455, TS 420

BIBLE READINGS

Psalm 49
Jeremiah 10.1–16
Romans 11.25–36
Luke 8.26–39

SINGING THE PSALM

Psalm 49 CWP, NPCW

ANTHEMS AND VOCAL MUSIC

Title	Composer	Voices	E/M/D	Book source	Single sheet publisher
UNISON/TWO PART/HIGH VOICES					
Creator God	Harper	U	E	CFTW	
Creator God	Rizza	U/SATB + descant#	E	ROP	
Let all creation sing	Ogden	U + descants	E	SFL2	
Praise, O praise	How	2 part	E	BC, MEA, NCAB	RSCM
There is a longing	Quigley	U/SATB#	E	CH4, LAU, SG	OCP
THREE/FOUR PARTS					
Achieved is the glorious work (Creation)	Haydn	SATB	M	FSB9	Novello
All creatures of our God and King	Harris	SATB	M		RSCM
For the gifts of life and love	Nardone	SATB	M	SC	
God omnipotent reigneth	Wood	SATB	E	SBS1	RSCM
O King all glorious	Willan	SATB unacc	E/M	ETAS	
O Lord our Governor	Barry Rose	SATB	M	MTP	
Rejoice, the Lord is king	Archer	SATB	M		Mayhew
Rejoice, the Lord is king	Kelly	SATB	M/D	NNAB, MTH1	
Song of the Creator	Weaver	SATB	M	SBS1	
The Doctrine of Wisdom	Mathias	SATB	M		OUP
The heavens are telling (Creation)	Haydn	SATB	M		Novello
We cannot measure how you heal (g)	Bell arr Archer	SATB	E	BC	RSCM
Where shall wisdom be found?	Carter	SATB	M/D		OUP
FIVE OR MORE PARTS					
Lord, let me know mine end	Greene	SSATB	M		Novello
Rejoice, the Lord is king	Weaver	SSAATB	M	SC	
O where shall wisdom be found?	Boyce	SSATB	M		Novello
The Lord is King	Radcliffe	SATBB	M		Encore

ORGAN MUSIC

PRELUDES

Clucas H.   **Schmücke dich** in *A Coldridge Organ Book* (Animus) E*

Dupré M.   **Ut queant laxis** Op.38/14 from *Le Tombeau de Titelouze* Op.38 (Gray) M

Stanford C.V.   **Allegretto in F** No.1 of *Six Short Preludes and Postludes* (Set 1) Op.101 (Stainer); also in *Preludes and Postludes* (Mayhew) E/M

Tomkins T.   **Voluntary in D minor** in *Nine Organ Pieces* (Stainer) M*

Vierne L.   **Lied** from *24 Pièces en Style Libre* Bk.2 (Masters, Durand) E/M

POSTLUDES

Dyson G.   **Voluntary in D** in *An Album of Praise* (OUP) E/M

Etherington C.   **Carillon** in *The IAO Millenium Organ Book* (IAO) M

Wesley S.   **Spiritoso** from **Voluntary IV in G** Op.6 No.4 in *Twelve Voluntaries for Organ* Op.6 Bk.1 (Fagus) E*

Wood C.   **Newtoun Tune** ('London New') No.6 of *Sixteen Preludes on Melodies from the English and Scottish Psalters* Vol.1 (FitzSimons) M

PROPER 8 (SUNDAY BETWEEN 26 JUNE AND 2 JULY INCLUSIVE) YEAR B

HYMNS AND SONGS

	pos	rdg	AMNS	CAON	CFE	CH4	CH5	CP	H&P	HTC	LAU	MP	NEH	SG	SOF	TS
All I once held dear		g		18		506						799		562	646	11
All people that on earth do dwell	ga		100	21	22	63	683	369	1	14	466	20	334	77	13	13
All that I am, all that I do		g		23	23	505					600					
Awake, awake: fling off the night!		n	342	57	64		334				851					
By your side I would stay		n		90								810			55	60
Come with all joy to sing to God	ga	o								16						
Dear Lord and Father of mankind		n	115	144	143	485	549	411	673	356	934	111	353	497	79	79
Filled with the Spirit's power		g	359	170			298	425	314	233				593		
For the fruits of his/all creation		n	457	185	178	231	39	254	342	286	731	153	*621*	299	1234	685
For the healing of the nations		n	361	186	179	706	496	427	402		886			261	1235	
From heaven you came, helpless babe		g		195	187	374	219	432			749	162		632	120	114
God has spoken – by his prophets		o					381		64	248	742	831		225		
God is working his purpose out		n		221	217	235	481	444	769	191	86	189	495	451	135	128
Hark, a herald/thrilling voice is calling/trumpet call is sounding		n	24	263	243		126	26		192	92		5	436		
I come with joy		g	473	304		656	421	305	610	408	649		*623*	469		
I will worship with all of my heart		o										991		213	859	270
I, the Lord of sea and sky (Here I am, Lord)		g		332	285	251	581	470			865	857		633	830	246
I'll follow my Lord		g												688		
Jesu, good above all other		g	378	350			585	487	732	96			387			
Miserere nobis/Holy Lord, have mercy (Taizé)											597			159		
My song is love unknown		g	63	463	503	399	231	112	173	136	752	478	86	384	400	897
Not far beyond the sea, nor high		o	401					528	477							
O Day of God, draw nigh		n	405				33									
O God of earth and altar		n		492	527			358	426		935			492		
Revive thy work/your church, O Lord!		o					308		780	515		578				
Soldiers of Christ, arise		n	219	606		515	487	571	719	533		604	449	643	506	
Sun of my soul	ev		11	621			72	21	646			618	251			
The kingdom is upon you!		g	512					590					*650*			
Thy/Your kingdom come! On bended knee		n	178	690		473		608					500			
Ubi caritas/Living charity (Taizé)		n		946		801	530				245				1573	
When I needed a neighbour		n	433	736	800	544	499				888				1604	
Will you come and follow me		g		752	812	533	605	622			877		647	634	1120	

SONGS FOR CHILDREN

Lord, you've promised CAON 864, CH 150, KS 244
Step by step, on and on CAON 885, CH 191

BIBLE READINGS

Psalms [52 and] 53
Jeremiah 11.1–14
Romans 13.1–10
Luke 9.51–62

SINGING THE PSALM

Psalm 52 CWP, NPCW
Psalm 53 CWP, NPCW

ANTHEMS AND VOCAL MUSIC

Title	Composer	Voices	E/M/D	Book source	Single sheet publisher
UNISON/TWO PART/HIGH VOICES					
Christ has no body now but yours	Ogden	U + descant#	E	CFAP, LOL	RSCM
Faith, hope and love	Ogden	2 part	E	SBS1	RSCM
I give you a new commandment	Aston	2 part	E	NOEAB, EAC2	RSCM
Love one another	S.S.Wesley	S	E	BC	RSCM
The Call (Come, my Way)	Vaughan Williams	U	E	NEP	S&B
When I needed a neighbour	Carter arr Burt	2 part	M	SFL1	
THREE/FOUR PARTS					
A new commandment	Anon arr Wilson	SATB	E	AWS	
A new commandment	Parshall	SATB unacc	E	WFC	
Greater love	Ireland	SATB	M	AC4	S&B
I give to you a new commandment	Nardone	SATB	E/M	SBS1	RSCM
I give you a new commandment	Shepherd	TTBB unacc	E		CMS/OUP
I give you my hands, Lord	Tambling	SAMen unacc	M	NAB2	
Lead me, Lord	S.S.Wesley	SATB	E	AC1, NCAB, NOEAB, NSAC1	Novello
O for a closer walk with God (g)	Stanford	SATB	E/M	AC1, ASA, BC, OBFA, AOAN1 (SAMen)	RSCM
The Lord bless you and keep you	Rutter	SATB	E/M	EAC1, JRA, WFC, OBFA (SAMen)	OUP
The Summons (g)	Bell	SATB	E	AWS	
Ubi caritas	Ives	SATB unacc	M	SC	
Ubi caritas	Lauridsen	SATB unacc	M		Faber
When I needed a neighbour	Carter arr Rose	SATB	E	MTH1	
FIVE OR MORE PARTS					
Love one another	Carter	SSAATTBB	M/D		OUP
Ubi caritas	Berkeley	SSATB unacc	D		Chester
Ubi caritas	Duruflé	SAATTBB unacc	M		Durand
When I needed a neighbour	Carter arr Rose	SATB + SATB	E/M	MTH1	

ORGAN MUSIC

PRELUDES

Bach J.S. **Adagio** from BWV 564 in Novello Vol.9, Bärenreiter Vol.6, Peters Vol.3 E/M
Bédard D. **Prélude** from *Suite* (Cheldar) M
Darke H. **Interlude** in *The Hovingham Sketches* (Banks) E/M
Dubois T. **Méditation in E flat** in *Douze Pièces* (Leduc, Bärenreiter) E/M
Joubert J. **Prelude on Old 100th** (OUP) M

POSTLUDES

Archer M. **Merton** in *25 Hymn Preludes: A Year of Praise* and in *40 Christmas Preludes* (both Mayhew) M
Campbell S. **Canterbury Improvisations: No. 1 Impromptu** (Novello); also in *Canterbury Organ Album* (Novello) M
Phillips G. **Procession** from *Tower Hill Suite* (Animus) E/M
Rawsthorne N. **Postlude** in *Twelve Miniatures for Festive Occasions* (Mayhew; manuals-only edition also available) E(*)

PROPER 9 (SUNDAY BETWEEN 3 AND 9 JULY INCLUSIVE) YEAR B

HYMNS AND SONGS

	pos	rdg	AMNS	CAON	CFE	CH4	CH5	CP	H&P	HTC	LAU	MP	NEH	SG	SOF	TS
A charge to keep I have		n							785							
Almighty Father, who for us thy Son didst give		n	338					374	401							
At/In the name of Jesus		n	148	54	59	458	94	380	74	172	762	41	338	317	32	33
Blessed are the ones I call the poor (HSNW p.86)		o														
Blest are the pure in heart		o	238	77	88		630	391	724	110	908		341	372		
Blest are they, the poor in spirit		o			89	341					814					
Come, let us use the grace divine		n							649							
Come, now is the time to worship	ga	n				196						1040		10	1203	662
Crown him with many crowns		g	147	137	139	459	263	166	255	174	321	109	352	321	77	77
Father of mercy, God of consolation		n					511						323			
Filled with compassion		g										828			716	105
For the fruits of his/all creation		g	457	185	178	231	39	254	342	286	731	153	*621*	299		685
Glorious things of thee are spoken		g	172	205	195	738	646	435	817	494	827	173	362	35	127	691
Go forth and tell!	se	g		238			478	437	770	505		178		596	738	
God is my great desire		1ps		218	216						912					
He that is down needs fear no fall		g	218						676							
How long, O Lord, will you forget		o				7						848		651		
In God alone my soul (Taizé)		n													813	
I've found a friend (Fragar)		n														251
Jesus lives! Thy terrors now		n	82	354			272	148	198	156		373	112	409	296	
Jesus, where'er thy people meet/ Lord Jesus, when your people	ga	n	162	367			336	492	549	371			390	16		844
Join all the glorious names		g				460			493	78	214		392	*639*	46	313	848
Look, ye saints, the sight is glorious		n				439	275	171	201	179		426			349	869
Love divine, all loves excelling		g	131	428	398	519	634	516	267	217	801	449	408	179	377	343
My God! I know, I feel thee mine		o							740							
O Lord, hear my prayer (Taizé)		o		938	542		620				929	908		246	423	394
Rock of ages (Kendrick)		n													1507	951
Rock of ages, cleft for me		n	135	584	624	554	557	565	273	593		582	445	150	488	950
Send me out from here	se	g											594		996	
The kingdom is upon you!		n	512					590					*650*			
The kingdom of God is justice and joy		g		646	701			591	139	333	821	651		184		
We hail thy presence glorious		n	266	714									310			

SONGS FOR CHILDREN

O Lord, I want to sing your praises MP 904, SOF 961
Sent by the Lord am I CFE 638, CG 105, CH4 250, IECS, LAU 855, SBTL, SG 616

BIBLE READINGS

Psalms [63 and] 64
Jeremiah 20.1–11a
Romans 14.1–17
Luke 10.1–11,16–20

SINGING THE PSALM

Psalm 63 CRP, CWP, LAU, NPCW, PFS
    Bell *O God, you are my God alone* CG, CH4, PPP
    Haugen *Your love is finer than life* CFE, LAU (GIA)#
    Hurd *My heart is searching* C#
    Taizé *Jesus, your Spirit in us* C#
    Walker *O Lord, I will sing* OOD (OCP)#
Psalm 64 CWP, NPCW

ANTHEMS AND VOCAL MUSIC

Title	Composer	Voices	E/M/D	Book source	Single sheet publisher
UNISON/TWO PART/HIGH VOICES					
A Song of Peace and Joy	Mawby	U + descant + instr	E	VFLS	
At the name of Jesus	Walker	U/SATB#	E	ATNJ	OCP
Sent by the Lord am I (g)	Trad arr Weaver	2 part	E/M	BC	
Shalom chaverim (g)	Trad arr Weaver	U	E	SFL1, VFLS	
Song of Consolation	Jones	U#	E	VE	
Surgens Jesus (g)	Monteverdi	SSA unacc	M	AC3	
Unless a grain of wheat	Farrell	U/SATB#	E	CFE, LAU, RITH, WYP	OCP
THREE/FOUR PARTS					
Blest are the pure in heart	Walford Davies	SATB unacc	E	MTH1, NCAB	RSCM
Christus factus est	Anerio	SATB unacc	M	AWTE, CM1, ESM	
Christus factus est	Ridout	SATB unacc	E		Encore
Go forth and tell!	Ogden	SATB	E	SBS2	RSCM
Go forth into the world in peace	Rutter	SATB	E/M	JRA	OUP
Go in peace	Schiavone	SATB#	E	C	
How beauteous are their feet	Stanford	SATB	M	ASA, NNAB, SC, AOAN1 (SAMen)	
How beautiful upon the mountains	Stainer	SATB	M	AOAN1 (SAMen), BC, NNAB	RSCM
Make me a channel of your peace	Temple arr Wilson	SATB	E	AWS	
May the peace of God the Father	Trad arr Harper	SATB#	E	BC, LOL	
O pray for the peace of Jerusalem	Goss	SATB	E	AC1	
O pray for the peace of Jerusalem	Howells	SATB	M		OUP
The peace of God	Rutter	SATB	E		OUP
The Prayer of Peace	Carter	SATB	M/D	EAC1	OUP
Trust in the Lord	Moore	SATB	M		Encore
FIVE OR MORE PARTS					
Deep peace	Carter	SSATB + solo SA	M	ACA, WFC	OUP
I was glad	Parry	SSAATTBB	M/D		RSCM
Surgens Jesus	Lassus	SSATB unacc	M/D		Mapa Mundi
Surgens Jesus	Philips	SSATB unacc	M/D	NCAB	
The Song of Christ's Glory	Ives	SSAATTBB unacc	M	WOTC	

ORGAN MUSIC

PRELUDES

Archer M.   **Franconia** in *25 Hymn Preludes: A Year of Praise* (Mayhew) E
Bédard D.   **Invocation** from *Triptyque* (Cheldar) E/M
Berlioz H.   **Hymne pour l'élévation** from **Three Pieces** in *Organ Music for Manuals Only* (Dover) E*
Dienel O.   **Wer nur den lieben Gott** Op.52/3 in *Berliner Orgelmusik des 19 Jahrhunderts* (Breitkopf) E
Elgar E.   **Cantique** Op.3/1 in *Elgar Organ Album* Bk.1 (Novello) E/M

POSTLUDES

Berlioz H.   **Toccata** from **Three Pieces** in *Organ Music for Manuals Only* (Dover) E/M*
Dienel O.   **Scherzando** Op.27 in *Berliner Orgelmusik des 19 Jahrhunderts* (Breitkopf) M
Ives G.   **Intrada** in *The Modern Organist* Bk.1 (Banks) E/M
Nixon J.   **St Albinus** in *Hymn Tune Preludes* (Fagus) E/M

PROPER 10 (SUNDAY BETWEEN 10 AND 16 JULY INCLUSIVE) YEAR B

HYMNS AND SONGS

	pos	rdg	AMNS	CAON	CFE	CH4	CH5	CP	H&P	HTC	LAU	MP	NEH	SG	SOF	TS
All my hope on God is founded		ap	336	19	21	192	10	368	63	451	959	16	333	525		620
Almighty Father, who for us thy Son didst give		g	338					374	401							
Be thou my vision/Lord, be my vision		o,ap	343	70	74/75	465	643	386	378	545	970	51	339	669	42	50
Beyond all mortal praise		o,ap		71									340			
Facing a task unfinished		n										126		88		
Father in heaven, grant to your children/Loving Creator		g				116			3	2	313		200			
Father of all whose laws have stood		g								539			664			
For I'm building a people of power		n		181	174							151			111	109
Great is thy faithfulness		o		249		153	80	453	66	260		200	636	39	147	138
Happy are they, they that love God		o	176	262			649	456	711	473			369			
Hark, my soul! It is the Lord/Christian, do you hear		g	244	264			569	457	521	472		209	637			
Help us to help each other/Jesus, united by thy grace		g	374	275			523	461	773	540						
I bind unto myself today/Christ be with me		ap		302	274	639	322	203	695	5	312		159/278			757
Immortal, invisible, God only wise		ap	199	314	301	132	6	474	9	21	725	327	377	44	234	220
Jesus is Lord! Creation's voice proclaims it		n		352	326		96	170	260	S 17	324	367			290	284
Jesus, Lord, we look to thee		g	380					489	759				481			
Laudate omnes gentes/Sing praises, all you peoples (Taizé)		ps									478				1515	
Let there be love shared among us		g		386	358		525					411			329	317
Let us sing to the Lord (Taizé)		ps									689					
My God, accept my heart this day		g	279	455	495			338	701	551	872		318	559		
Put thou thy trust in God/Commit thou all thy ways		o	223	576		270	563	562	672							
Ubi caritas/Living charity (Taizé)		g		946		801	530				245				1573	
We have a gospel to proclaim		n	431	716	778	363	491	612	465	519	852	728	486	331	1583	
When I needed a neighbour		g	433	736	800	544	499				888				1604	
Who can measure heaven and earth?		ap							27							
Who can sound the depths of sorrow		g		747								766		257	604	579
Who would true valour see/He who would valiant be		g	212	281	248	535	662	621	688	590	862	224	372	639	174	
You rescued me		g										1020			1142	605

SONGS FOR CHILDREN

When I needed a neighbour AMNS 433, CAON 736, CAP 65, CFE 800, CH 229, CH4 544, CH5 499, JP 275, LAU 888, SOF 1604

Would you walk by on the other side? CAP 70, CH5 500, JP 498

BIBLE READINGS

Psalm 66*

Job 4.1; 5.6–27 *or* Ecclesiasticus 4.11–31

Romans 15.14–29

Luke 10.25–37

SINGING THE PSALM

Psalm 66* CWP, NPCW, PAME

ANTHEMS AND VOCAL MUSIC

Title	Composer	Voices	E/M/D	Book source	Single sheet publisher
UNISON/TWO PART/HIGH VOICES					
He came singing love	Gibson	2 part	E	VFLS	
Lift on high the name of Jesus	Ogden	U/SATB#	E		WLP
Love one another (g)	S.S.Wesley	S	E	BC	RSCM
Out of darkness	Walker	U/SATB#	E	CFE, LAU, OOD	OCP
Prayer of St Benedict (g)	Payne	2 part	E	VFLS	
Sent by the Lord am I	Trad arr Weaver	2 part	E	BC	
The Good Samaritan (g)	Rusbridge	U	E		WLP
THREE/FOUR PARTS					
A Prayer of St Richard of Chichester	Archer	SATB	E		RSCM
Blessed is he that considereth the poor (g)	Wise	SATB	M	NCAB	
Give almes of thy goods (g)	Tye	SATB unacc	E	AC1, OBTA	OUP
Go forth and tell!	Ogden	SATB	E/M	SBS2	RSCM
Go forth into the world in peace	Rutter	SATB	E/M	JRA	OUP
Greater love	Ireland	SATB	M	AC4	S&B
I give to you a new commandment (g)	Nardone	SATB	E/M	SBS1	RSCM
Let all the world	Dyson	SATB	E	MTH1	Novello
Let all the world in every corner sing	Leighton	SATB	M/D	EAC1	Novello
Let all the world in every corner sing	Vaughan Williams	SATB	M		S&B
Now abideth faith, hope and charity (g)	Howells	SATB	D		Novello
The Spirit of the Lord	Elgar	SATB	M	SAEE	RSCM
Though I speak with the tongues of men (g)	Bairstow	SATB	M	NCAB, WFC	OUP
Ubi caritas (g)	Ives	SATB unacc	M	SC	
When I needed a neighbour (g)	Carter arr Whitbourn	SATB	E	AWS	
FIVE OR MORE PARTS					
Let the people praise thee, O God	Mathias	SSAATTBB	M/D	WFC	OUP
Ubi caritas (g)	Berkeley	SSATB unacc	D		Chester
Ubi caritas (g)	Duruflé	SAATTBB unacc	M		Durand
When I needed a neighbour	Carter arr Rose	SATB + SATB	E/M	MTH1	

ORGAN MUSIC

PRELUDES

Alwood R. **Voluntary** in *The Mulliner Book* (Stainer) E/M*

Drayton P. **Pavane** in *A Second Easy Album* (OUP) E

Gárdonyi Z. **Be thou my vision** in *Jazz Inspirations* (Bärenreiter) E/M

Vierne L. **Entrée** from *Messe Basse* Op.8 on 3-staves in *A Graded Anthology for Organ* Bk.5 (Cramer) E/M*

Watson R. **Immortal, invisible** in *At Your Service* (Fagus) E

POSTLUDES

Alain J. **Postlude pour l'office de Complies** in *Complete Works* Bk.3 (Leduc) E/M

Du Mage P. **Basse de trompette** from *Première Livre d'Orgue* (Kalmus) E/M*

Stanford C.V. **On an old Irish church melody** No.5 of *Six Short Preludes and Postludes* (Set 1) Op.101 (Stainer); also in *Preludes and Postludes* (Mayhew) E/M

Thalben-Ball G. **Gopsal** No.32 of *113 Variations on Hymn Tunes* (Novello) E

PROPER 11 (SUNDAY BETWEEN 17 AND 23 JULY INCLUSIVE) YEAR B

HYMNS AND SONGS

	pos	rdg	AMNS	CAON	CFE	CH4	CH5	CP	H&P	HTC	LAU	MP	NEH	SG	SOF	TS
All hail the power of Jesus' name		n	140	16	19	457	250	163	252	587	323	13	332	24	9	7
As the deer pants for the water		n		45	54	550	606				965	37			27	27
At/In the name of Jesus		n	148	54	59	458	94	380	74	172	762	41	338	317	32	33
Bless the Lord, my soul (Taizé)				923	81		1				813			105	676	56
By your side I would stay		g		90								810			55	60
Christ triumphant, ever reigning		n		104	113	436	259	398		173	763	77	*613*	319	62	655
Come, let us anew our journey pursue		ap							354							
Come, sing the praise of Jesus		n								208		101	320			
Heaven shall not wait		n		272		362										151
How deep the Father's love		n				549	224					988	193		780	185
How long, O Lord, will you forget		o				7						848	651			
I want to walk with Jesus Christ		g					580			S 16		302			261	
I will worship with all of my heart		g										991	213		859	270
In God alone my soul (Taizé)														813		
Jesus is the name we honour		n				481						870	122		870	285
Jesus shall take the highest honour		g		360								378	123		302	296
Join all the glorious names		n				460		493	78	214		392	639	46	313	848
Lord, as I wake I turn to you		o	485				56		634	267	672		236	561		
Lord, teach us how to pray aright		o	227	418		545	619	98	551	367			406			
Now is eternal life		n	402	470			392	152	203				114			
O heaven is in my heart		n		499											416	388
O let the Son of God enfold you		n		506								502			419	392
O love divine, how sweet thou art		g	124				621	541					424			
Praise to the holiest in the height		n	117	572	606	378	108	557	231	140	788	563	439	58	469	
The Lord is my light (Taizé)		n		944												
To be in your presence		g		694								951	523		1067	524
When you've been broken		o													1115	
Where high the heavenly temple stands		n	130			451	291			184						
With joy we meditate the grace		n	530					624	235			774				

SONGS FOR CHILDREN
Come, children, join and sing CH4 185

BIBLE READINGS

Psalm 73*

Job 13.13 - 14.6 *or* Ecclesiasticus 18.1–14

Hebrews 2.5–18

Luke 10.38–42

SINGING THE PSALM

Psalm 73* CWP, NPCW

ANTHEMS AND VOCAL MUSIC

Title	Composer	Voices	E/M/D	Book source	Single sheet publisher
UNISON/TWO PART/HIGH VOICES					
Calm me, Lord (g)	Rizza	U/SATB#	E	CAON, CAS, FOLO	
Centre of my life	Inwood	U/SATB#	E	CFE, CSF, LAU, SG	OCP
Dear Lord and Father of mankind	Parnell	SS	M		Encore
Listen (g)	Nazareth arr Archer	2 part	E	BC	
Prayer of St Benedict	Payne	2 part	E	VFLS	
Silent, surrendered (g)	Rizza	U/SATB#	E	CAON, CAS, FOL, TS	
THREE/FOUR PARTS					
Angels	Lole	SATB	M		Encore
Be still, my soul (g)	Sibelius	SATB	E		Breitkopf & Hartel
Be still, my soul(g)	Whitlock	SATB	M		Banks
Christ our God descends from heaven	Bullard	SAMen	E	SBS2	
Christus factus est	Anerio	SATB unacc	M	AWTE, CM1, ESM	
Christus factus est	Bruckner	SATB unacc	M/D	ESM	RSCM
Greater love	Ireland	SATB	M	AC4	S&B
Jesu, the very thought of thee	Bairstow	SATB unacc	E/M		OUP
King of all ages, throned on high	Isom	SATB	E	NOEAB	
Lead me, Lord	S.S.Wesley	SATB	E	AC1, NCAB, NOEAB, NSAC1	Novello
Man that is born of a woman (Funeral Sentences)	Purcell	SATB	M		S&B, Novello
O clap your hands	Vaughan Williams	SATB	M/D	AC4	OUP
O for a closer walk with God (g)	Stanford	SATB	M	AC1, ASA, BC, OBFA, AOAN1 (SAMen)	RSCM
The Song of Christ's Glory	P.Moore	SATB	E		RSCM
FIVE OR MORE PARTS					
Christe adoramus te	Monteverdi	SSATB unacc	M	ESM	
Homo natus de muliere	Wilbye	SSAATB unacc	M		Banks
Let all mortal flesh keep silence	Bairstow	SSAATTBB unacc	D	AC4	S&B
The Song of Christ's Glory	Ives	SSAATTBB unacc	M	WOTC	
Walk softly (g)	Chilcott	SAATBB	M	BCA	OUP

ORGAN MUSIC

PRELUDES

Elgar E.	**No.2** *and/or* **No.4** from *Vesper Voluntaries* (Faber) E/M(*)
Harris W.H.	**Fantasy Prelude** in *Retrospection* (Novello) M/D
Harwood B.	**Praise, my soul** No.6 of *8 Short Pieces Op.58* in *Complete Works* Vol.2 (Stainer) E/M
Lloyd Webber W.S.	**Communion** 2-stave in *Prayer and Praise* (Paxton), 3-stave in *Aria* (Mayhew) E(*)
Whitlock P.	**Andante tranquillo** from *Five Short Pieces* in *Whitlock: Complete Shorter Works* (OUP) E/M

POSTLUDES

Jacob G.	**Festal Flourish** in *An Album of Praise* (OUP) E/M
Lloyd Webber W.S.	**Choral March** in *Prayer and Praise* (Paxton) E/M(*)
Nixon J.	**Procession on 'Salzburg'** in *Easter Glory* (Mayhew) M
Willan H.	**Postlude on 'Miles Lane'** in *36 Short Preludes and Postludes* Set 1 (Peters) M

PROPER 12 (SUNDAY BETWEEN 24 AND 30 JULY INCLUSIVE) YEAR B

HYMNS AND SONGS

	pos	rdg	AMNS	CAON	CFE	CH4	CH5	CP	H&P	HTC	LAU	MP	NEH	SG	SOF	TS
A debtor to mercy alone		n								449						
Alleluia! Sing to Jesus		n	262	12	37	445	398	278	592	170	644	207	271	458	153	616
Bless the Lord, my soul (Taizé)				923	81		1				813			105	676	56
Christ triumphant, ever reigning		n		104	113	436	259	398		173	763	77	*613*	319	62	655
Come to us, creative Spirit		ap				612	453		377	308				621		
Draw near/nigh and take the body of the Lord	cm	n			150		411	296		401	628		281			
Father God, I wonder		g		159		186						128		107	92	91
Father of heaven, whose love profound		g	97	165	163	483	319	421	519	359		827	358	144		1201
Great is thy faithfulness		g		249		153	80	453	66	260		200	*636*	39	147	138
Hark! The voice of love and mercy		n					221			128				382		1234
Help us, O Lord, to learn		n	373				382	460	474	493			370	226		
How sweet the name of Jesus sounds		o,n	122	297		461	92	467	257	211		251	374	42	194/782	190/1273
I know that my Redeemer lives, what joy		o		311			270		196	169		278		406		
Jesus shall take the highest honour		n		360								378		123	302	296
Join all the glorious names		n				460		493	78	214		392	*639*	46	313	848
Lord Jesus Christ, you have come to us		g	391	411	383		429	505	617	417	772	435	297	670	357	
Lord, teach us how to pray aright		g	227	418		545	619	98	551	367			406			
My God, how wonderful thou art		o	102	457	497		7	523	51	369	727	468	410	202	395	896
One thing I ask		g				199						913			440	407
Seek ye first the kingdom of God		g		590	633	641	596		138		820	590			493	447
Shout for joy and sing your praises		o		596								927			496	450
Son of God, eternal Saviour		g	132			468	527	573		102			498			
The Lord ascendeth up on high		n				440		173	210				135			
Thou art/You are the way		n	128	682			115	600	234	113		695	464			
Thy/Your kingdom come, O God		g	177	691			509	607	783	334		949	499	269		
We hail thy presence glorious		n	266	714									310			
Where high the heavenly temple stands		n	130			451	291			184						
With joy we meditate the grace		o	530					624	235			774				
Within our darkest night (Taizé)				950												

SONGS FOR CHILDREN

Caribbean Lord's Prayer CAON 544, CAP 51, CFE 584, CH 167, IECS, JP 192, MP 557, SG 247
God's not dead CAON 810, CH 72, JP 60, KS 85, TS 133

BIBLE READINGS

Psalm 74*

Job 19.1–27a *or* Ecclesiasticus 38.24–34

Hebrews 8

Luke 11.1–13

SINGING THE PSALM

Psalm 74* CWP, NPCW

ANTHEMS AND VOCAL MUSIC

Title	Composer	Voices	E/M/D	Book source	Single sheet publisher
UNISON/TWO PART/HIGH VOICES					
Settings of the Lord's Prayer (g)	Various	U	E	MCW1	
I will worship (g)	Dyson	U	M	HP	
I know that my Redeemer lives	Ogden	U + descant	E		WLP
King of glory, King of peace	Sanders	SSAA	M/D		Encore
Our Father (g)	Carter	U/cong	E	NCAB	
Pater noster (g)	Plainsong	U	E	C	
The Lord's Prayer (African Sanctus) (g)	Fanshawe	U/SATB	E		Faber
THREE/FOUR PARTS					
Above all praise	Mendelssohn	SATB	E	NCAB, OEAB	RSCM
Christus vincit	Mawby	SATB	D		Mayhew
Ecce sacerdos magnus	Bruckner	SATB + 3 trombones	M/D		Peters
Give us, Lord, a new heart	Farrell	SATB/U#	M	LAU, RITH, SLG	OCP
Greater love	Ireland	SATB	M	AC4	S&B
I know that my Redeemer liveth	Morley	SATB	M		Fagus
King of all ages, throned on high	Isom	SATB	E	NOEAB	
King of glory, King of peace	Ives	SATB	M	SBS1	RSCM
Notre Père (g)	Duruflé	SATB unacc	E		Durand
O God, the King of glory	Purcell	SATB unacc	E	APA, ETAS	OUP
Pater noster (g)	Stravinsky	SATB	M	RCM	B&H
Rejoice, the Lord is king	Archer	SATB	M		Mayhew
Rejoice, the Lord is king	Kelly	SATB	M/D	NNAB, MTH1	
Scio enim quod Redemptor	Lassus	SATB unacc	M	CM5	Chester
The Lord's Prayer (g)	Tchaikovsky	SATB unacc	E	RCM	
FIVE OR MORE PARTS					
Otche nash (g)	Arensky	SAATBB unacc	M	ESM	
Pater noster (g)	Stanford	SSAATTBB unacc	M		RSCM

ORGAN MUSIC

PRELUDES

Bach J.S.	**Vater unser in Himmelreich** BWV 683 in Novello Vol.16, Peters Vol.5 and Bärenreiter Vol.4 E/M*
Hylton Stewart C.	**St Peter** from *Five Short and Easy Pieces on Hymn Tunes* (Novello) E
Lang C.S.	**St Peter** No.4 of *Twenty Hymn-Tune Preludes for Manuals Only* Set 1 (OUP) E*
Richter E.F.	**Vater unser im Himmelreich** Op.29/2 in *Organ Music of the Classical & Early Romantic Periods* Vol.6 (Bärenreiter) M
Willan H.	**St James** in *36 Short Preludes and Postludes* Set 3 (Peters) E/M

POSTLUDES

Buxtehude D.	**Vater unser im Himmelreich** BuxWV 207 in *Complete Works* Vol.5 (Bärenreiter) M/D
Darke H.	**Prelude on 'Darwall's 148th'** No.2 of *Three Chorale Preludes* Op.20 (Novello) M
Du Mage P.	**Grand jeu** from *Première Livre d'Orgue* (Kalmus) E/M*
Willan H.	**Prelude on 'Hyfrydol'** in *Ten Hymn Preludes* Set 1 (Peters) E/M

PROPER 13 (SUNDAY BETWEEN 31 JULY AND 6 AUGUST INCLUSIVE) YEAR B

HYMNS AND SONGS

	pos	rdg	AMNS	CAON	CFE	CH4	CH5	CP	H&P	HTC	LAU	MP	NEH	SG	SOF	TS
All I once held dear		n		18		506						799		562	646	11
Almighty Father, who for us thy Son didst give		n	338					374	401							
Author of faith, eternal Word		n						381	662							
Be thou my vision/Lord, be my vision	o,g		343	70	74/75	465	643	386	378	545	970	51	339	669	42	50
Bless the Lord, my soul (Taizé)				923	81		1				813			105	676	56
Ere God had built the mountains		o							32							
For all the saints who from their labours rest		n	305	177	176	740	459	232	814	567	371	148	197	636	109	684
For all thy saints, O Lord		n	308	179			461	215					224			
Give me/us the wings of faith		n	324	204			463	216	815				225			
God of grace and God of glory		g	367	225			533	448	712	324		192		574	139	
Have faith in God, my heart		n	372	268			458	675	431							
He that is down needs fear no fall		g	218						676							
Immortal, invisible, God only wise	ga	o	199	314	301	132	6	474	9	21	725	327	377	44	234	220
Lord, it belongs not to my care		n	242					224	679		916		402			
Moses, I know you're the man		n		451	491				450		888					
My faith looks up to thee		n		453			590	522	683			469	72			1437
O Lord, hear my prayer (Taizé)				938	542		620				929	908		246	423	
O Lord of heaven and earth and sea		o	287				363	540	337	287			422	306		
O Lord, your tenderness		g		515								511		569	433	402
(O) worship the Lord in the beauty of holiness		g	49	552	560	201	196	89	505	344	169	529	52	204	457	426
Rejoice! Rejoice! Christ is in you		n			618						818	572			480	438
Take my life and let it be		g	249	625	677	502	597	581	705	554	874	624		678	519	468
The God of Abraham praise		n	331	642		162	323	586	452	9	712	645	148	66	530	975
The head that once was crowned with thorns		n	141	644	696	438	285	172	209	182	290	647	134	442	531	979
The works of the Lord are created in wisdom		o						266		26						
We give immortal praise		n	520	713				206	18	11						
We rest on thee/trust in you, our shield and our defender		n								446		735		510	587	1043
Who can measure heaven and earth		o							27							
With wonder, Lord, we see your works		o	531					269	353					316		

SONGS FOR CHILDREN

Don't be lazy SOF 701

Moses, I know you're the man CAON 451, CFE 491, H&P 450, LAU 868

BIBLE READINGS

Psalm 88*
Job 28 *or* Ecclesiasticus 42.15–25
Hebrews 11.17–31
Luke 12.13–21

SINGING THE PSALM

Psalm 88* CWP, FGP, NPCW

ANTHEMS AND VOCAL MUSIC

Title	Composer	Voices	E/M/D	Book source	Single sheet publisher
UNISON/TWO PART/HIGH VOICES					
A Song of Wisdom	Stanford	U	M		RSCM
Freedom is coming	Trad arr Perona-Wright	SSAA unacc	E	RTF	
Give us the wings of faith	Blatchly	SS	M	HP	
Let my people go	Trad arr Weaver	2 part	E	RTF	
Long since in Egypt's plenteous land	Parry	S + solo SS	E	NSAC1	
My eyes for beauty pine	Howells	U	E/M	NCAB, NOEAB	OUP
O Lord, my heart is not proud	Rizza	U/SATB#	E	CAON, CAS, FOL, TS	
THREE/FOUR PARTS					
Ach arme Welt (g)	Brahms	SATB unacc	M/D	ESM	Breitkopf & Hartel
Be thou my vision	Chilcott	SATB + solo S	E/M	BCA, NOEAB	OUP
Fairest Lord Jesus	Trad arr How	SAMen	E	BC, TEA	RSCM
Firmly I believe and truly	Shephard	SAMen	E	SFL2	
Lord, give me faith	Robson	SATB	E		RSCM
O hearken thou	Elgar	SATB	M	MTP	
O Lord, increase our faith	Loosemore	SATB (unacc)	E	NCAB, SBS1	RSCM
The Doctrine of Wisdom	Mathias	SATB	M		Banks
To be a pilgrim	Burt	SAMen	E/M	OBFA	RSCM
Where shall wisdom be found?	Carter	SATB	M/D		OUP
FIVE OR MORE PARTS					
Delight thou in the Lord	Thurlow	SSAATTBB	M/D		Encore
Go down, Moses (5 Spirituals from 'A Child of Our Time')	Trad arr Tippett	SSAATTBB unacc	M/D		Schott
In exitu Israel	S.Wesley	SATB + SATB	M		Novello
Jesu meine Freude (g)	J.S. Bach	SSATB unacc	D		Novello
Lord, let me know mine end	Greene	SSATB	M		Novello
O where shall wisdom be found?	Boyce	SSATB	M		Novello

ORGAN MUSIC

PRELUDES

Andriessen H.   **3rd movement of Suite** (Zengerinck) E/M

Benoist F.   **Pièce No.12** in *Benoist: Pièces pour Orgue* (Chanvrelin) E/M

Bonighton R.   **St Denio** in *100 Hymn Preludes* and in *Hymn Preludes for the Church Year* Bk.2 (both Mayhew) E

Dubois T.   **Petite Pastorale Champenoise** p.88 in *Complete Works* Vol.1 (Bärenreiter) E/M

Marsh J.   **Voluntary VI** of *Eighteen Voluntaries* Vol.1 (Animus) E*

POSTLUDES

Andriessen H.   **4th movement of Suite** (Zengerinck) E/M

Bédard D.   **Variations sur 'Sine nomine'** (Cheldar) M

Tomkins T.   **A Fantasy** in *Early Organ Music* Vol.2 (Faber) and in *Early English Organ Music* Vol.2 (OUP) M/D*

Weymann J.   **Festival Movement** Op.12/5 in *Praise and Thanks* (Bärenreiter) E/M

PROPER 14 (SUNDAY BETWEEN 7 AND 13 AUGUST INCLUSIVE) YEAR B

HYMNS AND SONGS

	pos	rdg	AMNS	CAON	CFE	CH4	CH5	CP	H&P	HTC	LAU	MP	NEH	SG	SOF	TS
At/In the name of Jesus		g	148	54	59	458	94	380	74	172	762	41	338	317	32	33
Beneath the cross of Jesus		n		65			561	105	165			55			39	45
Children of the heavenly King		g	213							566			344			
Christ is the King! O friends rejoice		n,g	345				86	165		492			345	31		
Father, we praise you now the night is over	mo	n			168	209	53	3	633				149			
Fight the good fight		n	220	169	171	517	566	423	710	526	860	143	359	635	107	
For all the saints who from their labours rest		n	305	177	176	740	459	232	814	567	371	148	197	636	109	684
For all thy saints, O Lord		n	308	179			461	215					224			
Give me/us the wings of faith		n	324	204			463	216	815				225			
Glorious things of thee are spoken		g	172	205	195	738	646	435	817	494	827	173	362	35	127	691
Glory in the highest to the God of heaven		n					693	300		582			363	37		
God who spoke in the beginning		o	468													
Hark, a herald/thrilling voice is calling/trumpet call is sounding		g	24	263	243		126	26		192	92		5	436		
He gave his life in selfless love		n					417			405		214		467		
He that is down needs fear no fall		g	218						676							
How shall I sing that majesty		o	472	296		128	468	466	8				373/699			
In Christ alone my hope is found		n										1072			1346	1311
In heavenly love abiding		g		323		551		478	678	458		331	331	*638*	238	782
O let the Son of God enfold you		n		506								502			419	392
Praise ye the Lord! 'Tis good to raise		o							338							
Thanks be to God who gives us the victory		n											637		521	
The Church's one foundation		n	170	636	688	739	528	585	515	501	830	640	484	581	525	477
The Lord is my light (Taizé)				944												
The works of the Lord are created in wisdom		o						266		26						
Thou/God, whose almighty word		o	180	684	738	112	324	267	29	506	887	699	466	597	557	
Thy/Your kingdom come! On bended knee		g	178	690		473		608					500			
Wait for the Lord (Taizé)				949	762	276					88				1575	
Who can measure heaven and earth?		o								27						
With wonder, Lord, we see your works		o	531				269	353					316			
Ye holy angels bright		n	198	755		179	376	626	20	353			783	475	76	619

SONGS FOR CHILDREN

Don't be lazy SOF 701
O when the saints CAON 876, CFE 571, CH 163, JP 195, RTF

BIBLE READINGS

Psalm 91*
Job 39.1 - 40.4 *or* Ecclesiasticus 43.13–33
Hebrews 12.1–17
Luke 12.32–40

SINGING THE PSALM

Psalm 91* CRP, CWP, FGP, LAU, MCW1, NEP, NPCW
 Bell *Whoever lives beside the Lord* CG, PPP
 Haugen *Be with me, Lord* C (GIA)#
 Joncas *On eagle's wings* CFE, LAU (OCP)#
 O'Hara *Be with me, Lord* CRP#

ANTHEMS AND VOCAL MUSIC

Title	Composer	Voices	E/M/D	Book source	Single sheet publisher
UNISON/TWO PART/HIGH VOICES					
Settings of the Te Deum	Various	U	E	MCW1	
Gaudent in coelis	Dering	2 part	M	AC2, SFL2	Schott
Let all creation sing	Ogden	U + descants#	E	SFL2	
Look at the world	Rutter	U/SATB	E	JRA	OUP
Maranatha, alleluia! (g)	Ogden	U + descant	M	SFL2 (SAMEN), ACB, CFL	RSCM
THREE/FOUR PARTS					
A Gaelic Blessing	Rutter	SATB	E	NCAB	RSCM
Fear not, O land	Elgar	SATB	M		Novello
For the beauty of the earth	Carter	SATB	M	NOEAB	OUP
For the gifts of life and love	Nardone	SATB	M	SC	
For all thy saints	Bullard	SATB	E/M	NOEAB	
Fight the good fight	Gardner	SATB	M	MTH1	OUP
Hail, glorious spirits, heirs of light	Tye	SATB unacc	E		RSCM
Holy is the true light	Harris	SATB	E/M	FSB7, NCAB, SL(ATTB)	Novello
In the city of the Lord	Harper	SATB	M/D	LOL	
O quam gloriosum	Byrd	SATB unacc	M	OBTA	
O quam gloriosum	Victoria	SATB unacc	M	ESM, NCAB	Chester
O thou the central orb (g)	Wood	SATB	M	AC4, AFC, SC	RSCM
O what their joy and their glory must be	Harris	SATB	M	ETAS	OUP
Song of the Creator	Weaver	SATB	M	SBS1	
The Church triumphant	Shephard	SATB	E	SBS1	RSCM
The heavens are telling (Creation)	Haydn	SATB	M		Novello
The true glory (g)	Aston	SATB	M		RSCM
Thou visitest the earth	Greene	SATB + solo T	E	BC, FAB1, NSAC2, NCAB, AOAN1 (SAB)	Novello
When the saints go marching in	Trad arr Rutter	SATB	M		OUP
FIVE OR MORE PARTS					
Vigilate (g)	Byrd	SATBB unacc	D		Chester

ORGAN MUSIC

PRELUDES

Betteridge L.   **Gregorian Prelude** (Paraclete) E/M
Marchand L.   **Trio** and **Récit** from *Quatrième Livre* in *Organ Compositions* (Kalmus K4148) E*
Near G.   **Moscow** in *Choraleworks* Set 1 (Aureole) E/M
Stanford C.V.   **Lento in G** No.3 of *Six Short Preludes and Postludes* (Set 2) Op.105 (Stainer); also in *Preludes and Postludes* (Mayhew) E/M
Tambling C.   **Chorale on 'York'** in *An Organ Miscellany* (Mayhew) E/M

POSTLUDES

Bédard D.   **Variations sur 'Sine nomine'** (Cheldar) M
Callaerts J.   **No.3 of Three Inventions** in *St Cecilia Organ Library* Vol.1 (Cramer) E/M
Lidon J.   **Sonata de 1º tono** in *Silva Ibérica* (Schott) E*
Lloyd Webber W.S.   **Festal March** in *Aria* (Mayhew) E/M

PROPER 15 (SUNDAY BETWEEN 14 AND 20 AUGUST INCLUSIVE) YEAR B

HYMNS AND SONGS

	pos	rdg	AMNS	CAON	CFE	CH4	CH5	CP	H&P	HTC	LAU	MP	NEH	SG	SOF	TS
All my hope on God is founded		n	336	19	21	192	10	368	63	451	959	16	333	525		620
Author of faith, eternal Word		g						381	662							
Be still, for the presence of the Lord		o		67	72	189	325	383			720	50	629	7	40	47
Beauty for brokenness		n		60		259	494				806			263	664	37
Christ be the Lord of all our days		n								256			630			
Christ is alive! Let Christians sing		g		96		416	260	140	190		272			32		
Christ is the King! O friends rejoice		n	345				86	165		492			345	31		
Christ's is the world in which we move		n		101	115	724					882			252	685	1165
Confitemini Domino (Taizé)				925	137						701					
Help us to help each other/Jesus, united by thy grace		g	374	275			523	461	773	540						
How shall I sing that majesty		o	472	296		128	468	466	8				373/ 699			
How sweet the name of Jesus sounds		n	122	297		461	92	467	257	211		251	374	42	194/ 782	190/ 1273
I, the Lord of sea and sky (Here I am, Lord)		o		332	285	251	581	470			865	857		633	830	246
Jesus, these eyes have never seen		n	245	365				491					389			
Jesus, where'er thy people meet/ Lord Jesus, when your people	ga	o	162	367			336	492	549	371			390	16		844
Jubilate Deo omnis terra (Taizé)		2ps			336						691					
My God, how wonderful thou art		o	102	457	497		7	523	51	369	727	468	410	202	395	896
O Christe Domine Jesu (Taizé)					519						757					
O God beyond all praising		n		489			362			36	728		644	53	953	
O Lord, the clouds are gathering		g				708	538					509		255	429	399
O my soul, arise and bless your Maker		n										1095			1481	1460
O thou who camest from above		g	233	541	557	625	639	191	745	596		525	431	560	451	416
Praise to Christ, the Lord incarnate		n										1104		327	1503	1486
Thanks/Praise to God whose word was spoken		o	423			605	387	584	483	255			438	229		
This is the place (Holy ground)		o													1061	1008
Who can sound the depths of sorrow		g		747								766		257	604	579

SONGS FOR CHILDREN

Jesus will never, ever CAON 853, CH 128, JP 412
Jubilate everybody CAON 371, CFE 338, CH 130, CH4 65, CH5 701, JP 145, LAU 471, MP 394, SOF 315
The voice from the bush said CAON 896, CH 199

BIBLE READINGS

Psalms [92 and] 100
Exodus 2.23 - 3.10
Hebrews 13.1–15
Luke 12.49–56

SINGING THE PSALM

Psalm 92 CH4, CRP, CWP, NPCW
Psalm 100 CH4, CRP, CWP, FGP, H&P, LAU, MCW1, NEP, NPCW, PAME
Berthier *Laudate Dominum* TSFP#
Deiss *All the earth* C, CFE, LAU #
Rizza *Cantate Domino* AIL#
Wardle *Enter his gates with thanksgiving* PIW

ANTHEMS AND VOCAL MUSIC

Title	Composer	Voices	E/M/D	Book source	Single sheet publisher
UNISON/TWO PART/HIGH VOICES					
All are welcome (Let us build a house)	Haugen	U#	E	CG, CH4, LAU	GIA
Bread for the world	Farrell	U#	E	GBAN	OCP
Community of Christ	Farrell	U + descant#	E	GBU	
Freedom is coming	Trad arr Perona-Wright	SSAA unacc	E	RTF	
I lift up my eyes	Ogden	U	E		WLP
I will lift up mine eyes	Mawby	S	E		RSCM
Let my people go	Trad arr Weaver	2 part	E	RTF	
Long since in Egypt's plenteous land	Parry	S + solo SS	E	NSAC1	
Send us as your blessing, Lord	Walker	U/SSATB#	M	HIG	OCP
The bread which you do not use	Moore	2 part	M	BFH	
THREE/FOUR PARTS					
Ad te levavi oculos meos	Palestrina	SATB unacc	M	TFM	OUP
Be still, for the presence of the Lord	Evans arr Shephard	SAMen	E	OBFA	
Blessed is he that considereth the poor	Wise	SATB	M	NCAB	
Blest are the pure in heart	Walford Davies	SATB unacc	E	NCAB, MTH1	RSCM
Christ the beginning	P.Moore	SATB	M		Encore
Dives and Lazarus	Trad arr Carter	SATB	M		OUP
Give almes of thy goods	Tye	SATB unacc	E	AC1, OBTA	
Greater love	Ireland	SATB	M	AC4	S&B
I will lift up my eyes (Requiem)	Howells	SATB unacc	M/D		Novello
I will lift up mine eyes	Rutter	SATB	M		OUP
Jesus Christ, yesterday, today and forever	Toolan	SATB	E	LAU	
Like as the hart	Howells	SATB	M/D	AC4	OUP
The Beatitudes	Pärt	SATB	D		Universal
FIVE OR MORE PARTS					
Go down, Moses (5 Spirituals from 'A Child of Our Time')	Trad arr Tippett	SSAATTBB unacc	M/D		Schott
In exitu Israel	S.Wesley	SATB + SATB	M		Novello
Steal away	Trad arr Blackwell	SAATBB unacc	M	SFC	

ORGAN MUSIC

PRELUDES

Darke H. **Andantino** from *A Little Organ Book for Hubert Parry* (Banks) E/M
Dunstable J. **Sub tuam protectionem** (3 movements) from *The Buxheimer Orgelbuch* Vol. 2 (Hinrichsen) E/M*
Lang C.S. **St Peter** No.4 of *Twenty Hymn-Tune Preludes for Manuals Only* Set 1 (OUP) E*
Rawsthorne N. **Gelobet sei Gott** in *Easter Glory* (Mayhew) E/M
Wesley S.S. **Andante in G (1864)** No.6 in *English Organ Music* Vol.10 (Novello) M

POSTLUDES

Farrar E. **Chorale Prelude on 'Lord, thee I'll praise'** Op.7/3 (Animus) E/M
Kellner J.P. **Präludium und Fugette in G minor** in *Orgelmusik um J.S.Bach* Vol.2 (Breitkopf) E/M
Kunkel L. **Postludium** in *Jazz Inspirations 2* (Bärenreiter) E/M
Sumsion H. **Quiet Postlude** (RSCM) M

PROPER 16 (SUNDAY BETWEEN 21 AND 27 AUGUST INCLUSIVE) YEAR B

HYMNS AND SONGS

	pos	rdg	AMNS	CAON	CFE	CH4	CH5	CP	H&P	HTC	LAU	MP	NEH	SG	SOF	TS
All hail the power of Jesus' name		o	140	16	19	457	250	163	252	587	323	13	332	24	9	7
Baptized in water		g			67	636				381	407			492		
Behold the servant of the Lord		n							788					668		
Bless the Lord, my soul (Taizé)		g		923	81		1				813			105	676	56
Broken for me, broken for you	cm	g		87			404	287		S 6		66		485	53	58
Come, let us use the grace divine		n							649							
Faithful Shepherd, feed me	cm	n		156			644		29				282	498		
Freedom and life are ours		o,g								544				171		
God of freedom, God of justice		o		224		263		447								
Great Shepherd of thy people, hear		n	164	250			614	454	490	363				238		
Jesus, where'er thy people meet/Lord Jesus, when your people	ga	n	162	367			336	492	549	371			390	16		844
Lord, I was blind, I could not see		g							423	437		433				
Make way, make way, for Christ the king		o		438	479	279	134				819	457			384	349
O bless the God of Israel		o					706			599						
O Christ the healer, we have come		g				717	513	346			430			489		
O Christe Domine Jesu (Taizé)					519						757					
O thou, who at thy Eucharist didst pray/O Christ	of	n	265	540	556	669	438	318	779	420	833		302	476		
The God of Abraham praise		o	331	642		162	323	586	452	9	712	645	148	66	530	975
The King of love my Shepherd is		n	126	649	699	462	20	589	69	44	804	649	457	205	533	984
The kingdom is upon you!		o	512					590					650			
The Lord my pasture shall prepare		n	111	653				593					458			
The Lord's my shepherd		n	426	654	706	14–16	21	594	70	591	806	660	459	207	537	486
The Lord's my shepherd (Townend)		n										1008		206	1030	988
The Spirit lives to set us free		o		666			490				771	664			1555	
Thine arm/Your hands, O Lord, in days of old		g	285	671			347	397			431		324			
Thou who wast rich/Lord, you were rich		n				318	168	72		63		700		356		1018
You rescued me												1020			1142	605

SONGS FOR CHILDREN

Freedom is coming CFE 526, IECS, RTF
Make way, make way CAON 438, CFE 479, CH4 279, CH5 134, JP 427, KS 249, LAU 819, MP 457, SOF 384, TS 349
The voice from the bush CAON 896, CH 199

BIBLE READINGS

Psalm 116*
Exodus 4.27 - 5.1
Hebrews 13.16–21
Luke 13.10–17

SINGING THE PSALM

Psalm 116* CH4, CRP, CWP, FGP, H&P, MCW1, NEH, NPCW, PAME, PFS
Dean *How can I repay the Lord* HIG (OCP)#
Haugen *I will walk in the presence of God* C, LAU (GIA)#

ANTHEMS AND VOCAL MUSIC

Title	Composer	Voices	E/M/D	Book source	Single sheet publisher
UNISON/TWO PART/HIGH VOICES					
Freedom is coming	Trad arr Perona-Wright	SSAA unacc	E	RTF	
He shall feed his flock (Messiah)	Handel	U	M		Novello
Let my people go	Trad arr Weaver	2 part	E	RTF	
Psalm 23	How	U/SSS	M		Weinberger
Psalm 23	Mawby	U	M		RSCM
The Lord is my shepherd	Kelly	S	M		Encore
The Lord is my shepherd	Schubert	SSAA	M/D	ESM	
THREE/FOUR PARTS					
In olden time and distant land (g)	Trad arr Mold	SATB	E		Encore
Jesus, you are the way	Rizza	SATB + solo S#	E	FOL	Mayhew
Loving Shepherd of thy sheep	Ledger	SATB	E	NOEAB	
Now the God of peace	Knight	SATB	E	SBS1, FSB5	RSCM
Our lives are laid open before you	March	SATB	E	SBS2	
The God of love (Elegy)	Thalben-Ball arr Seivewright	SATB	M		Banks
The Lord is my shepherd	Berkeley	SATB	D	MTP	Chester
The Lord is my shepherd	Carter	SATB	M	ACA	OUP
The Lord is my shepherd	Goodall	SATB	E		Faber
The Lord is my shepherd	Radcliffe	SATB unacc	M		Encore
The Lord is my shepherd (Requiem)	Rutter	SATB	M		OUP
The Lord is my shepherd	Stanford	SATB	M/D	ASA, MTP	Novello
We cannot measure how you heal (g)	Bell arr Archer	SATB	E	BC	RSCM
FIVE OR MORE PARTS					
Go down, Moses (5 Spirituals from 'A Child of Our Time')	Trad arr Tippett	SSAATTBB unacc	M/D		Schott
Haec dies (g)	Byrd	SSATTB unacc	D	OBTA	OUP
Haec dies (g)	Howells	SSSATB unacc	D		OUP
I love the Lord	Harvey	SATB + solo SSATB unacc	D	EAC1, MTP	Novello

ORGAN MUSIC

PRELUDES

Ashdown F.   **Pastor pastorum** from *Two Meditations on the 23rd Psalm* E/M
Dubois T.   **Thème Provençal Varié** in *Douze Pièces Nouvelles* (Masters, Leduc) M
Lloyd R.   **Reverie** in *New Music for Organ* Bk.2 (Mayhew) E
Vierne L.   **Complainte** No.3 of *24 Pièces en Style Libre* Bk.1 (Masters, Durand) E(*)
Willan H.   **Song 1** in *36 Short Preludes and Postludes* Set 2 (Peters) E

POSTLUDES

Boëllmann L.   **Sortie** No.5 from *Heures Mystiques* Op.29 (Kalmus, Enoch, Bärenreiter) E*
Lang H.   **Festival Postlude** in *Praise and Thanks* (Bärenreiter) E/M
Near G.   **Leoni** in *Choraleworks* Set 2 (Aureole) E/M
Palmer C.   **Thema Ostinata** in *Canterbury Organ Album* (Novello) M

PROPER 17 (SUNDAY BETWEEN 28 AUGUST AND 3 SEPTEMBER INCLUSIVE) YEAR B

HYMNS AND SONGS

	pos	rdg	AMNS	CAON	CFE	CH4	CH5	CP	H&P	HTC	LAU	MP	NEH	SG	SOF	TS
All hail the Lamb		o			18							12			8	6
All heaven declares		o		17	20	426					760	14		420	10	8
All ye who seek for sure relief/a comfort sure		n	64	26	31		101				212		63			
As the deer pants for the water		n		45	54	550	606				965	37			27	27
At even, ere the sun was set		n	9	50			65	12	142	315		43	243	487		
At the Lamb's high feast we sing		o	81	53	58		254	138			269		104			
Bless the Lord, my soul (Taizé)				923	81		1				813			105	676	56
Come with me, come wander (HSNW p.84)		n														
Eat this bread/Jesus Christ, bread of life (Taizé)		n		926	151	661					633				1221	
Give me/us the wings of faith		o	324	204			463	216	815				225			
Hail, thou once despisèd Jesus		o		258			268	168	222	175		203			149	
Happy the home that welcomes you		o							366	300						
He is exalted		n		273		437						217		117	164	156
How bright these glorious spirits shine!		o	306			745	467	221		572			227			
Jesus Christ is waiting		n		349	323	360					889			624	1381	1360
Jesus, come! for we invite you		n								109						
Jesus, Lord, we pray		n	475				342	365		302	413					
Jesus, thy blood and righteousness		o					671	111	225	460				177		841
Just as I am, without one plea		o	246	374	339	553	587	308	697	440		396	294	507	316	306
Led like a lamb to the slaughter		o		380			273					402		424	322	312
Lord, enthroned in heavenly splendour	of	o	263	408	379		431	311	616	416	769	431	296	52	352	870
Make me a channel of your peace		n		437	478	528	503	519	776	S 19	898	456		691	381	348
Now in reverence and awe	ps,n											902	232	1468		
Now lives the Lamb of God		o					703			159			413			
Put peace into each other's hands		n		575		659	507							479		1489
Songs of thankfulness and praise		n	53	609	661		197	90		98	172		56	376		
The day of resurrection		o	75	637	690	413	283	157	208	161	283		117	415		
The Lamb's high banquet we await		o											101			
Thine arm/Your hands, O Lord, in days of old		n	285	671			347	397			431		324			
We come as guests invited	hc	n					451			602	630	723				

SONGS FOR CHILDREN

Jesus' hands were kind hands CH4 351, CH5 213, H&P 393, JP 134, KS 194
You are salt for the earth CFE 821, LAU 854

BIBLE READINGS

Psalm 119.1–16*
Exodus 12.21–27
Matthew 4.23 - 5.20

SINGING THE PSALM

Psalm 119.1–16* CRP, CWP, MCW1, NPCW, PAME
Dean *A lamp for my steps* HG#
Dean *You have laid down your precepts* HG#
Walker *Teach me, O God* ATNJ (OCP)#

ANTHEMS AND VOCAL MUSIC

Title	Composer	Voices	E/M/D	Book source	Single sheet publisher
UNISON/TWO PART/HIGH VOICES					
Christ is the world's true light	Stanton	2 part	E	OEAB	
Light of the world	Dankworth	U	E	HP	
Make me a light	Wilby	U/2 part	E	HP, EAC2	
My lips shall speak of thy praise	Greene	SS	M		OUP
The Lord is my light	Bell	U	E	VFLS	
THREE/FOUR PARTS					
Amen, amen, it shall be so!	Bell	SATB + cantor	E	LAA	
Blest are the pure in heart	Walford Davies	SATB unacc	E	NCAB, MTH1	RSCM
Christ whose glory fills the skies	Darke	SATB	M	SBS1	RSCM
Light of the world	Elgar	SATB	M/D	AWTE	Novello
Lighten our darkness	Stanford	SATB	E/M		RSCM
O thou the central orb	Wood	SATB	M	AC4, SC, AFC	RSCM
O Trinity, most blessed light	Turner	SATB	E	AC1	
Phos hilaron	Flood	SATB	M/D	ETAS	
Teach me, O Lord	Moger	SAB	E		RSCM
Teach me, O Lord	Attwood	SATB	E	NOEAB	RSCM
Teach me thy way, O Lord	Fox	SATB unacc	E	FSB7, SBS1	RSCM
The Beatitudes	Chilcott	SATB	M		OUP
The Beatitudes	Pärt	SATB	D		Universal
The Beatitudes	Watson Henderson	SATB	M	SC	RSCM
The Lord is my light and my salvation	Noon	SATB	M	SBS1	RSCM
The Lord is my light and my salvation	Rutter	SATB + clarinet	M		OUP
FIVE OR MORE PARTS					
Beati mundo corde	Byrd	SSATB unacc	M/D	ETAS	CMS/OUP
Os justi	Bruckner	SSATTBB unacc	M/D	ESM	Peters
Sing joyfully	Byrd	SAATB unacc	M	OBTA	OUP
Teach me, O Lord	Byrd	SAATB	M	OBTA	OUP

ORGAN MUSIC

PRELUDES

Cameron J.G. **On a tune by O. Gibbons** (Song 67) in *Six Preludes on Hymn Tunes* (Novello) E/M
Darke H. **In Green Pastures** in *An Easy Album* Bk.1 (OUP) E
Nagel M. **Groovy Meditation** in *Jazz Inspirations 2* (Bärenreiter) E/M*
Nixon J. **Saffron Walden** in *Hymn Tune Preludes* (Fagus) E/M
Peeters F. **O blessed day when first was poured** ('Angelus') in *Hymn Preludes for the Liturgical Year* Op.100 Bk.1 (Peters) E

POSTLUDES

Archer M. **Noel nouvelet** in *Fifty Hymn Preludes* and in *Preludes on the Great Hymns of Lent, Holy Week and Easter* (both Mayhew) E/M
Bédard D. **Toccatina** from *Triptyque* (Cheldar) M
Near G. **Salzburg** in *Choraleworks* Set 1 (Aureole) E/M
Moore P. **Ellacombe** in *Preludes on the Great Hymns of Lent, Holy Week and Easter* (Mayhew) E/M

PROPER 18 (SUNDAY BETWEEN 4 AND 10 SEPTEMBER INCLUSIVE) YEAR B

HYMNS AND SONGS

	pos	rdg	AMNS	CAON	CFE	CH4	CH5	CP	H&P	HTC	LAU	MP	NEH	SG	SOF	TS
At the Lamb's high feast we sing		o	81	53	58		254	138			269		104			
Be still, for the presence of the Lord		n		67	72	189	325	383			720	50	*629*	7	40	47
Be thou my guardian/O Lord, our guardian/Lord, be my guardian		o	217	69			635	385					64			
Be thou my vision/Lord, be my vision		n	343	70	74/75	465	643	386	378	545	970	51	339	669	42	50
Behold us, Lord, a little space		n							376							
Christian, dost thou see them		n	55										65			
Come, Holy Spirit, descend on us		n				589					304	818		19		1168
Father God in heaven, Lord most high		n								358			236			
Father, hear the prayer we offer		n	113	161	158	255	645	416	436	360	933	132	357	237	1229	
Forth in thy name, O Lord, I go	se		239	188	184	529	567	430	381	306	861	159	235	623	1237	
God is our strength and refuge		o		219			12	443		527		188		650		699
Great Shepherd of thy people, hear		n	164	250			614	454		490	363		238			
Jesus, where'er thy people meet/Lord Jesus, when your people	ga	n	162	367			336	492	549	371			390	16		844
Jesus, remember me (Taizé)				931		775	617				253				875	294
King of glory, King of peace		n	194	375	343		358	494	499	603	715	397	391	178		
Lead us, heavenly Father, lead us		o	224	379	351		652	496	68	595	315	400	393	640	321	311
Light of the minds that know him	se	n		397			588	501		477			400	626		
Lord, as I wake I turn to you	ga	n	485				56			634	267	672		236	561	
Now is the healing time decreed		n											59			
O/Our God, our help in ages past		o	99	494	528	161	537	537	358	37	955	498	417	542	415	905
O Lord, hear my prayer (Taizé)		n		938	542		620				929	908	246		423	394
Prayer is the soul's sincere desire		n				546	625	561	557	372			567	442		
Rejoice in God's saints		n	508			742		227					675			
Soldiers of Christ, arise		n	219	606		515	487	571	719	533		604	449	643	506	
The day thou gavest, Lord, is ended	ev		16	638	691	220	73	22	648	280	679	641	252	65	527	
The God of Abraham praise		o	331	642		162	323	586	452	9	712	645	148	66	530	975
The Lamb's high banquet we await		o											101			
The Spirit came as promised		n					313			244			450			
There is no moment of my life		n					19		428				185			
Through the night of doubt and sorrow		o	211	687			661	605	441	466		948	468	544		
You rescued me		o										1020			1142	605

SONGS FOR CHILDREN

Caribbean Lord's Prayer CAON 544, CAP 51, CFE 584, CH 167, IECS, JP 192, MP 557, SG 247
The Church is wherever God's people are praising CH4 522

BIBLE READINGS

Psalm 119.41–56*
Exodus 14.5–31
Matthew 6.1–18

SINGING THE PSALM

Psalm 119.41–56* CWP, NPCW

ANTHEMS AND VOCAL MUSIC

Title	Composer	Voices	E/M/D	Book source	Single sheet publisher
UNISON/TWO PART/HIGH VOICES					
Canticle of Moses	Gibbons	U + descant	M		WLP
I will sing to the Lord	Various	U	E	RE	
Evening Psalm (O Lord, let my prayer rise; Psalm 141)	Inwood	U	E	CSF, MCW1	OCP
Prayer responses	Various	U/SATB	E	MCW1, SBS2	
Settings of the Lord's Prayer	Various	U	E	C, MCW1	
Song of Moses	Various	U	E	CWP, MCW1	
THREE/FOUR PARTS					
A Prayer of St Patrick	Rutter	SATB unacc	E/M		OUP
Give alms of thy goods	Tye	SATB unacc	E	AC1, OBTA	
Hear my prayer	Batten	SATB + solo B	E		OUP
Hear my prayer	Mendelssohn	SATB	M		RSCM
Let my prayer	Blow	SATB unacc	E	AC1	
Let thy merciful ears, O Lord	Mudd	SATB	E	NCAB, OBTA	OUP
Lord, I call upon thee	Bairstow	SATB	M/D	MTP	
Morning Prayers (Three Prayers of Dietrich Bonhoeffer)	P.Moore	SATB + solo A unacc	M/D		B&H
Notre Père	Duruflé	SATB unacc	E		Durand
Pater noster	Stravinsky	SATB	M	RCM	B&H
The Lord's Prayer	Tavener	SATB unacc	E	RCM	
FIVE OR MORE PARTS					
A Prayer of King Henry VI	G. Jackson	SSATB unacc	M	CN	
Go down, Moses (5 Spirituals from 'A Child of Our Time')	Trad arr Tippett	SSAATTBB unacc	M/D		Schott
Hear my prayer	Purcell	SSAATTBB unacc	M	APA	Faber, Novello
Let my prayer rise	Chesnokov	SATTB unacc	M	RCM	
Otche nash	Arensky	SAATBB unacc	M	ESM	
Pater noster	Stanford	SSAATTBB unacc	M		RSCM
Wade in the water	Trad arr Adams	SSAATTBB	M/D	SFC	

ORGAN MUSIC

PRELUDES

Bach J.S. **Vater unser in Himmelreich** BWV 636 from the *Orgelbüchlein* (many editions) E/M

Bach J.S. **Vater unser in Himmelreich** BWV 737 in Novello Vol.19, Peters Vol.7 and Bärenreiter Vol.3 E

Boëllmann L. **Moderato amabile** Op.post. in *Complete Works* Vol.2 (Bärenreiter) M

Buxtehude D. **Vater unser im Himmelreich** BuxWV 219 in *Complete Works* Vol.5 (Bärenreiter) E/M

Willan H. **Prelude on 'Wareham'** in *Ten Hymn Preludes* Set 2 (Peters) E/M

POSTLUDES

Dyson G. **Forth in thy name, O Lord, I go** in *Variations on Old Psalm Tunes* Bk.1 (Novello) E/M

Herbig C. **Canzon 'Vater unser im Himmelreich'** in *German Organ and Keyboard Music of the 17th C First Editions* Vol. 2 (Bärenreiter) E/M(*)

Noble T.T. **Chorale Prelude 'St Ann'** (OUP reprint) M

Parry C.H.H. **Chorale Prelude 'Old 104th'** in *Seven Chorale Preludes* Set 1 (Novello); also in *Preludes and Postludes* (Mayhew) M

HYMNS AND SONGS

	pos	rdg	AMNS	CAON	CFE	CH4	CH5	CP	H&P	HTC	LAU	MP	NEH	SG	SOF	TS
Blessed Jesus, at your word/Dearest Jesu, we are here		n	269	143	87		410	294								
Come, let us sing for joy to the Lord	ga	o													71	1171
Come, worship God who is worthy of honour	ga	o					690			18						
Confitemini Domino (Taizé)				925	137						701					
Faithful Shepherd, feed me	cm	n		156			644		29				282	498		
Father God in heaven, Lord most high		n								358				236		
God has spoken to his people		o					380			S 13	472	182			131	
Hark, my soul! It is the Lord/Christian, do you hear		o	244	264			569	457	521	472		209	*637*			
I will sing the wondrous story		n		337					223	212		315		43	278	821
I, the Lord of sea and sky (Here I am, Lord)		o		332	285	251	581	470			865	857		633	830	246
Jesu, the very thought of thee		n	120	368	321	560	101	485	265	478	798	386	385	534	308	
Jesu, thou joy of loving hearts		n	255	369		662	425	486	258	413		383	292	471		839
Lord, as I wake I turn to you	ga	n	485				56		634	267	672		236	561		
Lord, I lift your name on high		n				558						881	126		897	330
Loving Shepherd of thy sheep		n	134	434	475		655	517		305	802	888				
Make way, make way, for Christ the king	ga	o		438	479	279	134				819	457			384	349
Master, speak! Thy servant heareth		o							535			459			386	
O Jesu, King most wonderful		n	120ii				106	539	269	484			386			
O Lord, hear my prayer (Taizé)		o		938	542		620				929	908		246	423	394
Open our eyes, Lord		o		532								545			443	1468
Praise and thanksgiving, Father, we offer		n	415	558			44	272	350							
Rejoice today with one accord	ga				620					347			444			
Seek ye first the kingdom of God		n		590	633	641	596		138		820	590			493	447
Speak, Lord, in the stillness		o					624			253		608				
The God of love my shepherd is		n	110	643			587	43					77			
The Lord's my shepherd		n	426	654	706	14–16	21	594	70	591	806	660	459	207	537	486
The Lord's my shepherd (Townend)		n										1008		206	1030	988
Thy way, not mine, O Lord		n		692								950				
To God be the glory		n		695	745	512	373	609	463	584	719	708		71	559	526
Will you come and follow me		o		752	812	533	605	622			877		*647*	634	1120	

SONGS FOR CHILDREN

Make way, make way CAON 438, CFE 479, CH4 279, CH5 134, JP 427, KS 249, LAU 819, MP 457, SOF 384, TS 349
Praise and thanksgiving let everyone bring CAON 878, CH 174, JP 447

BIBLE READINGS

Psalm 119.73–88*
Exodus 18.13–26
Matthew 7.1–14

SINGING THE PSALM

Psalm 119.73–88* CWP, NPCW

ANTHEMS AND VOCAL MUSIC

Title	Composer	Voices	E/M/D	Book source	Single sheet publisher
UNISON/TWO PART/HIGH VOICES					
Alleluia fontium	Inwood	4 part + cantor	E	WYP	
O for a closer walk with God	Caesar	SSA	M/D	EAC2	
Sizohamba naye/We are on the Lord's road	Trad arr Weaver	U	E	IECS, SFL1	
THREE/FOUR PARTS					
Blessed are those that are undefiled in the way	Greene	SATB + SS	M/D		CMS/OUP
Fight the good fight	Gardner	SATB	E	MTH1	OUP
For the gifts of life and love	Nardone	SATB	M	SC	
He shall feed his flock (Messiah)	Handel arr Hand	SAMen	M	AOAN1	
Jesu dulcis memoria	Pott	SATB + solo S unacc	M/D	CN	
Jesu dulcis memoria	Shephard	SATB	E/M		RSCM
Jesu dulcis memoria	Victoria	SATB unacc	M	ESM, NSAC1, NCAB	CMS
Jesu, the very thought of thee	Bairstow	SATB unacc	E/M	FSB7	OUP
Jesu, the very thought of thee	K.Beaumont	SATB unacc	E/M		Encore
Lead me, Lord	S.S.Wesley	SATB	E	AC1, NCAB, NOEAB, NSAC1	Novello
Lord, for thy tender mercy's sake	Hilton/Farrant	SATB unacc	E	AWTE, NCAB, FAB1, NOEAB, OBTA	OUP
O for a closer walk with God	Ives	SATB	M		RSCM
O for a closer walk with God	Stanford	SATB	M	AC1, BC, OBFA (SAB)	RSCM
O Master, let me walk with thee	Ledger	SATB	M		Encore
Seek him out	Bryden	SATB + solo S	E/M		Encore
Seek ye first	Lafferty arr Wilson	SATB	E	AWS	
The light of the world	Carter	SATB	M	ACA	OUP
FIVE OR MORE PARTS					
Beati quorum via	Stanford	SSATBB unacc	M	ASA, WFC	RSCM
I want Jesus to walk with me	Trad arr Willams	SSATB	M	SFC	
Jesu dulcis memoria	Villette	SSAATTBB unacc	M/D		UMP
Seek ye the Lord	Varley Roberts	SSATB	M	FAB1	Novello

ORGAN MUSIC

PRELUDES

Armstrong Gibbs C.   **Lyric Melody** No.1 of *Six Sketches* Bk.1 (OUP) E/M

Boëllmann L.   **Offertoire** in *Complete Works* Vol.1 (Bärenreiter) E/M*

Karg-Elert S.   **Liebster Jesu, wir sind hier** No.11 of *20 Preludes and Postludes* Op.78 (Breitkopf) E/M

Nixon J.   **Crimond** in *Hymn Tune Preludes* (Fagus) E/M

Widor C-M   **Adagio** from *5th Symphonie* (Hamelle, Kalmus, Dover) E/M

POSTLUDES

Andriessen H.   **Premier Choral** (Zengerinck) M

Bach J.S.   **Allein Gott in der Höh' sei Ehr'** BWV 716 in Novello Vol.18, Peters Vol.6 E/M

Frescobaldi G.   **Canzona post il Communio** No.18 in *Fiori Musicali* (Bärenreiter, Peters) E/M*

Reger M.   **Komm, O komm, du Geist des Lebens** Op.67/23 in *Complete Chorale Preludes* (Breitkopf) E/M

HYMNS AND SONGS

	pos	rdg	AMNS	CAON	CFE	CH4	CH5	CP	H&P	HTC	LAU	MP	NEH	SG	SOF	TS
Be still, for the presence of the Lord		o		67	72	189	325	383			720	50	629	7	40	47
Be still, my soul		n		68	73	691	666	384					625			49
Blest are the pure in heart		o	238	77	88		630	391	724	110	908		341	372		
Can I ascend the hill of the Lord?		o													683	63
Child of the stable's secret birth		n						47	124	53			43			
Eternal Father, strong to save		n	292	153	152	260	612	413	379	285	963	122	354	235	1222	
Fierce raged the tempest		n	225							144						
God is our strength and refuge		n		219			12	443		527		188		650		699
Head of thy church triumphant		o							818							
In the cross of Christ I glory		n		327		397	225	480	167			338	379			
Inspired by love and anger		n		325	311	253										
Jesus calls us: o'er the tumult		n	312	347		509	584	233	141	104		359	200	668		
Jesus, restore to us again		o,n										873			876	295
Lead us, heavenly Father, lead us		n	224	379	351		652	496	68	595	315	400	393	640	321	311
Let us go up to the house of God		o												887		
My Jesus, my Saviour		n		461		531						1003		129	935	367
Nada te turbe/Nothing can trouble (Taizé)				937							947		659			
O bless the God of Israel		o					706			599						
O changeless Christ, for ever new		n			518					108	745		374			
Rejoice! The Lord is king		o	139	580	619	449	281	563	243	180	326	575	443	440	482	948
Sweet Sacrament divine	cm	n		622	674			324			663		307			
The Lord is king! Lift up thy voice		o,n	107	650		129	8	592	58	183		656		98		
Thine arm/Your hands, O Lord, in days of old		n	285	671				347	397		431		324			
Though I feel afraid		n													1063	522
Walk with me, oh my Lord		n			765						966					
We cannot measure how you heal		n		712	772	718	514	348			433		490			
When peace, like a river		n										757				574
Will your anchor hold in the storms of life		n		753		737	680		689			770				
Within our darkest night (Taizé)				950												

SONGS FOR CHILDREN

Calm me, Lord CAON 924, CAS, FOLO
Tell me the stories of Jesus CH5 110, H&P 153, JP 228, MP 629, TS 152
Who's the King of the jungle? CH 236, JP 289, KS 388, SOF 1625

BIBLE READINGS

Psalm 119.137–152*

Exodus 19.10–25

Matthew 8.23–34

SINGING THE PSALM

Psalm 119.137–152* CWP, NPCW

Walker *You, O Lord, are close* C#

ANTHEMS AND VOCAL MUSIC

Title	Composer	Voices	E/M/D	Book source	Single sheet publisher
UNISON/TWO PART/HIGH VOICES					
Calm me, Lord	Rizza	U/SATB#	E	CAON, CAS, FOLO	
I'm goin' up a yonder	Hawkins	2 part	E	RTF	
Sing of the Lord's goodness	Sands	U + descant#	E	CFE, CG, CH4, CH5, LAU, SFL1, SG, SLG	OCP
THREE/FOUR PARTS					
A Gaelic Blessing	Rutter	SATB	E	NCAB	RSCM
Be still, for the presence of the Lord	Evans arr Shephard	SAMen	E	OBFA	
Be still, my soul	Sibelius	SATB	E		Breitkopf & Hartel
Be still, my soul	Whitlock	SATB	M		Banks
Be thou my vision	Chilcott	SATB + S solo	E/M	BCA, NOEAB	OUP
Be thou my vision	Rutter	SATB	M		OUP
Christ whose glory fills the skies	Darke	SATB	M	SBS1	RSCM
For lo, I raise up	Stanford	SATB	D		Cathedral
God hath spoken	Gibbs	SATB	M		RSCM
God omnipotent reigneth	Wood	SATB	E	SBS1	RSCM
How can I keep from singing?	Lowry arr Weaver	SAB	E	SFL2	
Immortal invisible, God only wise	Mold	SATB	M		Banks
My eyes for beauty pine	Howells	SATB	E	NOEAB	OUP
On this mountain	Ridout	SAMen	M	AOAN1	
Praise to the Lord, the Almighty	Stanford	SATB	M	ASA	
There is a land of pure delight	Ives	SATB	M		RSCM
They that go down to the sea in ships	Sumsion	SATB	M		RSCM
FIVE OR MORE PARTS					
Ascendente Jesu in naviculum	De Wert	SSATTB unacc	D		Mapa Mundi
Deep peace	Carter	SSATB + solo SA	M	ACA, WFC	OUP
O Lord our Governor	Hawes	SATB + SATB	M		Novello

ORGAN MUSIC

PRELUDES

Bach J.S.	**Liebster Jesu, wir sind hier** BWV 706(i), BWV 730 or BWV 731 in Novello Vol.18, Bärenreiter Vol.3, Peters Vol.5 E
Brahms J.	**Mein Jesu, der du mich** No.1 of *Eleven Chorale Preludes* Op.122 (many editions) M
Bridge F.	**Allegretto grazioso** No.1 of *Six Organ Pieces* (Boosey) M
Karg-Elert S.	**Es ist das Heil** No.13 of *20 Preludes and Postludes* Op.78 (Breitkopf) E/M
Lloyd R.	**Melita** in *Hymn Preludes for the Church Year* Bk.2 (Mayhew) E

POSTLUDES

Dubois T.	**Fantaisie (in E)** in *Douze Pièces* (Leduc, Bärenreiter) M
Guilain J-A.	**Basse de trompette** from *Suite de Magnificat du Premier Ton* (Kalmus) E/M*
Krebs J.L.	**Fantasia sopra 'Wer nur den lieben Gott'** in *Complete Works* Vol.3 (Breitkopf) M
Tambling C.	**Toccata** in *New Music for Organ* Bk.2 (Mayhew) E/M

PROPER 21 (SUNDAY BETWEEN 25 SEPTEMBER AND 1 OCTOBER INCLUSIVE) YEAR B

HYMNS AND SONGS

	pos	rdg	AMNS	CAON	CFE	CH4	CH5	CP	H&P	HTC	LAU	MP	NEH	SG	SOF	TS
At even ere the sun was set	ev	n	9	50			65	12	142	315		43	243	487		
Author of faith, eternal Word		o						381	662							
Be still, for the presence of the Lord		o		67	72	189	325	383			720	50	629	7	40	47
Bless the Lord, my soul (Taizé)				923	81		1				813			105	676	56
Blessing and honour (Ancient of days)		o				442						976		106	675	54
Christ whose glory fills the skies	mo		4	105			578	52	2	457	266	670	79	234	170	1200
Cleanse me from my sin, Lord		n										82				
Come, O thou/O come, though all-victorious Lord		n							418	441						
God forgave my sin in Jesus' name		n		212	209		480			S 12	849	181		129		123
How shall I sing that majesty		o	472	296		128	468	466	8				373/699			
I hunger and I thirst		n						306	730	409				470		
I'm accepted, I'm forgiven		n										321			229	217
King of kings, majesty		o										1000			1404	309
Lord Jesus, think on me		n	129	412	384	491/2	554	97	533	316	204		70			
Majesty, worship his majesty		o		436	477		276				767	454			379	346
Nada te turbe/Nothing can trouble (Taizé)				937							947		659			
O bless the God of Israel		o					706			599						
O Christ the healer, we have come		n				717	513	346			430		489			
O for a heart to praise my God	o,n		230	484			638	533	536	483		495	74	149	411	904
O for a thousand tongues to sing		n	125	485		352	104	534	744	219		496	415	55	412	383/1452
O God, by whose almighty plan			406					204	396							
O God, you search me and you know me		n				97						779		514		1454
These are the days of Elijah		o					141					1012			1047	503
Thine arm/Your hands, O Lord, in days of old		n	285	671				347	397		431		324			
'Tis/It's/How good, Lord, to be here		o	318					248	156		209		178			
We cannot measure how you heal		n		712	772	718	514	348			433		490			
When God of old came down from heaven		o	90					199								
When I needed a neighbour		n	433	736	800	544	499				888				1604	
You are before me, God/Thou art before me, Lord		n				96			543							
You, living Christ, our eyes behold		o	533				333						487			

SONGS FOR CHILDREN

Our God is a great big God TS 1475
When I needed a neighbour AMNS 433, CAON 736, CAP 65, CFE 800, CH 229, CH4 544, CH5 499, JP 275, LAU 888, SOF 1604

BIBLE READINGS

Psalms 120 and 121
Exodus 24
Matthew 9.1–8

SINGING THE PSALM

Psalm 120 CWP, NPCW
Psalm 121 CH4, CRP, CWP, H&P, MCW1, NEP, NPCW, PAME, PFS
  Bell *Lifting my eyes up to the hills* PPP
  Haugen *I lift up my eyes (Pilgrim's Song)* C (GIA)#

ANTHEMS AND VOCAL MUSIC

Title	Composer	Voices	E/M/D	Book source	Single sheet publisher
UNISON/TWO PART/HIGH VOICES					
All that is hidden	Farrell	U/SATB#	E	CFE, LAU, RITH, SFTL	OCP
Glory of the God of Israel	Fletcher	2 part	M		Mayhew
God of the living	Tamblyn	U/SATB#	E	SFTL	
THREE/FOUR PARTS					
Almighty and everlasting God	Gibbons	SATB unacc	M	FAB1, NCAB, NSAC1, OBTA	OUP
Asperges me	Victoria	SATB unacc	E/M		Joed
Be thou my vision	Chilcott	SATB + S solo	E/M	BCA, NOEAB	OUP
Be thou my vision	Rutter	SATB	M		OUP
Dear Lord and Father of mankind	Carter	SATB	M	ACA	OUP
For lo, I raise up	Stanford	SATB	D		Cathedral
Glorious and powerful God	Wood	SATB	E/M	SC	Cathedral
God omnipotent reigneth	Wood	SATB	E	SBS1	RSCM
Here, O my Lord, I see thee	Barry Rose	SATB	E	MTH2	
Hide not thou thy face	Farrant	SATB unacc	E/M	BC, FAB1, NCAB, OBFA (SAMen), OBTA	RSCM
Immortal invisible, God only wise	Mold	SATB	M		Banks
My eyes for beauty pine	Howells	SATB	E	NOEAB	OUP
O Lord that seest	Wood	SATB	E/M	SBS1	RSCM
On this mountain	Ridout	SAMen	M	AOAN1	
Purge me, O Lord	Tallis	SATB unacc	E/M	SBS1, TA	OUP, RSCM
Turn thy face from my sins	Attwood	SATB	E/M	BC, FAB1, NCAB, TEA	RSCM
There's a wideness in God's mercy	Bevan	SATB	E	LD, MTH1, NEP, NOEAB	
We cannot measure how you heal	Bell arr Archer	SATB	E	BC	RSCM
FIVE OR MORE PARTS					
Lo! God is here!	P.Moore	SSAATTBB	M/D		Faber
Prayer to the Father of heaven	Vaughan Williams	SAATTBB unacc	D		OUP
Remember, remember not, Lord	Purcell	SSATB unacc	M	APA	Faber

ORGAN MUSIC

PRELUDES

Alberti J.   **Herzlich lieb hab ich dich, O Herr** in *80 Chorale Preludes* (Peters) E
Bédard D.   **Récit** from *Suite du Premier Ton* (Cheldar) E/M
Groves R.   **Richmond** in *12 Hymn-Tune Preludes* Set 1 (Novello) E(*)
Thalben-Ball G.   **Elegy No.2** from *A Little Organ Book for Hubert Parry* (Banks) M
Weelkes T.   **Two Voluntaries** in *Early Organ Music* Vol.2 (Faber) E*

POSTLUDES

Clucas H.   **Melita** in *A Coldridge Organ Book* (Animus) E*
Dupré M.   **Thou splendor and power** Op.38/15 from *Le Tombeau de Titelouze* Op.38 (Gray) M/D
Peeters F.   **Stars of the morning (Trisagion)** No.5 in *Hymn Preludes for the Liturgical Year* Op.100 Vol.4 (Peters) E/M
Zipoli D.   **Canzona** in *Organ Music for Manuals* Bk.2 (OUP) E/M*

PROPER 22 (SUNDAY BETWEEN 2 AND 8 OCTOBER INCLUSIVE) YEAR B

HYMNS AND SONGS

	pos	rdg	AMNS	CAON	CFE	CH4	CH5	CP	H&P	HTC	LAU	MP	NEH	SG	SOF	TS
Christ be my leader		o							709							
God forgave my sin in Jesus' name		n		212	209		480			S 12	849	181			129	123
God's Spirit is (deep) in my heart		n		231	227				315		864					
Guide me, O thou great Jehovah/Redeemer		o	214	252	233	167	647	455	437	528	960	201	368	638	148	708
Happy are they, they that love God		n	176	262			649	456	711	473			369			
He that is down needs fear no fall		n	218						676							
How shall they hear who have not heard		n										250		598		
Judge eternal, throned in splendour		o		372		264	535	356	409	329		395	490	600		
Let saints on earth/Come, let us join our friends		o	182	384				222	812	574		409	396	578		
Let the round world with songs rejoice		n											214			
Lord Jesus, think on me		o	129	412	384	491/2	554	97	533	316	204		70			
Lord of all hopefulness		o	394	413	386	166	618	507	552	101	969	882	239	509	902	
May the mind of Christ my Saviour		n		447		536	636	521	739	550		463		671	1448	887
O Lord of heaven and earth and sea		n	287				363	540	337	287			422	306		
O praise our great and glorious Lord		o			548						664					
Saints of God! Lo, Jesu's people		n											179			
Send me out from here	se	n										594			996	
Shall we gather at the river		o		594			677									1497
Son of God, eternal Saviour		n	132			468	527	573		102			498			
Thanks be to God whose love	ga				715						946		3			
The eternal gifts of Christ the King		n	297	639							374		213			
The kingdom is upon you!		n	512					590					*650*			
The Lord is my light (Taizé)		n		944												
There is a land of pure delight		o	190				681	597	822	575			460			
Thine/Yours be the glory		o	428	672	728	419	288	160	212	167	287	689	120	417	551	510
This little light of mine		n		901	736											
Thy/Your kingdom come, O God		o	177	691			509	607	783	334			949	499	269	
When peace, like a river		o										757				574
Who would true valour see/He who would valiant be		n	212	281	248	535	662	621	688	590	862	224	372	639	174	

SONGS FOR CHILDREN

God has chosen me CFE 212, LAU 858, MP 830, SFL1 24, SG 612
Sent by the Lord am I CFE 638, CG 105, CH4 250, IECS, LAU 855, SBTL, SG 616
This little light of mine CAON 901, CFE 736, CH 212, JP 258, VFLS 37

BIBLE READINGS

Psalms 125 and 126
Joshua 3.7–17
Matthew 10.1–22

SINGING THE PSALM

Psalm 125 CWP, NPCW
Psalm 126 CH4, CRP, CWP, H&P, LAU, MCW1, NEP, NPCW
Farrell *Those who sow in tears/What marvels* GBU, VE#
Smith *The Lord has done great things for us* (WLP)
Ward *What marvels the Lord worked for us!* VE#

ANTHEMS AND VOCAL MUSIC

Title	Composer	Voices	E/M/D	Book source	Single sheet publisher
UNISON/TWO PART/HIGH VOICES					
Lift on high	Ogden	U/SATB	E		WLP
O healing river	Joncas	U/SATB#	E	A, CFE	GIA
Send us as your blessing, Lord	Walker	U/SSATB#	E/M	CFE, HIG	OCP
Sent by the Lord am I	Trad arr Weaver	2 part	E	BC, IECS	RSCM
Vox ultima crucis	Harris	U	E	OEAB	RSCM
THREE/FOUR PARTS					
At the river	Copland arr Wilding-White	SATB	E/M	SC	B&H
Deep river	Trad arr Hart	SATB	M	SFC	
Freedom is coming	Trad arr Ogden	SAB	E	SFL2	
Give me the wings of faith	Leighton	SATB	D		Novello
Give us the wings of faith	Bullock	SATB	M	AC4, FSB10	OUP
Go forth into the world in peace	Rutter	SATB	M	JRA	OUP
Hamba nath'inkululi wethu (Go with us, Lord)	Trad arr Weaver	SAB	E	SFL2	
Judge eternal	Archer	SATB	E/M		Mayhew
Light of the lonely pilgrim's heart	Nardone	SATB	E		B&H
Take up your cross	Corp	SATB	E	SBS1, WOTC	RSCM
There is a land of pure delight	Ives	SATB	M		RSCM
To be a pilgrim	Burt	SAMen	E/M	OBFA	
FIVE OR MORE PARTS					
Deep river (5 Spirituals from 'A Child of our Time')	Tippett	SATB + solo SATB unacc	M/D		Schott
Down to the river to pray	Trad arr Lawson	SATTBB unacc	E/M		Hal Leonard
The Twelve	Walton	SSAATTBB	D		OUP

ORGAN MUSIC

PRELUDES

Ahle J.   **Vater unser im Himmelreich** in *120 Chorale Preludes of the 17C & 18C* (Peters) E*
Beauvarlet-Charpentier J.J.   **Quartetto** in *Pièces pour Orgue* (Chanvrelin) E/M
Groves R.   **Dundee** in *12 Hymn-Tune Preludes* Set 1 (Novello) E(*)
Howells H.   **Intrata No.2** in *Three Pieces for Organ* (Novello) M
Whitlock P.   **Canzona** from *Sonata in C minor* (Ramsey) M/D

POSTLUDES

Guilmant A.   **Paraphrase on 'Judas Maccabeus'** from *18 Nouvelles Pièces* Op.90 (Schott); also in *Complete Works* Vol.4 (Belwin-Mills) E/M
Marchand L.   **Dialogue** p.84 in *Selected Compositions* Vol.1 (Kalmus) E
Rheinberger J.   **Fughetta in D** in *The Progressive Organist* Bk.6 (Novello) E/M
Vierne L.   **Offertoire** from *Messe Basse* (Schola Cantorum) M*

HYMNS AND SONGS

	pos	rdg	AMNS	CAON	CFE	CH4	CH5	CP	H&P	HTC	LAU	MP	NEH	SG	SOF	TS
All ye who seek for sure relief/a comfort sure		n	64	26	31			101			212		63			
Alleluia! Sing to Jesus	of	n	262	12	37	445	398	278	592	170	644	207	271	458	153	616
Beauty for brokenness		n		60		259	494					806		263	664	37
Come to me, come to me		n				759										
Disposer supreme and judge of the earth	o		298	149				214					216			
Father of mercy, God of consolation		n					511						323			
For all the saints who from their labours rest	o		305	177	176	740	459	232	814	567	371	148	197	636	109	684
Forth in thy name, O Lord, I go	se	n	239	188	184	529	567	430	381	306	861	159	235	623	1237	
Happy are they, they that love God		n	176	262			649	456	711	473			369			
Hark, what a sound, and too divine		n				127	28	236					*600*			
How sweet the name of Jesus sounds		n	122	297		461	92	467	257	211		251	374	42	194/782	190/1273
I danced in the morning (Lord of the dance)		n	375	305	275	404	93	468			765		375		1310	
I heard the voice of Jesus say		n	247	310		540	576	469	136		795	275	376		215	206
In God alone my soul (Taizé)		n											813			
In heavenly armour we'll enter the land	o											639			237	228
Join all the glorious names	o					460		493	78	214		392	639	46	313	848
Just as I am, without one plea	n		246	374	339	553	587	308	697	440		396	294	507	316	306
Mine eyes have seen the glory	o			449	488	476			242		987					
Nada te turbe/Nothing can trouble (Taizé)				937							947			659		
Now come to me, all you who seek		n			510											
Onward, Christian soldiers	o		333		581	514	659	549	718	532		543	435		442	
Rejoice! Rejoice! Christ is in you	o				618						818	572			480	438
Soldiers of Christ, arise	o		219	606		515	487	571	719	533		604	449	643	506	
Stand up, stand up for Jesus	o		221	617			488	578	721	535		617	453	644	513	1517
We are marching in the light of God	o			709	768	516	152					954		551	1076	539
We rest on thee/We trust in you	o									446		735		510	587	1043
With joy we meditate the grace		n	530					624	235			774				

SONGS FOR CHILDREN

Jesus before me, Jesus beside me CH4 576

Siya hamba (We are marching in the light of God) CAON 709, CFE 768, CG 139, CH 218, CH4 516, CH5 152, IECS, KS 350, MP 954, SFL1 12, SG 551, SOF 1076, TS 539

BIBLE READINGS

Psalms 127 [and 128]

Joshua 5.13 - 6.20

Matthew 11.20–30

SINGING THE PSALM

Psalm 127 CWP, H&P, NPCW, PAME

Psalm 128 CRP, CWP, FGP, NPCW, PAME

Dean *O blest are they* VE#

Inwood *O blessed are those* LAU, LMOL, VE#

ANTHEMS AND VOCAL MUSIC

Title	Composer	Voices	E/M/D	Book source	Single sheet publisher
UNISON/TWO PART/HIGH VOICES					
Dear Lord and Father of mankind	Parnell	SS	E/M		Encore
He shall feed his flock (Messiah)	Handel	U	M		Novello
Song of Consolation	Jones	U#	E	VE	
There is a longing in our hearts	Quigley	U/SATB#	E	CH4, LAU, SG	OCP
THREE/FOUR PARTS					
A Clare Benediction	Rutter	SATB (unacc)	E	JRA, OBFA (SAMen)	OUP
A touching place (Christ's is the world)	Bell	SATB	E	CG, IAMB, LFB, WGIR, WIS	GIA
As water to the thirsty	Coleman arr Barnard	SATB	E	SC, WIS	
Except the Lord build the house (Three Motets No.3)	Rubbra	SATB unacc	M		Lengnick
Fight the good fight	Gardner	SATB	M	MTH1	
He shall feed his flock (Messiah)	Handel arr Hand	SAMen	M	AOAN1	
His yoke is easy (Messiah)	Handel	SATB	D		Novello
I heard the voice of Jesus say	Shephard	SATB	M		RSCM
Jesus, fount of consolation	Freylinghausen	SATB	E	MTH1	
Just as I am	Chilcott	SATB	E	BCA	OUP
O Lord, heal us	Walker	SATB + descant	E	ATNJ	
The Lord bless you and keep you	Rutter	SATB	E	JRA, EAC1, WFC, OBFA (SAMen)	OUP
The secret of Christ	Shephard	SATB	M	NCAB	RSCM
We cannot measure how you heal	Bell arr Archer	SATB	E	BC	RSCM
FIVE OR MORE PARTS					
Joshua fit the battle of Jericho	Trad arr Barnett	SSAATTBB unacc	D	SFC	

ORGAN MUSIC

PRELUDES

Atkinson G.   **Elegy on a Scottish Fiddle Tune** (Fagus) E/M

Boëllmann L.   **Prélude** No.1 of *Douze Pièces* Op.16 (Leduc, Masters); also in *Complete Works* Vol.1 (Bärenreiter) M

Clérambault L-N.   **Fugue** from *Livre d'Orgue: Suite du Premier Ton* (Schola Cantorum, Kalmus) E/M*

Thiman E.   **Intermezzo** from *Eight Interludes* Set 3 (Novello) E/M

POSTLUDES

Anon.   **Voluntary in A minor** in *Old English Organ Music for Manuals* Bk.6 (OUP) E*

Behnke J.   **Siyahamba** in *Three Global Songs* (Hope) M

Elgar E.   **No.8** from *Vesper Voluntaries* (Faber) E/M

Peeters F.   **Scherzo** from *Modale Suite* Op.43 (Lemoine) M

Nixon J.   **Hyfrydol** in *Hymn Tune Preludes* (Fagus) E/M

PROPER 24 (SUNDAY BETWEEN 16 AND 22 OCTOBER INCLUSIVE) YEAR B

HYMNS AND SONGS

	pos	rdg	AMNS	CAON	CFE	CH4	CH5	CP	H&P	HTC	LAU	MP	NEH	SG	SOF	TS
Adoramus te, Domine (Taizé)				921	11		345				667			208		
All my hope on God is founded		o	336	19	21	192	10	368	63	451	959	16	333	525		620
All praise to thee, for thou, O King divine		n	337	22			684	372	253	204			335			
Be still, my soul		o		68	73	691	666	384					625			49
Bread of life, hope of the world	cm	n			95	663					78			484		
Come, let us join our cheerful songs	ga		144	120			332	401	810	206		93	349	33	70	
Come, let us with our Lord arise	mo	n	449				142	575	375			254				
From heaven you came, helpless babe		n		195	187	374	219	432			749	162		632	120	114
Glory, love, and praise, and honour	pc	n	461	207				436	35				287			
Great is thy faithfulness		o		249		153	80	453	66	260		200	636	39	147	138
Guide me, O thou great Jehovah/ Redeemer		o	214	252	233	167	647	455	437	528	960	201	368	638	148	708
Hail, thou source of every blessing		n											51			
Happy are they, they that love God		o	176	262			649	456	711	473			369			
I danced in the morning (Lord of the dance)		n	375	305	275	404	93	468			765		375		1310	
I'll follow my Lord		n											688			
I'm not ashamed to own/name my Lord		n		316		645			677	448		323		532		
Jehovah Jireh, my provider		o										354			284	
Jesus, hope of every nation		n								58			336			
May the mind of Christ my Saviour		n		447		536	636	521	739	550		463		671	1448	887
My Lord, you wore no royal crown		n								118			628			
O Christe Domine Jesu (Taizé)					519						757					
O God of Bethel/Jacob		o	216	491		268	657	536	442	35		907	416	241		
O/Our God, our help in ages past		o	99	494	528	161	537	537	358	37	955	498	417	542	415	905
Praise to the Lord, the almighty	ga	o	207	573	608	124	365	558	16	40	706	564	440	59	470	945
The day thou gavest, Lord, is ended	ev		16	638	691	220	73	22	648	280	679	641	252	65	527	
Through all the changing scenes of life		o	209	686	740		372	604	73	46		702	467	654	1566	1561
Through the darkness of the ages		o											538			
Through the night of doubt and sorrow		o	211	687			661	605	441	466		948	468	544		
Thy/Your hand, O God, has guided		o	171	689	741	511	529	606	784	536	876	705	485	649	1065	
With joy we meditate the grace		n	530				624	235			774					

SONGS FOR CHILDREN

Jesus went to worship CH5 483
Step by step, on and on CAON 885, CH 191

BIBLE READINGS

Psalm 141

Joshua 14.6–14

Matthew 12.1–21

SINGING THE PSALM

Psalm 141 CWP, LAU, MCW1, NPCW

Inwood *Evening Psalm/Let my prayer rise before you* CSF

Trad arr Dean *Let my prayer, O Lord* C

Walker *Let my prayer rise* C, CIH (OCP)#

ANTHEMS AND VOCAL MUSIC

Title	Composer	Voices	E/M/D	Book source	Single sheet publisher
UNISON/TWO PART/HIGH VOICES					
A Prayer of St Richard of Chichester	Allain	2 part	E	VFLS	
A Prayer of St Richard of Chichester	White	2 part	E	BC, OBFA, OEAB	OUP
Christ be with me	Rawsthorne	U	E	SBS2	
Christ has no body now but yours	Ogden	2 part	E	LOL, CFAP	RSCM
Day by day	How	U + 2 part	E	BC	RSCM
Jesu, by thy wounded feet	Ferguson	S	E		Encore
O God, you search me	Farrell	U/SATB#	E	CBL, CH4, LAU, MCW1, SG, TS	OCP
Teach us, good Lord	Nicholson	SS	E		RSCM
This day was made by the Lord	Walker	U/SAB#	E	OOD	OCP
When I survey the wondrous cross	R.Jones	2 part#	E	MHWE	
THREE/FOUR PARTS					
A Prayer of St Richard of Chichester	Archer	SATB	E		RSCM
Christus factus est	Anerio	SATB unacc	M	AWTE, CM1, ESM	
Haec dies	Arcadelt	SATB unacc	E	NCAB, CM5	
Haec dies	Palestrina	SATB unacc	M		OUP
The Song of Christ's Glory	P.Moore	SATB	E		RSCM
To be a pilgrim	Burt	SAMen	E/M	OBFA	
We cannot measure how you heal	Bell arr Archer	SATB	E	BC	RSCM
FIVE OR MORE PARTS					
Haec dies	Byrd	SSATTB unacc	D	OBTA	OUP
Haec dies	Howells	SSATB unacc	D		OUP
The Song of Christ's Glory	Ives	SSAATTBB unacc	M	WOTC	

ORGAN MUSIC

PRELUDES

Bairstow E.   **No.1** of *Three Short Preludes* (Banks) E/M

Bédard D.   **Communion** from *Suite Liturgique* (Cheldar) E

Buck D.   **Chorale Prelude 'St Anne'** in *Six Chorale Preludes* Op.49 (Warner) E

Krebs J.L.   **Herzlich lieb hab ich dich, O Herr** No.10 in *Complete Works* Vol.3 (Breitkopf) E/M

POSTLUDES

Anon.   **Was Gott tut, das ist wohlgetan** in *Orgelmusik um J.S.Bach* Vol.2 (Breitkopf) M

Barr J.   **Prelude on 'Cwm Rhondda'** in *Three Preludes on Hymn Tunes* (Gray) M

Bennett J.   **Trumpet Voluntary from Voluntary I** in *Ten Voluntaries* Bk.1 (Fagus) E*

Groves R.   **St Anne** in *12 Hymn-Tune Preludes* Set 2 (Novello) E(*)

Seifert U.   **Fantasia on 'Sollt ich meinem Gott nicht singen?'** in *Praise and Thanks* (Bärenreiter) E/M

PROPER 25 (SUNDAY BETWEEN 23 AND 29 OCTOBER INCLUSIVE) YEAR B

HYMNS AND SONGS

	pos	rdg	AMNS	CAON	CFE	CH4	CH5	CP	H&P	HTC	LAU	MP	NEH	SG	SOF	TS
Abide with me	ev	o	13	2	9	580	62	10	665	425	907	4	331	495	2	2
All praise to thee, for thou, O King divine		g	337	22			684	372	253	204			335			
Amazing grace – how sweet the sound		g		29	40	555	642	375	215	28	846	31	626	26	19	18
Awake, my soul, and with the sun	mo,ga	o	1	58		210	51	1	632	264			804	232	618	
Christ's is the world in which we move		g		101	115	724					882			252	685	1165
Come down, O love divine		g	156	114	125	489	294	175	281	231	303	89	137	663	1202	71
Disposer supreme and judge of the earth		n	298	149				214					216			
Eternal light, shine in my heart		o					613	415		339						
Fight the good fight		n	220	169	171	517	566	423	710	526	860	143	359	635	107	
God, we praise you! God, we bless you!		g				120	696	450		341				38		
I will sing the wondrous story		g		337					223	212			315	43	278	821
Immortal, invisible, God only wise	ga	o	199	314	301	132	6	474	9	21	725	327	377	44	234	220
King of glory, King of peace		g	194	375	343		358	494	499	603	715	397	391	178		
Name of all majesty		g		465			102	525		218		481		324	939	
New every morning is the love	mo	o	2	467		214	59	6	636	270		480	238			
O God beyond all praising		o		489			362			36	728			53	953	
O/Our God, our help in ages past		o	99	494	528	161	537	537	358	37	955	498	417	542	415	905
Oft in danger/Christian soldiers		n	210	487				547	715	524		533	434			
Onward, Christian soldiers		n	333		581	514	659	549	718	532		543	435		442	
Ostende nobis, Domine (Taizé)		g		583							839					
Powerful in making us wise to salvation		o							479	252				228		
Soldiers of Christ, arise		n	219	606		515	487	571	719	533		604	449	643	506	
Soldiers who are Christ's below		n	302	607				228					450			
Stand up, stand up for Jesus		n	221	617		488	578	721	535			617	453	644	513	1517
Teach me, my God and King		o	240	629			601	583	803				456			
Tell out, my soul		g	422	631	684	286	712	362	86	42	880	631	186	62	520	471
The Lord is my light (Taizé)				944												
To him we come		n								518		709		679	1569	
We rest on thee/We trust in you		n								446		735		510	587	1043
Will your anchor hold in the storms of life?		o		753		737	680		689			770				
Ye that know the Lord is gracious		g	175			642	493	628					477			

SONGS FOR CHILDREN

Be bold, be strong JP 14, KS 17, MP 49, SOF 37, TS 38

BIBLE READINGS

Psalm 119.121–136
Ecclesiastes 11, 12
2 Timothy 2.1–7
Luke 18.9–14

SINGING THE PSALM

Psalm 119.121–136 CWP, NPCW, PAME

ANTHEMS AND VOCAL MUSIC

Title	Composer	Voices	E/M/D	Book source	Single sheet publisher
UNISON/TWO PART/HIGH VOICES					
Settings of Kyrie eleison/Lord, have mercy	Various	U/SATB	E	C, LAU, MCW1, RE	
Bambelela (You must never give up)	Trad South African	U/SATB	E	C	
Be strong in the Lord	Nicholson	SS	E		Curwen
Creator God	Rizza	U/SATB + descant#	E	ROP	
Give me strength	Chilcott	2 part	E	VFLS	
THREE/FOUR PARTS					
Be strong and of good courage	Campbell	SATB	M	FSB7	
Fight the good fight	Gardner	SATB	E	MTH1	OUP
God is our hope and strength	Stanford	SATB	M		Novello
Greater love	Ireland	SATB	M	AC4	S&B
Jesu, grant me this I pray	Gibbons	SATB	E/M	AWTE	
Let thy merciful ears O Lord (g)	Mudd	SATB	E	NCAB, OBTA	OUP
Lord, for thy tender mercy's sake (g)	Hilton/Farrant	SATB unacc	E	AWTE, NCAB, FAB1, NOEAB, OBTA	OUP
Merciful Lord (g)	March	SATB unacc	M	SBS2	
Morning Prayers (Three Prayers of Dietrich Bonhoeffer)	P.Moore	SATB + solo A unacc	M/D		B&H
O most merciful (g)	Bullock	ATTB	E	SL	
O most merciful (g)	Wood	SATB	E	NSAC2	RSCM
Prayers in Time of Distress (Three Prayers of Dietrich Bonhoeffer) (g)	P.Moore	SATB unacc	M/D		B&H
Solus ad victimam	Leighton	SATB	M	AC1, NCAB, SC	Banks
There's a wideness in God's mercy	Bevan	SATB	E	LD, MTH1, NEP, NOEAB	
Wondrous cross	Wilby	SATB	E	OBFA, WOTC	
FIVE OR MORE PARTS					
Deus noster refugium	Hassler	SAATTB unacc	M/D		CMS/OUP
God is our hope and strength	Blow	SSAATTBB	M		Banks
Let the people praise thee, O God (g)	Mathias	SSAATTBB	M/D	WFC	OUP
Miserere mei (g)	Byrd	SATBB unacc	M/D	OBTA	OUP
Prayer to the Holy Trinity	Tavener	SATB + SSAAA unacc	M		Chester

ORGAN MUSIC

PRELUDES

Brewer A.H.	**Elegy** No.2 of *Three Pieces* (Banks) E/M	
Flor C.	**Ein feste Burg** in *80 Chorale Preludes* (Peters) E*	
Mendelssohn F.	**Prelude** from *Prelude and Fugue in G* Op.37/2 (many editions) E/M	
Shearing G.	**Amazing grace** in *Sacred Sounds from George Shearing* (SMP) E/M	
Willan H.	**Prelude on 'Melcombe'** in *Ten Hymn Preludes* Set 1 (Peters) E	

POSTLUDES

Buxtehude D.	**Ein feste Burg ist unser Gott** BuxWV 184 in Peters Vol.2 and Bärenreiter Vol.4 E/M	
Groves R.	**St Anne** in *12 Hymn-Tune Preludes* Set 2 (Novello) E(*)	
Thiman E.	**Postlude in the 18th C Style** from *Eight Interludes* Set 3 (Novello) E/M	
Walcha H.	**Ein' feste Burg ist unser Gott** in *Choralvorspiele I* (Peters) E/M	

THE LAST SUNDAY AFTER TRINITY (IF OBSERVED AS BIBLE SUNDAY) YEAR B

(For the Dedication Festival, see Year A, page 120.)

HYMNS AND SONGS

	pos	rdg	AMNS	CAON	CFE	CH4	CH5	CP	H&P	HTC	LAU	MP	NEH	SG	SOF	TS
All for Jesus, all for Jesus		n		13	16			277	251	469			272	661		
Angel voices, ever singing		n	163	37	45	498	346	377	484	307	724	34	336	27	24	
Christ is our cornerstone		g	161	98			327	395		564			206	14		
Come down, O love divine		n	156	114	125	489	294	175	281	231	303	89	137	663	1202	71
Father of mercies, in thy word		s	167							247			224			
God has spoken – by his prophets		s					381		64	248	742	831		225		
God of glory, we exalt your name		g										191			137	130
God of grace and God of glory		g	367	225			533	448	712	324		192		574	139	
God, who has caused to be written		s	467							472						
Help us, O Lord, to learn		n	373				382	460	474	493			370	226		
How sure the Scriptures are!		s								249			227			
In the Lord I'll be ever thankful (Taizé)				929	308	772					944	865		656	817	
Jesus shall reign where'er the sun		n	143	359		470	97	490	239	516	322	379	388	45	301	1376
Let all the world in every corner sing		n	202	382	357	122	360	497	10	342	716	404	394	47	879	
Lord, be thy word/make your word my rule		s	232				383	209		250						
Lord, I have made thy word my choice		s	490					504	475							
Lord, thy word abideth/your word shall guide us		s	166	420	390		384	515	476	251	977/8	446	407			
May the mind of Christ my Saviour		n		447		536	636	521	739	550		463		671	1448	887
Not far beyond the sea, nor high		s	401					528	477							
O for a thousand tongues to sing		g	125	485		352	104	534	744	219		496	415	55	412	383/1452
Open thou mine eyes		s										546				
Powerful in making us wise to salvation		s							479	252				228		
Rise and hear! The Lord is speaking		s	509				385	321								
Thanks/Praise to God whose word was spoken		s	423			605	387	584	483	255			438	229		
Thou/God, whose almighty word		s	180	684	738	112	324	267	29	506	887	699	466	597	557	
We have a gospel to proclaim		s	431	716	778	363	491	612	465	519	852	728	486	331	1583	
Will you come and follow me	se	g		752	812	533	605	622			877		647	634	1120	
Your word is a lamp unto my feet		s												234		

SONGS FOR CHILDREN

Spirit of God, unseen as the wind CG 117, CH4 600, CH5 386, SG 233
The word of the Lord is planted in my heart JP 473, KS 338

BIBLE READINGS

Psalm 119.1–16
2 Kings 22
Colossians 3.12–17
Luke 4.14–30

SINGING THE PSALM

Psalm 119.1–16 CRP, CWP, NPCW, PAME

Dean *A lamp for my steps* HG#
Dean *You have laid down your precepts* HG#
Walker *Teach me, O God* ATNJ (OCP)#

ANTHEMS AND VOCAL MUSIC

Title	Composer	Voices	E/M/D	Book source	Single sheet publisher
UNISON/TWO PART/HIGH VOICES					
God the singer	Ogden	U + descant	E	VFLS	
He came singing love	Gibson	2 part	E	VFLS	
I will sing a song of love	Bell	U	E	VFLS	
May the Word of God strengthen us	Walker	U/2 part#	E	C	
Praise to you, O Christ our Saviour	Farrell	U#	E	CFE, LAU, RITH, WYP	OCP
When in our music God is glorified	Haugen	U#	E		GIA
THREE/FOUR PARTS					
Angel voices	Shephard	SATB	M	SC	RSCM
Blessed be the God and Father	S.S.Wesley	SATB	M	FAB1, NCAB, SC	RSCM
Cantate Domino	Pitoni	SATB unacc	E	AC1, NCAB, NSAC1, NOEAB, SC	
I will praise God because of his word	Purcell	SATB	E/M	TPS	
I will sing of the Lord's great love	McKinley	SATB	M	SC	
Let all the world	Vaughan Williams	SATB	M/D		S&B
O for a thousand tongues to sing	Shephard	SATB	M/D		RSCM
O sing joyfully	Batten	SATB unacc	E	SCAB, WFC	RSCM
Teach me, O God	Camidge	SAB	E	CHM	
Teach me, O Lord	Attwood	SATB	E	NOEAB	RSCM
The peace of God	Rutter	SATB	E	JRA, NOEAB	OUP
The Spirit of the Lord	Elgar	SATB	M	SAEE	RSCM
Thy word is a lantern	Purcell	SATB	M	APA	Novello
Waiting for the word	Skellern	SATB	E/M		RSCM
FIVE OR MORE PARTS					
Beati quorum via	Stanford	SSATBB unacc	M	ASA, WFC	RSCM
Cantate Domino	Monteverdi	SSATTB	M	ESM	OUP
Os justi	Bruckner	SSATTB unacc	M/D	ESM	Peters
Sing joyfully	Byrd	SAATB unacc	M	OBTA	OUP
Teach me, O Lord	Byrd	SAATB	M	OBTA	OUP

ORGAN MUSIC

PRELUDES

Bach J.S. **Gottes Sohn ist kommen** ('Ravenshaw') BWV 703 in Novello Vol.18, Bärenreiter Vol.3, Peters Vol.5 E*
Buxtehude D. **Erhalt uns Herr bei deinem Wort** BuxWV 185 in *Complete Works* Vol.4 (Bärenreiter) E/M
Peeters F. **Lord keep us steadfast in thy word** in *Ten Chorale Preludes* Op.68 (Peters) E/M
Rinck J. **Gottes Sohn ist kommen** ('Ravenshaw') in *Hier Preisen auf der Erd* Vol.1 (Breitkopf) E
Walther J.G. **Herr Jesu Christ, dich zu uns wend** in *The Progressive Organist* Bk.5 (Novello) E/M

POSTLUDES

Bach J.S. **Herr Jesu Christ, dich zu uns wend** BWV 709 in Novello Vol.18, Bärenreiter Vol.3, Peters Vol.5 E/M
Karg-Elert S. **O Ewigkeit, du Donnerwort** No.42 from *Choral-Improvisationen* Op.65 and in the anthology
14 Choral-Improvisationen (Breitkopf) E/M
Walther J.G. **Erhalt uns, Herr, bei deinem Wort** No.11 in *Orgelchoräle* (Barenreiter), in *80 Chorale Preludes* (Peters) and
120 Chorale Preludes of the 17C & 18C (Peters) E

Suitable before or after: Movements from Böhm G. **Partita 'Herr Jesu Christ, dich zu uns wend'** in *The Complete Works*
(Breitkopf) E-M(*)

THE FOURTH SUNDAY BEFORE ADVENT
YEAR B

(For All Saints' Day, see Year A, page 122.)

HYMNS AND SONGS

	pos	rdg	AMNS	CAON	CFE	CH4	CH5	CP	H&P	HTC	LAU	MP	NEH	SG	SOF	TS
Adoramus te, Domine (Taizé)				921	11		345				667			208		
All heaven declares		n		17	20	426					760	14		420	10	8
Alleluia! Sing to Jesus		n	262	12	37	445	398	278	592	170	644	207	271	458	153	616
Beyond all mortal praise		o		71									340			
Blessing and honour (Ancient of days)		o				442						976		106	675	54
Blest are the pure in heart		g	238	77	88		630	391	724	110	908		341	372		
Glory in the highest to the God of heaven		o					693	300		582			363	37		
God moves in a mysterious way		o	112	222		158	13	445	65			193	365			700
God, we praise you! God, we bless you!		o				120	696	450		341				38		
Here is love (Bewes verses)		o												174		
How bright these glorious spirits shine		n	306				745	467	221		572			227		
Jerusalem the golden		n	184	340	317	747	670	482		573	991		381			
Lord of the Church, we pray for our renewing		n					303			499		442		577	1433	
Majesty, worship his majesty		n		436	477		276				767	454			379	346
Misericordias Domini/From age to age (Taizé)					489											
My God, how wonderful thou art		n	102	457	497		7	523	51	369	727	468	410	202	395	896
O for a thousand tongues to sing		n	125	485		352	104	534	744	219		496	415	55	412	383/1452
Prayer is the soul's sincere desire		o				546	625	561	557	372		567	442			
Purify my heart		g		574			640					921		163	475	436
Such love, pure as the whitest snow		n		620								619		216	514	465
The Church's one foundation		n	170	636	688	739	528	585	515	501	830	640	484	581	525	477
The day thou gavest, Lord, is ended	ev	o	16	638	691	220	73	22	648	280	679	641	252	65	527	
There is a higher throne		n										1116			1541	1538
We come as guests invited		g					451			602	630	723				
Who are these, like stars appearing		n	323	746			475	229					231			
Ye/You servants of God, your master proclaim		n	149	756	819	130	492	627	278	520		784	476	75	620	1074

SONGS FOR CHILDREN

All heaven declares CAON 17, CFE 20, CH4 426, KS 4, LAU 760, MP 14, SG 420, SOF 10, TS 8
Great is he MP 1048, SOF 1254, TS 705
Have you heard the raindrops CAON 817, CH 78, CAP 2, CH4 525, JP 71, KS 99

BIBLE READINGS

Psalm 145*

Daniel 2.1–48 (*or* 1–11, 25–48)

Revelation 7.9–17

Matthew 5.1–12

SINGING THE PSALM

Psalm 145* CH4, CRP, CWP, FGP, H&P, LAU, NEH, NPCW, PAME, PFS

    Gelineau *There can be no greater love* TSFP#

    Walker *I will bless your name* ATNJ

ANTHEMS AND VOCAL MUSIC

Title	Composer	Voices	E/M/D	Book source	Single sheet publisher
UNISON/TWO PART/HIGH VOICES					
Settings of the Te Deum	Various	U	E	MCW1	
Alleluia! Raise the Gospel (g)	Farrell	U/SATB#	E	C, GBU	OCP
Benedictus/The Beatitudes (g)	Rizza	U/SATB#	E	ROP	
Blest are they (g)	Haas	U	E	CFE, CH4, LAU	GIA
Gaudent in coelis	Dering	2 part	M	AC2, SFL2	Schott
Let the bright seraphim	Handel	U	M/D		Novello
The Song of the Tree of Life	Vaughan Williams	2 part	E	AC2	OUP
THREE/FOUR PARTS					
And I saw a new heaven	Archer	SATB	M	NOEAB	
And I saw a new heaven	Bainton	SATB	M/D	FSB4	Novello
And I saw another angel	Stanford	SATB + solo T	M		Cathedral, Novello
Blessed are the pure in heart (g)	Walford Davies	SATB unacc	E	MTH1, NCAB	RSCM
I beheld, and lo, a great multitude	Blow	SATB + SATB soli	D		OUP
In the city of the Lord	Harper	SATB	M/D	LOL	
Lo, round the throne a glorious band	Ley	SATB	E	NCAB	Novello
O quam gloriosum	Byrd	SATB unacc	M	OBTA	Banks
O quam gloriosum	Vaet	SATB unacc	M	ETAS	
O quam gloriosum	Victoria	SATB unacc	M	ESM, NCAB	Chester
The Beatitudes (g)	Chilcott	SATB	M		OUP
The Beatitudes (g)	Pärt	SATB	D		Universal
The Beatitudes (g)	Watson Henderson	SATB	M	SC	RSCM
Worthy is the Lamb (Messiah)	Handel	SATB	M		Novello
FIVE OR MORE PARTS					
Alleluia, I heard a voice	Weelkes	SATBB unacc	M/D	OBTA	OUP
Beati mundo corde (g)	Byrd	SSATB unacc	M/D	ETAS	CMS/OUP
Glorious in heaven	Whitlock	SATBB unacc	E/M	ETAS	

ORGAN MUSIC

PRELUDES

Coleman H.   **Franconia** in *Ten Hymn Tune Voluntaries* Bk.2 (Stainer) E

Guridi J.   **Capriccio** No.2 in *Escuela Española de Organo* (UME) E/M

Edwards P.   **Improvisation on 'St Clement'** from *Northampton Miniatures* (Fagus) E*

Langlais J.   **Le Paradis** No.1 of *Huit Chants de Bretagne* (Bornemann) M

Stanford C.V.   **Intermezzo on an Irish Air** Op.189/4 (Novello); also in *The Victorian Collection* (McAfee) E/M

POSTLUDES

Lloyd Webber W.S.   **Trumpet Minuet** in *Prayer and Praise* (Paxton) E*

Pierné G.   **Prélude** No.1 of *Trois Pièces* Op.29 (Durand) E/M

Rutter J.   **Toccata in seven** in *A Second Easy Album* (OUP) E/M

Vaughan Williams R.   **Prelude on 'Hyfrydol'** in *Three Preludes on Welsh Hymn Tunes* (Stainer) M

HYMNS AND SONGS

	pos	rdg	AMNS	CAON	CFE	CH4	CH5	CP	H&P	HTC	LAU	MP	NEH	SG	SOF	TS
All hail the power of Jesus' name		o	140	16	19	457	250	163	252	587	323	13	332	24	9	7
By your side I would stay		n		90								810			55	60
Christ is the world's light		n	440	99	111		87	213	455	321	744			591		
Come down, O love divine		n	156	114	125	489	294	175	281	231	303	89	137	663	1202	71
Crown him with many crowns		o	147	137	139	459	263	166	255	174	321	109	352	321	77	77
From thee/you all skill and science flow		o	286				512	345	389	310						
God is working his purpose out		o		221	217	235	481	444	769	191	86	189	495	451	135	128
How sweet the name of Jesus sounds		n	122	297		461	92	467	257	211		251	374	42	194/782	190/1273
Jerusalem, my happy home/thou city blest		n	187	339			481		569	373		228				
Judge eternal, throned in splendour		o		372		264	535	356	409	329		395	490	600		
Light of the minds that know him	se	n		397			588	501		477			400	626		
Lord, enthroned in heavenly splendour	of	o	263	408	379		431	311	616	416	769	431	296	52	352	870
May the mind of Christ my Saviour		o		447		536	636	521	739	550		463		671	1448	887
Nada te turbe/Nothing can trouble (Taizé)		n		937							947			659		
O Day of God, draw nigh		o	405				33									
O thou who camest from above		n	233	541	557	625	639	191	745	596		525	431	560	451	416
Spirit divine, attend our prayers		o				583	341	195	327	240		614				
Such love, pure as the whitest snow		n		620								619		216	514	465
The kingdom of God is justice and joy		o		646	701			591	139	333	821	651		184		
Thou art the way: by thee alone/You are the way		n	128	682			115	600	234	113		695	464			
Thy/Your hand, O God, has guided		n	171	689	741	511	529	606	784	536	876	705	485	649	1065	
Thy/Your kingdom come, O God		o	177	691			509	607	783	334		949	499	269		
Thy/Your kingdom come! On bended knee		o	178	690		473		608					500			
To God be the glory		n		695	745	512	373	609	463	584	719	708		71	559	526
To him we come		n								518		709		679	1569	
When the music fades		n										1016		222	1113	576

SONGS FOR CHILDREN

And everyone beneath the vine and fig tree CAON 774, CAP 149, CH 17
Give me peace, O Lord CAON 802, CFE 191

BIBLE READINGS

Psalms 46 [and 82]
Isaiah 10.33 - 11.9
John 14.1–29 (*or* 23–29)

SINGING THE PSALM

Psalm 46 CH4, CWP, H&P, NPCW, PAME
Psalm 82 CWP, NPCW

ANTHEMS AND VOCAL MUSIC

Title	Composer	Voices	E/M/D	Book source	Single sheet publisher
UNISON/TWO PART/HIGH VOICES					
A Song of Peace	Stanford	U	M		RSCM
A Song of Peace and Joy	Mawby	U + descant + instr	E	VFLS	
Christ is the world's true light	Stanton	U + descant	E	OBFA, OEAB	Banks
He came singing love	Gibson arr Weaver	2 part	E	VFLS	
If there is to be peace	Shephard	2 part	E/M	VFLS	
Let nothing trouble you	Farrell	U#	E	CBL	
O for a closer walk with God	Caesar	SSA	M/D	EAC2	
THREE/FOUR PARTS					
A tender shoot	Goldschmidt	SATB	M	AFC, TCB	RSCM
And the glory of the Lord (Messiah)	Handel	SATB	M		Novello
Come down, O love divine	Harris	SATB	E/M	FSB9, NCAB, MTH2	Novello
Come down, O love divine	Tadman-Robins	SAMen	E	OBFA	
E'en so Lord Jesus, quickly come	Manz	SATB unacc	M	AFC	Morning Star
Holy Spirit, truth divine	Carter	SATB	E	ETAS, NOEAB	OUP
I will not leave you comfortless	Joule	SATB	M/D		RSCM
If ye love me	Tallis	SATB unacc	E	FAB1, NOEAB, NSAC1, OBTA, TA, SL (AATB)	OUP
O for a closer walk with God	Ives	SATB	M		RSCM
O for a closer walk with God	Stanford	SATB	M	AC1, ASA, BC, OBFA, AOAN1 (SAMen)	RSCM
O Lord, give thy Holy Spirit	Tallis	SATB unacc	E/M	TA, SCAB	OUP
Spirit of the Lord, come down	Harper	SA(T)B	E	SBS1, SOTL	RSCM
The Lord bless you and keep you	Rutter	SATB	E	JRA, EAC1, WFC, OBFA (SAMen)	OUP
Virga Jesse floruit	Bruckner	SATB unacc	D	AFC, CHMO	Peters
FIVE OR MORE PARTS					
If ye love me	Chilcott	SSATBB unacc	M	BCA, WFC	
Non vos relinquam	Byrd	SSATB unacc	M/D		S&B (in Gradualia)

ORGAN MUSIC

PRELUDES

Harwood B.	**Rest** No.4 of *8 Short Pieces* Op.58 in *Complete Works* Vol.2 (Stainer) E/M	
Lang C.S.	**Chorale Prelude on 'Irish'** No.1 of *Three Chorale Preludes* Op.77 (OUP Archive) E/M	
Langlais J.	**Chant de Paix** No.3 from *Neuf Pièces* (Bornemann, Leduc) E	
Marchand L.	**Trio** p.64 in *Selected Compositions* Vol.1 (Kalmus) E/M*	
Vann S.	**St James** from *Fifty Hymn Preludes* (Mayhew) E/M	

POSTLUDES

Dupré M.	**Before the ending of the day** No.5 in *Le Tombeau de Titelouze* (Gray) E/M
Peeters F.	**Now thank we all our God** No.1 of *Ten Chorale Preludes* Op.69 (Peters) E/M
Wesley S.	**Fugue 'Non nobis Domine'** from *Voluntary IV in G* Op.6 No.4 in *Twelve Voluntaries for Organ* Op.6 Bk.1 (Fagus) E*
Willan H.	**Postlude on 'Miles Lane'** in *36 Short Preludes and Postludes* Set 1 (Peters) M

THE SECOND SUNDAY BEFORE ADVENT YEAR B

HYMNS AND SONGS

	pos	rdg	AMNS	CAON	CFE	CH4	CH5	CP	H&P	HTC	LAU	MP	NEH	SG	SOF	TS
All hail the power of Jesus' name		s	140	16	19	457	250	163	252	587	323	13	332	24	9	7
Alleluia! Alleluia! Hearts to heaven		n	80	9		427	251	137		151			103	398		
Christ is the King! O friends rejoice		S	345			86	165			492			345	31		
Christ triumphant, ever reigning		s		104	113	436	259	398		173	763	77	*613*	319	62	655
Crown him with many crowns		s	147	137	139	459	263	166	255	174	321	109	352	321	77	77
For all the saints who from their labours rest		n	305	177	176	740	459	232	814	567	371	148	197	636	109	684
God forgave my sin in Jesus' name		n		212	209		480			S 12	849	181			129	123
Happy are they, they that love God		n	176	262			649	456	711	473			369			
How firm a foundation		o		292						430		243				186
I'm not ashamed to own/name my Lord		o		316		645			677	448		323/992		532		
Jerusalem the golden		n	184	340	317	747	670	482		573	991		381			
Jesus, remember me (Taizé)				931		775	617				253				875	294
Jesus shall reign where'er the sun		s	143	359		470	97	490	239	516	322	379	388	45	301	1376
Jesus shall take the highest honour		s		360								378		123	302	296
Jesus, stand among us in thy risen power		o		362			338		530	364		380			304	
Judge eternal, throned in splendour		s		372		264	535	356	409	329		395	490	600		
Let us sing to the Lord (Taizé)		ps									689					
Majesty, worship his majesty		s		436	477		276				767	454			379	346
O worship the King, all glorious above	ga	s	101	551	559	127	34	546	28	24	683	528	433	90	456	425
Palms of glory, raiment bright		n	307				226						230			
Rejoice! The Lord is king		s	139	580	619	449	281	563	243	180	326	575	443	440	482	948
The day thou gavest, Lord, is ended	ev	n	16	638	691	220	73	22	648	280	679	641	252	65	527	
The kingdom of God is justice and joy		n		646	701			591	139	333	821	651		184		
Thy/Your kingdom come, O God		s	177	691			509	607	783	334			949	499	269	
Thy/Your kingdom come! On bended knee		s	178	690		473	608						500			
Ye/You servants of God, your master proclaim		o	149	756	819	130	492	627	278	520		784	476	75	620	1074

SONGS FOR CHILDREN

Come and praise the Lord our king CAP 21, CFE 121, HTC S8, JP 34
Let us sing to the God of salvation SG 86

BIBLE READINGS

Psalm 95
Daniel 3 (*or* 3.13–30)
Matthew 13.24–30,36–43

SINGING THE PSALM

Psalm 95 CH4, CRP, CWP, FGP, H&P, LAU, MCW1, NPCW, PAME
Berthier *Let us sing to the Lord* TSFP#
Inwood *Ring out your joy* CSF#
O'Hara *O that today you would listen* CRP#
Trad arr Foster *Come, ring out your joy* C

ANTHEMS AND VOCAL MUSIC

Title	Composer	Voices	E/M/D	Book source	Single sheet publisher
UNISON/TWO PART/HIGH VOICES					
All you works of God	Haugen	U	E	CH4	GIA
Daniel Jazz	Chappell	U	E		Novello
Now the green blade riseth	Tamblyn	SSAA	M	EAC2	
Now the green blade riseth	Trad arr Bullard	2 part	E	OBFA	
Rejoice, the Lord is king	Weaver	2 part	E/M	CFAP	
Send down the fire of your justice	Haugen	U#	E	C, TS	GIA
Take the word of God with you	Walker	U/SAB#	E	CFE, CIH, LAU	OCP
Unless a grain of wheat	Farrell	U/SATB#	E	CFE, LAU, RITH, WYP	OCP
THREE/FOUR PARTS					
Cantate Domino	Hassler	SATB unacc	M	CM4	
Cantate Domino	Pitoni	SATB unacc	E	AC1, NCAB, NSAC1, NOEAB, SC	OUP
God hath spoken	Gibbs	SATB	M		RSCM
Now the green blade riseth	Trad arr Lindley	SATB	E/M	AWTE	Banks
Now the green blade riseth	Trad arr Lumsden	SATB	M		Encore
O how glorious is the kingdom	Harwood	SATB	M/D		Banks
Rejoice, the Lord is king	Kelly	SATB	M/D	NNAB, MTH1	
Rejoice, the Lord is king	Weaver	SATB	M	SC	
FIVE OR MORE PARTS					
Cantate Domino	Monteverdi	SSATTB	M	ESM	OUP

ORGAN MUSIC

PRELUDES

Brewer A.H. **Cloister Garth** in *Gloucester Organ Album* (Novello) M
Guilmant A. **Communion No.1 in G** Op.15 No.1 in *Complete Works* Vol.1 (McAfee) and in *An Organ Miscellany* (Mayhew) E
Hingeston J. **Double Voluntary** in *Early English Organ Music* Vol.2 (OUP) E/M*
Howells H. **Tranquillo, ma con moto** No.1 of *Six Short Pieces* (Novello) E/M
Karg-Elert S. **In modo dorico** No.1 from *Sempre Semplice* Bk.1 Op.142 (Cathedral Music) E/M

POSTLUDES

Lebègue N. **Offertoire du 5ème ton** p.12 in *Offertoires from Troisième Livre d'Orgue* (Hawthorns); also p.178 in *Complete Works* Vol.3 (Kalmus) E/M(*)
Lloyd Webber W.S. **Solemn Procession** in *Aria* (Mayhew) and *Fanfares and Processionals* (Novello) M
Mendelssohn F. **Fugue** from *6th Sonata* (many editions) E/M
Rheinberger J. **Monologue in C** Op.162/1 in *Monologues* (Carus) and *Free Organ Music for the Worship Service* (Carus) E/M

CHRIST THE KING (THE SUNDAY NEXT BEFORE ADVENT) YEAR B

HYMNS AND SONGS

	pos	rdg	AMNS	CAON	CFE	CH4	CH5	CP	H&P	HTC	LAU	MP	NEH	SG	SOF	TS
A mighty fortress/A safe stronghold/God is our fortress	o		114		3	454	668	366	661	523	958	2		637	25	
Adoramus te, Domine (Taizé)				921	11		345				667			208		
All hail the power of Jesus' name		s	140	16	19	457	250	163	252	587	323	13	332	24	9	7
All heaven declares	gr			17	20	426					760	14		420	10	8
Alleluia! Sing to Jesus	of	s	262	12	37	445	398	278	592	170	644	207	271	458	153	616
At/In the name of Jesus		s	148	54	59	458	94	380	74	172	762	41	338	317	32	33
Blessing and honour (Ancient of days)		s				442						976		106	675	54
Bread of heaven, on thee we feed		n	271	82				284		398			276	464		
Bread of life, hope of the world	cm				95	663					78			484		
Break thou the bread of life		n					379	286	467			64			50	
Christ is the King! O friends rejoice		s	345				86	165		492			345	31		
Christ triumphant, ever reigning		s		104	113	436	259	398		173	763	77	*613*	319	62	655
Crown him with many crowns		s	147	137	139	459	263	166	255	174	321	109	352	321	77	77
Faithful Shepherd, feed me	cm	n		156			644			29			282	498		
I am the bread of life		n		299	271/2		420				629	261			200	
Jesus shall reign where'er the sun		s	143	359		470	97	490	239	516	322	379	388	45	301	1376
Jesus shall take the highest honour		s		360								378		123	302	296
Jesus, we enthrone you		s													310	300
Judge eternal, throned in splendour		s		372		264	535	356	409	329		395	490	600		
King of kings, majesty		s										1000		1404		309
Majesty, worship his majesty		s		436	477		276				767	454			379	346
Make way, make way for Christ the King	ga	s		438	479	279	134				819	457			384	349
O Christe Domine Jesu (Taizé)					519						757					
O worship the King, all glorious above	ga	s	101	551	559	127	34	546	28	24	683	528	433	90	456	425
Rejoice! The Lord is king		s	139	580	619	449	281	563	243	180	326	575	443	440	482	948
The kingdom of God is justice and joy		s		646	701			591	139	333	821	651		184		
The Lord ascendeth up on high		s				440		173	210				135			
Thy/Your kingdom come, O God		s	177	691			509	607	783	334			949	499	269	
Thy/Your kingdom come! On bended knee		s	178	690		473		608				500				

SONGS FOR CHILDREN

All heaven declares CAON 17, CFE 20, CH4 426, KS 4, LAU 760, MP 14, SG 420, SOF 10, TS 8
He is the King of kings CAON 818, CH 80, TS 1244
Make way, make way CAON 438, CFE 479, CH4 279, CH5 134, JP 427, KS 249, LAU 819, MP 457, SOF 384, TS 349
Two little fishes CH4 504

BIBLE READINGS

Morning Psalms 29 and 110
Evening Psalm 72*
Daniel 5
John 6.1–15

SINGING THE PSALM

Psalm 29 CRP, CWP, NEP, NPCW, PAME
    Feeley *The Lord will bless his people with peace* VE
    Gregory Murray, Gelineau *The Lord will bless his people with peace* VE
    Rees *The Lord will bless his people with peace* PCMG
Psalm 110 CRP, CWP, NPCW
Psalm 72* CH4, CRP, CWP, H&P, MCW1, NPCW, PAME
    Haugen *Every nation on earth* (GIA)#

ANTHEMS AND VOCAL MUSIC

Title	Composer	Voices	E/M/D	Book source	Single sheet publisher
UNISON/TWO PART/HIGH VOICES					
Bread for the world	Farrell	U#	E	GBAN	
Let all mortal flesh keep silence	Trad arr Cleobury	2 part	E	AFC	
Let all mortal flesh keep silence	Trad arr Greening	2 part	E	TEA	
O sacrum convivium	Leighton	S/SS	M/D	EAC2	
Panis angelicus	Franck	SS	M		Ashdown
THREE/FOUR PARTS					
Adoramus te, Christe	Lassus	SATB unacc	M	ESM, AWTE	Chester
Adoramus te, Christe	Palestrina	SATB unacc	M	NCAB	Banks
Christ, our God, descends from heaven	Bullard	SAB	E/M	SBS2	
Let all mortal flesh keep silence	Trad arr Covey-Crump	SATB unacc	M	MTH1	
Let all the world	Dyson	SATB	E	MTH1	Novello
Let all the world	Halsey	SATB	E	BC	RSCM
Let all the world	Leighton	SATB	M/D	EAC1	Novello
Let all the world	Vaughan Williams	SATB	M/D		S&B
Lord, I trust thee	Handel	SATB	E	NCAB, NOEAB	
O sacrum convivium	Byrd	SATB unacc	M	SBS2	
O sacrum convivium	Messiaen	SATB unacc	D		UMP
O sacrum convivium	P.Moore	SATB unacc	E	TNA	
Panis angelicus	Franck	SATB	M	ESM, OBFA, WFC	RSCM
Panis angelicus	Saint-Saëns	SATB	E	NCAB	
FIVE OR MORE PARTS					
Christe adoramus te	Monteverdi	SSATB unacc	M	ESM	
Let all mortal flesh keep silence	Bairstow	SSAATTBB unacc	M/D	AC4	S&B
O sacrum convivium	Tallis	SAATB unacc	M/D	TA	OUP

ORGAN MUSIC

PRELUDES

Boëly A.P.F.   **Domine Deus, Rex Cœlestis** p.13 in *The Liturgical Service* Bk.1 (Kalmus) E/M*
Falcinelli R.   **Choral-Prelude No.2 à l'introit de la Messe de Christ-Roi** in *Préludes à l'Introït* (Schola Cantorum) M
Ridout A.   **Praise, my soul** in *100 Hymn Preludes* (Mayhew) E/M
Thalben-Ball G.   **Gopsal** No.32 of *113 Variations on Hymn Tunes* (Novello) E

POSTLUDES

Burkhardt M.   **Diademata** No.1 of *5 Easter Season Hymn Improvisations* (Morning Star) E/M
Manz P.   **Praise, my soul, the king of heaven** in *Two Pieces for Festive Occasions* (Morning Star) M
Marsh J.   **Christ triumphant** in *The Organist's Liturgical Year* (Mayhew) E/M
Sechter S.   **Wunderbarer König** in *18 Choralvorspiele* Op. 90 (Doblinger) E*

Suitable before or after: Movements from Callahan C. **Partita on 'Diademata'** (Morning Star) E/M-M

YEAR C

THE FIRST SUNDAY OF ADVENT YEAR C

HYMNS AND SONGS

	pos	rdg	AMNS	CAON	CFE	CH4	CH5	CP	H&P	HTC	LAU	MP	NEH	SG	SOF	TS
All hail the power of Jesus' name		n	140	16	19	457	250	163	252	587	323	13	332	24	9	7
Awake, awake: fling off the night!	ga	s	342	57	64			334			851					
Bless the Lord, my soul (Taizé)				923	81		1				813			105	676	56
Christ is coming! Let creation		s				475										
Christ triumphant, ever reigning		n		104	113	436	259	398		173	763	77	*613*	319	62	655
Come, thou long-expected Jesus		s	31	128	133	472	119	24	81	52	100	102	3	335		
Creator of the stars of night/ starry height		s	23	135	138	288	121	25			87		1			
Fear not, rejoice and be glad		o			169						144				106	
Great is the darkness		s									835			264	742	136
Hark, a herald/thrilling voice is calling/trumpet call is sounding		s	24	263	243		126	26		192	92		5	436		
He came down that we may have love		g				359								116		
Hills of the North, rejoice		s	470	282	255		128	29	237		983		7			
How lovely on the mountains (Our God reigns)		s		295	268		129				768	249			192	189
I cannot tell why he, whom angels worship		n		303				54	238	194		266		437	205	199
I'm accepted, I'm forgiven		g										321			229	217
Immortal love, for ever full		g	133	315			211	475	392	105		328	378	176		
In Christ alone my hope is found		s,g									1072				1346	1311
Lo, he comes with clouds descending/Jesus comes		s	28	405	373	477	132	31	241	196	109	424	9	438	347	324
Longing for light (Christ, be our light)		s				543					883					1409
Make way, make way, for Christ the king		s		438	479	279	134				819	457			384	349
Name of all majesty		g		465			102	525		218		481		324	939	
The Lord will come and not be slow		s	29	655			140	37	245				15			
To God be the glory!		g		695	745	512	373	609	463	584	719	708		71	559	526
Wake, O wake/Wake, awake/ Sleepers, wake!		s	32	703	763	278	142	39	249	199	91		16			
Waken, O sleeper		s		702			143									
We give immortal praise		g	520	713				206	18	11						
Ye/You servants of the Lord		s	150	757			145	40	248	598			18			

SONGS FOR CHILDREN

Alleluia! Hurry, the Lord is near CH4 280, TCB 2
Christmas is coming CH4 282, LAU 93
He came down that we may have love CH4 359, SG 116, VE

BIBLE READINGS

Psalm 9*
Joel 3.9–21
Revelation 14.13 - 15.4
John 3.1–17

SINGING THE PSALM

Psalm 9* CH4, CWP, NPCW

ANTHEMS AND VOCAL MUSIC

Title	Composer	Voices	E/M/D	Book source	Single sheet publisher
UNISON/TWO PART/HIGH VOICES					
Be peace on earth	Crotch	SS	M	OEAB	
King of glory, King of peace	Sanders	SSAA	M/D		Encore
Let all mortal flesh keep silence	Trad arr Greening	2 part	E	TEA	
Let all mortal flesh keep silence	Trad arr Cleobury	2 part	E	AFC	
Maranatha, alleluia!	Ogden	U + descant	E	ACB, CFL, SFL2 (SAMen)	RSCM
Rejoice, the Lord is king	Weaver	2 part	E/M	CFAP	
Soon and very soon	Crouch arr Iliff	U/SATB	E	TCB	
THREE/FOUR PARTS					
And I saw a new heaven	Bainton	SATB	M/D	FSB4	Novello
And I saw a new heaven	Archer	SATB	M	NOEAB	
And the glory of the Lord (Messiah)	Handel	SATB	M	AOAN1 (SAB)	Novello
Christ our God descends from heaven	Bullard	SAMen	E	SBS2	RSCM
God omnipotent reigneth	Wood	SATB	E	SBS1	RSCM
God so loved the world (g)	Chilcott	SATB + solo S unacc	M	BCA, AWTE	OUP
God so loved the world (g)	Goss	SATB unacc	E	NCAB	
God so loved the world (g)	Ley	ATTB	M	SL	S&B
God so loved the world (g)	Stainer	SAB unacc	E/M	AOAN1	
God so loved the world (g)	Stainer	SATB unacc	E/M	AWTE, FAB1, MHWE, NOEAB, NSAC1	Novello, RSCM
King of all ages, throned on high	Isom	SATB	E	NOEAB	
Let all mortal flesh keep silence	Trad arr Covey-Crump	SATB unacc	M	MTH1	
Rejoice, the Lord is king	Archer	SATB	M		Mayhew
Rejoice, the Lord is king	Kelly	SATB	M/D	NNAB, MTH1	
Rejoice, the Lord is king	Weaver	SATB	M	SC	
FIVE OR MORE PARTS					
Let all mortal flesh keep silence	Bairstow	SSAATTBB unacc	M	AC4	S&B
Lord, thou hast been our refuge	Vaughan Williams	SATB + SATB	M		Curwen
So God loved the world (g)	Gibbons	SAATB	M		Novello

ORGAN MUSIC

PRELUDES

Berthier J.	**Variations on 'Wachet auf'** in *Variations on Six Chorales* (Mayhew) E/M
Near G.	**Nun komm, der Heiden Heiland** in *Choraleworks* Set 1 (Aureole) E/M
Oldroyd G.	**Conditor alme siderum** No.2 of *Three Liturgical Improvisations* (OUP) E/M
Peeters F.	**Wachet auf** in *Ten Chorale Preludes* Op.68 (Peters) M
Vetter N.	**Nun komm, der Heiden Heiland** in *80 Chorale Preludes* (Peters) E(*)

POSTLUDES

Bach J.S. **Nun komm, der Heiden Heiland** BWV 661 in Novello Vol.17, Bärenreiter Vol.2, Peters Vol.7 M

Herbig C. **Canzon sopra 'Nun komm, der Heiden Heiland'** in *German Organ and Keyboard Music of the 17th C First Editions* Vol. 2 (Bärenreiter) E/M(*)

Reger M. **Wachet auf** Op.67/43 in *Complete Works* Vol.7 (Breitkopf) M

Mawby C. **Rorate caeli desuper** in *Gregorian Calendar* (Mayhew) E/M

THE SECOND SUNDAY OF ADVENT YEAR C

HYMNS AND SONGS

	pos	rdg	AMNS	CAON	CFE	CH4	CH5	CP	H&P	HTC	LAU	MP	NEH	SG	SOF	TS
All ye who seek for sure relief/a comfort sure		o	64	26	31			101			212		63			
Come, thou long-expected Jesus		s	31	128	133	472	119	24	81	52	100	102	3	335		
Comfort, comfort now/ye my people		o				274	120				97					
Creator of the stars of night/starry height		s	23	135	138	288	121	25			87		1			
Faithful Shepherd, feed me	cm	o		156			644			29			282	498		
God has spoken – by his prophets		o				381		64	248	742	831		225			
Great is the darkness		s									835		264	742	136	
Hark the glad sound! The Saviour comes		s	30	265		277	124	27	82	193		210	6	435	154	
Hark what a sound, and too divine		s					127	28	236				600			
Heaven shall not wait		s		272		362										151
Hills of the North, rejoice		s	470	282	255		128	29	237		983		7			
How beauteous/gracious are their feet		o	301					220	449							
How lovely on the mountains (Our God reigns)		o		295	268		129				768	249			192	189
I cannot tell why he, whom angels worship		s		303				54	238	194		266		437	205	199
Immortal, invisible, God only wise	ga	o	199	314	301	132	6	474	9	21	725	327	377	44	234	220
Jesus shall reign where'er the sun		s	143	359		470	97	490	239	516	322	379	388	45	301	1376
Judge eternal, throned in splendour		s		372		264	535	356	409	329		395	490	600		
Lord of the Church, we pray for our renewing		s					303			499		442		577	1433	
O comfort my people		o		481	523						99					
O Day of God, draw nigh		s	405				33									
On Jordan's bank, the Baptist's cry		o	27	527	575	334	136	34	84	601	94	538	12	339		
Restore, O Lord, the honour		o		582		469						579		274	483	439
The advent of our God/King	gr	s	25	633			36						14			
The kingdom of God is justice and joy		s		646	701			591	139	333	821	651		184		
The Lord will come and not be slow		s	29	655			140	37	245				15			
These are the days of Elijah		o					141					1012			1047	503
Thou/God, whose almighty word		s	180	684	738	112	324	267	29	506	887	699	466	597	557	
Thy/Your kingdom come, O God		o	177	691			509	607	783	334		949	499	269		
Wait for the Lord (Taizé)		s		949	762	276					88				1575	

SONGS FOR CHILDREN

Hey! Hey! Anybody listening? JP2 362
When the time is right CAON 913, KS 379

BIBLE READINGS
Psalms 75 [and 76]
Isaiah 40.1–11
Luke 1.1–25

SINGING THE PSALM
Psalm 75 CWP, NPCW
Psalm 76 CWP, NPCW

ANTHEMS AND VOCAL MUSIC

Title	Composer	Voices	E/M/D	Book source	Single sheet publisher
UNISON/TWO PART/HIGH VOICES					
Settings of the Benedictus (The Song of Zechariah)	Various	U	E	CWP, MCW1, NEP	
Hark! a messenger is calling	Kelly	3 part	E/M	CFL	
He shall feed his flock (Messiah)	Handel	U	M		Novello
How beautiful are the feet (Messiah)	Handel	S	M		Novello
Prepare ye the way of the Lord	Schwartz arr Ogden	2 part	E	SFL1	
Song of Consolation	Jones	U	E	VE	
The Spirit of the Lord is upon me	Corp	2 part	E	VFLS	
THREE/FOUR PARTS					
And the glory of the Lord (Messiah)	Handel	SATB	M		Novello
Benedictus	Stanford	SATB	M	AFC	
Canite tuba	Guerrero	SATB unacc	M	AFC	
Fuit homo missus a Deo	Palestrina	SATB unacc	M	AFC	
Hark, the glad sound	Walford Davies	SATB	E		RSCM
He shall feed his flock (Messiah)	Handel arr Hand	SAMen	M	AOAN1	
How beauteous are their feet	Stanford	SATB	M	AOAN1 (SAMen), ASA, NNAB, SC	Novello
How beautiful upon the mountains	Stainer	SATB	M	AOAN1 (SAMen), BC	RSCM
How lovely are the messengers	Mendelssohn	SATB	M	AFC	Novello
I look from afar	Piccolo	SATB	M/D		RSCM
Kindle a light to lighten the darkness	Lloyd	SATB	M		Encore
Now the God of peace	Knight	SATB	E	SBS1	RSCM
This is the record of John	Gibbons	SATB + solo A	M/D	OBTA	OUP
This is the record of John	Ives	SATB	M/D	AFC	
Vox clamantis	Esquivel	SATB unacc	M/D		Mapa Mundi
FIVE OR MORE PARTS					
Canite tuba	Palestrina	SSATB unacc	M	CM12	
Rorate coeli	Byrd	SSATB unacc	M/D		Joed, OUP
Vox dicentis, clama	Naylor	SATB + SATB unacc	D		Curwen

ORGAN MUSIC

PRELUDES
Bach J.S.   **Lob sei dem allmächtigen Gott** (Fughetta) BWV 704 in Novello Vol.18, Bärenreiter Vol.3, Peters Vol.5 E/M*
Fish A.   **Advent Aria** in *The Organist's Liturgical Year* (Mayhew) E
Hunt W.   **Franconia** from *Six Choral Preludes* (Cramer) M
Trevor C.H.   **Study on 'Franconia'** in *The Progressive Organist* Bk.5 (Novello) E
Watson R.   **Immortal, invisible** in *At Your Service* (Fagus) E

POSTLUDES
Archer M.   **Bristol** in *25 Hymn Preludes: A Year of Praise* (Mayhew) and in *40 Christmas Preludes* (Mayhew) E/M
Cameron J.G.   **Bristol** in *Six Preludes on Hymn Tunes* (Novello) M
Guilmant A.   **Sortie sur 'Creator alme siderum'** from *Liturgical Organist* Op.65 Bk.5 (Masters, Schott) or in *Complete* Works Vol.6 (Belwin Mills) M
Whitlock P.   **Hymn Prelude 'St Denio'** in *Whitlock: Complete Shorter Works* (OUP) M/D

HYMNS AND SONGS

	pos	rdg	AMNS	CAON	CFE	CH4	CH5	CP	H&P	HTC	LAU	MP	NEH	SG	SOF	TS
Be bold, be strong	o											49			37	38
Christ is the King! O friends rejoice	s	345				86	165		492			345	31		
Christ whose glory fills the skies	n	4	105		578	52	2	457	266	670	79	234	170	1200	
Creator of the stars of night/ starry height	s	23	135	138	288	121	25			87		1			
Hark, a herald/thrilling voice is calling/trumpet call is sounding	s	24	263	243		126	26		192	92		5	436		
Hills of the North, rejoice	o	470	282	255		128	29	237		983		7			
How lovely on the mountains (Our God reigns)	s		295	268		129				768	249			192	189
I hunger and I thirst	o						306	730	409			470			
In the Lord I'll be ever thankful (Taizé)	o		929	308	772					944	865		656	817	
Let the desert sing	o								198						
Lo, in the wilderness a voice	s	384										170			
Longing for light (Christ, be our light)	s				543					883				1409	
O bless the God of Israel	n					706			599						
O come, O come, Emmanuel	s	26	480	522	273	135	32	85	66	112	493	11	338	410	
O Day of God, draw nigh	s	405				33									
O for a thousand tongues to sing	o	125	485		352	104	534	744	219		496	415	55	412	383/ 1452
On Jordan's bank, the Baptist's cry	s	27	527	575	334	136	34	84	601	94	538	12	339		
Prepare the way for the Lord	s											342			
Rejoice! The Lord is king	s	139	580	619	449	281	563	243	180	326	575	443	440	482	948
The kingdom of God is justice and joy	s		646	701			591	139	333	821	651		184		
The Lord is my song (Taizé)	o		651												
The Lord my pasture shall prepare	o	111	653			593						458			
The Lord will come, and not be slow	o	29	655			140	37	245				15			
There's a light upon the mountains	s								246		679				
Wait for the Lord (Taizé)	s		949	762	276					88				1575	
When the King shall come again	o			806					200	90					
You shall go out with joy	o		766	831	804	377				878	796			640	609

SONGS FOR CHILDREN

Alleluia! Hurry, the Lord is near CH4 280, TCB 2

Be bold, be strong JP 14, KS 17, MP 49, SOF 37, TS 38

Christmas is coming CH4 282, LAU 93

BIBLE READINGS

Psalms 50.1–6 [and 62]
Isaiah 35
Luke 1.57–66[67–80]

SINGING THE PSALM

Psalm 50.1–6 CH4, CWP, NPCW
  Bell *Let the giving of thanks* PPP
Psalm 62 CH4, CRP, CWP, FGP, NPCW
  Bell *On God alone I wait silently* C, PPP, TIOAU
  Berthier *In God alone* C, TSFP#
  Daniels *I rest in God alone* MP, PIW#
  Rizza *In God alone* LIOD#

ANTHEMS AND VOCAL MUSIC

Title	Composer	Voices	E/M/D	Book source	Single sheet publisher
UNISON/TWO PART/HIGH VOICES					
Advent Prose	Trad arr Cleobury	U	E	AFC	
Rejoice, the Lord is king	Weaver	2 part	E/M	CFAP	
There is a longing	Quigley	U/SATB#	E	CH4, LAU, SG	OCP
THREE/FOUR PARTS					
And the glory of the Lord (Messiah)	Handel	SATB	M	AOAN1 (SAB)	Novello
Confortamini et iam	Lassus	SATB unacc	M		Joed
On Jordan's bank	Trad arr Archer	SATB	E	AFC	
Rejoice in the Lord alway	Anon arr Le Huray	SATB unacc	E	AFC	OUP
Rejoice in the Lord alway	Carter	SATB	M/D	ACA	OUP
Rejoice in the Lord always	Purcell	SATB	E	NCAB	Novello
Rejoice, the Lord is king	Archer	SATB	M		Mayhew
Rejoice, the Lord is king	Kelly	SATB	M/D	NNAB, MTH1	
Rejoice, the Lord is king	Weaver	SATB	M	SC	
Rorate coeli	Handl	SATB unacc	M		Mapa Mundi
The bells of waiting Advent ring	Trad arr Iliff	SATB/U	E	TCB	
The Wilderness	Goss	SATB	M		Banks
We wait for thy loving kindness	McKie	SATB	E/M	AC4, NSAC2	OUP
Zion, at thy shining gates	Trad arr Guest	SATB	E	AFC	
FIVE OR MORE PARTS					
Canite tuba	Palestrina	SSATB unacc	M	CM12	
Gaudete omnes	Praetorius	SATTB unacc	D		Chester
Laetentur caeli	Byrd	SSATB unacc	M/D	OBTA	
Rorate coeli	Byrd	SSATB unacc	M/D		Joed, OUP

ORGAN MUSIC

PRELUDES

Guilmant A.   **Noël pour le temps de l'Avent** in *Guilmant Selected Works* Vol.4 (Bärenreiter) E/M
Oldroyd G.   **Verbum supernum prodiens** No.3 of *Three Liturgical Improvisations* (OUP) E/M
Shearing G.   **I love thee, my Lord** in *Sacred Sounds from George Shearing* (SMP) E/M
Sowerby L.   **Veni, veni Emmanuel** in *Advent to Whitsuntide* (Hinrichsen reprint) M
Walther J.G.   **Mach's mit mir** ('Eisenach') in *120 Chorale Preludes of the 17C & 18C* (Peters) M

POSTLUDES

Atkinson G.   **Postlude on 'Veni Emmanuel'** (Fagus) E/M
Krebs J.L.   **Von Gott will ich nicht lassen** No.11 in *Complete Works Vol.4: Clavierübung* (Breitkopf) E/M*
Lang C.S.   **Voluntary on 'Winchester New'** in *Festal Voluntaries: Advent* (Novello) M/D
Murray G.   **Processional on 'O come, Emmanuel'** in *New Music for Organ* Bk.2 (Mayhew) M

THE FOURTH SUNDAY OF ADVENT YEAR C

HYMNS AND SONGS

	pos	rdg	AMNS	CAON	CFE	CH4	CH5	CP	H&P	HTC	LAU	MP	NEH	SG	SOF	TS
Adoramus te, Domine (Taizé)				921	11		345				667		208			
All hail the power of Jesus' name		o,n	140	16	19	457	250	163	252	587	323	13	332	24	9	7
Behold the servant of the Lord		n							788				668			
Come, thou long-expected Jesus		n	31	128	133	472	119	24	81	52	100	102	3	335		
Come, thou Redeemer of the earth		n					153	49					19			
Crown him with many crowns		o	147	137	139	459	263	166	255	174	321	109	352	321	77	77
Emmanuel, Emmanuel		n										121			83	675
God is working his purpose out		o		221	217	235	481	444	769	191	86	189	495	451	135	128
Immanuel, O Immanuel		n										326			233	219
In heavenly armour we'll enter the land		o										639			237	228
Jesus, the name high over all		n		364			99		264	213		385		323	307	298
Let earth and heaven combine		n							109							1394
Long ago, prophets knew		o	484	406	375		133	58	83		116		10			867
Magnificat (Taizé)		s									335				1445	
Magnificat (Rizza)		s		935												
Mary, blessed teenage mother		n		442												
No wind at the window		n				287										
O come, O come, Emmanuel		o,n	26	480	522	273	135	32	85	66	112	493	11	338	410	
O Day of God, draw nigh		o	405					33								
People look east, the time is near		n		557		281		35								
Spirit divine, attend our prayers		o				583	341	195	327	240		614				
The darkness turns to dawn		n								68			363			
Thy/Your kingdom come! On bended knee		o	178	690		473		608					500			
To the name of our/that brings salvation		n	121	698	749	471	117	610	80	222			470	72		
When came in flesh the incarnate Word		n,s											17			
Where is this stupendous stranger?		n	527					75					41			
Ye who own the faith of Jesus/All who keep/claim		n		759	29			231			359		188			

SONGS FOR CHILDREN

Christmas is coming CH4 282, LAU 93

Soon and very soon CH4 749, CH5 138, JP 221, MP 605, SOF 1007, TCB 20, TS 460

BIBLE READINGS

Psalms 123 [and 131]
Isaiah 10.33 - 11.10
Matthew 1.18–25

SINGING THE PSALM

Psalm 123 CRP, CWP, NPCW
Psalm 131 CRP, CWP, FGP, NPCW

Bell *For you, the pride from my heart is banished* CH4, PPP
Deiss *My soul is longing for your peace* CFE, LAU
Rizza *O Lord, my heart is not proud* CAS, FOL#
Smith *Guard my soul* (WLP)#
Walker *Like a child rests* LAU, OOD (OCP)#

ANTHEMS AND VOCAL MUSIC

Title	Composer	Voices	E/M/D	Book source	Single sheet publisher
UNISON/TWO PART/HIGH VOICES					
A Song of Peace	Stanford	U	M		RSCM
A tender shoot	Goode	SSA unacc + cello	D	CFL	
Ave regina caelorum	Dufay	SAA unacc	M	AC3	
Hymn to the Virgin	Verdi	SSAA	D	AC3	
I sing of a maiden	Halsey	2 part	M	CFL	
My soul in stillness waits	Haugen	U#	E	CFE, LAU	GIA
There is no Rose	Britten	SSA	M	CC3	
THREE/FOUR PARTS					
A tender shoot	Goldschmidt	SATB	M	AFC, TCB	RSCM
Angelus ad virginem	Trad arr Carter	SATB	E/M	AFC	
Angelus ad virginem	Trad arr Willcocks	SATB	M	CC3	
Beata virgo	Byrd	SATB unacc	M	CHMO	
Dostoino yest	Tchaikovsky	SATB unacc	M/D	ESM	
Ecce concipies	Handl	SATB unacc	M	AFC	
Es ist ein Ros' entsprungen	Cashmore/Praetorius	SATB unacc	M	AFC	
I sing of a maiden	Berkeley	SATB unacc	E/M	AFC, N	Chester
The Angel Gabriel	Trad arr Rutter	SATB unacc	E	CC3	OUP
The Angel Gabriel	Trad arr Pettman	SATB unacc	E	ACB, TCB	Banks
The Spirit of the Lord	Elgar	SATB	M	SAEE	RSCM
There is a flow'r sprung of a tree	Vann	SATB unacc	M	AFC	RSCM
There is no Rose	Bax arr Dawkes	SATB	D	N	
There is no Rose	Joubert	SATB unacc	M	N	Novello
Virga Jesse floruit	Bruckner	SATB unacc	D	AFC, CHMO	Peters
FIVE OR MORE PARTS					
Hymn to the Mother of God	Tavener	SSAATTBB unacc	M/D	EAC1	Chester
Hymn to the Virgin	Britten	SSAATTBB unacc	M		B&H
Of a Rose, a lovely Rose	Rutter	SSATB	M		OUP
Unser lieben Frauen Traum	Reger	SSATBB unacc	D	ESM	

Anthems suggested for Year B (page 141) are also appropriate.

ORGAN MUSIC

PRELUDES

Brahms J.	**Es ist ein' Ros'** No.8 of *Eleven Chorale Preludes* Op.122 (many editions) E/M
Bunk G.	**Es kommt ein Schiff** in *Choralimprovisationen* (Butz) E/M
Dallier H.	**O clemens! O pia!** No.2 of *Cinq Invocations* (Lemoine) M
Gibbs A.	**Virgin-born, we bow before thee** from *Peacehaven Preludes* (Bardic) E(*)
Hesford B.	**Meditations 'Our Lady Victorious'** in *St Cecilia Organ Library* Vol.1 (Cramer) E

POSTLUDES

Dallier H.	**Electa ut sol** No.5 of *Cinq Invocations* (Lemoine) M
Dupré M.	**Virgo Dei genitrix** No.2 of *Eight Short Preludes on Gregorian Themes* (Summy-Birchard) M*
Pachelbel J.	**Magnificat Fugue II** in *A Graded Anthology for Organ* Bk.2 (Cramer) E*
Schiefferdecker C.	**Meine seele erhebet den Herren** in *Choralbearbeitungen des Norddeutschen Barocks* (Breitkopf) E/M

(For Christmas Day, see Year A, page 10.)

THE FIRST SUNDAY OF CHRISTMAS YEAR C

HYMNS AND SONGS

	pos	rdg	AMNS	CAON	CFE	CH4	CH5	CP	H&P	HTC	LAU	MP	NEH	SG	SOF	TS
A great and mighty wonder		s	43	4			146	41	90	49			21			
A noble flower of Juda		s			5						126					
All hail the power of Jesus' name		n	140	16	19	457	250	163	252	587	323	13	332	24	9	7
All my heart this night rejoices		s						43	91	76						
Beauty for brokenness		o		60		259	494					806		263	664	37
Behold the amazing gift of love		n,s				478		389	666							
Behold, the great Creator makes		s	44	62		308		46		50			23			
Child in the manger		s		93	105	314	151			51	141	71				
Child of the stable's secret birth		s						47	124	53			43			
Christ is the world's true light		n	346	100		456	501	396	456	323			494	432		
Cloth for the cradle		s		107												
From east to west, from shore to shore		s		193					99				20			
Gloria/Glory to God (Taizé)		g		960		760								110		119
Glory in the highest to the God of heaven		n,s					693	300		582			363	37		
God of glory, we exalt your name		o										191			137	130
He came down that we may have love		s				359							116			
In the bleak midwinter		s	42	326	305	305	162	55	107	600	144	337	28	353	243	789
Joy to the world!		s		370	335	320	166	57	77	197	156	393		340	314	305
Jubilate Deo, alleluia (Taizé)					337											
Let earth and heaven combine		s							109							1394
Lord, who left the highest heaven		s								97						
Love came down at Christmas		s		427	397	316	170	59	105	62		451		376		
O Christ the same, through all our story's pages		NY		477			103			263			258			
Of the Father's heart/love/God of God		s	33/325	486	562	319	175	64/65	79	56	160		33	337		
Thou didst leave thy throne		s	250	683			114	601	154			697	465		555	1015
Thou who wast rich/Lord, you were rich		s				318	168	72		63		700		356		1018
Who would think that what was needed		s		750		295		78								

Hymns and songs particularly appropriate for the New Year are marked NY.

SONGS FOR CHILDREN

He came down that we may have love CH4 359, IECS, SG 116, VE
Long ago and far away CH5 167
The Virgin Mary had a baby boy CAON 670, CAP 121, CFE 717, CH4 300, HTC S25, JP 251, SOF 1050

BIBLE READINGS

Psalm 132
Isaiah 61
Galatians 3.27 - 4.7
Luke 2.15–21

SINGING THE PSALM

Psalm 132 CWP, NPCW

ANTHEMS AND VOCAL MUSIC

Title	Composer	Voices	E/M/D	Book source	Single sheet publisher
UNISON/TWO PART/HIGH VOICES					
At the name of Jesus	Walker	U/SATB#	E	ATNJ	OCP
Glory to God/While shepherds watched (g)	Haugen	U/SATB#	E	VE	
Lift on high	Ogden	U/SATB	E		WLP
Many are the lightbeams	Haugen	U	E		GIA
The Spirit of the Lord is upon me	Corp	2 part	E	VFLS	
THREE/FOUR PARTS					
For him all stars have shone	Chilcott	SATB + upper voices	E	BCC	OUP
Go tell it on the mountain	Trad arr Burton	SATB	M/D	CSFC	
Jesu dulcis memoria	Pott	SATB + solo S unacc	M/D	CN	
Jesu dulcis memoria	Shephard	SATB	E/M		RSCM
Jesu dulcis memoria	Victoria	SATB unacc	M	ESM, NSAC1, NCAB	CMS
No small wonder/Small wonder the star	Edwards	SATB	E/M	TCB, N	
Quem vidistis, pastores (g)	Poulenc	SATB unacc	M/D		Salabert
Shepherd's Pipe Carol (g)	Rutter	SATB	M	CC2, JRC	OUP
Song of the Angels	Rizza	SATB#	E/M	ROP	
The Lamb	Tavener	SATB unacc	M/D	N	Chester
The little road to Bethlehem (g)	Head	SATB	E		B&H
The Spirit of the Lord	Elgar	SATB	M	SAEE	RSCM
FIVE OR MORE PARTS					
All hail the power of Jesu's name	Greenhill	SATBB	E/M		Novello
Hodie nobis caelorum rex	Lobo	SATB + SATB unacc	D		Mapa Mundi
Jesu dulcis memoria	Villette	SSAATTBB unacc	M/D		UMP
O nomen Jesu	Philips	SSATB unacc	M		Mapa Mundi
O ye little flock	Amner	SSAATB	M		CMS/OUP
Quem vidistis, pastores (g)	Lassus	SSATB unacc	M		Mapa Mundi

Music listed for Years A and B (pages 13 and 143) is also suitable.

ORGAN MUSIC

PRELUDES

Albrechtsberger J.G.	**Pastorale** in *Sechs Pastoralestücke* (Doblinger) E/M	
Groves R.	**Divinum mysterium** No.5 of *Six Plainsong Preludes* (Novello) E(*)	
Milford R.	**Prelude on 'Unto us a boy is born'** No.13 of *Three Christmas Pieces* (Cathedral Music or OUP reprint) M	
Lloyd Webber W.S.	**Interlude on 'The Coventry Carol'** in *The Oxford Book of Christmas Music* and in *Songs without Words* (Music Sales) E	
Sumsion H.	**Prelude on 'The Coventry Carol'** *or* **Prelude on 'The Holly and the Ivy'** (RSCM) E/M	

POSTLUDES

Cavazzoni G.	**Christe redemptor omnium** in *First Organ Book* (Schott) and *Early Organ Music* Vol.16 (Faber) M*	
Clucas H.	**Nativity** ('Quem pastores') in *A Coldridge Organ Book* (Animus) E*	

Suitable before or after: Movements from Callahan C. **Partita on 'Adeste fideles'** (Concordia) E/M-M *or* Self A. **Variations on 'Divinum mysterium'** (Animus) E/M-M

THE SECOND SUNDAY OF CHRISTMAS YEAR C

HYMNS AND SONGS

	pos	rdg	AMNS	CAON	CFE	CH4	CH5	CP	H&P	HTC	LAU	MP	NEH	SG	SOF	TS
A great and mighty wonder		s	43	4			146	41	90	49			21			
All my hope on God is founded		NY	336	19	21	192	10	368	63	451	959	16	333	525		620
Angels from the realms of glory	of	s	39	36		324	147	44	92	77	131	35		344	23	631
Child of the stable's secret birth		s						47	124	53			43			
Christ be the Lord of all our days		NY								256			630			
Christians, awake! Salute the happy morn		n	36	94				48	96	78		80	24	347	59	653
From east to west, from shore to shore		s		193					99				20			
Glorious things of thee are spoken		NY	172	205	195	738	646	435	817	494	827	173	362	35	127	691
God is working his purpose out		NY		221	217	235	481	444	769	191	86	189	495	451	135	128
Great is thy faithfulness		NY		249		153	80	453	66	260		200	636	39	147	138
I cannot tell why he, whom angels worship		n		303				54	238	194		266		437	205	199
In the bleak midwinter	cm	s	42	326	305	305	162	55	107	600	144	337	28	353	243	789
King of glory, King of peace		o	194	375	343		358	494	499	603	715	397	391	178		
Let earth and heaven combine		s							109							1394
Lord, for the years		NY		409		159	81	81		328	942	428	619	602	892	327
Lord, I come to you		NY										880		689	895	329
Lord, who left the highest heaven										97						
Love came down at Christmas		n		427	397	316	170	59	105	62		451			376	
O Christ the same, through all our story's pages		NY		477			103			263			258			
O/Our God, our help in ages past		NY	99	494	528	161	537	537	358	37	955	498	417	542	415	905
Of the Father's love/heart/God of God		s	33/325	486	562	319	175	64/65	79	56	160		33	337		
Once in royal David's city	ga		46	521	577	315	177	66	114	67	128	539	34	359	438	404
Take my life and let it be		NY	249	625	677	502	597	581	705	554	874	624		678	519	468
The first Nowell	of	s		641	692	323	198		119	93	150	644	36		529	974
Thou didst leave thy throne	of		250	683			114	601	154			697	465		555	1015
Thou who wast rich/Lord, you were rich						318	168	72		63		700		356		1018
Through all the changing scenes of life		NY	209	686	740		372	604	73	46		702	467	654	1566	1561
Ubi caritas/Living charity (Taizé)		n		946		801	530				245				1573	
Where is this stupendous stranger?			527					75					41			
Within our darkest night (Taizé)		g		950												

Hymns and songs particularly appropriate for the New Year are marked NY.

SONGS FOR CHILDREN

God made a boomerang CAON 806, KS 82
He came down that we may have love CH4 359, IECS, SG 116, VE

BIBLE READINGS

Psalm 135*
1 Samuel 1.20–28
1 John 4.7–16
Matthew 2.13–23

SINGING THE PSALM

Psalm 135* CWP, NPCW

ANTHEMS AND VOCAL MUSIC

Title	Composer	Voices	E/M/D	Book source	Single sheet publisher
UNISON/TWO PART/HIGH VOICES					
Faith, hope and love	Ogden	2 part	E	SBS1	RSCM
I give you a new commandment	Aston	2 part	E	TBC, NOEAB	RSCM
Jesu, Jesu, fill us with your love	Trad arr Weaver	2 part	E	SFL1	
Life through him	Inwood	U/2 part	E		OCP
Love one another	S.S.Wesley	S	E	BC	RSCM
Out of darkness	Walker	U/SATB#	E	CFE, LAU, OOD	OCP
Ubi caritas	Lole	SS	E		Encore
When I needed a neighbour	Carter arr Burt	2 part	M	SFL1	
THREE/FOUR PARTS					
A new commandment	Shephard	SATB	E	AWTE	RSCM
A new commandment	Parshall	SATB unacc	E	WFC	
And didst thou travel light	Shephard	SATB	E/M	BC	RSCM
Greater love	Ireland	SATB	M	AC4	S&B
I give to you a new commandment	Nardone	SATB	E/M	SBS1	RSCM
In the heart where love is abiding	Barnard	SATB	E	AWTE, BC	RSCM
Love divine	Goodall	SATB	E		Faber
Love divine	Ledger	SATB	E		Dean
Love divine	Willcocks	SATB	E	NOEAB	
Though I speak with the tongues of men	Bairstow	SATB	M	FSB10, NCAB, WFC	OUP
Ubi caritas	Ives	SATB unacc	M	SC	
Ubi caritas	Lauridsen	SATB unacc	M		Faber
Ubi caritas	Mawby	SATB	E		Mayhew
FIVE OR MORE PARTS					
Love one another	Carter	SSAATTBB	M/D		OUP
Ubi caritas	Duruflé	SAATTBB unacc	M		Durand
Ubi caritas	Berkeley	SSATB unacc	D		Chester
When I needed a neighbour	Carter arr Rose	SATB + SATB	E/M	MTH1	

For anthems related to the Gospel see Years A and B (pages 15 and 145).

ORGAN MUSIC

PRELUDES

Buxtehude D.   **Gelobet seist du, Jesu Christ** BuxWV 189 in Complete Works Vol.4 (Bärenreiter) M
Hand C.   **Angels from the realms of glory** in *40 Christmas Preludes* (Mayhew) M
Peeters F.   **All glory be to God on high** No.2 of *Ten Chorale Preludes* Op.69 (Peters) E/M*
Rowley A.   **The Little Prayers** or **Mary's Song** from *3 Scenes from the Boyhood of Christ* (Novello) E-E/M
Vetter N.   **Allein Gott in der Höh sei Ehr'** in *80 Chorale Preludes* (Peters) E*

POSTLUDES

Bach W.F.   **Wir Christenleut** in *W.F.Bach Organ Works* Bk.2 (Peters) E/M
Karg-Elert S.   **Gelobet sei'st du, Jesu Christ** No.6 from *Choral-Improvisationen* Op.65 Bk.1 (Breitkopf) M
Krebs J.L.   **Prelude and Fugetta on 'Allein Gott'** No.1 in *Complete Works Vol.4: Clavierübung* (Breitkopf) E/M*
Peeters F.   **King Jesus hath a garden** (variations) Op.39/10 in *Ten Organ Chorales* Op.39 (Schott) M/D

THE BAPTISM OF CHRIST (THE FIRST SUNDAY OF EPIPHANY) YEAR C

(For Epiphany, see Year A, page 16.)

HYMNS AND SONGS

	pos	rdg	AMNS	CAON	CFE	CH4	CH5	CP	H&P	HTC	LAU	MP	NEH	SG	SOF	TS
All who are thirsty, come to the Lord		o												546		
Awake, awake: fling off the night!		s	342	57	64		334				851					
Baptized in water	gr	g			67	636				381	407			492		
Be thou my vision/Lord, be my vision		s	343	70	74/75	465	643	386	378	545	970	51	339	669	42	50
Bless the Lord, my soul (Taizé)		n		923	81		1				813			105	676	56
Break thou the bread of life	cm	o,g					379	286	467			64			50	
Christ, when for us you were baptized		g	442					92	129							
Come down, O love divine	ga	g	156	114	125	489	294	175	281	231	303	89	137	663	1202	71
Do not be afraid, for I have redeemed you		s		150	147	191					972	115			1213	1183
Father of mercies, in thy/your word		o	167							247				224		
Fear not, for I am with you		s													105	
God has spoken to his people/Open your ears		s					380			S 13	472	182			131	
Great is the darkness		n									845			264	742	136
Hail to the Lord's anointed		g	142	259	241	474	125	87	125	190	102	204	55		150	709
How firm a foundation		s		292						430		243				186
In Christ alone my hope is found		n										1072			1346	1311
Lord of the Church, we pray		s					303			499		442		577	1433	
Lord, be thy word/make your word my rule		o	232				383	209		250						
Lord, thy word abideth/your word shall guide us	gr	o	166	420	390		384	515	476	251	977/8	446	407			
Name of all majesty		s		465			102	525		218		481		324	939	
Now is eternal life		n	402	470			392	152	203				114			
O thou who camest from above		s	233	541	557	625	639	191	745	596		525	431	560	451	416
Out of the flowing river		g				335										
Songs of thankfulness and praise		s	53	609	661		197	90		98	172		56	376		
Spirit divine, attend our prayers		g				583	341	195	327	240		614				
Spirit of the living God (Iverson)	gr	g		615	666	619	310		295	S 23	306	613			510	462
The sinless one to Jordan came		s					200						58			
There is a river		s			722											
To the name of our/that brings salvation		g	121	698	749	471	117	610	80	222			470	72		
When Jesus came to Jordan		g	526				204	93	132							

Seasonal hymns and songs listed for Years A and B (pages 18 and 146) are also appropriate.

SONGS FOR CHILDREN

Light a flame CH 255, SOF 339
We're a bright light together CAON 906, KS 362, TS 1040

BIBLE READINGS

Psalms 46 and 47

Isaiah 55.1–11

Romans 6.1–11

Mark 1.4–11

SINGING THE PSALM

Psalm 46 CH4, CWP, H&P, NPCW, PAME

Psalm 47 CH4, CRP, CWP, FGP, H&P, NEH, NPCW, PAME, PFS

Bell *Clap your hands all you nations* CG, MCW1, PPP, SG

ANTHEMS AND VOCAL MUSIC

Title	Composer	Voices	E/M/D	Book source	Single sheet publisher
UNISON/TWO PART/HIGH VOICES					
Give us, Lord, a new heart	Farrell	U/SATB#	E/M	LAU, RITH, SLG	OCP
Ho! everyone who thirsts	Haugen	U#	E	LAU	GIA
The Song of the Tree of Life	Vaughan Williams	U/2 part	M	AC2	OUP
Unless a grain of wheat	Farrell	U/SATB#	E	CFE, LAU, RITH, WYP	OCP
Water of life	Dean	U#	E	CFE, CSF, LAU, NEP	OCP
THREE/FOUR PARTS					
And didst thou travel light	Shephard	SATB	E	BC	RSCM
As water to the thirsty	Coleman arr Barnard	SATB	E	SC	
Christus factus est	Anerio	SATB unacc	M	AWTE, CM1, ESM	
Christus factus est	Ridout	SATB unacc	E		Encore
Come down, O love divine	Harris	SATB	E/M	FSB9, NCAB, MTH2	Novello
Come down, O love divine	Tadman-Robins	SAMen	E	OBFA	
Greater love	Ireland	SATB	M	AC4	S&B
Holy Spirit, ever dwelling	Howells	SATB	E/M	ETAS	
Listen sweet dove	Ives	SATB	M	EAC1, SC	RSCM
Now is eternal life	Lloyd	SAMen	E/M	AOAN1	
O for a closer walk with God	Ives	SATB	M		RSCM
O for a closer walk with God	Stanford	SATB	M	AC1, ASA, BC, OBFA, AOAN1 (SAMen)	RSCM
O Saviour of the world	Goss	SATB	M	NCAB, NOEAB	
Out of the stillness	Shephard	SATB	E/M	SBS2	RSCM
The Song of Christ's Glory	P.Moore	SATB	E		RSCM
The Spirit of the Lord	Elgar	SATB	M/D	SAEE	RSCM
Tomorrow shall be my dancing day	Gardner	SATB	M	N	OUP
FIVE OR MORE PARTS					
Come down, O love divine	Rutter	SSAATTBB unacc	D		OUP
In splendente nube	Philips	SSATB unacc	M/D		Mapa Mundi
The Song of Christ's Glory	Ives	SSAATTBB unacc	M	WOTC	

See also the anthems listed for Years A and B (pages 19 and 147).

ORGAN MUSIC

PRELUDES

Groves R.   **The Rosy Sequence** No.2 of *Six Plainsong Preludes* (Novello) E/M(*)

Harker C.   **Pastorale: The Rosy Sequence** in *Three Pieces based on Plainsong Themes* (Bosworth) E/M

Karg-Elert S. **O Lamm Gottes, unschuldig** No.20 from Vol.2 of *Choral-Improvisationen* Op.65 (Breitkopf) M

Near G.   **Baptism of the Lord** in *A Gregorian Liturgical Year* Vol.1 (Aureole) E

Telemann G.P. **O Lamm Gottes unschuldig** in *12 Easy Chorale Preludes* (Kalmus, Peters) E*

POSTLUDES

Bach J.S.   **O Lamm Gottes unschuldig** BWV 656 in Novello Vol.17, Bärenreiter Vol.2, Peters Vol.7 M/D

Bunk G.   **Christ, unser Herr, zum Jordan kam** in *Choralimprovisationen* (Butz) E

Peeters F.   **Deus tuorum militum** in *30 Chorale Preludes on Gregorian Hymns* Bk.2 (Peters) M

Purvis R.   **What child is this?** in *The Oxford Book of Christmas Music* (OUP) E/M

THE SECOND SUNDAY OF EPIPHANY YEAR C

HYMNS AND SONGS

	pos	rdg	AMNS	CAON	CFE	CH4	CH5	CP	H&P	HTC	LAU	MP	NEH	SG	SOF	TS
Be still and know I (John Bell)		o												18	672	
Be still and know II (John Bell)		o			70	754							242			
Be still and know that I am God		o		66	71	755	608				909	48			41	48
Brightest and best of the sons of the morning		s	47	85	99	327	190	84	123	338		65	49	346		
Christ, from whom all blessings flow		n								764	491					
Christ is the King! O friends rejoice		n	345				86	165		492			345	31		
Dear Lord and Father of mankind		o	115	144	143	485	549	411	673	356	934	111	353	497	79	79
Father, Lord of all creation		n	356	163	161		318	418								
Forth in the peace of Christ we go	se		458	187	183	646	454	429		542	853		361	594		
Give me/us the wings of faith		n	324	204			463	216	815				225			
Hail to the Lord's anointed		s	142	259	241	474	125	87	125	190	102	204	55		150	709
Head of the church, our risen Lord		n								547						
Hushed was the evening hymn		o							523			253				
I cannot tell why he, whom angels worship		g		303				54	238	194		266		437	205	199
I come with joy		g	473	304		656	421	305	610	408	649		623	469		
I, the Lord of sea and sky (Here I am, Lord)	se	g		332	285	251	581	470			865	857		633	830	246
I will offer up my life		g				503						990		565	851	265
In Christ alone my hope is found		g										1072			1346	1311
In Christ there is no east or west		n	376	319	303	624	522	477	758	322	831	329	480	575		
Jesus calls us: o'er the tumult		g	312	347		509	584	233	141	104		359	200	668		
Jesus, stand among us in thy risen power		n		362			338		530	364		380			304	
Let earth and heaven combine		s							109							1394
Let there be love shared among us		n		386	358		525					411			329	317
Lord, speak to me that I may speak		o					589	512	553	510		444				
O Christe Domine Jesu (Taizé)					519						757					
One is the body		n				679							280			
Revive thy work/your church, O Lord!		n					308		780	515		578				
Songs of thankfulness and praise		s	53	609	661		197	90		98	172		56	376		
Speak, Lord, in the stillness		o					624			253		608				
The Church's one foundation		n	170	636	688	739	528	585	515	501	830	640	484	581	525	477
The race that long in darkness/The people who in darkness		s	52	656	711	290	199	38	89	71	168		57			
Why, impious Herod		s											46			
Will you come and follow me	se	g		752	812	533	605	622			877		647	634	1120	
You are the King of glory		g		762	822							790		627		

SONGS FOR CHILDREN

Far and near, hear the call KS 49, MP 982, SG 610, SOF 709, TS 90

Give me joy in my heart/Give me oil in my lamp AMNS 459, CAON 201, CAP 43, CFE 190, CH 55, CH5 570, CP 433, H&P 492, HTC S11, JP 50, KS 66, LAU 722, MP 167, SOF 728

BIBLE READINGS

Psalm 96
1 Samuel 3.1–20
Ephesians 4.1–16
John 1.29–42

SINGING THE PSALM

Psalm 96 CRP, CWP, FGP, H&P, MCW1, NPCW, PAME, PIW
Dean *Proclaim the wonders of the Lord* HG#
Walker *Save us, Lord our God* ATNJ (OCP)

ANTHEMS AND VOCAL MUSIC

Title	Composer	Voices	E/M/D	Book source	Single sheet publisher
UNISON/TWO PART/HIGH VOICES					
Settings of the Lamb of God/Agnus Dei	Various	U/SATB	E	C, MCW1	
Christ has no body now but yours	Ogden	U + descant	E	CFAP, LOL	RSCM
Here I am, Lord	Schutte arr Weaver	2 part	E	SFL1	
O God, you search me	Farrell	U/SATB#	E	CBL, CH4, LAU, MCW1, SG, TS	OCP
Sent by the Lord am I	Trad arr Weaver	2 part	E	BC	
Take my gifts	Farrell	U#	E	GBU	
The Call (Come, my Way)	Vaughan Williams	U	E	NEP	S&B
You have called us	Farrell	U#	E	C	OCP
THREE/FOUR PARTS					
A Prayer of St Richard of Chichester	Archer	SATB	E		RSCM
Behold the Lamb of God (Messiah)	Handel	SATB	M		Novello
Christ be my beginning	Moore	SATB	M		Encore
Come, my Way, my Truth, my Life	Rawsthorne	SAB	E/M		Mayhew
Expectans expectavi	Wood	SATB	M		Banks
Go forth and tell!	Ogden	SATB	E/M	SBS2	RSCM
Go forth into the world in peace	Rutter	SATB	E/M	JRA	OUP
Here I am, Lord	Schutte arr Archer	SATB	E	MTH1	
I waited for the Lord	Mendelssohn	SATB	M		Novello
Lead me, Lord	S.S.Wesley	SATB	E	AC1, FAB1, NCAB, NOEAB, NSAC1	Novello
O Lamb of God	Taverner	SAB	E	SETA	
Take this moment	Bell	SATB	E	CG, IAMB, LFB, OITB, WIS	GIA
The Call	Lloyd	SATB unacc	M		RSCM
The Lamb	Tavener	SATB unacc	M/D	N	Chester
FIVE OR MORE PARTS					
The Twelve	Walton	SSAATTBB	D		OUP

ORGAN MUSIC

Bach J.S.	**In dich hab' ich gehoffet, Herr** BWV 640 from the *Orgelbüchlein* (many editions) E/M	
Gigault N.	**Fugue pour L'Agnus Dei** p.27 in *Organ Book* Vol.1 (Kalmus) E*	
Nixon J.	**Cross of Jesus** in *Hymn Tune Preludes* (Fagus) E/M	
Piutti C.	**Christe, du Lamm Gottes** (3 strophes) in *Choralvorspiele* Op.34 Vol.1 (Bärenreiter) E	
Richter E.F.	**Jesu meine Freude** Op.20/4 in *Organ Music of the Classical & Early Romantic Periods* Vol.6 (Bärenreiter) M	

POSTLUDES

Bach J.S.	**Wer nur den lieben Gott lässt walten** BWV 642 from the *Orgelbüchlein* (many editions) E/M
Gigault N.	**Fugue à 3 sur L'Agnus** p.48 in *Organ Book* Vol.1 (Kalmus) E*
McKelvey M.	**Thornbury (Intrada, Alla Siciliana, Finale)** in *Preludes on Favourite Hymns* (Mayhew; 2-stave and 3-stave editions available) E/M
Near G.	**Epiphany 2** in *A Gregorian Liturgical Year* Vol.1 (Aureole) E/M

THE THIRD SUNDAY OF EPIPHANY YEAR C

HYMNS AND SONGS

	pos	rdg	AMNS	CAON	CFE	CH4	CH5	CP	H&P	HTC	LAU	MP	NEH	SG	SOF	TS
At/In the name of Jesus		g	148	54	59	458	94	380	74	172	762	41	338	317	32	33
Be still, for the presence of the Lord		g		67	72	189	325	383			720	50	629	7	40	47
Christ, from whom all blessings flow		n,u							764	491						
Christ, when for us you were baptized		n	442				92	129								
Come, see this glorious light		n												1208		
Firmly I believe and truly		g	118	174	173		320	426		429	962		360	287		
God is love, and where true love is		u	465		214		520	441	757		242		513			
I come with joy	of	u	473	304		656	421	305	610	408	649		623	469		
I give you all the honour		g		308			574					271			210	203
Jesus Christ is waiting		g		349	323	360					889		624			1360
Jesus, Lord, we look to thee	gr	u	380				489	759				481				
Jesus, the name high over all		g		364			99		264	213		385		323	307	
Jesus, united by thy grace		u							773							298
Lord of the Church, we pray	of	u					303			499		442		577	1433	
O for a thousand tongues to sing		g	125	485		352	104	534	744	219		496	415	55	412	383/ 1452
O thou, who at thy Eucharist didst pray/O Christ	of	u	265	540	556	669	438	318	779	420	833		302	476		
One is the body	gr	u				679							280			
The Church's one foundation		u	170	636	688	739	528	585	515	501	830	640	484	581	525	477
The price is paid		n										663			540	487
There is a Redeemer		g		658		559	112					673		396	544	492
Thine arm/Your hands, O Lord, in days of old		g	285	671			347	397			431		324			
To God be the glory!		n		695	745	512	373	609	463	584	719	708		71	559	526
Wait for the Lord (Taizé)		s		949	762	276						88			1575	
Why, impious Herod		s											46			

Hymns and songs especially suitable for celebrations of the Week of Prayer for Christian Unity are marked 'u'.

SONGS FOR CHILDREN
Come and praise the Lord our king CAP 21, CFE 121, HTC S8, JP 34
He paid a debt JP 77

BIBLE READINGS

Psalm 33
Numbers 9.15–23
1 Corinthians 7.17–24
Mark 1.21–28

SINGING THE PSALM

Psalm 33 CRP, CWP, FGP, H&P, LAU, NEH, NPCW, PAME, PFS
Walker *Lord, be with us* OOD#

ANTHEMS AND VOCAL MUSIC

Title	Composer	Voices	E/M/D	Book source	Single sheet publisher
UNISON/TWO PART/HIGH VOICES					
Alleluia, raise the Gospel (alternative text)	Farrell	U/SATB#	E	GBU	OCP
Litany to the Holy Spirit (In the hour of my distress)	Hurford	U/SATB	E	AC2, NEP (U), NSAC1, NOEAB	OUP
Lord, be thy word my rule	J.H.Wood	2 part	E	SEA2	Novello
My lips shall speak of thy praise	Greene	SS	M		Banks
Praise to you, O Christ our Saviour	Farrell	U#	E	CFE, LAU, RITH, WYP	OCP
Sent by the Lord am I	Trad arr Weaver	2 part	E	BC	
THREE/FOUR PARTS					
Be thou my vision	Chilcott	SATB + solo S	E/M	BCA, NOEAB	OUP
Christ the Word	Vann	SATB	M	STS	
I will praise God because of his word	Purcell	SATB	E/M	TPS	
In God's word will I rejoice	Purcell	SAB	M	TPS, SFL2	
O Lord, increase our faith	Loosemore	SATB (unacc)	E	SBS1, NCAB	RSCM
O most merciful	Wood	SATB	E	NSAC2	RSCM
Teach me, O Lord	Attwood	SATB	E	NOEAB	RSCM
Teach me thy way, O Lord	Purcell	SATB	M	TPS	
The Doctrine of Wisdom	Mathias	SATB	M		OUP
Thou art the way	Steel	SATB	M	NNAB, MTH2	
Thy word is a lantern	Purcell	SATB	M	APA	Novello
Waiting for the word	Skellern	SATB	E		RSCM
Where shall wisdom be found?	Carter	SATB	M/D		Banks
Word of God	Farrell	SATB unacc	E	GBU	
FIVE OR MORE PARTS					
Beati quorum via	Stanford	SSATBB unacc	M	ASA, WFC	RSCM
In medio Ecclesiae	Joubert	SSAATBB unacc	D	CN	OUP
Open thou mine eyes	Rutter	SSATBB unacc	M		OUP
Teach me, O Lord	Byrd	SAATB	M	OBTA	OUP

ORGAN MUSIC

PRELUDES

Bach J.S.   **Herr Christ, der ein'ge Gottes-Sohn** BWV 601 from the *Orgelbüchlein* (many editions) M
Couperin F.   **Dialogue sur la voix humaine** No.XI from *Messe pour les Couvents* (Kalmus) E*
Dubois T.   **Interlude from Seven Pieces** (Butz, Kalmus); also in *Complete Works* Vol.1 (Bärenreiter) E/M
Kerll J.K.   **Toccata IV cromatica con durezza, e ligature** No.4 in *Faber Early Organ* Vol.15 E/M*
Moore P.   **Prelude on 'St Botolph'** in *New Music for Organ* Bk.2 (Mayhew) E

POSTLUDES

Buxtehude D.   **Herr Christ, der einig Gotts Sohn** BuxWV 192 in *Complete Works* Vol.4 (Bärenreiter) E/M
Elgar E.   **No.7** *and/or* **No.6** from *Vesper Voluntaries* (Faber) E/M(*)
De Grigny N.   **A solis ortus/Crudelis Herodes** 2 settings in *Livre d'Orgue* (Kalmus, Schott) M-D
Ropartz G.   **Sur un thème breton** from *Trois Pièces* (Schola Cantorum) M

HYMNS AND SONGS

	pos	rdg	AMNS	CAON	CFE	CH4	CH5	CP	H&P	HTC	LAU	MP	NEH	SG	SOF	TS
All-creating heavenly Giver		o								489				662		
Angel voices, ever singing		o	163	37	45		346	377	484	307	724	34	336	27	24	
Bless the Lord, my soul (Taizé)				923	81		1				813			105	676	56
Bright the vision that delighted		o	96	86			316	392	445	578			343	29		
Come to the waters and I will give you rest		g										104				
Come, thou/O fount of every blessing		g						406	517	337						663
Confitemini Domino (Taizé)				925	137						701					
Glorious things of thee are spoken		g	172	205	195	738	646	435	817	494	827	173	362	35	127	691
God is here! As we his people		o,g	464				330	301	653	560	470					
God of glory, we exalt your name		o											191		137	130
Holy Spirit, truth divine	gr	g		289		626		184	289	235						
How sweet the name of Jesus sounds		g	122	297		461	92	467	257	211		251	374	42	194	190
I cannot tell why he, whom angels worship		g		303				54	238	194		266		437	205	199
I heard the voice of Jesus say		g	247	310		540	578	469	136		795	275	376		215	206
I'm accepted, I'm forgiven		g										321			229	217
Immortal, invisible, God only wise	ga	o	199	314	301	132	6	474	9	21	725	327	377	44	234	220
Jesu, lover of my soul		g	123	343	319	490	553	96	528	438	797	372	383	201	297	838
Jesu, the very thought of thee		g	120	368	321	560	101	485	265	478	798	386	385	534	308	
Jesu, thou joy of loving hearts	of/cm	g	255	369		662	425	486	258	413		383	292	471		839
Jesus, where'er thy people meet/Lord Jesus, when your people	ga	n,g	162	367			336	492	549	371			390	16		844
Now thank we all our God		o	205	474	512	182	361	530	566	33	945	486	413	54	405	
O Lord of heaven and earth and sea		o	287				363	540	337	287			422	306		
Songs of thankfulness and praise		s	53	609	661		197	90		98	172		56	376		
Through all the changing scenes of life		ps	209	686	740		372	604	73	46		702	467	654	1566	1561
Water of life, cleanse and refresh us		g			401							512		655		
Why, impious Herod		s											46			

SONGS FOR CHILDREN

God is good CAON 214, CH4 178, JP 55, KS 74, MP 185, SOF 132, TS 124
I will offer up my life CH4 503, KS 186, MP 990, SG 565, SOF 851, TS 265

BIBLE READINGS

Psalm 34
1 Chronicles 29.6–19
Acts 7.44–50
John 4.19–29a

SINGING THE PSALM

Psalm 34 C, CRP, CWP, FGP, H&P, LAU, MCW1, NPCW, PAME
Bell *I will always bless the Lord* C, CH4, IAMB, OITB
Dean *Taste and see* CFE, WYP#
Ogden *Taste and see* (WLP)
Rizza *I will bless the Lord* LIOD#
Schutte *Ever on my lips* C (OCP)#
Walker *Taste and see* CSF (OCP)#

ANTHEMS AND VOCAL MUSIC

Title	Composer	Voices	E/M/D	Book source	Single sheet publisher
UNISON/TWO PART/HIGH VOICES					
Eins bitte ich vom Herren	Schütz	2 part	M	AC2	
I was glad	Hubbard	SA	M	SFJ	Banks
I was glad	Warren arr How	U	E	SWAMS	
THREE/FOUR PARTS					
Angel voices	Shephard	SATB	M	SC	RSCM
Behold, the tabernacle of God	Harris	SATB	E/M		RSCM
Behold, the tabernacle of God	Rutter	SATB	M/D		OUP
Blessed city, heavenly Salem	Bairstow	SATB	D		Banks
Christ is our cornerstone	Ogden	SATB	E/M	SBS2	RSCM
Christ is our cornerstone	Rawsthorne	SATB	M		Mayhew
Christ is our cornerstone	Thorne	SATB	E/M	NOEAB	
Holy Spirit, truth divine (g)	Carter	SATB	E/M	ETAS, NOEAB	OUP
How lovely are thy dwellings	Brahms	SATB	M/D		RSCM
How lovely are thy dwellings	Self	SAB	E		RSCM
If ye love me (g)	Tallis	SATB unacc	E	FAB1, NCAB, NOEAB, NSAC1, OBTA, TA, SL (AATB)	OUP
O Lord our Governor	Barry Rose	SATB	M	MTP	
O pray for the peace of Jerusalem	Goss	SATB	M	AC1	
O pray for the peace of Jerusalem	Howells	SATB	M		OUP
Surely thou hast tasted that the Lord is good	Bernard Rose	SATB unacc	D	EAC1	Cathedral
The Church triumphant	Shephard	SATB	E/M	SBS1	RSCM
The Lord is my light and my salvation	Noon	SATB	M	SBS1	RSCM
Yours is the greatness	How	SATB	E	SBS2	
FIVE OR MORE PARTS					
Behold, O God our defender	Howells	SSAATTBB	M/D	MTP	Novello
If ye love me (g)	Chilcott	SSATB unacc	M	BCA, WFC	
If ye love me (g)	Wilby	SSATB	E		Banks
Lo! God is here!	P.Moore	SSAATTBB	M/D		Faber

ORGAN MUSIC

PRELUDES

Bonighton R.   **St Denio** in *100 Hymn Preludes* and *Hymn Preludes for the Church Year* Bk.2 (both Mayhew) E
Clérambault L-N.   **Récit de Nazard** from *Livre d'Orgue: Suite du Deuxième Ton* (Schola Cantorum, Kalmus) E/M
Howells H.   **Psalm-Prelude** Set 1 No.1 (Novello) M
Langlais J.   **Tiento** from *Suite Médiévale* (Salabert) M
Wesley S.   **Air in C minor** No.15 in *Organ Works* Vol.10 (Fagus) E/M*

POSTLUDES

Dubois T.   **Grand Choeur in B flat** in *Douze Pièces* (Leduc, Bärenreiter) M
Fletcher A.   **Blaenwern** in *Preludes on Favourite Hymns* (Mayhew; 2-stave and 3-stave editions available) E/M
Near G.   **St Denio** in *Choraleworks* Set 2 (M) *or* **Nun danket** in *Choraleworks* Set 1 (E/M) (both Aureole)
Piroye C.   **La Béatitude: Dialogue à deux choeurs** in *18th C Pieces for Manuals* (Novello) E/M*

PROPER 1 (SUNDAY BETWEEN 4 AND 10 FEBRUARY INCLUSIVE) YEAR C

(if earlier than the Second Sunday before Lent)

(For the Presentation of Christ in the Temple, see Year A, page 26.)

HYMNS AND SONGS

	pos	rdg	AMNS	CAON	CFE	CH4	CH5	CP	H&P	HTC	LAU	MP	NEH	SG	SOF	TS
Alleluia! Alleluia! Hearts to heaven		n	80	9		427	251	137		151			103	398		
As a fire is meant for burning		g				252					828					
Before Jehovah's aweful/ awesome throne/Sing to the Lord with joyful voice	ga	g	197					387	61	15						
Before the throne of God above		e				466		283		453		975		169	1187	643
Brother, sister, let me serve you/ Will you let me be your servant		n		88	813	694	517	393			924			619	54	
Captains of the saintly band		g	299	91				212					215			
Christ is alive! Let Christians sing		e		96		416	260	140	190		272			32		
Christ is the King! O friends rejoice		g	345				86	165		492			345	31		
Christ is the world's true light		n	346	100		456	501	396	456	323			494	432		
Come, let us with our Lord arise	m	n	449					142	575	375			254			
Fear not, rejoice and be glad		g			169							144			106	
Firmly I believe and truly		n	118	174	173		320	426		429	962		360	287		
God has spoken – by his prophets		g					381		64	248	742	831		225		
God, we praise you! God, we bless you!		n				120	696	450		341				38		
Here I am, wholly available		g										229			167	161
Here in this place (Gather us in)		g		253	623						475			4		
In Christ there is no east or west		n	376	319	303	624	522	477	758	322	831	329	480	575		
In heavenly love abiding		n		323		551		478	678	458		331	638		238	782
Jesus bids us shine		g		845			482									
Jesus lives! Thy terrors now		n	82	354			272	148	198	156		373	112	409	296	
Let all mortal flesh keep silence	cm	n	256	381	355	666	427	309	266	61	607		295	472	1413	
Longing for light (Christ, be our light)		g				543						883				1409
My God, accept my heart this day		n	279	455	495			338	701	551	872		318	559		
O lift us up, strong Son of God		o						427								
O Lord, you are the centre of my life		g			543						423			543		
O Lord, your tenderness	cm	n		515								511		569	433	402
Psallite Domino (Taizé)		ps			614											
Purify my heart		n		574			640					921		163	475	436
The/All earth was dark (Lights to the world)		g										8/643				
Thou/God, whose almighty word		g	180	684	738	112	324	267	29	506	887	699	466	597	557	
Who can measure heaven and earth		ap								27						

SONGS FOR CHILDREN

Jesus bids us shine CAON 845, CH5 482, JP 128, KS2 588

Lord, I pray, if today CH4 541

You are salt for the earth LAU 854

BIBLE READINGS

Psalms [1 and] 2
Wisdom 6.1–21 *or* Hosea 1
Colossians 3.1–22
Matthew 5.13–20

SINGING THE PSALM

Psalm 1 CH4, CRP, CWP, FGP, H&P, MCW1, NPCW, PAME, PIW
    Bell *Happy is the one* PPP
Psalm 2 CWP, NPCW, PAME

ANTHEMS AND VOCAL MUSIC

Title	Composer	Voices	E/M/D	Book source	Single sheet publisher
UNISON/TWO PART/HIGH VOICES					
Settings of the Jubilate	Various	U/SATB	E	CWP, MCW1	
Bless, O Lord, us thy servants	Harper	U/SATB	E	PSA	RSCM
God the singer	Ogden	U + descant	E	VFLS	
He came singing love	Gibson	2 part	E	VFLS	
I will sing a song of love	Bell	U	E	VFLS	
Let the bright seraphim (Samson)	Handel	S	D		Novello
O praise the Lord	Greene	S	M		Novello
When, in our music, God is glorified	Haugen	U#	E		GIA
THREE/FOUR PARTS					
Angel voices	Shephard	SATB	M	SC	RSCM
Cantate Domino	Pitoni	SATB unacc	E	AC1, NCAB, NSAC1, NOEAB, SC	
Go forth and tell!	Ogden	SATB	E	SBS2	RSCM
I will sing of the Lord's great love	McKinley	SATB	M	SC	
I will sing with the spirit	Goodenough	SATB	E	SBS2	
I will sing with the spirit	Rutter	SATB	M	JRA	OUP
If ye love me (g)	Tallis	SATB unacc	E	FAB1, NCAB, NOEAB, NSAC1, OBTA, TA, SL (AATB)	OUP
Jubilate!	Ogden	SATB unacc	M	SC	RSCM
O sing joyfully	Batten	SATB unacc	E	SCAB, WFC	RSCM
Sing we merrily	Campbell	SATB	M	MTP	Novello
When in our music God is glorified	Carter	SATB unacc	M/D		OUP
When music wakes my sleeping heart	Bonighton	SAMen	M	AOAN1	
FIVE OR MORE PARTS					
Cantate Domino	Monteverdi	SSATTB	M	ESM	
If ye love me	Chilcott	SSATBB unacc	M	BCA, WFC	OUP
Jubilate Deo	G.Gabrieli	SSAATTBB unacc	M/D	ESM	OUP
Jubilate Deo	Walton	SATB + SATB	M		OUP
O clap your hands	Gibbons	SSAATTBB unacc	D	OBTA	OUP
Sing joyfully	Byrd	SAATB unacc	M/D	OBTA	OUP

ORGAN MUSIC

PRELUDES

Bach J.S.	**Liebster Jesu, wir sind hier** BWV 633 or 634 from the *Orgelbüchlein* (many editions) E/M
Couperin F.	**Duo sur les tierces** No.VIII from *Messe pour les Paroisses* (Kalmus) E⋆
Peeters F.	**Aria** (Heuwekmeijer) E/M
Sumsion H.	**Sarabande & Interlude** in *A Second Easy Album* (OUP) E/M
Vierne L.	**Communion** from *Messe Basse* (Schola Cantorum); also in *French Masterworks* (Belwin Mills) E/M

POSTLUDES

Edwards P.	**Meditation in the Dorian Mode** from *Northampton Miniatures* (Fagus) E⋆
Joubert J.	**Picardy** in *Six Short Preludes on English Hymn Tunes* Op.125 (Novello) E/M⋆
Nagel M.	**Give us peace (Jazz Variations)** in *Jazz Inspirations* (Bärenreiter) E/M
Thiman E.	**Trumpet Tune on 'Moscow'** in *Five Hymn Tune Variants* (Curwen) E/M

PROPER 2 (SUNDAY BETWEEN 11 AND 17 FEBRUARY INCLUSIVE) YEAR C
(if earlier than the Second Sunday before Lent)

HYMNS AND SONGS

	pos	rdg	AMNS	CAON	CFE	CH4	CH5	CP	H&P	HTC	LAU	MP	NEH	SG	SOF	TS
A/The new commandment		g		35	4		515			S 26	920	1			22	23
All praise to thee, for thou, O King divine		n	337	22			684	372	253	204			335			
And can it be that I should gain		n		32	43	396	218	376	216	588	790	33	*627*	168	21	21
Brother, sister, let me serve you/Will you let me be your servant		n		88	813	694	517	393			924			619	54	
Christ, when for us you were baptized		n	442					92	129							
Christ whose glory fills the skies	mo		4	105		578	52	2	457	266	670	79	234	170	1200	
Father of all, whose laws have stood		g								539				664		
Freedom and life are ours		n								544				171		
God is love, and where true love is	gr	g	465		214		520	441	757		242		513			
Jesu, lover of my soul		ap	123	343	319	490	553	96	528	438	797	372	383	201	297	838
Lord, as I wake I turn to you	mo	ps	485				56		634	267	672		236	561		
Lord, make us servants of your peace		g				527										
Lord of all power, I give you my will/Lord of creation		n	395				500	594	508	699	547	869	440			
Make me a channel of your peace		g		437	478	528	503	519	776	S 19	898	456		691	381	348
Make way, make way, for Christ the king		n		438	479	279	134				819	457			384	349
Miserere nobis/Holy Lord, have mercy (Taizé)	o										597					
O for a thousand tongues to sing		n	125	485		352	104	534	744	219		496	415	55	412	383/1452
O Jesu, King most wonderful		n	120ii				106	539	269	484			386			
O Lord, hear my prayer (Taizé)		ps		938	542		620				929	908		246	423	394
O Son of God, eternal love		n											428			
O Trinity, most/of blessed light	ev		5	542									54			
Restore, O Lord, the honour	o			582		469							579	274	483	439
The kingdom is upon you!	ap,n		512				590						*650*			
The price is paid		n									663				540	487
What shall our greeting be		g							806					584		
Who can measure heaven and earth		ap								27						
Ye that know the Lord is gracious		n	175			642	493	628					477			

SONGS FOR CHILDREN
Do what you know is right CAON 791, CH 38, KS2 448
Our God is a God who makes friends CH4 792

BIBLE READINGS

Psalms [5 and] 6
Wisdom 11.21 - 12.11 *or* Hosea 10.1–8,12
Galatians 4.8–20
Matthew 5.21–37

SINGING THE PSALM

Psalm 5 CH4, CWP, NPCW, PFS
Psalm 6 CWP, NPCW
Bell *Hear me, Lord, and draw near* LFB, PPP

ANTHEMS AND VOCAL MUSIC

Title	Composer	Voices	E/M/D	Book source	Single sheet publisher
UNISON/TWO PART/HIGH VOICES					
Settings of Kyrie eleison/Lord, have mercy (g)	Various	U/SATB	E	C, LAU, MCW1, RE	
Carol of the Atonement (g)	Trad arr Greening	2 part	E	TEA	
Give ear unto me	Marcello	SS	M	AC2	
In thee, O Lord, I put my trust	Handel	2 part	E		RSCM
Listen	Nazareth arr Archer	2 part	E	BC	
My song is in sighing	Dalby	S	M/D	HP	Novello
Ponder my words	Walmisley	SSAA	M		RSCM
THREE/FOUR PARTS					
Blessed are they	S.S.Wesley	SAB	E		S&B
Hear my prayer	Batten	SATB + solo B	E		OUP
Hear my prayer	Mendelssohn	SATB	M		RSCM
Lead me, Lord	S.S.Wesley	SATB	E	AC1, FAB1, NCAB, NOEAB, NSAC1	Novello
O God of my righteousness	Greene	SATB + solo ST	M/D		CMS/OUP
O hearken thou	Elgar	SATB	M	MTP, SAEE	Novello
O most merciful	Bullock	SATB	E	NNAB	
O most merciful	Wood	SATB	E	NSAC2	RSCM
Prayer before the Crucifix (g)	P. Moore	SATB	M		Banks
Seek him out	Bryden	SATB + solo S	E/M		Encore
Seek ye the Lord	Varley Roberts	SATB + solo T	M	FAB1	Novello
FIVE OR MORE PARTS					
Delight thou in the Lord	Thurlow	SSAATTBB + T unacc	M/D		Encore
For this mortal must put on immortality	S.S.Wesley	SSATTB	M		OUP
Hear my prayer	Purcell	SSAATTBB unacc	M	APA	Faber/Novello
O Lord in thy wrath	Gibbons	SSAATB	M	OBTA	OUP
Turn thee, O Lord	Croft	SSATTBB			Novello

ORGAN MUSIC

PRELUDES

Anon.	**Ich ruf zu dir, Herr Jesu Christ** in *Orgelmusik um J.S.Bach* Vol.2 (Breitkopf) E/M
Guilmant A.	**Trois Oraisons: No.2** Op.94 in *Selected Works* Vol.3 (Bärenreiter) E/M
Homilius G.A.	**Herr Jesu Christ, du höchstes Gut** in *Chorale Preludes* (Breitkopf) M
Salomé T.	**En forme de canon** in *St Cecilia Organ Library* Vol.1 (Cramer) E/M(*)
Warren N.	**A New Commandment** in *Preludes on Favourite Hymns* and *Preludes on Favourite Hymns for Manuals* (Mayhew) E(*)

POSTLUDES

Brewer A.H.	**Carillon** No.3 in *A Little Organ Book for Hubert Parry* (Banks) M
De Grigny N.	**Dialogue 'Amen'** p.30 in *Livre d'Orgue* (Kalmus, Schott) E/M(*)
Guridi J.	**Salida** No.7 in *Escuela Española de Organo* (UME) E
Viner A.	**Richmond** in *Hymn Preludes for the Church Year* Bk.2 (Mayhew) E/M

PROPER 3 (SUNDAY BETWEEN 18 AND 24 FEBRUARY INCLUSIVE) YEAR C
(if earlier than the Second Sunday before Lent)

HYMNS AND SONGS

	pos	rdg	AMNS	CAON	CFE	CH4	CH5	CP	H&P	HTC	LAU	MP	NEH	SG	SOF	TS
As the bridegroom to his chosen		o	340						30							
Bless the Lord, my soul (Taizé)				923	81		1				813			105	676	56
Come, let us to the Lord our God		o				482	206	402	33							
Come, now is the time to worship	ga					196						1040		10	1203	662
Father, hear our prayer		g												157		93
Father, hear the prayer we offer		g	113	161	158	255	645	416	436	360	933	132	357	237	1229	
Father, we praise thee now the night is over	ga				168	209	53	3	633				149			
Fight the good fight		n	220	169	171	517	566	423	710	526	860	143	359	635	107	
Forgive our sins as we forgive			362	180	182	486	550	428	134	111	845		66	145		
Forth in thy name, O Lord, I go	se		239	188	184	529	567	430	381	306	861	159	235	623	1237	
Give me/us the wings of faith		n	324	204			463	216	815				225			
Happy are they, they that love God		n	176	262			649	456	711	473			369			
I am trusting thee, Lord Jesus		g		300						433		258			202	
Lord, as I wake I turn to you	mo		485				56		634	267	672		236	561		
Lord, teach us how to pray aright		g	227	418		545	619	98	551	367			406			
Master, speak! Thy servant heareth		g							535			459			386	
Not for our sins alone		g	229													
O God, by whose almighty plan		n	406					204	396							
O Lord, hear my prayer (Taizé)				938	542		620				929	908		246	423	394
Prayer is the soul's sincere desire		g				546	625	561	557	372		567	442			
Rejoice, O land, in God thy might		g	296	579			539	359		331			493			
Spirit divine, attend our prayers		o				583	341	195	327	240		614				
The steadfast love of the Lord never ceases		o										666			549	505

SONGS FOR CHILDREN
Father God, I wonder CAON 159, CH4 186, JP 337, KS 52, MP 128, SG 107, SOF 92, TS 91
Praise him, praise him (God is love) CAON 563, CH5 367, H&P 565, HTC S21, JP 201

BIBLE READINGS

Psalms [11 and] 13
Hosea 14
Galatians 5.2–10
Matthew 6.1–8

SINGING THE PSALM

Psalm 11 CWP, NPCW
Psalm 13 CWP, NPCW, PAME
  Haugen *How long, O God* (GIA)#

ANTHEMS AND VOCAL MUSIC

Title	Composer	Voices	E/M/D	Book source	Single sheet publisher
UNISON/TWO PART/HIGH VOICES					
Examine me, O Lord	Boyce	SS	E/M		Novello
Give us, Lord, a new heart	Farrell	U/SATB#	E/M	LAU, RITH, SLG	OCP
Love will find out the way	Goodall	2 part	E/M	SFL2	RSCM
O for a closer walk with God	Caesar	SSA	M/D	EAC2	
THREE/FOUR PARTS					
As truly as God is our Father	Mathias	SATB	M/D	ETAS	OUP
Blessed are those that are undefiled in the way	Greene	SATB + solo SS	M/D		CMS/OUP
Give alms of thy goods (g)	Tye	SATB unacc	E	AC1, OBTA	OUP
Holy God	March	SATB unacc	E	SBS2	
Lord, for thy tender mercy's sake	Hilton/Farrant	SATB unacc	E	AWTE, NCAB, FAB1, NOEAB, OBTA	OUP
Love of love	Moore	SATB	E/M		Encore
O for a closer walk with God	Ives	SATB	M		RSCM
O for a closer walk with God	Stanford	SATB	M	AC1, ASA, BC, OBFA, AOAN1 (SAMen)	RSCM
O Master, let me walk with thee	Ledger	SATB	M/D		Encore
Purest and highest	Stanford	SATB	E	ASA	RSCM
FIVE OR MORE PARTS					
A Prayer of King Henry VI	G. Jackson	SSATB unacc	M	CN	
Ah, mine heart	G.Jackson	SSAATB unacc	M		OUP
Beati quorum via	Stanford	SSATBB unacc	M	ASA, WFC	RSCM
Cast me not away from thy presence	S.S.Wesley	SSATB	M	MTP	Novello
I want Jesus to walk with me	Trad arr Willams	SSATB	M	SFC	OUP
Turn thee unto me, O Lord	Boyce	SSATB	E/M		CMS/OUP

ORGAN MUSIC

PRELUDES

Bédard D.	**Adagio** (Cheldar) M	
Chaminade C.	**Marche Funèbre** in *La Nef Sacrée* (Enoch) E/M(*)	
Dubois T.	**Chant pastorale** in *Douze Pièces Nouvelles* (Masters, Leduc) E/M	
Karg-Elert S.	**O Gott, du frommer Gott** No.43 from *Choral-Improvisationen* Op.65 (Breitkopf) M	
Willan H.	**Prelude on 'Wareham'** in *Ten Hymn Preludes* Set 2 (Peters) E/M	

POSTLUDES

Dyson G.   **Forth in thy name, O Lord, I go** in *Variations on Old Psalm Tunes* Bk.1 (Novello) E/M
Krebs J.L.   **O Gott, du frommer Gott** in *Complete Works* Vol.3 (Breitkopf) E/M
Lebègue N.   **Offertoire (G minor)** p.5 in *Offertoires from Troisième Livre d'Orgue* (Hawthorns) or p.171 in *Complete Works*
        Vol.3 (Kalmus) E/M(*)
Plum J-M.   **Préambule** in *Niederländisch-belgische Orgelromantik* (Breitkopf) E/M(*)

THE SECOND SUNDAY BEFORE LENT YEAR C

HYMNS AND SONGS

	pos	rdg	AMNS	CAON	CFE	CH4	CH5	CP	H&P	HTC	LAU	MP	NEH	SG	SOF	TS
All creatures of our God and King	ga	o	105	6	15	147	24	250	329	13	694	7	263	23	645	614
All things bright and beautiful		n	116	25	27	137	25	251	330	283	685	23	264	294	14	14
All you works of God						151										
Come, let us join our cheerful songs	ga		144	120			332	401	810	206		93	349	33	70	
Come, let us with our Lord arise	mo		449				142	575	375				254			
Come, ye faithful/Alleluia, raise the anthem	ga	o	145	131			84	409	813	205		103	351	25		
Fill your hearts with joy and gladness		ps		172		103				30	703	147		80	717	
For the fruits of his/all creation			457	185	178	231	39	254	342	286	731	153	*621*	299	1234	685
Give to our God immortal praise			460	203			353	434	22	31		171		83		
God who made the earth, the air		n		235			4									
God who spoke in the beginning		o	468													
God, whose farm is all creation			370	236		226	41	271	344	282	733			302		
Immortal, invisible, God only wise	ga	o	199	314	301	132	6	474	9	21	725	327	377	44	234	220
Jesus is Lord! Creation's voice				270	326		96	170	260	S 17	324	367			290	284
'Jesus is Lord' – the cry that echoes		o										1078			1387	1367
Let us sing to the Lord (Taizé)											689					
Lord of beauty, thine the splendour			106	415			29	258					265			
Lord of the boundless curves of space			493				31	210	335				405			
Morning has broken	mo	o		450	490	212	58	260	635	265	671	467	237		393	
New every morning is the love			2	467		214	7	6	636	270		480	238			
O Lord, my God (How great thou art)				511	568	154	32	262			721	506		56	425	396
O Lord of heaven and earth and sea			287					540	337	287			422	306		
Praise the Lord of heaven				568					507							
Seek ye first the kingdom of God	gr	n		590	633	641	596		138		820	590			493	447
The earth is the Lord's (Kendrick)												642			528	
The spacious firmament on high		o	103	665		148	35	265	339				267			
Think of a world without any flowers				900		155	50		572							
This is the day the Lord has made (Milligan)													618			
Thou/God, whose almighty word		o	180	684	738	112	324	267	29		506	887	699	466	597	557
Touch the earth lightly						243										
Who can measure heaven and earth?		o								27						
With wonder, Lord, we see your works		o	531					269	353					316		

Some of the hymns and songs listed for Years A and B (pages 34 and 160) are also appropriate.

SONGS FOR CHILDREN

God, who made the earth CAON 325, CAP 10, CH5 4, JP 63
Seek ye first CAON 590, CFE 633, CH 184, CH4 641, CH5 596, H&P 138, JP 215, LAU 820, MP 590, SOF 493, TS 447
When your Father made the world CAON 914, CAP 73, CH 232, CH4 239
Who put the colours in the rainbow? CAON 915, CAP 12, CH 235, CH4 143, JP 288, KS 386, SOF 1624

BIBLE READINGS

Psalm 147*
Genesis 1.1 - 2.3
Matthew 6.25–34

SINGING THE PSALM

Psalm 147* CRP, CWP, H&P, MCW1, NPCW, PAME, SC
Bell *Sing to God with joy* MCW1, PPP

ANTHEMS AND VOCAL MUSIC

Title	Composer	Voices	E/M/D	Book source	Single sheet publisher
UNISON/TWO PART/HIGH VOICES					
All things bright and beautiful	Rutter	2 part	E		OUP
Be cool	Chilcott	U	E	CFTW	
Creator God	Rizza	U/SATB#	E	ROP	
Let all creation sing	Ogden	U + descants	E	SFL2	
Let nothing trouble you	Farrell	U#	E	CBL	
Look at the world	Rutter	U/SATB	E	JRA	OUP
Morning has broken	Trad arr Nelson	SSA	E		Banks
Song of the Sun	Orff	SSSA	M	AC3	Schott
The fruits of the land	Ogden	U	E	BC, SFL1	WLP
THREE/FOUR PARTS					
A Gaelic Blessing	Rutter	SATB	E	NCAB	RSCM
Achieved is the glorious work (Creation)	Haydn	SATB	M	FSB9	Novello
Christ be with me	Pachelbel	SAMen	E	AOAN1	
Fairest Lord Jesus	Trad arr How	SAMen	E	TEA	RSCM
For the beauty of the earth	Carter	SATB	M	NOEAB	OUP
For the beauty of the earth	Rutter	SATB	E	JRA	OUP
God omnipotent reigneth	Wood	SATB	E	SBS1	RSCM
How can I keep from singing?	Lowry arr Weaver	SAMen	E	SFL2	
Immortal, invisible	Mold	SATB	M		Banks
O Lord, our Governor	Barry Rose	SATB	M	MTP	
Song of the Creator	Weaver	SATB	M	SBS1	
The Canticle of Brother Sun	Ives	SATB	M		OUP
The heavens are telling (Creation)	Haydn	SATB	M		Novello
FIVE OR MORE PARTS					
O sing unto the Lord	Hinde	SSATB + solo SSATB	M/D	MTP	

ORGAN MUSIC

PRELUDES

Alain J.	**Choral dorien** in *Deux Chorals* (Philippo) E/M
Clérambault L-N.	**Flutes** *and/or* **Plein jeu** from *Livre d'Orgue: Suite du Deuxième Ton* (Schola Cantorum, Kalmus) E(*)
Karg-Elert S.	**God of heaven and earth** No.35 from *Choral-Improvisationen* Op.65 Vol.4 (Breitkopf) M
Parry C.H.H.	**Chorale Prelude 'Melcombe'** in *Seven Chorale Preludes* Set 1 (Novello) and in *Preludes and Postludes* (Mayhew) E
Watson R.	**All things bright and beautiful** in *At Your Service* (Fagus) E

POSTLUDES

Couperin G.F.	**Offertoire in G minor** in *Couperin: Pièces pour Orgue* (Chanvrelin) M(*)
Gaze N.	**Scimieso on 'Monkland'** in *Avenales (Cheerful Organ Pieces for Harvest)* (Fagus) M/D
Leighton K.	**Fanfare** in *Easy Modern Organ Music* Bk.1 (OUP) E/M
Willan H.	**Prelude on 'London New'** in *36 Short Preludes and Postludes* Set 2 (Peters) E

HYMNS AND SONGS

	pos	rdg	AMNS	CAON	CFE	CH4	CH5	CP	H&P	HTC	LAU	MP	NEH	SG	SOF	TS
Adoramus te, Domine (Taizé)		o		921	11		345				667			208		
As now the sun's declining rays	ev	n		43			11						242			
Be still, for the presence of the Lord	gr	o		67	72	189	325	383			720	50	629	7	40	47
Be thou my vision/Lord, be my vision			343	70	74/75	465	643	386	378	545	970	51	339	669	42	50
Bright the cloud and bright the glory						353										
Christ upon/Jesus on the mountain peak	gr		441	357			205		155	115			177	322		
Christ whose glory fills the skies	mo		4	105		578	52	2	457	266	670	79	234	170	1200	
Come, living God, when least expected		o				609		403								
Come, praise the name of Jesus										538						
From glory to glory advancing	se		276	194				299					286			
Here in this place (Gather us in)	ga				253	623					475			4		
I, the Lord of sea and sky (Here I am, Lord)	se	o		332	285	251	581	470			865	857		633	830	246
Immortal, invisible, God only wise	ga		199	314	301	132	6	474	9	21	725	327	377	44	234	220
Jesus, these eyes have never seen	cm		245	365			491						389			
Jesus, where'er thy people meet/Lord Jesus, when your people		o	162	367			336	492	549	371			390			844
Jesus, you are changing me													389		311	
Lift high the cross		n	72	394	363		484	499	170	508	389	417	641	601	1418	
Lord, the light of your love is shining				419	388	448	195	513			770	445		614	362	335
Meekness and majesty				448	487	356	228				751	465		395	390	353
My God, how wonderful thou art			102	457	497		7	523	51	369	727	468	410	202	395	896
Name of all majesty				465			102	525		218		481		324	939	
O my Saviour, lifted		n	248	519			237					516			437	
O raise your eyes on high and see				502		551		544			208					
O splendour of God's glory bright								7	461							
O vision blest of heavenly light													176			
Stay, Master, stay upon this heavenly hill									158							
The brightness of God's glory										221						
The Lord is my light (Taizé)		n		944												
Thee we adore, O hidden Saviour	of/cm		254	640			449	329					308			
'Tis/It's/How good, Lord, to be here	gr		318					248	156		209		178			
Unless a (single) grain of wheat		n			754	347					748					
We declare your majesty		o										726			577	544
You, living Christ, our eyes behold		o	533				333						487			

Some of the hymns and songs listed for Years A and B (pages 36 and 162) are also appropriate.

SONGS FOR CHILDREN

Moses, I know you're the man CAON 451, CFE 491, H&P 450, LAU 868
The voice from the bush said CAON 896, CH 199

BIBLE READINGS

Psalm 89.1–18*
Exodus 3.1–6
John 12.27–36a

SINGING THE PSALM

Psalm 89.1–18* CH4, CRP, CWP, NPCW, PAME

Codona *I will sing forever* VE#
Haugen *I will sing forever* (GIA)#
Ogden *I will sing* (WLP)#
Ogden *I will sing forever* (WLP)#
Tamblyn *I will sing for you* VE
Walker *O Lord, I will sing* OOD (OCP)#

ANTHEMS AND VOCAL MUSIC

Title	Composer	Voices	E/M/D	Book source	Single sheet publisher
UNISON/TWO PART/HIGH VOICES					
Ex ore innocentium	Ireland	SS	M/D	NSAC2	B&H
Give us, Lord, a new heart	Farrell	U/SATB#	E/M	LAU, RITH, SLG	OCP
Lift on high the name of Jesus	Ogden	U/SATB#	E		WLP
My song is love unknown	Archer	SS	M	EAC2	RSCM
O bone Jesu	Dering	SS	M	HP	
Unless a grain of wheat	Farrell	U#	E	CFE, LAU, RITH, WYP	OCP
THREE/FOUR PARTS					
Adoramus te, Christe	Lassus	SATB unacc	M	ESM, AWTE	Chester
Adoramus te, Christe	Palestrina	SATB unacc	M	NCAB	Banks
As Moses lifted up the serpent	Bairstow	SATB	E/M		Banks
Be still, for the presence of the Lord	Evans arr Shephard	SATB + flute	E	OBFA	
Christus factus est	Anerio	SATB unacc	E/M	ESM, CM1, AWTE	
Christus factus est	Bruckner	SATB unacc	M/D	ESM	RSCM
Dear Lord, who bore our weight of woe	Kellam	SATB	M		RSCM
Greater love	Ireland	SATB	M	AC4	S&B
Here, O my Lord, I see thee	Barry Rose	SATB	E/M	MTH2	
Here, O my Lord, I see thee	Whitlock	SATB	E	NSAC2	OUP
I am the bread of life	Toolan arr Wilson/ Thurlow	SATB	E	AWS/SWAMS	
In a world where people walk in darkness	Trad arr Harper	SATB	E	LOL	
Jesus Christ (Once again)	Redman arr Tambling	SATB	M	WSCC1	
Lead, kindly light	F.Walker	SATB	E		Banks
Prayer before the Crucifix	P. Moore	SATB	M		Banks
Solus ad victimam	Leighton	SATB	M	NCAB, AC1, SC	
The sacrifice of God	Wills	SATB	M/D		RSCM
The secret of Christ	Shephard	SATB	M	NCAB	RSCM
Verily, verily I say unto you	Tallis	SATB unacc	E	AC1, SBS2, TA	OUP
FIVE OR MORE PARTS					
Christe adoramus te	Monteverdi	SSATB unacc	M	ESM	Novello
Lo! God is here!	P.Moore	SSAATTBB	D		Faber

ORGAN MUSIC

PRELUDES

Boëllmann L.   **Lento-Allegro con moto** Op.post. in *Complete Works* Vol.2 (Bärenreiter) M
Chaminade C.   **Offertoire ou Communion** No.2 in *La Nef Sacrée* (Enoch) E/M(*)
Gárdonyi Z.   **Be thou my vision** in *Jazz Inspirations* (Bärenreiter) E/M
Rheinberger J.   **Visione** Op.156 No.5 in *12 Pieces* Op.156 (Carus) and in *Free Organ Music for the Worship Service* (Carus) E/M
Wesley S.   **Diapason Piece** p.12 in *Ten Short Pieces for Organ* (Animus) E*

POSTLUDES

Coleman H.   **Prelude on 'Darwall's 148th'** from *10 Hymn Tune Voluntaries* (Stainer) M
Lebègue N.   **Offertoire in C minor** p.30 in *Offertoires from Troisième Livre d'Orgue* (Hawthorns) or p.194 in *Complete Works* Vol.3 (Kalmus) E/M(*)
Nixon J.   **Carlisle** in *Hymn Tune Preludes* (Fagus) E/M

Suitable before or after: Movements from Callahan C. **Partita on ' Slane'** (Concordia) E-M

THE FIRST SUNDAY OF LENT YEAR C
(For Ash Wednesday, see Year A, page 38.)

HYMNS AND SONGS

	pos	rdg	AMNS	CAON	CFE	CH4	CH5	CP	H&P	HTC	LAU	MP	NEH	SG	SOF	TS
All praise to thee, for thou, O King divine		n	337	22			684	372	253	204			335			
Amazing grace – how sweet the sound		n		29	40	555	642	375	215	28	846	31	626	26	19	18
And can it be that I should gain		n		32	43	396	218	376	216	588	790	33	627	168	21	21
Be thou my guardian/O Lord, our guardian/Lord, be my guardian		s	217	69			635	385		374			64	512		
Be thou my vision/Lord, be my vision		s	343	70	74/75	465	643	386	378	545	970	51	339	669	42	50
Christ's is the world in which we move		n		101	115	724					882			252	685	1165
Cleanse me from my sin, Lord		o										82				
Come down, O love divine		n	156	114	125	489	294	175	281	231	303	89	137	663	1202	71
Come, let us to the Lord our God		o				482	206	402	33							
Father of heaven, whose love profound		n	97	165	163	483	319	421	519	359			827	358	144		1201
Forgive our sins as we forgive		o	362	180	182	486	550	428	134	111	845		66	145		
Forty days and forty nights		s	56	190	185	337	207	95	130	103	206	160	67	381		
God forgave my sin in Jesus' name		o		212	209		480			S 12	849	181			129	123
God, who stretched the spangled heavens		o					27							625		
I will sing the wondrous story		n		337					223	212		315		43	278	821
Jesu, lover of my soul		n	123	343	319	490	553	96	528	438	797	372	383	201	297	838
Just as I am, without one plea		n	246	374	339	553	587	308	697	440		396	294	507	316	306
King of glory, King of peace		n	194	375	343		358	494	499	603	715	397	391	178		
Lead us, heavenly Father, lead us		s	224	379	351		652	496	68	595	315	400	393	640	321	311
Lift up your hearts! We lift them	of	n	241	395		518		500	405	366			398			
Lord Jesus, think on me		s	129	412	384	491/2	554	97	533	316	204		70			
Name of all majesty		n		465			102	525		218		481		324	939	
Now is the healing time decreed		s											59			
O Lord, hear my prayer (Taizé)		n		938	542		620				929	908		246	423	394
Praise, my soul, the King of heaven	ga	n	192	565	602	160	366	555	13	38	807	560	436	93	466	433
Safe in the shadow of the Lord		o			626	55	595			445	953	583		516	991	
Tell out, my soul		n	422	631	684	286	712	362	86	42	880	631	186	62	520	471
The love of God comes close		o										940		186		1533
Through the night of doubt and sorrow	se	s	211	687			661	605	441	466			948	468	544	
We sing the praise of him who died		o	138	723		405	248	125	182	146			738	94	390	
When all thy mercies, O my God		o	109	732			374	617	573	39			751	472	73	
Ye that know the Lord is gracious	of	n	175			642	493	628					477			

SONGS FOR CHILDREN

Grace is when God gives us CH4 163, JP 355, KS 92
Kyrie eleison VFLS 3

BIBLE READINGS

Psalm 119.73–88

Jonah 3

Luke 18.9–14

SINGING THE PSALM

Psalm 119.73–88 CWP, NPCW

ANTHEMS AND VOCAL MUSIC

Title	Composer	Voices	E/M/D	Book source	Single sheet publisher
UNISON/TWO PART/HIGH VOICES					
Settings of Kyrie eleison/Lord, have mercy	Various	U/SATB	E	C, LAU, MCW1, RE	
Christ has no body now but yours	Ogden	2 part	E	LOL, CFAP	RSCM
Jonah Man Jazz	M.Hurd	U	E		Novello
O God, you search me	Farrell	U/SATB#	E	CBL, CH4, LAU, MCW1, SG, TS	OCP
Teach us, good Lord	Nicholson	SS	E		RSCM
The Servant Song	Gillard arr Ogden	2 part	E	SFL1	
When I survey the wondrous cross	R.Jones	2 part#	E	MHWE	
THREE/FOUR PARTS					
A Prayer of King Henry VI	Ley	SATB unacc	E	NSAC2	OUP
And didst thou travel light	Shephard	SATB	E	BC	RSCM
Be thou my vision	Chilcott	SATB	E/M	BCA, NOEAB	OUP
Be thou my vision	Rutter	SATB	M		OUP
Fight the good fight	Gardner	SATB	E	MTH1	OUP
King of glory, King of peace	J.S.Bach arr Harris	SATB	E	NCAB	OUP
King of glory, King of peace	Ives	SATB	M/D	SBS1	RSCM
King of glory, King of peace	Lloyd	SATB unacc	M/D		Encore
Light of the lonely pilgrim's heart	Nardone	SATB	E		B&H
Lord, for thy tender mercy's sake	Hilton/Farrant	SATB unacc	E	AWTE, FAB1, NCAB, NOEAB, OBTA	OUP
Lord, in thy mercy	Mendelssohn	SAMen	E	OBFA	
O for a closer walk with God	Stanford	SATB	M	AC1, ASA, BC, AOAN1, OBFA (SAMen)	RSCM
O Master, let me walk with thee	Ledger	SATB	M/D		Encore
O most merciful	Bullock	ATBB	E	SL	
Take up your cross	Corp	SATB	E	SBS1, WOTC	RSCM
There's a wideness in God's mercy	Bevan	SATB	E	LD, NEP, NOEAB, MTH1	
View me, Lord	Lloyd	SATB unacc	E	NNAB, SEA2	Novello
FIVE OR MORE PARTS					
Hear my prayer	Purcell	SSAATTBB	M	APA	Faber, Novello
Prayer to the Holy Trinity	Tavener	SATB + SSAAA unacc	M		Chester

ORGAN MUSIC

PRELUDES

Atkinson G.   **A Scots Lullaby** ('Dream Angus') (Fagus) E

Gant A.   **Amazing grace** in *Preludes on Favourite Hymns* and in *Preludes on Favourite Hymns for Manuals* (both Mayhew) E/M(*)

Hand C.   **Southwell** in *Hymn Preludes for Lent, Holy Week and Easter* (Mayhew) E/M

Tallis T.   **Ecce tempus idoneum** or **Ex more docti mistico** in *Complete Keyboard Works* (Hinrichsen) E*

Thiman E.   **Chorale Prelude 'Abridge'** in *Six Pieces for Organ* Set 1 (Curwen) E

POSTLUDES

Archer J.S.   **Three Short Variations on 'Heinlein'** in *Variations on Well-known Hymn Tunes* (Novello) E/M*

Shearing G.   **Amazing grace** in *Sacred Sounds from George Shearing* (SMP) E/M

Sumsion H.   **Chorale Prelude on 'Down Ampney'** (Paraclete) E/M

Thomas M.   **Lledrod** in *Six Preludes on Welsh Hymn Tunes* (Mansel Thomas Trust) E/M

Music listed for Ash Wednesday is also suitable (pages 39 and 367).

THE SECOND SUNDAY OF LENT YEAR C

HYMNS AND SONGS

	pos	rdg	AMNS	CAON	CFE	CH4	CH5	CP	H&P	HTC	LAU	MP	NEH	SG	SOF	TS
All that I am, all that I do		n		23	23	505					600					
Father, hear the prayer we offer		s	113	161	158	255	645	416	436	360	933	132	357	237	1229	
Forgive our sins as we forgive		s	362	180	182	486	550	428	134	111	845		66	145		
God be in my head	cm	n	236	211	205	538	631	439	694	543	914		328	666		
God of freedom, God of justice		o		224		263		447								
I bind unto myself today/Christ be with me		n		302	274	639	322	203	695	5	312		159/278			757
I heard the voice of Jesus say		n	247	310		540	576	469	136		795	275	376		215	206
I will offer up my life		n				503						990		565	851	265
Jesus Christ is waiting		o		349	323	360					889			624	1381	1360
Light of the minds that know him	se	n		397			588	501		477			400	626		
Lord Jesus, think on me		s	129	412	384	491/2	554	97	533	316	204		70			
Lord of our life and God of our salvation		s		417						529		441	404			
Miserere nobis/Holy Lord, have mercy (Taizé)		s									597					
My Jesus, my Saviour		s		461		531						1003		129	935	367
O God of Bethel/Jacob		s	216	491		268	657	536	442	35		907	416	241		
O Jesus, I have promised	se	n	235	503	536	644	593	538	704	531	875	501	420	676	418	391
O Lord, your tenderness		n		515								511		569	433	402
O worship the King, all glorious above	ga	n	101	551	559	127	34	546	28	24	683	528	433	90	456	425
Praise to the holiest in the height		n	117	572	606	378	108	557	231	140	788	563	439	58	469	
Send down the fire of your justice		o														1495
Take up thy cross, the Saviour said		n	237	626		402	599	582		114		935	76	645		
There's a wideness in God's mercy/Souls of men/ Restless souls		s	251	662		187	9	598	230	443	810	607/683	461/700	188		
What does the Lord require?		o	432		796		498		414		893					
Who would true valour see/He who would valiant be		s	212	281	248	535	662	621	688	590	862	224	372	639	174	
Will you come and follow me	se	n		752	812	533	605	622			877		647	634	1120	
You are before me, God/Lord		o				96			543							

SONGS FOR CHILDREN

Do what you know is right CAON 791, CH 38, KS2 448
The journey of life CAP 45, JP 468

BIBLE READINGS

Psalm 135*
Jeremiah 22.1–9,13–17
Luke 14.27–33

SINGING THE PSALM

Psalm 135* CWP, NPCW

ANTHEMS AND VOCAL MUSIC

Title	Composer	Voices	E/M/D	Book source	Single sheet publisher
UNISON/TWO PART/HIGH VOICES					
A Prayer of St Richard of Chichester	Allain	2 part	E	VFLS	
A Prayer of St Richard of Chichester	White	2 part	E	BC, OBFA, OEAB	OUP
Christ be with me	Rawsthorne	U	E	SBS2	
Christ has no body now but yours	Ogden	2 part	E	LOL, CFAP	RSCM
Day by day	How	U + 2 part	E	BC	RSCM
He came singing love	Gibson	2 part	E	VFLS	
Jesu, by thy wounded feet	Ferguson	S	E		Encore
Teach us, good Lord, to serve thee	Nicholson	2 part	E		RSCM
When I survey the wondrous cross	R.Jones	2 part#	E	MHWE	
THREE/FOUR PARTS					
A Prayer of St Richard of Chichester	Archer	SATB	E		RSCM
And didst thou travel light	Shephard	SATB	E	BC	RSCM
Be thou my vision	Chilcott	SATB	M	BCA, NOEAB	OUP
Fight the good fight	Gardner	SATB	E	MTH1	OUP
Go forth and tell!	Ogden	SATB	E	SBS2	RSCM
Here I am, Lord	Schutte arr Archer	SATB	E	MTH1	
I give you my hands, Lord	Tambling	SAMen unacc	M	AOAN1	
Light of the lonely pilgrim's heart	Nardone	SATB	E		B&H
O for a closer walk with God	Ives	SATB	M		RSCM
O for a closer walk with God	Stanford	SATB	M	AC1, ASA, BC, OBFA, AOAN1 (SAMen)	RSCM
O Master, let me walk with thee	Ledger	SATB	M/D		Encore
Take up your cross	Corp	SATB	E	SBS1. WOTC	RSCM
The Grail Prayer	Rizza	SATB + solo S	E	FOLO, LUE	Mayhew
To be a pilgrim	Burt	SAMen	E/M	OBFA	
Wondrous cross	Wilby	SATB	E	OBFA, WOTC	

ORGAN MUSIC

PRELUDES

Lang C.S. **Martyrdom** No.2 of *Twenty Hymn-Tune Preludes for Manuals Only* Set 1 (OUP) E*
Peeters F. **O what their joy and their glory must be** in *Hymn Preludes for the Liturgical Year* Op.100 Bk.21 (Peters) E
Reger M. **Straf mich nicht** Op.67/39 in *Complete Chorale Preludes* (Breitkopf) M
Thiman E. **Meditation on 'Breslau'** in *Five Hymn Tune Variants* (Curwen) E/M
Walther J.G. **Ach Gott und Herr** in *80 Chorale Preludes* (Peters) E/M

POSTLUDES

Andriessen H. **Thema met varietes** (Zengerinck) M
Bach J.S. **Es ist das Heil uns kommen her** BWV 638 from the *Orgelbüchlein* (many editions) E/M
Piutti C. **Herr und Aelster deiner Kreuzegemeinde** in *Choralvorspiele* Op.34 Vol.2 (Bärenreiter) E/M

Suitable before or after: Movements from Böhm G. **Partita 'Auf meinen lieben Gott'** in *Complete Works* (Breitkopf) E–M(*)

HYMNS AND SONGS

	pos	rdg	AMNS	CAON	CFE	CH4	CH5	CP	H&P	HTC	LAU	MP	NEH	SG	SOF	TS
As Jacob with travel was weary one day		o	435	775				378	444							
Be thou my guardian/O Lord, our guardian/Lord, be my guardian		s	217	69			635	385		374			64	512		
Behold the Lamb of God (Bell)		n			78						598			190		1145
Beneath the cross of Jesus		o		65			561	105	165			55			39	45
Blessèd assurance		o		74	84	561	562	390	668			59			44	52
How sweet the name of Jesus sounds		s	122	297		461	92	467	257	211		251	374	42	194/782	190/1273
I cannot tell why he, whom angels worship		n		303				54	238	194		266		437	205	199
I come with joy		n	473	304		656	421	305	610	408	649		623	469		
I will offer up my life		n				503						990		565	851	265
If you would follow me		s,n			299						743					
I'll follow my Lord		n												688		
Immortal love, for ever full		s	133	315			211	475	392	105		328	378	176		
In Christ alone my hope is found		n										1072			1346	1311
In heavenly love abiding		s		323		551		478	678	458		331	638		213	782
Jesus calls us: o'er the tumult		n	312	347		509	584	233	141	104		359	200	668		
Jesus, where'er thy people meet/Lord Jesus, when your people	ga	o	162	367			336	492	549	371			390	16		844
Just as I am, without one plea		n	246	374	339	553	587	308	697	440		396	294	507	316	306
Lead, kindly light		o	219	378	348		653	495	67		961	399	392			
Lo, God is here! Let us adore		o							531				209			
Nearer, my God, to thee		o		466			656	526	451			482				372
O God of Bethel/Jacob		o	216	491		268	657	536	442	35		907	416	241		
Timeless love! We sing the story		o						268	60	47		707		100		
Wait for the Lord (Taizé)				949	762	276					88				1575	
We love the place, O God		o	160	718			343	211		558		731	471			
Will you come and follow me	se	n		752	812	533	605	622			877		647	634	1120	

SONGS FOR CHILDREN

As Jacob with travel was weary AMNS 435, CAON 775, CP 378, H&P 444
Step by step, on and on CAON 885, CH 191

BIBLE READINGS

Psalms 12 and 13
Genesis 28.10–19a
John 1.35–51

SINGING THE PSALM

Psalm 12 CWP, NPCW
Psalm 13 CH4, CWP, NPCW, PAME
Haugen *How long, O God* (GIA)#

ANTHEMS AND VOCAL MUSIC

Title	Composer	Voices	E/M/D	Book source	Single sheet publisher
UNISON/TWO PART/HIGH VOICES					
Settings of Agnus Dei/Lamb of God	Various	U/SATB	E	C, LAU, MCW1	
Christ has no body now but yours	Ogden	U + descant	E	CFAP, LOL	RSCM
O God, you search me	Farrell	U/SATB#	E	CBL, CH4, LAU, MCW1, SG, TS	OCP
Send down the fire of your justice	Haugen	U/SATB	E	C, TS	GIA
The Call (Come, my Way)	Vaughan Williams	U	E	NEP	S&B
You have called us	Farrell	U#	E	C	
THREE/FOUR PARTS					
A Prayer of St Richard of Chichester	Archer	SATB	E		RSCM
Angels	Lole	SATB	M		Encore
Angel voices	Shephard	SATB	M	SC	RSCM
Behold the Lamb of God (Messiah)	Handel	SATB	M		Novello
Christ be my beginning	P.Moore	SATB	M		Encore
Come, my Way, my Truth, my Life	Archer	SAB	E/M	AOAN1	Mayhew
Go forth and tell!	Ogden	SATB	E/M	SBS2	RSCM
Here I am, Lord	Schutte arr Archer	SATB	E	MTH1	
I waited for the Lord	Mendelssohn	SATB	M		Novello
Jesus, Lamb of God, Redeemer	Elgar	SATB	E	OBFA	
Just as I am	Chilcott	SATB	M	BCA	OUP
Lead me, Lord	S.S.Wesley	SATB	E	AC1, FAB1, NCAB, NOEAB, NSAC1	Novello
O Lamb of God	Taverner	SAB	E	SETA	
The Call	Lloyd	SATB unacc	M		RSCM
The Lamb	Tavener	SATB unacc	M/D		Chester
The Spirit of the Lord	Elgar	SATB	M	SAEE	RSCM
FIVE OR MORE PARTS					
The Angels	Harvey	SATB + SATB unacc	D		Faber

ORGAN MUSIC

PRELUDES

Bridge F.	**Adagio in E** from *Three Pieces 1905* (Novello) M	
Couperin F.	**Basse de trompette** No.IX from *Messe pour les Couvents* (Kalmus) E/M*	
Hanff J.N.	**Ach Gott, vom Himmel** in *Choralvorspiele alter Meister* (Peters) E/M	
Krebs J.L.	**Ach Gott, vom Himmel sieh darein** No.5 in *Complete Works Vol.4: Clavierübung* (Breitkopf) E/M*	
Widor C-M.	**Andante cantabile** 2nd movement of *4th Symphonie* (Kalmus, Hamelle) E/M	

POSTLUDES

Bach J.S.	**Ach Gott, vom Himmel sieh darein** BWV 741 in Bärenreiter Vol.3, Peters Vol.9 M	
Couperin F.	**Fugue sur la Trompette** No.II from *Messe pour les Couvents* (Kalmus) E/M*	
Lang C.S.	**Procession** from *Album of Postludes* (OUP) E/M	
Widor C-M.	**Toccata in F minor** 1st movement of *4th Symphonie* (Kalmus, Hamelle) M	

THE FOURTH SUNDAY OF LENT YEAR C

HYMNS AND SONGS

	pos	rdg	AMNS	CAON	CFE	CH4	CH5	CP	H&P	HTC	LAU	MP	NEH	SG	SOF	TS
All my hope on God is founded		o	336	19	21	192	10	368	63	451	959	16	333	525		620
Amazing grace – how sweet the sound		s		29	40	555	642	375	215	28	846	31	626	26	19	18
As the deer pants for the water		o		45	54	550	606				965	37			27	27
Behold the amazing gift of love		g				478		389	666							
Come, my Way, my Truth, my Life		g		123		579	610	405	254		911		633			
Fight the good fight		n	220	169	171	517	566	423	710	526	860	143	359	635	107	
Give me/us the wings of faith		o	324	204			463	216	815				225			
God of freedom, God of justice		g		224		263		447								
Great is thy faithfulness		s		249		153	80	453	66	260		200	636	39	147	138
Guide me, O thou great Jehovah/Redeemer		n	214	252	233	167	647	455	437	528	960	201	368	638	148	708
How deep the Father's love		s				549	224				988			193	780	185
I heard the voice of Jesus say		o	247	310		540	576	469	136		795	275	376		215	206
Inspired by love and anger		n		325	311	253										
It is a thing most wonderful		g	70	333			226	109	224	131		346	84	557	252	801
Jesus, the name high over all		g		364			99		264	213		385		323	307	298
Light of the minds that know him	se	g		397			588	501		477			400	626		
Now is the healing time decreed		s											59			
O God of Bethel/Jacob		o	216	491		268	657	536	442	35		907	416	241		
Rejoice! The Lord is king		n	139	580	619	449	281	563	243	180	326	575	443	440	482	948
Rock of ages (Kendrick)		s													1507	951
Rock of ages, cleft for me		s	135	584	624	554	557	565	273	593		582	445	150	488	950
Safe in the shadow of the Lord		o			626	55	595			445	953	583		516	991	
There is a Redeemer		g		658		559	112					673		396	544	492
Thine arm/Your hands, O Lord, in days of old		g	285	671				347	397		431		324			
Those who wait on the Lord		o														1013
Wait for the Lord (Taizé)		o		949	762	276					88			1575		
We cannot measure how you heal		s,g		712	772	718	514	348			433			490		
Who would true valour see/He who would valiant be		n	212	281	248	535	662	621	688	590	862	224	372	639	174	
Ye/You holy angels bright		n	198	755		179	376	626	20	353		783	475	76	619	
You who dwell in the shelter of the Lord		o			832						952					

SONGS FOR CHILDREN

Do what you know is right CAON 791, CH 38, KS2 448
They that wait upon the Lord MP 688

BIBLE READINGS

Psalm 30
Prayer of Manasseh *or* Isaiah 40.27 - 41.13
2 Timothy 4.1–18
John 11.17–44
[Principal Service readings may be used
if Mothering Sunday provisions displace
them at the Principal Service itself.]

SINGING THE PSALM

Psalm 30 CH4, CRP, CWP, NEP, NPCW
Inwood *I will praise you, Lord* CSF (OCP)#
O'Carroll *I will praise you, Lord* RE
Ogden *Keep me by your side, Lord* (WLP)#
Ridge *I will praise you, Lord* RE#

ANTHEMS AND VOCAL MUSIC

Title	Composer	Voices	E/M/D	Book source	Single sheet publisher
UNISON/TWO PART/HIGH VOICES					
Christ has no body now but yours	Ogden	U + descant	E	CFAP, LOL	RSCM
On eagle's wings	Joncas	U#	E	CFE, LAU	OCP
We will rise again	Haas	U#	E		GIA
THREE/FOUR PARTS					
A Garland of Praise	Lloyd	SATB	M		Encore
As Moses lifted up the serpent	Bairstow	SATB	M		Banks
Be not afraid (Elijah)	Mendelssohn	SATB	M		Novello
Blessed are they	S.S.Wesley	SAB	E		S&B
Come out, Lazar! (g)	Spicer	SATB	D	EAC1	
Fight the good fight	Gardner	SATB	E	MTH1	OUP
Give us the wings of faith	Bullock	SATB	E	AC4	OUP
God so loved the world (g)	Bullard	SAMen	E	OBFA	
God so loved the world (g)	Chilcott	SATB + solo S unacc	M	AWTE, BCA	OUP
God so loved the world (g)	Stainer	SAB unacc	E/M	AOAN1	
God so loved the world (g)	Stainer	SATB unacc	E/M	AWTE, FAB1, MHWE, NOEAB, NSAC1	RSCM
Lead me, Lord	S.S.Wesley	SATB	E	AC1, NCAB, NOEAB, NSAC1	Novello
Lord, in thy mercy	Mendelssohn	SAMen	E	OBFA	
O God of my righteousness	Greene	SATB + solo ST	M		CMS/OUP
O Lord, increase our faith	Loosemore	SATB (unacc)	E	NCAB, SBS1	RSCM
The Raising of Lazarus	Willaert	SATB unacc	M		Ricordi
Verily, verily I say unto you (g)	Tallis	SATB unacc	E	AC1, TA, SBS2	OUP
FIVE OR MORE PARTS					
For this mortal must put on immortality	S.S.Wesley	SSATB	M		OUP
Ich bin der Auferstehung und das Leben	Schütz	SATB + SATB	M		Peters

ORGAN MUSIC

PRELUDES

Beechey G.   **Petra** in *The Cross of Christ* (Fagus) E
Buxtehude D.   **Canzonetta** BuxWV 172 in *Complete Works* Vol.3 (Bärenreiter) E/M*
Callahan C.   **Prelude on 'Michael'** in *Two English Voluntaries* (Concordia) E/M
Cameron J.G.   **On a Tune by O. Gibbons** (Song 67) in *Six Preludes on Hymn Tunes* (Novello) E/M
Willan H.   **Prelude on 'Tunbridge'** in *Ten Hymn Preludes* Set 3 (Peters) E/M

POSTLUDES

Bach J.S.   **Ich hab' mein' Sach' Gott heimgestellt** BWV 707 in Novello Vol.18 and Peters Vol.6 E/M
Barr J.   **Prelude on 'Cwm Rhondda'** in *Three Preludes on Hymn Tunes* (Gray) M
Couperin F.   **Dialogue** No.IX from *Messe pour les Paroisses* (Kalmus) E/M(*)
Young G.   **Prelude in Classic Style** (SMP) E/M

THE FIFTH SUNDAY OF LENT YEAR C
(Passiontide begins)

HYMNS AND SONGS

	pos	rdg	AMNS	CAON	CFE	CH4	CH5	CP	H&P	HTC	LAU	MP	NEH	SG	SOF	TS
An upper room did our Lord prepare	ga/of	n	434	38	42		399	130	594		248					
And now, O Father, mindful of the love	of/cm	s	260	34			400	279	593	392			273	459		
Come, bless the Lord	ev	o										88			68	
Come, wounded healer		s		130											1210	1176
Glory be to Jesus		n	66	206	197		220	108		126	750		83	146		
Here is love, vast as the ocean		s					222					987		174	168	164
How deep the Father's love		s				549	224					988		193	780	185
I know a place (At the cross)		s										851			802	209
In the cross of Christ I glory		s		327		397	225	480	167			338	379			
It is a thing most wonderful		s	70	333			226	109	224	131		346	84	557	252	801
Jesus Christ (Once again)		s										995		394	865	274
Jesus, remember me (Taizé)		s		931		775	617				253				875	294
Lift high the cross, the love of Christ proclaim		s	72	394	363		484	499	170	508	389	417	641	601	1418	
Morning glory, starlit sky/Open are the gifts		s	496			390		259					608			
My song is love unknown		s	63	463	503	399	231	112	173	136	752	478	86	384	400	897
No scenes of stately majesty		s											427	1463	375	
O love divine, how sweet thou art		s	124				621	541					424			
O love, how deep, how broad, how high	of	s	119	516		354	214	118	229				425			
Praise to the holiest in the height		s	117	572	606	378	108	557	231	140	788	563	439	58	469	
Rock of ages (Kendrick)		s													1507	951
Rock of ages, cleft for me		s	135	584	624	554	557	565	273	593		582	445	150	488	950
Take up thy cross, the Saviour said		s	237	626		402	599	582		114		935	76	645		
The royal banners forward go		s	58	663	712		243	122	179		252		79			
Thou didst leave thy throne		s	250	683			114	601	154			697	465		555	1015
We sing the praise of him who died		s	138	723		405	248	125	182	146		738	94	390		
What kind of love is this?		s										750			1111	568
When I survey the wondrous cross		s	67	738	801	392	247	127	180	147	756	755/1126	95	680	596	572

SONGS FOR CHILDREN
I'm special JP 106, KS 162, MP 325, SOF 236, TS 222
Jesus is a friend of mine JP 136, KS 195

BIBLE READINGS

Psalm 35*
2 Chronicles 35.1–6,10–16
Luke 22.1–13

SINGING THE PSALM

Psalm 35* CWP, NPCW

ANTHEMS AND VOCAL MUSIC

Title	Composer	Voices	E/M/D	Book source	Single sheet publisher
UNISON/TWO PART/HIGH VOICES					
Ex ore innocentium	Ireland	SS	M/D	NSAC2	B&H
Gethsemane	Rizza	U/SATB	E	ROP	
No greater love	Joncas	U/SATB	E/M	MHWE	GIA
THREE/FOUR PARTS					
An upper room	Trad arr Whibourn	SATB	E	AWS	
Come, Lord Jesus	Hubbard	SATB unacc	E	GAW	Banks
Greater love	Ireland	SATB	M	AC4	S&B
It is a thing most wonderful	P.Moore	SATB	M	SC, WOTC	RSCM
Jesus Christ (Once again)	Redman arr Tambling	SATB	M	WSCC1	
O sacrum convivium	Byrd	SATB unacc	M	SBS2	
O sacrum convivium	Messiaen	SATB unacc	D		UMP
O sacrum convivium	P.Moore	SATB unacc	E	TNA	
Solus ad victimam	Leighton	SATB	M	AC1, NCAB, SC	Banks
Timor et tremor	Poulenc	SATB	M/D		Salabert
Verily, verily, I say unto you	Tallis	SATB unacc	E	AC1, TA, SBS2	OUP
What wondrous love is this?	Trad arr Weaver	SAB	E	LOL, SFL2	
Wondrous cross	Wilby	SATB	E	OBFA, WOTC	
FIVE OR MORE PARTS					
O sacrum convivium	Tallis	SAATB unacc	M/D	TA	OUP
O sacrum convivium	Villette	SSAATTBB unacc	D		Leduc
Salvator mundi	Blow	SSATB	D		CMS/OUP
Salvator mundi	Tallis	SAATB unacc	M/D	OBTA, SC, TA	RSCM

ORGAN MUSIC

PRELUDES

Bach J.S.	**Erbarm' dich** BWV 721 in Novello Vol.18 and Bärenreiter Vol.3 E
Homilius G.A.	**Ach Herr, mich armen Sünder** in *Chorale Preludes* (Breitkopf) M/D
Lloyd R.	**Caswall** in *Hymn Preludes for Lent, Holy Week and Easter* (Mayhew) E/M
Walther J.G.	**Herzlich thut mich verlangen** in *Organ Music for Manuals* Bk.1 (OUP) E*
Willan H.	**Rockingham** in *36 Short Preludes and Postludes* Set 1 (Peters) E

POSTLUDES

Bach J.S.   **Christus, der uns selig macht** BWV 620 from the *Orgelbüchlein* (many editions) M

Brahms J.   **Herzlich thut mich verlangen** No.9 of *Eleven Chorale Preludes* Op.122 E/M

Pachelbel J.   **Ach Herr, mich armen Sünder** No.5b in *Selected Works* Vol.3 (Kalmus); also p.65 in *Organ Works* (Dover) E/M(*)

Smith A.   **Recessional on 'Love Unknown'** (Escorial) E/M

PALM SUNDAY YEAR C

(Readings for the Liturgy of Palms are found only in the Principal Service Lectionary.)

HYMNS AND SONGS

	pos	rdg	AMNS	CAON	CFE	CH4	CH5	CP	H&P	HTC	LAU	MP	NEH	SG	SOF	TS
Ah, holy Jesu, how hast thou offended		n		5	13	381	215	100	164	123			62	378		
All praise to thee, for thou, O King divine		n	337	22			684	372	253	204			335			
And now, O Father, mindful of the love	of/cm	n	260	34			400	279	593	392			273	459		
Broken for me, broken for you	cm	n		87			404	287		S 6		66		485	53	58
From heaven you came, helpless babe		n		195	187	374	219	432			749	162		632	120	114
Hail, thou once despisèd Jesus		n		258			268	168	222	175		203		149		
He gave his life in selfless love		n					417			405		214	467			
Here is love, vast as the ocean		n					222					987		174	168	164
How deep the Father's love		n				549	224					988		193	780	185
I am the vine and you the branches (LFB p.52)		o														
I cannot tell why he, whom angels worship		s		303				54	238	194		266		437	205	199
I know a place (At the cross)		n										851			802	209
I will sing the wondrous story		s		337					223	212		315		43	278	821
In the cross of Christ I glory		n		327		397	225	480	167			338	379			
It is a thing most wonderful		n	70	333			226	109	224	131		346	84	557	252	801
Jesus Christ (Once again)		n										995		394	865	274
Jesus, remember me (Taizé)		s		931		775	617				253			875	294	
Meekness and majesty		n		448	487	356	228			751	465		395	390	353	
Morning glory, starlit sky/Open are the gifts			496			390		259					*608*			
My Lord, what love is this		n		462	500		230					476		194	398	370
My Lord, you wore no royal crown		s								118			628			
My song is love unknown		n	63	463	503	399	231	112	173	136	752	478	86	384	400	897
No scenes of stately majesty		n											427	1463	375	
O Lord, hear my prayer (Taizé)		s		938	542		620				929	908		246	423	394
O love divine, how sweet thou art			124				621	541				424				
O love, how deep, how broad, how high		s	119	516		354	214	118	229			425				
O sacred head		n	68	535	552	382	235	119/120	176	139	237	520	90	385	446	928
Praise to the holiest in the height		n	117	572	606	378	108	557	231	140	788	563	439	58	469	
Thou didst leave thy throne		s	250	683			114	601	154			697	465		555	1015
We sing the praise of him who died		n	138	723		405	248	125	182	146		738	94	390		
When I survey the wondrous cross		n	67	738	801	392	247	127	180	147	756	755/1126	95	680	596	572
Who is this, so weak and helpless		n		748									474			
You are the vine (Daniels)		o										792			629	
You are the vine (O'Hara)		o			824											

SONGS FOR CHILDREN

Each of us is a living stone CAON 793, CH 41

BIBLE READINGS

Psalm 69.1–20
Isaiah 5.1–7
Luke 20.9–19

SINGING THE PSALM

Psalm 69.1–20 CRP, CWP, H&P, NPCW, PAME

ANTHEMS AND VOCAL MUSIC

Title	Composer	Voices	E/M/D	Book source	Single sheet publisher
UNISON/TWO PART/HIGH VOICES					
Christ has no body now but yours	Ogden	U + descant	E	CFAP, LOL	RSCM
Ex ore innocentium	Ireland	SS	M/D	NSAC2	B&H
I see his blood upon the rose	Ogden	U	M	SFL2	
My song is love unknown	Archer	SS	M	EAC2	RSCM
When I survey the wondrous cross	R.Jones	2 part#	E	MHWE	
THREE/FOUR PARTS					
Christus factus est	Anerio	SATB unacc	M	ESM, CM1, AWTE	
Christus factus est	Bruckner	SATB unacc	M/D	ESM	RSCM
Christus factus est	Ridout	SATB unacc	E		Encore
God so loved the world	Bullard	SAMen	E	OBFA	
It is a thing most wonderful	P.Moore	SATB	M	SC, WOTC	RSCM
Jesu, grant me this I pray	Gibbons	SATB	E/M	AWTE	
O Saviour of the world	Goss	SATB	M	FAB1, NCAB, NOEAB	
O Saviour of the world	Somervell	SATB	E	NCAB	
Solus ad victimam	Leighton	SATB	M	AC1, NCAB, SC	Banks
Surely thou hast tasted that the Lord is good	Bernard Rose	SATB unacc	M/D	EAC1	
The Lamentation	Bairstow	SATB	M	AWTE	OUP
The Song of Christ's Glory	P.Moore	SATB	E		RSCM
What wondrous love is this?	Trad arr Weaver	SAB	E	LOL, SFL2	
Wondrous cross	Wilby	SATB	E	OBFA, WOTC	
FIVE OR MORE PARTS					
Crucifixus a 6	Lotti	SSAATB	M	WOTC	
Crucifixus pro nobis	Leighton	SATB div	D		Novello
Salvator mundi	Blow	SSATB	D		CMS/OUP
Salvator mundi	Tallis	SAATB unacc	M/D	OBTA, SC, TA	RSCM
Vinea mea electa	Gesualdo	SSATTB unacc	M/D		Carus
Vinea mea electa	Poulenc	SATBB unacc	D		Salabert

Settings of 'God so loved the world' listed for the Fourth Sunday of Lent (page 287) are also suitable.

ORGAN MUSIC

PRELUDES

Bach J.S. **Hilf Gott, dass mir's gelinge** BWV 624 from the *Orgelbüchlein* (many editions) M/D

Brahms J. **O Welt, ich muß dich lassen** No.11 of *Eleven Chorale Preludes* Op.122 E/M

Bridge F. **Andante con moto in D flat** No.IV of *Six Organ Pieces* (Boosey) M

Walther J.G. **O Welt, ich muß dich lassen** in *80 Chorale Preludes* (Peters) E

POSTLUDES

Bunk G. **Herzlich tut mich verlangen** in *Choralimprovisationen* (Butz) and *Niederländisch-belgische Orgelromantik* (Breitkopf) E/M

De Grigny N. **Dialogue 'Qui tollis peccata'** p.23 in *Livre d'Orgue* (Kalmus, Schott) E/M(*)

Dubois T. **Entrée** No.1 of *Ten Pieces* (Schirmer); also in *Complete Works* Vol.1 (Bärenreiter) M

Stanford C.V. **Song 24** No.4 of *Six Short Preludes and Postludes* (Set 2) Op.105 (Stainer) and in *Preludes and Postludes* (Mayhew) E/M

Suitable before or after: Movements from Bach J.S. **Partita 'Sei gegrüsset'** BWV 768 in Novello Vol.19, Bärenreiter Vol.1, Peters Vol.5 E-D

EASTER DAY YEAR C
(For Good Friday, see Year A, page 52.)

HYMNS AND SONGS

	pos	rdg	AMNS	CAON	CFE	CH4	CH5	CP	H&P	HTC	LAU	MP	NEH	SG	SOF	TS
Alleluia, alleluia, give thanks to the risen Lord	gr	s		8	32		252	136	250	S 3	268	30			6	4
Alleluia! Alleluia! Hearts to heaven	of	s	80	9		427	251	137		151			103	398		
Alleluia, alleluia, Jesus, risen Lord of life	gr	s				428				262				421		1102
Away with gloom, away with doubt!		s	437			418			187							
Christ is alive, with joy we sing		s			107						270					
Christ the Lord is risen again		s	79	103			258	141	192	153			105	400		1166
Come, ye faithful/Alleluia, raise the anthem	ga	s	145	131			84	409	813	205		103	351	25		
Come, ye faithful, raise the strain/ Spring has come	ga	s	76	132		414	262	143	194	160			106			
Comes Mary to the grave		g				407				152				401		
From the very depths of darkness		g		198												
God, we praise you! God, we bless you!		s				120	696	450		341				38		
Good Christians all, rejoice and sing		s	85	241	230			145	191	154			107	404		
Good Joseph had a garden		g					265	146	195							
Hail thee, festival day (Easter)	ga	s		257							255		109			
He has risen		s										839			753	155
He is Lord, he is Lord		s		274	246	443	91		256	S 7	761	220			165	158
Jesus Christ is risen today/Christ the Lord	ga	s	77	348	322	410	271	147	193	155	267	357	110	408	285	276
Jesus lives! Thy terrors now		s	82	354			272	148	198	156		373	112	409	296	
Led like a lamb to the slaughter		g		380			273					402		424	322	312
Most glorious Lord of life		s		452		215		151					255			
Now is eternal life	se	s	402	470			392	152	203				114			
Now the green blade riseth		g	501	475	513	417	278	153	204		278		115	414		
O sons and daughters, let us sing/ Alleluia!		g	74			431	279	154	205		280		125			
See, what a morning!		g										1105				1494
Sing alleluia to the Lord	gr				647		109			S 22		601			499	
Surrexit Dominus vere (Taizé)		s				794										
The day of resurrection		s	75	637	690	413	283	157	208	161	283		117	415		
The Lamb's high banquet we await		s											101			
The strife is o'er/past		s	78	667		412	286	159	214	163	275	670	119	416		
These are the facts		s								162		687		284		
Thine/Yours be the glory	se	s	428	672	728	419	288	160	212	167	287	689	120	417	551	510
Walking in a garden		g		705			290						123			
When Easter to the dark world came		g							200							
Ye/You choirs of new Jerusalem		s	73	754	818		292	162	823	168	279		124	419		

Seasonal hymns and songs listed for Years A and B (pages 54 and 176) are also appropriate.

SONGS FOR CHILDREN
All in an Easter garden CAON 768
Breathe on me, Spirit of Jesus SOF 677
Risen! Risen! KS 289

BIBLE READINGS

Morning Psalms 114 and 117
Evening Psalms 105 *or* 66.1–11
Isaiah 43.1–21
1 Corinthians 15.1–11 *or* John 20.19–23

SINGING THE PSALM

Psalm 114 CFE, CWP, NPCW, PAME
Psalm 117 CRP, CWP, FGP, NPCW
    Bell *Praise your Maker* PPP
    Berthier *Laudate Dominum* CAON, CFE, CH4, CH5, LAU, TSFP#
    Inwood *Holy is God* HIG, LAU #
    Jakob *Go out to the whole world* C
Psalm 105 CRP, CWP, NPCW, PAME
    Dean *He, the Lord, is our God* VE
Psalm 66.1–11 CRP, CWP, NPCW
    Deiss *All you nations* CFE

ANTHEMS AND VOCAL MUSIC

Title	Composer	Voices	E/M/D	Book source	Single sheet publisher
UNISON/TWO PART/HIGH VOICES					
Settings of the Creed	Various	U/SATB	E	MCW1	
Breathe on me	Hubbard	U	E	SFJ	Banks
I have loved you with an everlasting love	Ogden	U	E		WLP
Surgens Jesus	Monteverdi	SAA unacc	M	AC3	
The peace of God	Rutter	SSA	E		OUP
Prayer for Peace	Rizza	U/SATB#	E	ROP	
THREE/FOUR PARTS					
A Gaelic Blessing	Rutter	SATB	E	NCAB	RSCM
Blessed be the God and Father	S.S.Wesley	SATB	M	FAB1, NCAB, SC	RSCM
Deep peace	Carter	SATB + cong	M	ACA, WFC	OUP
Easter	Vaughan Williams	SATB + solo B	M		S&B
Easter Morning	Ferguson	SATB unacc	E/M		RSCM
If ye be risen again with Christ	Gibbons	SATB + solo SSA	M		Novello
Jesus came when the doors were shut	Tomkins	SATB + solo AB	M		Cathedral
O for a thousand tongues	Shephard	SATB	M/D		OUP
Out of the stillness	Shephard	SATB	E	SBS2	RSCM
Since by man came death (Messiah)	Handel	SATB	M		Novello
The world itself keeps Easter day	Trad arr Halsey	SATB unacc	M		Encore
This joyful Eastertide	Trad arr Wood	SATB unacc	E	NOEAB	Banks
This joyful Eastertide	Trad arr Ledger	SATB	E	AWTE	
This joyful Eastertide	Trad arr Harris	SATB	E	MTH1	Novello
Walking by faith	Marsh	SAB	E	AOAN1	
FIVE OR MORE PARTS					
As one who has slept	Tavener	SSATB + SATB	M/D		Chester
Death is swallowed up	Tomkins	SAATB + solo SSAABB	M		Cathedral
Dum transisset Sabbatum	Taverner	SATBB unacc	D		S&B
Surgens Jesus	Lassus	SSATB unacc	M/D		Mapa Mundi
Surgens Jesus	Philips	SSATB unacc	M/D	NCAB	
Surrexit Christus	O'Regan	SSAATTBB unacc	D	CN	

ORGAN MUSIC

PRELUDES

Bach J.S.   **Christ lag in Todesbanden** BWV 695 in Novello Vol.18, Bärenreiter Vol.3, Peters Vol.6 M(*)
Herbig C.   **Canzon supra 'Christ lag in Todesbanden'** in *German Organ and Keyboard Music of the 17th C First Editions* Vol. 2 (Bärenreiter) E/M(*)
Karg-Elert S.   **Jesus, meine Zuversicht** No.10 of *20 Preludes and Postludes* Op.78 (Breitkopf) E
Telemann G.P.   **Christ lag in Todesbanden** in *Seasonal Chorale Preludes for Manuals* Bk.2 (OUP) E*
Vann S.   **Variations on 'Eya! Resurrexit Jesus Christus'** in *Today in Paradise* (Mayhew) E/M*

POSTLUDES

Berthier J.   **Variations on 'Mit Freuden zart'** in *Variations on Six Chorales* (Mayhew) M
Guilmant A.   **Offertoire sur 'O filii'** Op.49/2 in *Complete Works* Vol.5 (Belwin-Mills) and *Selected Works* Vol.3 (Bärenreiter) M
Krebs J.L.   **Praeambulum 'Christ lag in Todesbanden'** No.4 in *Complete Works Vol.4: Clavierübung* (Breitkopf) E/M*

Suitable before or after: Movements from Spedding A. **Victimae paschali laudes** (Banks) E/M-M/D

THE SECOND SUNDAY OF EASTER YEAR C

HYMNS AND SONGS

	pos	rdg	AMNS	CAON	CFE	CH4	CH5	CP	H&P	HTC	LAU	MP	NEH	SG	SOF	TS
Abide with me		n	13	2	9	580	62	10	665	425	907	4	331	495	2	2
Alleluia! Jesus is risen		n				429										
As we walked home at close of day		n					253									
Be known to us in breaking bread		n					401	282	597						669	
Bless the Lord, my soul (Taizé)				923	81		1				813			105	676	56
Bread of heaven, on thee we feed		o	271	82				284		398			276	464		
Broken for me, broken for you		o,n		87			404	287		S 6		66		485	53	58
Christ is risen! Raise your voices		s												399		
Christ triumphant, ever reigning		o		104	113	436	259	398		173	763	77	613	319	62	655
Come, ye faithful/Alleluia, raise the anthem	ga	s	145	131			84	409	813	205		103	351	25		
Crown him with many crowns		o	147	137	139	459	263	166	255	174	321	109	352	321	77	77
Eat this bread, drink this cup (Taizé)		n		926	151	661					633			1221		
God, we praise you! God, we bless you!		s				120	696	450		341			38			
Hail, thou once despisèd Jesus/our once rejected Jesus!		o		258			268	168	222	175		203		149		
He was pierced for our transgressions		o										222			173	169
How deep the Father's love		o				549	224					988		193	780	185
I am the bread of life		n		299	272		420		611		629	261			200	
Jesu, thou joy of loving hearts		n	255	369		662	425	486	258	413		383	292	471		839
Jesus lives! Thy terrors now		s	82	354			272	148	198	156		373	112	409	296	
Jesus, stand among us at the meeting of our lives		n		361			424					381		303		
Let there be love shared among us		s		386	358		525					411			329	317
Light of the minds that know him	se	n		397			588	501		477			400	626		
Look, ye saints, the sight is glorious		o				439	275	171	201	179		426			349	
Love's redeeming work is done/Christ the Lord is risen/All creation		s	83	433		411	277	150	193	150		76	113	412		
O thou who this mysterious bread		n							621							
Sing of one who walks beside us	ev	n									285					
The day of resurrection		s	75	637	690	413	283	157	208	161	283		117	415		
The head that once was crowned with thorns		o	141	644	696	438	285	172	209	182	290	647	134	442	531	979/1528
The Lamb's high banquet we await		s											101			
The strife is o'er/past		o,s	78	667		412	286	159	214	163	275	670	119	416		
We give immortal praise		o	520	713				206	18	11						

SONGS FOR CHILDREN

Haven't you heard that Jesus is risen? CG 46, CH4 433
No more weeping SG 426

BIBLE READINGS

Psalm 16
Isaiah 52.13 - 53.12 *or* 53.1–6,9–12
Luke 24.13–35

SINGING THE PSALM

Psalm 16 CH4, CRP, CWP, FGP, H&P, LAU, NPCW, PAME, RE
Bell *Keep me, Lord* OITB
Inwood *Keep me safe, O God* EM, LAU #
Inwood *O Lord, you are the centre of my life* CFE, CSF, LAU, SG (OCP)#
Rizza *It is the spirit of love* AIL#
Soper *You will show me the path of life* C#
Walker *Preserve me, God* LMOL, RE#

ANTHEMS AND VOCAL MUSIC

Title	Composer	Voices	E/M/D	Book source	Single sheet publisher
UNISON/TWO PART/HIGH VOICES					
I am the bread of life	Lole	U + descant	E	BC	RSCM
Jesus, you are the bread	Farrell	U/SATB#	E	C, RITH	
Shepherd of souls	Barnard	2 part	E	BFH	
The Servant Song	Gillard arr Ogden	2 part	E	SFL1	
THREE/FOUR PARTS					
Alleluia, cognoverunt	Byrd	SATB unacc	M		Novello
Bread is blessed and broken	Bell	SATB	E	CG, LFB, WIS	
Christ was the Word	Maxim	SATB unacc	E	SBS2	
Christus factus est	Anerio	SATB unacc	M	AWTE, CM1, ESM	
Christus factus est	Bruckner	SATB unacc	M/D	ESM	RSCM
Christus factus est	Ridout	SATB unacc	E		Encore
Ego sum panis vivus	Byrd	SATB unacc	M		OUP
Ego sum panis vivus	Palestrina	SATB unacc	M	CM1	
God so loved the world	Bullard	SAMen	E	OBFA	
God so loved the world	Chilcott	SATB + solo S unacc	M	AWTE, BCA	OUP
God so loved the world	Goss	SATB unacc	E	NCAB	
God so loved the world	Ley	ATTB	M	SL	S&B
God so loved the world	Stainer	SATB unacc	E/M	AOAN1 (SAB), AWTE, FAB1, MHWE, NOEAB, NSAC1	RSCM
Here, O my Lord, I see thee	Barry Rose	SATB	E/M	MTH2	
Here, O my Lord, I see thee	Whitlock	SATB	E/M	NSAC2	OUP
I am the bread of life	Lole	SATB	E	SBS1, WIS	
O taste and see	Vaughan Williams	SATB	E	AC4, NOEAB, NSAC1	OUP
The Song of Christ's Glory	P.Moore	SATB	E/M		RSCM
FIVE OR MORE PARTS					
Abendlied	Rheinberger	SSATTB unacc	M	ESM	Carus-Verlag
Ich bin der Auferstehung und das Leben	Schütz	SATB + SATB	M		Peters
In nomine Jesu	Handl	SAATB unacc	M		RSCM
The Song of Christ's Glory	Ives	SSAATTBB unacc	M	WOTC	

ORGAN MUSIC

PRELUDES

Anon.	**Christ ist erstanden** *and/or* **Christus resurrexit** from *The Buxheimer Orgelbuch* Vol. 1 (Hinrichsen) E*
Bach J.S.	**Ach bleib bei uns** BWV 649 in Novello Vol.16, Bärenreiter Vol.1, Peters Vol.7 M
Cavazzoni G.	**Hymnus 'Ad coenam agni providi'** in *Organ Works* (Schott) E*
Walther J.G.	**Jesus, meine Zuversicht** in *80 Chorale Preludes* (Peters) E/M
Willan H.	**Chorale Prelude on a melody by M.Vulpius** No.4 of *Six Chorale Preludes* (OUP) M

POSTLUDES

Bonighton R.	**Gelob't sei Gott** in *Preludes on Favourite Hymns* (Mayhew; 2-stave and 3-stave editions available) E/M
Dandrieu J.F.	**Offertoire** ('O filii et filiae') p.1 in *Offertoires from Premier Livre d'Orgue* (Hawthorns) M*
Lasky D.	**Trumpet Tune on 'Lyra Davidica'** ('Easter Hymn') in *An Album of Trumpet Tunes* (Warner) E/M
Walther J.G.	**Erschienen ist der herrlich Tag** 5 settings in *Orgelchoräle* (Barenreiter) E/M(*)

HYMNS AND SONGS

	pos	rdg	AMNS	CAON	CFE	CH4	CH5	CP	H&P	HTC	LAU	MP	NEH	SG	SOF	TS
All people that on earth do dwell	ga	o	100	21	22	63	683	369	1	14	466	20	334	77	13	13
Christ is the King! O friends rejoice		o	345				86	165		492			345	31		
Come, ye faithful/Alleluia, raise the anthem	ga	s	145	131			84	409	813	205		103	351	25		
Confitemini Domino (Taizé)				925	137						701					
God, we praise you! God, we bless you!		s				120	696	450		341				38		
Hark, my soul! It is the Lord/Christian, do you hear		n	244	264			569	457	521	472		209	637			
He is Lord, he is Lord		s		274	246	443	91		256	S 7	761	220			165	158
I am the bread of life		n		299	272		420		611		629	261			200	
I cannot tell why he, whom angels worship		n		303			54	238	194			266		437	205	199
I danced in the morning		n	375	305	275	404	93	468			765		375		1310	
Jesus lives! Thy terrors now		s	82	354			272	148	198	156		373	112	409	296	
Jesus, the name high over all		n		364			99		264	213		385		323	307	298
Jesus, thy blood and righteousness		n					671		225	460				177		841
Let us sing to the Lord (Taizé)		o									689					
Light of the minds that know him	se	n		397			588	501		477			400	626		
Misericordias Domini/From age to age (Taizé)		o			489											
Most glorious Lord of life		s		452		215		151					255			
Now is eternal life	se	s	402	470			392	152	203				114			
Praise him on the trumpet		o		561	600		364					558			464	
Rejoice! Rejoice! Christ is in you		n			618						818	572			480	438
Rejoice! The Lord is king		o	139	580	619	449	281	563	243	180	326	575	443	440	482	948
Revive thy work/your church, O Lord!		n	362				308		780	515		578				
The Lamb's high banquet we await		s											101			
The Lord is risen from the dead		s				797										
The Lord is risen indeed!		s	84	652				158					118			
We give immortal praise		n	520	713				206	18	11						
Ye choirs of new Jerusalem		s	73	754	818		292	162	823	168	279		124	419		

SONGS FOR CHILDREN

Christ is risen as he said CH5 256
I danced in the morning AMNS 375, CAON 305, CAP 22, CFE 275, CH 96, CH4 404, CH5 93, CP 468, JP 91, LAU 765, NEH 375, SOF 1310
The Lord is risen from the dead CH4 797

BIBLE READINGS

Psalm 86

Isaiah 38.9–20

John 11.[17–26]27–44

SINGING THE PSALM

Psalm 86 CRP, CWP, FGP, H&P, NPCW, PAME

ANTHEMS AND VOCAL MUSIC

Title	Composer	Voices	E/M/D	Book source	Single sheet publisher
UNISON/TWO PART/HIGH VOICES					
He came singing love	Gibson arr Weaver	2 part	E	VFLS	
I will sing a song of love	Bell	U	E	VFLS	
Let all the world	Lang	2 part	M		OUP
Sing of the Lord's goodness	Sands	U + descant#	E	CFE, CG, CH4, CH5, LAU, SFL1, SG, SLG	OCP
Unless a grain of wheat	Farrell	U/SATB#	E	CFE, LAU, RITH, WYP	OCP
THREE/FOUR PARTS					
A Garland of Praise	Lloyd	SATB	M		Encore
As Moses lifted up the serpent	Bairstow	SATB	M		Banks
Come out, Lazar!	Spicer	SATB	D	EAC1	
God so loved the world	Bullard	SAMen	E	OBFA	
God so loved the world	Chilcott	SATB + solo S unacc	M	AWTE, BCA	OUP
God so loved the world	Goss	SATB unacc	E	NCAB	
God so loved the world	Ley	ATTB	M	SL	S&B
God so loved the world	Stainer	SATB unacc	E/M	AOAN1 (SAB), AWTE, FAB1, MHWE, NOEAB, NSAC1	RSCM
I am the bread of life	Toolan arr Wilson/ Thurlow	SATB	E	AWS/SWAMS	
Let all the world	Halsey	SATB	E	BC	RSCM
Let all the world	Leighton	SATB	M/D	EAC1	Novello
Let all the world	Vaughan Williams	SATB	M		S&B
O Lord, increase our faith	Loosemore	SATB (unacc)	E	NCAB, SBS1	RSCM
The raising of Lazarus	Willaert	SATB unacc	M		Ricordi
Verily, verily I say unto you	Tallis	SATB unacc	E	AC1, SBS2, TA	OUP
FIVE OR MORE PARTS					
I am the Resurrection and the Life	Gibbons	SAATB	M		Banks
Ich bin der Auferstehung und das Leben	Schütz	SATB + SATB	M		Peters

ORGAN MUSIC

PRELUDES

Buxtehude D. **Jesus Christus, unser Heiland, der den Tod** BuxWV 198 in *Complete Works* Vol.4 (Bärenreiter) E/M*

Dyson G. **O Prince of Peace** in *Variations on Old Psalm Tunes* Bk.3 (Novello) E/M

Homilius G.A. **Jesus, meine Zuversicht** No.19 in *Chorale Preludes* (Breitkopf) M

Krebs J.L. **Herr Gott, dich loben per canonem** No. 6 in *Complete Works* Vol.3 (Breitkopf) E

Walther J.G. **Erschienen ist der herrlich Tag** in *A Graded Anthology for Organ* Bk.3 (Cramer) E*

POSTLUDES

Herzog J.G. **Easter Sonata: Maestoso** in *Passiontide and Easter* (Bärenreiter) E/M

Peeters F. **Deus tuorum militum** in *30 Chorale Preludes on Gregorian Hymns* Bk.2 (Peters) M/D

Purcell H. **Old 100th** in *120 Chorale Preludes of the 17C & 18C* (Peters) and in *Complete Works* (Novello) M*

Wiedemann E. **Auf, auf, mein Herz, mit Freuden** in *Passiontide and Easter* (Bärenreiter) E/M

HYMNS AND SONGS

	pos	rdg	AMNS	CAON	CFE	CH4	CH5	CP	H&P	HTC	LAU	MP	NEH	SG	SOF	TS
Alleluia, alleluia, give thanks		s		8	32		252	136	250	S 3	268	30			6	4
Alleluia! Alleluia! Hearts to heaven		n	80	9		427	251	137		151			103	398		
Bless the Lord, my soul (Taizé)				923	81		1				813			105	676	56
Christ is the King! O friends rejoice		s	345				86	165		492			345	31		
Christ triumphant, ever reigning		n		104	113	436	259	398		173	763	77	*613*	319	62	655
Come, ye faithful/Alleluia, raise the anthem		n	145	131			84	409	813	205		103	351	25		
Crown him with many crowns		n	147	137	139	459	263	166	255	174	321	109	352	321	77	77
Father of mercies, in thy word		n	167							247			224			
From heaven you came, helpless babe		n		195	187	374	219	432			749	162		632	120	114
God forgave my sin in Jesus' name		n		212	209		480			S 12	849	181			129	123
God is love, let heaven adore him		o	365	217		123	3	442	36		811	187	364			
Good Christians all, rejoice and sing		n	85	241	230		145	191		154			107	404		
Here is love, vast as the ocean		o					222					987		174	168	164
How deep the Father's love		n				549	224					988		193	780	185
How lovely on the mountains (Our God reigns)		n		295	268		129				768	249		192	189
How sure the Scriptures are!		n								249			227			
I know that my Redeemer lives, glory, hallelujah!		s				423										
I know that my Redeemer lives, what joy		s		311			270		196	169		278		406		
Jesu, good above all other		o	378	350			585	487	732	96			387			
Join all the glorious names		n				460		493	78	214		392	639	46	313	848
Laudate omnes gentes/Sing praises, all you peoples (Taizé)											478			1515		
Loving Shepherd of thy sheep		n	134	434	475		655	517		305	802	888				
O for a thousand tongues to sing		n	125	485		352	104	534	744	219		496	415	55	412	383/1452
O sons and daughters, let us sing/Alleluia!		n	74			431	279	154	205		280		125			
Saviour, again to thy dear name we raise	ev	n	15	587		221	71	20	643	281		584	250			
The Lamb's high banquet we await		s											101			
The Lord is risen indeed		s	84	652			158						118			
The strife is o'er/past		s	78	667		412	286	159	214	163	275	670	119	416		
When all thy mercies, O my God		o	109	732			374	617	573	39		751	472	73		
You are merciful to me		o										1018		166	1124	593

SONGS FOR CHILDREN

Christ is risen as he said CH5 256
From the rising of the sun JP 49, MP 163, SOF 121, TS 1215

BIBLE READINGS

Psalms 113 and 114
Isaiah 63.7–14
Luke 24.36–49

SINGING THE PSALM

Psalm 113 CH4, CRP, CWP, NPCW
Deiss Give praise to the Lord CFE
Psalm 114 CFE, CWP, NPCW, PAME

ANTHEMS AND VOCAL MUSIC

Title	Composer	Voices	E/M/D	Book source	Single sheet publisher
UNISON/TWO PART/HIGH VOICES					
A Song of St Francis	Hurd	SSA	M/D	EAC2	
Easter Anthems I & II	Harper	U/2 part	E	MCW1	
How beautiful are the feet (Messiah)	Handel	U	E/M		Novello
I know that my Redeemer lives	Dean	U	E		Decani
I know that my Redeemer lives	Ogden	U	E		WLP
O Lord, I will sing	Walker	U/SATB#	E	OOD	OCP
Prayer for Peace	Rizza	U/SATB#	E	ROP	
Surgens Jesus	Monteverdi	SAA unacc	M	AC3	
THREE/FOUR PARTS					
A Gaelic Blessing	Rutter	SATB	E	NCAB	RSCM
Come, ye faithful	Thatcher	SATB	E	NCAB, OEAB	Banks
Et resurrexit	Dalby	SATB	D	NNAB	
God be merciful unto us	Carter	SATB	M		Banks
I know that my Redeemer liveth	Morley	SATB	M		Fagus
Lord, make me an instrument of your peace	Aston	SATB	E/M		RSCM
May the peace of God the Father	Trad arr Harper	SATB	E	BC, LOL	
Now go in peace	Trad arr Jeffcoat	SATB	E	PSA, SC	
O God, thou art my God	Purcell	SATB	M	APA, SC	
Prayer of St Francis	Kelly	SATB	M/D		Encore
The Lord bless you and keep you	Rutter	SATB	E	EAC1, JRA, WFC, OBFA (SAMen)	OUP
The peace of God	Rutter	SATB	E	JRA, NOEAB	OUP
The Prayer of Peace	Carter	SATB	M	EAC1	OUP
FIVE OR MORE PARTS					
Deep peace	Carter	SSATB	M	ACA, WFC	OUP
Let the people praise thee, O God	Mathias	SSAATTBB	M/D	WFC	OUP
Surgens Jesus	Lassus	SSATB unacc	M/D		Mapa Mundi
Surgens Jesus	Philips	SSATB unacc	M/D	NCAB	

ORGAN MUSIC

PRELUDES

Bach J.S. **Du Friedefürst, Herr Jesu Christ** BWV 1102 in *Neumeister Chorale Preludes* (Bärenreiter) E/M*
Homilius G.A. **Mache dich, mein Geist, bereit** in *Chorale Preludes* (Breitkopf) E/M
Kellner J.P. **Was Gott tut, das ist wohlgethan** in *Choralvorspiele alter Meister* (Peters) E/M
Peeters F. **Wer nur den lieben** No.4 of *Ten Chorale Preludes* Op.69 (Peters) E/M
Piutti C. **Mein Friedefürst, dein freundliches Regieren** in *Choralvorspiele* Op.34 Vol.2 (Bärenreiter) E

POSTLUDES

Buxtehude D. **Es ist das Heil uns Kommen her** BuxWV 186 in *Complete Works* Vol.4 (Bärenreiter) E/M
Guilmant A. **Choral, Variations and Fugue on 'Was Gott thut, das ist wohlgethan'** in *Guilmant Selected Works* Vol.4 (Bärenreiter) M
Viner A. **Cwm Rhondda** in *100 Hymn Preludes* (Mayhew) E

Suitable before or after: Movements from Pachelbel J. **Partita 'Was Gott tut, das ist wohlgetan'** in *Selected Works* Vol.4 (Kalmus) E/M-M*

THE FIFTH SUNDAY OF EASTER YEAR C

HYMNS AND SONGS

	pos	rdg	AMNS	CAON	CFE	CH4	CH5	CP	H&P	HTC	LAU	MP	NEH	SG	SOF	TS
At dawn the women made their way		n				408										
Be bold, be strong		o										49			37	38
Christ the Lord is risen again		n	79	103			258	141	192	153			105	400		1166
Christus resurrexit (Taizé)		s									265					
Come, ye faithful/Alleluia, raise the anthem	ga	s	145	131			84	409	813	205		103	351	25		
Come, ye faithful, raise the strain/Spring has come	ga	s	76	132		414	262	143	194	160			106			
Do not be afraid, for I have redeemed you		o		150	147	191					972	115			1213	1183
God, we praise! God, we bless you!		s				120	696	450		341				38		
Good Christians all, rejoice and sing		n	85	241	230			145	191	154			107	404		
He has risen		n											839		753	155
Here in this place (Gather us in)		o			253	623					475			4		
In heavenly armour we'll enter the land		o										639			237	228
Jesus lives! Thy terrors now		n	82	354			272	148	198	156		373	112	409	296	
Laudate Dominum/Sing, praise and bless the Lord (Taizé)		ps		933	346	77	359				698				1514	458
Love's redeeming work is done/Christ the Lord is risen/All creation		n	83	433		411	277	150	193	150		76	113	412		
Most glorious Lord of life		n		452		215		151					255			
Now is eternal life	se	s	402	470			392	152	203				114			
Sing of the Lord's goodness		o			654	157	368				713			61		
Stand up, stand up for Jesus		o	221	617			488	578	721	535		617	453	644	513	1517
The day of resurrection		n	75	637	690	413	283	157	208	161	283		117	415		
The Lamb's high banquet we await		s											101			
The Lord is risen indeed		n	84	652			158						118			
The strife is o'er/past		n	78	667		412	286	159	214	163	275	670	119	416		
Thine/Yours be the glory	se	n	428	672	728	419	288	160	212	167	287	689	120	417	551	510
Through all the changing scenes of life		o	209	686	740		372	604	73	46		702	467	654	1566	1561
Walk with me, oh my Lord		o			765						966					
Who would true valour see/He who would valiant be		o	212	281	248	535	662	621	688	590	862	224	372	639	174	
Ye/You choirs of new Jerusalem		n	73	754	818		292	162	823	168	279		124	419		

SONGS FOR CHILDREN

Christ is risen as he said CH5 256
I danced in the morning AMNS 375, CAON 305, CAP 22, CFE 275, CH 96, CH4 404, CH5 93, CP 468, JP 91, LAU 765, NEH 375, SOF 1310
Praise him, praise him in the morning CAON 564, CAP 40, CFE 601, CH 177, H&P 506, JP 202

BIBLE READINGS

Psalm 98
Daniel 6.[1–5]6–23
Mark 15.46 - 16.8

SINGING THE PSALM

Psalm 98 BC, CH4, CRP, CWP, FGP, H&P, MCW1, NEH, NPCW, PAME, PFS

Bell *Sing a new song to the Lord* (GIA)
Berthier *Psallite Deo* TSFP#
Berthier *Sing to God* TSFP#
Foster *All the ends of the earth* VE
Haas, Haugen *All the ends of the earth* CFE, LAU, VE (GIA)#
Moore *All the ends of the earth* PCMG
Wright *All the ends of the earth* VE

ANTHEMS AND VOCAL MUSIC

Title	Composer	Voices	E/M/D	Book source	Single sheet publisher
UNISON/TWO PART/HIGH VOICES					
Daniel Jazz	Chappell	U	E		Novello
Didn't my Lord deliver Daniel?	Trad arr Weaver	2 part	E	RTF	
I know that my Redeemer lives	Dean	U	E		Decani
Let all creation sing (Easter verses)	Ogden	U + descant	E	SFL2	WLP
Out of darkness	Walker	U/SATB#	E	CFE, LAU, OOD	OCP
Song of the Risen One	Haas	U/SATB#	E/M		GIA
THREE/FOUR PARTS					
Christ the Lord is risen again	Rutter	SATB	M	AC1, AWTE	OUP
Comes Mary to the grave	N.Warren	SATB	E	WIS	
Here, O my Lord, I see thee	Barry Rose	SATB	E/M	MTH2	
Here, O my Lord, I see thee	Whitlock	SATB	E/M	NSAC2	OUP
Love's redeeming work is done	Ogden	SATB/U	E	SBS1	RSCM
O filii et filiae	Trad arr Sanger	SATB	M/D		Banks
O sons and daughters, let us sing	Trad arr Walford Davies	SATB	E	MTH2	RSCM
O voice of the beloved	Ives	SATB	M	SBS2	RSCM
Out of the stillness	Shephard	SATB	M	SBS2	RSCM
Sing choirs of heaven!	Shephard	SATB	E	AWTE, BC, NEP	RSCM
Sing ye to the Lord	Bairstow	SATB	M/D	NNAB	Novello
The strife is o'er	Armstrong Gibbs	SATB	M	OEAB	Banks
The strife is o'er	Ley	SATB	E	NCAB	OUP
The strife is o'er	Shephard	SATB	M		OUP
When Mary through the garden went	Stanford	SATB unacc	E	ASA	S&B
Ye choirs of new Jerusalem	Shephard	SATB	D	EAC1	OUP
Ye choirs of new Jerusalem	Stanford	SATB	M	AC1, AWTE, FAB1	RSCM
FIVE OR MORE PARTS					
Didn't my Lord deliver Daniel?	Trad arr Hart	SSAATTBB (unacc)	M/D	SFC	
Easter Propers	Byrd	SSATB unacc	M/D		Chester
Surrexit Christus hodie	Scheidt	SATB + SATB (unacc)	M/D	AWTE	Collegium

ORGAN MUSIC

PRELUDES

Anon. **Verse** No.6 in *Organ Music in Restoration England* (OUP) E/M*
Bach J.S. **Jesus, meine Zuversicht** BWV 728 in Novello Vol.18, Bärenreiter Vol.3, Peters Vol.5 E*
Couperin F. **Tierce en taille** No.XVIII from *Messe pour les Couvents* (Kalmus) E/M
Bédard D. **Andantino** (Cheldar) E/M
Vann S. **Savannah** in *Preludes on the Great Hymns of Lent, Holy Week and Easter* (Mayhew) E

POSTLUDES

Beechey G. **Gelobt sei Gott** in *Easter Preludes* (Fagus) E
Bridge F. **Andante moderato in C minor** No.1 of *Three Pieces 1905* (Novello) M
Gibbs A. **Easter Toccata 'The strife is o'er'** No.5 of *Five Hymn Preludes* (Bardic) M/D
Moore P. **Ellacombe** in *Preludes on the Great Hymns of Lent, Holy Week and Easter* (Mayhew) E/M

HYMNS AND SONGS

	pos	rdg	AMNS	CAON	CFE	CH4	CH5	CP	H&P	HTC	LAU	MP	NEH	SG	SOF	TS
Alleluia, alleluia, give thanks to the risen Lord	gr	n		8	32		252	136	250	S 3	268	30			6	4
Alleluia, alleluia, Jesus, risen Lord	gr	n				428					262			421		1102
Be bold, be strong		o										49			37	38
Christ is alive! Let Christians sing		n		96		416	260	140	190		272			32		
Christ is alive, with joy we sing		n			107						270					
Christ is the King! O friends rejoice		o	345				86	165		492			345	31		
Christ triumphant, ever reigning		n		104	113	436	259	398		173	763	77	*613*	319	62	655
Come, ye faithful/Alleluia, raise the anthem	ga	n	145	131			84	409	813	205		103	351	25		
Come, ye faithful, raise the strain/Spring has come	ga	n	76	132		414	262	143	194	160			106			
Comes Mary to the grave		n				407				152				401		
God, we praise you! God, we bless you!		s				120	696	450		341				38		
Good Christians all, rejoice and sing		n	85	241	230			145	191	154			107	404		
Hail thee, festival day (Easter)	ga	s		257							255		109			
He has risen		n										839			753	155
He is Lord, he is Lord		n			246	443			256	S 7		220			165	158
I know that my Redeemer lives, glory, hallelujah!		s				423										
I know that my Redeemer lives, what joy		s		311		423	270		196	169		278		406		
In the Lord I'll be ever thankful (Taizé)		o		929	308	772					944	865		656	817	
Jesus lives! Thy terrors now	se	s	82	354			272	148	198	156		373	112	409	296	
Lord, enthroned in heavenly splendour		s	263	408	379		431	311	616	416	769	431	296	52	352	870
Love's redeeming work is done/Christ the Lord is risen/All creation		s	83	433		411	277		193			76	113			
Now is eternal life	se	s	402	470			392	152	203				114			
Our Lord Christ hath risen		n				421	280									
Rejoice! Rejoice! Christ is in you		o			618						818	572			480	438
Rejoice! The Lord is king		o	139	580	619	449	281	563	243	180	326	575	443	440	482	948
Surrexit Christus (Taizé)		s		943	672		282/711				266					
The Lamb's high banquet we await		s											101			
Thine be the glory	se	s	428	672	728	419	288	160	212	167	287	689	120	417	551	510
Ye choirs of new Jerusalem		s	73	754	818		292	162	823	168	279		124	419		

SONGS FOR CHILDREN

Be bold, be strong JP 14, KS 17, MP 49, SOF 37, TS 38
Come and praise the Lord our king CAP 21, CFE 121, HTC S8, JP 34
Haven't you heard that Jesus is risen? CG 46, CH4 433
Go out to the whole world LAU 998

BIBLE READINGS

Psalms 126 and 127
Zephaniah 3.14–20
Matthew 28.1–10,16–20

SINGING THE PSALM

Psalm 126 CH4, CRP, CWP, H&P, LAU, MCW1, NEP, NPCW
  Farrell *Those who sow in tears/What marvels* GBU, VE#
  Smith *The Lord has done great things for us* (WLP)
  Ward *What marvels the Lord worked for us!* VE#
Psalm 127 CWP, H&P, NPCW, PAME

ANTHEMS AND VOCAL MUSIC

Title	Composer	Voices	E/M/D	Book source	Single sheet publisher
UNISON/TWO PART/HIGH VOICES					
Alleluia to the end of time	Inwood	U#	E		OCP
God the singer	Ogden	U + descant	E	VFLS	
I know that my Redeemer lives	Dean	U	E		Decani
I know that my Redeemer lives	Ogden	U	E		WLP
Rejoice greatly (Messiah)	Handel	U	M/D		Novello
Rejoice, the Lord is king	Weaver	2 part	E/M	CFAP	
Sing of the Lord's goodness	Sands	U + descant#	E	CFE, CG, CH4, CH5, LAU, SFL1, SG, SLG	OCP
The angel rolled the stone away	Trad arr Weaver	2 part	E	SFL1	
THREE/FOUR PARTS					
Comes Mary to the grave	N.Warren	SATB	E	WIS	
Easter morning	Ferguson	SATB unacc	E/M		RSCM
I know that my Redeemer liveth	Morley	SATB	M		Fagus
Love's redeeming work is done	Ogden	SATB/U	E	SBS1	RSCM
O filii et filiae	Trad arr Sanger	SATB	M/D		Banks
O sing joyfully	Batten	SATB unacc	E	SCAB, WFC	RSCM
O sing joyfully	Campbell	SATB	M	MTP	Novello
O sons and daughters, let us sing	Trad arr Walford Davies	SATB	E	MTH2	RSCM
Rejoice, the Lord is king	Archer	SATB	M		Mayhew
Rejoice, the Lord is king	Kelly	SATB	M/D	NNAB, MTH1	
Rejoice, the Lord is king	Weaver	SATB	M	SC	
When Mary through the garden went	Stanford	SATB unacc	E	ASA	S&B
Ye choirs of new Jerusalem	Shephard	SATB	D	EAC1	OUP
Ye choirs of new Jerusalem	Stanford	SATB	M	AC1, AWTE, FAB1	RSCM
FIVE OR MORE PARTS					
Dum transisset sabbatum	Taverner	SATBB	M/D		Banks
Sing joyfully	Byrd	SAATB unacc	M/D	OBTA	OUP
Victimae Paschali	Victoria	SATB + SATB unacc	M/D		Joed

ORGAN MUSIC

PRELUDES

Dubois T.   **Elévation** No.6 of *Ten Pieces* (Schirmer); also in *Complete Works* Vol.1 (Bärenreiter) E
Langlais J.   **No.1** of *Trois Offertoires* (Combre) E/M
Pierné G.   **Cantilène** No.2 of *Trois Pièces* Op.29 (Durand) E/M
Sechter S.   **O wie selig seid ihr doch** in *18 Choralvorspiele* Op. 90 (Doblinger) E*
Widor C.-M.   **Andante** (3rd movement) from *2ème Symphonie* (Hamelle, Kalmus, Dover) M

POSTLUDES

Beechey G.   **Salve, festa dies** in *Easter Preludes* (Fagus) M
Bonighton R.   **Gelob't sei Gott** in *Preludes on Favourite Hymns* (Mayhew; 2-stave and 3-stave editions available) E/M
Guilmant A.   **Paraphrase on 'Judas Maccabeus'** Op.90/16 from *18 Nouvelles Pièces* Op.90 (*Complete Works* Vol.4; Belwin-Mills) E/M
Moore P.   **St Fulbert** in *Preludes on the Great Hymns of Lent, Holy Week and Easter* (Mayhew) E/M

THE SEVENTH SUNDAY OF EASTER (THE SUNDAY AFTER ASCENSION DAY) YEAR C

(For Ascension Day, see Year A, page 66.)

HYMNS AND SONGS

	pos	rdg	AMNS	CAON	CFE	CH4	CH5	CP	H&P	HTC	LAU	MP	NEH	SG	SOF	TS
All hail the power of Jesus' name		s	140	16	19	457	250	163	252	587	323	13	332	24	9	7
All over the world the Spirit is moving		o		20						984		18			12	12
Alleluia! Sing to Jesus	of	s	262	12	37	445	398	278	592	170	644	207	271	458	153	616
Blessèd be the name of the Lord (Daniels, Prosch)		o										808			46	53
Blessing and honour (Ancient of days)		s				442						976		106	675	54
Christ, from whom all blessings flow		n							764	491						
Christ is the King! O friends rejoice		n	345				86	165		492			345	31		
Christ triumphant, ever reigning		n		104	113	436	259	398		173	763	77	*613*	319	62	655
Crown him with many crowns		n	147	137	139	459	263	166	255	174	321	109	352	321	77	77
Father, Lord of all creation		n	356	163	161		318	418								
God has spoken – by his prophets		o					381		64	248	742	831		225		
Hail the day that sees him rise		g	87	255	240		266	167	197	176	291	202	130	434		
In Christ there is no east or west		n	376	319	303	624	522	477	758	322	831	329	480	575		
In the Lord I'll be ever thankful (Taizé)		o		929	308	772					944	865		656	817	
Jesus shall reign where'er the sun	se		143	359		470	97	490	239	516	322	379	388	45	301	1376
Jesus shall take the highest honour				360								378		123	302	296
Jesus, stand among us in thy risen power		n		362			338		530	364		380			304	
Jesus, we enthrone you		s										388			310	300
King of kings, majesty		s									1000			1404	309	
Let there be love shared among us		n		386	358		525					411			329	317
Lord, enthroned in heavenly splendour		n	263	408	379		431	311	616	416	769	431	296	52	352	870
Majesty, worship his majesty		s		436	477		276				767	454			379	346
Make way, make way for Christ the King	ga			438	479	279	134				819	457			384	349
My hope is built on nothing less		o								462		473		537		365
O for a heart to praise my God		o	230	484			638	533	536	483		495	74	149	411	904
One is the body		n				679								280		
Psallite Domino (Taizé)					614											
Rejoice! The Lord is king		n	139	580	619	449	281	563	243	180	326	575	443	440	482	948
Revive thy work/your church, O Lord!		n					308		780	515		578				
The Church's one foundation		n	170	636	688	739	528	585	515	501	830	640	484	581	525	477
The head that once was crowned with thorns		g	141	644	696	438	285	172	209	182	290	647	134	442	531	979/ 1528
The Lord ascendeth up on high		g				440		173	210				135			

SONGS FOR CHILDREN

Have you heard the raindrops CAON 817, CH 78, CAP 2, CH4 525, JP 71, KS 99

I am the church! CH4 204, CH5 521, JP 367

Make way, make way CAON 438, CFE 479, CH4 279, CH5 134, JP 427, KS 249, LAU 819, MP 457, SOF 384, TS 349

BIBLE READINGS

Psalm 68*
Isaiah 44.1–8
Ephesians 4.7–16
Luke 24.44–53

SINGING THE PSALM

Psalm 68* CH4, CRP, CWP, NPCW, PAME

ANTHEMS AND VOCAL MUSIC

Title	Composer	Voices	E/M/D	Book source	Single sheet publisher
UNISON/TWO PART/HIGH VOICES					
Lift on high	Ogden	U/SATB	E		WLP
Like the murmur of the dove's song	A.Smith	2 part	E	OBFA	
O breath of life	Trad arr Bullard	2 part	E	OBFA	
O Holy Spirit	Hubbard	U	E	SFJ	Banks
Spirit of God	Farrell	U#	E	GBAN, LAU	
Water of life	Dean	U#	E	CFE, CSF, LAU, NEP	OCP
THREE/FOUR PARTS					
Angel voices	Shephard	SATB	M	SC	RSCM
Come, let us join our cheerful songs	Bullard	SAB	M		RSCM
Fill thou my life	Lloyd	SAMen	E	AOAN1	
Grow in grace	Archer	SATB	E/M	SBS1	RSCM
Holy Spirit, ever dwelling	Howells	SATB	E	ETAS	
Let God arise (ps)	Locke	ATB	M	AMV	OUP
O for a closer walk with God	Ives	SATB	M		RSCM
O for a closer walk with God	Stanford	SATB	M	AC1, ASA, BC, OBFA, AOAN1 (SAMen)	RSCM
O Spirit all-embracing	Martinson	SATB	M	ETAS	
Take this moment	Bell	SATB	E	CG, IAMB, LFB, OITB, WIS	GIA
Spiritus intus alit	B.Ferguson	SATB	M	ETAS	
Spirit of holiness	Trad arr Barnard	SATB	E	WIS	
The Grail Prayer	Rizza	SATB + solo S	E	FOLO, LUE	Mayhew
Veni Sancte Spiritus	Fenton	SATB	M		B&H
Veni Sancte Spiritus	Harper	SATB (unacc)	E	SOTL	
Veni Sancte Spiritus	Kelly	SATB	D	EAC1	
FIVE OR MORE PARTS					
Veni Sancte Spiritus	Rutter	SSAATTBB unacc	M/D	CN	OUP
Veni Sancte Spiritus	Victoria	SATB + SATB unacc	M		Joed

See also the anthems listed for Ascension Day (page 67).

ORGAN MUSIC

PRELUDES

Jongen J.   **Petite Pièce** in *Jongen Organ Album* (OUP) E/M
Karg-Elert S.   **Sollt ich meinem Gott nicht singen?** No.22 in *Choral-Improvisationen* Op.65 and in the anthology
                14 Choral-Improvisationen (Breitkopf) E
Kauffmann G.   **Man lobt dich in der Stille** in *A Graded Anthology for Organ* Bk.5 (Cramer) M
Krebs J.L.   **Herzlich lieb hab ich dich, O Herr** No.10 in *Complete Works* Vol.3 (Breitkopf) E/M
Scronx G.   **Echo Fantasia** in *Organ Music for Manuals* Bk.6 (OUP) E/M*

POSTLUDES

Coleman H.   **Prelude on 'Hyfrydol'** in *Hymn Tune Voluntaries* (OUP) E/M
Hurford P.   **Exurgat Deus** from *Suite: Laudate Dominum* (OUP) M
Willan H.   **Prelude on 'Ebenezer'** in *Ten Hymn Preludes* Set 2 (Peters) M
Whitlock P.   **Sortie** (Ps. 68) No.7 of *Seven Sketches from the Psalms* (OUP) M/D

DAY OF PENTECOST (WHIT SUNDAY) YEAR C

HYMNS AND SONGS

	pos	rdg	AMNS	CAON	CFE	CH4	CH5	CP	H&P	HTC	LAU	MP	NEH	SG	SOF	TS
Adoramus te, Domine (Taizé)				921	11		345				667			208		
All over the world the Spirit is moving		o		20							984	18			12	12
Be still, for the presence of the Lord	gr			67	72	189	325	383			720	50	*629*	7	40	47
Breathe on me, breath of God		o	157	84	98	596	293	174	280	226	302	67	342	554	51	57
Christ on whom the Spirit rested		s								228						
Christians, lift up your hearts (Praise for the Spirit)		s	444	95				399		229						
Come down, O love divine	ga	s	156	114	125	489	294	175	281	231	303	89	137	663	1202	71
Come, gracious Spirit, heavenly dove		g	153	116		587	295	176					347			
Come, Holy Ghost, our souls inspire	ga	g	93	118		586	296	178	283	589		90	138	555		
Come, O thou Traveller unknown		o	243					407	434				350			
Come, thou most/O Holy Spirit, come		g	92	127			297	180	284	227			139	20		
Creator Spirit, by whose aid		s							285							
Gracious Spirit, hear our pleading		s				613										
Hail thee, festival day! (Pentecost)		s				581			302		255					
Holy Spirit, come, confirm us	se	g	471	288		640	299	183	288		311		140			
Holy Spirit, ever dwelling/living		n				615			303				141			
Jesus, you are changing me		n										389			311	
Like the murmur of the dove's song		s				592		185						17		
Lord of the Church, we pray		s					303			499			442		577	1433
Lord, the light of your love is shining		n		419	388	448	195	513			770	445		614	362	335
Love divine, all loves excelling		n	131	428	398	519	634	516	267	217	801	449	408	179	377	343
O breath of life, come sweeping through us	gr			476		595	305		777	237		488			407	379
O King enthroned on high		s	158	504				189	311				421			
O Lord, your tenderness		n		515								511		569	433	402
O thou who camest from above		s	233	541	557	625	639	191	745	596		525	431	560	451	416
On the day of Pentecost		s	504					192								
Our Lord, his Passion ended		s	91					194	323				*611*			
Sing to him in whom creation		n							324				142			
Speak, Lord, in the stillness		o					624			253	608					
Spirit of God within me		g		612	665			196	294	243	310			677		
Spirit of mercy, truth and love		o	89	613				197					143			
Spirit of the living God (Iverson)	gr	s		615	666	619	310		295	S 23	306	613			510	462
The Spirit lives to set us free		n		666			490				771	664			1555	
Wind of God, dynamic Spirit		s												681		

Seasonal hymns and songs listed for Years A and B (pages 70 and 190) are also appropriate.

SONGS FOR CHILDREN

Holy Spirit, fill our hearts CH4 611
Holy Spirit (pour your power) KS 515
Jesus is Lord, alleluia! LAU 294
Wa wa wa emimimo A 103, IECS, MAG, SFL1 13

BIBLE READINGS

Morning Psalms 36.5–10 and 150
Evening Psalm 33.1–12
Exodus 33.7–20
2 Corinthians 3.4–18
John 16.4b-15

SINGING THE PSALM

Psalm 36.5–10 CH4, CWP, NPCW, PAME
    Taizé *With you, O Lord* TSFP#
    Wardle *Your love, O Lord, reaches to the heavens* PIW
Psalm 150 CH4, CWP, H&P, LAU, MCW1, NEP, NPCW, PIW
    Berthier *Let us sing to the Lord* TSFP#
Psalm 33.1–12 CRP, CWP, FGP, H&P, LAU, NEH, NPCW, PAME, PFS
    Walker *Lord, be with us* OOD#

ANTHEMS AND VOCAL MUSIC

Title	Composer	Voices	E/M/D	Book source	Single sheet publisher
UNISON/TWO PART/HIGH VOICES					
I'm gonna sing	Trad arr Jones	3 part + descant	E	VFLS	
Like the murmur of a dove's song	A.Smith	2 part	E	OBFA	
O breath of life	Trad arr Bullard	2 part	E	OBFA	
Psalm 150	Britten	3 part	M/D		B&H
Psalm 150	Harper	2 part	E		OUP
THREE/FOUR PARTS					
Every time I feel the Spirit	Trad arr Chilcott	SATB	M/D	SFC	
Exsultate justi	Viadana	SATB	E/M	ESM, SL (ATTB)	
Grow in grace	Archer	SATB	E/M	SBS1	RSCM
I will sing with the spirit	Goodenough	SATB	E	SBS2	
If ye love me	Tallis	SATB unacc	E	FAB1, NCAB, NOEAB, NSAC1, OBTA, TA, SL (AATB)	OUP
Listen sweet dove	Ives	SATB	M	EAC1, SC	RSCM
Love divine	Lloyd	SAMen	E	AOAN1	
Love divine	Willcocks	SATB	E	NOEAB	
O for a closer walk with God	Ives	SATB	M		RSCM
O for a closer walk with God	Stanford	SATB	M	AC1, ASA, BC, OBFA, AOAN1 (SAMen)	RSCM
O Lord, give thy Holy Spirit	Harper	SATB	E	SBS2	
O praise God in his holiness	Bernard Rose	SATB	M	MTP	
O praise God in his holiness	Chilcott	SAMen	E/M	OBFA	
O praise God in his holiness	Weldon	SAMen	E	OBFA	
Praise ye the Lord	Rutter	SATB	E/M	AC1	OUP
FIVE OR MORE PARTS					
If ye love me	Chilcott	SSATBB unacc	M	BCA, WFC	
Veni Sancte Spiritus	Rutter	SSAATTBB unacc	M/D	CN	OUP
Veni Sancte Spiritus	Victoria	SATB + SATB unacc	M		Joed

ORGAN MUSIC

PRELUDES

Albrechtsberger J.G.   **Fugue 'Komm Heiliger Geist'** in *Albrechtsberger Vier Fugen* (Doblinger) M(*)
Gigout E.   **Introduction and Interlude on 'Veni Creator'** in *An Organ Album for Manuals Only* (Banks) E*
Göttsche G.M.   **Komm, Gott Schöpfer, Heiliger Geist** in *Jazz Inspirations* (Bärenreiter) E/M
Saint-Saëns C.   **Feria Pentecostes** No.2 of *Sept Improvisations* Op.150 (Durand) or (Butz) M

POSTLUDES

Bédard D.   **Fantaisie sur 'Veni Creator'** (Cheldar) M/D
Böhm G.   **Nun bitten wir den Heiligen Geist** in *Complete Works* (Breitkopf) E/M
Ridout A.   **Spirit** from *Canticle of the Rose* (Mayhew) E/M
Thiman E.   **Postlude for Whitsunday** in *Times and Seasons* Bk.1 (Novello) E/M
Vann S.   **Prelude on 'Down Ampney'** in *Six Preludes* (Mayhew) E/M

TRINITY SUNDAY YEAR C

HYMNS AND SONGS

	pos	rdg	AMNS	CAON	CFE	CH4	CH5	CP	H&P	HTC	LAU	MP	NEH	SG	SOF	TS
Angel voices, ever singing		o	163	37	45	498	346	377	484	307	724	34	336	27	24	
Be still, for the presence of the Lord		o		67	72	189	325	383			720	50	629	7	40	47
Born by the Holy Spirit's breath		n							279	225		61	446			
Christ for the world we sing!		n	344					394	789							
Confitemini Domino (Taizé)				925	137						701					
Father eternal, Lord of the ages		s								1			356			
Father, I place into your hands		n		162	159		565				971	133			97	97
Father most holy, merciful and tender/loving		s	94	164	162			419	5	3			144			
Father of heaven, whose love profound		n	97	165	163	483	319	421	519	359		827	358	144		1201
Father, we adore you, lay our lives	cm	s		166	164		568	297		S 5	718	139			99	
Father, we love you, we worship		s		167	167		348					142			102	103
Give to our God immortal praise		n	460	203			353	434	22	31		171		83		
God, we praise you! God, we bless you!		s				120	696	450		341			38			
He came down that we may have love		n				359							116			
Holy, holy, holy, Lord God almighty	mo	s	95	286	259	111	321	202	7	594	468	237	146	290	183	177
How shall I sing that majesty		s	472	296		128	468	466	8				373/699			
I bind unto myself today/Christ be with me		s		302	274	639	322	203	695	5	312		159/278			757
I, the Lord of sea and sky (Here I am, Lord)	se	o		332	285	251	581	470			865	857		633	830	246
Immortal, invisible, God only wise		s	199	314	301	132	6	474	9	21	725	327	377	44	234	220
Immortal love, for ever full		n	133	315			211	475	392	105		328	378	176		
Jesus, where'er thy people meet/Lord Jesus, when your people	ga	o	162	367			336	492	549	371			390	16		844
Lead us, heavenly Father, lead us		s	224	379	351		652	496	68	595	315	400	393	640	321	311
May the grace of Christ our Saviour	gr	s	181	446			524	520	762	370			298	579		
Name of all majesty		n		465			102	525		218		481		324	939	
Thanks/Praise to God whose word was spoken		o	423			605	387	584	483	255			438	229		
The God of Abraham praise		o	331	642		162	323	586	452	9	712	645	148	66	530	975
Thou/God, whose almighty word		s	180	684	738	112	324	267	29	506	887	699	466	597	557	
Through all the changing scenes of life		o	209	686	740		372	604	73	46		702	467	654	1566	1561
We give immortal praise		n	520	713				206	18	11						

SONGS FOR CHILDREN

Because of who he is KS 18, TS 642
Father in heaven/Loving Creator CH4 116, H&P 3, HTC 2, LAU 313, SBTL, SG 200
The voice from the bush CAON 896, CH 199

BIBLE READINGS

Morning Psalm 29
Evening Psalm 73.1–3,16–28
Exodus 3.1–15
John 3.1–17

SINGING THE PSALM

Psalm 29 CRP, CWP, NEP, NPCW, PAME
    Feely *The Lord will bless his people with peace* VE
    Gregory Murray, Gelineau *The Lord will bless his people with peace* VE
    Rees *The Lord will bless his people with peace* PCMG
Psalm 73.1–3, 16–28 CWP, NPCW

ANTHEMS AND VOCAL MUSIC

Title	Composer	Voices	E/M/D	Book source	Single sheet publisher
UNISON/TWO PART/HIGH VOICES					
Give us, Lord, a new heart	Farrell	U/SATB#	E/M	LAU, RITH, SLG	OCP
Inpoured Spirit	Rizza	U/SATB#	E	ROP	
O for a closer walk with God	Caesar	SSA	M/D	EAC2	
O God, you search me	Farrell	U/SATB#	E	CBL, CH4, LAU, MCW1, SG, TS	OCP
THREE/FOUR PARTS					
As Moses lifted up the serpent	Bairstow	SATB	M		Banks
As water to the thirsty	Coleman arr Barnard	SATB	E	SC, WIS	
Be still, for the presence of the Lord	Evans arr Shephard	SATB + flute	E	OBFA	
Every time I feel the spirit	Trad arr Chilcott	SATB	M	SFC	
God so loved the world	Bullard	SAMen	E	OBFA	
God so loved the world	Chilcott	SATB + solo S unacc	M	AWTE, BCA	OUP
God so loved the world	Goss	SATB unacc	E	NCAB	
God so loved the world	Ley	ATTB	M	SL	S&B
God so loved the world	Stainer	SAB unacc	E/M	AOAN1	
God so loved the world	Stainer	SATB unacc	E/M	AWTE, FAB1, MHWE, NOEAB, NSAC1	RSCM
Here, O my Lord, I see thee	Barry Rose	SATB	E/M	MTH2	
Here, O my Lord, I see thee	Whitlock	SATB	E	NSAC2	Novello
Holy Spirit, truth divine	Carter	SATB	E	ETAS, NOEAB	OUP
O for a closer walk with God	Stanford	SATB	M	AC1, BC, ASA, OBFA, AOAN1 (SAMen)	RSCM
Verily, verily I say unto you	Tallis	SATB unacc	E	AC1, TA, SBS2	OUP
FIVE OR MORE PARTS					
In splendente nube	Philips	SSATB unacc	M/D		Mapa Mundi
Lo! God is here!	P.Moore	SSAATTBB	D		Faber
O holy and glorious Trinity	Palestrina	SSATB unacc	M		CMS/OUP
O lux, beata Trinitas	Halsey	SATB + SATB unacc	M		Encore
So God loved the world	Gibbons	SAATB	M		Novello
With all our hearts	Tallis	SAATB unacc	M	ETAS	

Anthems suggested for Years A and B (pages 73 and 193) are also suitable.

ORGAN MUSIC

PRELUDES

Bach J.S.   **Wir glauben all' an einen Gott, Schöpfer** (fughetta) BWV 681 in Novello Vol.16, Bärenreiter Vol.4, Peters Vol.7 E/M

Buxtehude D.   **Gott der Vater wohn uns bei** BuxWV 190 in *Complete Works* Vol.4 (Bärenreiter) E/M

Lugge J.   **Gloria tibi Trinitas** 6 settings in *Collected Works of J.Lugge* (Novello) E–M*

Tallis T.   **Antiphon–Gloria tibi Trinitas** in *Complete Keyboard Works* (Hinrichsen) E*

Telemann G.M.   **Allein Gott in der Höh' sei Ehr'** in *Organ Music for Manuals* Bk.4 (OUP) E*

POSTLUDES

Groves R.   **Nicea** in *12 Hymn-Tune Preludes* Set 1 (Novello) E(*)

Langlais J.   **Le Saint Esprit** No.3 of *Trois Méditations sur la Sainte Trinité* (Combre) M/D

Peeters F.   **Alta Trinita beata** No.7 in *Hymn Preludes for the Liturgical Year* Op.100 Vol.5 (Peters) E/M

Tomkins T.   **Gloria tibi Trinitas** in *English Organ Music* Vol.2 (Novello) M*

HYMNS AND SONGS

	pos	rdg	AMNS	CAON	CFE	CH4	CH5	CP	H&P	HTC	LAU	MP	NEH	SG	SOF	TS
Captains of the saintly band		n	299	91				212					215			
Christ is the King! O friends rejoice		n	345				86	165		492			345	31		
Christ is the one who calls		n										813				
Disposer supreme and judge of the earth		n	298	149				214					216			
Do not be afraid, for I have redeemed you		n		150	147	191					972	115			1213	1183
Drop, drop, slow tears		o		151			548	106					82			
Faithful one, so unchanging		ps					2					825		547	89	89
Father eternal, Lord of the ages		n								1			356			
Glory be to Jesus		o	66	206	197		220	108		126	750		83	146		
Go forth and tell!		n		238			478	437	770	505		178			596	738
God, we praise you! God, we bless you!		n				120	696	450		341				38		
Hark, my soul! It is the Lord/ Christian, do you hear		n	244	264			569	457	521	472		209	637			
I, the Lord of sea and sky (Here I am, Lord)		n		332	285	251	581	470			865	857		633	830	246
Inspired by love and anger		n			311	253										
Jesus calls us: o'er the tumult		n	312	347		509	584	233	141	104		359	200	668		
King of glory, King of peace		o	194	375	343		358	494	499	603	715	397	391	178		
Let the round world with songs rejoice		n											214			
Most glorious Lord of life		n		452		215		151					255			
O Lord, hear my prayer (Taizé)		ps		938	542		620				929	908		246	423	394
Praise to Christ, the Lord incarnate		n										1104		327	1503	1486
Restore, O Lord, the honour		o		582		469						579		274	483	439
Saints of God! Lo, Jesu's people		n											179			
The day thou gavest/you gave us, Lord, is ended	ev		16	638	691	220	73	22	648	280	679	641	252	65	527	
The Spirit lives to set us free		n		666			490				771	664			1555	
Will you come and follow me		n		752	812	533	605	622			877		647	634	1120	

SONGS FOR CHILDREN

Jesus' hands were kind hands CH4 351, CH5 213, H&P 393, JP 134, KS 194

Tell me the stories of Jesus CH5 110, H&P 153, JP 228, MP 629, TS 1521

BIBLE READINGS

Psalm 39
Genesis 4.1–16
Mark 3.7–19

SINGING THE PSALM

Psalm 39 CWP, NPCW

ANTHEMS AND VOCAL MUSIC

Title	Composer	Voices	E/M/D	Book source	Single sheet publisher
UNISON/TWO PART/HIGH VOICES					
God has chosen me	Farrell arr Weaver	2 part	E	SFL1	
King of glory, King of peace	Sanders	SSAA	M/D		Encore
Out of darkness	Walker	U/SATB#	E	CFE, LAU, OOD	OCP
The Call (Come, my Way)	Vaughan Williams	U	E	NEP	S&B
The Spirit of the Lord is upon me	Corp	2 part	E	VFLS	
You are Peter	Aston	2 part	E		RSCM
You have called us by our name	Farrell	U#	E	C	OCP
THREE/FOUR PARTS					
Christ, the way of life	Warren	SAMen	E	AOAN1	
Come, my Way, my Truth, my Life	Archer	SAB	E/M	AOAN1	Mayhew
Come, my Way, my Truth, my Life	Rawsthorne	SAB	E/M		Mayhew
Come, my way	Rizza	SATB/U#	E	ROP	
Go forth and tell!	Ogden	SATB/U	E	SBS2	
Go forth into the world in peace	Rutter	SATB	E/M	JRA	OUP
Hymn to St Peter	Britten	SATB	D		B&H
King of glory, King of peace	Ives	SATB	M	SBS1	RSCM
King of glory, King of peace	Walford Davies	SATB	M	SC, MTH2	
O Master, let me walk with thee	Ledger	SATB	M		Encore
The Call	Lloyd	SATB unacc	M		RSCM
The Spirit of the Lord	Elgar	SATB	M	SAEE	RSCM
Tu es Petrus	Duruflé	SATB unacc	M		Durand
Tu es Petrus	Hassler	SATB unacc	M	CM4	
FIVE OR MORE PARTS					
O Lord, in thy wrath	Gibbons	SSAATB	M	OBTA	OUP
The Twelve	Walton	SSAATTBB + solo SATB	D		OUP
Tu es Petrus	Palestrina	SSATBB unacc	M/D	ESM	Joed

ORGAN MUSIC

PRELUDES

Du Mage P.	**Trio** *and/or* **Duo** from *Première Livre d'Orgue* (Kalmus) E/M⋆
Edwards P.	**Improvisation on 'St Clement'** from *Northampton Miniatures* (Fagus) E⋆
Hurford P.	**Chorale Prelude 'Caswall'** in *The Church Year* (Cramer) and *Five Chorale Preludes* (OUP) E
Peeters F.	**University College** No.3 in *Hymn Preludes for the Liturgical Year* Op.100 Vol.5 (Peters) E/M

POSTLUDES

Armstrong Gibbs C.	**Jubilate Deo** No.3 of *Six Sketches* Bk.1 (OUP) E/M
Bridge F.	**Allegro marziale e ben marcato** No.3 of *Six Organ Pieces* (Boosey) M
Rawsthorne N.	**Exultemus** in *Twelve Miniatures for Festive Occasions* (Mayhew; manuals-only edition also available) E(⋆)
Thalben-Ball G.	**Gwalchmai** *or* **Woodlands** in *113 Variations on Hymn Tunes* (Novello) E
Archer M.	**Merton** in *25 Hymn Preludes: A Year of Praise* and in *40 Christmas Preludes* (both Mayhew) M

PROPER 5 (SUNDAY BETWEEN 5 AND 11 JUNE INCLUSIVE) YEAR C

(if after Trinity Sunday)

HYMNS AND SONGS

	pos	rdg	AMNS	CAON	CFE	CH4	CH5	CP	H&P	HTC	LAU	MP	NEH	SG	SOF	TS
Captains of the saintly band		n	299	91				212					215			
Come, let us use the grace divine		o							649							
Glory, love, and praise, and honour	se	o	461	207				436	35				287			
God has spoken – by his prophets		n					381		64	248	742	831		225		
God, who made the earth, declared it good		o				228										
God who made the earth, the air		o		235			4									
Great is thy faithfulness		o		249		153	80	453	66	260		200	636	39	147	138
Great Shepherd of thy people, hear		n	164	250			614	454	490	363			238			
Hands that have been handling	pc	n	278				303									
Help us, O Lord, to learn		n	373				382	460	474	493			370	226		
I have loved you with an everlasting love (Henry)		o													798	
I have loved you with an everlasting love (Joncas)		o			276						775					
Jesus calls us: o'er the tumult		n	312	347		509	584	233	141	104		359	200	668		
Lord, in thy name thy servants plead		o											126			
Lord of beauty, thine the splendour		o	106	415			29	258					265			
Lord of the changing year		o								261				303		
Lord, thy word abideth/your word shall guide us		n	166	420	390		384	515	476	251	977/8	446	407			
Misericordias Domini/From age to age (Taizé)				489												
Nada te turbe/Nothing can trouble (Taizé)				937							947			659		
O bless the God of Israel		o					706			599						
O love that wilt not let me go		o		517		557	592	542	685	486		515			434	917
O praise our great and glorious/gracious Lord		o			548						664		116			
Open our eyes, Lord		n		532								545		443	1468	
Send your word, O God		n														958
Strengthen for service, Lord/Make strong	pc	n	421	619			446	323	626	423			306	473		
Thanks/Praise to God whose word was spoken		n	423			605	387	584	483	255			438	229		
Through the darkness of the ages		o											538			
Through our God we shall do valiantly		ps									703				558	1562
Thy/Your kingdom come, O God		n	177	691			509	607	783	334		949	499	269		
Touch the earth lightly		o				243										
Who put the colours in the rainbow?		o		915		143									1624	
Your word is a lamp unto my feet		n											234			

SONGS FOR CHILDREN

Colours of day CAP 55, CFE 118, CH 33, JP 28, KS2 433, LAU 764, MP 1039, SOF 64, TS 69

God almighty set a rainbow CAON 804, CH 64

In our lives plant seeds of hope CH4 349

Who put the colours in the rainbow? CAON 915, CAP 12, CH 235, CH4 143, JP 288, KS 386, SOF 1624

BIBLE READINGS

Psalm 44*
Genesis 8.15 - 9.17
Mark 4.1–20

SINGING THE PSALM

Psalm 44* CWP, NPCW

ANTHEMS AND VOCAL MUSIC

Title	Composer	Voices	E/M/D	Book source	Single sheet publisher
UNISON/TWO PART/HIGH VOICES					
Alleluia, raise the Gospel (alternative text)	Farrell	U/SATB#	E	GBU	OCP
Captain Noah and his floating Zoo	Horovitz	U/SATB	E/M		Novello
Give ear unto me	Marcello	SS	E/M	AC2	
Listen	Nazareth arr Archer	U	E	BC	
Listen to the Spirit	Dean	U#	E	C	
Take the word of God with you	Walker	U/SAB#	E	CFE, CIH, LAU	OCP
THREE/FOUR PARTS					
Blessed be the God and Father	S.S.Wesley	SATB	M	NCAB, FAB1	RSCM
Christ the Word	Vann	SATB	M	STS	
Christ was the Word	Maxim	SATB unacc	E	SBS2	
In God's word	Purcell	SAB	M	TPS, SFL2	
Lead me, Lord	S.S.Wesley	SATB	E	AC1, NCAB, NOEAB, NSAC1	Novello
Lord of our fathers	Mawby	SAMen	E	AOAN1	
The Spirit of the Lord	Elgar	SATB	M	SAEE	RSCM
Thy word is a lantern	Purcell	SATB	M	APA	Novello
Waiting for the word	Skellern	SATB	E/M		RSCM
FIVE OR MORE PARTS					
Teach me, O Lord	Byrd	SAATB	M	OBTA	OUP

ORGAN MUSIC

PRELUDES

Alcock W.G.	**Rather slowly** No.10 in *A Little Organ Book for Hubert Parry* (Banks) E/M
Walther J.G. (Bach)	**Chorale Prelude 'Ach Gott und Herr'** included as Bach BWV 692 in Novello Vol.18 E*
Buxtehude D.	**Ach Gott und Herr** BuxWV 177 in *Complete Works* Vol.4 (Bärenreiter) E
Dupré M.	**Sacris solemniis** No.4 of *Eight Short Preludes on Gregorian Themes* (Summy-Birchard) E/M*
Sechter S.	**Die Christen gehn in dieser Welt** in *18 Choralvorspiele* Op. 90 (Doblinger) E/M*

POSTLUDES

Altnickol J.	**Ricercar in C** in *Orgelmusik um J.S.Bach* (Breitkopf) E/M
Delvincourt C.	**Marche d'Église** No.1 of *Trois Pièces* (Durand) M
Piutti C.	**Aus meines Herzens Grunde** in *Choralvorspiele* Op.34 Vol.1 (Bärenreiter) E

Suitable before or after: Movements from Willan H. **Partita on 'St Flavian'** in *Ten Hymn Preludes* Set 1 (Peters) E/M-M

PROPER 6 (SUNDAY BETWEEN 12 AND 18 JUNE INCLUSIVE) YEAR C

(if after Trinity Sunday)

HYMNS AND SONGS

	pos	rdg	AMNS	CAON	CFE	CH4	CH5	CP	H&P	HTC	LAU	MP	NEH	SG	SOF	TS
Almighty God, thy/your word is cast		n					378		466							
As a tree planted	cm	n			50						370					
Be still and know I (John Bell)		n												18	672	
Be still and know II (John Bell)		n			70	754								242		
Be still and know that I am God		n		66	71	755	608				909	48			41	48
Be still, for the presence of the Lord		n		67	72	189	325	383			720	50	629	7	40	47
Come, let us to the Lord our God		n				482	206	402	33							
Dear Lord and Father of mankind		n	115	144	143	485	549	411	673	356	934	111	353	497	79	79
Eternal Father, strong to save		n	292	153	152	260	612	413	379	285	963	122	354	235	1222	
Fierce raged the tempest		n	225						144							
For the fruits of all/his creation		n	457	185	178	231	39	254	342	286	731	153	*621*	299	1234	685
Glorious things of thee are spoken	o		172	205	195	738	646	435	817	494	827	173	362	35	127	691
Holy Spirit, truth divine		n		289		626	300	184	289	235						
In our lives plant seeds of hope		n				349										
Jesus calls us: o'er the tumult		n	312	347		509	584	233	141	104		359	200	668		
Lead, kindly light	o		215	378	348		653	495	67		961	399	392			
Lord Jesus, once you spoke to men		n	392							112						
Misericordias Domini/From age to age (Taizé)					489											
Now the green blade riseth		n	501	475	513	417	278	153	204		278		115	414		
O God of Bethel/Jacob	o		216	491		268	657	536	442	35		907	416	241		
O Jesus, I have promised		n	235	503	536	644	593	538	704	531	875	501	420	676	418	391
One bread, one body	cm	n			578	665	440				832					
Praise to the Lord, the almighty	ga	n	207	573	608	124	365	558	16	40	706	564	440	59	470	945
Rise and hear! The Lord is speaking		n	509				385	321								
Tell out, my soul	o		422	631	684	286	712	362	86	42	880	631	186	62	520	471
The God of Abraham praise	o		331	642		162	323	586	452	9	712	645	148	66	530	975
The kingdom of God is justice and joy		n		646	701		591	139	333		821	651		184		
Timeless love! We sing the story		n					268	60	47				707	100		
Unless a (single) grain of wheat shall fall		n			754	347					748					
Wait for the Lord (Taizé)				949	762	276						88			1575	
When can I go and meet with God?	o														1112	

SONGS FOR CHILDREN

Calm me, Lord CAON 924, CAS, FOLO
In our lives plant seeds of hope CH4 349
Who's the King of the jungle? CH 236, JP 289, KS 388, SOF 1625

BIBLE READINGS

Psalms 52 [and 53]

Genesis 13

Mark 4.21–41

SINGING THE PSALM

Psalm 52 CWP, NPCW

Psalm 53 CWP, NPCW

ANTHEMS AND VOCAL MUSIC

Title	Composer	Voices	E/M/D	Book source	Single sheet publisher
UNISON/TWO PART/HIGH VOICES					
All that is hidden	Farrell	U/SATB#	E	CFE, LAU, RITH, SFTL	OCP
Calm me, Lord	Rizza	U/SATB#	E	CAON, CAS, FOLO	
Dear Lord and Father of mankind	Parnell	SS	E/M		Encore
Listen	Nazareth arr Archer	2 part	E	BC	
Listen to the Spirit	Dean	U#	E	C	
Now the green blade riseth	Tamblyn	SSAA	M	EAC2	
Take the word of God with you	Walker	U/SAB#	E	CFE, CIH, LAU	OCP
THREE/FOUR PARTS					
A Gaelic Blessing	Rutter	SATB	E	NCAB	RSCM
Be still, my soul	Sibelius	SATB	E		Breitkopf & Hartel
Be still, my soul	Whitlock	SATB	M		Banks
Dear Lord and Father of mankind	Carter	SATB	M	ACA	OUP
Deep peace	Carter	SATB	M	ACA, WFC	OUP
How can I keep from singing	Lowry arr Weaver	SAB	E	SFL2	
The Lord is my light and my salvation	Noon	SATB	M	SBS1	RSCM
The Lord is my light and my salvation	Rutter	SATB + clarinet	D		OUP
Now the green blade riseth	Trad arr Lindley	SATB	E/M	AWTE	
Now the green blade riseth	Trad arr Lumsden	SATB	M		Encore
They that go down to the sea in ships	Sumsion	SATB	M		RSCM
FIVE OR MORE PARTS					
Ascendente in naviculum	De Wert	SSATB unacc	D		Mapa Mundi
Now the green blade riseth	Trad arr Moore	SAATBB unacc	M/D		Encore

ORGAN MUSIC

PRELUDES

Burtonwood S.   **Air** (Fagus) E/M

d'Indy V.   **Prélude in E flat minor** Op.66 (Durand); 2-stave edition in *Organ Music for Manuals Only* (Dover) M(*)

Jackson F.   **Prelude on 'East Acklam'** in *Five Preludes on English Hymn Tunes* (Banks) M

Lloyd R.   **Melita** in *Hymn Preludes for the Church Year* Bk.2 (Mayhew) E

Sechter S.   **Lobe den Herren** No.9 of *18 Choralvorspiele* Op. 90 (Doblinger) E/M*

POSTLUDES

Bédard D.   **Fantaisie** (Cheldar) M

Couperin G.F.   **Coriphé et chœur** in *Couperin: Pièces pour Orgue* (Chanvrelin) E/M(*)

Dubois T.   **Canon No.5** in *Douze Pièces Nouvelles* (Masters, Leduc) M

Willan H.   **Prelude on 'Rouen'** in *Ten Hymn Preludes* Set 3 (Peters) E/M

PROPER 7 (SUNDAY BETWEEN 19 AND 25 JUNE INCLUSIVE) YEAR C

(if after Trinity Sunday)

HYMNS AND SONGS

	pos	rdg	AMNS	CAON	CFE	CH4	CH5	CP	H&P	HTC	LAU	MP	NEH	SG	SOF	TS
A stranger once did bless the earth		n	335													
Abide with me	ev		13	2	9	580	62	10	665	425	907	4	331	495	2	2
Be still and know I (John Bell)		n												18	672	
Be still and know II (John Bell)		n			70	754							242			
Be still and know that I am God		n		66	71	755	608				909	48			41	48
Bless the Lord, my soul (Taizé)		o		923	81		1				813			105	676	56
Christ, from whom all blessings flow		o							764	491						
Confitemini Domino (Taizé)		n		925	137						701					
Eternal Ruler of the ceaseless round		o	353	154		269		181					355			
Father, hear the prayer we offer		o	113	161	158	255	645	416	436	360	933	132	357	237	1229	
Father of mercy, God of consolation		n					511						323			
He that is down needs fear no fall		o	218						676							
Heal me, hands of Jesus		n								319				488		
Healer of our every ill		n									427					
I am trusting thee, Lord Jesus		o		300						433		258			202	
I heard the voice of Jesus say		n	247	310		540	576	469	136		795	275	376		215	206
Immortal love, for ever full		n	133	315			211	475	392	105		328	378	176		
Lord, be thy word/make your word my rule		o	232				383	209		250						
Lord, I was blind, I could not see		n							423	437		433				
Lord Jesus Christ, lover of all		n									437					
O Christ the healer, we have come		n				717	513	346			430			489		
O for a thousand tongues to sing		n	125	485		352	104	534	744	219		496	415	55	412	383/1452
Ostende nobis, Domine (Taizé)		n			583						839					
Reach out and touch the Lord		n										569				
River, wash over me		n										581			487	441
Set my spirit free		n										595			494	
Thine arm/Your hands, O Lord, in days of old		n	285	671			347	397		431		324				
Thine/Yours for ever, God of love		o	234	673			660	599		556		972	463			
We cannot measure how you heal		n		712	772	718	514	348			433			490		
When Jesus the healer passed through		n				350			151							

SONGS FOR CHILDREN

Jesus' hands were kind hands CH4 351, CH5 213, H&P 393, JP 134, KS 194

My God is so big/Our God is so great CAON 547/865/872, CH 169, JP 169, KS 255, SOF 1455, TS 420

BIBLE READINGS

Psalms [50 and] 57
Genesis 24.1–27
Mark 5.21–43

SINGING THE PSALM

Psalm 50 CRP, CWP, NPCW, PAME
Bell *Let the giving of thanks* PPP
Psalm 57 CWP, NPCW, PIW

ANTHEMS AND VOCAL MUSIC

Title	Composer	Voices	E/M/D	Book source	Single sheet publisher
UNISON/TWO PART/HIGH VOICES					
Amazing grace	Trad arr Jones	U + descant	E	RTF, VFLS	
Listen to the Spirit	Dean	U#	E	C	
Litany to the Holy Spirit (In the hour of my distress)	Hurford	U	E	AC2, NEP	OUP
On eagle's wings	Joncas	U#	E	CFE, LAU	OCP
There is a longing in our hearts	Quigley	U/SATB#	E	CH4, LAU, SG	OCP
THREE/FOUR PARTS					
A touching place (Christ's is the world)	Bell	SATB	E	CG, IAMB, LFB, WGIR, WIS	
As water to the thirsty	Coleman arr Barnard	SATB	E	SC, WIS	
Evening Prayers (Three Prayers of Dietrich Bonhoeffer)	P.Moore	SATB unacc	D		B&H
Hear my prayer	Batten	SATB + solo B	E		OUP
Hear my prayer	Mendelssohn	SATB	M		RSCM
I heard the voice of Jesus say	Shephard	SATB	M		RSCM
In a world where people walk in darkness	Trad arr Harper	SATB unacc	E	LOL	
In olden time and distant land	Mold	SATB	E		Encore
Just as I am	Chilcott	SATB	E	BCA	OUP
Litany to the Holy Spirit	Hurford	SATB	E	NOEAB, NSAC1	OUP
Now go in peace	Trad arr Jeffcoat	SATB	E	PSA, SC	
O Lord, heal us	Walker	SATB + descant	E	ATNJ	
O most merciful	Wood	SATB	E		RSCM
Strengthen ye the weak hands	Harris	SATB	M		Novello
There's a wideness in God's mercy	Bevan	SATB	E/M	LD, MTH1, NEP, NOEAB	
Thou God of truth and love	Archer	SATB	M		Mayhew
We cannot measure how you heal	Bell arr Archer	SATB	E	BC	RSCM
With loving hands	Tredinnick	SATB	E	WIS	
FIVE OR MORE PARTS					
Blessing	Allwood	SATBB unacc	E	NSAC2	

ORGAN MUSIC

PRELUDES

Delvincourt C.	**Méditation** No.2 of *Trois Pièces* (Durand) M
Elgar E.	**No.3** from *Vesper Voluntaries* (Faber) E/M(*)
Parry C.H.H.	**Chorale Prelude 'Eventide'** in *Seven Chorale Preludes* Set 1 (Novello) or *Preludes and Postludes* (Mayhew) E/M
Tambling C.	**Chorale on 'York'** in *An Organ Miscellany* (Mayhew) E/M
Wood C.	**Prelude on 'Surrey'** No.4 of *Sixteen Preludes on Melodies from the English and Scottish Psalters* Vol.2 (FitzSimons) M

POSTLUDES

Ridout A.	**Scherzo** in *A Second Easy Album* (OUP) E/M
Sumsion H.	**Introduction and Theme** (RSCM) M/D
Valente A.	**La Romanesca** in *Silva Ibérica* (Schott) E*
Willan H.	**Prelude on 'Richmond'** in *Ten Hymn Preludes* Set 1 (Peters) M

PROPER 8 (SUNDAY BETWEEN 26 JUNE AND 2 JULY INCLUSIVE) YEAR C

HYMNS AND SONGS

	pos	rdg	AMNS	CAON	CFE	CH4	CH5	CP	H&P	HTC	LAU	MP	NEH	SG	SOF	TS
At even ere the sun was set		n	9	50			65	12	142	315		43	243	487		
Blessing and honour (Ancient of days)		o				442						976		106	675	54
Come with me, come wander (HSNW p.84)		n														
God's Spirit is (deep) in my heart		n		231	227				315		864					
Have faith in God, my heart		n	372	268			458	675	431							
I'll praise my Maker while I've breath		o					357	473	439	20		320		84		
Inspired by love and anger		n		325	311	253										
King of glory, King of peace		n	194	375	343		358	494	499	603	715	397	391	178		
Let your word go forth among the nations		n														320
Lord God, who blessed our fathers here (LUR 12)		o														
Lord of all hopefulness		n	394	413	386	166	618	507	552	101	969	882	239	509	902	
Make way, make way, for Christ the king		n		438	479	279	134				819	457			384	349
Miserere nobis/Holy Lord, have mercy (Taizé)										597				159		
O Christ, the Master Carpenter		n								135				673		
O for a thousand tongues to sing	se	n	125	485		352	104	534	744	219		496	415	55	412	383/1452
O God of Bethel/Jacob		o	216	491		268	657	536	442	35		907	416	241		
Ostende nobis, Domine (Taizé)					583						839					
Praise, my soul, the King of heaven	ga	o	192	565	602	160	366	555	13	38	807	560	436	93	466	433
Send me out from here	se	n										594			996	
Send me, Lord (Thuma mina)					636	800							694			
Shepherd divine, our wants relieve		o	228					566	558							
Songs of thankfulness and praise		n	53	609	661		197	90		98	172		56	376		
The God of Abraham praise		o	331	642		162	323	586	452	9	712	645	148	66	530	975
The Son of God his glory hides		n					595									
Thine arm/Your hands, O Lord, in days of old		n	285	671			347	397			431		324			
We have a gospel to proclaim		n	431	716	778	363	491	612	465	519	852	728	486	331	1583	
We'll walk the land		n		717								743		617	583	551
When the Lord in glory comes		n								201		758				

SONGS FOR CHILDREN

Jesus is greater CAON 847, CH 122, KS 196, TS 282
Sent by the Lord am I CFE 638, CG 105, CH4 250, IECS, LAU 855, SBTL, SG 616

BIBLE READINGS

Psalms [59.1–6,18–20 and] 60

Genesis 27.1–40

Mark 6.1–6

SINGING THE PSALM

Psalm 59.1–6,18–20 CWP, NPCW

Psalm 60 CWP, NPCW

ANTHEMS AND VOCAL MUSIC

Title	Composer	Voices	E/M/D	Book source	Single sheet publisher
UNISON/TWO PART/HIGH VOICES					
Settings of the Creed	Various	U/SATB	E	MCW1	
Give us the wings of faith	Blatchly	SS	M	HP	
Send us as your blessing, Lord	Walker	U/SSATB#	E/M	HIG	OCP
Sent by the Lord am I	Trad arr Weaver	2 part	E	BC	
We believe	Walker	U/SATB#	E	HIG, LAU	
We walk by faith	Haugen	U#	E	CFE, LAU	GIA
While faith is with me	Hubbard	U	E	SFJ	Banks
THREE/FOUR PARTS					
Be thou faithful unto death (St Paul)	Mendelssohn	SATB	M		Novello
Firmly I believe and truly	Shephard	SAMen	E	SFL2	
Give me the wings of faith	Leighton	SATB	D		Novello
Give us the wings of faith	Bullock	SATB	M	AC4, FSB10	OUP
Go forth and tell!	Ogden	SATB	E	SBS2	RSCM
If God is building when we build	Trad arr Barnard	SATB	E	SBS2	
If you believe and I believe	Trad Zimbabwean	SATB unacc	E	C, CG, CH4, IECS, RTF, SBTL	
Light of the world	Elgar	SATB	M/D	AWTE, SAEE	Novello
Lord, give me faith	Robson	SATB	E		RSCM
Lord of all hopefulness	Trad arr Rose	SATB + solo S	E/M	MTH2	
Now go in peace	Trad arr Jeffcoat	SATB	E	PSA, SC	
O Lord, increase our faith	Loosemore	SATB (unacc)	E	NCAB, SBS1	RSCM
Summa	Pärt	SATB unacc	M		Universal
Though you do not now see Christ	Ferguson	SATB unacc	M		Encore
Walking by faith	Marsh	SAMen	E	AOAN1	
FIVE OR MORE PARTS					
Os justi	Bruckner	SSATTB unacc	M	ESM	Peters

ORGAN MUSIC

PRELUDES

Bédard D.   **Communion sur 'Lauda Sion'** No.3 of *Six Paraphrases Grégoriennes* (Cheldar) E

Boëllmann L.   **Adagietto** No.11 of *Douze Pièces* Op.16 (Leduc, Masters) or *Complete Works* Vol.1 (Bärenreiter) E/M

Groves R.   **Praise, my soul** in *12 Hymn-Tune Preludes* Set 1 (Novello) E(*)

Stanford C.V.   **No.3** of *Six Short Preludes and Postludes* (Set 1) Op.101 (Stainer); also in *Preludes and Postludes* (Mayhew) E/M

Wesley S.S.   **Voluntary - Grave and Andante** (Animus) E/M

POSTLUDES

Bach C.P.E.   **Fantasie and Fugue in C minor** in *Complete Works* Vol.2 (Peters) M

Edwards P.   **Okehampton Trumpet Tune** (Fagus) E

Pasquini B.   **Partite sopra la Aria della Folia da Espagna** in *Silva Ibérica* Vol.1 (Schott) E*

West J.E.   **Festal Song** in *English Romantic Classics* (Belwin) E/M

HYMNS AND SONGS

	pos	rdg	AMNS	CAON	CFE	CH4	CH5	CP	H&P	HTC	LAU	MP	NEH	SG	SOF	TS
All people that on earth do dwell	ga		100	21	22	63	683	369	1	14	466	20	334	77	13	13
Awake, my soul, and with the sun	mo,ga		1	58		210	51	1	632	264		804	232	618		
Captains of the saintly band		n	299	91				212					215			
Father God in heaven, Lord most high		n								358				236		
Glorious things of thee are spoken			172	205	195	738	646	435	817	494	827	173	362	35	127	691
Glory to thee my God, this night/All praise	ev		10	208	200	223	63	14	642	274		176	244	502		
Go forth and tell!		n		238			478	437	770	505		178		596	738	
God moves in a mysterious way		n	112	222		158	13	445	65			193	365			700
God's Spirit is (deep) in my heart		n		231	227				315		864					
How beauteous/gracious are their feet		n	301					220	449							
How bright these glorious spirits shine		n	306			745	467	221		572			227			
Jesus calls us: o'er the tumult		n	312	347		509	584	233	141	104		359	200	668		
Lead us, heavenly Father, lead us		o	224	379	351		652	496	68	595	315	400	393	640	321	311
Lo, in the wilderness a voice		n	384										170			
Lord of all hopefulness		n	394	413	386	166	618	507	552	101	969	882	239	509	902	
O Christ the same, through all our story's pages		o		477			103			263			258			
O God of Bethel/Jacob		n	216	491		268	657	536	442	35		907	416	241		
(O) worship the Lord in the beauty of holiness	ga	n	49	552	560	201	196	89	505	344	169	529	52	204	457	426
Pray for the church, afflicted and oppressed		n						559	556				267			
Put thou thy trust in God/Commit thou all thy griefs		n	223	576		270	563	562	672							
Shepherd divine, our wants relieve		o	228					566	558							
Sing we the praises of the great forerunner		n	315					234								
The Lord is my song (Taizé)				651							929					
Walk with me, O my Lord		o			765						966					
When the Lord in glory comes		n								201		758				
Will you come and follow me		n		752	812	533	605	622			877		647	634	1120	
Within our darkest night (Taizé)		n		950												

SONGS FOR CHILDREN

Jesus is greater CAON 847, CH 122, KS 196, TS 282
Sent by the Lord am I CFE 638, CG 105, CH4 250, IECS, LAU 855, SBTL, SG 616

BIBLE READINGS

Psalms 65 [and 70]
Genesis 29.1–20
Mark 6.7–29

SINGING THE PSALM

Psalm 65 CH4, CWP, H&P, NEP, NPCW, PAME, PFS
Psalm 70 CWP, NPCW, PAME

ANTHEMS AND VOCAL MUSIC

Title	Composer	Voices	E/M/D	Book source	Single sheet publisher
UNISON/TWO PART/HIGH VOICES					
Give us the wings of faith	Blatchly	SS	M	HP	
God has chosen me	Farrell arr Weaver	2 part	E	SFL1	
Sent by the Lord am I	Trad arr Weaver	2 part	E	BC	
The Call (Come, my Way)	Vaughan Williams	U	E	NEP	S&B
THREE/FOUR PARTS					
Benedictus	Stanford	SATB	M	AFC	
Canite tuba	Guerrero	SATB unacc	M	AFC	
For I went with the multitude	Aston	SATB	M	EAC1	Novello
Fuit homo missus a Deo	Palestrina	SATB unacc	M	AFC	
Give me the wings of faith	Leighton	SATB	D		Novello
Give us the wings of faith	Bullock	SATB	M	AC4, FSB10	OUP
Go forth and tell!	Ogden	SATB	E/M	SBS2	RSCM
Hail, glorious spirits, heirs of light	Tye	SATB unacc	E		RSCM
Holy is the true light	Harris	SATB	E/M	FSB7, NCAB, NSAC2, SL(ATTB)	Novello
How beauteous are their feet	Stanford	SATB	M	AOAN1 (SAMen), ASA, NNAB, SC	Novello
How lovely are the messengers	Mendelssohn	SATB	M	AFC	Novello
On Jordan's bank	Trad arr Archer	SATB	E	AFC	
Prepare ye the way of the Lord (Godspell)	Schwartz	SATB	M		Faber
Take up your cross	Corp	SATB	E	SBS1, WOTC	RSCM
This is the record of John	Gibbons	SATB + solo A	M/D	OBTA	OUP
This is the record of John	Ives	SATB	M/D	AFC	
Vox clamantis	Esquivel	SATB unacc	M/D		Mapa Mundi
FIVE OR MORE PARTS					
Canite tuba	Palestrina	SSATB unacc	M	CM12	
The Twelve	Walton	SSAATTBB	D		OUP
Vox dicentis, clama	Naylor	SATB + SATB unacc	D		Curwen

ORGAN MUSIC

PRELUDES

Bach J.S. — **Gott ist mein Heil** BWV 1106 in *Neumeister Chorale Preludes* (Bärenreiter) M*
Bridge F. — **Allegro comodo** No.2 of *Six Organ Pieces* (Boosey) E/M
De Grigny N. — **Dialogue de flûtes pour l'Élévation** p.43 in *Livre d'Orgue* (Kalmus, Schott) E(*)
Dupré M. — **No.2** of *Trois Élévations* (Combre) E
Nixon J. — **Mannheim** in *Meditation* (Mayhew) E/M

POSTLUDES

Bédard D. — **Sortie** from *Suite Liturgique* (Cheldar) M/D
Thalben-Ball G. — **Woodlands** in *113 Variations on Hymn Tunes* (Novello) E
Walmisley T.A. — **Prelude and Fugue in E minor** in *Tallis to Wesley* Vol. 36 (Hinrichsen) M
Wesley S. — **Allegretto in B flat** No.5 in *Organ Works* Vol.10 (Fagus) E*

PROPER 10 (SUNDAY BETWEEN 10 AND 16 JULY INCLUSIVE) YEAR C

HYMNS AND SONGS

	pos	rdg	AMNS	CAON	CFE	CH4	CH5	CP	H&P	HTC	LAU	MP	NEH	SG	SOF	TS
All ye who seek for sure relief/a comfort sure		n	64	26	31			101			212		63			
Blest are the pure in heart		n	238	77	88		630	391	724	110	908		341	372		
Come, O thou Traveller unknown		o	243					407	434				350			
Create in me a clean heart, O God		n										108			76	
Dear Lord and Father of mankind		n	115	144	143	485	549	411	673	356	934	111	353	497	79	79
Drop, drop, slow tears		n		151			548	106					82			
Here, O my Lord, I see thee face to face	cm	o	274	279		664	418	304	608	406		230		468		
Just as I am, without one plea		n	246	374	339	553	587	308	697	440		396	294	507	316	306
Lift up your hearts! We lift them	of	n	241	395		518		500	405	366			398			
Lord Jesus, think on me		n	129	412	384	491/2	554	97	533	316	204		70			
Love divine, all loves excelling		n	131	428	398	519	634	516	267	217	801	449	408	179	377	343
My God, accept my heart this day		n	279	455	495			338	701	551	872		318	559		
My God, how wonderful thou art		n	102	457	497		7	523	51	369	727	468	410	202	395	896
My Lord, what love is this		n		462	500		230					476		194	398	370
O come, thou/Come, O thou all-victorious Lord		n							418	441						
O for a heart to praise my God		n	230	484			638	533	536	483		495	74	149	411	904
O lift us up, strong Son of God		n							427							
O Lord, hear my prayer (Taizé)		o		938	542		620				929	908		246	423	394
O love that wilt not let me go		o		517		557	592	542	685	486		515			434	917
Praise, my soul, the King of heaven	ga	o	192	565	602	160	366	555	13	38	807	560	436	93	466	433
Purify my heart		n		574			640					921		163	475	436
River, wash over me		n										581			487	441
Rock of ages (Kendrick)		n												1507	951	
Rock of ages, cleft for me		n	135	584	624	554	557	565	273	593		582	445	150	488	950
Shepherd divine, our wants relieve		o	228				566	558								
Such love, pure as the whitest snow		n		620								619		216	514	465
Take this moment, sign and space		n			680	501	598				850					

SONGS FOR CHILDREN
Lord, you've promised CAON 864, CH 150, KS 244

BIBLE READINGS

Psalm 77*
Genesis 32.9–30
Mark 7.1–23

SINGING THE PSALM

Psalm 77* CH4, CWP, H&P, NPCW

ANTHEMS AND VOCAL MUSIC

Title	Composer	Voices	E/M/D	Book source	Single sheet publisher
UNISON/TWO PART/HIGH VOICES					
Eins bitte ich vom Herren	Schütz	2 part	M	AC2	
God of the living	Tamblyn	U	E/M		OCP
I was glad	Hubbard	SA	M	SFJ	Banks
THREE/FOUR PARTS					
A Gaelic Blessing	Rutter	SATB	E	NCAB	RSCM
And when the builders	Shephard	SATB	M/D		Banks
Behold, the tabernacle of God	Harris	SATB	E		RSCM
Behold, the tabernacle of God	Rutter	SATB	M/D		OUP
Christ is our cornerstone	Ogden	SATB	E	SBS2	
Christ is our cornerstone	Thorne	SATB	E/M	NOEAB	
Christians, shout for joy and gladness	Trad German	SAB	E	OBFA	
God is our hope and strength	J.S.Bach	SATB	E	AC1	
God is our hope and strength	Stanford	SATB	M		Novello
Jesus and the traders	Kodaly	SATB unacc	D		Universal Edition
Judge eternal	Archer	SATB	E/M		Mayhew
O pray for the peace of Jerusalem	Blow	SATB	M	FSB2	OUP
O pray for the peace of Jerusalem	Howells	SATB	M		OUP
Pray that Jerusalem	Chilcott	SATB	E/M		OUP
Pray that Jerusalem	Stanford	SATB	E	ASA	RSCM
Peace be to this congregation	Cadden arr Grindle	SATB	E/M		Encore
Surely thou hast tasted that the Lord is good	Bernard Rose	SATB unacc	D	EAC1	
There's a wideness in God's mercy	Bevan	SATB	E/M	LD, MTH1, NEP, NOEAB	
FIVE OR MORE PARTS					
Civitas sancti tui	Byrd	SAATBB unacc	M		Chester
God is our hope and strength	Blow	SSAATTBB	M		Banks

ORGAN MUSIC

PRELUDES

Clérambault L-N.   **Duo** *and/or* **Trio** from *Livre d'Orgue: Suite du Premier Ton* (Schola Cantorum, Kalmus) E*

Dubois T.   **Offertoire in A flat** p.11 in *Complete Works* Vol.1 (Bärenreiter) M

Floyd A.E.   **Chorale Prelude on 'Petra'** in *Musical Miniatures* and *Hymn Preludes for the Church Year* Bk.2 (both Mayhew) E/M

Sumsion H.   **Pastoral** in *A Book of Simple Organ Voluntaries* (OUP Archive) E/M

Willan H.   **Southwell** in *36 Short Preludes and Postludes* Set 3 (Peters) E

POSTLUDES

Adams T.   **Final movement** from *Voluntary No.1* in *Organ Works Vol.5: Six Organ Voluntaries* (Fagus) M(*)

Karg-Elert S   **Postludio festivo** No.12 from *Sempre Semplice* Op.142 Bk.2 (Cathedral Music) E/M

Oortmerssen J.van   **Psalm 77** from *Five Chorale Preludes* (Tactus) M

Thalben-Ball G.   **Love divine** No.51 of *113 Variations on Hymn Tunes* (Novello) E/M

HYMNS AND SONGS

	pos	rdg	AMNS	CAON	CFE	CH4	CH5	CP	H&P	HTC	LAU	MP	NEH	SG	SOF	TS
All praise to thee, for thou, O King divine		n	337	22			684	372	253	204			335			
Blest are the pure in heart		o,n	238	77	88		630	391	724	110	908		341	372		
Come, sinners, to the gospel feast	cm	n							460							
Come, thou/O fount of every blessing		g						406	517	337						663
Glorious things of thee are spoken		g	172	205	195	738	646	435	817	494	827	173	362	35	127	691
Glory to thee my God, this night/All praise to thee	ev		10	208	200	223	63	14	642	274		176	244	502		
God is here, as we his people		g	464				330	301	653	560	470					
God of freedom, God of justice		o		224		263		447								
Here, O my Lord, I see thee face to face	cm	n	274	279		664	418	304	608	406		230		468		
How sweet the name of Jesus sounds		g	122	297		461	92	467	257	211		251	374	42	194/782	190/1273
I cannot tell why he, whom angels worship		g		303			54	238	194			266		437	205	199
I heard the voice of Jesus say		n,g	247	310		540	576	469	136		795	275	376		215	206
I vow to thee, my country		n	295		286	704		355					*620*			
I'll praise my Maker while I've breath							357	473	439	20		320		84		
I'm accepted, I'm forgiven		g										321			229	217
Jesu, lover of my soul		g	123	343	319	490	553	96	528	438	797	372	383	201	297	838
Jesu, thou joy of loving hearts		g	255	369		662	425	486	258	413		383	292	471		839
Laudate Dominum/Sing, praise and bless the Lord (Taizé)		ps		933	346	77	359				698				1514	458
Lord of the Church, we pray for our renewing		g					303			499		442		577	1433	
Lord, speak to me that I may speak		o				542	589	512	553	510		444				
Meekness and majesty		n		448	487	356	228				751	465		395	390	353
Morning glory, starlit sky/Open are the gifts		n	496			390		259					*608*			
Nada te turbe/Nothing can trouble (Taizé)		n		937							947			659		
O/Our God our help in ages past		o	99	494	528	161	537	537	358	37	955	498	417	542	415	905
O soul, are you weary (Turn your eyes)		n										712				1470
Thanks/Praise to God whose word was spoken		o	423			605	387	584	483	255			438	229		
There's a wideness in God's mercy/Souls of men/ Restless souls		n	251	662		187	9	598	230	443	810	683	461/*700*	188		
Water of life, cleanse and refresh us		g			401							512	*655*			
When prison walls extend their reach (LUR 155)		o														

SONGS FOR CHILDREN

God speaks/Is it spooky? CH4 602, KS 172

BIBLE READINGS

Psalm 81
Genesis 41.1–16,25–37
1 Corinthians 4.8–13
John 4.31–35

SINGING THE PSALM

Psalm 81 CRP, CWP, FGP, NPCW

ANTHEMS AND VOCAL MUSIC

Title	Composer	Voices	E/M/D	Book source	Single sheet publisher
UNISON/TWO PART/HIGH VOICES					
As the deer longs	Hurd	U/SATB#	E	CFE, CG, CH4, LAU	OCP
He shall feed his flock (Messiah) (g)	Handel	S	M		Novello
I am the bread of life	Lole	U + descant	E	BC	RSCM
Joseph and the Amazing Technicolor Dreamcoat	Lloyd Webber	U	E		Novello
Like as the hart (g)	Goode	SSS	M		Encore
Sing we merrily	Symons	SS	M	AC2	
Water of life	Dean	U#	E	CFE, CSF, LAU, NEP	OCP
THREE/FOUR PARTS					
Amen, amen, it shall be so!	Bell	SATB + cantor	E	LAA	
Blessed are they	S.S.Wesley	SAB	M		S&B
Blest are the pure in heart	Gower	SATB	E		Encore
Blest are the pure in heart	Walford Davies	SATB unacc	E	MTH1, NCAB	RSCM
Here, O my Lord, I see thee	Barry Rose	SATB	E/M	MTH2	
Here, O my Lord, I see thee	Whitlock	SATB	E/M	NSAC2	OUP
I am the bread of life	Lole	SATB	E	SBS1, WIS	RSCM
Just as I am	Chilcott	SATB	M	BCA	OUP
Like as the hart (g)	Howells	SATB	M	AC4	
Morning glory, starlit sky	Barry Rose	SATB + solo S/T	E/M	MTH2	
Sicut cervus (g)	Palestrina	SATB unacc	M	ESM	Chester
Sing we merrily	Batten	SATB	E/M		Novello
Take up your cross	Corp	SATB	E	SBS1, WOTC	RSCM
The Beatitudes	Chilcott	SATB	M		OUP
The Beatitudes	Pärt	SATB	D		Universal
The Beatitudes	Watson Henderson	SATB	M	SC	RSCM
FIVE OR MORE PARTS					
Beati mundo corde (g)	Byrd	SSATB unacc	M/D	ETAS	CMS/OUP
Exultate Deo	Poulenc	SSAATTBB unacc	D		Salabert

ORGAN MUSIC

PRELUDES

Bibl R.	**2nd movement** of *Sonata No.1 in D minor* (Doblinger) M	
Couperin F.	**Tierce en taille** No.XI from *Messe pour les Paroisses* (Kalmus) E/M	
Dupré M.	**No.3** of *Trois Élévations* (Combre) E	
Frescobaldi G.	**Canzona** in *Organ Music for Manuals* Bk.3 (OUP) E*	
Sumsion H.	**Canzona** (RSCM) M	

POSTLUDES

Archer J.S.	**Improvisation on 'Blaenwern'** (Novello) M/D	
Bédard D.	**Grand jeu** from *Suite du Premier Ton* (Cheldar) E/M	
Bibl R.	**3rd movement** of *Sonata No.1 in D minor* (Doblinger) M	
Lloyd Webber W.S.	**Postlude** in *Prayer and Praise* (Paxton) E(*)	

PROPER 12 (SUNDAY BETWEEN 24 AND 30 JULY INCLUSIVE) YEAR C

HYMNS AND SONGS

	pos	rdg	AMNS	CAON	CFE	CH4	CH5	CP	H&P	HTC	LAU	MP	NEH	SG	SOF	TS
A mighty fortress/A safe stronghold/God is our fortress		o	114		3	454	668	366	661	523	958	2		637	25	
Be still, my soul		o		68	73	691	666	384					625			49
Bread of heaven, on thee we feed		n	271	82				284		398			276	464		
Bread of life, hope of the world	cm	n			95	663					78			484		
Bread of the world in mercy broken	cm	n	270	83	97		403	285	599	396			277	465		
Eat this bread/Jesus Christ, bread of life (Taizé)		n		926	151	661					633				1221	
For all the saints who from their labours rest		g	305	177	176	740	459	232	814	567	371	148	197	636	109	684
Glorious things of thee are spoken		n	172	205	195	738	646	435	817	494	827	173	362	35	127	691
God forgave my sin in Jesus' name		g		212	209		480			S 12	849	181			129	123
God moves in a mysterious way		o	112	222		158	13	445	65				193	365		700
Great is thy faithfulness		o		249		153	80	453	66	260		200	636	39	147	138
Guide me, O thou great Jehovah/Redeemer		n	214	252	233	167	647	455	437	528	960	201	368	638	148	708
Happy are they, they that love God	o,g		176	262			649	456	711	473			369			
I come with joy		n	473	304		656	421	305	610	408	649		623	469		
I hunger and I thirst		n						306	730	409			470			
Jehovah Jireh, my provider		o										354			284	
Jerusalem the golden		g	184	340	317	747	670	482		573	991		381			
Jesus, remember me (Taizé)		g		931		775	617				253				875	294
Lord, I have made thy word my choice		g	490				504	475								
Lord Jesus, once you spoke to men		g	392							112						
Now the green blade riseth		g	501	475	513	417	278	153	204			278	115	414		
O Lord, hear my prayer (Taizé)		ps		938	542		620				929	908	246	423	394	
Praise to the Lord, the almighty	ga	o	207	573	608	124	365	558	16	40	706	564	440	59	470	945
Seek ye first the kingdom of God		g		590	633	641	596		138		820	590			493	447
The kingdom of God is justice and joy		g		646	701			591	139	333	821	651		184		
Through the night of doubt and sorrow		n	211	687			661	605	441	466		948	468	544		
Who can sound the depths of sorrow		n		747							766			257	604	579

SONGS FOR CHILDREN

In our lives plant seeds of hope CH4 349
When the road is rough and steep JP 279, SOF 1612

BIBLE READINGS
Psalm 88*
Genesis 42.1–25
1 Corinthians 10.1–24
Matthew 13.24–30[31–43]

SINGING THE PSALM
Psalm 88* CWP, FGP, NPCW

ANTHEMS AND VOCAL MUSIC

Title	Composer	Voices	E/M/D	Book source	Single sheet publisher
UNISON/TWO PART/HIGH VOICES					
Bread for the world	Farrell	U#	E	GBAN	OCP
Bread of life	Farrell	U/SATB#	E	CFE, CH4, HIG, LAU, RITH, SG	OCP
Joseph and the Amazing Technicolor Dreamcoat	Lloyd Webber	U	E		Novello
O sacrum convivium	Leighton	S/SS	M/D	EAC2	
Take the word of God with you (g)	Walker	U/SAB#	E	CFE, CIH, LAU	OCP
The blessing cup that we bless	Ogden	U	E		WLP
Unless a grain of wheat (g)	Farrell	U/SATB#	E	CFE, LAU, RITH, WYP	OCP
THREE/FOUR PARTS					
Bread of the world	Scottish trad arr Bullard	SAMen	E	OBFA	
Bread of the world in mercy broken	Baldwin	SAMen	E	SBS2	
Christ, our God, descends from heaven	Bullard	SAB	E/M	SBS2	
Ego sum panis vivus	Byrd	SATB unacc	M		Chester
Ego sum panis vivus	Palestrina	SATB unacc	M	CM1	Chester
Let all mortal flesh keep silence	Trad arr Covey-Crump	SATB unacc	M	MTH1	
Lord, I trust thee	Handel	SATB	E	NCAB, NOEAB	
Now the green blade riseth (g)	Trad arr Lindley	SATB	E/M	AWTE	
O sacrum convivium	Byrd	SATB unacc	M	SBS2	
O sacrum convivium	Messiaen	SATB unacc	D		UMP
O taste and see	Vaughan Williams	SATB unacc	E	AC4, NOEAB, NSAC1	OUP
Panis angelicus	Franck	SATB	M	ESM	
Shepherd of souls	Barnard	SATB	E/M	SC	RSCM
Take and eat	Ogden	SATB unacc	E		WLP
Verily, verily I say unto you	Tallis	SATB unacc	E	AC1, SBS2, TA	OUP
FIVE OR MORE PARTS					
Let all mortal flesh keep silence	Bairstow	SSAATTBB unacc	M/D	AC4	S&B
O sacrum convivium	Tallis	SAATB unacc	M/D	TA	OUP
Panis angelicus	Villette	SSAATTBB unacc	M/D		UMP

ORGAN MUSIC

PRELUDES
Boëllmann L.   **Communion/Elévation No.1 in E flat** in *St Cecilia Organ Library* Vol.1 (Cramer) and *Heures Mystiques* Bk.1 Op.29 (Kalmus, Enoch) E/M*

Dvorak A.   **Prelude in A minor** in *Complete Works* (Supraphon) E/M

Feroci F.   **Elevazione** in *Italian Organ Music of the 18th C* (Flammer) E/M(*)

Nagel M.   **Ballade in D** in *The Organ Funeral Album* (Bärenreiter) E*

POSTLUDES
Berthier J.   **Variations on 'Lobe den Herren'** in *Variations on Six Chorales* (Mayhew) M*

Dvorak A.   **Fugue in G minor** in *Complete Works* (Supraphon) M

Bédard D.   **Fantaisie 'Ein feste Burg'** (Cheldar) M

Reger M.   **Ein feste Burg** Op.79 No.2 in *Complete Works* Vol.7 or *Hier Preisen auf der Erd* Vol.1 (Breitkopf) E/M

Walther J.G.   **Ein feste Burg** in *Seasonal Chorale Preludes for Manuals* Bk.2 (OUP) and *A Graded Anthology for Organ* Bk.4 (Cramer) E/M*

HYMNS AND SONGS

	pos	rdg	AMNS	CAON	CFE	CH4	CH5	CP	H&P	HTC	LAU	MP	NEH	SG	SOF	TS
Born by the Holy Spirit's breath		n							279	225		61		446		
Breathe on me, breath of God		n	157	84	98	596	293	174	280	226	302	67	342	554	51	57
Bring to the Lord a glad new song		n				106				336	705			78		
Come down, O love divine		n	156	114	125	489	294	175	281	231	303	89	137	663	1202	71
Eternal Father, strong to save		g	292	153	152	260	612	413	379	285	963	122	354	235	1222	
Father, Lord of all creation		n	356	163	161		318	418								
Fierce raged the tempest		g	225						144							
For the music of creation		n												36		
God is good all the time!		n									984				1244	125
Gracious Spirit, Holy Ghost/Holy Spirit, gracious guest		n	154	245		627	312	182	301	474		198	367	556		
Holy Spirit, come, confirm us		n	471	288		640	299	183	288		311		140			
Holy Spirit, ever dwelling/living		n				615				303			141			
Holy Spirit, truth divine		n		289		626	300	184	289	235						
In the Lord I'll be ever thankful (Taizé)		o		929	308	772					944	865		656	817	
Lord, thy word abideth/your word shall guide us	gr	g	166	420	390		384	515	476	251	977/8	446	407			
Misericordias Domini/From age to age (Taizé)		n			489											
O breath of life, come sweeping through us		n		476		595	305		777	237		488			407	379
O/Our God our help in ages past		o	99	494	528	161	537	537	358	37	955	498	417	542	415	905
O sing a song of Bethlehem		g	413	536				545								
O strength and stay	ev	o	7	537			70	18					248			
She sits like a bird (Enemy of apathy)		n			640	593					305					
Sing of the Lord's goodness		n			654	157	368				713			61		
Spirit of the living God, fall afresh on me		n		615	666	619/620	310		295	S 23/24		306	613		510	462
The Lord is my song (Taizé)		n		651							929					
Through the night of doubt and sorrow		o	211	687			661	605	441	466		948	468	544		
Thy/Your hand, O God, has guided		o	171	689	741	511	529	606	784	536	876	705	485	649	1065	
Walk with me, oh my Lord		g			765						966					
When in our music God is glorified		n		737	802	203	458	618			729					

SONGS FOR CHILDREN

Give thanks with a grateful heart CAON 202, CFE 189, CH 57, CH4 180, CH5 352, KS 68, MP 170, SG 108, SOF 124, TS 118

God is good, we sing and shout it CAON 214, CH4 178, JP 55, KS 74, MP 185, SOF 132, TS 124

BIBLE READINGS

Psalm 107.1–32*
Genesis 50.4–26
1 Corinthians 14.1–19
Mark 6.45–52

SINGING THE PSALM

Psalm 107.1–32* CH4, CRP, CWP, H&P, NPCW

ANTHEMS AND VOCAL MUSIC

Title	Composer	Voices	E/M/D	Book source	Single sheet publisher
UNISON/TWO PART/HIGH VOICES					
Calm me, Lord (g)	Rizza	U/SATB#	E	CAON, CAS, FOLO	
God the singer	Ogden	U + descant	E	VFLS	
He came singing love	Gibson	2 part	E	VFLS	
I'm gonna sing	Trad arr Jones	3 part + descant	E	VFLS	
I will sing a song of love	Bell	U	E	VFLS	
Let all the world	Lang	2 part	M		OUP
O hear us, Lord	Piccolo	SS	M/D	EAC2	
THREE/FOUR PARTS					
A Gaelic Blessing (g)	Rutter	SATB	E	NCAB	RSCM
Almighty and everlasting God	Gibbons	SATB unacc	E	NCAB, OBTA	OUP
Be still my soul (g)	Sibelius	SATB	E		Breitkopf & Hartel
Bless, O Lord, us thy servants	Harper	U/SATB (unacc)	E	PSA	RSCM
Call to remembrance	Farrant	SATB unacc	E	NCAB, OBTA	OUP
Cantate Domino	Pitoni	SATB unacc	E	AC1, NCAB, NSAC1, NOEAB, SC	
How can I keep from singing?	Lowry arr Weaver	SAMen	E	SFL2, SBS1	
I will sing with the spirit	Goodenough	SATB	E	SBS2	
I will sing with the spirit	Rutter	SATB	M	JRA	OUP
Let all the world	Leighton	SATB	M/D	EAC1	Novello
Let all the world	Vaughan Williams	SATB	M		S&B
Lord, for thy tender mercy's sake	Hilton/Farrant	SATB unacc	E	AWTE, FAB1, NOEAB, OBTA, NCAB	OUP
O sing joyfully	Batten	SATB	E	SCAB, WFC	RSCM
O sing joyfully	Campbell	SATB	M	MTP	Novello
Take this moment	Bell	SATB	E	CG, IAMB, LFB, OITB, WIS	GIA
There's a wideness in God's mercy	Bevan	SATB	E	LD, MTH1, NEP, NOEAB	
They that go down to the sea in ships (g)	Sumsion	SATB	M		RSCM
FIVE OR MORE PARTS					
Cantate Domino	Monteverdi	SSATTB	M	ESM	OUP
Sing joyfully	Byrd	SAATB unacc	M/D	OBTA	OUP

ORGAN MUSIC

PRELUDES

Chauvet A.	**Andante con moto** No.6 of *20 Morceaux* (Publimuses) M
Dubois T.	**Offertoire in B flat** No.1 in *Complete Works* Vol.1 (Bärenreiter) E/M
Fauré G.	**Pavane** (Cramer) M
Sumsion H.	**Chorale Prelude on 'Down Ampney'** (Paraclete)
Wesley S.	**Allegretto in E flat** No.33 in *Organ Works* Vol.10 (Fagus) E*

POSTLUDES

Bédard D.	**Toccata** from *Suite* (Cheldar) M/D
Sceats G.	**Introduction, Fugato & Coda** from *Miniature Suite* (Hinrichsen) E/M
Whitlock P.	**Chanty** from *Plymouth Suite* in *Whitlock: Complete Shorter Works* (OUP) E/M(*)
Zachau F.	**Komm, Heiliger Geist, Herre Gott** in *80 Chorale Preludes* and *Choralvorspiele alter Meister* (both Peters) E/M*

HYMNS AND SONGS

	pos	rdg	AMNS	CAON	CFE	CH4	CH5	CP	H&P	HTC	LAU	MP	NEH	SG	SOF	TS
A debtor to mercy alone		n								449						
All ye who seek for sure relief/a comfort sure		n	64	26	31		101				212		63			
Be bold, be strong		o										49			37	38
Bless the Lord, my soul (Taizé)				923	81		1			813				105	676	56
Christ is the King! O friends rejoice		o	345				86	165		492			345	31		
Dear Lord and Father of mankind		g	115	144	143	485	549	411	673	356	934	111	353	497	79	79
Father of mercies, in thy word		n	167							247			224			
Father of mercy, God of consolation		n					511						323			
Glorious things of thee are spoken		o	172	205	195	738	646	435	817	494	827	173	362	35	127	691
God is our strength and refuge		o		219			12	443		527		188		650		699
How lovely on the mountains (Our God reigns)		o		295	268		129				768	249			192	189
I believe in Jesus (Nelson)		g		301								264		333	203	195
I heard the voice of Jesus say		g	247	310		540	576	469	136		795	275	376		215	206
Lord, enthroned in heavenly splendour	of	o	263	408	379		431	311	616	416	769	431	296	52	352	870
May the mind of Christ my Saviour		n		447		536	636	521	739	550		463		671	1448	887
Misericordias Domini/From age to age (Taizé)		o			489											
My God, accept my heart this day		n	279	455	495			338	701	551	872		318	559		
O comfort my people		o		480	523						99					
O for a thousand tongues to sing		g	125	485		352	104	534	744	219		496	415	55	412	383/1452
O let the Son of God enfold you		g		506								502			419	392
O my Saviour, lifted		g	248	519			237					516			437	
O strength and stay	ev	o	7	537			70	18					248			
Rejoice! The Lord is king		o	139	580	619	449	281	563	243	180	326	575	443	440	482	948
Restore, O Lord, the honour		g		582		469						579		274	483	439
Sing praise to God who reigns above		n	193					569	511			447				
The Lord is my light (Taizé)				944												
Thou/God, whose almighty word		g	180	684	738	112	324	267	29	506	887	699	466	597	557	
To God be the glory		o		695	745	512	373	609	463	584	719	708		71	559	526
We come as guests invited	hc	n					451			602	630	723				

SONGS FOR CHILDREN

Be bold, be strong JP 14, KS 17, MP 49, SOF 37, TS 38
God is so good JP 53, KS 78, SOF 732, TS 1223

BIBLE READINGS

Psalms 108 [and 116]
Isaiah 11.10 - 12.6
2 Corinthians 1.1–22
Mark 7.24–30

SINGING THE PSALM

Psalm 108 CWP, NPCW
Psalm 116 CH4, CRP, CWP, FGP, H&P, MCW1, NEH, NPCW, PAME, PFS
    Dean *How can I repay the Lord* HIG (OCP)#
    Haugen *I will walk in the presence of God* C, LAU (GIA)#

ANTHEMS AND VOCAL MUSIC

Title	Composer	Voices	E/M/D	Book source	Single sheet publisher
UNISON/TWO PART/HIGH VOICES					
Be strong in the Lord	Nicholson	SS	E		Curwen
Dear Lord and Father of mankind	Parnell	SS	E/M		Encore
God beyond all names	Farrell	U/SATB#	E	CFE, GBAN, LAU	OCP
Like a child rests in its mother's arms	Walker	U#	E	LAU, OOD	OCP
Loving God	Aston	2 part	E	BC	
Song of Consolation	Jones	U	E	VE	
There is a longing in our hearts	Quigley	U/SATB#	E	CH4, LAU, SG	OCP
THREE/FOUR PARTS					
A Clare Benediction	Rutter	SATB (unacc)	E	JRA, OBFA (SAMen)	OUP
A touching place (Christ's is the world) (g)	Bell	SATB	E	CG, IAMB, LFB, WGIR, WIS	GIA
Be strong and of good courage	Campbell	SATB	M	FSB7	
God is our hope and strength	J.S. Bach	SATB	E/M	FSB4, AC1	
God is our hope and strength	Stanford	SATB	M		Novello
He shall feed his flock (Messiah)	Handel arr Hand	SAMen	M	AOAN1	
I heard the voice of Jesus say	Shephard	SATB	M		RSCM
Jesus, fount of consolation	Freylinghausen	SATB	E	MTH1	
Just as I am	Chilcott	SATB	E	BCA	OUP
O Lord, heal us	Walker	SATB + descant#	E	ATNJ	
Rejoice, the Lord is king	Archer	SATB	M		Mayhew
Rejoice, the Lord is king	Kelly	SATB	M/D	NNAB, MTH1	
Strengthen ye the weak hands	Harris	SATB	M		Novello
The Lord bless you and keep you	Rutter	SATB	M	EAC1, JRA, WFC, OBFA (SAMen)	OUP
The secret of Christ (g)	Shephard	SATB	M	NCAB	RSCM
We cannot measure how you heal (g)	Bell arr Archer	SATB	E	BC	RSCM
FIVE OR MORE PARTS					
Deus noster refugium	Hassler	SAATTB unacc	M		RSCM

ORGAN MUSIC

PRELUDES

Darke H.   **Interlude** in *The Hovingham Sketches* (Banks) E/M
Langlais J.   **Prélude No.1** in *Organ Book* (Elkan-Vogel) E*
Nixon J.   **St Bernard** in *Hymn Tune Preludes* (Fagus) E/M
Spedding A.   **Elegy** ('St Peter') in *Recuerdos* (IAO) E

POSTLUDES

Callahan C.   **Fanfare on 'Abbot's Leigh'** in *Two English Voluntaries* (Concordia) E/M
Dubois T.   **Entrée: Grand Chœur** p.93 in *Complete Works* Vol.1 (Bärenreiter) M
Nixon J.   **St Helen** in *Hymn Tune Preludes* (Fagus) E/M
Smart H.   **March in G** in *50 Victorian Pieces* (Mayhew) E/M
Vierne L.   **Cortège** No.2 of *24 Pièces en Style Libre* Bk.1 (Masters, Durand) M(*)

PROPER 15 (SUNDAY BETWEEN 14 AND 20 AUGUST INCLUSIVE) YEAR C

HYMNS AND SONGS

	pos	rdg	AMNS	CAON	CFE	CH4	CH5	CP	H&P	HTC	LAU	MP	NEH	SG	SOF	TS
Above all powers		n										1022			1151	611
All praise to thee, for thou, O King divine		n	337	22			684	372	253	204			335			
Christ is made the sure foundation/Blessèd city		o	332ii	97	109	200	326	207/208	485	559	456	73	205	572	1199	654
Christ is our cornerstone		o	161	98			327	395		564			206	14		
Empty he came		n								127			622			
Forth in thy name, O Lord, I go	se	g	239	188	184	529	567	430	381	306	861	159	235	623	1237	
Give thanks with a grateful heart		n		202	189	180	352					170		108	124	118
Glorious things of thee are spoken		o	172	205	195	738	646	435	817	494	827	173	362	35	127	691
God has spoken – by his prophets		o					381		64	248	742	831		225		
Great is thy faithfulness		g		249		153	80	453	66	260		200	636	39	147	138
Lead us, heavenly Father, lead us		g	224	379	351		652	496	68	595	315	400	393	640	321	311
Let earth and heaven combine		n							109							1394
May the mind of Christ my Saviour		g		447		536	636	521	739	550		463		671	1448	887
Morning glory, starlit sky/Open are the gifts		n	496			390		259					*608*			
Nada te turbe/Nothing can trouble (Taizé)				937							947			659		
Praise to the holiest in the height		g	117	572	606	378	108	557	231	140	788	563	439	58	469	
Such love, pure as the whitest snow		g		620								619		216	514	465
Thanks/Praise to God whose word was spoken		o	423			605	387	584	483	255			438	229		
The Lord is king! Lift up thy voice		g	107	650		129	8	592	58	183		656		98		
Thou who wast rich/Lord, you were rich		n				318	168	72		63		700		356		1018
Through all the changing scenes of life		g	209	686	740		372	604	73	46		702	467	654	1566	1561
Where is this stupendous stranger?		n	527				75						41			
With joy we meditate the grace		g	530					624	235			774				
Ye that know the Lord is gracious		o	175			642	493	628					477			

SONGS FOR CHILDREN

Each of us is a living stone CAON 793, CH 41
Give thanks with a grateful heart CAON 202, CFE 189, CH 57, CH4 180, CH5 352, KS 68, MP 170, SG 108, SOF 124, TS 118

BIBLE READINGS

Psalm 119.17–32*
Isaiah 28.9–22
2 Corinthians 8.1–9
Matthew 20.1–16

SINGING THE PSALM

Psalm 119.17–32* CWP, NPCW

Dean *You have laid down your precepts* HG#
Walker *Teach me, O God* ATNJ (OCP)#

ANTHEMS AND VOCAL MUSIC

Title	Composer	Voices	E/M/D	Book source	Single sheet publisher
UNISON/TWO PART/HIGH VOICES					
A Prayer of St Richard of Chichester	White	2 part	E	BC, OBFA, OEAB	OUP
Day by day	How	U + 2 part	E	BC	RSCM
Take my gifts	Farrell	U#	E	GBU	
Take my hands, Lord	Rizza	U/SATB#	E	CAS	
THREE/FOUR PARTS					
A Prayer of St Richard of Chichester	Archer	SATB	E		RSCM
Christ be with me	Pachelbel arr Rawsthorne	SAMen	E	AOAN1	
Christ is our cornerstone	Ogden	SATB	E/M	SBS2	RSCM
Christ is our cornerstone	Thorne	SATB	E/M	NOEAB	
For the gifts of life and love	Nardone	SATB	M	SC	
I give you my hands, Lord	Tambling	SAMen unacc	M	AOAN1	
Jesus, you are the way	Rizza	SATB + solo S#	E	FOL	Mayhew
Listen sweet dove	Ives	SATB	M	EAC1, SC	RSCM
Love divine	Ledger	SATB	E		Dean
Love of love	Moore	SATB	E/M		Encore
O God my King (g)	Amner	SATB unacc	E	AC1	
Surely thou hast tasted that the Lord is good	Bernard Rose	SATB unacc	M/D	EAC1	
Take this moment	Bell	SATB	E	CG, IAMB, LFB, OITB, WIS	GIA
Teach me, O Lord	Attwood	SATB	E	NOEAB	RSCM
The Grail Prayer	Rizza	SATB + solo S	E	FOLO, LUE	Mayhew
FIVE OR MORE PARTS					
Christ is all in all	Beaumont	SSATB unacc	M/D		Encore
Lo! God is here!	P.Moore	SSAATTBB	D		Faber
Teach me, O Lord	Byrd	SAATB	M	OBTA	OUP

ORGAN MUSIC

PRELUDES

Bach J.S.	**Liebster Jesu, wir sind hier** BWV 706(i), BWV 730 or BWV 731 in Novello Vol.18, Bärenreiter Vol.3, Peters Vol.5 E
Dubois T.	**Prélude** from *Seven Pieces* (Butz, Kalmus); also in *Complete Works* Vol.1 (Bärenreiter) E/M
Fletcher A.	**Mannheim** in *100 Hymn Preludes* and in *Hymn Preludes for the Church Year* Bk.2 (both Mayhew) E
Nixon J.	**Trio on 'Harewood'** in *50 Hymn Preludes* (Mayhew) E/M
Young G.	**Flourish** or **Sarabande** from *Suite Mediévale* (Flammer) E

POSTLUDES

Bennett J.	**Voluntary No.8 in G minor** in *Ten Voluntaries* Bk.1 (Fagus) M*
Dupré M.	**Antiphon II** No.2 of *Fifteen Pieces on Antiphons* Op.18 (Gray, Masters) M
Merkel G.	**Fugue** Op.124/2 in *The Progressive Organist* Bk.7 (Novello) E/M
Thalben-Ball G.	**Wiltshire** No.110 of *113 Variations on Hymn Tunes* (Novello) E

PROPER 16 (SUNDAY BETWEEN 21 AND 27 AUGUST INCLUSIVE) YEAR C

HYMNS AND SONGS

	pos	rdg	AMNS	CAON	CFE	CH4	CH5	CP	H&P	HTC	LAU	MP	NEH	SG	SOF	TS
All my hope on God is founded		n	336	19	21	192	10	368	63	451	959	16	333	525		620
At/In the name of Jesus		g	148	54	59	458	94	380	74	172	762	41	338	317	32	33
Be still, my soul		o		68	73	691	666	384					625			49
Christ is the King! O friends rejoice		g	345				86	165		492			345	31		
Christ triumphant, ever reigning		g		104	113	436	259	398		173	763	77	613	319	62	655
Crown him with many crowns		g	147	137	139	459	263	166	255	174	321	109	352	321	77	77
For the fruits of all/his creation		n	457	185	178	231	39	254	342	286	731	153	621	299	1234	685
Glory, love, and praise, and honour	pc	n	461	207				436	35				287			
God of mercy, God of grace		n	179	227			695	449		293			366	5		
Great is thy faithfulness		n		249		153	80	453	66	260		200	636	39	147	138
I am trusting thee, Lord Jesus		o		300						433		258			202	
I bind unto myself today/Christ be with me		o		302	274	639	322	203	695	5	312		159/278			757
In the Lord I'll be ever thankful (Taizé)				929	308	772					944	865		656	817	
Lo, in the wilderness a voice		g	384										170			
Lord Jesus, think on me		o	129	412	384	491/2	554	97	533	316	204		70			
Lord, you are more precious than silver		o										447			368	339
Loving Shepherd of thy sheep		o	134	434	475		655	517		305	802	888				
My heart is filled with thankfulness		n														1438
My spirit longs for thee		o	57				99						299			
Now thank we all our God		n	205	474	512	182	361	530	566	33	945	486	413	54	405	
O God, you search me and you know me		o				97					779			514		1454
O Jesus, I have promised		o	235	503	536	644	593	538	704	531	875	501	420	676	418	391
Praise, O praise our God and King		n	288	566			45	273	359							
Rejoice! The Lord is king		g	139	580	619	449	281	563	243	180	326	575	443	440	482	948
Son of God, eternal Saviour		n	132			468	527	573		102			498			
The kingdom of God is justice and joy		g		646	701			591	139	333	821	651	184			
The Lord is my song (Taizé)		ps		651							929					
There is a Redeemer		n,g		658		559	112					673		396	544	492

SONGS FOR CHILDREN

Give thanks with a grateful heart CAON 202, CFE 189, CH 57, CH4 180, CH5 352, KS 68, MP 170, SG 108, SOF 124, TS 118

God is so good JP 53, KS 78, SOF 732, TS 1223

BIBLE READINGS

Psalm 119.49–72*
Isaiah 30.8–21
2 Corinthians 9
Matthew 21.28–32

SINGING THE PSALM

Psalm 119.49–72* CWP, NPCW

ANTHEMS AND VOCAL MUSIC

Title	Composer	Voices	E/M/D	Book source	Single sheet publisher
UNISON/TWO PART/HIGH VOICES					
Look at the world	Rutter	U/SATB	E	JRA	OUP
Send down the fire of your justice	Haugen	U/SATB#	E	C, TS	GIA
Take my gifts	Farrell	U#	E	GBU	
Thanks be to God	Dean	U/SATB	E	CFE, LAU, SG	OCP
The Call (Come, my Way)	Vaughan Williams	U	E	NEP	S&B
THREE/FOUR PARTS					
Alleluia, alleluia, give thanks	Fishel	SATB	E	SWAMS	
And thank him then	Chilcott	SATB	E	BCA	OUP
Come, my Way, my Truth, my Life	Archer	SAMen	E	AOAN1	Mayhew
Come, my Way, my Truth, my Life	Harris	SATB	M	NNAB	
Come, my Way, my Truth, my Life	Rawsthorne	SAB	E/M		Mayhew
For the gifts of life and love	Nardone	SATB	M	SC	
Go forth and tell!	Ogden	SATB/U	E	SBS2	
Go forth into the world in peace	Rutter	SATB	E/M	JRA	OUP
I give you my hands, Lord	Tambling	SAMen unacc	M	AOAN1	
Irish Blessing	Chilcott	SATB	E	BCA	OUP
Jesu, joy of man's desiring	J.S.Bach	SATB	E	FAB1, NCAB, NOEAB, NSCA1, WFC	RSCM
Let the people praise thee, O God	Harwood	SATB	M		Novello
Praise to God, immortal praise	Vann	SAMen	E	AOAN1	
The Lord bless you and keep you	Rutter	SATB	E	JRA, EAC1, WFC, OBFA (SAMen)	OUP
The Spirit of the Lord	Elgar	SATB	M	SAEE	RSCM
Thou art the way	Steel	SATB	M	NNAB, MTH2	
FIVE OR MORE PARTS					
Blessing	Allwood	SATBB unacc	E	NSAC2	

ORGAN MUSIC

PRELUDES

Berthier J.	**Hommage à Du Mont I** *and/or* **II** from *Ten Liturgical Meditations* (Mayhew) E*
Lloyd Webber W.S.	**Andantino alla Cantilena** in *Eight Varied Pieces* (Bosworth) E/M
Peeters F.	**St Patrick's Breastplate** in *Hymn Preludes for the Liturgical Year* Op.100 Bk.3 (Peters) E
Willan H.	**Southwell** in *36 Short Preludes and Postludes* Set 3 (Peters) E

POSTLUDES

Berthier J.	**Conversation** from *Ten Liturgical Meditations* (Mayhew) E/M*
Howells H.	**Epilogue** in *The Hovingham Sketches* (Banks) M
Smart H.	**Allegro in D** in *50 Victorian Pieces* (Mayhew) E/M
Stanford C.V.	**On an old Irish church melody** No.5 of *Six Short Preludes and Postludes* (Set 1) Op.101 (Stainer); also in *Preludes and Postludes* (Mayhew) E/M

Suitable before or after: Movements from Callahan C. **Partita on 'Diademata'** (MorningStar) E/M–M

PROPER 17 (SUNDAY BETWEEN 28 AUGUST AND 3 SEPTEMBER INCLUSIVE) YEAR C

HYMNS AND SONGS

	pos	rdg	AMNS	CAON	CFE	CH4	CH5	CP	H&P	HTC	LAU	MP	NEH	SG	SOF	TS
All heaven declares		o		17	20	426					760	14		420	10	8
As I come into your presence		o														634
As the bridegroom to his chosen		n	340						30							
Author of faith, eternal Word		n					381		662							
Breathe on me, breath of God		n	157	84	98	596	293	174	280	226	302	67	342	554	51	57
Christ is surely coming		o										75				
Come, see the beauty of the Lord		o										100			74	
Crown him with many crowns		n	147	137	139	459	263	166	255	174	321	109	352	321	77	77
Eternal light, shine in my heart		n					613	415		339						
Fairest Lord Jesus		o				463	88			209		823	634	199		680
From heaven you came, helpless babe		n		195	187	374	219	432			749	162		632	120	114
Go labour on, spend and be spent		n							794							
Here, O my Lord, I see thee face to face	cm	n	274	279		664	418	304	608	406		230		468		
Holy, holy, holy, Lord God almighty	mo	n	95	286	259	111	321	202	7	594	468	237	146	290	183	177
Jesus, these eyes have never seen		o	245	365				491					389			
Judge eternal, throned in splendour		o		372		264	535	356	409	329		395	490	600		
King of glory, King of peace		o	194	375	343		358	494	499	603	715	397	391	178		
Lord of beauty, thine the splendour		o	106	415			29	258					265			
May the mind of Christ my Saviour	o,n			447		536	636	521	739	550		463		671	1448	887
My God, how wonderful thou art		o	102	457	497		7	523	51	369	727	468	410	202	395	896
Now is eternal life		n	402	470			392	152	203				114			
O changeless Christ, for ever new		n			518					108	745			374		
O Christ the same through all our story's pages		n		477			103			263			258			
O Christ, the great foundation		n								502	829					
O God, you search me and you know me		n				97					779			514		1454
O love divine, how sweet thou art		n	124				621	541				424				
O thou who camest from above		n	233	541	557	625	639	191	745	596		525	431	560	451	416
The Lord is my song (Taizé)				651							929					
Thine for ever, God of love		n	234	673			660	599		556		972	463			
This is the mystery, that Christ		n									947			1060	519
Wait for the Lord (Taizé)				949	762	276					88			1575	

SONGS FOR CHILDREN

He is the King of kings CAON 818, CH 80, TS 1244

1st Sept 2013   2nd 194 (102 (1st)
3rd. 234   402 last,

BIBLE READINGS

Psalm 119.81–96*
Isaiah 33.13–22
John 3.22–36

SINGING THE PSALM

Psalm 119.81–96* CWP, NPCW

ANTHEMS AND VOCAL MUSIC

Title	Composer	Voices	E/M/D	Book source	Single sheet publisher
UNISON/TWO PART/HIGH VOICES					
Settings of the Te Deum	Various	U/SATB	E	CWP, MCW1	
King of glory, King of peace	Sanders	SSAA	M/D		Encore
Life through him	Inwood	U/2 part	E		OCP
O God, you search me	Farrell	U/SATB#	E	CBL, CH4, LAU, MCW1, SG, TS	OCP
Rejoice, the Lord is king	Weaver	2 part	E/M	CFAP	
THREE/FOUR PARTS					
Ascribe unto the Lord	Travers	SATB + solo TB	M		Novello
Ascribe unto the Lord	S.S.Wesley	SATB	M		Banks, Novello
Fairest Lord Jesus	Trad arr How	SAMen	E	TEA	RSCM
Fuit homo missus a Deo	Palestrina	SATB unacc	M	AFC	
Give unto the Lord	Elgar	SATB	D		Novello
God hath spoken	Gibbs	SATB	M		RSCM
How lovely are the messengers	Mendelssohn	SATB	M	AFC	Novello
In the city of the Lord	Harper	SATB	M/D	LOL	
Judge eternal	Archer	SATB	M		Mayhew
Now is eternal life	Lloyd	SAMen	E/M	AOAN1	
O clap your hands	Rutter	SATB	M/D	AC4	OUP
O clap your hands	Vaughan Williams	SATB	M/D	AC4	OUP
O God, the King of glory	Purcell	SATB unacc	E	APA, ETAS	OUP
Oculi omnium	Wood	SATB unacc	E	NSAC1	RSCM
Rejoice, the Lord is king	Archer	SATB	M		Mayhew
Rejoice, the Lord is king	Kelly	SATB	M/D	NNAB, MTH1	
Zion, at thy shining gates	Trad arr Guest	SATB	E	AFC	
FIVE OR MORE PARTS					
Lift up your heads, O ye gates	Leighton	SSATB	M		Novello
O clap your hands	Gibbons	SSAATTBB unacc	D	OBTA	OUP
The Lord is King	Radcliffe	SATBB	M		Encore

ORGAN MUSIC

PRELUDES

Adams T.   **Larghetto from Voluntary No.3** in *Organ Works Vol.5: Six Organ Voluntaries* (Fagus) M*
Moore P.   **Fantasie-Aria 'St Elisabeth'** in *The Recitalist's Repertoire* Bk.1 (Mayhew) M/D
Vierne L.   **Canon No.6** in *24 Pièces en Style Libre* Bk.1 (Masters, Durand) E/M(*)
Willan H.   **Prelude on 'Nicea'** in *36 Short Preludes and Postludes* Set 1 (Peters) E*
Young G.   **Benedictus on 'Sicilian Mariners'** in *Eight Organ Voluntaries* (Presser) E/M

POSTLUDES

Adams T.   **Fugue from Voluntary No.3** in *Organ Works Vol.5: Six Organ Voluntaries* (Fagus) M*
Nixon J.   **Carlisle** in *Hymn Tune Preludes* (Fagus) E/M
Thalben-Ball G.   **Gwalchmai** No.33 of *113 Variations on Hymn Tunes* (Novello) E
Thiman E.   **Postlude on 'Regent Square'** in *Five Hymn Tune Variants* (Curwen) E/M

PROPER 18 (SUNDAY BETWEEN 4 AND 10 SEPTEMBER INCLUSIVE) YEAR C

HYMNS AND SONGS

	pos	rdg	AMNS	CAON	CFE	CH4	CH5	CP	H&P	HTC	LAU	MP	NEH	SG	SOF	TS
Adoramus te, Domine (Taizé)				921	11		345				667			208		
All I once held dear		n		18		506						799		562	646	11
All over the world the Spirit is moving		o		20							984	18			12	12
As water to the thirsty		n						252		470		803		553	659	
Break thou the bread of life	cm	n					379	286	467			64			50	
Come, my Way, my Truth, my Life	cm	n		123		579	610	405	254		911		633			
Father of mercies, in thy word		n	167							247				224		
God has spoken – by his prophets		n					381		64	248	742	831		225		
God of love, you freely give us		n		226												
Hark, my soul! It is the Lord/ Christian, do you hear		n	244	264			569	457	521	472		209	637			
Help us, O Lord, to learn		n	373				382	460	474	493			370	226		
How sure the Scriptures are		n								249				227		
Immortal, invisible, God only wise		n	199	314	301	132	6	474	9	21	725	327	377	44	234	220
In God alone my soul (Taizé)															813	
Jesus, restore to us again		n										873			876	295
Lord, for the years		o		409		159	81	81		328	942	428	619	602	892	327
May the mind of Christ my Saviour		n		447		536	636	521	739	550		463		671	1448	887
Not far beyond the sea, nor high		n	401					528	477							
O for a heart to praise my God		o	230	484			638	533	536	483		495	74	149	411	904
Peace is flowing like a river		o		553	595						902	554			458	
Praise the Lord of heaven (Dudley-Smith)		o		568					507							
Revive thy work/your church, O Lord!		o					308		780	515		578				
Rise and hear! The Lord is speaking		n	509				385	321								
Thanks/Praise to God whose word was spoken		n	423			605	387	584	483	255			438	229		
The heavens declare thy glory, Lord		n	168					264	481	254				230		
The prophets spoke in days of old		n	513					327								
This is the day the Lord hath made		n	22	677				9	577	379			257	70		
Thou/God, whose almighty word		n	180	684	738	112	324	267	29	506	887	699	466	597	557	
We believe in God the Father (Dudley-Smith)		n					363						286			
When the King shall come again		o		806						200	90					
Will you come and follow me		n		752	812	533	605	622				877	647	634	1120	

SONGS FOR CHILDREN

Have you heard the raindrops CAON 817, CH 78, CAP 2, CH4 525, JP 71, KS 99
Holy Spirit (pour your power) KS 515

2013   eP 267.
                405
                457
                533

BIBLE READINGS

Psalms [120 and] 121
Isaiah 43.14 - 44.5
John 5.30–47

SINGING THE PSALM

Psalm 120 CWP, NPCW
Psalm 121 CH4, CRP, CWP, H&P, MCW1, NEP, NPCW, PAME, PFS
    Bell *Lifting my eyes up to the hills* PPP
    Haugen *I lift up my eyes (Pilgrim's Song)* C (GIA)#

ANTHEMS AND VOCAL MUSIC

Title	Composer	Voices	E/M/D	Book source	Single sheet publisher
UNISON/TWO PART/HIGH VOICES					
Settings of the Benedictus (The Song of Zechariah)	Various	U/SATB	E	CWP, MCW1, NEP	
As the deer longs	Hurd	U/SATB#	E	CFE, CG, CH4, LAU	OCP
Come to the well	Farrell	U#	E	GBU	
Hark! a messenger is calling	Kelly	3 part	E/M	CFL	
Just like the deer	Ogden	U#	E/M		WLP
The Song of the Tree of Life	Vaughan Williams	2 part	E	AC2	OUP
Water of life	Dean	U#	E	CFE, CSF, LAU, NEP	OCP
Your love is finer than life	Haugen	U/SSA#	E	LAU	GIA
THREE/FOUR PARTS					
As water to the thirsty	Coleman arr Barnard	SATB	E	SC, WIS	
God has spoken	Trad arr Llewellyn	SATB	E	SWAMS	
How beauteous are their feet	Stanford	SATB	M	AOAN1 (SAMen), ASA, NNAB, SC	Novello
How beautiful upon the mountains	Stainer	SATB	M	AOAN1 (SAMen), BC, NNAB	RSCM
How lovely are the messengers	Mendelssohn	SATB	M	AFC	Novello
I heard the voice of Jesus say	Shephard	SATB	M		RSCM
Like as the hart	Croft	SAB	E	CHM	
Like as the hart	Howells	SATB	M	AC4	OUP
Like as the hart	Rawsthorne	SATB	E/M	AWTE	
O God, thou art my God	Purcell	SATB	M	SC	
On Jordan's bank	Trad arr Archer	SATB	E	AFC	
Sicut cervus	Palestrina	SATB unacc	M	ESM, SL(ATTB)	Chester
The dove descending breaks the air	Stravinsky	SATB	D		B&H
Thy word is a lantern	Purcell	SATB	M	APA	Novello
FIVE OR MORE PARTS					
Canite tuba	Palestrina	SSATB unacc	M	CM12	
Deus, Deus meus	R.Panufnik	SSAATTBB + solo S	D		Universal
Vox dicentis, clama	Naylor	SATB + SATB unacc	D		Curwen

ORGAN MUSIC

PRELUDES

Bairstow E.	**No.3** of *Three Short Preludes* (Banks) E/M
Reger M.	**Seelenbräutigam** Op.67/37 in *Complete Works* Vol.7 (Breitkopf) E/M
Stanford C.V.	**On an old Irish church melody** ('St Columba') No.6 of *Six Short Preludes and Postludes* (Set 1) Op.101 (Stainer); also in *Preludes and Postludes* (Mayhew) E
Warren N.	**Laetatus sum** in *Playing Them In & Playing Them Out* (Mayhew; 2 and 3-stave editions available) E(*)
Zipoli D.	**Canzona in D minor** in *Sonate d'Intavolature* (Süddeutscher Musikverlag) E/M*

POSTLUDES

Cameron J.G.	**Fantasia on 'St Denio'** (Novello) M
Gibbs A.	**Exuberance** from *Peacehaven Preludes* (Bardic) E/M*
Manz P.	**Joyful, joyful we adore thee** ('Ode to Joy') in *Two Pieces for Festive Occasions* (MorningStar) E/M
Piutti C.	**Sollt ich meinem Gott nicht singen?** in *Praise and Thanks* (Bärenreiter) E/M

PROPER 19 (SUNDAY BETWEEN 11 AND 17 SEPTEMBER INCLUSIVE) YEAR C

HYMNS AND SONGS

	pos	rdg	AMNS	CAON	CFE	CH4	CH5	CP	H&P	HTC	LAU	MP	NEH	SG	SOF	TS
All my heart this night rejoices		o						43	91	76						
Author of life divine	cm	n	258	56				281	596	395			274			
Awake, awake: fling off the night!		o	342	57	64			334			851					
Be known to us in breaking bread/O Lord, you gave	cm	n					401	282	597		410				669	
Behold, the darkness (Arise, shine)		o										36			38	
Bless the Lord, my soul (Taizé)				923	81		1				813			105	676	
Bread of heaven, on thee we feed		n	271	82				284		398			276	464		
Bread of life, hope of the world	cm	n			95	663				78			484			
Bread of the world in mercy broken	cm	n	270	83	97		403	285	599	396			277	465		
Break thou the bread of life	cm	n					379	286	467		64				50	
Broken for me, broken for you		n		87			404	287		S 6	66			485	53	58
Come, ye faithful/Alleluia, raise the anthem			145	131			84	409	813	205		103	351	25		
Darkness like a shroud (Arise, shine)		o										110			78	
Draw near/nigh and take the body of the Lord	cm	n			150		411	296		401	628		281			
Eat this bread/Jesus Christ, bread of life (Taizé)		g		926	151	661					633				1221	
Faithful Shepherd, feed me	cm	n		156			644		29				282	498		
Great is the darkness		o										835		264	742	136
I am the bread of life		n		299	271/2		420		611		629	261		200		
I come with joy		n	473	304		656	421	305	610	408	649		623	469		
Light's abode, celestial Salem		o	185	398			672	502					401			
Longing for light (Christ, be our light)		o				543					883					1409
Lord, enthroned in heavenly splendour	of	n	263	408	379		431	311	616	416	769	431	296	52	352	870
My God, and/now is thy table spread?		n	259	456	496		433	313		418	651			474		
Now is eternal life		n	402	470			392	152	203				114			
Now let us from this table rise	pc	n	403	472		675	436	315	619	419	647			475		
Spread, O spread, thou mighty word		o											482			
The Lord is my light (Taizé)				944												
The people that in darkness/The race that long		o	52	656	711	290	199	38	89	71	168		57			
This is the body of Christ		n				799										
To him we come		o								518		709		679	1569	
Ye that know the Lord is gracious		o	175			642	493	628					477			

SONGS FOR CHILDREN

I am a lighthouse JP 87, KS 114, SOF 196
Jesus the Lord said, 'I am the bread' H&P 137, LAU 746, MP 384

BIBLE READINGS

Psalms 124, 125
Isaiah 60
John 6.51–69

SINGING THE PSALM

Psalm 124 CH4, CWP, NPCW, PAME
Psalm 125 CWP, NPCW

ANTHEMS AND VOCAL MUSIC

Title	Composer	Voices	E/M/D	Book source	Single sheet publisher
UNISON/TWO PART/HIGH VOICES					
Arise, shine for thy light is come	How	2 part + cong	E/M		Ionian
Arise, shine!	Haugen	2 part + instrs	E		GIA
Ave verum	Poulenc	SSA	M/D		Salabert
Bread for the world	Farrell	U#	E	GBAN	OCP
Holy manna from above	Trad arr Warner	U	E	C	
One in body, heart and mind	Walker	U/SATB#	E	ATNJ, SFL2 (SAB)	OCP
THREE/FOUR PARTS					
Arise, shine	Rutter	SATB	M/D		OUP
Arise, shine	Shephard	SATB	E/M	SBS1	RSCM
Arise, shine, for your light has come	Mathias	SATB	M		Banks
Arise, shine, O Jerusalem	Palestrina arr Jackson, Moore	SATB	E	ETAS	
Arise, shine, O Zion	Greene	SATB	M		Banks
Ave verum	Byrd	SATB unacc	M	NCAB, NSAC2, OBTA	OUP
Ave verum	Elgar	SATB	M	BC, NCAB	RSCM
Ave verum	Mozart	SATB	M	MHWE, NCAB, NOEAB, NSAC1	RSCM
Christ, our God, descends from heaven	Bullard	SAMen	E	SBS2	
Ego sum panis vivus	Byrd	SATB unacc	M		Chester
Ego sum panis vivus	Palestrina	SATB unacc	M	CM1	Chester
Panis angelicus	Franck	SATB	M	ESM, FAB4	
Panis angelicus	Saint-Saëns	SATB	E	NCAB	
Take and eat	Ogden	SATB unacc	E		WLP
The Holy Eucharist	Harris	SATB	E		Banks
Verily, verily I say unto you	Tallis	SATB unacc	E	AC1, SBS2, TA	OUP
FIVE OR MORE PARTS					
Christ is the morning star	Carter	SSAATTBB	D		OUP
Surge illuminare	Palestrina	SATB + SATB unacc	M		Chester
Surge illuminare	Simpson	SSAATTBB unacc	M/D	CN	

ORGAN MUSIC

PRELUDES

Bach J.S.   **Adagio** from BWV 564 in Novello Vol.9, Bärenreiter Vol.6, Peters Vol.3 E/M
Pachelbel J.   **Wo Gott der Herr nicht bei uns hält** in *Manual Miscellany* Bk.2 (Elkin) E*
Vaughan Williams R.   **Prelude on 'Rhosymedre'** in *Three Preludes on Welsh Hymn Tunes* (OUP) E/M
Vierne L.   **Matines** from *Triptyque* Op.58 (Lemoine) E/M
Walford Davies H.   **Interlude in C** (Ramsey) M

POSTLUDES

Adlung J.   **Christus, der ist mein Leben** in *Orgelmusik um J.S.Bach* (Breitkopf) E/M
Hanff J.N.   **Wär Gott nicht mit uns diese Zeit** in *Choralvorspiele alter Meister* (Peters) M
Lebègue N.   **Offertoire** (Basse de trompette) p.1 in *Offertoires from Troisième Livre d'Orgue* (Hawthorns) E/M*
Young G.   **Plein jeu à la Couperin** from *Baroque Suite* (Flammer) M

PROPER 20 (SUNDAY BETWEEN 18 AND 24 SEPTEMBER INCLUSIVE) YEAR C

HYMNS AND SONGS

	pos	rdg	AMNS	CAON	CFE	CH4	CH5	CP	H&P	HTC	LAU	MP	NEH	SG	SOF	TS
Angel voices, ever singing		o	163	37	45	498	346	377	484	307	724	34	336	27	24	
At/In the name of Jesus		n	148	54	59	458	94	380	74	172	762	41	338	317	32	33
Christ is made the sure foundation/Blessèd city		o	332ii	97	109	200	326	207/208	485	559	456	73	205	572	1199	654
Christ is our cornerstone		o	161	98			327	395		564			206	14		
Christ triumphant, ever reigning		n		104	113	436	259	398		173	763	77	613	319	62	655
Come, my Way, my Truth, my Life	cm	n		123		579	610	405	254		911		633			
Father eternal, Lord of the ages		n								1			356			
God is here, as we his people		o	464				330	301	653	560	470					
Happy are they, they that love God		n	176	262			649	456	711	473			369			
Help us, O Lord, to learn		n	373				382	460	474	493			370	226		
Jesu, my Lord, my God, my all (Collins)	cm	n					583	483		476			384			
Jesus, hope of every nation		n								58				336		
Jesus is the name we honour		n				481						870		122	870	285
Jesus shall take the highest honour		n		360									378	123	302	296
Jesus, stand among us at the meeting of our lives		n		361			424						381		303	
Jesus, stand among us in thy risen power		n		362			338		530	364			380		304	
Jesus, the name high over all		n		364			99		264	213			385	323	307	298
Let us build a house (All are welcome)		o				198					458					
O changeless Christ, for ever new		n			518					108	745			374		
O Christ the same through all our story's pages		n		477			103			263			258			
O Christe Domine Jesu (Taizé)		n			519						757					
Open our eyes, Lord		n		532								545			443	1468
There is a Redeemer		n		658		559	112					673		396	544	492
Thou art the Christ, O Lord		n	317					236					172			
To the name of our/that brings salvation		n	121	698	749	471	117	610	80	222			470	72		
We love the place, O God		o	160	718			343	211		558		731	471			
You are the King of glory		n		762	822								790		627	
You, living Christ, our eyes behold		n	533				333						487			

SONGS FOR CHILDREN

Holy Spirit (pour your power) KS 515
Jesus before me, Jesus beside me CH4 576

22 Sept 2013

BIBLE READINGS

Psalms [128 and] 129
Ezra 1
John 7.14–36

SINGING THE PSALM

Psalm 128 CRP, CWP, NPCW, PAME
  Dean *O blest are they* VE#
  Inwood *O blessed are those* LAU, LMOL, VE#
Psalm 129 CWP, NPCW

ANTHEMS AND VOCAL MUSIC

Title	Composer	Voices	E/M/D	Book source	Single sheet publisher
UNISON/TWO PART/HIGH VOICES					
I am the bread of life	Lole	U + descant	E	BC	RSCM
I was glad	Hubbard	SA	M	SFJ	Banks
We love the place, O God	Brahms	SS	M		Novello
THREE/FOUR PARTS					
And when the builders	Shephard	SATB	M/D		Banks
Angel voices	Shephard	SATB	E/M	SC	RSCM
Behold, the tabernacle of God	Harris	SATB	E/M		RSCM
Behold, the tabernacle of God	Rutter	SATB	M/D		OUP
Blessed city, heavenly Salem	Bairstow	SATB	D		Banks
Christ is our cornerstone	Ogden	SATB	E	SBS2	RSCM
Christ is our cornerstone	Thorne	SATB	E/M	NOEAB	
How lovely are thy dwellings	Brahms	SATB	M/D		RSCM
How lovely are thy dwellings	Self	SAB	E		RSCM
How lovely is your dwelling place	Hubbard	SATB	M	GAW	Banks
I am the bread of life	Lole	SATB	E	SBS1, WIS	RSCM
Locus iste	Bruckner	SATB unacc	E/M	NCAB, ESM	RSCM
Locus iste	O'Regan	SATB unacc	M		OUP
O how amiable	Vaughan Williams	SATB	E/M	NCAB, AC4, OEAB	OUP
O pray for the peace of Jerusalem	Goss	SATB	M	AC1	
O pray for the peace of Jerusalem	Howells	SATB	M		OUP
The Church triumphant	Shephard	SATB	E/M	SBS1	RSCM
We love the place, O God	Sumsion	SATB	M/D		RSCM
FIVE OR MORE PARTS					
Behold, O God our defender	Howells	SSAATTBB	M/D	MTP	Novello
I was glad	Parry	SATB + SATB	M/D		RSCM

ORGAN MUSIC

PRELUDES

Gigault N.   **Benedictus** p.44 in *Organ Book* Vol.1 (Kalmus) E(*)
Milford R.   **Chorale Prelude 'St Columba'** in *A Book of Wedding Pieces* (OUP) E/M
Nixon J.   **Caswall** in *Hymn Tune Preludes* (Fagus) E/M
Stanford C.V.   **Pastorale** Op.189/1 (Novello) M

POSTLUDES

Fletcher A.   **Blaenwern** in *Preludes on Favourite Hymns* (Mayhew; 2 and 3-stave editions available) E/M
Guilmant A.   **Tempo di Minuetto in C** Op.45/4 in *Complete Works* Vol.2 (Belwin) and in *An Organ Miscellany* (Mayhew) M
Smith A.   **Recessional on 'Love unknown'** (Escorial) E/M
Thalben-Ball G. **Oriel** No.70 of *113 Variations on Hymn Tunes* (Novello) E/M
Wesley S.   **Voluntary in C** No.11 in *Organ Works* Vol.10 (Fagus) E/M*

HYMNS AND SONGS

	pos	rdg	AMNS	CAON	CFE	CH4	CH5	CP	H&P	HTC	LAU	MP	NEH	SG	SOF	TS
And can it be that I should gain		n		32	43	396	218	376	216	588	790	33	*627*	168	21	21
And did those feet in ancient time		o	294	33	44			353					488			
At even ere the sun was set	ev	n	9	50			65	12	142	315		43	243	487		
Bread of life, hope of the world	cm	n			95	663				78			484			
Children of the heavenly King		o	213							566			344			
Christ is the world's true light		n	346	100		456	501	396	456	323			494	432		
Eternal ruler of the ceaseless round		n	353	154		269		181					355			
Freedom and life are ours		n								544				171		
How beauteous/gracious are their feet		o	301					220	449							
How lovely on the mountains (Our God reigns)		o		295	268		129				768	249			192	189
I vow to thee, my country		o	295		286	704		355					*620*			
Jesu, the very thought of thee		n	120	368	321	560	101	485	265	478	798	386	385	534	308	
Laudate omnes gentes/Sing praises, all you peoples (Taizé)											478				1515	
Lord, for the years		o		409		159	81	81		328	942	428	*619*	602	892	327
Lord, the light of your love is shining		n		419	388	448	195	513			770	445		614	362	335
Make way, make way, for Christ the king		n		438	479	279	134				819	457			384	349
My Lord, you wore no royal crown		n								118				628		
O Jesu, King most wonderful		n	120ii				106	539	269	484			386			
O Son of God, eternal love		n											428			
Prayer is the soul's sincere desire		o				546	625	561	557	372		567	442			
Psallite Domino (Taizé)		ps			614											
Restore, O Lord, the honour		o		582		469						579		274	483	439
Rise and hear! The Lord is speaking		n	509				385	321								
Saviour, again to thy dear name we raise	ev		15	587		221	71	20	643	281		584	250			
The God of Abraham praise		n	331	642		162	323	586	452	9	712	645	148	66	530	975
The kingdom is upon you!		n	512					590					*650*			
There's a wideness in God's mercy/Souls of men/ Restless souls		n	251	662		187	9	598	230	443	810	683	461/ *700*	188		
Thou didst leave thy throne		n	250	683			114	601	154			697	465		555	1015

SONGS FOR CHILDREN

Make way, make way CAON 438, CFE 479, CH4 279, CH5 134, JP 427, KS 249, LAU 819, MP 457, SOF 384, TS 349
Sent by the Lord am I CFE 638, CG 105, CH4 250, IECS, LAU 855, SBTL, SG 616

BIBLE READINGS
Psalms 134, 135*
Nehemiah 2
John 8.31–38,48–59

SINGING THE PSALM
Psalm 134 CWP, LAU, MCW1, NPCW
    White *Praise the Lord, all ye servants of the Lord* CH4
Psalm 135* CWP, NPCW

ANTHEMS AND VOCAL MUSIC

Title	Composer	Voices	E/M/D	Book source	Single sheet publisher
UNISON/TWO PART/HIGH VOICES					
A Prayer of St Richard of Chichester	White	2 part	E	BC, OEAB	OUP
Centre of my life	Inwood	U/SATB#	E	CFE, CSF, LAU, SG	OCP
Christ whose glory fills the skies	Knight	S	M		RSCM
Day by day	How	U + 2 part	E	BC	RSCM
Give us the wings of faith	Blatchly	SS	M	HP	
O rest in the Lord (Elijah)	Mendelssohn	U	M		Novello
You are the centre	Rizza	U/SATB#	E	FOL	Mayhew
THREE/FOUR PARTS					
A Prayer of St Richard of Chichester	Archer	SATB	E		RSCM
Christ is our cornerstone	Thorne	SATB	E/M	NOEAB	
Christ whose glory fills the skies	Darke	SATB	M	SBS1	RSCM
Firmly I believe and truly	Shephard	SAMen	E	SFL2	
Give us the wings of faith	Bullock	SATB	M	AC4, FSB10	OUP
Go forth and tell!	Ogden	SATB	E	SBS2	RSCM
Grow in grace	Archer	SATB	E/M	SBS1	RSCM
Holy Spirit, truth divine	Carter	SATB	E/M	ETAS, NOEAB	OUP
If ye love me	Tallis	SATB unacc	E	FAB1, NCAB, NOEAB, NSAC1, OBTA, TA, SL (AATB)	OUP
My soul, there is a country	Parry	SATB unacc	D	SC	RSCM
O God the King of glory	Purcell	SATB	E/M	ETAS, APA	OUP
O Lord, increase our faith	Loosemore	SATB (unacc)	E	SBS1, NCAB	RSCM
The Song of Christ's Glory	P.Moore	SATB	E		RSCM
Thou God of truth and love	Archer	SATB	M		Mayhew
Thou, O Jehovah, abideth forever	Copland	SATB unacc	M/D		B&H
Though you do not now see Christ	Ferguson	SATB unacc	M		Encore
To be a pilgrim	Burt	SAMen	E/M	OBFA	
FIVE OR MORE PARTS					
The Song of Christ's Glory	Ives	SSAATTBB unacc	M/D	WOTC	

ORGAN MUSIC

PRELUDES
Boëllmann L.   **Prélude pastorale** from *Deuxième Suite* (Kalmus, Butz, Durand); also in *Complete Works* Vol.2 (Bärenreiter) E/M

Bonighton R.   **Song 1** in *Preludes on Favourite Hymns* and in *Preludes on Favourite Hymns for Manuals* (both Mayhew) E/M(*)

Fink C.   **Freu' dich sehr** Op.32/1 in *The Mendelssohn School* (McAfee) M

Guilmant A.   **Adagio from 3rd Sonata** Op.56 (Schott, Willemsen, Belwin-Mills, Dover, Bärenreiter); also 2-stave version in *Organ Music for Manuals* (Dover) E/M

Watson S.   **Pastorale** in *An Easy Album* Bk.1 (OUP) E/M

POSTLUDES
Fischer M.G.   **Fugue in D for full organ** in *Easy Organ Pieces from the 19th C* (Bärenreiter) E/M*

Karg-Elert S.   **Sollt ich meinem Gott nicht singen?** No.17 of *20 Preludes and Postludes* Op.78 (Breitkopf) M

Guilmant A.   **Preludio from 3rd Sonata** Op.56 (Schott, Willemsen, Belwin-Mills, Dover, Bärenreiter); also 2-stave version in *Organ Music for Manuals* (Dover) M

Spedding A.   **Carillon** ('Leoni') in *Recuerdos* (IAO) E/M

PROPER 22 (SUNDAY BETWEEN 2 AND 8 OCTOBER INCLUSIVE) YEAR C

HYMNS AND SONGS

	pos	rdg	AMNS	CAON	CFE	CH4	CH5	CP	H&P	HTC	LAU	MP	NEH	SG	SOF	TS
Amazing grace		n		29	40	555	642	375	215	28	846	31	*626*	26	19	18
Awake, awake, fling off the night		n	342	57	64			334			851					
Beauty for brokenness		o		60		259	494					806		263	664	37
Christ is the world's true light		n	346	100		456	501	396	456	323			494	432		
Christ whose glory fills the skies	m	n	4	105		578	52	2	457	266	670	79	234	170	1200	
Come, Holy Ghost, our souls inspire		n	93	118		586	296	178	283	589		90	138	555		
Father of mercies, in thy word		n	167							247			224			
God of freedom, God of justice		o		224		263		447								
He gave his life in selfless love		n					417			405		214		467		
I heard the voice of Jesus say		n	247	310		540	576	469	136		795	275	376		215	206
I'll praise my Maker while I've breath		n					357	473	439	20		320		84		
Immortal, invisible, God only wise	ga	o	199	314	301	132	6	474	9	21	725	327	377	44	234	220
In heavenly love abiding		n		323		551		478	678	458		331	*638*		238	782
Inspired by love and anger		o		325	311	253										
Jesu, the very thought of thee		n	120	368	321	560	101	485	265	478	798	386	385	534	308	
Judge eternal, throned in splendour		o		372		264	535	356	409	329		395	490	600		
Lord, I was blind, I could not see		n							423	437		433				
Lord, we long for you (Heal our nation)		o										448		254	365	337
My song is love unknown		n	63	463	503	399	231	112	173	136	752	478	86	384	400	897
O for a thousand tongues to sing		n	125	485		352	104	534	744	219		496	415	55	412	383/1452
O Jesu, King most wonderful		n	120ii				106	539	269	484			386			
O Lord, hear my prayer (Taizé)				938	542		620					929	908		246	423	394
Praise, my soul, the King of heaven	ga	o	192	565	602	160	366	555	13	38	807	560	436	93	466	433
Restore, O Lord, the honour		o		582		469						579		274	483	439
Tell out, my soul		o	422	631	684	286	712	362	86	42	880	631	186	62	520	471
The/All earth was dark (Lights to the world)		s										8/643				
The Lord will come, and not be slow		o	29	655			140	37	245				15			
Thou/God, whose almighty word		n	180	684	738	112	324	267	29	506	887	699	466	597	557	
Thy/ Your kingdom come! On bended knee		o	178	690		473		608					500			
To God be the glory!		n		695	745	512	373	609	463	584	719	708		71	559	526

SONGS FOR CHILDREN

Colours of day CAP 55, CFE 118, CH 33, JP 28, KS2 433, LAU 764, MP 1039, SOF 64, TS 69

Jesus the Lord said, 'I am the bread' H&P 137, IECS, LAU 746, MP 384

Open our eyes, Lord CAON 532, KS 278, MP 545, SOF 443, TS 1468

BIBLE READINGS
Psalm 142
Nehemiah 5.1–13
John 9

SINGING THE PSALM
Psalm 142 CWP, NPCW

ANTHEMS AND VOCAL MUSIC

Title	Composer	Voices	E/M/D	Book source	Single sheet publisher
UNISON/TWO PART/HIGH VOICES					
Amazing grace	Trad arr Jones	U + descant	E	RTF	
Be light for our eyes	Haas	U/SAB#	E	CFE	GIA
Bread of life (Lent verses)	Farrell	U/SATB#	E	HIG, RITH	OCP
Christ, be our light	Farrell	U#	E	CBL, CG, CH4, LAU, TS	OCP
Lift on high	Ogden	U/SATB#	E		WLP
Make me a light	Wilby	SS	E	EAC2, HP	Chester
Out of darkness	Walker	U/SATB#	E	CFE, LAU, OOD	OCP
The Spirit of the Lord is upon me	Corp	2 part	E	VFLS	
Word of God, burn within us	Hurd	U#	E	C	
THREE/FOUR PARTS					
Ad te levavi oculos meos	Palestrina	SATB unacc	M		OUP
Be thou my vision	Chilcott	SATB	M	NOEAB, BCA	OUP
Be thou my vision	Rutter	SATB	M		OUP
I heard the voice of Jesus say	Shephard	SATB	M		RSCM
In a world where people walk in darkness	Trad arr Harper	SATB	E	LOL	
O for a thousand tongues	Shephard	SATB	M/D		RSCM
O thou the central orb	Wood	SATB	M	AC4, AFC, SC	RSCM
Oculi omnium	Wood	SATB unacc	E	ETAS, NSAC1	RSCM
Open our eyes	Reith	SATB (unacc)	E	C	
The Lord is my light and my salvation	Noon	SATB	M	SBS1	RSCM
The Lord is my light and my salvation	Rutter	SATB + solo T + clarinet	M		OUP
The Spirit of the Lord	Elgar	SATB	M	SAEE	RSCM
We cannot measure how you heal	Bell arr Archer	SATB	E	BC	RSCM
Wings of the morning	Rutter	SATB	M		OUP
FIVE OR MORE PARTS					
Oculi omnium	Cleobury	SSAATTBB unacc	M		Encore
Open thou mine eyes	Rutter	SSATB unacc	M		OUP

ORGAN MUSIC

PRELUDES
Anon.   **Double Voluntary** in *Early English Organ Music* Vol.2 (OUP) M*
Du Mage P.   **Tierce en taille** from *Première Livre d'Orgue* (Kalmus) E/M
Groves R.   **Praise, my soul** in *12 Hymn-Tune Preludes* Set 1 (Novello) E(*)
Langlais J.   **Pastoral Song** No.II from *Organ Book* (Elkan-Vogel); also in *A Graded Anthology for Organ* Bk.3 (Cramer) E
Ropartz G.   **No.2** of *Trois Méditations* (Durand) E/M

POSTLUDES
Manz P.   **Praise, my soul, the king of heaven** in *Two Pieces for Festive Occasions* (MorningStar) M
Telemann G.P   **Fugue No.10** in *The Progressive Organist* Bk.5 (Novello) E/M
Watson R.   **Toccatina** *or* **Trumpet Tune** from *Suite for Mrs Thing* (Fagus) E
Wesley S.   **Voluntary III in C minor** Op.6 No.3 in *Twelve Voluntaries for Organ* Op.6 Bk.1 (Fagus) E/M*

HYMNS AND SONGS

	pos	rdg	AMNS	CAON	CFE	CH4	CH5	CP	H&P	HTC	LAU	MP	NEH	SG	SOF	TS
A/The new commandment		n		35	4		515			S 26	920	1			22	23
Be bold, be strong		o										49			37	38
Be still and know I (John Bell)		n												18	672	
Be still and know II (John Bell)		n			70	754								242		
Be still and know that I am God		n		66	71	755	608				909	48			41	48
Be thou my vision/Lord, be my vision		o	343	70	74/75	465	643	386	378	545	970	51	339	669	42	50
Come down, O love divine		n	156	114	125	489	294	175	281	231	303	89	137	663	1202	71
Deck thyself, my soul, with gladness/Soul, array thyself		n	257	146			445	295	606	400			280			
Do not be afraid, for I have redeemed you		o		150	147	191					972	115			1213	1183
Fear not, for I am with you		o													105	
For all the saints who from their labours rest		o	305	177	176	740	459	232	814	567	371	148	197	636	109	684
Forth in the peace of Christ we go	se	n	458	187	183	646	454	429		542	853		361	594		
God is love, and where true love is		n	465		214		520	441	757		242		513			
God is our strength and refuge		o		219			12	443		527		188		650		699
God of grace and God of glory		o	367	225			533	448	712	324		192		574	139	
Great/Lord God, your love has called us here		n	489	246		484	416	133	500	480						
Here is love, vast as the ocean		n					222					987		174	168	164
I come with joy		n	473	304		656	421	305	610	408	649		623	469		
In Christ alone my hope is found		o										1072			1346	1311
In heavenly love abiding		n		323		551		478	678	458		331	638		238	782
In the Lord I'll be ever thankful (Taizé)				929	308	772					944	865		656	817	
Lord, I come to you (Power of your love)		n										880	689		895	329
Love divine, all loves excelling		n	131	428	398	519	634	516	267	217	801	449	408	179	377	343
Sing of the Lord's goodness		o			654	157	368				713			61		
The Son of God proclaim		n	427				328	627	415	650			482			
There's a spirit in the air		n	515	661		616	314	198	326	245				69		
Ubi caritas/Living charity (Taizé)		n		946		801	530				245				1573	
What a friend we have in Jesus		n		727		547	627		559	373		746		646	593	566
Who would true valour see/He who would valiant be		o	212	281	248	535	662	621	688	590	862	224	372	639	174	

SONGS FOR CHILDREN

Be bold, be strong JP 14, KS 17, MP 49, SOF 37, TS 38
Come on and celebrate CAON 125, CH 35, CH5 328, JP 325, KS 34, MP 99, SOF 73, TS 75
Our God is a God who makes friends CH4 792

BIBLE READINGS
Psalm 144
Nehemiah 6.1–16
John 15.12–27

SINGING THE PSALM
Psalm 144 CWP, NPCW

ANTHEMS AND VOCAL MUSIC

Title	Composer	Voices	E/M/D	Book source	Single sheet publisher
UNISON/TWO PART/HIGH VOICES					
A Song of St Francis	Hurd	SSA	M/D	EAC2	
Faith, hope and love	Ogden	2 part	E	SBS1	RSCM
God is always there	Plainsong arr Bullard	2 part	E	OBFA	
Jesu, Jesu, fill us with your love	Trad arr Weaver	2 part	E	IECS, SFL1	
Love one another	S.S.Wesley	S	E	BC	
Prayer of St Benedict	Payne	2 part	E	VFLS	
The Father's love	Lole	SS	E/M	EAC2	RSCM
The Servant Song	Gillard arr Ogden	2 part	E	SFL1	
Ubi caritas	Lole	SS	M		Encore
THREE/FOUR PARTS					
Anima mea	M. de Rivafrecha	SATB unacc	E/M	CM3	Chester
Arise, my love	Martinson	SATB unacc	M/D	WFC	
Beloved, let us love	Aston	SATB unacc	D		RSCM
Greater love	Ireland	SATB	M	AC4	S&B
In the heart where love is abiding	Barnard	SATB	E	AWTE, BC	RSCM
Love divine	Willcocks	SATB	E	NOEAB	
Love one another	Carter	SATB	D		OUP
Lord, make me an instrument of your peace	Aston	SATB	E/M		RSCM
My beloved is mine	Lole	SATB unacc	M		Encore
O voice of the beloved	Ives	SATB	M	SBS2	RSCM
Set me as a seal	Walton	SATB	M/D	AC4, WFC	OUP
Strengthen ye the weak hands	Harris	SATB	M		Novello
Though I speak with the tongues of men	Bairstow	SATB	M	FSB10, NCAB, WFC	OUP
Thy perfect love	Rutter	SATB	E/M	NOEAB	OUP
Ubi caritas	Ives	SATB unacc	M	SC	
FIVE OR MORE PARTS					
Ubi caritas	Berkeley	SSATB unacc	D		Chester
Ubi caritas	Duruflé	SAATTBB unacc	M		Durand

ORGAN MUSIC

PRELUDES
Armstrong Gibbs C.   **Quiet Thoughts** No.1 of *Six Sketches* Bk.2 (OUP) E/M
De Grigny N.   **Récit de tierce en taille** p.17 in *Livre d'Orgue* (Kalmus, Schott) M
Slater G.   **Prelude 'St Botolph'** (OUP archive) E
Sumsion H.   **Variations on a Folk Tune** (RSCM) M
Valeri G.   **Sonata No.6: Siciliano** in *Italian Organ Music of the 18th C* (Flammer) E/M*

POSTLUDES
Armstrong Gibbs C.   **Processional March** No.3 of *Six Sketches* Bk.2 (OUP) E/M
Bach A.W.   **Fantasie in G minor** in *Berliner Orgelmusik des 19 Jahrhunderts* (Breitkopf) M
Tambling C.   **Processional** in *An Organ Miscellany* (Mayhew) E/M
Zipoli D.   **Al Post Communio** in *Sonate d'Intavolature* (Süddeutscher Musikverlag) E/M*

PROPER 24 (SUNDAY BETWEEN 16 AND 22 OCTOBER INCLUSIVE) YEAR C

HYMNS AND SONGS

	pos	rdg	AMNS	CAON	CFE	CH4	CH5	CP	H&P	HTC	LAU	MP	NEH	SG	SOF	TS
Come down, O love divine		n	156	114	125	489	294	175	281	231	303	89	137	663	1202	71
Come, gracious Spirit, heavenly dove		n	153	116		587	295	176					347			
Come, Holy Ghost, our souls inspire		n	93	118		586	296	178	283	589		90	138	555		
Come, Holy Spirit, descend on us		n				589					304	818		19		1168
Come, my Way, my Truth, my Life	cm	o		123		579	610	405	254		911		*633*			
Father of mercies, in thy word		o	167							247				224		
God has spoken – by his prophets		o					381		64	248	742	831		225		
God, who has caused to be written		o	467					472								
Holy Spirit, come, confirm us		n	471	288		640	299	183	288		311		140			
Holy Spirit, ever dwelling/living		n				615			303				141			
Holy Spirit, truth divine		n		289		626	300	184	289	235						
How sure the Scriptures are		o								249				227		
Jesus, restore to us again		o									873				876	295
Laudate Dominum/Sing, praise and bless the Lord (Taizé)				933	346	77	359				698				1514	458
Let us sing to the Lord (Taizé)											689					
Lord, be thy word/make your word my rule		o	232				383	209		250						
Lord, I have made thy word my choice		o	490					504	475							
Lord, thy word abideth/your word shall guide us		o	166	420	390		384	515	476	251	977/8	446	407			
Not far beyond the sea, nor high		o	401					528	477		112					
O thou who camest from above		n	233	541	557	625	639	191	745	596		525	431	560	451	416
Powerful in making us wise to salvation		o							479	252				228		
Spirit divine, attend our prayers		n				583	341	195	327	240		614				
Spirit of God within me		n		612	665			196	294	243	310			677		
Spirit of God, unseen as the wind		n				600	386						*612*	233		
Spirit of holiness, wisdom and faithfulness		n					576			246		611		449	1010	
Spirit of mercy, truth and love		n	89	613			197						143			
Spirit of the living God (Iverson)		n		615	666	619	310		295	S 23	306	613			510	462
Thanks/Praise to God whose word was spoken		o	423			605	387	584	483	255			438	229		
Thou/God, whose almighty word		o	180	684	738	112	324	267	29	506	887	699	466	597	557	
We have a gospel to proclaim		o	431	716	778	363	491	612	465	519	852	728	486	331	1583	
Your word is a lamp unto my feet		o												234		

SONGS FOR CHILDREN

Ho, ho, ho, hosanna CAON 821, CH 86, KS 109
Jesus, send me the helper JP 409, KS 213

BIBLE READINGS

Psalms [146 and] 149
Nehemiah 8.9–18
John 16.1–11

SINGING THE PSALM

Psalm 146 CRP, CWP, H&P, MCW1, NPCW, PAME
   Dean *Come, Lord, and save us* VE#
   Farrell *Common Psalm* CBL#
   Foster *Come, Lord* VE
Psalm 149 CWP, NPCW, PAME
   Trad *Blest be God* OITB

ANTHEMS AND VOCAL MUSIC

Title	Composer	Voices	E/M/D	Book source	Single sheet publisher
UNISON/TWO PART/HIGH VOICES					
Breathe on me	Hubbard	S	E	SFJ	Banks
Litany to the Holy Spirit (In the hour of my distress)	Hurford	U	E	AC2, NEP	OUP
O breath of life	Trad arr Bullard	2 part	E	OBFA	
Veni Sancte Spiritus	Walker	U + cantor#	E	WYP	OCP
THREE/FOUR PARTS					
Breathe on me, breath of God	Wilby	SATB	E/M		RSCM
Come down, O love divine	Harris	SATB	E/M	FSB9, NCAB, MTH2	Novello
Come down, O love divine	Tadman-Robins	SAMen	E	OBFA	
Come, Holy Ghost	Attwood	SATB	E	FAB1, NCAB, NSAC2, NNAB, AOAN1 (SAB)	Novello
Come, Holy Ghost, our souls inspire	Carter	SATB	D		OUP
Every time I feel the spirit	Trad arr Chilcott	SATB	M/D	SFC	
I will sing with the spirit	Goodenough	SATB	E	SBS2	
I will sing with the spirit	Rutter	SATB	E/M	JRA	OUP
If ye love me	Tallis	SATB unacc	E	FAB1, NCAB, NOEAB, NSAC1, OBTA, TA, SL (AATB)	OUP
Listen sweet dove	Ives	SATB	M	EAC1, SC	RSCM
O Holy Spirit, Lord of grace	Tye	SATB unacc	E	NCAB	RSCM
O Lord, give thy Holy Spirit	Harper	SATB	E	SBS2, SOTL	
Song 34: To the Holy Spirit	Gibbons	SATB	E	AC1, MEA (SAB)	
Spirit of the Lord, come down	Harper	SA(T)B	E	SBS1, SOTL	RSCM
The Spirit's gift	McKinley	SATB	M/D	LOL	
Veni Sancte Spiritus	Fenton	SATB	M		B&H
Veni Sancte Spiritus	Kelly	SATB	D	EAC1	
FIVE OR MORE PARTS					
Come down, O love divine	Rutter	SATB + SATB unacc	M/D		OUP
Come, Holy Ghost	Harvey	SSAATTBB unacc	D		Faber
If ye love me	Chilcott	SSATBB unacc	M	WFC, BCA	OUP
Veni Sancte Spiritus	Rutter	SSAATTBB unacc	M/D	CN	OUP
Veni Sancte Spiritus	Victoria	SATB + SATB unacc	M		Joed

ORGAN MUSIC

PRELUDES

Burtonwood S.   **Adagio** (Fagus) E/M
Buxtehude D.   **Nun bitten wir den Heligen Geist** BuxWV 209 in *Complete Works* Vol.5 (Bärenreiter) E/M
Karg-Elert S.   **Was Gott tut, das ist wohlgetan** No.61 from *Choral-Improvisationen* Op.65 Vol.6 and in *14 Choral-Improvisationen* (both Breitkopf) E/M
Lebègue N.   **Elévation in G** p.244 in *Complete Works* Vol.3 (Kalmus) E/M(*)
Rawsthorne N.   **Veni Creator** in *36 Miniatures* (3-stave) and *Twelve Miniatures for Quiet Occasions* (2-stave) (both Mayhew) E(*)

POSTLUDES

Bach W.F.   **Was mein Gott will** in *W.F.Bach Organ Works* Bk.2 (Peters) E/M
Beauvarlet-Charpentier J.J.   **Trio de grosse tierce** in *Pièces pour Orgue* (Chanvrelin) E*
De Grigny N.   **Veni Creator en taille** p.53 in *Livre d'Orgue* (Kalmus, Schott) M
Scheidt S.   **Komm, Gott Schöpfer, Heiliger Geist** in *The Church Year* (Cramer) E/M

PROPER 25 (SUNDAY BETWEEN 23 AND 29 OCTOBER INCLUSIVE) YEAR C

HYMNS AND SONGS

	pos	rdg	AMNS	CAON	CFE	CH4	CH5	CP	H&P	HTC	LAU	MP	NEH	SG	SOF	TS
A/The new commandment		g		35	4		515			S 26	920	1			22	23
Abide with me	ev	o	13	2	9	580	62	10	665	425	907	4	331	495	2	2
Awake, my soul, and with the sun	mo,ga	o	1	58		210	51	1	632	264		804	232	618		
Come down, O love divine		g	156	114	125	489	294	175	281	231	303	89	137	663	1202	71
Disposer supreme and judge of the earth		n	298	149			214						216			
Eternal light, shine in my heart		o					613	415		339						
Father of heaven, whose love profound		g	97	165	163	483	319	421	519	359		827	358	144		1201
Fight the good fight		n	220	169	171	517	566	423	710	526	860	143	359	635	107	
For the healing of the nations		g	361	186	179	706	496	427	402		886			261	1235	
Hail to the Lord's anointed		g	142	259	241	474	125	87	125	190	102	204	55		150	709
Immortal, invisible, God only wise	ga	o	199	314	301	132	6	474	9	21	725	327	377	44	234	220
In the Lord I'll be ever thankful (Taizé)				929	308	772					944	865		656	817	
Let there be love shared among us		g		386	358		525					411			329	317
Lord of all power, I give you my will/Lord of creation		g	395			500	594	508	699	547	869	440				
Make me a channel of your peace		g		437	478	528	503	519	776	S 19	898	456		691	381	348
New every morning is the love	mo	o	2	467		214	59	6	636	270		480	238			
O God beyond all praising		o		489			362			36	728			53	953	
O/Our God our help in ages past		o	99	494	528	161	537	537	358	37	955	498	417	542	415	905
Oft in danger/Christian soldiers		n	210	487			547		715	524		533	434			
Onward, Christian soldiers		n	333		581	514	659	549	718	532		543	435		442	
Powerful in making us wise to salvation		o							479	252				228		
Soldiers of Christ, arise		n	219	606		515	487	571	719	533		604	449	643	506	
Soldiers who are Christ's below		n	302	607			228						450			
Stand up, stand up for Jesus		n	221	617		488	578	721	535			617	453	644	513	1517
Take my life and let it be		g	249	625	677	502	597	581	705	554	874	624		678	519	468
Teach me, my God and King		o	240	629			601	583	803				456			
The Lord is my song (Taizé)				651							929					
To him we come		n								518		709		679	1569	
We rest on thee/We trust in you		n								446		735		510	587	1043
Will your anchor hold in the storms of life?		o		753		737	680		689			770				

SONGS FOR CHILDREN

Be bold, be strong JP 14, KS 17, MP 49, SOF 37, TS 38

BIBLE READINGS

Psalm 119.1–16
Ecclesiastes 11, 12
2 Timothy 2.1–7
Matthew 22.34–46

SINGING THE PSALM

Psalm 119.1–16 CRP, CWP, MCW1, NPCW, PAME

Dean *A lamp for my steps* HG#
Dean *You have laid down your precepts* HG#
Walker *Teach me, O God* ATNJ (OCP)#

ANTHEMS AND VOCAL MUSIC

Title	Composer	Voices	E/M/D	Book source	Single sheet publisher
UNISON/TWO PART/HIGH VOICES					
Bambelela (You must never give up)	Trad South African	U/SATB	E	C	
Be strong in the Lord	Nicholson	SS	E		Curwen
Christ has no body now but yours	Ogden	U + descant#	E	CFAP, LOL	RSCM
Creator God	Rizza	U/SATB#	E	ROP	
Ex ore innocentium	Ireland	SS	M/D	NSAC2	B&H
Give me strength	Chilcott	2 part	E	VFLS	
I give you a new commandment	Aston	2 part	E	BC, EAC2, NOEAB	RSCM
No greater love	Joncas	U/SATB	E/M	MHWE	GIA
THREE/FOUR PARTS					
A new commandment (g)	Parshall	SATB unacc	E	WFC	
Be strong and of good courage	Campbell	SATB	M	FSB7	Novello
Fight the good fight	Gardner	SATB	E	MTH1	OUP
God is our hope and strength	Stanford	SATB	M		Novello
Greater love	Ireland	SATB	M	AC4	S&B
I give to you a new commandment (g)	Nardone	SATB	E/M	SBS1	RSCM
Jesu, grant me this I pray	Gibbons	SATB	E/M	AWTE	
Prayer before the Crucifix	P. Moore	SATB	E/M		Banks
Solus ad victimam	Leighton	SATB	M	NCAB, AC1, SC	Banks
There's a wideness in God's mercy	Bevan	SATB	E	LD, MTH1, NOEAB, NEP	
Ubi caritas (g)	Ives	SATB unacc	M	SC	
Ubi caritas (g)	Mawby	SATB	E		Mayhew
Wondrous cross	Wilby	SATB	E	OBFA, WOTC	
FIVE OR MORE PARTS					
Deus noster refugium	Hassler	SAATTB unacc	M/D		CMS/OUP
God is our hope and strength	Blow	SSAATTBB	M		Banks
Ubi caritas (g)	Duruflé	SAATTBB unacc	M		Durand
Ubi caritas (g)	Berkeley	SSATB unacc	D		Chester

ORGAN MUSIC

PRELUDES

Beauvarlet-Charpentier J.J.   **Récit de flûte** (2 pieces) in *Pièces pour Orgue* (Chanvrelin) E*
Harwood B.   **2nd movement** from *1st Sonata* (Schott); also in *Complete Works* Vol.1 (Stainer) E/M
Peeters F.   **University College** in *Hymn Preludes for the Liturgical Year* Op.100 Vol.5 (Peters) E/M
Popplewell R.   **Prelude on 'Down Ampney'** in *The Modern Organist* (Banks) E/M
Rheinberger J.   **Cantilena** from *11th Sonata* (Amadeus, Carus or Novello) E/M

POSTLUDES

Peeters F.   **Built on a rock the Church doth stand** in *Hymn Preludes for the Liturgical Year* Op.100 Bk.10 (Peters) E/M
Walther J.G.   **Ein' feste Burg** in *Orgelchoräle* (Bärenreiter) M
Wood C.   **Old 104th Psalm** in *Sixteen Preludes on Melodies from the English and Scottish Psalters* Vol.2 (FitzSimons) M

Suitable before or after: Movements from Callahan C. **Partita on 'Slane'** (Concordia) E–M

THE LAST SUNDAY AFTER TRINITY (IF OBSERVED AS BIBLE SUNDAY) YEAR C

(For the Dedication Festival, see Year A, page 120.)

HYMNS AND SONGS

	pos	rdg	AMNS	CAON	CFE	CH4	CH5	CP	H&P	HTC	LAU	MP	NEH	SG	SOF	TS
At/In the name of Jesus		n	148	54	59	458	94	380	74	172	762	41	338	317	32	33
Christ is the world's light		n	440	99	111		87	213	455	321	744			591		
Father of all whose laws have stood		g								539				664		
Father of heaven, whose love profound		g	97	165	163	483	319	421	519	359		827	358	144		1201
Father of mercies, in thy word		s	167							247				224		
Go forth and tell!		n		238			478	437	770	505		178		596	738	
God has spoken – by his prophets		s					381		64	248	742	831		225		
God, who has caused to be written		s	467						472							
How shall they hear who have not heard		n										250		598		
How sure the Scriptures are!		s								249				227		
How sweet the name of Jesus sounds		n	122	297		461	92	467	257	211		251	374	42	194/782	190/1273
I'm not ashamed to own/name my Lord		n		316		645			677	448	323/992			532		
Jesu, the very thought of thee		n	120	368	321	560	101	485	265	478	798	386	385	534	308	
Lord, be thy word/make your word my rule		s	232				383	209		250						
Lord, I have made thy word my choice		s	490				504	475								
Lord, thy word abideth/your word shall guide us		s	166	420	390		384	515	476	251	977/8	446	407			
May the mind of Christ my Saviour		s		447	447	536	636	521	739	550		463		671	1448	887
Name of all majesty		n		465			102	525		218		481		324	939	
Not far beyond the sea, nor high		s	401				528	477		112						
Powerful in making us wise to salvation		s						479	252					228		
Saviour, again to thy dear name we raise	ev	n	15	587			71	20	643	281		584	250			
Seek ye first the kingdom of God		s		590	633	641	596		138		820	590			493	447
Take my life and let it be		g	249	625	677	502	597	581	705	554	874	624		678	519	468
Thanks/Praise to God whose word was spoken		s	423			605	387	584	483	255			438	229		
The Lord is my light (Taizé)				994												
The prophets spoke in days of old		o	513					327								
Thou/God, whose almighty word		s	180	684	738	112	324	267	29	506	887	699	466	597	557	
To the name of our/that brings salvation		n	121	698	749	471	117	610	80	222			470	72		
We have a gospel to proclaim		s	431	716	778	363	491	612	465	519	852	728	486	331	1583	
Your word is a lamp unto my feet		s												234		

SONGS FOR CHILDREN

Spirit of God, unseen as the wind CG 117, CH4 600, CH5 386, NEP 612, SG 233
The word of the Lord is planted in my heart JP 473, KS 338

BIBLE READINGS

Psalm 119.1–16
Jeremiah 36.9–32
Romans 10.5–17
Matthew 22.34–40

SINGING THE PSALM

Psalm 119.1–16 CRP, CWP, MCW1, NPCW, PAME

Dean *A lamp for my steps* HG#
Dean *You have laid down your precepts* HG#
Walker *Teach me, O God* ATNJ (OCP)#

ANTHEMS AND VOCAL MUSIC

Title	Composer	Voices	E/M/D	Book source	Single sheet publisher
UNISON/TWO PART/HIGH VOICES					
At the name of Jesus	Walker	U/SATB#	E	ATNJ	OCP
How beautiful are the feet (Messiah)	Handel	S	M		Novello
I love the name of Jesus	Thomerson arr Wilson	U/SATB	E	AWS	
Lift on high the name of Jesus	Ogden	U/SATB#	E		WLP
When I needed a neighbour (g)	Carter arr Burt	2 part	M	SFL1	
THREE/FOUR PARTS					
Go forth and tell!	Ogden	SATB	E/M	SBS2	RSCM
How beauteous are their feet	Stanford	SATB	M	AOAN1 (SAMen), ASA, NNAB, SC	
I will praise God because of his word	Purcell	SATB	E/M	TPS	
In God's word will I rejoice	Purcell arr Patrick	SAMen	E	SFL2,TPS	
In nomine Jesu	Handl	SATB unacc	M		Chester
King of glory, King of peace (g)	J.S.Bach arr Harris	SATB	E		OUP
King of glory, King of peace (g)	Ives	SATB	M	SBS1	RSCM
King of glory, King of peace (g)	Walford Davies	SATB	M	MTH2, SC	RSCM
O sing joyfully	Batten	SATB unacc	E	SCAB, WFC	RSCM
Teach me, O Lord	Attwood	SATB	E	NOEAB	RSCM
The Spirit of the Lord	Elgar	SATB	M	SAEE	RSCM
Thee will I love	Howells	SATB	D		Novello
FIVE OR MORE PARTS					
All hail the power of Jesu's name	Greenhill	SATBB	E/M		Novello
Beati quorum via	Stanford	SSATBB unacc	M	ASA, WFC	RSCM
Christe adoramus te	Monteverdi	SSATB unacc	M	ESM	
I love the Lord (g)	Harvey	SATB + solo SSATB unacc	D	EAC1, MTP	Novello
If ye love me (g)	Chilcott	SSATBB unacc	M	BCA, WFC	
O nomen Jesu	Philips	SSATB unacc	M		Mapa Mundi
Sing joyfully	Byrd	SAATB unacc	M	OBTA	OUP
The Song of Christ's Glory	Ives	SSAATTBB unacc	M/D	WOTC	

ORGAN MUSIC

PRELUDES

Bach J.S.   **Gottes Sohn ist kommen** ('Ravenshaw') BWV 724 in Novello Vol.18, Bärenreiter Vol.3, Peters Vol.6 E/M
Nixon J.   **Ravenshaw** in *Hymn Tune Preludes* (Fagus) E/M
Pachelbel J.   **Es spricht der Unweisen Mund wohl** No.10 in *Orgelwerke* Vol.2 (Peters) E/M*
Reger M.   **Herr Jesu Christ, dich zu uns wend** Op.135/11 in *Complete Chorale Preludes* (Breitkopf) E
Thomas Q.   **Ravenshaw** in *100 Hymn Preludes* and in *Hymn Preludes for the Church Year* Bk.2 (both Mayhew) E

POSTLUDES

Bach J.S.   **Herr Jesu Christ, dich zu uns wend** BWV 655 in Novello Vol.17, Bärenreiter Vol.2, Peters Vol.6 D
Buttstedt J.   **Gottes Sohn ist kommen** ('Ravenshaw') in *120 Chorale Preludes of the 17C & 18C* (Peters) E/M
Near G.   **Erhalt uns, Herr, bei deinem Wort** in *Choraleworks* Set 1 (Aureole) E/M
Walther J.G.   **Herr Jesu Christ, dich zu uns wend** in *A Graded Anthology for Organ* Bk.5 (Cramer) M*

THE FOURTH SUNDAY BEFORE ADVENT
YEAR C

(For All Saints' Day, see Year A, page 122.)

HYMNS AND SONGS

	pos	rdg	AMNS	CAON	CFE	CH4	CH5	CP	H&P	HTC	LAU	MP	NEH	SG	SOF	TS
As the deer pants for the water (Nystrom)		o		45	54	550	606				965	37			27	27
Bless the Lord, my soul (Taizé)				923	81		1				813			105	676	56
Every morning that breaks		o														1193
For all the saints who from their labours rest	s		305	177	176	740	459	232	814	567	371	148	197	636	109	684
Give me/us the wings of faith	s		324	204			463	216	815				225			
Great is thy faithfulness		o		249		153	80	453	66	260		200	636	39	147	138
Hark, my soul! It is the Lord/ Christian, do you hear		n	244	264			569	457	521	472		209	637			
How shall I sing that majesty	s		472	296		128	468	466	8				373/ 699			
I am the bread of life		n		299	272		420		611		629	261			200	
I cannot tell why he, whom angels worship		n		303				54	238	194		266		437	205	199
Jesu, thou joy of loving hearts		o	255	369		662	425	486	258	413		383	292	471		839
Jesus, the name high over all		n		364			99		264	213		385		323	307	298
Jesus, thy blood and righteousness		n					671		225	460				177		841
Light of the minds that know him	se	n		397			588	501		477			400	626		
Lord, as I wake I turn to you		o	485				56		634	267	672		236	561		
Misericordias Domini/From age to age (Taizé)					489											
New every morning is the love	mo	o	2	467		214	59	6	636	270		480	238			
O/Our God, our help in ages past		o	99	494	528	161	537	537	358	37	955	498	417	542	415	905
Rejoice! Rejoice! Christ is in you		n			618						818	572			480	438
Revive thy work/your church, O Lord!		n					308		780	515		578				
The steadfast love of the Lord never ceases		o										666			549	505
There is a land of pure delight	s		190				681	597	822	575			460			
There's a place (Because of you)	s										1011			457	1041	498
Through all the changing scenes of life		o	209	686	740		372	604	73	46		702	467	654	1566	1561
We give immortal praise		n	520	713				206	18	11						
When all thy mercies, O my God		o	109	732			374	617	573	39		751	472	73		
Who are these, like stars appearing	s		323	746			475	229					231			
Ye watchers and ye holy ones	s		532	758			476	230					478			

SONGS FOR CHILDREN

God our Father gave us life CAON 807, CH 68, KS2 485

BIBLE READINGS

Psalm 145*
Lamentations 3.22–33
John 11.[1–31]32–44

SINGING THE PSALM

Psalm 145* CH4, CRP, CWP, FGP, H&P, LAU, NEH, NPCW, PAME, PFS
  Gelineau *There can be no greater love* TSFP#
  Walker *I will bless your name* ATNJ

ANTHEMS AND VOCAL MUSIC

Title	Composer	Voices	E/M/D	Book source	Single sheet publisher
UNISON/TWO PART/HIGH VOICES					
As the deer longs	Hurd	U/SATB#	E	CFE, CG, CH4, LAU	OCP
It is good to give thanks to you	Ogden	U	E		WLP
Morning has broken	Trad arr Nelson	SSA	E		Banks
THREE/FOUR PARTS					
Almighty God, which hast me brought	Ford	SATB unacc	E	AC1, NCAB	
Brightest and best	Thiman	SATB	E	MTH1	
Christ is the morning star	Jakob	SATB	E	C	
Come out, Lazar!	Spicer	SATB	D	EAC1	
God so loved the world	Chilcott	SATB + solo S unacc	M	BCA, AWTE	OUP
God so loved the world	Goss	SATB unacc	E	NCAB	
God so loved the world	Stainer	SATB unacc	E/M	AWTE, FAB1, MHWE, NOEAB, NSAC1, AOAN1 (SAB)	RSCM
Like as the hart	Croft	SAB	E	CHM	
Like as the hart	Howells	SATB	M	AC4	OUP
Like as the hart	Rawsthorne	SATB	E/M	AWTE	
Morning glory, starlit sky	Barry Rose	SATB + solo S/T	E/M	MTH2	
Morning Prayers (Three Prayers of Dietrich Bonhoeffer)	P.Moore	SATB + solo A unacc	M/D		B&H
The raising of Lazarus	Willaert	SATB unacc	M		Ricordi
Wings of the morning	Rutter	SATB	M		OUP
FIVE OR MORE PARTS					
Ich bin der Auferstehung und das Leben	Schütz	SATB + SATB	M		Peters

ORGAN MUSIC

PRELUDES

Gigault N.   **Tu solus altissimus** p.22 in *Organ Book* Vol.1 (Kalmus) E(*)
Mendelssohn F.   **Theme and Variations in D** No.17 in *Complete Organ Works* Vol.1 (Bärenreiter) M
Noble T.T.   **Chorale Prelude 'Melcombe'** (OUP reprint) E/M
Pachelbel J.   **Gott Vater, der du deine Sonn** No.18 in *Selected Works* Vol.3 (Kalmus); also p.102 in *Organ Works* (Dover) E/M(*)
Thiman E.   **Andante tranquillo in E flat** No.4 of *Six Pieces* Set 1 (Curwen) E/M

POSTLUDES

Archer J.S.   **Improvisation on 'St Anne'** in *Variations on Well-known Hymn Tunes* (Novello) E/M*
Nixon J.   **Carlisle** in *Hymn Tune Preludes* (Fagus) E/M
Parry C.H.H.   **Prelude on 'Croft's 136'** in *Seven Chorale Preludes* Set 2 (Novello) and in *Preludes and Postludes* (Mayhew) M/D
Paix J.   **Phantasia primi toni** in *The Progressive Organist* Bk.4 (Novello) E

THE THIRD SUNDAY BEFORE ADVENT YEAR C

HYMNS AND SONGS

	pos rdg	AMNS	CAON	CFE	CH4	CH5	CP	H&P	HTC	LAU	MP	NEH	SG	SOF	TS
All my hope on God is founded	g	336	19	21	192	10	368	63	451	959	16	333	525		620
Be thou my vision/Lord, be my vision	o	343	70	74/75	465	643	386	378	545	970	51	339	669	42	50
Father, I place into your hands	o		162	159		565				971	133			97	97
Glorious things of thee are spoken	g	172	205	195	738	646	435	817	494	827	173	362	35	127	691
God is love, let heaven adore him	n	365	217		123	3	442	36		811	187	364			
God moves in a mysterious way	n	112	222		158	13	445	65			193	365			700
God of grace and God of glory	o	367	225			533	448	712	324		192		574	139	
Gracious Spirit, Holy Ghost/ Holy Spirit, gracious guest	n	154	245		627	312	182	301	474		198	367	556		
He lives in us, the Christ of God	n								457				173		
In the Lord I'll be ever thankful (Taizé)			929	308	772					944	865		656	817	
Jesus is King and I will extol him	n										366		289	283	
Jesus shall reign where'er the sun	g	143	359		470	97	490	239	516	322	379	388	45	301	1376
Lord God, you love us (Taizé)	o,n									782					
Lord, I lift your name on high	g				558						881		126	897	330
Lord, teach us how to pray aright	n	227	418		545	619	98	551	367			406			
Lord, teach us to pray	o										884				
Name of all majesty	g		465			102	525		218		481		324	939	
Nothing shall separate us	n										900		947	377	
Now is eternal life	n	402	470			392	152	203			114				
O for a heart to praise my God	n	230	484			638	533	536	483		495	74	149	411	904
Oft in danger/Christian soldiers	n	210	487			547	715	524		533	434				
Rejoice! The Lord is king	g	139	580	619	449	281	563	243	180	326	575	443	440	482	948
Show me your ways	o			642											
Spirit of God within me	n		612	665			196	294	243	310			677		
The kingdom of God is justice and joy	g		646	701			591	139	333	821	651		184		
Thou art the way: by thee alone/ You are the way	n	128	682			115	600	234	113		695	464			
We have a gospel to proclaim	g	431	716	778	363	491	612	465	519	852	728	486	331	1583	
Who can measure heaven and earth	o								27						
Ye that know the Lord is gracious	g	175			642	493	628					477			

SONGS FOR CHILDREN

Father, I place into your hands CAON 162, CFE 159, CH 44, CH5 565, JP 42, KS2 457, LAU 971, MP 133, SOF 97, TS 97

God's love is for everybody CH4 765

BIBLE READINGS

Psalm 40
1 Kings 3.1–15
Romans 8.31–39
Matthew 22.15–22

SINGING THE PSALM

Psalm 40 C, CH4, CRP, CWP, FGP, H&P, NPCW, PAME
   Bell *I waited, I waited on the Lord* HSNW, SG
   Bell *I waited patiently for God* CG, CH4, PPP

ANTHEMS AND VOCAL MUSIC

Title	Composer	Voices	E/M/D	Book source	Single sheet publisher
UNISON/TWO PART/HIGH VOICES					
At the name of Jesus	Walker	U/SATB#	E	ATNJ	OCP
I will sing forever of your love, O Lord	Ogden	U	E		WLP
O Lord, I will sing	Walker	U/SATB	E	OOD	OCP
O worship the Lord	Travers	U	E		RSCM
Sing of the Lord's goodness	Sands	U#	E	CFE, CG, CH4, CH5, LAU, SFL1, SG, SLG	OCP
THREE/FOUR PARTS					
Ascribe unto the Lord	Travers	SATB + solo TB	M		Novello
Ascribe unto the Lord	S.S.Wesley	SATB	M		Banks, Novello
Be thou my vision	Chilcott	SATB + solo S	M	NOEAB, BCA	OUP
Give unto the Lord	Elgar	SATB	D		Novello
I will sing of the Lord's great love	McKinley	SATB	M	SC	
Jesu dulcis memoria	Pott	SATB + solo S unacc	M/D	CN	
Jesu dulcis memoria	Shephard	SATB	E/M		RSCM
Jesu dulcis memoria	Victoria	SATB unacc	M	ESM, NSAC1, NCAB	CMS
Jesu, joy of man's desiring	J.S. Bach	SATB	E	FAB1, NCAB, NOEAB, NSAC1, WFC	RSCM
Judge eternal	Archer	SATB	M		Mayhew
Love divine	Willcocks	SATB	E	NOEAB	
Purest and highest	Stanford	SATB	E	ASA	RSCM
Rejoice, the Lord is king	Kelly	SATB	M/D	NNAB, MTH1	
Though you do not now see Christ	Ferguson	SATB unacc	E/M		Encore
FIVE OR MORE PARTS					
All hail the power of Jesu's name	Greenhill	SATBB	E/M		Novello
Christe adoramus te	Monteverdi	SSATB unacc	M	ESM	
Jesu dulcis memoria	Villette	SSAATTBB unacc	M/D		UMP
O nomen Jesu	Philips	SSATB unacc	M		Mapa Mundi

ORGAN MUSIC

PRELUDES

Archer M.	**Capetown 'Gracious Spirit'** in *25 Hymn Preludes: A Year of Praise* (Mayhew) E
Callahan C.	**Prelude on 'Michael'** in *Two English Voluntaries* (Concordia) E/M
Langlais J.	**Boys Town, lieu de paix** in *Mosaïque* Vol.1 (Combre) E/M
Peeters F.	**University College** No.3 in *Hymn Preludes for the Liturgical Year* Op.100 Vol.5 (Peters) E/M
Vierne L.	**Prélude** No.5 of *24 Pièces en Style Libre* Bk.1 (Masters, Durand) M(*)

POSTLUDES

Chauvet A.	**Grand Choeur in C** No.1 of *20 Morceaux* (Publimuses) E/M
Kauffmann G.	**Chorale Prelude 'Nun danket'** in *A Graded Anthology for Organ* Bk.3 (Cramer) and *80 Chorale Preludes* (Peters) E*
Mendelssohn F.	**Trio in F** in *Complete Organ Works* Vol.1 (Bärenreiter) M
Piutti C.	**Jerusalem, du hochgebaute Stadt** in *Choralvorspiele* Op.34 Vol.2 (Bärenreiter) E/M
Stein B.	**Prelude in D** in *Praise and Thanks* (Bärenreiter) E/M

THE SECOND SUNDAY BEFORE ADVENT
YEAR C

HYMNS AND SONGS

	pos	rdg	AMNS	CAON	CFE	CH4	CH5	CP	H&P	HTC	LAU	MP	NEH	SG	SOF	TS
Adoramus te, Domine (Taizé)				921	11		345				667			208		
All hail the power of Jesus' name		s	140	16	19	457	250	163	252	587	323	13	332	24	9	7
Be bold, be strong		o										49			37	38
Christ is the King! O friends rejoice		s	345				86	165		492			345	31		
Christ triumphant, ever reigning		s		104	113	436	259	398		173	763	77	613	319	62	655
Crown him with many crowns		s	147	137	139	459	263	166	255	174	321	109	352	321	77	77
Do not be afraid, for I have redeemed you		o		150	147	191					972	115			1213	1183
Here in this place (Gather us in)		o			253	623					475			4		
In heavenly armour we'll enter the land		o										639			237	228
Judge eternal, throned in splendour		s		372		264	535	356	409	329		395	490	600		
Rejoice! The Lord is king		s	139	580	619	449	281	563	243	180	326	575	443	440	482	948
Rise and hear! The Lord is speaking		n	509				385	321								
Send me, Lord (Thuma mina)		n			636	800								694		
Sent by the Lord am I	se	n			638	250					855			616		
Sing of the Lord's goodness		o			654	157	368				713			61		
Soldiers of Christ, arise		o	219	606		515	487	571	719	533		604	449	643	506	
Stand up, stand up for Jesus		o	221	617			488	578	721	535		617	453	644	513	1517
The kingdom is upon you!		s	512					590					650			
The kingdom of God is justice and joy		s		646	701			591	139	333	821	651		184		
Through all the changing scenes of life		o	209	686	740		372	604	73	46		702	467	654	1566	1561
Thy/Your kingdom come, O God		s	177	691			509	607	783	334		949	499	269		
Thy/Your kingdom come! On bended knee		s	178	690		473		608					500			
Walk with me, oh my Lord		o			765						966					
We have a gospel to proclaim		n	431	716	778	363	491	612	465	519	852	728	486	331	1583	
Who would true valour see/He who would valiant be		o	212	281	248	535	662	621	688	590	862	224	372	639	174	
Ye/You servants of God, your master proclaim		n	149	756	819	130	492	627	278	520		784	476	75	620	1074
Your word is a lamp unto my feet		n												234		

SONGS FOR CHILDREN

Be bold, be strong JP 14, KS 17, MP 49, SOF 37, TS 38
Colours of day CAP 55, CFE 118, CH 33, JP 28, KS2 433, LAU 764, MP 1039, SOF 64, TS 69
In our lives plant seeds of hope CH4 349
Sent by the Lord am I CFE 638, CG 105, CH4 250, IECS, LAU 855, SBTL, SG 616

BIBLE READINGS
Psalms [93 and] 97
Daniel 6
Matthew 13.1–9,18–23

SINGING THE PSALM
Psalm 93 CH4, CRP, CWP, H&P, MCW1, NEP, NPCW, PAME
Psalm 97 CRP, CWP, FGP, MCW1, NPCW, PAME

ANTHEMS AND VOCAL MUSIC

Title	Composer	Voices	E/M/D	Book source	Single sheet publisher
UNISON/TWO PART/HIGH VOICES					
All you works of God	Haugen	U	E	CH4	GIA
Daniel Jazz	Chappell	U	E		Novello
Didn't my Lord deliver Daniel?	Trad arr Weaver	2 part	E	CFAP	
Give ear unto me	Marcello	SS	E/M	AC2	
Listen	Nazareth arr Archer	U	E	BC	
Sent by the Lord am I	Trad arr Weaver	2 part	E	BC, CFAP	
Take the word of God with you	Walker	U/SAB#	E	CFE, CIH, LAU	OCP
THREE/FOUR PARTS					
Blessed be the God and Father	S.S.Wesley	SATB	M	FAB1, NCAB, SC	RSCM
Christ was the Word	Maxim	SATB unacc	E	SBS2	
Fight the good fight	Gardner	SATB	M	MTH1	OUP
Judge eternal	Archer	SATB	E/M		Mayhew
Lift up your heads (Messiah)	Handel	SATB	M		Novello
Lift up your heads	Handel arr Hand	SA	M/D	AOAN1	
Lift up your heads	Mathias	SATB	M/D	AC1	OUP
Thy word is a lantern	Purcell	SATB	M	APA	Novello
To be a pilgrim	Burt	SAMen	E/M	OBFA	
Waiting for the word	Skellern	SATB	E/M		RSCM
We wait for thy loving kindness	McKie	SATB	E	AC4, NSAC2	OUP
FIVE OR MORE PARTS					
Didn't my Lord deliver Daniel?	Trad arr Hart	SSAATTBB (unacc)	M/D	SFC	
Open thou mine eyes	Rutter	SSATB unacc	M		OUP

ORGAN MUSIC

PRELUDES
Bach W.F. **Christe, der du bist Tag und Licht** in *W.F.Bach Organ Works* Bk.2 (Peters) E/M
Karg-Elert S. **O Gott, du frommer Gott** No.16 from *20 Preludes and Postludes* Op.78 (Breitkopf) E/M
Michel J.M. **Now thank we all our God (Calypso)** in *Jazz Inspirations* (Bärenreiter) E/M
Quarles C. **Voluntary in F minor** in *An Organ Album for Manuals Only* Bk.2 (Banks) M*
Willan H. **Matins** from *Two Pieces* (Peters) E

POSTLUDES
Nagel M. **The Strong-Tower-Postlude** (Ein' feste Burg) in *Jazz Inspirations* (Bärenreiter) E/M
Vierne L. **Allegretto** Op.1 (Masters); also in *French Masterworks* (Belwin Mills) and on *French Romantic Organ Music* (CD-ROM) M/D
Walther J.G. **Herzlich lieb hab ich dich** No.18 in *Orgelchoräle* (Bärenreiter) E/M
Wesley S. **Preludium and Arietta** from *Voluntary in C minor for T.Adams* (Fagus) E/M(*)

CHRIST THE KING (THE SUNDAY NEXT BEFORE ADVENT) YEAR C

HYMNS AND SONGS

	pos	rdg	AMNS	CAON	CFE	CH4	CH5	CP	H&P	HTC	LAU	MP	NEH	SG	SOF	TS
Adoramus te, Domine (Taizé)				921	11		345				667			208		
All hail the power of Jesus' name		s	140	16	19	457	250	163	252	587	323	13	332	24	9	7
All heaven declares	gr			17	20	426					760	14		420	10	8
Alleluia! Sing to Jesus	of	s	262	12	37	445	398	278	592	170	644	207	271	458	153	616
At/In the name of Jesus		s	148	54	59	458	94	380	74	172	762	41	338	317	32	33
Blessing and honour (Ancient of days)		s				442						976		106	675	54
Christ is the King! O friends rejoice		s	345				86	165		492			345	31		
Christ triumphant, ever reigning		s		104	113	436	259	398		173	763	77	613	319	62	655
Crown him with many crowns		s	147	137	139	459	263	166	255	174	321	109	352	321	77	77
From heaven you came, helpless babe		n		195	187	374	219	432			749	162		632	120	114
Jesus shall reign where'er the sun		s	143	359		470	97	490	239	516	322	379	388	45	301	1376
Jesus shall take the highest honour		s		360								378		123	302	296
Jesus, we enthrone you		s										388		310	300
Judge eternal, throned in splendour		o		372		264	535	356	409	329		395	490	600		
King of kings, majesty		s										1000			1404	309
Lord, enthroned in heavenly splendour		n	263	408	379		431	311	616	416	769	431	296	52	352	870
Majesty, worship his majesty		s		436	477		276				767	454			379	346
Make way, make way for Christ the King	ga			438	479	279	134				819	457			384	349
Meekness and majesty		n		448	487	356	228				751	465		395	390	353
Morning glory, starlit sky/Open are the gifts		n	496			390		259					608			
O Christe Domine Jesu (Taizé)					519						757					
O God of earth and altar		o		492	527			358	426		935		492			
O worship the King, all glorious above	ga	s	101	551	559	127	34	546	28	24	683	528	433	90	456	425
Rejoice! The Lord is king		s	139	580	619	449	281	563	243	180	326	575	443	440	482	948
The head that once was crowned with thorns		n	141	644	696	438	285	172	209	182	290	647	134	442	531	979/1528
The kingdom of God is justice and joy		s		646	701			591	139	333	821	651		184		
The Lord ascendeth up on high		s				440		173	210				135			
Thy/Your kingdom come, O God		s	177	691			509	607	783	334		949	499	269		
Thy/Your kingdom come! On bended knee		s	178	690		473		608					500			

SONGS FOR CHILDREN

All heaven declares CAON 17, CFE 20, CH4 426, KS 4, LAU 760, MP 14, SG 420, SOF 10, TS 8
He is the King of kings CAON 818, CH 80, TS 1244
Make way, make way CAON 438, CFE 479, CH4 279, CH5 134, JP 427, KS 249, LAU 819, MP 457, SOF 384, TS 349

BIBLE READINGS

Morning Psalms 29 and 110
Evening Psalm 72*
1 Samuel 8.4–20
John 18.33–37

SINGING THE PSALM

Psalm 29 CRP, CWP, NEP, NPCW, PAME
  Feeley *The Lord will bless his people with peace* VE
  Gregory Murray, Gelineau *The Lord will bless his people with peace* VE
  Rees *The Lord will bless his people with peace* PCMG
Psalm 110 CRP, CWP, NPCW
Psalm 72* CRP, CWP, H&P, MCW1, NPCW, PAME
  Haugen *Every nation on earth* (GIA)#

ANTHEMS AND VOCAL MUSIC

Title	Composer	Voices	E/M/D	Book source	Single sheet publisher
UNISON/TWO PART/HIGH VOICES					
Settings of the Te Deum	Various	U/SATB	E	CWP, MCW1	
At the name of Jesus	Walker	U/SATB#	E	ATNJ	OCP
My song is love unknown	Archer	SS	M	EAC2	RSCM
THREE/FOUR PARTS					
Above all praise	Mendelssohn	SATB	E	NCAB, OEAB	RSCM
Adoramus te Christe	Lassus	SATB unacc	M	ESM, AWTE	Chester
Adoramus te Christe	Palestrina	SATB unacc	M	NCAB	Banks
Christus factus est	Anerio	SATB unacc	M	AWTE, CM1, ESM	
Christus factus est	Bruckner	SATB unacc	M/D	ESM	RSCM
Christus factus est	Ridout	SATB unacc	E		Encore
Christus vincit	Mawby	SATB	D		Mayhew
King of all ages, throned on high	Isom	SATB	E	NOEAB	
No scenes of stately majesty	Kendrick arr Tambling	SATB	E	WSCC1	
O God, the King of glory	Purcell	SATB unacc	E	APA, ETAS	OUP
O Saviour of the world	Goss	SATB	M	FAB1, NCAB, NOEAB	
O Saviour of the world	Somervell	SATB	E	NCAB	
The Song of Christ's Glory	P.Moore	SATB	E		RSCM
Vexilla regis	Bruckner	SATB unacc	M		Peters
What wondrous love is this?	Trad arr Weaver	SAB	E	LOL, SFL2	
With loving hands	Tredinnick	SATB	M	WIS	
Wondrous cross	Wilby	SATB	E	OBFA, WOTC	
Worthy is the Lamb (Messiah)	Handel	SATB	M		Novello
FIVE OR MORE PARTS					
All hail the power of Jesu's name	Greenhill	SATBB	E/M		Novello
Crucifixus	Caldara	SSSSAAAATTTTBBBB	M		OUP
Crucifixus	Lotti	SSAATTBB unacc	M/D	ESM, NSAC1	RSCM
The Song of Christ's Glory	Ives	SSAATTBB unnac	M	WOTC	

ORGAN MUSIC

PRELUDES

Boëly A.P.F.	**Quoniam tu solus** p.16 in *The Liturgical Service* Bk.1 (Kalmus) M
Dienel O.	**Es ist gewißlich an der Zeit** in *Hier Preisen auf der Erd* Vol.1 (Breitkopf) E
Groves R.	**Praise, my soul** in *12 Hymn-Tune Preludes* Set 1 (Novello) E(*)
Oortmerssen J.van	**Psalm 72** from *Five Chorale Preludes* (Tactus) E/M

POSTLUDES

Guilmant A.	**March on a theme of Haendel** Op.15/2 (Schott); also in *Complete Works* Vol.1 (Belwin) M/D
Piutti C.	**Wunderbarer König** in *Choralvorspiele* Op.34 Vol.3 (Bärenreiter) E/M
Gigault N.	**Fugue à 2 Domine Deus** p.38 in *Organ Book* Vol.1 (Kalmus) E*
Hurford P.	**Scherzo** or **Processional** from *Suite: Laudate Dominum* (OUP) E/M* and E/M

Suitable before or after: Movements from Hobby R. **Partita 'Praise, my soul, the king of heaven'** (Concordia) E/M

SUPPLEMENTARY ORGAN MUSIC

CHRISTMAS DAY YEARS A, B, C

ORGAN MUSIC

PRELUDES

Archer M.   **Humility, Corde natus** *or* **Cranham** in *25 Hymn Preludes: A Year of Praise* (Mayhew) and in *40 Christmas Preludes* (both Mayhew) E/M

Bédard D.   **Noël Huron** No.1 of *Deux Noëls* (Cheldar) E/M

Beechey G.   Pieces from *Six Preludes on Carol Melodies* and *Six More Easy Carol Preludes* (both Fagus) E-E/M

Bonnal J.   **Noël landais** in *A Graded Anthology for Organ* Bk.5 (Cramer) E/M

Buxtehude D.   **Der Tag, der ist so freudenreich** BuXWV 182 in *Complete Works* Vol.4 (Bärenreiter) E/M

Carter A.   **Chanson de la Vierge Pensive** in *A Carter Organ Album* (OUP) E/M

Chaminade C.   **Pastorale No.1 pour la Messe de Minuit** in *La Nef Sacrée* (Enoch) E/M(*)

Doyen H.   **Noël ancien** in *Christmas Music by Various French Composers* (Kalmus) E/M

Fox V.   **In dulci jubilo** in *At the Organ with Virgil Fox* (Gray) E/M

Harwood B.   **The shepherds at the manger** No.8 of *8 Short Pieces* Op.58 in *Complete Works* Vol.2 (Stainer) M

Ireland J.   **The Holy Boy** in *The Oxford Book of Christmas Organ Music* (OUP) E/M

Nixon J.   **The first nowell** in *Hymn Preludes for the Church Year* Bk.1 (Mayhew) E

Villard J.   **Noël Poitevin** in *Christmas Music by Various French Composers* (Kalmus) M

Watkinson J.   **Prelude on 'Divinum mysterium'** in *A Christmas Collection* (Novello) E/M

Yon P.   **Pastorale 'Gesù Bambino'** ('Adeste fideles') in *Oxford Book of Christmas Organ Music* (OUP) E/M

POSTLUDES

Bach J.S.   **In dulci jubilo** BWV 729 in Novello Vol.18, Bärenreiter Vol.3, Peters Vol.5   E/M

Bédard D.   **Toccata sur 'Il est né, le divin Enfant'** No.2 of *Deux Noëls* (Cheldar) E/M

Bédard D.   **Variations on 'In dulci jubilo'** (Cheldar) E/M

Behnke J.   **Go tell it on the mountain** (swing) in *Jazz Inspirations* (Bärenreiter) E/M

Berthier J.   **Variations on 'In dulci jubilo'** in *Variations on Six Chorales* (Mayhew) M*

Cook J.   **Paean on 'Divinum mysterium'** in *Festal Voluntaries: Christmas and Epiphany* (Novello) M

Faulkes W.   **Fantasia on old Christmas carols** in *Romantic Organ Music for Christmas and Advent* (Animus) M

Franck C.   **Noël angevin** or **Sortie in G** Nos.52 and 56 in *L'Organiste* (UMP, Kalmus, Schott)

Liszt F.   **The shepherds at the manger** (In dulci jubilo) in *Organ Music for Manuals Only* (Dover) and *At the Organ with Virgil Fox* (Gray) E/M*

Lloyd Webber W.S.   **Noël nouvelet** from *Six Interludes on Christmas Carols* (Novello) and in *Songs without Words* (Music Sales) E/M

Séjan N.   Three **Noëls** in *Séjan: Pièces pour Orgue* (Chanvrelin) E/M(*)

Spedding A.   **Carols** or **Nowell** in *Recuerdos* (IAO) E/M

Sumsion H.   **Prelude on 'Adeste fideles'** or **Prelude on 'Unto us is born a Son'** (both RSCM) E/M

Thiman E.   **Postlude on 'Adeste fideles'** in *A Christmas Collection* (Novello) M

Stanford C.V.   **At Christmas-tide** No.1 of *Six Occasional Preludes* Op.182 Set 1 (Stainer); also in *Preludes and Postludes* (Mayhew) M

Wills A.   **And suddenly there was with the angel** No.2 from *Christmas Meditations* (Novello) E/M

Suitable before or after: Pieces from the collections of noëls (<u>mostly without pedals</u>) by **Balbastre, C.** (2 books), **Corrette G.**, **Dandrieu J-F.**, **D'Aquin L-C.** and **Lebègue N.**, *The Holly and the Ivy* **Rawsthorne N.**, (Mayhew; 2 and 3 stave editions available), *Noëls traditionels* **Bouvard J.** (Lemoine) and *Christmas Music* **Guilmant A.** (Leupold) contain many useful carol preludes, interludes and postludes.

THE EPIPHANY (6 JANUARY) YEARS A, B, C

ORGAN MUSIC

PRELUDES

Anon.	**Herr Christ, der einig Gotts Soh**n in *120 Chorale Preludes of the 17C & 18C* (Peters) E*
Archer M.	**Stuttgart** in *25 Hymn Preludes: A Year of Praise* (Mayhew) and in *40 Christmas Preludes* (Mayhew) M
Armstrong Gibbs C.	**Lullay, thou little tiny child** in *A Christmas Album* (OUP) E/M
Bach J.S.	**Herr Christ, der ein'ge Gottes Sohn** BWV 698 in Novello Vol.18, Bärenreiter Vol.3, Peters Vol.5 E/M*
Dubois T.	**Marche des Rois Mages** in *Douze Pièces* (Leduc, Bärenreiter) E/M
Duruflé M.	**Prélude sur l'Introït de l'Épiphanie** in *Préludes à l'Introït* (Schola Cantorum) M
Fletcher A.	**We three kings of orient are** in *40 Christmas Preludes* (Mayhew) E/M
Glière R.	**Fugue on the Theme of a Russian Noël ('We three kings')** in *Organ Music for Manuals Only* (Dover) E/M*
Krebs J.L.	**Wie schön leuchtet der Morgens**tern in *Complete Works* Vol.3 (Breitkopf) E/M
Milford R.	**Variations on the 'Coventry Carol'** No.2 of *Three Christmas Pieces* (Cathedral Music or OUP reprint) M
Pachelbel J.	**Wie schön leuchtet der Morgenstern** No.26 in *Selected Works* Vol.3 (Kalmus), also p.141 in *Organ Works* (Dover) E/M
Peeters F.	**How lovely shines the morning star** No.7 of *Ten Chorale Preludes* Op.68 (Peters) M
Reger M.	**Wie schön leuchtet der Morgenstern** Op.135a/29 in *The Church Year* (Cramer) E/M
Telemann G.P.	**Wie schön leuchtet der Morgenstern** in *The Church Year* (Cramer) E
Thiman E.	**Chorale Prelude 'Stuttgart'** in *Progressive Organist* Bk.3 (Elkin) E

POSTLUDES

Bach J.S.	**Wie schön leuchtet der Morgenstern** BWV 739 in Novello Vol.19, Peters Vol.9 M/D
Buttstedt J.H.	**Vom Himmel kam der Engel Schar** in *Choralvorspiele alter Meister* (Peters) E/M
Buxtehude D.	**Herr Christ, der einig Gotts Sohn** BuxWV 191 in *Complete Works* Vol.4 (Bärenreiter) E/M
Buxtehude D.	**Wie schön leuchtet der Morgenstern** BuxWV 223 in *Complete Works* Vol.5 (Bärenreiter) M
Cavazzoni G.	**In Epiphania: Crudelis Herodes** in *Second Organ Book* (Schott, Kalmus) E*
Chauvet A.	**The Epiphany of Our Lord** in *Noëls for the Time of Christmas* (Concordia) E/M*
De Grigny N.	**A solis ortus/Crudelis Herodes** 2 settings in *Livre d'Orgue* (Kalmus, Schott) M-D
Peeters F.	**Prelude 'Brightest and best'** in *Hymn Preludes for the Liturgical Year* Op.100 Bk.1 (Peters) E/M
Peeters F.	**Chorale Prelude on 'Stuttgart'** in *Festal Voluntaries: Christmas & Epiphany* (Novello) M
Piutti C.	**Jesu, meine Freude** in *Choralvorspiele* Op.34 Vol.2 (Bärenreiter) E
Reger M.	**Wie schön leucht uns der Morgenstern** Op.67/51 in *Complete Organ Works* Vol.7 (Breitkopf) M
Telemann G.P.	**Wie schön leucht uns der Morgenstern** 2 settings in *Chorale Preludes* (Bärenreiter or A-R Edition) E*/M*
Titelouze J.	**A solis ortus/Crudelis Herodes** 3 settings in *Hymnes de l'Église* (Kalmus, Schott) E-M

Suitable before or after: Movements from Walther J.G. **Partita 'Jesu, meine Freude'** in *Choralvorspiele alter Meister* (Peters) M*

THE PRESENTATION OF CHRIST IN THE TEMPLE (CANDLEMAS, 2 FEBRUARY) YEARS A, B, C

ORGAN MUSIC

PRELUDES

Bach J.C.	**Mit Fried' und Freud'** in *80 Chorale Preludes* (Peters) E*
Bach J.S.	**Mit Fried' und Freud'** BWV 616 from the *Orgelbüchlein* (many editions) E/M
Bach J.S.	**Ein Kinderlein so löbelich** BWV 719 in *Neumeister Choral Preludes* (Bärenreiter) E*
Boëly A.	**Voici la première entrée** in *14 Preludes on Carols by Denizot* (Fentone) E
Drischner M.	**Schönster Herr Jesu** in *The Organ Funeral Album* (Bärenreiter) E*
Dupré M.	**Herr Gott, nun schleuss den Himmel auf** or **Mit Fried' und Freud'** Nos.31 & 56 of *79 Chorales* Op.28 (Gray) E
Fischer M.G.	**Mit Fried' und Freud'** in *The Organ Funeral Album* (Bärenreiter) E*
Gibbs A.	**Virgin-born, we bow before thee** from *Peacehaven Preludes* (Bardic) E(*)
Guilmant A.	**Offertoire 'Lumen ad revelationem'** No.1 in *The Liturgical Organist* Op.65 (Masters, Schott) and in *Complete Works* Vol.6 (Belwin Mills) M
Harwood B.	**Invocation** No.1 of *8 Short Pieces* Op.58 in *Complete Works* Vol.2 (Stainer) E/M
Moore P.	**Light of the nations** in *The Organist's Liturgical Year* (Mayhew) E
Peeters F.	**In peace and joy I now depart** in Vol.4 of *Hymn Preludes for the Liturgical Year* Op.100 (Peters) E/M
Reger M.	**Mit Fried' und Freud'** Op.79b/ No.5 & No.10 in *Complete Works* Bk.7 (Breitkopf) E/M & M/D
Whitlock P.	**Fidelis** from *Plymouth Suite* in *Whitlock: Complete Shorter Works* (OUP) E/M
Wills A.	**For mine eyes have seen thy salvation** No.5 from *Christmas Meditations* (Novello) E/M
Wood C.	**Nunc dimittis** No.7 in Vol.2 of *Sixteen Preludes on Melodies from the English and Scottish Psalters* (Fitzsimons) M
Wood C.	**Song of Symeon** No.2 of *Three Preludes founded upon Melodies from the Genevan Psalter* (Stainer) E/M

POSTLUDES

Bach J.S.	**Herr Gott, nun schleuss** BWV 617 from the *Orgelbüchlein* (many editions) M
Bach J.S.	**Herr Gott, nun schleuß** BWV 1092 In *Neumeister Choral Preludes* (Bärenreiter) E/M*
Buxtehude D.	**Mit Fried' und Freud'** BuxWV 76 in *Complete Works* Vol.5 (Bärenreiter) M/D
Dubois T.	**Fiat lux** In *Douze Pièces Nouvelles* (Masters, Leduc) M/D
Dupré M.	**Lumen ad revelationem** No.3 of *Six Antiennes pour le Temps de Noël* Op.48 (Bornemann) D
Dyson G.	**I was glad** in *Variations on Old Psalm Tunes* Bk.3 (Novello) M
Eldridge G.	**Fanfare** In *Fanfares and Processionals* (Novello) E/M
Gibbs A.	**Lumen et gloriam** No.3 of *Five Hymn Preludes* (Bardic) M
Near G.	**Westminster Abbey** in *Choraleworks* Set 1 (Aureole) E/M
Nixon J.	**Procession on 'Salzburg'** in *Easter Glory* (Mayhew) M
Nixon J.	**Variations on a French folk tune** in *The Organist's Liturgical Year* (Mayhew) M
Purvis	**What child is this?** in *The Oxford Book of Christmas Music* (OUP) E/M
Wills A.	**For mine eyes have seen thy salvation** No.5 from *Christmas Meditations* (Novello) E/M

ASH WEDNESDAY YEARS A, B, C

ORGAN MUSIC

PRELUDES (continued)

Leighton K.	**Aus der Tiefe** No.2 from *Six Fantasies on Hymn Tunes* Op.72 (Ramsey) M
Near G.	**Aus tiefer Not** in *Choraleworks* Set 2 (Aureole) E
Nixon J.	**Meditation for Ash Wednesday** in *The Organist's Liturgical Year* (Mayhew) E/M
Parry C.H.H.	**Chorale Prelude 'Martyrdom'** in *Seven Chorale Preludes* Set 2 (Novello) and in *Preludes and Postludes* (Mayhew) M
Peeters F.	**Christian, dost thou see them?** in *Hymn Preludes for the Liturgical Year* Op.100 Bk.2 (Peters) E
Reger M.	**Aus tiefer Not** Op.67/3 in *Complete Organ Works* Vol.7 (Breitkopf) M
Willan H.	**Prelude on 'Aberystwyth'** in *Ten Hymn Preludes* Set 1 (Peters) E/M

POSTLUDES

Andriessen H.	**De Profundis 'Aus der Tiefe'** in *Advent to Whitsuntide* (Hinrichsen reprint) M
Anon.	**Ach Gott, vom Himmel** in *Choralvorspiele alter Meister* (Peters) E/M
Bach J.S.	**Aus tiefer Not** BWV 687 in Novello Vol.16, Bärenreiter Vol.4, Peters Vol.6 M*
Bach J.S.	**Aus tiefer Not** BWV 1099 in *Neumeister Chorale Preludes* (Bärenreiter) E/M
Bach J.S.	**Jesu, meines Lebens Leben** BWV 1107 in *Neumeister Chorale Preludes* (Bärenreiter) E/M
Darke H.	**Fugue on 'Heinlein'** from *Chorale Prelude and Fugue on 'Heinlein'* (Anglo-American) M
Ley H.G.	**Fantasia on 'Aberystwyth'** (OUP) D
Oortmerssen J.van	**Ach, was soll ich Sünder machen?** from *Five Chorale Preludes* (Tactus) E
Pachelbel J.	**Aus tiefer Not** in *Orgelwerke* Vol.2 (Peters) or Vol.3 (Kalmus)* E/M(*)
Peeters F.	**From depths of woe I cry to thee** No.7 of *Ten Chorale Preludes* Op.69 (Peters) M
Piutti C.	**Aus tiefer Not** in *Choralvorspiele* Op.34 Vol.1 (Bärenreiter) E
Richter E.F.	**Aus tiefer Not** Op.20/6 in *Organ Music of the Classical & Early Romantic* Vol.6 (Bärenreiter) E/M
Zachau F.	**Aus tiefer Not** in *80 Chorale Preludes* (Peters) E*

Suitable before or after: Movements from Böhm G. **Partita 'Aus tiefer Not'** in *Complete Works* (Breitkopf) E-M(*) or Pachelbel J. **Partita 'Ach, was soll ich Sünder machen?'** in *Selected Works* Vol.4 (Kalmus) E/M-M(*)

GOOD FRIDAY YEARS A, B, C

ORGAN MUSIC (MORNING)

PRELUDES

(it is preferred that the organ remain silent)

Bach J.S.	**O Mensch, bewein'** BWV 622 from the *Orgelbüchlein* (many editions) E/M
Bach J.S.	**O Jesu, wie ist dein Gestalt** BWV 1094 in *Neumeister Chorale Preludes* (Bärenreiter) E*
Brahms J.	**Herzlich thut mich verlangen** No.4 or No.10 of *Eleven Chorale Preludes* Op.122 E/M
Callahan C.	**Improvisation on 'Were you there?'** from *A Lenten Suite* (Morning Star) E
Hurford P.	**Chorale Prelude 'Caswall'** in *The Church Year* (Cramer) and *Five Chorale Preludes* (OUP) E
Lloyd Webber W.S.	**There is a green hill far away** from *Six Interludes on Passion Hymns* (Novello) E/M
Mawby C.	**Crux fidelis** in *Gregorian Calendar* (Mayhew) E
Thiman E.	**Canzonetta on 'Horsley'** in *Festal Voluntaries: Lent, Passiontide & Palm Sunday* (Novello) M
Vann S.	**Cross of Jesus** in *Preludes on Favourite Hymns* (Mayhew; 2-stave and 3-stave editions available) E/M(*)

POSTLUDES

(the organ should remain silent)

ORGAN MUSIC (EVENING)

PRELUDES

(it is preferred that the organ remain silent)

Bach J.S.	**Herzlich thut mich verlangen** BWV 727 in Novello Vol.18, Bärenreiter Vol.3, Peters Vol.5 E
Bach J.S.	**Final chorus of St Matthew Passion** in *Passiontide and Easter* (Bärenreiter) M
Benoit P.	**Offertoire 'Ecce lignum'** No.1 of *Sept Pièces* (Consortium) E/M*
Bunk G.	**Herzlich tut mich verlangen** in *Choralimprovisationen* (Butz) E/M
Fletcher A.	**Were you there?** in *Hymn Preludes for the Church Year* Bk.2 (Mayhew) E
Howells H.	**Psalm-Prelude Set 2 No.1** (Novello) M/D
Mendelssohn F.	**Variations on 'Herzlich thut mich verlangen'** No.12 in *Complete Organ Works* Vol.1 (Bärenreiter) E/M
Oldroyd G.	**Prie-Dieu** in *A Book of Simple Organ Voluntaries* (OUP Archive) E
Vann S.	**It is finished** in *The Organist's Liturgical Year* (Mayhew) E/M
Vann S.	**Via crucis** in *Today in Paradise* (Mayhew) E*

POSTLUDES

(the organ should remain silent)

ASCENSION DAY YEARS A, B, C

ORGAN MUSIC

PRELUDES

Archer M.	**St Magnus** in *100 Hymn Preludes* (Mayhew) E/M	
Archer M.	**Llanfair** in *25 Hymn Preludes: A Year of Praise* (Mayhew) E/M	
Bach J.S.	**Nun freut euch** BWV 734 in Novello Vol.18, Bärenreiter Vol.3, Peters Vol.7 M	
Coleman H.	**Hyfrydol** in *24 Interludes based on Communion Hymns* (Optional Pedal) (OUP archive) E(*)	
de Klerk A.	**Salutis humanae Sator** No.4 of *Octo Fantasiae* (Zengerinck) E*	
Duruflé M.	**Méditation 'Cum jubilo'** (Durand) M	
Ives G.	**Processional** in *Ceremonial Music* (OUP) M	
Mawby C.	**Salutis humanae Sator II** in *Gregorian Calendar* (Mayhew) E/M	
Peeters F.	**Jesu, nostra redemptio** No.7 of *Ten Chorale Preludes on Gregorian Hymns* Bk.2 Op.76 (Peters) E/M	
Whitlock P.	**Plymouth Suite: Fidelis** in *Whitlock: Complete Shorter Works* (OUP) E/M	

POSTLUDES

Ashdown F.	**Trumpet Voluntary on 'Llanfair'** in *An Album of Trumpet Tunes* (Warner) E/M	
Bach J.S.	**Heut' triumphiret Gottes Sohn** BWV 630 from the *Orgelbüchlein* (many editions) E/M	
Bédard D.	**Variations sur 'Lasst uns erfreuen'** (Cheldar) E/M	
Beechey G.	**Salve, festa dies** in *Easter Preludes* (Fagus) M	
Benoit P.	**Fugue sur 'Ascendit Deus'** No.2 of *Sept Pièces* (Consortium) E/M(*)	
Cavazzoni G.	**In Ascensione Domini** in *Second Organ Book* (Schott, Kalmus) E/M	
Edwards P.	**Fanfare for Ascension** (Fagus) M	
Hand C.	**Miles Lane** in *100 Hymn Preludes* and in *Hymn Preludes for the Church Year* Bk.2 (both Mayhew) E/M	
Harwood B.	**Short Postlude for Ascensiontide** Op.15/4 in *Complete Works* Vol. 2 (Stainer) M	
Langlais J.	**Canzona** from *Folkloric Suite* (FitzSimons) M	
Marsh J.	**Christ triumphant** in *The Organist's Liturgical Year* (Mayhew) E/M	
Peeters F.	**Chorale Fantasie 'Lasst uns erfreuen'** in *Festal Voluntaries: Easter* (Novello) M	
Peeters F.	**Lasst uns erfreuen** in *Hymn Preludes for the Liturgical Year* Op.100 Bk.3 (Peters) M	
Piutti C.	**Chorale Prelude 'Heut triumphiret Gottes Sohn'** in *Choralvorspiele* Op.34 Vol.2 (Bärenreiter) and *Leipziger Orgelmusik des 19 C* (Breitkopf) E	
Thiman E.	**Postlude on 'Llanfair'** No.6 of *Six Pieces* Set 2 (Curwen) E/M	
Willan H.	**Prelude on 'Deo gracias'** in *Ten Hymn Preludes* Set 2 (Peters) M	
Willan H.	**Postlude on 'Miles Lane'** in *36 Short Preludes and Postludes* Set 2 (Peters) M	

DEDICATION FESTIVAL YEARS A, B, C

(Observed on the First Sunday in October or the last Sunday after Trinity
if the date is not known)

ORGAN MUSIC

PRELUDES

Bach J.S.	**Fughetta 'Allein Gott in der Höh sei Ehr'** BWV 677 in Novello Vol.16, Bärenreiter Vol.4, Peters Vol.6 E/M*
Gant A.	**Quam dilecta** in *Fifty Hymn Preludes* (Mayhew) E
Groves R.	**Urbs beata Jerusalem** No.6 of *Six Plainsong Preludes* (Elkin) E(*)
Harker C.	**Prelude on 'Westminster Abbey'** (Bosworth) E/M
Hopkins E.J.	**Allegretto con grazia** in *An Organ Miscellany* (Mayhew) M
Kauffmann G.	**Chorale Prelude 'Nun danket'** in *A Graded Anthology* Bk.3 (Cramer) and in *80 Chorale Preludes* (Peters) E*
Lloyd R.	**Near Mordiford Bridge** ('Hereford') in *Inspiration* (Mayhew; manuals-only edition also available) E
Nixon J.	**Trio on 'Harewood'** in *50 Hymn Preludes* (Mayhew) E/M
Spedding A.	Movements from **Urbs beata** (Banks) E/M
Telemann G.P.	**Allein Gott in der Höh sei Ehr** in *Seasonal Chorale Preludes for Manuals* Bk.1 (OUP) E*
Thiman E.	**Gloria in excelsis** No.6 of *Six Pieces* Set 1 (Curwen) E/M
Viner A.	**Intrada** from *100 Processionals and Recessionals* (Mayhew) E/M
Walther J.G.	**Chorale Prelude 'Mach's mit mir, Gott'** in *A Graded Anthology for Organ* Bk.3 (Cramer) E*

POSTLUDES

Bach J.S.	**Chorale Prelude 'Nun danket'** BWV 657 in Novello Vol.6, Bärenreiter Vol.6, Peters Vol.6 M/D
Bach/Beechey	**Chorale Prelude 'Nun danket'** BWV 192/3 (Fagus) E/M
Berthier J.	**Variations on 'Lobe den Herren'** in *Variations on Six Chorales* (Mayhew) M*
Faulkes W.	**Fantasia on Urbs beata** (Novello) M
Guilmant A.	**Sortie (for the dedication of churches)** Op.65 No.51 in *Complete Works* Vol.6 (Belwin-Mills) and *Selected Works* Vol.3 (Bärenreiter) E/M
Karg-Elert S.	**Lobe den Herren, O meine Seele** No.28 from *Choral-Improvisationen* Op.65 and in the anthology *14 Choral-Improvisationen* (Breitkopf) M
Karg-Elert S.	**Nun danket alle Gott: Marche triomphale** No.59 from *Choral-Improvisationen* Op.65 (many editions) M
Lloyd Webber W.S.	**Dedication March** in *Eight Varied Pieces* (Bosworth) M/D
Lloyd Webber W.S.	**Triumphant March** in *Prayer and Praise* (Paxton) E(*)
Peeters F.	**Festival Voluntary** Op.87 in *An Album of Praise* (OUP) E/M
Reger M.	**Dankpsalm** Op.145/2 (Breitkopf) M/D
Smith A.	**Trumpet Tune on 'Westminster Abbey'** in *Ten Hymn-Tune Preludes* (Animus) E/M
Willan H.	**Urbs Hierusalem beata** from *Five Preludes on Plainchant Melodies* (OUP Archive complete or singly) M
Willcocks D.	**Processional** (on 'Westminster Abbey') (Roger Dean) M

ALL SAINTS' DAY (1 NOVEMBER) YEARS A, B, C

ORGAN MUSIC

PRELUDES

Archer M.	**Dundee** in *25 Hymn Preludes: A Year of Praise* and in *40 Christmas Preludes* (both Mayhew) E/M	
Beechey G.	**Prelude on 'Placare Christe servulis'** (Fagus) E/M	
Brahms J.	**O wie selig seid ihr doch** No.6 of *Eleven Chorale Preludes* Op.122 E★	
d'Indy V.	**Verset 'Volo Pater'** in *St Cecilia Organ Library* Vol.1 (Cramer) E/M	
Dupont G.	**Pour le Toussaint** (Eschig/MDS) M	
Harker C.	**Iste confessor** (Angers) in *Three Pieces Based on French Church Melodies* (Novello) E/M	
Karg-Elert S.	**Before the image of a saint** No.8 from *Sempre Semplice* Op.142 (Breitkopf, Butz) E/M	
Nixon J.	**Ad tuum nomen** in *Hymn Tune Preludes* (Fagus) E/M	
Oortmerssen J.van	**For all the saints** from *Five Chorale Preludes* (Tactus) E/M	
Peeters F.	**Sine nomine** in *Hymn Preludes for the Liturgical Year* Op.100 Bk.5 (Peters) E/M	
Peeters F.	**Aeterna Christi munera** No.2 of *Thirty Chorale Preludes on Gregorian Themes* Op.76 (Peters) E	
Saint-Saëns C.	**Pro martyribus** No.5 of *Sept Improvisations* Op.150 (Durand, Butz) E/M	
Shearing G.	**There is a happy land** in *Sacred Sounds from George Shearing* (SMP) E/M	
Tournemire C.	Movements from **Festum Omnium Sanctorum** in *Petites Fleurs Musicales* Op.66 (Universal Edition) E★	
Tallis T.	**Iste confessor** in *Complete Keyboard Works* (Hinrichsen) E★	
Willan H.	**Prelude on 'Newbury'** in *Ten Hymn Preludes* Set 3 (Peters) E/M	

POSTLUDES

Bédard D.	**Variations sur 'Sine nomine'** *or* **Variations sur 'Lasst uns erfreuen'** (Cheldar) M	
Callahan C.	**Voluntary on 'Engelberg'** (Morning Star) M	
Chaminade C.	**Offertoire (All Saints)** *or* **Offertoire (All Souls)** in *La Nef Sacrée* (Enoch) E/M(★)	
Choveaux N.	**No.3** of *Three Pieces* (Lengnick) M/D	
Darke H.	**Prelude on 'Darwall's 148th'** No.2 of *Three Chorale Preludes* Op.20 (Novello)	
Dupré M.	**Placare Christe servulis** from *Le Tombeau de Titelouze* Op.38 (Bornemann) D	
Grace H.	**Toccatina on 'Kings Lynn'** in *Ten Compositions* Vol.1 (Schott) M	
Parry C.H.H.	**Chorale Prelude 'Old 104th'** in *Seven Chorale Preludes* Set 1 (Novello) and in *Preludes and Postludes* (Mayhew) M	
Redford J.	**Iste confessor with a meane** in *The Mulliner Book* (Stainer) E/M★	
Stanford C.V.	**Fantasia (In Festo Omnium Sanctorum)** Op.121 No.1 (Fitzjohn) M/D	
Willan H.	**Prelude on 'Iste confessor'** in *Ten Hymn Preludes* Set 3 (Peters) M	

Suitable before or after: Movements from Edwards P. **Partita 'Iste confessor'** Op.379 (Fagus) E-M or Self A. **Variations on 'Iste confessor'** (Animus) E/M-M

SECOND SERVICE LECTIONARY: ABBREVIATIONS

Books and collections

A	*Agape* (OUP), over 100 hymns, songs and chants from around the world
AC1–4	*Anthems for Choirs* (OUP), books 1 and 4: SATB, books 2 and 3: SA
ACA	*Andrew Carter Anthems* (OUP), 10 anthems for SATB choirs
ACB	*Advent Carol Book* (RSCM), a service and resource book compiled and edited by Trevor Jarvis
AFC	*Advent for Choirs* (OUP), 52 pieces in a range of styles, edited by Archer and Cleobury
AIL	*Awakening in Love* (Mayhew), 13 songs and chants by Margaret Rizza
AMNS	*Hymns Ancient & Modern, New Standard Edition* (Canterbury Press)
AMV	*Anthems for Men's Voices* (OUP), mainly renaissance and baroque anthems for ATB
AOAN1	*Anthems Old and New for SAMen 1* (Mayhew), 100 settings for smaller choirs, SAMen
APA	*A Purcell Anthology* (OUP), 15 anthems for four or more parts
ASA	*A Stanford Anthology* (OUP), 18 anthems and motets for SATB and organ
ATNJ	*At the Name of Jesus* (OCP), service music and songs by Christopher Walker
AWS	*Anthems from Worship Songs* (RSCM), 16 songs arranged for SATB
AWTE	*Ash Wednesday to Easter for Choirs* (OUP), over 50 anthems, mostly SATB, with organ
BC	*The Bronze Collection* (RSCM), 34 songs and anthems at Bronze standard in the *Voice for Life* scheme
BCA	*Bob Chilcott Anthems* (OUP), 10 anthems for SATB choirs
BCC	*Bob Chilcott Carols* (OUP), 9 carols for mixed voices
BFH	*Bread for the Hungry* (RSCM), festival service for upper or mixed voices
C	*Cantate* (Decani), chants, short songs and psalms for all kinds of worship
CAON	*Complete Anglican Hymns Old and New* (Mayhew)
CAP	*Come and Praise* (BBC), volumes 1, 2 and combined volume
CAS	*Chants and Songs* (Mayhew), 16 of Margaret Rizza's songs in simplified arrangements
CAYP	*Come All You People* (Wild Goose), collection of chants and responses from the Iona Community
CBL	*Christ Be Our Light* (OCP), songs and service music by Bernadette Farrell
CC1–4	*Carols for Choirs* (OUP), four volumes of carols, vols.1–3: SATB; vol.4: upper voices
CFAP	*Called for a Purpose* (RSCM), festival service for upper or mixed voices
CFE	*Celebration Hymnal for Everyone* (McCrimmon)
CFL	*Carols for Life* (RSCM), 42 songs and carols for unison, upper-voice and equal-voice choirs
CFTW	*Care for the World* (RSCM), festival service for upper or mixed voices
CG	*Common Ground* (St Andrew Press)
CH	*Children's Hymn Book* (Mayhew)
CH4	*Church Hymnary: Fourth Edition* (Canterbury Press)
CH5	*Church Hymnal: Fifth Edition* (Oxford University Press)
CHM	*Choise Musick* (RSCM), collection of 12 anthems for SAB choirs
CHMO	*Christmas Motets* (OUP), mainly from the 16th–18th centuries for advanced choirs, edited by John Rutter
CIH	*Christ is Here* (OCP), songs and service music by Christopher Walker
CM1–12	*Chester Motets* (Chester), volumes 1–12, unaccompanied European renaissance motets
CN	*Cantica Nova* (OUP), 18 motets for mixed voices by contemporary British composers
CP	*Common Praise* (Canterbury Press)
CRP	*Complete Responsorial Psalter* (McCrimmon), responsorial Psalms using Grail translation
CSF	*Come to Set Us Free* (OCP/Thomas More), collection of pieces by contemporary Catholic composers
CSFC	*Christmas Spirituals for Choirs* (OUP), 12 arrangements of carols in a gospel style for SATB choirs
CV	*Christmas Voices* (Novello), 14 new carols for SATB choirs by various composers
CWP	*Common Worship Psalter* (RSCM), pointed version of the psalter with chants
EAC1/2	*English Anthem Collection* (RSCM), twentieth century anthems, book 1: SATB, book 2: SA
EM	*Easter Mysteries* (OCP), songs and liturgical music for Holy Week and Easter
EOA	*Enemy of Apathy* (Wild Goose), songs for Easter to Pentecost from Iona

ESM	*European Sacred Music* (OUP), 50 motets and anthems, edited by John Rutter	
ETAS	*Epiphany to All Saints* (OUP), 50 anthems and liturgical pieces for SATB choirs	
FAB1	*Favourite Anthem Book One* (Mayhew), 25 anthems for SATB choirs	
FGP	*Forty-one Gelineau Psalms* (GIA)	
FOL	*Fountain of Life* (Mayhew), 12 songs and chants by Margaret Rizza	
FOLO	*Fire of Love* (Mayhew), 14 songs and chants by Margaret Rizza	
FSB1–10	*Festival Service Books* (RSCM)	
GAW	*Great and Wonderful* (Banks), 19 anthems by Ian Hubbard for SATB choirs	
GBAN	*God Beyond All Names* (OCP), songs and service music by Bernadette Farrell	
GBU	*Go Before Us* (OCP), songs by Bernadette Farrell, some with sign language pictures	
HG	*Holy Gifts* (OCP/Thomas More), songs and service music by Stephen Dean	
HIG	*Holy is God* (OCP/Thomas More), collection of pieces by contemporary Catholic composers	
H&P	*Hymns & Psalms* (Methodist Publishing House)	
HP	*High Praise* (Novello), 28 anthems for upper voices, edited by Barry Rose	
HSNW	*Heaven Shall Not Wait* (Wild Goose), songs of creation and incarnation from Iona	
HTC	*Hymns for Today's Church* (Hodder)	
IAMB	*Iona Abbey Music Book* (Wild Goose), songs from the *Iona Abbey Worship Book*	
IECS	*In Every Corner Sing* (RSCM), music from the world church	
JP	*Junior Praise* (Marshall Pickering), volumes 1, 2 and combined volume	
JRA	*John Rutter Anthems* (OUP), 11 anthems for SATB choirs	
JRC	*John Rutter Carols* (OUP), 10 carols for SATB choirs	
KS	*Kidsource* (Mayhew), volumes 1 & 2	
LAA	*Love and Anger*, (Wild Goose), 19 songs of lively faith and social justice from the Iona Community	
LAU	*Laudate* (Decani Music)	
LD	*Love Divine: Four Extended Hymns* (CMS/OUP), settings for SATB choirs	
LFB	*Love from Below* (Wild Goose), songs celebrating the seasons of life, from Iona	
LIOD	*Light in our Darkness* (Mayhew), 10 psalms and chants by Margaret Rizza	
LMOL	*Lead me, O Lord* (OCP), collection of pieces by contemporary Catholic composers	
LOL	*Light Of Life* (RSCM), 75th anniversary book with anthems, readings and service music	
LUE	*Lent Until Easter* (Mayhew), 26 seasonal anthems for SATB choirs	
LUR	*Light Upon the River* (St Matthias Press), hymn texts by Christopher Idle	
MAG	*Many and Great* (Wild Goose), songs of the world church	
MCW1	*Music for Common Worship I* (RSCM), a resource book for Sunday services	
MEA	*More Easy Anthems* (RSCM), 13 anthems for unison or small SAB/SATB choirs	
MHWE	*Music for Holy Week and Easter* (McCrimmons), seasonal songs, hymns, anthems and liturgical music	
MP	*Complete Mission Praise* (2005 edition; numbers are consistent with all previous versions)	
MTH1/2	*More Than Hymns* (Novello), hymn anthems for mixed voice choirs	
MTP	*More Than Psalms* (Novello), 24 anthems on texts from the Psalms for mixed voices	
MUC	*Ubi Caritas* (OCP), liturgical music and songs based on plainsong melody by Bob Hurd	
N	*Noel* (Novello), 47 carols and anthems for Advent, Christmas and Epiphany for SATB choirs	
NCAB	*New Church Anthem Book* (OUP), 100 anthems from the Renaissance to the present	
NEH	*New English Hymnal* (Canterbury Press), with numbers above 600 (italicized) from NEP	
NEP	*New English Praise* (Canterbury Press), hymns, psalms and liturgical settings, a supplement to NEH	
NNAB	*The New Novello Anthem Book* (Novello), 41 classic and modern anthems	
NOEAB	*New Oxford Easy Anthem Book* (OUP), 63 easy anthems for the church's year	
NPCW	*New Psalms for Common Worship* (Mayhew), responsorial settings of all *Common Worship* Psalms	
NSAC1/2	*The Novello Short Anthem Collections* (Novello), two volumes for smaller SATB choirs	
OBFA	*Oxford Book of Flexible Anthems* (OUP), 60 anthems which can be sung in a variety of parts	
OBTA	*Oxford Book of Tudor Anthems* (OUP), 34 anthems from the sixteenth century	
OEAB	*Oxford Easy Anthem Book* (OUP), 50 anthems, 1 to 4 parts	
OITB	*One is the Body* (Wild Goose), songs of unity and diversity from the Iona Community	
OOD	*Out of Darkness* (OCP), songs and service music by Christopher Walker, mainly for Easter	
PAME	*Psalms and Music for the Eucharist* (McCrimmon), responsorial Psalms for CW Lectionary (Year A)	
PCMG	*Psalms for the Church Choir and Music Group* (Mayhew), 27 Psalms with congregational response	

PFS	*Psalms for Singers* (RSCM), 26 responsorial Psalms for congregational use	
PIW	*Psalms in Worship* (RSCM), 25 Psalm settings in a variety of styles	
PPP	*Psalms of Patience, Protest and Praise* (Wild Goose), Psalms in varied styles by John Bell	
PSA	*Psallam* (RSCM), 80th anniversary book with music by composers from the RSCM worldwide	
PSRB	*Palm Sunday Resource Book* (RSCM), modern Passiontide anthems for choirs	
RCM	*Russian Choral Masterpieces* (Novello), 15 unaccompanied pieces for choirs	
RE	*Resurrexit* (Decani), songs and liturgical music for Lent, Holy Week and Easter	
RITH	*Restless is the Heart* (OCP), songs and liturgical music by Bernadette Farrell	
ROP	*River of Peace* (Mayhew), 14 songs and chants by Margaret Rizza	
RTF	*Road to Freedom* (RSCM), festival service with readings and songs for upper or mixed voices	
SAEE	*Seven Anthems: Edward Elgar* (Novello), 7 anthems for mixed voice choirs and organ	
SBS1	*Sunday by Sunday Collection Vol.1* (RSCM), 30 photocopiable anthems for all seasons of the year	
SBS2	*Sunday by Sunday Collection Vol.2* (RSCM), 30 photocopiable anthems for use at the Sunday Eucharist	
SBTL	*Sent by the Lord* (Wild Goose), songs of the world church	
SC	*The Silver Collection* (RSCM), 30 anthems at Silver standard in the *Voice for Life* scheme	
SCAB	*Sixteenth Century Anthem Book* (OUP), collection of Renaissance unaccompanied pieces for SATB choirs	
SEA1/2	*Short and Easy Anthems* (Novello), 14 anthems in each volume for small choirs	
SETA	*Six Easy Three-Part Anthems* (RSCM), short and simple pieces for SAB	
SFC	*Spirituals for Choirs* (OUP), 20 arrangements for advanced choirs compiled by Bob Chilcott	
SFJ	*Shout for Joy* (Banks), 14 anthems by Ian Hubbard for upper voice choirs	
SFL1	*Songs for Life 1* (RSCM), songbook for children and adult beginners	
SFL2	*Songs for Life 2* (RSCM), songs in unison, 2 part and 3 part, SAMen	
SFTL	*Search for the Lord* (OCP/Thomas More), collection of pieces by contemporary Catholic composers	
SG	*Sing Glory* (Mayhew)	
SL	*Sing Low* (Novello), 30 anthems for lower voices, edited by Barry Rose	
SLG	*Sing of the Lord's Goodness* (OCP/Thomas More), songs and service music by Catholic composers	
SOF	*Songs of Fellowship*, volumes 1, 2 & 3 (Kingsway)	
SOS	*Songs of the Spirit* (RSCM), 10 arrangements of traditional sacred songs by Martin How	
SOTL	*The Spirit of the Lord* (RSCM), festival service book with a Holy Spirit theme	
SSJ	*Stories and Songs of Jesus* (OCP), 15 children's songs by Christopher Walker	
SWAMS	*Sing With All My Soul* (RSCM), 52 worship songs arranged for SATB choirs	
TA	*A Tallis Anthology* (OUP), 17 anthems and motets	
TCB	*The Carol Book* (RSCM), resources for the seasons of Advent, Christmas and Epiphany	
TEA	*Twelve Easy Anthems* (RSCM), anthems in unison, 2 or 3 parts	
TIOAU	*There is One Among Us* (Wild Goose), collection of chants and responses from the Iona Community	
TNA	*Ten New Anthems for Mixed Voices* (Mayhew), pieces by Archer, Rawsthorne, Bertalot and others	
TPS	*The Purcell Selection* (RSCM), 20 anthems by Henry Purcell arranged for small choirs	
TS	*The Source*, volumes 1, 2 & 3 (Mayhew)	
TSFP	*Taizé: Songs for Prayer* (GIA), collection of Taizé music, instrumental parts available	
VE	*Veni Emmanuel* (Decani), liturgical music, songs and psalm settings for Advent and Christmastide	
VFLS	*Voice for Life Songbook* (RSCM), 40 songs and anthems for choirs at beginner or intermediate levels	
WFC	*Weddings for Choirs* (OUP), 40 pieces, sacred and secular, for SATB choirs on themes of love and praise	
WGIR	*When Grief is Raw* (Wild Goose), 25 songs for times of sorrow and bereavement from Iona	
WIS	*Worship in Song* (RSCM), 34 worship songs arranged for SATB choirs	
WOTC	*Way of the Cross* (RSCM), sequence of music and readings for Passiontide	
WSCC1/2	*Worship Songs for the Church Choir* (Mayhew), 20 arrangements for SATB by Tambling in each volume	
WYP	*We are Your People* (OCP/Thomas More), songs and liturgical music by Catholic composers	